FOUNDATION PRESS

CONSTITUTIONAL LAW STORIES

SECOND EDITION

Edited By

MICHAEL C. DORF

Cornell University Law School

FOUNDATION PRESS

2009

THOMSON REUTERS

© 2004 FOUNDATION PRESS

© 2009 By THOMSON REUTERS/FOUNDATION PRESS
      195 Broadway, 9th Floor
      New York, NY 10007
      Phone Toll Free 1–877–888–1330
      Fax (212) 367–6799
      foundation–press.com
Printed in the United States of America

ISBN 978–1–59941–169–9

ACKNOWLEDGMENTS

This second edition of *Constitutional Law Stories* was the product of a collaborative effort by the chapter authors and others. Paul Caron cleverly persuaded me to edit the first edition of this book, at a time when I did not yet realize that I was thereby making a lifetime commitment. John Bloomquist and Jim Coates of Foundation Press were ever so patient as some of the chapter authors and I missed successive deadlines. Silvia Babikian and Neil Kelly did a great job as research assistants on the new and revised chapters in this book, building on the work of their predecessors on the first edition: Karessa Cain, Akiva Goldfarb, John Laufer, Scott Martin, Renee Paradis, and Zachary Tripp. Richard Banks was the victim of my own poor planning in asking him to write about a non-canonical case for the first edition: to make room for one of the new chapters in the second edition, I reluctantly cut his terrific chapter. Sherry Colb provided wise counsel on just about every aspect of this project. Finally, thanks to the protagonists of *Constitutional Law Stories*, living and dead—many of whom never chose to become the center of a great national controversy.

MICHAEL C. DORF

Ithaca 2009

*

CONSTITUTIONAL LAW STORIES

Part III: Liberty and the Constitution

FOUNDATION PRESS

CONSTITUTIONAL LAW STORIES

*

Introduction

Michael C. Dorf

Putting the people back in "We the People"

Selecting a mere fifteen of the hundreds of cases that comprise the constitutional law canon[1] to include in *Constitutional Law Stories* was a daunting challenge. My choices are just that—*my own* idiosyncratic effort to put together a selection of interesting tales that provide a deeper understanding of the project of constitutional law as a whole. Few readers will agree that every case I included belongs in this book or that all of my omissions were justified. I nonetheless begin by explaining how I chose the cases to include and exclude in the hope that my explanation will shed some light on the overall aims of this book.

In winnowing the constitutional cases in the *United States Reports*, I relied in part on the conventions of the law school curriculum. Landmarks like *Mapp v. Ohio*,[2] *Gideon v. Wainwright*,[3] and *Miranda v. Arizona*[4] are relegated to criminal procedure courses; *Pennoyer v. Neff*,[5] Goldberg v. Kelly,[6] and *Mathews v. Eldridge*[7] are covered in civil procedure; and important Takings Clause decisions such as *Pennsylvania Coal Co. v. Mahon*,[8] *Lucas v. South Carolina Coastal Council*,[9] and *Nollan v.*

---

[1] *See* J.M. Balkin & Sanford Levinson, *The Canons of Constitutional Law*, 111 Harv. L. Rev. 963 (1998).

[2] 367 U.S. 643 (1961).

[3] 372 U.S. 335 (1963).

[4] 384 U.S. 436 (1966).

[5] 95 U.S. 714 (1877).

[6] 397 U.S. 254 (1970).

[7] 424 U.S. 319 (1976).

[8] 260 U.S. 393 (1922).

[9] 505 U.S. 1003 (1992).

California Coastal Comm'n[10] are typically reserved to the course in property. These disciplinary lines undoubtedly partake of considerable arbitrariness, but as *Constitutional Law Stories* is meant to serve (in one of its capacities) as a companion text to the typical first year law school course in constitutional law, I confined my choices to the main currents of such a course: structural issues of separation of powers and federalism; equal protection; and individual rights (including First Amendment rights).

The first edition of this book omitted perhaps the most-closely-followed and controversial Supreme Court case in decades, *Bush v. Gore*.[11] As a number of commentators have observed, the Court's purported treatment of that case as *sui generis*,[12] calls to mind the notion of adjudication "as a restricted railroad ticket, good for this day and train only."[13] However, the initial omission of *Bush v. Gore* from *Constitutional Law Stories* was less the result of my judgment that the case would lack doctrinal legs than my sense that, in the first term of the Presidency of George W. Bush, the case was sufficiently fresh in our collective memory that its story did not need to be rehearsed. Now, as the Bush administration fades into history, some objectivity with respect to *Bush v. Gore* is both possible and necessary. Michael Gerhardt provides that, and more, in Chapter 4.

Likewise, the first edition omitted any cases or materials directly arising out of the terrorist attacks of September 11, 2001, the domestic response, or the military actions in Afghanistan and Iraq. Here too, the immediate background facts were still fresh in memory, and here too the time is now ripe for a retrospective view. Yet as Benjamin Wittes and Hannah Neprash show in Chapter 15 of this second edition, even today the core issues posed by the detention of designated enemy combatants at Guantanamo Bay Naval Base and elsewhere remain largely unanswered. So too, as Neil Gotanda notes in opening Chapter 7, "*Korematsu v. United States*[14] refuses to join history."

---

[10] 483 U.S. 825 (1987).

[11] 531 U.S. 98 (2000).

[12] *See id.* at 109 ("Our consideration is limited to the present circumstances, for the problem of equal protection in election processes generally presents many complexities.")

[13] Smith v. Allwright, 321 U.S. 649, 669 (1944). *See, e.g.*, Philip P. Frickey, *Doctrine, Context, Institutional Relationships, and Commentary: The Malaise of Federal Indian Law Through the Lens of Lone Wolf*, 38 Tulsa L. Rev. 5, 34 (2002) (invoking the metaphor of a restricted railroad ticket); Linda Greenhouse, *Thinking About the Supreme Court After Bush v. Gore*, 35 Ind. L. Rev. 435, 436 (2002) (same); Pamela S. Karlan, *Exit Strategies In Constitutional Law: Lessons for Getting the Least Dangerous Branch out of the Political Thicket*, 82 B.U. L. Rev. 667, 696 (2002) (same).

[14] 323 U.S. 214 (1944).

Perhaps reflecting my own view of the limited relevance of the original understanding to contemporary constitutional debates,[15] *Constitutional Law Stories* has something of a presentist bias. Only two founding era cases—*Marbury v. Madison*[16] and *McCulloch v. Maryland*[17] —are discussed in separate chapters. One could certainly tell a ripping yarn about how, prior to the Supreme Court's decision in *Gibbons v. Ogden*,[18] New York and New Jersey nearly went to war over steamboat rights on the Hudson River.[19] Likewise, President Andrew Jackson's angry reaction to the opinion of Chief Justice John Marshall in *Worcester v. Georgia*[20] would make for another fine tale. But I opted to include more cases that are directly relevant to modern doctrine.

This is not to say that I have only chosen cases that are exemplars of "good law." On the contrary, other than *Marbury* and *McCulloch*, the only nineteenth century cases I have included are *Dred Scott v. Sandford*[21] and *Plessy v. Ferguson*,[22] both of which are offered as cautionary tales. Moreover, three of the twentieth century cases—*Lochner v. New York*,[23] *Whitney v. California*,[24] and *Korematsu*—serve much the same purpose, although, as David Bernstein explains in Chapter 9, a wave of recent scholarship has begun to reconsider the vilification of *Lochner* and its progeny. Conversely, to some readers *Roe v. Wade*[25] will seem a cautionary tale, though that is certainly not how Lucinda Finley portrays it in Chapter 10. Finally, even cases that are good law in the sense that their holdings remain in effect, are often presented in the pages that follow as wrongly decided or resting on faulty reasoning.

---

[15] *See* Michael C. Dorf, *Integrating Normative and Descriptive Constitutional Theory: The Case of Original Meaning*, 85 Geo. L.J. 1765, 1767 (1997).

[16] 5 U.S. (1 Cranch) 137 (1803).

[17] 17 U.S. (4 Wheat.) 316 (1819).

[18] 22 U.S. (9 Wheat.) 1 (1824).

[19] For a colorful account, see David Lear Buckman, *Old Steamboat Days on the Hudson River* 37–42 (1907).

[20] 31 U.S. (6 Pet.) 515 (1832). Jackson reportedly said "John Marshall has made his decision, now let him enforce it." 1 Charles Warren, *The Supreme Court in United States History*, 759 n. 53 (revised ed. 1926). Though the story is probably apocryphal, the true story is itself quite interesting. See Barry Friedman, *The History of the Countermajoritarian Difficulty, Part One: The Road to Judicial Supremacy*, 73 N.Y.U. L. Rev. 333, 399–401 (1998).

[21] 60 U.S. (19 How.) 393 (1856).

[22] 163 U.S. 537 (1896).

[23] 198 U.S. 45 (1905).

[24] 274 U.S. 357 (1927).

[25] 410 U.S. 113 (1973).

By including a fair number of poorly reasoned or morally obtuse decisions in this book I aim to combat a common impulse among both students and scholars of constitutional law—the tendency to treat the story of American constitutionalism as the unfolding manifest destiny of the ideals announced in the Declaration of Independence and inscribed in the Constitution. This mythic narrative treats the Founding as a kind of divinely inspired event—the "The Miracle at Philadelphia"—sacralyzing both the Constitution[26] and its authoritative interpretation by the oracular Supreme Court.[27] Even those thoughtful voices that recognize that the Constitution was conceived in the original sin of slavery[28] nonetheless tend to see its subsequent evolution as a march of progress.[29] To be sure, few deny that the country and the Court have, from time to time, deviated from the true path—as when the Southern Redemption of the 1870s delayed (by nearly a century) the implementation of the Reconstruction Amendments,[30] or when (during much of the same period) the Supreme Court and state high courts invoked contract and property rights to block much progressive legislation—but these periods are seen as deviant.

The tendency of Americans to fetishize the Constitution and the Supreme Court that speaks in its name is exacerbated by the tendency of lawyers and law students in the common law tradition to try to rationalize cases. In response to legal realist and other critical accounts of constitutional doctrine, I myself have frequently asked my students to formulate their points in a way that could be put into a brief. The conventions of legal argument require lawyers to treat cases that are good law as more than brute facts but as correct in a deeper sense. Consequently, law students and lawyers must constantly rationalize even bad decisions. As Ronald Dworkin explains, common lawyers interpret authoritative text and prior precedent so as to put the law as a whole in its best light.[31] It is theoretically possible to maintain that one is putting a set of harmful decisions in their best light, but the human mind tends to recoil from cognitive dissonance, and thus the lawyerly imperative to rationalize points in the same, celebratory direction as our

---

[26] See Michael Kammen, *A Machine That Would Go of Itself* (1986).

[27] See Henry P. Monaghan, *Our Perfect Constitution*, 56 N.Y.U. L. Rev. 353 (1981).

[28] See Thurgood Marshall, *Reflections on the Bicentennial of the United States Constitution*, 101 Harv. L. Rev. 1, 2–5 (1987).

[29] See *id.* at 5 (describing the Constitution's "promising evolution through 200 years of history").

[30] See Eric Foner, *Reconstruction: America's Unfinished Revolution*, 1863–1877 (Perennial Library ed. 1989).

[31] See Ronald Dworkin, *Law's Empire* 167–75, 186–224 (1986).

constitutional culture more broadly. The cautionary tales contained in these pages should dampen the celebratory impulse.

Nonetheless, one must be careful not to err in the other direction and demonize the Court. Some opinions are justly celebrated. The two free speech cases addressed in *Constitutional Law Stories*—*Whitney v. California* and *West Virginia State Board of Education v. Barnette*[32]—are illustrative. Here and elsewhere, the book aims to go deeper than the materials of the ordinary constitutional law or First Amendment casebook in explaining what and why we celebrate. In Chapter 11, Ashutosh Bhagwat shows how the free speech philosophy of Justice Brandeis differed from that of Justice Holmes and why the Brandeisian conception fits better with American democratic traditions than does the Holmesian metaphor of the marketplace of ideas. In Chapter 12, Vincent Blasi and Seana Shiffrin argue that the value of the right not to speak lies not so much in the ability not to be misunderstood by an external audience as in avoiding the internal interference with idea formation that can result from compelled affirmation.

What to celebrate in constitutional law is, of course, contested territory, and knowing the composition of the anti-canon is not always helpful in constructing an affirmative account of constitutional law. For example, in laying bare the story of *Plessy v. Ferguson* in Chapter 6, Cheryl Harris leaves one wondering how it could have remained the law of the land for nearly six decades. Yet she also shows how its core assumptions have not so much been repudiated as they have been reconfigured. Knowing that we as a nation are now *against* "separate but equal" does not tell us what we are *for*. (The first) Justice Harlan's *Plessy* dissent articulates, in consecutive sentences, both the principle that the Equal Protection Clause condemns a caste system *and* the principle of colorblindness.[33] Yet much of the most urgent contemporary debate over the meaning of constitutional equality pits these principles against one another. Do programs of race-based affirmative action which violate the colorblindness principle but are designed to combat racial caste hierarchy violate the Constitution? Neither Harlan's *Plessy* dissent nor *Brown v. Board of Education*[34]—which repudiates *Plessy* in the realm of public education but says little more—answers this question. And the formalism of the modern doctrine of "colorblindness," Harris argues, has clear antecedents in the formalism of *Plessy* itself.

---

[32] 319 U.S. 624 (1943).

[33] *See Plessy*, 163 U.S. at 559 (Harlan, J., dissenting) ("There is no caste here. Our constitution is color-blind. . . .").

[34] 347 U.S. 483 (1954).

The contest over *Brown*'s legacy and the *Law Stories* concept as a whole could be taken to exemplify the observation of Justice Holmes in his *Lochner* dissent that "general propositions do not decide concrete cases."[35] That line is of a piece with the oft-quoted fourth sentence of Holmes' *The Common Law*: "The life of the law has not been logic: it has been experience."[36] Human affairs are messy and law, rather than invariably imposing order on life's untidiness, often simply reflects it. Thus, to understand the law, it is not enough to learn general, often platitudinous nostrums. Whether the subject is the common law or constitutional law, abstract statements like "no man may profit from his own wrong,"[37] or "racial classifications are permissible only if necessary and narrowly tailored to achieve a compelling interest,"[38] at best identify the considerations relevant to a judicial decision; the actual decision is based on a range of additional factors that can only be comprehended by deep familiarity with the social facts surrounding the case.

This approach to law is "pragmatic" in the philosophical sense of the term. Some critics of pragmatism associate the term with a kind of act-consequentialism: to be a pragmatic judge, in this view, is to "simply decide cases in whatever way will produce the best future results."[39] However, philosophical pragmatism in the American tradition of Charles Sanders Pierce, Henry James, and John Dewey is not merely oriented toward consequences; it is also against grand theory and abstraction; it is for bottom-up rather than top-down ways of understanding and responding to the world. *Constitutional Law Stories* is pragmatic in this way: It suggests that to understand the enterprise of constitutional law, we do better to learn the rich details of the people whose lives were

---

[35] *Lochner*, 198 U.S. at 76 (Holmes, J., dissenting).

[36] Oliver Wendell Holmes, Jr., *The Common Law* 1 (1881).

[37] Ronald Dworkin, *Taking Rights Seriously* 22–24 (1977) (finding this principle to be dispositive in *Riggs v. Palmer*, 22 N.E. 188 (N.Y. 1889)).

[38] *Metro Broadcasting, Inc. v. F.C.C.*, 497 U.S. 547, 602 (1990) (O'Connor, J., dissenting).

[39] Richard H. Fallon, Jr., *How to Choose a Constitutional Theory*, 87 Calif. L. Rev. 535, 564 (1999). Ronald Dworkin, another critic of what he calls pragmatism, also uses the term as a synonym for consequentialism. *See* Dworkin, *supra* note 31, at 160 ("Pragmatism ... says that judges should follow whichever method of deciding cases will produce what they believe to be the best community for the future."). Although the law-and-economics movement that Judge Richard Posner played an important role in founding could be said to reduce judging and other legal activities to utilitarian calculations, Posner's own work rejects the act-consequentialist account of pragmatism. *See, e.g.,* Richard A. Posner, *Pragmatism Versus Purposivism in First Amendment Analysis*, 54 Stan. L. Rev. 737, 738 (2002) (pragmatism "is easily derided as unprincipled, ad hoc, and 'political'; but it is these things only if it is thought to entail the disregard of the systemic as well as immediate consequences of judicial decisions, which no pragmatist judge worth his salt believes.")

altered by the process of constitutional adjudication than we would by constructing a synthetic overarching theory about how the Constitution is or should be interpreted.

But there is no need to be dogmatically bottom-up. After all, even Holmes—the law's Ur-pragmatist[40]—was not resolutely against abstraction or for bottom-up approaches. Indeed, in *The Path of the Law*, Holmes tells a charming story about a justice of the peace, who, faced with a suit between two farmers over a broken churn that one had lent the other, ruled for the defendant because he could find no law establishing an obligation not to break a churn.[41] The foolish justice of the peace had missed the point that the law is—or, according to Holmes, should be—organized in distinctly legal categories that abstract away distinctions between borrowed churns and other borrowed items. The challenge for students of Holmes is reconciling his belief in the primacy of situated experience over logic with his preference for legal as opposed to social or natural categories.[42]

Whether Holmes' thinking on these issues was internally consistent is not my concern here. However, there is a closely related puzzle that cannot be easily glossed. The problem lies at the heart of the Supreme Court's decision-making procedures. On the one hand, with almost complete control over their own docket,[43] the Justices do not sit as a court of error. The Court's rules make clear that, with a small number of exceptions, it will only take cases that present issues with implications for persons and institutions besides the parties.[44] On the other hand, the Court interprets the case-or-controversy language of Article III as precluding federal courts (including itself) from considering abstract questions of law divorced from concrete, ripe, adversarial settings.[45] What justifies these dual—almost contradictory—requirements?

The conventional answer goes something like this: (1) Absent control over its own docket, the Court would be swamped with unimportant

---

[40] On the relation of Holmes to Pierce, James and Dewey, see Louis Menand, *The Metaphysical Club: A Story of Ideas in America* (2001).

[41] *See* Oliver Wendell Holmes, Jr., *The Path of the Law*, 10 Harv. L. Rev. 457, 474–75 (1897).

[42] As Frederick Schauer observes, Holmes was not arguing for large abstract categories rather than small concrete ones, but for *legal* as opposed to social or natural categories. *See* Frederick Schauer, *Principles, Institutions, and the First Amendment*, 112 Harv. L. Rev. 84, 109 (1998) ("Juridical categories are not necessarily larger than the categories of the world. There are, after all, far more insects than there are torts.")

[43] The vast majority of the Court's cases come to it by writ of certiorari to the federal courts of appeals, *see* 28 U.S.C. § 1254, or state high courts, *see* 28 U.S.C. § 1257.

[44] *See* Sup. Ct. R. 10.

[45] *See* Allen v. Wright, 468 U.S. 737, 750–52 (1984).

work; (2) in selecting cases to review, the Court necessarily engages in a form of triage, taking just those controversies that have the greatest significance; (3) given the Court's lack of democratic accountability, it is reluctant to resolve constitutional or other pressing national issues that have not led to concrete cases or controversies; (4) the Court makes better decisions when it addresses cases as they arise in the real world rather than in the abstract; and therefore (5) within the universe of concrete justiciable cases and controversies, the Court chooses to hear those that present the most pressing general questions.

The principal difficulty with the foregoing argument is that step (4), while true of many issues, is false with respect to others. When the federal or state governments adopt statutes or regulations of dubious constitutionality, individuals and organizations facing high compliance costs have a strong interest in knowing as soon as possible whether in fact they must comply. The possibility of anticipatory and injunctive relief somewhat mitigates the costs from the delay between the time a legal rule is enacted and the time that the Supreme Court ultimately passes on its constitutionality, but that period is still typically measured in years. It is for that reason (among others) that most European constitutional courts are competent to review legislation in the abstract, rendering what, in the United States, would be barred as advisory opinions.[46]

In any event, the United States Supreme Court's preference for concrete cases sometimes seems a matter of form rather than substance. For example, as Garrett Epps explains in Chapter 13, en route to its conclusion that the Free Exercise Clause of the First Amendment does not entitle participants in religious rituals to exemptions from generally applicable laws not targeted at religion, the Supreme Court injected a question—whether the use of peyote was criminally proscribed in Oregon—that had previously played no role in the case. The Court apparently viewed the peyote litigation as a convenient vehicle with which to address the general question of religious exemptions, just as the Marshall Court saw the litigation over Mr. Marbury's entitlement to his justice of the peace commission as an opportunity to establish the Court's power of judicial review. In these instances and others, the Court treats the real messy facts as largely irrelevant: the particularities of the stories of Al Smith, William Marbury, and Norma McCorvey (the Jane Roe of *Roe v. Wade*) apparently concern the Court no more than Holmes thought a court should care whether a farmer borrowed a churn or a plow.

---

[46] *See* Vicki C. Jackson & Mark V. Tushnet, *Comparative Constitutional Law* 607 (1999) (noting "the prevalence of 'abstract' review in Europe").

If the Supreme Court does not seem to care about the stories behind the cases it decides, why should anyone other than the parties themselves? One reason is that the stories are fascinating. Each of the fifteen chapters in this volume is its own riveting drama of conflict and uneasy resolution. But *Constitutional Law Stories* is not merely useful as entertainment. It also facilitates evaluation of the Court's performance in constitutional cases.

Let us contrast the Anglo–American common-law method of adjudication that the Supreme Court has applied in constitutional cases with an admittedly stylized version of the method employed in a continental legal system. In the latter, judges understand their role as applying highly specific, comprehensive rules set out by the lawmakers to whatever facts come before them. Because the legislature—or, in the case of constitutional adjudication, the constitution maker—has, in principle, anticipated every circumstance, the judge's task is understood as largely mechanical. By contrast, common law judges are more ambitious. They customize legal rules and principles to particular cases. Relative to continental adjudication (as an ideal type), the common law has the advantage of flexibility.[47]

Of course, flexibility comes with its own costs. First, common-law development of legal principles poses a risk of myopia and path dependence. The presentation of important questions through particular parties and fact patterns can distort the decision-making process, as when the Court fashions a general rule based on peculiarly sympathetic or unsympathetic facts or when important interests are not represented.

In addition, the flexibility of the common-law method carries with it special dangers in constitutional adjudication as practiced in the United States. State common-law rules of contract, property, and tort are default rules, defeasible by majority vote in the legislature. By contrast, constitutional decisions of the United States Supreme Court can only be changed by the Court itself or by constitutional amendment. Given the Court's reluctance to overrule its own precedents and the difficulty of obtaining the two-thirds majority in each house of Congress plus ratification by three fourths of the state legislatures necessary for constitutional amendment, the Court's constitutional decisions are insulated from popular override to a much greater extent than common law decisions of state high courts. Add to this difference the fact that federal judges are appointed for life whereas state judges frequently must stand for elec-

---

[47] *See* Michael C. Dorf, *The Supreme Court, 1997 Term—Foreword: The Limits of Socratic Deliberation*, 112 Harv. L. Rev. 4, 7 (1998) (noting that adaptability is conventionally accepted as a feature of the common law).

tion, and we have what Alexander Bickel famously called the "counter-majoritarian difficulty"[48] associated with the practice of judicial review.

Given the risks of myopia, path dependence, and usurpation, it is appropriate to set the bar high in evaluating the work of the Court. To be justified, the common-law method of constitutional interpretation should at least deliver on its promise of customizing justice in the cases the Court considers. And the best way to see whether it delivers on that promise is to evaluate the Court's performance in detail, as the essays in this book do.

Accordingly, although *Constitutional Law Stories* is not a work of constitutional theory, it is highly relevant to the central theoretical questions of American constitutional law: whether the practice of judicial review can be justified and if so, what method or methods of constitutional interpretation should the Court employ?

Some of the chapters in *Constitutional Law Stories* address these issues expressly. In Chapter 1, Michael McConnell explains that, at the time *Marbury v. Madison* was decided, the courts' ability to override Congress was less controversial than Congressional ability to limit the power of the courts; in Chapter 8, Stephen Ansolabehere and Samuel Issacharoff evaluate the Court's decision in *Baker v. Carr*[49] to enter a "political thicket"[50] by expanding the scope of justiciability to encompass challenges to legislative malapportionment; and in Chapter 14, Mark Tushnet brings us full circle, treating *City of Boerne v. Flores*[51] as "a modern version of *Marbury*," in which the issue is no longer simply the power of the Court to reach an independent judgment of constitutionality, but the extent to which the Court is the exclusive organ of constitutional interpretation.

Likewise, with respect to interpretive method: in Chapter 2, Daniel Farber sees Chief Justice Marshall's broad strokes in *McCulloch v. Maryland* as setting the terms for debates over constitutional interpretation and the nature of the federal union that persist to this day; in Chapter 3, Jim Chen explores the question of judicial deference to Congress in such matters through the story of *Wickard v. Filburn*[52] and its continuing relevance in battles over the scope of federal power; and in Chapter 5, Christopher Eisgruber notes the association of *Dred Scott v. Sandford* with both the controversial doctrine of substantive due process

---

[48] Alexander M. Bickel, *The Least Dangerous Branch: The Supreme Court at the Bar of Politics* 16 (1962).

[49] 369 U.S. 186 (1962).

[50] *Colegrove v. Green*, 328 U.S. 549, 556 (1946) (opinion of Frankfurter, J.).

[51] 521 U.S. 507 (1997).

[52] 317 U.S. 111 (1942).

and the controversial claim that the Constitution should be interpreted to accord with the original understanding of those who framed and ratified it. Indeed, in an important sense, questions of legitimacy and methodology are at play in every chapter of *Constitutional Law Stories*.

Nonetheless, it would be a mistake to view constitutional law exclusively through the lens of questions about the legitimacy and scope of judicial review. Even if most of the Constitution were not justiciable, constitutional questions would hardly vanish; they would simply be addressed to other government officials. Important debates about the Constitution have taken place in non-judicial settings. *McCulloch* is a good example: nearly all of the arguments over the constitutionality of the Bank of the United States that figured in that case had previously been explored within the Washington Administration.

In organizing *Constitutional Law Stories* around fifteen judicial decisions, I do not mean to suggest that constitutional law is made exclusively by the courts. On the contrary, the chapters that follow show how the Supreme Court's contribution to a constitutional case is frequently less important than the framing of the question by others. Those others surely include government units and officials, but they also include private lawyers and the ordinary citizens they represent. With the exception of the Thirteenth Amendment, the Constitution only addresses government actors; yet the duties it assigns these actors correlate with rights and interests of real people. Ultimately, the point of *Constitutional Law Stories*—if there can be anything so reductionist as a single point conveyed by a book that is the joint product of nineteen authors of diverse viewpoints—is to put the "people," as individuals, back in the collectivity the Constitution names as "We the People."

*

1

Michael W. McConnell

The Story of *Marbury v. Madison*: Making Defeat Look Like Victory

One of the closest and most acrimonious elections in American history was followed by one of the most hotly debated constitutional decisions. Disputes over who won the election lasted months beyond Election Day. Although the two leading candidates generally behaved themselves with moderation and civility (and neither was an inspiring public speaker), their partisan supporters inflamed public opinion with charges of political and personal malfeasance. Each party viewed the other not as a legitimate democratic alternative, but as a deep-dyed danger to the Constitution. One party was accused of favoring the rich, of aggrandizing executive power at the expense of Congress, of fighting an illegal war unauthorized by Congress, of exaggerating national security concerns, of trampling freedom of speech and press, and of invading the rights of aliens in the interest of protecting the incumbent from dissent. The other party was accused of demagoguery, of "anarchy" and "sedition," of weakening America's military readiness, of lack of respect for religious and traditional constitutional values, of hostility to commerce and industry, and of dangerous naiveté—if not outright enthusiasm—about the worldwide revolution that had already brought terror to one major nation and could spread disorder to our own.

Judicial appointments and philosophy were a major issue in the campaign. The incumbent President and his predecessor had named federal judges who uniformly shared their conservative philosophy. The challenger criticized those judges for favoring creditors and large landowners and supporting the prosecution of newspaper editors and other critics of the administration. Some judges appointed by the incumbent asserted the authority of the federal courts to convict citizens for "crimes" not set forth in statutes passed by Congress. The challenger's party denounced the undemocratic implications of a life-tenured federal judiciary, insulated from democratic accountability and armed with the powers to make law and to override the popular will.

Early election returns produced a virtual tie in electoral votes, with the nation sharply split along regional lines. The result hinged on the outcome in one southern state, where it took weeks for authorities to determine who won. On December 12, the result was announced: the Republican candidate had been elected.

But that was not the end of the matter. Under the peculiar voting rules of that era, electors each would cast two votes for President with the leading candidate elected President and the runner-up Vice President. Because all the Republican electors cast their ballots for both the Republican candidates, Thomas Jefferson was tied with his running mate, Aaron Burr of New York. That threw the election into the lame duck House of Representatives, which was dominated by the Federalist Party of John Adams and Alexander Hamilton. That created a unique opportunity for a deal: Burr would be selected President, in defiance of the popular will, and he would return the favor by supporting the Federalists. (To their credit, neither Adams nor Hamilton supported the scheme.) For three months, the House was deadlocked. Federalist-dominated delegations from six states cast their ballots for Burr, Jefferson commanded eight state delegations, and two were split. It was as close as the nation would ever come to a coup, achieved in strict conformity to the forms of the Constitution. No wonder Jefferson denounced this plan as a usurpation, or that Virginia Governor James Monroe threatened to use the state militia to prevent Burr's ascension to the Presidency.

In the midst of this regime crisis, President Adams and the defeated Federalists sought to protect the nation from the radical measures of their successors by securing a powerful and independent judicial branch, staffed by life-tenured judges loyal to Federalist principles.[1]

Adams' opportunity to shape the courts received a boost when Oliver Ellsworth, the third Chief Justice of the United States, resigned, and Adams' first choice for his replacement, John Jay, declined the position. The President now turned to his most trusted cabinet officer, forty-five-year-old John Marshall of Virginia. More than any other person, Marshall was to shape the character of the federal judiciary. Though he had no prior judicial experience, Marshall had served with distinction

---

[1] Sources discussing the Election of 1800 include Richard E. Ellis, *The Jeffersonian Crisis: Courts and Politics in the Young Republic* (1971); James F. Simon, *What Kind of Nation?: Thomas Jefferson, John Marshall, and the Epic Struggle to Create a United States* (2002); Frank Van der Linden, *Turning Point: Jefferson's Battle for the Presidency* (2002).

as a soldier in the Revolution; as a delegate to the Virginia ratifying convention; as a member of the House of Representatives, where he was leader of the moderate wing of the Federalist Party; as envoy to France during the XYZ Affair; and as Secretary of State, in which position he was chief architect of Adams' successful policy of reconciliation with France. Marshall was an uncommonly able lawyer with an affable disposition that helped him to build coalitions and disarm his critics. Ominously, however, one of the few people with whom Marshall could not get along was his distant cousin, Thomas Jefferson, who had just defeated Adams for the presidency.[2]

Adams nominated Marshall as Chief Justice on January 20, 1801. After a one-week delay by high Federalist critics, Marshall was confirmed. In what now seems a bizarre mixture of roles, however, Marshall continued to serve as Acting Secretary of State for the remaining five weeks of Adams' presidency. In that capacity, he was to make a mistake, which precipitated the most famous constitutional decision of his career.

The next big move in President Adams' strategy to shore up the judiciary occurred precisely as the Jefferson–Burr contest reached its climax. On February 13, the Federalist Congress passed and Adams signed the Judiciary Act of 1801. The Act replaced an antiquated and inefficient federal judicial structure with a new system of circuit courts and extended the scope of federal jurisdiction. No longer would Supreme Court Justices have to endure the discomforts and hazards of riding circuit, with appeals from their circuit court decisions going to their own Court. That system had proven slow, inefficient, and arguably unfair. In its place, there would be six new circuit courts with sixteen new judges. Because these courts were capable of hearing cases regularly and conveniently throughout the nation, they enhanced the efficiency, fairness, and authority of the federal courts—and by the same token, their ability to compete with the state court system for prestige and authority.

Enactment of the Judiciary Act could be understood as good government reform, but the rushed circumstances of its passage in the lame duck Congress and the immediate nomination and rapid confirmation of sixteen new life-tenured judges, all of them staunch Federalists, gave the Judiciary Act a partisan odor. With Jeffersonians soon to be in control of both the executive and legislative branches, Federalists believed that preservation of the checks and balances of constitutional government required that the judiciary be in other hands: their own. To add insult to injury, the statute reduced the size of the Supreme Court as of the next vacancy, thus denying the new president (whoever it would be, Jefferson or Burr) his first appointment. Jefferson was quick to perceive the partisan implications: "[the Federalists] have retired into the Judiciary

---

[2] *See generally* Jean Edward Smith, *John Marshall: Definer of a Nation* (1996); R. Kent Newmyer, *John Marshall and the Heroic Age of the Supreme Court* (2001).

as a stronghold . . . and from that battery all the works of Republicanism are to be beaten down and erased."[3]

Four days after passage of the Judiciary Act, the Burr machinations came to an end. On the thirty-sixth presidential ballot, enough Federalist representatives cast blank ballots to enable the selection of Thomas Jefferson as the third President of the United States.

By this time, Adams's major restructuring of the federal judiciary was complete. But one relatively minor part of the strategy was yet to be put in place. On Friday, February 27, a week before his presidency was to end, Congress passed and Adams signed the Organic Act for the District of Columbia. This Act created the position of justice of the peace in the new District of Columbia. It should not be assumed that these were petty offices. The justices of the peace were the principal arm of local government in the two counties of the District, thus combining executive, judicial, legislative, and administrative power. Above all, they were responsible for maintaining public order. No one observing recent events in Paris could think that maintenance of public order in the national capital lacked political significance. The justices of the peace were to serve for five-year terms, conveniently extending just beyond the term of the new president.

Over the weekend, Adams collected names of promising appointees. He relied particularly on the recommendations of Benjamin Stoddert, his Secretary of the Navy and a leader of the moderate Federalists of Maryland, for the names of justices of the peace to serve in Washington County, which was carved out of Stoddert's state, and on Levan Powell, Federalist congressman from Virginia, for Alexandria County nominations. On Monday, he submitted forty-two names to the Senate. Contrary to some historians, the justice of the peace nominees were a bipartisan mix: six of Adams' twenty-three nominees in Washington County were Republicans. Among the nominees were such distinguished figures as six-term Maryland governor Thomas Sim Lee; former Senator Tristam Dalton; outgoing Secretary of the Navy Benjamin Stoddert himself; former Georgetown Mayor and U.S. Representative Uriah Forest; and Architect of the Capitol, William Thornton. Best known to posterity, however, is a 38–year-old Georgetown businessman who never ran for office: William Marbury.[4]

Marbury was an experienced public official as well as a self-made, successful banker and investor. He had served as Agent of the State of

---

[3] Letter from Thomas Jefferson to John Dickinson, Dec. 19, 1801, in 10 *The Writings of Thomas Jefferson* 302, 302 (Albert E. Bergh ed., 1907) [hereinafter "Writings of Jefferson"].

[4] Information in this and the following paragraph comes from David F. Forte, *Marbury's Travail: Federalist Politics and William Marbury's Appointment as Justice of the*

Maryland, the state's highest unelected official, responsible for organizing and collecting the debts of the state. During the Whisky Rebellion, he led the Annapolis militia to put down an uprising in western Maryland. Later, he was a principal in the Potomac Company, headed by George Washington, a company founded to build a canal linking the Potomac to the Ohio River. In 1798, Marbury moved from Annapolis to Georgetown, where he had been elected Director of the Bank of Columbia and hired by Stoddert as agent to the Washington Navy Yard, responsible for finance and procurement. Marbury's political loyalties are revealed in the name he chose for his youngest son: Alexander Hamilton Marbury. They are also evident in newspaper reports of his behavior the night Jefferson was proclaimed President-elect. Republican demonstrators marched through Georgetown compelling citizens to illuminate their houses to celebrate the event. Even some prominent Federalists succumbed to the pressure. The *Washington Gazette* reported, however, that Marbury defied the demonstrators, leaving his residence dark, and "the mob left him imprecating vengeance."[5]

By the close of business on Tuesday, March 3, 1801, the day before Jefferson was to take office, Adams' nominees to the position of justice of the peace were confirmed by the Senate—so quickly that some of them had not been informed of their nomination and declined to serve. Adams remained hard at work until about 9:00 p.m., signing commissions. He went to bed early, and arose at 4:00 a.m. to depart the capital without having to witness the awful event of Jefferson's inauguration. As Adams signed the papers, aides transported them to the Department of State, where the Acting Secretary of State—John Marshall himself—affixed the Great Seal.

Precisely what happened to the commissions is not clear. Some were delivered. Marshall's younger brother James—himself a newly commissioned Circuit Judge for the District of Columbia—delivered a few to appointees in Alexandria, where there were concerns about the possibility of disruptive political celebrations. Other commissions lay undelivered. Later, John Marshall explained that he was short-handed that night because two State Department aides were assisting the President. Besides, he considered delivery legally inconsequential, once the commissions had been signed and sealed.[6] That was a fateful error.

Peace, 45 Cath. U. L. Rev. 349 (1996). *See also* John A. Garraty, *The Case of the Missing Commissions*, in *Quarrels That Have Shaped the Constitution* (John A. Garraty ed., 1962).

[5] See Forte, supra note 4, at 397 n.253 (quoting Washington Gazette, Feb. 25, 1801) (in turn quoting a letter dated Feb. 18, 1801).

[6] Letter from John Marshall to James Marshall, Mar. 18, 1801, in 6 *The Papers of John Marshall* 90 (Charles F. Hobson & Fredrika J. Teute eds., 1990) [hereinafter "Marshall Papers"].

When Jefferson took office the next day, a sheaf of commissions was discovered in the offices of the Department of State. Among the commissions was that of William Marbury. Interestingly, James Madison, whose name graces Marbury's famous constitutional case, was still in Virginia, settling the estate of his father, who had died the week before. He did not take office until May.[7] Jefferson ordered his Acting Secretary of State, Attorney General Levi Lincoln, to withhold the undelivered commissions. It is likely that Jefferson had them destroyed. He also reduced the number of justices of the peace (as the statute allowed) and nominated Republicans in place of many of Adams' appointees, thus removing almost all the staunch Federalists from the position.

These actions attracted little attention at the time. In his inaugural address, Jefferson emphasized reconciliation between the parties—"We are all Republicans: we are all Federalists"—and the justices of the peace of the District of Columbia were small potatoes. Not until nine months later did Federalist strategists make an issue in court of Jefferson's disposition of the commissions.

Adams' appointees to the federal courts soon served notice that judicial independence would be a thorn in the side of the new administration. In *Wilson v. Mason*,[8] Marshall's first constitutional decision, the Supreme Court made clear that it would be the ultimate authority in land disputes between local settlers and nonresident land companies. This was one of the flashpoints in the Jeffersonian–Federalist war over the judiciary because small farmers and settlers (mostly Jeffersonians) preferred the more politically accountable state courts to the distant and more legalistic federal courts. In *The Schooner Betsy*,[9] the Court staked its claim to authority in matters of foreign affairs. In both cases, Marshall used his characteristic tactic (evident later in *Marbury v. Madison*[10]) of avoiding confrontation by coupling the assertion of authority, which the Jeffersonians feared, with a narrow result, which the Jeffersonians desired.

Perhaps more threatening was the decision of the new Circuit Court for the District of Columbia, by party-line vote, to order the prosecutor to initiate a libel prosecution against the editor of the Republican *National Intelligencer*, based solely on the common law. The editor had published a letter defending Jefferson and criticizing the courts. The judges voting for the order were James Marshall, the younger brother of the Chief Justice, and Abigail Adams's nephew, William Cranch. The

---

[7] *See* Simon, *supra* note 1, at 174.

[8] 5 U.S. (1 Cranch) 45 (1801).

[9] *Murray v. Schooner Charming Betsy*, 6 U.S. (2 Cranch) 64 (1804).

[10] 5 U.S. (1 Cranch) 137 (1803).

legal doctrine on which they based the prosecution—federal common law—implied that the federal courts could exert power even without authorization by Congress.[11] Although the Republican District Attorney declined to prosecute the case,[12] the episode made clear that the Federalists were prepared to use the circuit courts to their advantage.

Republican stalwarts—to some extent supported by their new President—were plotting a counter-strategy to undo the edifice of the Federalist judiciary. In June, Jefferson received a letter from his congressional ally, William Branch Giles:

> What concerns us most is the situation of the Judiciary as now organized. It is constantly asserted that the Revolution is incomplete, as long as that strong fortress is in possession of the enemy; and it is surely a most singular circumstance that the public sentiment should have forced itself into the Legislative and Executive Department, and that the Judiciary should not only not acknowledge its influence, but should pride itself in resisting its will, under the misapplied idea of "independence."[13]

Republicans proposed to attack judicial life tenure by removing the new circuit judges from office by statute and by threatening sitting judges with impeachment. They proposed to repeal the Judiciary Act of 1801 and thus to return to the weak and inefficient structure of the pre–1801 judiciary. They denied the authority of federal judges to act on the basis of common law in the absence of statutes, especially in criminal cases. Some of them even denied the power of the judiciary to review the decisions of Congress or the executive on constitutional or (in the case of the executive) other legal grounds.

The disagreement over the judiciary went to the heart of American constitutionalism. Was the Constitution, as the Republicans believed, principally an instrument of popular government, in which the will of the people should control even the question of constitutional meaning? Or was the Constitution, as the Federalists believed, principally an instrument of the rule of law, to be enforced by independent judges even in the face of popular opposition?

In his first annual message to Congress, on December 8, 1801, Jefferson laid down the gauntlet: "The Judiciary system of the United States, and especially that portion of it recently erected, will of course,

---

[11] See Simon, *supra* note 1, at 150.

[12] See 1 Charles Warren, *The Supreme Court in United States History 1789–1835* (Fred B. Rothman ed., 1987) (1926).

[13] Letter from William Branch Giles to Thomas Jefferson, June 1, 1801, quoted in Ellis, *supra* note 1, at 20–21.

present itself to the contemplation of Congress."[14] Republicans moved quickly to repeal the Judiciary Act of 1801. Debate in the Senate occupied the entire month of January 1802. It was one of the most heated constitutional debates in our history and the one most clearly directed to the constitutional role of the federal courts. Interestingly, it was the first Senate debate to be transcribed and published—and the contract to do so was given to the same editor threatened with libel prosecution by Judges Marshall and Cranch.

Shortly after Jefferson's message, on December 16, 1801, Charles Lee, a Virginia Federalist who had served as Attorney General under both Washington and Adams, appeared in John Marshall's Supreme Court to request a writ of mandamus to compel the Secretary of State, Madison, to deliver a copy of his commission to Marbury and three other Adams appointees to justice of the peace: Dennis Ramsay, William Harper, and Robert Townshend Hooe. Jefferson's Attorney General, Levi Lincoln, who happened to be in court, stated that he had no instructions regarding the case. After consulting with his colleagues, Marshall set the case for argument in the next Term of Court. No one could have expected this minor matter would make constitutional history. At the time, the debate over repeal of the Judiciary Act of 1801 commanded center stage.[15]

Federalists in Congress argued that the repeal would be unconstitutional, essentially on two grounds. First, they argued that the requirement of circuit riding by Supreme Court Justices in ordinary cases violated the provision of Article III granting the Supreme Court appellate jurisdiction in most cases and original jurisdiction in only a few, narrowly defined areas. *Hayburn's Case*[16] had already established that it was unconstitutional for Congress to assign the Court duties other than those prescribed by Article III, and Congress had acquiesced in that judgment. This could be seen as a variant on that principle. Second, Federalists argued that removal of the newly appointed circuit judges would violate the constitutional provision of life tenure for Article III judges. This, they stressed, was a direct threat to the principle of an independent judiciary. "What will be the effect of the desired repeal?" asked constitutional framer Gouverneur Morris, now Senator from New York. "Will it not be a declaration to the remaining judges that they hold their offices subject to your will and pleasure? And what will be the result of this? It will be, that the check established by the Constitution,

---

[14] Thomas Jefferson, Message to Congress, in 9 *Works of Thomas Jefferson* 321, 340 (Paul L. Ford ed., 1904).

[15] Much of the following account of the debate is based on James M. O'Fallon, *Marbury*, 44 Stan. L. Rev. 219 (1992).

[16] 2 U.S. (2 Dall) 408 (1792).

wished for by the people, and necessary in every contemplation of common sense, is destroyed."[17]

After a month of debate, the Senate approved the Repeal Act by a vote of 16–15 over the constitutional objections of the Federalists. The House followed suit by a vote of 59–32. Jefferson signed the bill in early March. Almost immediately, eleven of the judges who had lost their jobs petitioned Congress for redress—a reminder of the older view that Congress was the first line of defense for vindication of constitutional principles. They were rebuffed, quickly in the House and by a party line vote in the Senate.

Attention now turned to the judiciary and particularly to the Supreme Court. In cases in the 1790s, the Court had shown itself willing to address the constitutionality of Acts of Congress. Because the Judiciary Act repeal affected the judiciary itself, the matter fell within even the narrowest conception of judicial review, the conception that each branch could protect its own constitutional powers from the assaults of the other branches. The Supreme Court Justices could respond to the Repeal Act either by refusing to ride circuit or by holding that the removal of the new circuit judges had been unconstitutional.

In the resolution of these great issues, the *Marbury* litigation was a sideshow. Few people cared whether Adams' appointees were seated as justices of the peace. By the time the case was argued, Congress had stripped the office of much of its power and pay, and two of the five years of the term had already passed. It seems unlikely that, by this point, even the four petitioners cared much about the job. The great question of the day was whether the judiciary would defy the popular will and strike down the Judiciary Act repeal. Presumably to forestall such a decision, Congress passed another bill canceling the Supreme Court's June Term, thus postponing the next meeting of the Court for more than a year, to the second Monday of February 1803. "Are the gentlemen afraid of the judges?" asked Delaware Federalist James Bayard, a close friend of Marshall. "Are the gentlemen afraid that they will pronounce the repealing law void?"[18]

Whether Congress was afraid of the Judges, Republican members of Congress hoped to make the Judges afraid of the Congress. "If the Supreme Court shall arrogate this power to themselves, and declare our law to be unconstitutional," warned John Nicholas of Virginia, "it will then behoove us to act. Our duty is defined."[19] By postponing the next Term of the Supreme Court, Congress forced each of the Justices to decide, individually, whether to comply with the new law and return to

---

[17] 11 Annals of Cong. 38 (1802) (speech of Gov. Morris).

[18] Quoted in Simon, *supra* note 1, at 168.

[19] 12 Annals of Cong. 438 (1802).

circuit duty. This exposed each Justice, individually, to the wrath of Congress if he did not.

To drive home the point, the Jeffersonians opened a second front in their campaign against an independent and powerful judiciary. The week before the Supreme Court resumed its duties in February 1803, Republican House leaders commenced impeachment proceedings against Judge John Pickering of New Hampshire. Pickering was an inspired choice for the first judicial impeachment proceeding. He had committed no "high crime or misdemeanor." But he was a drunk and arguably insane, thus an ideal test case for the proposition that Congress could use the impeachment club in cases beyond the seemingly strict language of the Impeachment Clause. After convicting Judge Pickering, the Jeffersonians were expected to go after a bigger and more significant target, probably Supreme Court Justice Samuel Chase, the most uncompromising Federalist on the High Court. Between dismissing the circuit judges and mounting a credible threat of impeachment of the Supreme Court Justices, the Jeffersonians hoped to deflate the judiciary's arrogant pretensions to independence from the will of the people.

The Justices got the message. Marshall wrote a letter to each of his colleagues soliciting their views on the circuit-riding question. In his letter, he stressed that

> This is not a subject to be lightly resolved on. The consequences of refusing to carry the law into effect may be very serious. For myself personally I disregard them, and so I am persuaded does every other Gentleman on the bench when put in competition with what he thinks his duty. But the conviction of duty ought to be very strong before the measure is resolved on.[20]

Even Chase, the Court's most combative Federalist, commented that "[t]he burthen of deciding so momentous a question, under the present circumstances of our country, would be very great on all the Judges assembled, but an individual Judge, declining to take a Circuit, must sink under it."[21] By the time the Court met as a body, each of the Justices had ridden circuit, and four of them, including Marshall, had ruled against the claim that removal of the circuit judges by the Repeal Act had been unconstitutional. Far from reflecting a confident and assertive judiciary, therefore, *Marbury* must be understood as the product of a defeated and demoralized Court.

Marbury has been taught to generations of law students as establishing the authority of the courts to decline to enforce a statute they

---

[20] Letter from John Marshall to William Paterson, Apr. 19, 1802, in 6 *Marshall Papers* 108, 109.

[21] Letter from Samuel Chase to John Marshall, Apr. 24, 1802, in 6 *Marshall Papers* 109, 116.

deem to be unconstitutional. At the time, however, that proposition was not particularly controversial. After the Anti-federalist "Brutus" issued his prescient warnings about the anti-democratic implications of constitutional judicial review during the fight over ratification,[22] the proposition that courts could disregard unconstitutional legislation became more or less conventional wisdom during the 1790s.[23] Although not reflected in the text of Article III—an omission that some historians attribute to uncertainty and disagreement—debate at the Constitutional Convention and again in the First Congress over the Bill of Rights presupposed the authority of the courts to engage in some form of judicial review. Both Madison and Jefferson spoke in favor of judicial review during the early years. Indeed, Jeffersonians were disappointed that the courts were not more inclined, during the 1790s, to invalidate legislation they thought unconstitutional, such as the carriage tax or the Alien and Sedition Acts. When they were out of power, judicial review appeared to be a useful check. Only when the Jeffersonians assumed control over the legislative and executive branches and saw their political rivals in control of the judiciary did they entertain serious reservations about judicial review.

The scope of judicial authority to review the constitutionality of Acts of Congress surfaced repeatedly during the debate over the Repeal Act. Federalists tended to take an expansive view of that authority. According to them, judicial review is an essential part of the structure of the Constitution, and the courts' judgments are final. The judges "are intended to stand between the Legislature and the Constitution, between the Government and the people; they are intended to check the Legislature. Should the Legislature even surmount the barrier of the Constitution, it is the duty of the judges to repel it back within the bounds which limit its power," according to a North Carolina Federalist.[24] Gouverneur Morris stated that "[t]he decision of the Supreme Court is, and, of necessity, must be final. This, Sir, is the principle, and the source of the right for which we contend."[25]

During the Repeal Act debates, most Jeffersonians hewed to a moderate middle. Under this view, judicial review was an implication of the principle that each department of government had authority to make independent constitutional judgments in the course of discharging its

---

[22] Brutus, Essay XV, in 2 *The Complete Anti–Federalist* 437–42 (Herbert Storing ed., 1981).

[23] Much of the following is based on David E. Engdahl, *John Marshall's "Jeffersonian" Concept of Judicial Review*, 42 Duke L.J. 279 (1992), and O'Fallon, *supra* note 15.

[24] 11 Annals of Cong. 859 (1802) (speech by Rep. William Hill).

[25] Id. at 180 (speech by Sen. Gov. Morris).

own duties. Within the confines of a case or controversy, the courts had authority to determine which of two competing laws applicable to the case—the statute or an inconsistent constitutional provision—controlled the outcome. But this did not imply any special or final, let alone exclusive, power of "judicial" review. The other branches faced similar issues of legal and constitutional interpretation in the course of performing their duties. The Constitution was final and authoritative, but its meaning was to be determined by each branch within its own scope of authority, and ultimately by the people. This has become known as "departmentalism" or "co-ordinate review." A few years after *Marbury*, Jefferson put it this way:

> The Constitution intended that the three great branches of the government should be co-ordinate, and independent of each other. As to acts, therefore, which are to be done by either, it has given no control to another branch. . . . Where different branches have to act in their respective lines, finally and without appeal, under any law, they may give to it different and opposite constructions.[26]

Madison put it this way:

> I suppose an exposition of the Constitution may come with as much propriety from the Legislature, as any other department of the Government. . . . I acknowledge, in the ordinary course of Government, that the exposition of the laws and constitution devolves upon the Judiciary. But, I beg to know, upon what principle it can be contended, that any one department draws from the constitution greater powers than another, in marking out the limits of the powers of the several departments? . . . I do not see that any one of these independent departments has more right than another to declare their sentiments on that point.[27]

According to Jeffersonians, coordinate review gave triple security to individual rights. Any denial of life, liberty, or property required first that the legislative branch consider the limitation constitutional, second that the executive bring charges (which it would not do if the restriction were not constitutional), and third that the court—meaning both judge and jury—deem it constitutional. No one branch had authority to determine constitutionality for all. In 1820, Jefferson declared it "a very dangerous doctrine indeed" that judges would be deemed "the ultimate arbiters of all constitutional questions."[28]

---

[26] Letter from Thomas Jefferson to George Hay, June 2, 1807, in 11 *Writings of Jefferson* 213, 213–14.

[27] 1 Annals of Cong. 479, 520 (Joseph Gales ed., 1789) (speeches by Rep. James Madison).

[28] Letter from Thomas Jefferson to William C. Jarvis, Sep. 28, 1820, in 15 *Writings of Jefferson* 276, 277.

For the most part, Republicans in Congress parroted the Jeffersonian line on judicial review. A Maryland Republican, for example, declared that "judges ought to be the guardians of the Constitution, so far as questions were constitutionally submitted to them," but that the legislature, executive, and judiciary, each were "severally the guardians of the Constitution, so far as they were called on in their several departments to act." He added that he had "not supposed the judges were intended to decide questions not judicially submitted to them, or to lead the public mind in Legislative or Executive questions."[29]

Arch–Jeffersonian John Breckinridge of Kentucky was the first member of Congress to deny the power of courts to refuse to enforce an Act of Congress they deemed unconstitutional. The legislature, he said, "have the exclusive right to interpret the Constitution, in what regards the law-making power, and the judges are bound to execute the laws they make."[30] This was a minority view, even among Republicans. A Massachusetts Republican, for example, responded to Breckinridge:

> However I may differ in opinion from some with whom I have the honor generally to agree, I may not deny, but must frankly acknowledge the right of judicial officers of every grade to judge for themselves of the constitutionality of every statute on which they are called to act in their respective spheres. This is not only their right, but it is their indispensable duty thus to do. Nor is this the exclusive right and indispensable duty of the Judiciary department. It is equally the inherent and the indispensable duty of every officer, and I believe I may add, of every citizen of the United States.[31]

Federalists shrewdly responded that without judicial review, state governments would be at the mercy of the national Congress, and there would be no effectual protection against "consolidated [g]overnment."[32] This was a reminder that Jeffersonians, no less than Federalists, sought judicial protection when their cherished principles did not prevail in the political process.

The combination of broad judicial review with federal common law was particularly unsettling to Jeffersonian principles of popular sovereignty. Common law was judicial governance in the absence of legislation; judicial review was judicial governance in defiance of legislation. A life-tenured, unelected judiciary armed with both powers was dangerously close to an aristocracy. One Republican congressman worried:

---

[29] 11 Annals of Cong. 115 (1802) (speech by Sen. Robert Wright).

[30] *Id.* at 179 (speech by Sen. John Breckinridge).

[31] *Id.* at 982 (speech by Rep. John Bacon).

[32] *Id.* at 180 (speech by Sen. Gov. Morris).

Give the Judiciary this check upon the Legislature; allow them the power to declare your laws null and void; allow the common law, a system extending to all persons and all things, to be attached to the Constitution, as I understand it is contended; and in vain have the people placed you upon this floor to legislate. . . .[33]

From the vantage point of 200 years, it seems obvious that *Marbury* must be connected to this debate. But counsel's argument in *Marbury* had nothing to do with judicial review of legislation, and the holding of *Marbury* regarding judicial review was nothing out of the ordinary. It more or less reflected the consensus of Federalists and moderate Republicans. The real novelty of *Marbury* was its assertion of authority to issue affirmative commands to the executive.[34] Marshall's order to show cause implied the power of the courts to direct the President regarding his conduct of the executive office. DeWitt Clinton of New York accurately described the case at the time as "involving a right [of the Supreme Court] to control the Executive."[35] The Constitution charges the President—not the courts—with the duty to "take Care that the laws be faithfully executed."[36] Although the courts were a check against unconstitutional executive action, such as an unlawful prosecution or seizure of property, it was not obvious that the courts could order an executive officer to take an action, such as providing William Marbury with a copy of his commission. Under Jefferson's theory that each branch has the duty to decide constitutional and legal questions that fall within its own sphere of authority, the Court was overstepping its bounds if it told the President how to conduct his Article Two, Section Three power of commissioning officers of the United States.

Jefferson and Madison expressed their view of the illegitimacy of the proceeding in the most eloquent possible way. They did not bother to show up. Madison, the nominal defendant, went unrepresented: a dramatic way of showing that the Administration did not recognize the Court's jurisdiction over a cabinet officer in the exercise of his executive responsibilities.

Marbury was scheduled for trial on February 9, 1803. Also on the Court's docket was the far more important case, *Stuart v. Laird,*[37] a direct challenge to the constitutionality of the Repeal Act. *Marbury* did not seem of much consequence.

---

[33] *Id.* at 552–53 (speech by Rep. Thompson).

[34] *See* Michael J. Klarman, *How Great Were the "Great" Marshall Court Decisions?*, 87 Va. L. Rev. 1111, 1114–17 (2001).

[35] 12 Annals of Cong. 48 (1802) (speech by Sen. DeWitt Clinton).

[36] US Const. art. 2, § 3.

[37] 5 U.S. (1 Cranch) 299 (1803).

There ensued one of the oddest proceedings in the history of American litigation.[38] Only four of the six Justices attended the entire proceeding. The Court met in a cramped, sparsely furnished committee room in the Capitol, and later adjourned to Stelle's Hotel for the convenience of the ailing Justice Chase. The first order of business in the case was to establish that Marbury, Ramsay, Harper, and Hooe had been appointed and commissioned, but that the commissions had not been delivered. This was surprisingly difficult to prove. The Republican-dominated Senate had refused to provide them with an official record of their nomination and confirmation, and the State Department declined to provide the relevant documents. But what made the proceeding exceptionally odd was that the person most intimately acquainted with the facts—the person who would have been the best witness, the person responsible for the fiasco—was sitting in the presiding chair as Chief Justice. The nominal defendant, Madison, had nothing to do with the affair. Jefferson's Acting Secretary of State on the morning in question, Levi Lincoln, was now Attorney General. Everyone in court knew exactly what had happened, but no one could, or would, provide the formal evidence.

Charles Lee first called the two State Department clerks who had assisted with the commissions. After initially refusing to testify, the clerks coyly claimed not to know what had happened to the petitioners' commissions. Lee then called Levi Lincoln to the stand. Lincoln was reluctant to testify. He invoked the privilege against self-incrimination. (Did he fear that destruction of the commissions was a criminal offense?) More to the point, he warned that certain persons he "highly respect-ed"—presumably Jefferson and Madison—thought it improper for a cabinet secretary to be haled into court to testify "to facts which came to his knowledge officially." If either side had pressed the point, *Marbury* might have become a showdown over the unsettled question of executive privilege, anticipating Aaron Burr's treason trial[39] and the Nixon tapes case.[40] But Lee and Lincoln came to an accommodation. Lincoln agreed to consider written questions.

The next day, Lincoln answered three of the four questions Lee propounded. He stated that he had seen "a considerable number" of completed commissions in the State Department office the morning of March 4, but could not identify whether the petitioners' commissions were among them. He stated that he had not given the commissions to Madison, his successor. Chief Justice Marshall discreetly permitted Lin-

---

[38] The following description of the proceedings is primarily derived from Smith, *supra* note 2; Simon, *supra* note 1, and William Cranch's U.S. Reports.

[39] *United States v. Burr*, 25 F. Cas. 30 (No. 14,692–D) (C.C.D. Va. 1807).

[40] *United States v. Nixon*, 418 U.S. 683 (1974).

coln to decline to tell what actually happened to them. Based on affidavits from James Marshall and another clerk, however, Lee declared that he had "proved the existence of the commissions."

Lee then argued his legal points. Deliberately tailoring his argument to the Repeal Act controversy, Lee emphasized the theme of judicial independence. From the Federalists' perspective, Jefferson's refusal to allow Marbury to serve his five-year term as justice of the peace presented the same issue, in miniature, as the Repeal Act's displacement of life-tenured circuit judges. In both cases, the Administration was willing to defy the law in order to wrest control over the institutions of justice. Moreover, although Lee did not argue the point, the constitutional issue on which *Marbury* ultimately was decided was essentially the same as that posed by the return to circuit riding: whether it was constitutional for Congress to give Supreme Court Justices original jurisdiction beyond that authorized by Article III.

The Court then retired to consider its decision. The options did not appear propitious. If the Court decided in favor of Marbury, it was almost certain that Jefferson would refuse to comply. That would establish a precedent that the courts have no authority over the President. Moreover, it seemed likely that Congress would take this act of judicial impudence as an occasion for impeachment proceedings. The independent judiciary would be proven feckless, and then destroyed. On the other hand, if the Court decided against Marbury, it would reveal itself a paper tiger. Either way, Jefferson would emerge victorious.

Marshall's solution to this dilemma was strategically brilliant, even if not quite sound from a strictly legal point of view. He held, first, that Marbury was entitled to his commission. This was probably not correct. Justices of the peace were not Article III officers and did not have life tenure. The statute gave the president the right to determine the number of justices of the peace, and Jefferson had exercised that power by reducing the number from forty-three to thirty. Moreover, the Supreme Court was to hold more than 100 years later, all officers of the federal government exercising executive authority serve at the will of the president.[41] The statutory five year term of office for the justices of the peace was inconsistent with this, since it had the effect of requiring the President to submit new nominees (or reappoint old ones) every five years.

Marshall held, second, that Marbury was entitled to the writ of mandamus as a remedy for deprivation of his office. In modern constitutional pedagogy, this is generally passed over as an inconsequential feature of the opinion, but it may have been the most momentous and most questionable part. The writ of mandamus was available only for the

---

[41] *See Myers v. United States*, 272 U.S. 52, 163–64 (1926).

compulsion of "ministerial" duties. Was it merely "ministerial" for the Secretary of State to defy a direct order of the President, with regard to a matter (commissioning officers of the United States) committed to the President by Article II? Was it "ministerial" to commission a person to a job that was either eliminated or already filled? Moreover, even aside from these details, it was a significant step to hold that the courts have authority to issue affirmative orders to the executive. One might think the relations between the courts and the two other branches are symmetrical. While the courts have authority to refuse to give effect to Acts of Congress deemed unconstitutional, they have never been thought to have power to require the legislative branch to act—"ministerially" or otherwise. Why is the executive different? Jefferson believed that each branch of government was responsible for interpreting the law relevant to its own operations, and specifically that the President was charged with enforcement of the law within the executive branch. A few years after *Marbury*, Jefferson's Attorney General Caesar Rodney issued an opinion declaring that federal courts do not have authority to issue writs of mandamus to executive officers:

> Writs of this kind, if made applicable to officers indiscriminately, and acts purely ministerial, and executive in their nature, would necessarily have the effect of transferring the powers vested in one department to another department. If, in a case like the present, where the law vests a duty and a discretion in an executive officer, a court can not only administer redress against the misuse of the authority, but can previously direct the use to be made of it, it would seem that under the name of a judicial power, an executive function is necessarily assumed, and that part of the constitution perhaps defeated, which makes it the duty of the president to take care, that the laws be faithfully executed.[42]

Thus, the Jefferson Administration formally declared its intention not to comply with this holding of the Court. It was not until the 1840s that the Court would again assert the power to direct an executive officer to do his duty, and not until passage of the Administrative Procedure Act that this became routine.

Third, Marshall declared that it was unconstitutional for Congress to assign the mandamus power, a species of original jurisdiction, to the Supreme Court. This, too, was problematic. Textually, the holding was based on a strained reading of the Exceptions Clause of Article III, which appears to permit Congress to "make exceptions" to the original allocation of jurisdiction between original and appellate jurisdiction. Moreover, the power of the Court to issue writs of mandamus as a matter of

---

[42] Report of the Attorney General of the United States, July 15, 1808, in *Aurora General Advertiser*, No. 5464, at 2–3 (Aug. 9, 1808) (William J. Duane & Co., pub.).

original jurisdiction was imparted by the First Congress and had been exercised on several occasions during the 1790s. It is hard to square the holding that this was unconstitutional with the Court's unanimous holding, a week later, that establishment by the First Congress and subsequent acquiescence by the Court had legitimized the practice of circuit riding. Perhaps this was the Court's subtle way of suggesting that its latter holding was a bow to pressure rather than a decision of principle.

Marshall ended the opinion with the ringing defense of judicial review for which it is famous:

> It is emphatically the province and duty of the judicial department to say what the law is. Those who apply the rule to particular cases must of necessity expound and interpret that rule. If two laws conflict with each other, the courts must decide on the operation of each. So if a law be in opposition to the constitution; if both the law and the constitution apply to a particular case, so that the court must either decide that case conformably to the law, disregarding the constitution; or conformably to the constitution, disregarding the law; the court must determine which of these conflicting rules governs the case.[43]

None of this went beyond the well-accepted middle ground. Marshall did not assert the exclusive power of courts to interpret the Constitution, or even the finality of their decisions, outside of the "particular case." He was careful to limit the practice of judicial review to cases of a judicial nature. (The greater scope of judicial review authority today is not attributable to any change in constitutional theory, but to an expansion in the forms of action, such as the writ of injunction.) He suggested that, in the exercise of this power, courts should not act in doubtful cases, and should accord deference to the judgments of the politically accountable branches.

Marshall's discourse on judicial review seemed less momentous to his contemporaries than it appears to us today. Jefferson, for example, criticized the decision not for its exercise of judicial review, but for the Court's decision to reach questions on the merits despite the Court's admitted lack of jurisdiction and its criticism of his own decision to withhold the commissions. In the decades after *Marbury*, Jeffersonian critics attacked the Court not for striking down Acts of Congress, but for upholding them. (The most notable instance was *McCulloch v. Maryland*.[44]) Nor did *Marbury* lead to other overrulings. Not until 1857, in

---

[43] *Marbury*, 5 U.S. at 177–78.

[44] 17 U.S. (4 Wheat) 316 (1819).

Dred Scot v. Sandford,[45] would the Court again hold an Act of Congress unconstitutional, and, when that happened, the issue of judicial power returned to the center stage of national politics.

Marbury can best be understood as Marshall's oblique commentary on the Judiciary Act repeal, which he was powerless to confront directly. If it was illegal for Jefferson to dismiss a justice of the peace, who was to serve a five-year term, it must have been a far more serious breach for Congress to dismiss sixteen life-tenured Article III judges. If Congress could not assign mandamus jurisdiction to the Supreme Court, it must have been unconstitutional, as well, to assign circuit-riding duty. But by holding that the Supreme Court had no jurisdiction in the case (and blaming it on Congress), Marshall was spared the necessity of acting and the indignity of having his orders ignored. Jefferson and the Republican Congress might be annoyed, but there was no way for them to respond to a decision that, in the final analysis, did nothing.

Marbury was brilliant, then, not for its effective assertion of judicial power, but for its effective avoidance of judicial humiliation. Its bold, but empty, assertion of judicial power masked a quiet capitulation on all the issues that really mattered. A week after *Marbury*, the Supreme Court handed down its decision in *Stuart v. Laird*, a terse, unanimous opinion (Marshall not participating) upholding the Judiciary Act repeal and the return of the Justices to circuit riding duty. Ten years later, the Court handed down another unanimous opinion, *United States v. Hudson & Godwin*,[46] renouncing the power of federal courts to prosecute under the common law. The Jeffersonian counter-revolution had succeeded.

---

[45] 60 U.S. (19 How.) 393 (1857).

[46] 11 U.S. (7 Cranch) 32 (1812).

*

2

Daniel A. Farber

The Story of *McCulloch*: Banking on National Power

There is no denying the importance of *McCulloch v. Maryland*.[1] As of January 1, 2009, it had been cited in over 2,400 state and federal cases in the Westlaw computer database. Many scholars consider it the single most important opinion in the Court's history. Later national leaders have invoked John Marshall "whenever they needed authority to confirm the legitimacy of the national government deriving from the people of the United States, to defend the independence of the federal judiciary, to support broad constructions of Congress's Commerce Clause and Necessary and Proper Clause Powers, and to justify judicial construction of the Constitution to meet the pressing issues of the day."[2] And a number of lines from the opinion are second-nature to any constitutional lawyer, such as Marshall's definition of the "necessary and proper" clause and his dictum that "we must never forget that it is a Constitution we are expounding."[3]

But much less familiar is the historical setting of the decision. Chief Justice Marshall did not write on a clean slate in *McCulloch*, for the constitutionality of a national bank had been disputed since the early days of the Republic and involved deep questions of constitutional theory. To understand Marshall's opinion fully, we need to place it firmly into historical context. Only by doing so can we understand why *McCulloch* was such a controversial decision at the time. We may also be

---

[1] 17 U.S. (4 Wheat.) 316 (1819).

[2] Michael J. Gerhardt, *The Lives of John Marshall*, 43 Wm. & Mary L. Rev. 1399, 1443 (2002).

[3] 17 U.S. (4 Wheat.) at 407 (once amusingly paraphrased by a student on an exam as "we must never forget that it is a Constitution we are *expanding*.")

able to see how the Court's continuing debates over federalism relate to the vision Marshall articulated in *McCulloch*.[4]

How McCulloch *Got to the Supreme Court*

Often the interesting part of the development of a case relates to the lives and conduct of the parties, the litigation tactics of the lawyers, and the way that lower court proceedings contributed to the appellate decisions. With respect to *McCulloch*, however, the interesting history relates not to the earlier stages of the litigation but to its deep roots in American constitutional history. When Marshall ruled on the constitutionality of the Bank of the United States, he was continuing a debate that had begun even before the Constitution went into effect. He was also contributing to a discussion of the nature of the Union and the scope of federal power that had begun with Hamilton, Madison, and Jefferson. The extensive oral arguments in *McCulloch* were primarily concerned with linking the case to the broad constitutional themes of this ongoing debate, setting the stage for Marshall's historic opinion. Thus, Marshall was adding a chapter to a constitutional debate begun by others.

The Bank of the United States and the Founding Fathers

Controversy about a national bank arose even before the Constitution was adopted. The country emerged from the American Revolution with serious inflation, along with over $450 million in debt and little prospect of paying it off.[5] Between 1779 and 1781, congressional interest in chartering a bank rose, with the goal of stabilizing the currency on the basis of the bank's notes.[6] Robert Morris, the mastermind behind the bank plan, intended to keep the bank's notes in circulation indefinitely as a form of paper money.[7] After the Bank of North America was chartered by Congress,[8] Morris tried unsuccessfully to push through Congress his scheme to convert the existing national debt into circulating bank notes, but he was unable to secure adequate funding.[9] Nonethe-

---

[4] *See generally* John T. Noonan, Jr., *Narrowing the Nation's Power: The Supreme Court Sides with the States* 29–31, 117–19 (2002).

[5] *See* Janet A. Riesman, *Money, Credit, and Federalist Political Economy, in Beyond Confederation: Origins of the Constitution and American National Identity* 128, 130–31 (Richard Beeman et al. eds., 1987).

[6] *Id.* at 136–38.

[7] *Id.* at 140–42.

[8] *Id.* at 148.

[9] *Id.* at 144–46.

less, the Bank of North America was not a complete failure. Franklin, Jefferson, and Hamilton were among its investors and depositors, and the bank handled payments for the Continental Army.[10]

Even in this pre-Constitution period, the legality of a national bank was disputed. James Wilson, soon to be an important participant in the adoption of the new Constitution, made the case in favor of the bank.[11] He argued that "[w]henever an object occurs, to the direction of which no particular state is competent, the management of it must, of necessity, belong to the United States in congress assembled."[12] For "many purposes," he maintained, "the United States are to be considered as one undivided, independent nation; and as possessed of all the rights, and powers, and properties, by the law of nations incident to such."[13] Congress was warranted in establishing a bank for a variety of reasons. Such a bank provided a reliable source of nationwide paper currency. "To have a free, easy, and equable instrument of circulation is of much importance in all countries: it is of peculiar importance in young and flourishing countries, in which the demands for credit, and the rewards of industry, are greater than in any other."[14] A bank would also provide a ready source of funds in the event of war.[15] Wilson concluded "that in times of peace, the national bank will be highly advantageous; that in times of war, it will be essentially necessary, to the United States."[16]

When the Constitutional Convention met in the summer of 1787, the question of a national bank was still on the delegates' minds. During the debate on a proposal to empower Congress to build canals, Madison proposed that Congress also be given the power "to grant charters of incorporation where the interest of the U. S. might require & the legislative provisions of individual States may be incompetent."[17] Rufus King of Massachusetts, who was later to be a director of the first Bank of the United States,[18] objected that such a provision would be divisive: "In

---

[10] Paul Johnson, *A History of the American People* 214 (1997).

[11] James Wilson, *Consideration on the Bank of North America* (1785), *in Contexts of the Constitution: A Documentary Collection on Principles of American Constitutional Law* 368 (Neil H. Cogan ed., 1999).

[12] *Id.* at 373.

[13] *Id.*

[14] *Id.* at 380.

[15] *Id.* at 383.

[16] *Id.*

[17] Daniel A. Farber & Suzanna Sherry, *A History of the American Constitution* 141 (1990).

[18] *Id.* at 439.

Philada. & New York, It will be referred to the establishment of a Bank, which has been a subject of contention in those Cities. In other places it will be referred to mercantile monopolies."[19] James Wilson (already on record as supporting a bank prior to the Convention) responded that "[a]s to Banks he did not think with Mr. King that the power in that point of view would excite the prejudices & parties apprehended."[20] George Mason argued for giving Congress only the power to charter canal companies, because he was "afraid of monopolies of every sort" and "did not think they were by any means already implied by the Constitution as supposed by Mr. Wilson."[21] A vote was then taken on a modified motion, limiting the power to canals as suggested by Mason. The modified motion failed, killing the broader proposal as well.[22]

After the Constitution was ratified, Alexander Hamilton became the first Secretary of the Treasury. As one commentator observes, Hamilton's plan was a daring effort to jumpstart a foundering national economy:

> The scope and insight of Hamilton's political economy are breathtaking. Suppose you were appointed Treasury Secretary of a start-up country with a poor credit history, an enormous amount of delinquent debt, both local and national, unexploited natural resources, disconnected and rudimentary product markets, and disordered and illiquid financial markets? And suppose further that your new country was "possessed of little active wealth, or in other words, little moneyed capital," what would you do?[23]

Building on Robert Morris's earlier ideas, Hamilton put forward an ambitious scheme for the federal government to raise taxes through tariffs and then to refinance both the federal government's war debt and that of the states. Establishing a national bank was a key part of this scheme. Like Morris, Hamilton planned to use the bank's notes to expand the national money supply. Hamilton was successful in part of this plan. By establishing a dependable method of financing public debt, he put the country's credit on a firm footing for the first time.[24]

---

[19] *Id.* at 141.

[20] *Id.*

[21] *Id.*

[22] *Id.*

[23] David McGowan, *Ethos in Law and History: Alexander Hamilton, The Federalist, and the Supreme Court*, 85 Minn. L. Rev. 755, 796 (2001) (quoting Alexander Hamilton, *Report Relative to Provision for the Support of Public Credit* (Jan. 9, 1790), *reprinted in* 6 *The Papers of Alexander Hamilton* 51, 67 (Harold C. Syrett & Jacob E. Cook eds., 1962)).

[24] *Id.* at 804.

The bank was a critical part of Hamilton's scheme. It would be the government's chief fiscal agent, making it easier to collect taxes, make payments, and obtain short-term loans. Its notes would provide a national currency, and it would provide a source of capital for financing businesses.[25] This plan was modeled closely on the Bank of England, which had helped rescue Britain from the verge of bankruptcy.[26]

Opposition to the bank had several roots. Some opponents disagreed with Hamilton's view on the necessity of a strong currency, viewing national wealth as based solely on productivity rather than on the financial system.[27] Other attacks were from defenders of agrarian values, many of them former opponents of the Constitution. They rejected Hamilton's focus on commerce and feared his efforts to build national financial institutions. They believed that, like the Bank of England, an American national bank would create a powerful class of financiers, who would in turn co-opt the federal government and undermine the autonomy of the states. These agrarians were afraid that a national bank would bring on the kind of "corruption" (primarily in the form of undue influence on legislators) that they had long criticized in English society.[28] Finally, bank opponents such as Madison feared that if the bank were established in Philadelphia, this would strengthen the claim of that city to become the national capital, blocking their preferred locations on the Potomac and elsewhere.[29]

In Congress, opposition to the bank was led by Madison. He argued that the bank proposal was dubious as a policy matter. More importantly, he contended that it was unconstitutional. Congress had only limited enumerated powers. At most the bank would be convenient rather than necessary. Implication and construction could not be used to extend congressional power. Madison viewed the Bank of North America as distinguishable—technically illegal, but a wartime necessity.[30] In particular, Madison rejected the necessary and proper clause as a basis of authority for the bank:

> The essential characteristic of the government, as composed of limited and enumerated powers, would be destroyed: If instead of direct and incidental means, any means could be used, which in the

---

[25] See Stanley Elkins & Eric McKitrick, *The Age of Federalism* 226 (1993).

[26] *Id.* at 227–28.

[27] See Riesman, *supra* note 5, at 160–61.

[28] See Saul Cornell, *The Other Founders: Anti–Federalism and the Dissenting Tradition in America, 1788–1828,* at 176–81 (1999).

[29] Elkins & McKitrick, *supra* note 25, at 229.

[30] James Madison, Opinion on the Constitutionality of the Bill to Establish a National Bank (Feb. 2, 1791), *in Contexts of the Constitution, supra* note 11, at 527, 530–531.

language of the preamble to the bill, "might be conceived to be
conducive to the successful conducting of the finances; or might be
conceived to *tend* to give *facility* to the obtaining of loans." He
[Madison] urged an attention to the diffuse and ductile terms which
had been found requisite to cover the stretch of power contained in
the bill. He compared them with the terms *necessary* and *proper*,
used in the Constitution, and asked whether it was possible to view
the two descriptions as synonymous [sic], or the one as a fair and
safe commentary on the other.[31]

A few days later, he repeated much of his argument, this time stressing
how dangerous it would be to give Congress the power to create
corporations:

The power of granting Charters, he [Madison] observed, is a great
and important power, and ought not to be exercised, without we find
ourselves expressly authorized to grant them: Here he dilated on the
great and extensive influence that incorporated societies had on
public affairs in Europe: They are a powerful machine, which have
always been found competent to effect objects on principles, in a
great measure independent of the people.[32]

Madison's argument rested on a theory of interpretation that would
later be called originalism. He articulated three principles of constitutional interpretation: (1) an "interpretation that destroys the very characteristic of the government cannot be just"; (2) where the meaning is
clear, it must be accepted regardless of consequences; and (3) in "contro-
verted cases, the meaning of the parties to the instrument, if to be
collected by reasonable evidence, is a proper guide" and may be found
from "[c]ontemporary and concurrent expositions."[33]

In reply, supporters of the bank made three arguments. First, they
argued that establishing a bank was a "necessary incident to the entire
powers to regulate trade and revenue, and to provide for the public
credit and defense."[34] Second, they maintained (perhaps correctly) that
Madison was inventing new doctrines of interpretation that were not
sanctioned by leading authorities such as Blackstone. Finally, they
recalled that Federalist 44 (which was actually written by Madison
himself, though this was not known at the time) had expressly endorsed

---

[31] *Id.* at 531.

[32] James Madison, Opinion on the Constitutionality of the Bill to Establish a National
Bank (Feb. 8, 1791), *in Contexts of the Constitution, supra* note 11, at 536, 536–37.

[33] Madison, *supra* note 30, at 529.

[34] Elkins & McKitrick, *supra* note 25, at 231 (quoting 1 *Annals of Cong.* 1959 (Joseph
Gales ed., 1789)).

the doctrine of implied powers.[35] Madison apparently failed to persuade
his colleagues. Having passed the Senate already, the bank bill passed
the House by a vote of 39 to 20.[36]

Madison had several discussions about the bank with President
Washington, who was sufficiently concerned to tell Madison to prepare a
veto message for possible use. Washington then asked the Attorney
General, Edmund Randolph, and, more importantly, Secretary of State
Jefferson, to advise him about the constitutionality of the bill.[37]

Hamilton's economic schemes were anathema to Jefferson. Jefferson's vision of the American future was agrarian, and he was suspicious
of manufacturing, commerce, and finance. Like most Southern planters,
he was deeply hostile to banks.[38] Jefferson responded to Washington's
request with a vigorous attack on the constitutionality of the Bank.[39]

Jefferson began by cataloguing the ways in which the bank statute
might conflict with state laws, which it would preempt.[40] In his view, the
foundation of the Constitution was the Tenth Amendment's reservation
of power to the states: "To take a single step beyond the boundaries thus
specially drawn around the powers of Congress, is to take possession of a
boundless field of power, no longer susceptible of any definition."[41] He
then considered the possible sources of power. The bank could not be
justified under the power to tax for the purpose of paying federal debt,
because it did neither. Nor did it fit under the government's power to
borrow money, for the bank would be at complete liberty to decide
whether to loan any money to the federal government. And although the
Bank's bills and notes would trade in interstate commerce, issuing the
bills was not interstate commerce: "For the power given to Congress by
the Constitution, does not extend to the internal regulation of the
commerce of a state (that is to say of the commerce between citizen and
citizen) which remains exclusively with it's [sic] own legislature; but it's
[sic] external commerce only, that is to say, it's [sic] commerce with
another state, or with foreign nations or with the Indian tribes."[42]

---

[35] Id.

[36] *Id.* at 232.

[37] *Id.*

[38] Johnson, *supra* note 10, at 215.

[39] Thomas Jefferson, Opinion on the Constitutionality of the Bill to Establish a
National Bank (Feb. 15, 1791), *in Contexts of the Constitution, supra* note 11, at 540.

[40] *Id.*

[41] *Id.* at 541

[42] *Id.*

Jefferson also invoked the original intent:

> It is known that the very power now proposed *as a means*, was rejected *as an end*, by the Convention which formed the constitution. A proposition was made to them to authorize Congress to open canals, and an amendatory one to empower them to incorporate. But the whole was rejected, and one of the reasons of rejection urged in debate was that then they would have a power to erect a bank, which would render the great cities, where there were prejudices and jealousies on that subject adverse to the reception of the constitution.[43]

Jefferson in no uncertain terms rejected the necessary and proper clause as a basis for the Bank: "It has been much argued that a bank will give great facility, or convenience in the collection of taxes. Suppose this were true: yet the constitution allows only the means which are 'necessary' not those which are merely 'convenient' for effecting the enumerated powers."[44] "Can it be thought that the Constitution intended that for a shade or two of *convenience*, more or less," that "Congress should be authorised to break down the most antient and fundamental laws of the several states, such as those against Mortmain, the laws of alienage, the rules of descent, the acts of distribution, the laws of escheat and forfeiture, the laws of monopoly?"[45] A similar argument could be made to give Congress every non-enumerated power, for there "is no one [power] which ingenuity may not torture into a *convenience, in some way or other*, to *some one* of so long a list of enumerated powers."[46] To construe the clause so broadly "would swallow up all the delegated powers, and reduce the whole to one phrase."[47]

Somewhat surprisingly, Jefferson concluded by offering Washington an escape hatch. Unless Washington was "tolerably clear" that the bank bill was unconstitutional, he ought to defer to the legislature.[48] "[I]f the pro and the con hang so even as to balance his judgment, a just respect for the wisdom of the legislature would naturally decide the balance in favour of their opinion."[49]

---

[43] *Id.* at 542.

[44] *Id.*

[45] *Id.* at 543–44.

[46] *Id.* at 542.

[47] *Id.*

[48] *Id.* at 544.

[49] *Id.*

After receiving Jefferson's views, Washington asked Hamilton to respond.[50] Hamilton's response is particularly significant for present purposes, because John Marshall later "read, summarized, and reprinted" portions of the letter.[51] Although prepared in haste—it is dated only a week and a day later than Jefferson's[52]—Hamilton's response was cogent and powerful, anticipating in many ways the Court's opinion over three decades later in *McCulloch*.[53]

Hamilton began with a discourse on the nature of governmental powers. He laid down the general principle that every governmental power necessarily includes "a right to employ all the *means* requisite, and fairly *applicable* to the attainment of the *ends* of such power; and which are not precluded by restrictions & exceptions specified in the constitution; or not immoral, or not contrary to the essential ends of political society."[54] The division of powers between the federal government and the states did not alter this principle: with respect to the powers allocated to them, each was fully sovereign. After all, he pointed out, the Constitution limited the powers of the states (for example, by depriving them of the power to abrogate contracts), so if sovereignty implied unlimited power then neither the federal government nor the states could be considered sovereign.[55]

Hamilton particularly took issue with Jefferson's call for strict construction. He argued that constitutional powers, especially those relating to finances, trade, and defense, should be construed liberally, for the "means by which national exigencies are to be provided for, national inconveniencies [sic] obviated, national prosperity promoted, are of such infinite variety, extent and complexity, that there must, of necessity, be great latitude of discretion in the selection & application of those means."[56] Hamilton rejected the argument that broad construction was more appropriate at the state level than the federal level. If anything, he maintained, the opposite was true, because a wider range and more critical set of public necessities were entrusted to the federal government.[57]

---

[50] *See* Elkins & McKittrick, *supra* note 25, at 232.

[51] McGowan, *supra* note 23, at 854.

[52] *See* Alexander Hamilton, Opinion on the Constitutionality of the Bill to Establish a National Bank (Feb. 23, 1791), *in Contexts of the Constitution, supra* note 11, at 544; Jefferson, *supra* note 39, at 540.

[53] *See* Hamilton, *supra* note 52, at 544.

[54] *Id.* at 545.

[55] *Id.*

[56] *Id.* at 549.

[57] *Id.* at 550.

Hamilton also rejected Jefferson's reliance on original intent. So far as the record showed, the only actual decision made at the convention related to incorporating canal companies and was not germane to the bank issue. Participants disagreed about just what issue was debated. And in any event, original intent was not decisive:

> The Secretary of State will not deny, that whatever may have been the intention of the framers of a constitution, or of a law, that intention is to be sought for in the instrument itself, according to the usual & established rules of construction. Nothing is more common than for laws to *express* and *effect*, more or less than was intended. If then a power to erect a corporation, in any case, be deducible by fair inference from the whole or any part of the numerous provisions of the constitution of the United States, arguments drawn from extrinsic circumstances, regarding the intention of the convention, must be rejected.[58]

The only question, then, was whether incorporating a bank had the requisite relationship with any of the enumerated powers. With respect to the taxing power, a bank increased the circulation of money (remember, this was a period when currency was hard to come by), thereby providing the means for payment of taxes. Without the availability of the bank's notes as a means of payment, Hamilton said, the federal government might have been forced to accept bills from various private banks or even payment in kind.[59] Regarding the power of borrowing money, the existence of a national bank would provide a source of emergency loans in the event of war or other exigencies.[60] And in several respects, the bank would also relate to interstate commerce. "Money is the very hinge on which commerce turns."[61] Expanding the money supply would provide a "convenient medium" for trade and would also eliminate the need for shipping precious metals back and forth.[62] It was irrelevant whether other banks could also perform a similar function to some extent: the issue was the scope of congressional power, not the expediency of exercising it on any given occasion.[63]

Given later disputes about the scope of the Commerce Clause, Hamilton's response to Jefferson's argument is of some interest. Recall that Jefferson had drawn a sharp line between transactions within a

---

[58] *Id.* at 553.

[59] *Id.* at 560.

[60] *Id.* at 562.

[61] *Id.* at 563.

[62] *Id.*

[63] *See* McGowan, *supra* note 23, at 812.

state and interstate commerce, with the former being no concern of the federal government. Hamilton questioned this distinction:

> But what regulation of commerce does not extend to the internal commerce of every state? What are all the duties upon imported articles amounting to prohibitions, but so many bounties upon domestic manufactures affecting the interests of different classes of citizens in different ways? What are all the provisions of the coasting act, which relate to the trade between district and district of the same State? In short what regulation of trade between the States, but must affect the internal trade of each State? What can operate upon the whole but must extend to every part![64]

Two days after receiving Hamilton's opinion, Washington signed the bank bill.[65] This decision carried great weight: Washington had presided at the Constitutional Convention and was of course a revered national figure. Hamilton had prevailed in the debate. Even today, his letter seems more forceful and focused than the statements of his opponents.

Why was Hamilton's opinion more powerful than Madison's and Jefferson's? Two leading historians suggest that Hamilton, unlike Jefferson and Madison, was in the same position he had been when writing the Federalist. "Being on the offensive," they observe, "expounding the positive side of any argument, dealing with positive innovations, and being on top of one's subject all have more than a casual relation both to the energy of a person's convictions and to the effectiveness with which the case is made."[66] Arguing for broad construction comes easily "when convinced that a generous use of the government's powers will have a positive and salutary effect on the community, and a broad-construction opinion is likely to be of high quality when behind it is a sense of urgency about taking some kind of action."[67] Thus, as in the Federalist, Hamilton was still an institution-builder, arguing that public needs required bold actions.

In contrast, Jefferson and Madison were moving away from the position of the Federalist. They were at the turning point "at which one prefers to see the Constitution not as a sanction for achieving one's own ends but as a protection against those designs of others which have come to be seen as usurping and corrupting."[68] Jefferson was able to embrace strict construction with little strain, since he had never been an ardent

---

[64] Hamilton, *supra* note 53, at 564.

[65] Elkins & McKitrick, *supra* note 25, at 233.

[66] *Id.*

[67] *Id.*

[68] *Id.* at 234.

supporter of the Constitution, but Madison was being forced to reverse positions that he had taken in the Federalist. He saw around him an emerging world "dominated by moneyed men and merchants subservient to the interest of England and a British system," and he was forced into an awkward constitutional stance by the imperative of combating this perceived threat to American values.[69] For the time, however, the Bank issue was settled, and the battle with Hamilton moved on to other issues.

The Litigation and the Lawyers

The charter of the First Bank of the United States expired in 1811. It had become politically unpopular because of its association with the Federalist Party, opposition by the state banks, and the dominance of foreign investors among its shareholders.[70] But the War of 1812 soon drove home the desirability of a national bank, and a new charter was issued in 1816. The Second Bank of the United States was badly managed, and the Bank took the blame for a post-war financial collapse, resulting in intense hostility toward the bank everywhere except the Northeast. Between 1816 and 1820, Georgia, Indiana, Illinois, Kentucky, Maryland, North Carolina, Ohio, and Tennessee each enacted anti-Bank legislation.[71] In the meantime, further evidence of bank mismanagement came to light, with almost a $2 million loss in the Maryland branch (serious money in those days!).[72]

McCulloch began in 1818 as an action to collect a fine of $100 against James W. McCulloch, the cashier of the Maryland branch. This was the penalty for circulating a bank note without the required Maryland stamp (which could be avoided if the bank paid a $15,000 annual fee). By agreement between the state attorney general and federal officials, it became a test case on the constitutionality of the bank. The Maryland Court of Appeals upheld the Maryland state tax law in an unreported per curiam opinion, setting the stage for an appeal to the Supreme Court.[73]

The oral arguments lasted nine days and brought before the Court the leading constitutional lawyers in the country.[74] By way of background, something should be said about four of these lawyers: Daniel

---

[69] *Id.*

[70] 1 Charles Warren, *The Supreme Court in United States History* 504 (rev. ed. 1926).

[71] *Id.* at 505–06.

[72] *Id.* at 506.

[73] *Id.* at 506–07.

[74] *Id.*

Webster, William Wirt, William Pinkney, and Luther Martin. During this period, Supreme Court advocates played a particularly important role. The Court did not receive written briefs, making the oral arguments critical.[75] The leading lawyers also helped shape the legal disputes that ultimately reached the Court.

The best-remembered of the lawyers today was Daniel Webster, who argued for the Bank. He is said to have been the "most famous, the most controversial, and perhaps the most charismatic of all the leading Marshall Court advocates."[76] He was also the leading orator of his time.[77] His physical appearance was riveting: the "jet-black hair, ... the massive head, the huge, dark, piercing eyes, ... the sonorous voice, ... the imposing carriage—taken together, these features seemed more than striking; they seemed suggestive of a powerful inner force."[78] He argued many of the leading Marshall Court cases between 1819 and 1830, and lost only one major one.[79] Webster was particularly active in shaping the Court's agenda, and he was also devoted to propounding the Marshall Court's constitutional vision to the public.[80]

Also arguing on behalf of the bank was Attorney General William Wirt. He was in some ways an unlikely public figure, having no family connections or inheritance and being more inclined to literature than the law.[81] He was named Attorney General in 1817 by President Monroe and remained until 1829, when Jackson assumed the presidency.[82] During his career, he appeared before the Supreme Court 170 times, including almost all of the great constitutional cases of the era.[83]

The third notable advocate for the Bank was William Pinkney. Pinkney, though from humble origins, was renowned as a dandy for his elegant manner and fancy dress.[84] He was not just a lawyer but a diplomat. He had been involved in diplomatic missions beginning in the

---

[75] G. Edward White, *The Marshall Court and Cultural Change, 1815–1835*, at 247 (1988).

[76] Id. at 267.

[77] *Id.* at 276.

[78] *Id.* at 268.

[79] *Id.* at 275.

[80] *Id.* at 288.

[81] *Id.* at 255.

[82] *Id.* at 262.

[83] *Id.* at 264.

[84] *Id.* at 241.

Washington administration and was later minister to England.[85] Pinkney was not well-liked. For example, Wirt said he could "not love the man for he has no heart but for himself."[86] Though he was not personally popular, no one questioned his ability as a lawyer. Marshall reportedly said that he never knew Pinkney's "equal as a reasoner—so clear and luminous was his method of argumentation."[87] This was not idle praise: some of Marshall's opinions closely track Pinkney's arguments.[88]

In particular, portions of the *McCulloch* opinion essentially paraphrase Pinkney's oral argument.[89] If Justice Story is to be believed, Marshall's high regard for Pinkney was well-deserved. Of his three-day (!) oral argument, Story said:

> I never, in my whole life, heard a greater speech; it was worth a journey from Salem to hear it; his elocution was excessively vehement, but his eloquence was overwhelming. His language, his style, his figures, his arguments were most brilliant and sparkling. He spoke like a great statesman and patriot, and a sound constitutional lawyer. All the cobwebs of sophistry and metaphysics about State rights and State sovereignty he brushed away with a mighty besom [broom].[90]

The towering figure on the other side of the case was Luther Martin, the long-time Attorney General of Maryland.[91] In his younger days, he had been a delegate to the Constitutional Convention, where he defended the prerogatives of the small states and opposed expansive federal power.[92] He later became a Federalist, modifying his views in the process.[93] His personal manner and appearance were a stark contrast with Pinkney: he was known for his slovenly dress, overindulgence in alcohol, soiled clothing, rambling speech, and bad table manners.[94] His argument in *McCulloch* was said to be "characteristically long, rambling, and exhaustive," with much attention to the views of the Framers

---

[85] *Id.* at 245–46.

[86] *Id.* at 253.

[87] *Id.* at 243.

[88] *Id.* at 247.

[89] *Id.* at 248–50.

[90] Warren, *supra* note 70, at 507–08.

[91] White, *supra* note 75, at 235.

[92] *Id.* at 230.

[93] *Id.* at 230–31.

[94] *Id.* at 237.

(including Martin himself, of course).[95] At the end of Martin's argument, he read aloud some remarks that John Marshall had made years earlier at the Virginia convention to ratify the Constitution. When he finished, Marshall apparently took a deep breath; when Story asked him about it after the argument, Marshall said he was relieved that he had not said anything really foolish in the debate.[96] Martin suffered a major stroke weeks after the argument and never really recovered.[97] His closing days were spent as a boarder in the house of Aaron Burr, whom he had earlier defended against treason charges.[98]

The Oral Arguments

The oral arguments revealed three important divisions between the Bank's defenders and its attackers. These divisions related to the nature of the Union, the scope of the necessary and proper clause, and the extent of the state's power of taxation.

Most fundamentally, the two sides had different conceptions of the nature of the Union. Arguing for the bank, Pinkney contended that the Constitution "springs from the people" rather than the states in their corporate capacity.[99] In contrast, the state's lawyers argued that the Constitution is "a compact between the states, and all the powers which are not expressly relinquished by it, are reserved to the states."[100] The Constitution was founded, "not by the people of the United States at large, but by the people of the respective states."[101] The constitutional system "was established by reciprocal concessions and compromises between the state and federal governments."[102]

As to the scope of the necessary and proper clause, the Bank's defenders embraced a wide definition and relied heavily on nonjudicial precedent regarding the clause's application to the bank. Webster pointed out that the bank question had been fully explored in the early years of the republic, and that all three branches had been acting for over thirty years on the assumption that the bank was constitutional.[103] Such

---

[95] *Id.* at 238.

[96] Warren, *supra* note 70, at 507.

[97] White, *supra* note 75, at 240.

[98] *Id.*

[99] McCulloch, 17 U.S. (4 Wheat.) at 377.

[100] *Id.* at 363.

[101] *Id..*

[102] *Id.* at 371.

[103] *Id.* at 323.

a longstanding interpretation "must be considered as ratified by the voice of the people."[104] This construction, Pinkney said, was especially entitled to deference because it was contemporaneous with the Constitution and made by the authors of the Constitution themselves.[105] Indeed, by the time the bank was rechartered, the president (Madison himself) had admitted that the constitutional issue was no longer subject to dispute.[106]

In terms of the meaning of the clause itself, Webster continued that "necessary" and "proper" were to be considered synonymous, and meant only "such powers as are suitable and fitted to the object; such as are best and most useful in relation to the end proposed."[107] Whether Congress had chosen the best possible means was not for a court to decide.[108] Similarly, Wirts maintained that "necessary and proper" was "equivalent to needful and adapted," citing Johnson's Dictionary as support.[109] In any event, Wirts said, no one could deny that "banks, dispersed throughout the country, are appropriate means of carrying into execution" the federal government's powers.[110] The extent of federal power could not depend on a judgment by the court regarding the degree of necessity. Such a context-based standard would make the validity of federal policies "dependent for their being, on extrinsic circumstances, which, as these are perpetually shifting and changing, must produce correspondent changes in the essence of the powers on which they depend."[111] Rather, claimed Wirts, the degree of necessity "presents a mere question of political expediency, which, it is repeated, is exclusively for legislative consideration."[112] Pinkney emphasized the practical need for a broad construction, because it was impossible for the framers to have gone into every detail or to "foresee the infinite variety of circumstances, in such an unexampled state of society as ours, for ever changing and for ever improving."[113] Courts were incompetent to judge the degree of necessity[114]; they could merely confirm that "what has been done is not a mere evasive pretext."[115]

---

[104] *Id.* at 353.

[105] *Id.* at 378–79.

[106] *Id.* at 380.

[107] *Id.* at 324–25.

[108] *Id.* at 325.

[109] *Id.* at 356.

[110] *Id.* at 354.

[111] *Id.* at 355.

[112] *Id.* at 357.

[113] *Id.* at 385.

[114] *Id.* at 389–90.

[115] *Id.* at 387.

In response, the state's advocates minimized the significance of early practice and advocated a narrow interpretation of the clause. Admittedly, in an earlier era, a national bank may have been necessary for the purpose of the federal government, but necessity "has relation to circumstances which change; in a state of things which may exist at one period, and not at another."[116] In contrast to conditions when the Bank was rechartered in 1816, the situation had been much different in the early years of the Republic. When Hamilton argued on behalf of a national bank, "there were but three banks in the United States, with limited capitals, and contracted spheres of operation."[117] Moreover, the need to establish branches in states such as Maryland was even less clear, and that decision had been made by the bank itself rather than Congress. The state's lawyers also claimed that only Congress could make such a vital decision about overriding state preferences, because Congress was the only tribunal "which ... may be safely trusted; the only one in which the states to be affected by the measure, are all fairly represented."[118] Such a power could not be delegated to an essentially private corporation.[119]

Furthermore, the state drew a distinction between "means which are incidental to the particular power" in question and those "which may be arbitrarily assumed as convenient to the execution of the power, or usurped under the pretext of necessity."[120] Necessary, in this context, means "indispensably requisite."[121] Again, the state relied on the original intent: "The people never intended they [the federal government] should become bankers or traders of any description. They meant to leave to the states the power of regulating the trade of banking, and every other species of internal industry," subject merely to the regulation of interstate and foreign commerce by Congress.[122]

The taxation issue seemed to present the greatest difficulty for the defenders of the Bank. Pinkney viewed this as the "last and greatest, and only difficult question" in the case.[123] "If the states may tax the

---

[116] *Id.* at 331.

[117] *Id.* at 332.

[118] *Id.* at 336.

[119] *Id.*

[120] *Id.* at 365.

[121] *Id.* at 367.

[122] *Id.* at 368.

[123] *Id.* at 390.

bank," Webster asked, "to what extent shall they tax it, and where shall they stop?"[124] He added, in words echoed by Pinkney[125] and later by the Court, that the power to "tax involves, necessarily, a power to destroy."[126] If states could tax the bank, maintained Wirts, "they may tax the proceedings in the courts of the United States," and "nothing but their own discretion can impose a limit upon this exercise of their authority."[127] "But, surely," he added, "the framers of the constitution did not intend that the exercise of all of the powers of the national government should depend upon the discretion of the state governments"—for that "was the vice of the former confederation, which it was the object of the new constitution to eradicate."[128] Pinkney proclaimed that "[w]hatever the United States have a right to do, the individual states have no right to undo. The power of congress to establish a bank, like its other sovereign powers, is supreme, or it would be nothing."[129] It would be very difficult for a court to determine when the level of a tax had passed the threshold of reasonableness, and by the time the evidence of harm was sufficiently clear, it might be too late.[130] Nor was this a truly nondiscriminatory tax, for no other bank had a branch office in Maryland. And if Maryland's law was upheld, what could be done about Kentucky's imposition of a $60,000 annual tax on the bank?[131]

The state's advocates had several arguments on the taxation issue. They argued that the bank was essentially private, not a federal instrumentality, and therefore not entitled to any kind of sovereign immunity from taxation.[132] Moreover, a "sovereign putting his property within the territory and jurisdiction of another sovereign, and of course, under his protection, submits it to the ordinary taxation of the state, and must contribute fairly to the wants of the revenue."[133] And the defenders of the Constitution had said "again and again" in the ratification debates that the state's right of taxation was "sacred and inviolable."[134] The

---

124 *Id.* at 327.

125 *Id.* at 391.

126 *Id.* at 327.

127 *Id.* at 361–62.

128 *Id.* at 362.

129 *Id.* at 391.

130 *Id.* at 392.

131 *Id.* at 393.

132 *Id.* at 339–40.

133 *Id.* at 342.

134 *Id.* at 344.

"unlimited power of taxation results from state sovereignty."[135] The only limit placed by the Constitution on state taxation was the ban on imposts and tonnage duties.[136] True, the power to tax could be abused, but so could the federal government's powers; the Constitution could only function effectively so long as the states and the federal government maintained a cooperative relationship.[137] Only "mutual confidence, discretion and forbearance" can prevent clashes between the two levels of government.[138] Luther Martin conceded that abuse of the tax power, either by the states or by the federal government, was possible. But he viewed this risk as unavoidable, stemming from the inability of the Constitutional Convention (to which, recall, he was a delegate) to fully resolve the difficult issues posed by concurrent powers of taxation.[139]

Overall, the state stressed the extent to which the Bank was relying on implications piled on implications. First the power to create a bank was implied, then from that the power to create branches, and from that the immunity of the branches from taxation, the state's "most vital and essential power."[140] The argument for the bank was like the "famous fig tree of India", whose "branches shoot from the trunk to a considerable distance; then drop upon the earth, where they take root and become trees, from which also other branches shoot, and plant and propagate and extend themselves in the same way, until gradually a vast surface is covered, and everything perishes in the spreading shade."[141]

At the narrowest level, the dispute between the two sides involved questions of burden of proof and judicial competence. In terms of competence, at issue were whether a court had the capacity to review the aptness of Congress's choice of means under changing circumstances or the ability to determine the economic impact of a state tax on a federal instrumentality. Assuming that courts could not or should not draw such distinctions, a bright-line rule was needed, and the question was then which side to favor. The arguments for a rule favoring the federal government were based on the supremacy clause, the need for an effective central government, and the political safeguard provided by the representation of every state and its people in Congress. The arguments for favoring the state governments were the compact theory of the

---

[135] *Id.* at 370.

[136] *Id.* at 369.

[137] *Id.* at 349–50.

[138] *Id.* at 371.

[139] *Id.* at 376.

[140] *Id.* at 347.

[141] *Id.*

Constitution, state sovereignty, and the need to maintain enforceable limits on the enumerated federal powers. If the federal government got the benefit of the doubt, the Court would not review the actual necessity of congressional measures and would embrace a per se rule against state taxes of federal activities. If the state received the benefit of the doubt, the Court would determine whether a given congressional measure (at least one as extraordinary as chartering a bank) was really indispensable under current conditions and would rely on cooperation between levels of government to prevent abuse of the state's powers of taxation. The choices were to trust the courts to make factual determinations about legislative measures, to trust Congress to exercise its powers responsibly, or to trust the states to behave fairly toward the federal government. Which of these institutions to trust was the fundamental issue posed by the oral arguments.

The Supreme Court Decision

Only two of the Justices were Federalists. The other five were from the opposing party that had been founded by Madison and Jefferson in their struggle against Hamilton and his fellows.[142] Nevertheless, Webster anticipated a favorable decision.[143] It came only three days after the end of Pinkney's argument.[144]

Not surprisingly, the unanimous opinion was written by Marshall. To a greater extent than any other Chief Justice in history, Marshall dominated the Court during his tenure. He transformed the office of the chief justiceship.[145] He wrote nearly half of the majority opinions during his tenure as Chief Justice, including nearly every opinion in constitutional cases, and in his early days, he wrote almost all of the Court's opinions.[146] With the notable exception of Thomas Jefferson, nearly everyone he interacted with liked and admired him, a useful trait in the close-knit world of early Washington society.[147] His "humility, good humor, flexibility, and patience" were invaluable in persuading other Justices to adopt his views or at least suppress their dissents.[148] He is also said to have been "unquestionably one of the great legal reasoners

---

[142] Warren, *supra* note 70, at 508–09.

[143] *Id.*

[144] *Id.* at 510.

[145] White, *supra* note 75, at 367–68.

[146] *Id.*

[147] *Id.* at 372.

[148] *Id.* at 373.

of his time: contemporaries regularly testified to his ability to march from premise to conclusion."[149] What made his opinions "peculiarly authoritative" was his "invocation of the supposedly timeless principles of the founding age," on which constitutional language was founded.[150]

Marshall began his opinion in *McCulloch* by stressing the imperative need for the Court to resolve the issue. The magnitude of the issues and its practical significance might "essentially influence the great operations of the government."[151] But the question "must be decided peacefully, or remain a source of hostile legislation, perhaps, of hostility of a still more serious nature; and if it is to be so decided, by this tribunal alone can the decision be made."[152] His opinion is not notable for its originality; essentially every idea can be traced to the oral arguments and Hamilton's letter to Washington. But the opinion has a flow to it that makes the conclusions seem almost inevitable. Below, we consider his analysis of the three major questions posed by the case.

The Sovereignty Issue

In discussing the sovereignty issue, Marshall began with a paraphrase of the state's claims. The state maintained that in construing the Constitution, it was important to "consider that instrument, not as emanating from the people, but as the act of sovereign and independent states."[153] Hence, the powers of the federal government were "delegated by the states, who alone are truly sovereign; and must be exercised in subordination to the states, who alone possess supreme dominion."[154]

In Marshall's view, however, the states did not and could not create the federal government. The Constitution drew its power from the state ratification conventions, which represented the people.[155] The state sovereignties were competent to form a league, such as the old Articles of Confederation, but not to "change this alliance into an effective government, possessing great and sovereign powers, and acting directly on the people."[156] Deriving, as it did, its powers directly from the people, the federal government was necessarily "supreme within its sphere of ac-

---

[149] *Id.*

[150] *Id.* at 375.

[151] *McCulloch*, 17 U.S. (4 Wheat.) at 400.

[152] *Id.* at 400–01.

[153] *Id.* at 402.

[154] *Id.*

[155] *Id.* at 403.

[156] *Id.* at 404.

tion," though that sphere was limited to the extent of its delegated powers: "It is the government of all; its powers are delegated by all; it represents all, and acts for all."[157]

McCulloch derives federal power from "We the People," but does not address a longtime dispute about the nature of popular sovereignty. Are "We the People" one people, though voting within particular state boundaries, or multiple state peoples, each preserving its own group identity? Various theories have been offered on this point during American history. Lincoln believed that Americans were one nation from the moment of independence. Others have believed that the separate state peoples gave rise to one unified People when the Constitution was ratified, while still others maintain that the state peoples remain completely separate even today.[158] These distinctions seem somewhat fine, if not theological, like medieval disputes over the nature of the Trinity, but that has not prevented them from having large political implications at times in our history.

Marshall does not clearly address this question in *McCulloch*. He did say that the "government of the Union" is "emphatically and truly, a government of the people."[159] He continued: "In form, and in substance, it emanates from them. Its powers are granted by them, and are to be exercised directly on them, and for their benefit."[160] This language suggests the existence of a unitary national people. But earlier, in speaking of ratification, he had said that it was true that the people had assembled in their separate states. "No political dreamer was ever wild enough to think of breaking down the lines which separate the states, and of compounding the American people into one common mass. Of consequence, when they act, they act in their states."[161] That language may suggest that the American people have not actually fused into a single whole, though it can also be read to mean that the state peoples retain their own identities and provide a forum for action even though a unified American people *also* exists. *McCulloch*, however, does not seem to take a real position on the fine points of popular sovereignty (though Marshall did have more to say on the subject after the opinion came down). The opinion does make it clear, however, that true sovereignty does not reside in state governments and that those governments are subordinate to the federal government.

---

[157] *Id.* at 405.

[158] *See* Daniel A. Farber, *Lincoln's Constitution* ch.2 (2003).

[159] 17 U.S. (4 Wheat.) at 405.

[160] *Id.*

[161] *Id.* at 403.

Marshall's axiom that federal sovereignty is supreme over the state governments provides the underlying theme for the rest of the opinion. This axiom implies that ultimate trust is to be reposed in the judgment of Congress, not in the judgment of the state legislatures. This in turn supports a broad interpretation of the necessary and proper clause and a narrow construction of state powers over federal entities.

The Scope of Federal Power

Marshall began his argument about the scope of federal power, as had the Bank's lawyers, by referring to the long and consistent practice of the other branches of government. He did not deny "that a bold and daring usurpation might be resisted, after an acquiescence still longer and more complete than this."[162] But at least where the issue related to the allocation of powers among the people's delegates, rather than to individual rights, such governmental practice should receive considerable weight.[163]

McCulloch emphasizes the paramount importance of federal power and the need for broad construction. "A constitution, to contain an accurate detail of all the subdivisions of which its great powers will admit, and of all the means by which they may be carried into execution, would partake of the prolixity of a legal code, and could scarcely be embraced by the human mind."[164] Hence, the nature of the Constitution required "that only its great outlines should be marked, its important objects designated, and the minor ingredients which compose those objects, be deduced from the nature of the objects themselves."[165] In considering the scope of federal powers, then, "we must never forget that it is a *constitution* we are expounding."[166] And given the "ample powers" entrusted to the federal government—the "sword and the purse, all the external relations, and no inconsiderable portion of the industry of the nation"—it must be entrusted with equally "ample means."[167] It was "in the interest of the nation" to facilitate the exercise of this power; "[i]t can never be their interest, and cannot be presumed to have been their intention, to clog and embarrass its execution...."[168]

---

[162] *Id.* at 401.

[163] *Id.*

[164] *Id.* at 407.

[165] *Id.*

[166] *Id.*

[167] *Id.* at 407–08.

[168] *Id.* at 408.

The power to create a corporation was just a means, like any other means, to be used where appropriate.[169]

Marshall rejected the argument that the word "necessary" limited the Congress's discretion over the choice of means. He had already indicated that, even *without* the necessary and proper clause, Congress would have had broad discretion over means. Thus, the state's argument came down to the idea that the necessary and proper clause actually narrowed the discretion which Congress might otherwise have derived directly from the various enumerated powers. Marshall found that implausible, since the text treats the clause as an additional source of power rather than a limitation on powers already granted.[170] The word "necessary" was capable of a broad range of meanings, depending on context, and "frequently imports no more than that one thing is convenient, or useful, or essential to another."[171] Indeed, elsewhere the Constitution used the term "absolutely necessary."[172] A narrow construction would defeat "the execution of those great powers on which the welfare of a nation essentially depends."[173] In a Constitution "intended to endure for ages to come, and consequently, to be adapted to the various *crises* of human affairs," it would have made no sense to "provide, by immutable rules, for exigencies which, if foreseen at all, must have been seen dimly, and must be best provided for as they occur."[174]

In famous language, Marshall set out the parameters of congressional power: "Let the end be legitimate, let it be within the scope of the constitution, and all means which are appropriate, which are plainly adapted to the end, which are not prohibited, but consist with the letter and spirit of the constitution, are constitutional."[175]

Marshall found it clear that the Bank met this test:

Throughout this vast republic, from the St. Croix to the Gulf of Mexico, from the Atlantic to the Pacific, revenue is to be collected and expended, armies are to be marched and supported. The exigencies of the nation may require, that the treasure raised in the north should be transported to the south, that raised in the east, conveyed to the west, or that this order should be reversed. Is that construc-

---

[169] *Id.* at 409–11.

[170] *Id.* at 419–20.

[171] *Id.* at 413.

[172] *Id.* at 414.

[173] *Id.* at 415.

[174] *Id.*

[175] *Id.* at 421.

tion of the constitution to be preferred, which would render these operations difficult, hazardous and expensive?[176]

As to the practical utility of the Bank, Marshall relied on the consensus among the nation's financial authorities over time.[177] Nor was the existence of the state banks as an alternative relevant, as the state had contended. The federal government is not to be dependent on the states "for the execution of the great powers assigned to it."[178] In any event, "congress alone can make the election" between the "choice of means."[179]

Intergovernmental Immunity

This left only the question of whether Maryland could tax the activities of a lawful federal instrumentality such as the Bank. Like the Bank's lawyers, Marshall embraced the proposition that the power to tax is the power to destroy.[180] But, said Marshall, it is "of the very essence of supremacy, to remove all obstacles to its action within its own sphere, and so to modify every power vested in subordinate governments, as to exempt its own operations from their own influence."[181] (As with most of the premises of Marshall's argument, he cites no authority for this proposition—it is seemingly presented as a self-evident truth which only an idiot could deny.)

"No taxation without representation" is part of the founding American creed. Accordingly, Marshall begins his analysis of the tax issue by explaining that the only check against abuse of the tax power is "found in the structure of the government itself," because in "imposing a tax, the legislature acts upon its constituents."[182] But although the people of a state give their government the power to tax themselves, the power of taxation extends only to the "subjects over which the sovereign power of a state extends," and this does not include the federal government.[183] This standard—the tax power corresponds with the extent of sovereignty—provides an "intelligible standard," freeing the court from "the perplexing inquiry, so unfit for the judicial department, what degree of

---

[176] *Id.* at 408.

[177] *Id.* at 423–24.

[178] *Id.* at 424.

[179] *Id.*

[180] *Id.* at 427.

[181] *Id.*

[182] *Id.* at 428.

[183] *Id.* at 429.

taxation is the legitimate use, and what degree may amount to the abuse of the power."[184] It also eliminates the need to repose confidence in the government of each state. For why would "the people of any one state" be "willing to trust those of another with a power to control the operations of a government to which they have confided their most important and valuable interests?"[185]

Marshall rebuffed the claim that state taxation of the federal government and federal taxation of the state government were equivalent. His argument presages what later became known as the process theory of constitutional law. The critical passage encapsulated much of the opinion's rationale and is worth quoting at length:

> But the two cases are not on the same reason. The people of all the states have created the general government, and have conferred upon it the general power of taxation. The people of all the states, and the states themselves, are represented in congress, and, by their representatives, exercise this power. When they tax the chartered institutions of the states, they tax their constituents; and these taxes must be uniform. But when a state taxes the operations of the government of the United States, it acts upon institutions created, not by their own constituents, but by people over whom they claim no control. It acts upon the measures of a government created by others as well as themselves, for the benefit of others in common with themselves. The difference is that which always exists, and always must exist, between the action of the whole on a part, and the action of a part on the whole—between the laws of a government declared to be supreme, and those of a government which, when in opposition to those laws, is not supreme.[186]

All of Marshall's rationales stem from the lawyers' oral presentations. Given the shortness of time, it could hardly have been otherwise. But he hangs the arguments on a framework that seems all his own. His basic premises were that the federal government was entrusted with the most important powers of government by the people themselves and that it was necessarily supreme over the states, whose powers derived from only subsets of the people. Given these premises, Marshall's conclusions flowed inexorably.

---

[184] *Id.* at 429–30.

[185] *Id.* at 431.

[186] *Id.* at 435–36.

The Immediate Impact of McCulloch

McCulloch was seen as the most important case of the Term.[187] Response to the opinion was explosive, especially in the South and what was then the West (now the Midwest). A Mississippi paper said that the "last vestige of the sovereignty and independence of the individual States composing the National Confederacy is obliterated at one fell swoop."[188] In Tennessee, a newspaper said the decision had "awakened public attention to the aristocratical [sic] character of the Court, and must sooner or later bring down on the members of it the execration of the community," while a Kentucky paper said Marshall's principles "must raise an alarm throughout our widely-extended empire" because they "strike at the roots of State–Rights and State Sovereignty."[189]

The most significant attacks on *McCulloch* came in the form of anonymous essays by Virginia Judge Spencer Roane and another member of the inner circle of Virginia politics, probably Judge William Brockenbrough.[190] Virginia was not particularly anti-Bank, but it was a stronghold of the Jeffersonian states' rights ideology.[191] Thus, the attacks focused on the broad nationalist principles of the opinion rather than its specific holding concerning the Bank.

In the first of the critical essays to appear, the anonymous author pointed to "two principles" in the *McCulloch* opinion that "endanger the very existence of state rights."[192] One was "the denial that the powers of the federal government were delegated by the states"; the other was the claim that federal powers, especially the necessary and proper clause, "ought to be construed in a liberal, rather than a restricted sense."[193] As to the first, the Constitution was not ratified by the mass of the people but by "the people only within the limits of the respective sovereign states," whereby the states "in their sovereign capacity did delegate to the federal government its powers, and in so doing were parties to the compact."[194] As to the second, if Congress took full advantage of the Court's interpretation of its powers, "it is difficult to say how small

---

[187] *See* White, *supra* note 75, at 542.

[188] Warren, *supra* note 70, at 519.

[189] *Id.* at 520.

[190] Gerald Gunther, Introduction to *John Marshall's Defense of* McCulloch v. Maryland 1, 13 (Gerald Gunther, ed., 1969).

[191] *Id.* at 9.

[192] *A Virginian's "Amphictyon" Essays*, Rich. Enquirer, Mar. 30–Apr. 2, 1819, *reprinted in* Gunther, *supra* note 190, at 52, 54.

[193] *Id.* at 54–55.

[194] *Id.* at 56.

would be the remnant of power left in the hands of the state authorities."[195] The next essay in the series set out a parade of horribles: the federal government could "lay out ... money on roads and canals," "create boards for internal improvement," "build universities, academies, and school houses for the poor," "incorporate companies for the promotion of agriculture," and build churches and pay ministers.[196]

Roane's essays took a similar tack. He raised the alarm about the expansion of federal power: "That man must be a deplorable idiot who does not see that there is no earthly difference between an *unlimited* grant of power, and a grant limited in its terms, but accompanied with *unlimited* means of carrying it into execution."[197] The word "necessary" must be strictly construed, as Roane said it was in the common law and the law of nations.[198] The Court's interpretation would "even give congress a right to *disarm* the people, as nothing is more *conducive* to insurrection, than having the means to make it successful."[199] A similar breadth of interpretation had brought the Sedition Act into being.[200]

Roane also stressed that the Constitution is "a *compact* between the people of each state, and those of all the states, and it is nothing more than a compact."[201] "Can it be said, after this, that the constitution was adopted by the people of the United States as *one* people? Or can it be denied that it was adopted by the several states, by the people of the said states respectively, and are *they* not parties to the compact?"[202] Hence, he said, "[o]ur general government then ... is as much ... a 'league,' as was the former confederation. The only difference is, that the powers of this government are much *extended*."[203] Thus, "this government may be, in some sense, considered, as a continuation of the *former* federal government."[204]

Marshall was sufficiently alarmed to publish his own anonymous defenses of the decision. With respect to the necessary and proper clause,

---

[195] *Id.* at 55.

[196] *Id.* at 75.

[197] *Roane's "Hampden" Essays*, Rich. Enquirer, June 11–22, 1819, *reprinted in* Gunther, *supra* note 190, at 106, 110.

[198] *Id.* at 117–24.

[199] *Id.* at 134.

[200] *Id.*

[201] *Id.* at 127.

[202] *Id.* at 142.

[203] *Id.* at 146.

[204] *Id.*

he challenged Roane's analogies to other areas of the law. None of the circumstances "which might seem to justify rather a strict construction" in the situations cited by Roane "apply to a constitution":

> It is not a contract between enemies seeking each other's destruction, and anxious to insert every particular, lest a watchful adversary should take advantage of the omission. Nor is it a case where implications in favor of one man impair the vested rights of another. Nor is it a contract for a single object, everything relating to which, might be recollected and inserted. It is the act of a people, creating a government, without which they cannot exist as a people.[205]

But Marshall also denied that *McCulloch* had given Congress unlimited powers. "The reasoning of the judges," he said, "is opposed to that restricted construction which would embarrass congress, in the execution of its acknowledged powers; and maintains that such construction, if not required by the words of the instrument, ought not to be adopted of choice; but makes no allusion to a construction enlarging the grant beyond the meaning of its ends."[206]

Marshall staunchly rejected Roane's assertion that the United States remained a confederation, as it had been before the Constitution was adopted:

> Will [Roane] deny that there is such a people as the people of the United States? Have we no national existence? ... The United States is a nation; but a nation composed of states in many, though not in all, respects, sovereign. The people of these states are also the people of the United States.... [W]e are all citizens, not only of our particular states, but also of this great republic.[207]

Admittedly, Marshall said, the Constitution was adopted "by the people acting as states."[208] But he observed that a government's character depended on its constitution, not on its manner of adoption. The United Kingdom was a single nation, even though it came into being through the separate actions of the parliaments of England, Scotland, and Ireland.[209]

Unlike the Articles of Confederation, "our constitution is not a league" but a "government,"[210] and Marshall insisted that Americans

---

[205] *Marshall's "A Friend of the Constitution" Essays*, Alexandria Gazette, June 30–July 15, 1819, *reprinted in* Gunther, *supra* note 190, at 155, 170.

[206] *Id.* at 182.

[207] *Id.* at 195.

[208] *Id.* at 197.

[209] *Id.* at 197–98.

[210] *Id.* at 199.

should think twice before reducing the country to the chaos and weak-
ness it suffered under the Articles.[211] "Our constitution," maintained
Marshall,"is not a compact."[212] Rather, it is "the act of a single party. It
is the act of the people of the United States, assembling in their
respective states, and adopting a government for the whole nation."[213]
Hence, "[a]ll arguments founded on leagues and compacts, must be
fallacious when applied to a government like this."[214]

Some of the fallout over *McCulloch* was legal rather than political,
as states attempted other methods of attacking the Bank. A later case,
Osborn v. Bank of the United States,[215] gave Marshall the opportunity to
reemphasize some of his themes from the earlier opinion. Ohio had
passed a law imposing a $50,000 tax on each of the Bank's branches.
Pursuant to this law, Osborn, the state auditor, decided to seize the
funds from the bank. The Bank obtained a federal injunction against
collection of the tax, but state officials went ahead anyway. After being
refused payment of the tax, Osborn's assistant entered the bank's vault
and took everything he could find, to the tune of $120,000. The lower
federal court issued an order directing the return of the funds to the
bank.[216]

Today, *Osborn* is mostly known only to experts in the law of federal
jurisdiction, primarily because of the Court's holding that a federal court
could hear any suit brought by the Bank as a federal instrumentality.
For present purposes, however, the more important point was the
injunction against the state officers. Just as he had rejected state
authority to tax the bank, Marshall repudiated the claim that state
sovereign immunity shielded its officers' interference with the bank. He
stressed the possible impact of a contrary holding on federal supremacy:
state officers could "arrest the execution of any law in the United
States." If a state administrator imposed a fine or penalty on a federal
official, the official would be unable to obtain an injunction. The post-
man, the tax collector, the U.S. marshal, and the military recruiter
would all be at risk of ruinous penalties like those assessed against the
Bank. In short, Marshall said, a state would be "capable, at its will, of
attacking the nation, of arresting its progress at every step, of acting
vigorously and effectually in the execution of its designs, while the

---

[211] *Id.* at 199–200.

[212] *Id.* at 203.

[213] *Id.*

[214] *Id.*

[215] 22 U.S. (9 Wheat.) 738 (1824).

[216] Warren, *supra* note 70, at 528–30, 533.

nation stands naked, stripped of its defensive armour."[217] Once again, national supremacy was the prime imperative.

McCulloch, like *Osborn* after it, must be seen as part of the battle over states' rights that began with the Virginia and Kentucky Resolutions and ended at Appomattox Courthouse. Jefferson and Madison, in the Resolutions they drafted, embraced the compact theory of the Constitution and toyed with state interposition against the federal government. Roane himself had earlier used the same theories to argue that the state courts were not subject to appellate review by the Supreme Court, because one sovereign could not direct the actions of another. A little later, the compact theory formed the basis for John Calhoun's theory of nullification and, after that, for Southern secession. On the other side of this debate were figures such as Marshall, Webster (not only in *McCulloch* but in important public speeches), and later Lincoln. The debate over strict construction derived from this basic difference in how to conceptualize the Union. Was it merely a league of sovereign states, or was it a sovereign nation in its own right?[218]

The Continuing Importance of McCulloch *Today*

The Bank of the United States died an inglorious death at the hands of Andrew Jackson, who first vetoed a renewal of its charter and then brought it down by withdrawing all federal deposits.[219] Perhaps confirming the views of its supporters about genuine need for the Bank, the economy promptly went into a tailspin.[220] By the time Jackson left office, says one historian, "America was in the early stages of its biggest financial crisis to date."[221] But the Bank of the United States never rose again, though today the national bank system and the Federal Reserve serve much the same functions that Hamilton intended for the Bank.

Yet the significance of *McCulloch* far outlived the dispute that gave rise to the case. As the late Gerald Gunther explained:

> With his elaborate endorsement of constitutional flexibility and congressional discretion, Marshall unmistakably cast the Court's weight on the centralizing side in the recurrent struggle about allocation of authority between nation and states. With this opinion, the Court provided a reservoir of justifications for national action

---

[217] 22 U.S. (9 Wheat.) at 847–48, 857–58.

[218] See Farber, *supra* note 158, ch.3.

[219] See Johnson, *supra* note 10, at 353–55.

[220] *Id.* at 356–57.

[221] *Id.* at 357.

perhaps even fuller than Marshall intended—one repeatedly drawn on during the Era of Good Feelings and the Age of the Robber Barons and the New Deal and our civil rights crises by those who have sought to expand the area of national competence.[222]

To Gunther's list we might now add the strong measures taken by Congress and the Executive beginning in the fall of 2008, in an effort to stabilize the reeling national economy.

Despite the almost iconic stature of *McCulloch* in American constitutional law, its meaning and current significance are still contested on today's Supreme Court. As basic issues about the nature of federalism are once again being debated, some dissonance appears to exist between Marshall's nationalist vision and the inclinations of some of the current Justices.

The Supreme Court found occasion to debate again the nature of the Union in the 1995 *Term Limits* case, which involved a state's power to set term limits for members of Congress.[223] The majority view in *Term Limits* was that control over federal legislators pertained solely to the new government created by the Constitution rather than to any preexisting state authority, and hence was not "reserved" by the Tenth Amendment. Justice Stevens' majority opinion lays out the conventional modern view of state and federal sovereignty. Under the Articles of Confederation, Stevens said, "the States retained most of their sovereignty, like independent nations bound together only by treaties."[224] The new Constitution "reject[ed] the notion that the Nation was a collection of States, and instead creat[ed] a direct link between the National Government and the people of the United States."[225] Stevens' view harkened back to Daniel Webster's assertion that "[t]he people of the United States are one people."[226]

In contrast, Justice Thomas's dissent, joined by three of his colleagues, squarely rejected this vision of national sovereignty. "Because the majority fundamentally misunderstands the notion of 'reserved' powers," he said, "I start with some first principles."[227] The most basic of those first principles, according to Justice Thomas, was this: "The ultimate source of the Constitution's authority is the consent of the people of each individual State, not the consent of the undifferentiated

---

[222] Gunther, *supra* note 190, at 6.

[223] *U.S. Term Limits, Inc. v. Thornton*, 514 U.S. 779 (1995).

[224] *Id.* at 803 (quoting *Wesberry v. Sanders*, 376 U.S. 1, 9 (1964)).

[225] *Id.*

[226] Robert V. Remini, *Daniel Webster: The Man and His Time* 379 (1997).

[227] *U.S. Term Limits*, 514 U.S. at 846 (Thomas, J., dissenting).

people of the Nation as a whole."[228] Justice Thomas argued that under the Constitution "the people of each State retained their separate political identities" even after ratification.[229]

Justice Kennedy, who has generally sided with the Court's proponents of states' rights, refused to go along with Thomas's view of state sovereignty in *Term Limits*. In Kennedy's view, the basis of the federal government's legitimacy is "that it owes its existence to the act of the whole people who created it."[230] He denied that "the sole political identity of an American is with the State of his or her residence."[231] He disputed the view that "the people of the United States do not have a political identity as well, one independent of, though consistent with, their identity as citizens of the State of their residence." Like the states, Kennedy concluded, the national government is "republican in essence and in theory," drawing its power from the People.[232] Only four years later, however, in *Alden v. Maine*,[233] Justice Kennedy joined the four *Term Limits* dissenters in proclaiming that the states retain "a residuary and inviolable sovereignty" or at least, as he quickly added, "the dignity, though not the full authority, of sovereignty."[234] Apparently, the sovereignty issue remains unsettled, even today.

This is not surprising, because the Framers themselves apparently had no very clear conception about the location of sovereignty under the Constitution. As a leading historian explains, "no single vector neatly charted the course the framers took in allocating power between the Union and the states."[235] In Federalist 39, which refers to the origins of the Constitution in the "federal" action of the peoples of the various states, Madison concludes by speaking of the untidy, mixed nature of the new government. "The proposed Constitution," he said, "is, in strictness, neither a national nor a federal Constitution, but a composition of both."[236] It combines some features of each. "In its foundation," he said,

---

[228] *Id.*

[229] *Id.* at 849.

[230] *Id.* at 839 (Kennedy, J., concurring).

[231] *Id.* at 840.

[232] *Id.* at 839–42.

[233] 527 U.S. 706 (1999).

[234] *Id.* at 715.

[235] Jack N. Rakove, *Original Meanings: Politics and Ideas in the Making of the Constitution* (1996).

[236] *The Federalist* No. 39 (James Madison), *reprinted in The Federalist Papers* 254, 259 (Issac Kramnick ed., 1987).

"it is federal, not national."[237] But "in the sources from which the ordinary powers of the government are drawn, it is partly federal and partly national; in the operation of these powers, it is national, not federal; in the extent of them, again, it is federal, not national."[238] Finally, according to Madison, the amendment process "is neither wholly federal nor wholly national."[239] Thus, if there was a simple answer about the location of sovereignty after ratification, the Framers themselves apparently didn't know it. As a leading historian of the Framing period says, after 1789, "sovereignty itself would remain diffused—which is to say, it would exist everywhere and nowhere."[240]

If past experience is any guide, the ambiguity of the historical record is likely only to fuel the debate. Sovereignty remains a live issue in American law, almost two centuries after *McCulloch*. Not surprisingly, the meaning of *McCulloch* itself remains a bone of contention in these debates. Justice Thomas quoted *McCulloch* to the effect that no political dreamer ever thought of "compounding the American people into one common mass," in support of his theory that sovereignty remains with the separate populaces of each state.[241] Justice Kennedy, however, also quoted *McCulloch* to support the theory that the government derives its power from the people of America, not from the states.[242] Justice Thomas is probably right that Marshall viewed ratification as a state-by-state process.[243] But as his response to Roane shows, Marshall did not agree that the peoples of the states remained entirely separate; rather, he emphasized that ratification of the Constitution simultaneously created the People of the United States as an entity.

Thomas's dissent in *Term Limits*, plus the Court's recent interest in protecting state sovereign immunity from congressional or judicial interference, suggests a possible leaning toward the compact theory that was rejected by Marshall. But whatever uncertainties may exist about its theoretical substructure, the legal framework created by Marshall—one of broad national power untrammeled by potential resistance from state governments—remains firmly in place. Today's disputes take place at

---

[237] *Id.*

[238] *Id.*

[239] *Id.*

[240] Jack N. Rakove, *Making a Hash of Sovereignty, Part I*, 2 Green Bag 2d 35, 41 (1998); *see also* Jack N. Rakove, *Making a Hash of Sovereignty, Part II*, 3 Green Bag 2d 51 (1999).

[241] *U.S. Term Limits*, 514 U.S. at 849.

[242] *Id.* at 839.

[243] *See* Martin S. Flaherty, *John Marshall,* McCulloch v. Maryland, *and "We the People": Revisions in Need of Revising*, 43 Wm. & Mary L. Rev. 1339, 1370–79 (2002).

the margins of federal power, such as the ability of Congress to compel the affirmative assistance of state legislators and administrators.[244] Neither Thomas nor anyone else on the modern Supreme Court would argue that all federal powers must be construed as narrowly as possible or that states have the authority to hinder federal programs with which they disagree. Thus, the fundamental holding of *McCulloch* is now legal bedrock.

Conclusion

The breadth of Marshall's opinion is remarkable. He does discuss some details of the constitutional text, such as the contrast between "necessary" in the necessary and proper clause and "absolutely necessary" elsewhere in the Constitution. But he makes little reference to the specifics of the ratification debates, the legal authorities cited by the parties, or the specific reasons given in Congress for chartering a bank. Rather, he relied primarily on his understanding of the Constitution's "objects, ends, and nature."[245] In doing so, he drew on the structural points made by Webster, Pinkney, and Wirts in the oral argument, some of which traced all the way back to Hamilton. But he bound them together with an overriding theme: the federal government must be supreme as to any matter of common concern among the states, because it alone represented the people of the entire nation.

Constitutional law is generally thought to involve the interpretation of a text. But in *McCulloch*, it may be more accurate to say that Marshall was interpreting an *action*: the agreement of the peoples of the various states to transform the existing league into a nation, in the process transforming themselves from thirteen separate state peoples into "We, the People of the United States." By adopting the text of the Constitution, the people not only created a government but also a nation. The words they used can only be understood as a constituent part of this act of self-creation. It is this act that is probably the deepest message of the *McCulloch* opinion.

---

[244] *See Printz v. United States*, 521 U.S. 898 (1997).

[245] Sylvia Snowiss, *Text and Principle in John Marshall's Constitutional Law: The Cases of* Marbury *and* McCulloch, 33 J. Marshall L. Rev. 973, 1002 (2000).

*

3

Jim Chen*

The Story of *Wickard v. Filburn*: Agriculture, Aggregation, and Commerce

Introduction

The story of American constitutional law is in many respects an agrarian fable. Strikingly large chunks of constitutional law originate in America's rural past.[1] Numerous constitutional controversies have arisen from seemingly humble disputes over crop production, animal husbandry, and the processing of agricultural commodities.[2]

---

* The telling of this story owes a great deal to Mary Lou Filbrun Spurgeon, the daughter of Roscoe Curtiss Filbrun. I have drawn heavily from an August 30, 2002, letter from Mrs. Spurgeon [hereinafter Spurgeon Letter]. One item not covered in that letter is Roscoe Filburn's decision in the early 1950s to change the spelling of his family name to "Filbrun." Mrs. Spurgeon knew no specific reason for the spelling change. I shall refer to this chapter's protagonist as Roscoe *Filburn* when discussing his Supreme Court case, but as Roscoe *Filbrun* when discussing his later life.

The Ohio newspapers cited in this article and the Filburn family history cited in note 92 are available in the Dayton Metro Library. A version of this chapter was published as Filburn's *Legacy*, 52 Emory L.J. 1719 (2003).

[1] *Cf.* Jim Chen, *The Potable Constitution*, 15 Const. Comment. 1 (1998) (using cases involving milk and liquor to outline American constitutional law).

[2] *See, e.g., United States v. Carolene Prods. Co.*, 304 U.S. 144 (1938); *United States v. Butler*, 297 U.S. 1 (1936); *A.L.A. Schechter Poultry Corp. v. United States*, 295 U.S. 495 (1935); *Nebbia v. New York*, 291 U.S. 502 (1934); *The Slaughter–House Cases*, 83 U.S. (16 Wall.) 36 (1872). *See generally* Geoffrey P. Miller, *Public Choice at the Dawn of the Special Interest State: The Story of Butter and Margarine*, 77 Cal. L. Rev. 83 (1989); Geoffrey P. Miller, *The True Story of Carolene Products*, 1987 Sup. Ct. Rev. 397.

Wickard v. Filburn[3] bridges the illusory gap between agricultural and constitutional law. *Filburn*[4] addresses core issues of federalism, perhaps the "oldest question of constitutional law."[5] Nearly every case about civil liberties or governmental structure can be analyzed as "a case about federalism."[6] Among American innovations in government, "federalism was the unique contribution of the Framers."[7] If indeed the American founding "split the atom of sovereignty,"[8] then the New Deal sustained federalism's first chain reaction. In 1942, the year in which Enrico Fermi harnessed atomic fission, the Supreme Court decided *Wickard v. Filburn*.[9]

Filburn is at once a product of its era and a beacon across legal generations. The New Deal program in *Filburn* addressed agricultural complaints dating from the end of World War I. When Roscoe Filburn won his initial victory in court, the local newspaper divided its front page between that news and a war dispatch from the Dutch East Indies.[10] Like art deco architecture, the photography of Margaret Bourke–White[11] and Walker Evans,[12] and Christian Dior's exuberant designs,[13] *Filburn* bears the cultural marks of the Jazz Age, the Great Depression, and World War II. *Filburn*, so it seems, happened only yesterday.[14] By the same

---

[3] 317 U.S. 111 (1942).

[4] *Wickard v. Filburn*, of course, should be abbreviated as *Filburn* and not as *Wickard*. As Secretary of Agriculture, Claude Wickard was involved in far more cases than Roscoe Filburn, a private citizen. Once upon a time the Supreme Court understood this distinction and properly abbreviated *Filburn*. See, e.g., *Mandeville Island Farms v. American Crystal Sugar Co.*, 334 U.S. 219, 231 n.10 (1948) (referring twice to "the *Filburn* case"). A leading Warren Court decision, however, used *Wickard* as the short form, see *Maryland v. Wirtz*, 392 U.S. 183, 196 n.27 (1968), and by now all hope of restoring this traditional citation convention seems lost. See, e.g., *United States v. Lopez*, 514 U.S. 549, 556–58 (1995) (referring constantly to "*Wickard*").

[5] *New York v. United States*, 505 U.S. 144, 149 (1992); see also H. Jefferson Powell, *The Oldest Question of Constitutional Law*, 79 Va. L. Rev. 633 (1993).

[6] *Coleman v. Thompson*, 501 U.S. 722, 726 (1991).

[7] *United States v. Lopez*, 514 U.S. 549, 575 (1995) (Kennedy, J., concurring).

[8] *U.S. Term Limits, Inc. v. Thornton*, 514 U.S. 779, 838 (1995) (Kennedy, J., concurring).

[9] 317 U.S. 111 (1942).

[10] Compare *U.S. Court Voids Wheat Penalty*, Dayton Sunday J.-Herald, Mar. 15, 1942, at 1, with *Allies Concede Loss of 12 Warships Off Java but Bag 8 Enemy Vessels*, Dayton Sunday J.-Herald, Mar. 15, 1942, at 1.

[11] See generally *Margaret Bourke–White: Photographer* (Sean Callahan, Maryann Kornely & Debra Cohen eds., 1998).

[12] See generally James Agee & Walker Evans, *Let Us Now Praise Famous Men* (1939).

[13] See generally Marie–France Pochna, *Christian Dior: The Man Who Made the World Look New* (Joanna Savill trans., 1996).

[14] See Frederick Lewis Allen, *Only Yesterday: An Informal History of the 1920's* (rpt. 1997).

token, *Filburn* represents a pivotal moment in the Supreme Court's centuries-long effort to define the scope of Congress's power "[t]o regulate Commerce with foreign Nations, and among the several States, and with the Indian Tribes."[15]

Filburn and other New Deal cases involved two fiercely contested aspects of Commerce Clause jurisprudence. Each of these points of dispute can be traced to the language of the Constitution. One involved the definition of "Commerce"; the other, the significance of the phrase, "among the several States." Before the New Deal, the Supreme Court distinguished sharply between commerce and productive activities such as agriculture, manufacturing, and mining. "Commerce with foreign nations and among the States," wrote the Court in 1880, "consists in intercourse and traffic, including . . . navigation and the transportation and transit of persons and property, as well as the purchase, sale, and exchange of commodities."[16] At the same time, even the expectation that "products of domestic enterprise in agriculture or manufactures, or in the arts, may ultimately become the subjects of foreign [or interstate] commerce" did not entitle Congress to regulate the production of these articles.[17] The Court reasoned that such an expansive interpretation of Congress's power to regulate commerce would displace the traditional police power of the states over "not only manufactures, but also agriculture, horticulture, stock raising, domestic fisheries, mining–in short, every branch of human industry."[18]

In the twenty-first century, the federal government's regulatory power reaches each of these fields. The contemporary scope of Congress's power over foreign and interstate commerce draws its strength precisely from the expectation that "the wheat grower of the Northwest, and the cotton planter of the South, [would] plant, cultivate, and harvest his [or her] crop with an eye on the prices at Liverpool, New York, and Chicago."[19] Before the New Deal, the "delicate, multiform, and vital interests" in these fields of enterprise at one time seemed inherently "local in all the details of their successful management."[20] Today's Court, by contrast, treats the regulation of commodity markets as an appropriate, even routine, subject for federal legislation.

---

[15] U.S. Const. art. I, § 8, cl. 3.

[16] *County of Mobile v. Kimball*, 102 U.S. 691, 702 (1880); *accord Kidd v. Pearson*, 128 U.S. 1, 20–21 (1888).

[17] *Veazie v. Moor*, 55 U.S. (14 How.) 568, 573 (1853); *accord Carter v. Carter Coal Co.*, 298 U.S. 238, 298 (1936).

[18] *Kidd*, 128 U.S. at 21.

[19] *Id.*

[20] *Id.*

Filburn has also figured prominently in the Supreme Court's treatment of the line between intrastate and interstate commerce. The Court's Commerce Clause cases have always acknowledged that congressional power does not reach "those internal concerns ... which are completely within a particular State, which do not affect other States, and with which it is not necessary to interfere, for the purpose of executing some of the general powers of the [federal] government."[21] This division of responsibility does not mean, however, that "the power of Congress ... stop[s] at the jurisdictional lines of the several States."[22] Commerce Clause jurisprudence before the New Deal established that Congress's power to regulate "instruments of interstate commerce" inherently "embraces the right to control ... all [intrastate] matters having such a close and substantial relation to interstate traffic that [federal] control is essential or appropriate."[23] The fact that certain activities simultaneously affect intrastate and interstate commerce "does not derogate from the complete and paramount authority of Congress over the latter."[24]

Federal responses to agricultural crises during the early twentieth century triggered a dramatic struggle over the boundary between state and federal authority. Even before the New Deal, the Supreme Court endorsed congressional efforts to combat monopolistic threats to the free flow of livestock and grain.[25] Agricultural controversies helped the Court envision how "commerce among the States is not a technical legal conception, but a practical one, drawn from the course of business."[26] The New Deal's aggressive response to global depression, which dealt extraordinarily harsh blows to American agriculture, inspired unprecedented legislation at the frontiers of Congress's authority.

By virtue of its prominence in the New Deal's agricultural debate, *Wickard v. Filburn* assumed an even greater role in the ensuing constitutional transformation. Together with *United States v. Darby*[27] and *NLRB v. Jones & Laughlin Steel Corp.*,[28] *Wickard v. Filburn* is thought

---

[21] *Gibbons v. Ogden*, 22 U.S. (9 Wheat.) 1, 195 (1824).

[22] *Id.*

[23] *Houston, E. & W. Tex. Ry. v. United States (The Shreveport Rate Cases)*, 234 U.S. 342, 351 (1914).

[24] *Id.*

[25] *See, e.g., Board of Trade v. Olsen*, 262 U.S. 1, 32 (1923) (upholding provisions of the Grain Futures Act of 1922); *Stafford v. Wallace*, 258 U.S. 495, 516 (1922) (rejecting a challenge to the Packers and Stockyards Act).

[26] *Swift & Co. v. United States*, 196 U.S. 375, 398 (1905).

[27] 312 U.S. 100 (1941).

[28] 301 U.S. 1 (1937).

to have marked a turning point, perhaps even a high-water mark, in Commerce Clause jurisprudence.[29] The Rehnquist Court aggressively reinterpreted the Commerce Clause in "a mighty effort to put the states in what" today's Justices believe "to be their rightful place."[30] Given the apparent ideological allegiances of their successors, the death of Chief Justice Rehnquist and the retirement of Justice O'Connor do not appear likely to undermine the Court's reinvigorated resolve to define clear "distinction[s] between what is truly national and what is truly local."[31] *Filburn* has been thrown back into the constitutional fray. Should the 111th Congress and the Obama administration expand federal powers in response to the United States' economic problems, Filburn could come to play an important role in resolving the validity of those actions.

After providing a brief survey of American agriculture and its regulation between the World Wars, I shall describe the controversy over Roscoe Filburn's 1941 wheat crop. In its own time, *Wickard v. Filburn* represented merely one minor component of the New Deal Court's Commerce Clause jurisprudence. Greater turmoil over the Commerce Clause at the turn of the twenty-first century has breathed new life into *Filburn*. I shall therefore examine not only what *Filburn* meant when it was decided, but also what it represents today.

Background

American farmers suffered mightily during the Great Depression.[32] A mere generation earlier, American farmers were enjoying unmatched prosperity. The period immediately before World War I is memorialized as the "parity" period in federal agricultural law. "Parity" is the ratio of

---

[29] *See United States v. Morrison*, 529 U.S. 598, 608 (2000) ("[I]n the years since *NLRB v. Jones & Laughlin Steel Corp.*, Congress has had considerably greater latitude ... than our previous case law permitted." (citations omitted)); *United States v. Lopez*, 514 U.S. 549, 556 (1995) ("*Jones & Laughlin Steel, Darby*, and *Wickard* ushered in an era of Commerce Clause jurisprudence that greatly expanded the previously defined authority of Congress...."); *id.* at 573 (Kennedy, J., concurring) (describing *Jones & Laughlin* as "mark[ing] the Court's definitive commitment to the practical conception of the commerce power"); *Perez v. United States*, 402 U.S. 146, 151 (1971) (describing *Darby* and *Filburn* as cases that "restored" the "broader view of the Commerce Clause announced" in *Gibbons v. Ogden*, 22 U.S. (9 Wheat.) 1 (1824)); *Heart of Atlanta Motel, Inc. v. United States*, 379 U.S. 241, 257 (1964) (listing *Jones & Laughlin, Darby*, and *Filburn* among decisions upholding applications of the commerce power).

[30] John T. Noonan, Jr., *Narrowing the Nation's Power: The Supreme Court Sides with the States* 8 (2002); *see also* Philip P. Frickey & Steven S. Smith, *Judicial Review, the Congressional Process, and the Federalism Cases: An Interdisciplinary Critique*, 111 Yale L.J. 1707 (2002).

[31] *Lopez*, 514 U.S. at 567–68.

[32] *See, e.g.*, John Steinbeck, *The Grapes of Wrath* (1939).

current prices, wages, interest rates, and taxes paid by farmers relative
to "the general level of such prices, wages, rates, and taxes during the
period January 1910 to December 1914, inclusive."[33] The notion that the
government should preserve "the ratio of the prices farmers receive for
the products they sell to the prices they pay for goods and services" at a
level enjoyed during the "parity" period became a rallying point for
those "advocating increased income for farmers."[34]

The years before the Great War were in fact agriculture's golden
age. The 1920 census was the first to report a higher urban than rural
population; in the following decade, the urban population of the United
States would grow by an unprecedented 15 million:[35]

> In 1790, 1 out of every 20 of the 3,929,214 inhabitants of the United
> States was living in urban territory.... In every decade thereafter,
> with the exception of that from 1810 to 1820, the rate of growth of
> the urban population exceeded that of the rural population. By 1860,
> one out of five persons was included in the urban population. The
> process of urbanization continued in the following decades, and by
> 1920 the urban population exceeded the rural population.[36]

But raw population shifts concealed the true drivers of change. The
war that made the world safe for democracy rendered the American
countryside unfit for agriculture.[37] "The initial shock of war in 1914 ...
brought an overnight collapse in the foreign sales of wheat and cotton...."[38] American entry into the war drove commodity prices even
lower, as the urgent cultivation of 40 million new acres poured vast grain

---

[33] 7 U.S.C. § 1301(a)(1)(C) (2000); *see also United States v. Butler*, 297 U.S. 1, 54
(1936) (reporting the use of a "base period" of August 1909 through July 1914 in the
determination of price and income support levels under the Agricultural Adjustment Act of
1933). *See generally, e.g.*, George N. Peek & Hugh S. Johnson, *Equality for Agriculture*
(1922); William R. Camp, *The Organization of Agriculture in Relation to the Problem of
Price Stabilization*, 32 J. Pol. Econ. 282 (1924).

[34] Harold F. Breimyer, *Agricultural Philosophies and Policies in the New Deal*, 68
Minn. L. Rev. 333, 336 (1983); *see also* Peter H. Irons, *The New Deal Lawyers* 115–16
(1982) (describing the application of the parity principle in the drafting of the Agricultural
Adjustment Act of 1933).

[35] *See* 2 U.S. Dep't of Commerce, Bureau of the Census, *U.S. Census of Population:
1950*, at 12 (1953) (Characteristics of the Population / United States Summary) (reporting
an increase of 14,796,850 in the urban population of the United States between 1920 and
1930).

[36] *Id.*

[37] *See generally* Benjamin H. Hibbard, *Effects of the Great War upon Agriculture in the
United States and Great Britain* 22–67 (1919) (Carnegie Endow. for Int'l Peace, Div. of
Econ. & History, Preliminary Economic Studies of the War No. 11).

[38] Theodore Saloutos, *The American Farmer and the New Deal* 3 (1982).

harvests out of the Plains.[39] Meanwhile, wartime inflation devastated purchasing power on the farm.[40]

Macroeconomic turmoil coincided with technological revolution. "[T]he process of economic development and specialization" during the early twentieth century transformed "functions which are necessary to the total economic process of" agriculture into "separate and independent productive functions operated in conjunction with the agricultural function but no longer a part of it."[41] Systematic substitution of engines for organic horsepower simultaneously raised yields, increased dependence on purchased inputs, and decreased demand for feed grains.[42] Many farmers, especially wheat growers, were caught in a classic price squeeze:[43] depressed demand and prices for their products, coupled with unbearable increases in the cost of living.[44]

Nowhere was the transformation more dramatic than in the South. Full deployment of the mechanical cotton picker between the World Wars rendered "obsolete the sharecropper system" that had taken root after the Civil War.[45] Boll weevil infestation delivered the *coup de grâce* to the South's agrarian economy.[46] In "one of the largest and most rapid mass internal movements of people in history," six and a half million black Americans would eventually leave the rural South.[47] "[W]hen the

---

[39] *Id.*

[40] *See* A.B. Genung, *The Purchasing Power of the Farmer's Dollar from 1913 to Date*, 117 Annals Am. Acad. Pol. & Soc. Sci. 22, 22–23 (1925).

[41] *Farmers Reservoir & Irrig. Co. v. McComb*, 337 U.S. 755, 761 (1949).

[42] *See* Saloutos, *supra* note 38, at 6, 25.

[43] *See generally, e.g., Federal Power Comm'n v. Conway Corp.*, 426 U.S. 271, 279 (1976); *City of Anaheim v. Southern Cal. Edison Co.*, 955 F.2d 1373, 1376–78 (9th Cir. 1992); John E. Lopatka, *The Electric Utility Price Squeeze as an Antitrust Cause of Action*, 31 UCLA L. Rev. 563 (1984).

[44] For an explanation of the "agricultural treadmill," the farm-flavored variant of the price squeeze, see Willard W. Cochrane, *Farm Prices: Myth and Reality* 85–107 (1958); Willard C. Cochrane, *The Development of American Agriculture: A Historical Analysis* 378–95 (1979).

[45] Nicholas Lemann, *The Promised Land: The Great Black Migration and How It Changed America* 5 (1991).

[46] *See* 4 U.S. Dep't of Commerce, Bureau of the Census, *Fifteenth Census of the United States: 1930*, at 12 (1933) ("The boll weevil was probably responsible for more changes in the number of farms, farm acreage, and farm population [during the 1920s] than all other causes put together.").

[47] Lemann, *supra* note 45, at 6; *see also* Conrad Taeuber & Irene B. Taeuber, *The Changing Population of the United States* 109–11 (1958) (discussing the "dramatic speed" with which "Negroes [moved] out of the southern States" and into "very largely . . . urban areas").

migration ended" by the end of the 1960s, "black America was ... less than a quarter rural; 'urban' had become a euphemism for 'black.' "[48]

White or black, tenant or freehold, American farmers found no succor in peacetime. Triumph in the Great War paradoxically destroyed foreign markets. Transformed by victory from a global debtor into a creditor, the United States became a nation of importers. A rosy balance of payments made it very hard to restore American agricultural exports to prewar levels.[49] Political instability razed several significant European markets. Crushed by brutal reparation obligations and by hyperinflation,[50] Germany hiked tariffs and subsidized domestic grain production.[51] Fascist Italy likewise closed its markets.[52] The restructuring of Soviet agriculture all but barred imports.[53]

Catastrophically, the United States also embraced forbidding tariffs and agricultural autarky. The McNary–Haugen bills that nearly became law in 1927 and 1928 would have raised tariffs on agricultural imports in order to lift domestic commodity prices.[54] Herbert Hoover's election ended the McNary–Haugen plan,[55] but his administration implemented the notoriously protectionistic Smoot–Hawley Tariff Act.[56] As retaliatory tariffs rose all over the world, America's "most disastrous single mistake ... in international relations" completed the rout.[57] Domestic supplies

---

[48] Lemann, *supra* note 45, at 6.

[49] *See generally* E.G. Nourse, *The Trend of Agricultural Exports*, 36 J. Pol. Econ. 330 (1928); Rexford Guy Tugwell, *The Problem of Agriculture*, 39 Pol. Sci. Q. 549 (1924).

[50] *See generally* John Maynard Keynes, *The Economic Consequences of the Peace* 235–48 (1920) (warning, with tragic accuracy, of hyperinflation's dire consequences in Germany).

[51] *See* Leo Pasvolsky, *International Relations and Financial Conditions in Foreign Countries Affecting the Demand for American Agricultural Products*, 14 J. Farm Econ. 257, 260–62 (1932).

[52] *See id.* at 262–63; N.W. Hazan, *The Agricultural Program of Fascist Italy*, 15 J. Farm Econ. 489 (1933).

[53] *See* Mordecai Ezekiel, *European Competition in Agricultural Production, with Special Reference to Russia*, 14 J. Farm Econ. 267, 271–73 (1932). *But cf.* U.S. Dep't of Commerce, *Foreign Commerce and Navigation of the United States* 363 (1942) (reporting that the Soviet Union resumed its imports of American wheat and flour by the 1940s).

[54] *See* Gilbert C. Fite, *American Farmers: The New Minority* 42–47 (1981).

[55] *See* Kenneth Finegold & Theda Skocpol, *State and Party in America's New Deal* 75–81 (1995); Jon Lauck, Note, *Against the Grain: The North Dakota Wheat Pooling Plan and the Liberalization Trend in World Agricultural Markets*, 8 Minn. J. Global Trade 289, 293–97 (1999).

[56] Pub. L. No. 71–361, 46 Stat. 590 (1930) (codified as amended in scattered sections of 19 U.S.C.).

[57] Richard N. Cooper, *Trade Policy as Foreign Policy*, in *U.S. Trade Policies in a Changing World Economy* 291, 291 (Robert M. Stern ed., 1987).

soared, exports evaporated, and prices crashed.[58] In the halcyon days before World War I, American farmers might have unloaded their wheat abroad. But the new tariffs sealed off many overseas markets. Nor would war beyond America's shores restore agricultural prosperity. Foreign aid programs such as Lend–Lease and wartime increases in demand offered only modest and evanescent relief.[59]

The 1932 presidential campaign thus coincided with an important moment in American agricultural history: North and South at last were united in mutual misery.[60] Foreclosure auctions transferred one-quarter of the land in Mississippi on a single day in April 1932.[61] The Farmers' Holiday Association conducted violent demonstrations throughout the Midwest.[62] Agricultural relief became a central plank of Franklin D. Roosevelt's presidential campaign.[63]

But Roosevelt's earliest efforts to deliver price and income support and debt relief to farmers met constitutional defeat. After invalidating the Farm Bankruptcy Act of 1934,[64] the Supreme Court dealt an even harsher blow to the New Deal's agricultural agenda. The Agricultural Adjustment Act of 1933,[65] which Roosevelt hailed as "the most drastic and far-reaching piece of farm legislation ever proposed in time of peace,"[66] drew condemnation as an open door for "government's invasion

---

[58] *See* U.S. Dep't of Agric., *Agricultural Statistics* 10, 20, 22 (1942) (noting a two-thirds decline in wheat prices between 1929 and 1932 and additional price drops in 1938, 1940, and 1941); Robert L. Stern, *The Commerce Clause and the National Economy, 1933–1946 (Part II)*, 59 Harv. L. Rev. 883, 901 (1946) (same).

[59] *See* U.S. Dep't of Agric., *1943 Annual Report of the Secretary of Agriculture* 136 (1944) (reporting increases in demand for wheat as grain, as animal feed, and as a base for alcohol).

[60] *Cf.* Jim Chen, *Of Agriculture's First Disobedience and Its Fruit*, 48 Vand. L. Rev. 1261, 1316–19 (1995) (contrasting the Northern and Southern traditions in American agriculture); Paul S. Taylor, *Public Policy and the Shaping of Rural Society*, 20 S.D. L. Rev. 475, 476–80 (1975) (same).

[61] *See* William E. Leuchtenburg, *Franklin D. Roosevelt and the New Deal, 1932–1940*, at 23 (1963).

[62] *See* Fite, *supra* note 54, at 53–54.

[63] *See* Frank Freidel, *Franklin D. Roosevelt: The Triumph* 342–50 (1956); *cf.* Breimyer, *supra* note 34, at 342–43 (describing the "instrumental" role played by "the personality of Franklin D. Roosevelt" in the development of New Deal agricultural policy).

[64] *See* Frazier–Lemke Farm Bankruptcy Act, Pub. L. No. 73–486, 48 Stat. 1289 (1934); *Louisville Joint Stock Land Bank v. Radford*, 295 U.S. 555, 601–02 (1935).

[65] Agricultural Adjustment Act of 1933, Pub. L. No. 73–10, 48 Stat. 31 (codified as amended at 7 U.S.C. §§ 601–626 (2000)).

[66] Franklin D. Roosevelt, *"New Means to Rescue Agriculture"–The Agricultural Adjustment Act*, *in* 2 The Public Papers and Addresses of Franklin D. Roosevelt 74, 79 (1938).

of private business."[67] In the 1936 decision of *United States v. Butler*, the Supreme Court held that the Act's tax on agricultural processors unconstitutionally "invade[d] the reserved rights of the states" insofar as it purported "to regulate and control agricultural production, a matter beyond the powers delegated to the federal government."[68] This Tenth Amendment decision came on the heels of *A.L.A. Schechter Poultry Corp. v. United States*,[69] which invalidated the National Industrial Recovery Act. Both the National Industrial Recovery Act and the Agricultural Adjustment Act–the figurative hammer and sickle of Roosevelt's Hundred Days–lay in ruins.

Commerce Clause jurisprudence, however, was evolving rapidly in favor of expanded federal authority. In upholding the National Labor Relations Act, the 1937 case of *NLRB v. Jones & Laughlin Steel Corp.*[70] blurred the distinction between commerce and productive activities such as manufacturing and agriculture. Whether regulated entities are "engaged in production is not determinative," wrote Chief Justice Charles Evans Hughes.[71] Rather, *Jones & Laughlin* measured the federal commerce power according to a regulated activity's "effect upon interstate commerce."[72] Expanding the "stream of commerce" metaphor that dominated commerce cases before the New Deal,[73] *Jones & Laughlin* authorized Congress to remove "[b]urdens and obstructions . . . springing from other sources."[74]

This constitutional shift revitalized the New Deal's agricultural agenda. From 1935 to 1938, Congress passed four major statutes that reinstated earlier laws in all but name: the Frazier–Lemke Farm Bankruptcy Act of 1935,[75] the Soil Conservation and Domestic Allotment Act of 1936,[76] the Agricultural Marketing Agreement Act of 1937,[77] and the

---

[67] Gilbert C. Fite, *Farmer Opinion and the Agricultural Adjustment Act, 1933*, 48 Miss. Valley Hist. Rev. 656, 669 (1962).

[68] 297 U.S. 1, 68, 74–75 (1936).

[69] 295 U.S. 495 (1935).

[70] 301 U.S. 1 (1937).

[71] *Id.* at 40.

[72] *Id.*

[73] *See id.* at 34–36 (citing, *inter alia, Stafford v. Wallace*, 258 U.S. 495 (1922)).

[74] *Id.* at 36; *cf. Board of Trade v. Olsen*, 262 U.S. 1, 32 (1923) (characterizing grain futures transactions as "a constantly recurring burden and obstruction to [interstate] commerce," even though those transactions were "not in and of themselves interstate commerce").

[75] Pub. L. No. 74–384, 49 Stat. 942 (1935).

[76] Pub. L. No. 74–461, 49 Stat. 1148 (1936).

[77] Pub. L. No. 75–137, 50 Stat. 246 (1937) (codified as amended at 7 U.S.C. §§ 601–624, 671–674 (2000)).

monumental Agricultural Adjustment Act of 1938.[78] By 1939, the new
Farm Bankruptcy Act, the Agricultural Marketing Agreement Act, and
the new Agricultural Adjustment Act had all withstood constitutional
challenges.[79] The soil conservation law escaped scrutiny because "[n]o
one could challenge the value" or the constitutionality "of conservation."[80] Payments for planting "soil-conserving" crops achieved much of
the acreage reduction contemplated under the invalidated Agricultural
Adjustment Act of 1933.[81] The Supreme Court's decision to uphold a
tobacco inspection statute reinforced the Roosevelt administration's
growing sense of invulnerability.[82]

Among the cases in this sequence, *Mulford v. Smith*[83] was perhaps
the most significant. Even though the marketing quotas imposed by the
Agricultural Adjustment Act of 1938 intruded far more aggressively into
the tobacco industry than the 1933 Act's processing taxes, *Mulford*
approved the 1938 Act with little fanfare. Whereas the 1933 Act had
been condemned merely three years earlier as an unconstitutional "plan
to regulate and control agricultural production, a matter beyond the
powers delegated to the federal government,"[84] *Mulford* blessed the 1938
Act as a program "intended to foster, protect and conserve [interstate]
commerce."[85]

The shift in Commerce Clause jurisprudence made a manifest difference. In *Mulford*'s wake, a circuit court upheld cotton marketing quotas

---

[78] Pub. L. No. 75–430, 52 Stat. 31 (1938) (codified as amended at 7 U.S.C. §§ 1281–
1393 (2000)).

[79] *See United States v. Rock Royal Co-op., Inc.*, 307 U.S. 533, 562–81 (1939) (upholding
the Agricultural Marketing Agreement Act); *Mulford v. Smith*, 307 U.S. 38, 47–51 (1939)
(upholding the Agricultural Adjustment Act of 1938); *Wright v. Vinton Branch of the
Mountain Trust Bank*, 300 U.S. 440, 470 (1937) (upholding the Farm Bankruptcy Act); *see
also H.P. Hood & Sons v. United States*, 307 U.S. 588, 595 (1939) (regarding *Rock Royal* as
"determinative" of the constitutionality of the Agricultural Marketing Agreement Act).

[80] Breimyer, *supra* note 34, at 348; *cf. Mayo v. United States*, 319 U.S. 441, 446–48
(1943) (exempting fertilizer distributed by federal officials from a Florida inspection law
under the theory of intergovernmental immunity).

[81] *See* Fite, *supra* note 54, at 60; Breimyer, *supra* note 34, at 348–49 & n.65; Jim Chen,
*Get Green or Get Out: Decoupling Environmental from Economic Objectives in Agricultural
Regulation*, 48 Okla. L. Rev. 333, 343 (1995).

[82] *See Currin v. Wallace*, 306 U.S. 1 (1939) (upholding the Tobacco Inspection Act, ch.
623, 49 Stat. 731 (1935) (codified as 7 U.S.C. §§ 511–511q (2000))).

[83] 307 U.S. 38 (1939).

[84] *United States v. Butler*, 297 U.S. 1, 68 (1936).

[85] *Mulford*, 307 U.S. at 48.

imposed by the Agricultural Adjustment Act.[86] The Supreme Court endorsed Congress's power to fix commodity prices directly.[87] *United States v. Darby*,[88] which upheld the Fair Labor Standards Act of 1938, resolved most of the important remaining Commerce Clause issues. In addition to overruling *Hammer v. Dagenhart*,[89] the 1918 decision that had confined the commerce power "to articles which in themselves have some harmful or deleterious property,"[90] *Darby* renounced any judicial authority to question Congress's "motive and purpose" in framing legislation "to make effective the [federal] conception of public policy" for interstate commerce.[91] By 1941, the Roosevelt administration's struggle to reinvent the Commerce Clause in its image had been waged and won.

The Lower Court Decision

Roscoe Curtiss Filburn was born August 2, 1902, in Dayton, Ohio, to Martin and Mary Elizabeth Filburn.[92] He represented the fifth generation of an Ohio farm family.[93] His maternal grandparents, John and Susannah Smith, farmed a full section in Montgomery County.[94] The Smiths divided their 640 acres among seven children. Mary Elizabeth received the homestead, ninety-five acres of farmland, and nine additional wooded acres.[95] Roscoe Filburn's middle name, Curtiss, was the first name of the physician who saved the arm of his father, Martin, after a threshing accident.[96] A family biography provided a quote testifying to

---

[86] *See Troppy v. La Sara Farmers Gin Co.*, 113 F.2d 350, 350–52 (5th Cir. 1940).

[87] *See Sunshine Anthracite Coal Co. v. Adkins*, 310 U.S. 381, 393–94 (1940); *United States v. Rock Royal Co-op., Inc.*, 307 U.S. 533, 571 (1939); *cf. Carter v. Carter Coal Co.*, 298 U.S. 238, 312–16 (1936) (declining to review Congress's power to fix coal prices).

[88] 312 U.S. 100 (1941).

[89] 247 U.S. 251 (1918).

[90] *Darby*, 312 U.S. at 116–17 (overruling *Hammer*).

[91] *Id.* at 115.

[92] *See* Jerry Allen Filbrun et al., *A Fillbrunn Family History: Various Members of the Families Fillbrunn, Filbrun, Filburn, et al., 1570–1985*, at 176 (1985) [hereinafter *Filbrun Family History*].

[93] *See id.* at 174.

[94] *See* Spurgeon Letter, *supra* note * at 2.

[95] *See id.* at 3.

[96] *See Filbrun Family History*, *supra* note 92, at 174.

Roscoe Filburn's "sense of pride": "I never worked for another man in my life."[97]

Roscoe Filburn raised dairy cattle and poultry. His family welcomed "75 ... customers ... every day for milk and eggs."[98] Roscoe Filburn also planted winter wheat each fall and harvested the crop the following summer. Filburn sold part of his wheat crop, fed part to his cattle and poultry, ground part into flour for household consumption, and kept the rest as seed for the following season. Under the terms of the 1938 Act, he held an allotment to cultivate 11.1 acres of wheat at a normal yield of 20.1 bushels per acre. In fall 1940, Filburn planted not 11.1 but 23 acres. In July 1941, he harvested 462 bushels in all.[99] His extra 11.9 acres yielded 239 bushels.

Filburn's excess harvest violated his acreage allotment. Acreage limitations were the Agricultural Adjustment Act's primary tool for controlling the supply of federally subsidized crops. Supply control has always played a crucial role in agricultural regulation. Because excessive production can stretch the gap between a commodity's market price and the target price set in a government-sponsored support program, virtually every price support mechanism is paired with some sort of supply control.[100] The need for supply control increases dramatically when the government extends nonrecourse loans to producers, which effectively raise minimum commodity prices.[101] Before the 1941 planting season, it became evident that "[t]he low prices [for wheat] were obviously the result of the excessive supply."[102] Only stiffer penalties on excess production could prevent already overflowing stocks from surpassing the all-time high reached in 1940.[103] In spite of farmers' traditional opposition, acreage restrictions seemed inevitable.[104]

Fear of a wheat glut and an accompanying price crash turned the spotlight to the Agricultural Adjustment Act's supply control provisions. The Act directed the Secretary of Agriculture to proclaim a national acreage allotment for each year's wheat crop, to be apportioned among states, counties, and individual farms. Potential production limits were

---

[97] *Id.* at 176.

[98] Spurgeon Letter, *supra* note * at 7–8.

[99] *See Wheat Control Challenged*, Dayton J., July 15, 1941, at 1, 2.

[100] *See* J.W. Looney, *The Changing Focus of Government Regulation of Agriculture in the United States*, 44 Mercer L. Rev. 763, 787–88 (1993).

[101] *See, e.g., St. Paul Fire & Marine Ins. Co. v. Commodity Credit Corp.*, 646 F.2d 1064, 1067 (5th Cir. 1981).

[102] Stern, *supra* note 58, at 902.

[103] *See id.* at 901–02.

[104] *See* Fite, *supra* note 54, at 51–52.

triggered in any marketing year (beginning July 1) in which the Secretary projected that the total wheat supply would exceed normal domestic consumption and export by more than 35 percent. The Act required the Secretary to make a proclamation to that effect by May 15. After that proclamation, but before June 10, the Secretary had to conduct a referendum of affected farmers. A compulsory national marketing quota for wheat would take effect for the marketing year unless more than one-third of participating farmers voted to suspend the quota. When Filburn planted his 1941 crop, the Act's penalty for excess wheat was 15 cents per bushel.

During spring 1941, Secretary of Agriculture Claude Wickard projected a wheat surplus and proposed a marketing quota. He scheduled a national referendum for May 31. In a radio address on May 19, Secretary Wickard mentioned a pending bill before Congress, which would have raised the nonrecourse loan rate on wheat to 85 percent of parity. The resulting increase in wheat's effective minimum market price would prompt more production, which threatened to suppress real market prices and thereby to increase the government's price support obligations. The wheat program would have delivered "an average price . . . of about $1.16 a bushel" for 1941, "as compared with the world market price of 40 cents a bushel."[105]

During his May 19 address, Secretary Wickard announced: "Because of the uncertain world situation, we deliberately planted several million extra acres of wheat this year. . . . Farmers should not be penalized because they have provided insurance against shortages of food." He did not mention, however, that a pending amendment to the Agricultural Adjustment Act would increase the penalty on excess wheat from 15 cents per bushel to 49 cents (half of the parity loan rate, then 98 cents) and would subject a violating farm's crop to a lien in favor of the United States.

On May 26, Congress approved the pending amendment. On May 31, the Department of Agriculture conducted the wheat growers' referendum. Among those voting, 81 percent favored the marketing quota. Ohio farmers, however, voted against the quota.[106] Thanks to the overwhelming national vote, both the increase in the loan rate on wheat and the strengthened penalty for exceeding individual marketing quotas took effect.

Officials charged with administering the Agricultural Adjustment Act in Montgomery County assessed a penalty of 49 cents on each of Filburn's 239 excess bushels and imposed a lien on his entire wheat crop

---

[105] *Wickard v. Filburn*, 317 U.S. 111, 126 (1942).

[106] *See Wheat Control Challenged*, *supra* note 99, at 1.

against the $117.11 penalty. Pending payment, the county committee also withheld Filburn's marketing card, which he needed in order to sell his wheat.

In a suit filed in the U.S. District Court for the Southern District of Ohio, Filburn challenged his marketing excess penalty. The majority opinion in *Filburn v. Helke*[107] failed even to mention the Commerce Clause. Rather, District Judge John Druffel emphasized "the fact that the law increasing the penalty was approved only five days prior to the national referendum."[108] He reasoned that the case hinged on whether farmers "were unintentionally misled."[109] The court stressed how the May 26 amendment, which more than tripled the penalty for excess wheat, contradicted Secretary Wickard's purported pledge to safeguard farmers against unfair penalties.[110] The court reasoned that Secretary Wickard should have warned the farmers that "increased parity loans" would expose farmers "to increased penalties for the farm marketing excess."[111] The court concluded that the May 26 amendment "retroactively" effected "a taking of . . . property without due process."[112]

Judge Florence Allen, the lone dissenter, found "no equitable justification" for blocking "the fulfillment of the declared legislative will of the nation."[113] Judge Allen alone anticipated *Filburn*'s pivotal constitutional issue. Relying heavily on Supreme Court cases upholding New Deal agricultural programs[114] and quoting extensively from congressional findings of fact,[115] Judge Allen described the Agricultural Adjustment Act "as applied to wheat [as] a valid exercise of the federal commerce power."[116]

---

[107] 43 F.Supp. 1017 (S.D. Ohio), *rev'd sub nom. Wickard v. Filburn*, 317 U.S. 111 (1942). Carl Helke and other members of Montgomery County's agricultural committee were named as defendants.

[108] *Id.* at 1018. District Judge Robert Nevin joined Judge Druffel.

[109] *Id.* at 1019.

[110] *See id.*

[111] *Id.*

[112] *Id.* In the alternative, the court ruled "that the equities of the case . . . favor the plaintiff." *Id.*

[113] *Id.* at 1020 (Allen, J., dissenting).

[114] *See id.* at 1022–23 (citing, *inter alia*, *Mulford v. Smith*, 307 U.S. 38 (1939); *United States v. Rock–Royal Co-op., Inc.*, 307 U.S. 533 (1939)).

[115] *See id.* (quoting 7 U.S.C. § 1331).

[116] *Id.* at 1022.

The Briefs

The district court's decision to enjoin enforcement of the Agricultural Adjustment Act on constitutional grounds entitled Secretary Wickard to appeal directly to the Supreme Court. The Supreme Court noted probable jurisdiction.[117]

Three of the five questions presented by the government's initial brief focused on Secretary Wickard's May 19 radio address, the May 26 amendment, and the May 31 growers' referendum.[118] The fourth question raised the issue on which *Wickard v. Filburn* would ultimately hinge: "Whether the wheat marketing quota provisions of the Agricultural Adjustment Act of 1938, as amended on May 26, 1941, are within the commerce power of Congress."[119]

With respect to Congress's power to regulate interstate commerce, the government's brief made two crucial contributions. First, the government demonstrated that the district court could not have avoided the commerce question, at least insofar as that court's "disposition of the case . . . of necessity [was] inconsistent with appellee[] [Filburn's] position that [the disputed] regulation [was] not within the commerce power."[120] Because the Agricultural Adjustment Act's penalty on all wheat "marketed" in excess of a farm's allotted quota included wheat "dispose[d] of by feeding to poultry and livestock as well as by selling," Filburn attacked the Act on constitutional grounds to the extent that the Act "subject[ed] to penalties wheat used on the farm, such as that fed to livestock, as well as wheat which is sold."[121]

Second, the government's brief documented the duality of the wheat market. On one hand, the government described "[t]he vast extent of the interstate and foreign movements of wheat and flour."[122] On the other, the government distinguished wheat from tobacco, the crop at issue in *Mulford v. Smith*.[123] Unlike tobacco, wheat was "marketed by over a million farmers through almost innumerable outlets."[124] A "substantial

---

[117] See *Wickard v. Filburn*, 62 S.Ct. 919, 919 (1942).

[118] See Brief for the Appellants, at 2, *reprinted in* 39 *Landmark Briefs and Arguments of the Supreme Court of the United States: Constitutional Law* 677, 682 (Philip B. Kurland & Gerhard Casper eds., 1975) [hereinafter *Landmark Briefs*].

[119] *Id.* The fifth question challenged Filburn's ability to sue individual members of the agricultural conservation committees for Ohio and Montgomery County. *See id.* at 2, 53, *reprinted in Landmark Briefs, supra* note 118, at 682, 733.

[120] *Id.* at 38 n.7, *reprinted in Landmark Briefs, supra* note 118, at 718 n.7.

[121] *Id.*

[122] *Id.* at 12, *reprinted in Landmark Briefs, supra* note 118, at 692.

[123] 307 U.S. 38 (1939).

[124] Brief for the Appellant, at 45, *reprinted in Landmark Briefs, supra* note 118, at 725.

quantity" of that wheat would be consumed on the farm "as feed for livestock, as seed, and, to a slight extent, as food."[125] These traits complicated the regulation of wheat to an enormous degree. The government's emphasis on this unique combination of commercial significance and regulatory difficulty would prove pivotal.

Counsel for Filburn treated this aspect of the government's argument as an opportunity to distinguish *Mulford* and other decisions upholding the New Deal's agricultural programs.[126] The appellee's brief concluded with what it considered a fatal concession by the government: "practically all farmers sell locally, indicating that wheat does not come within the category of milk and other farm products that are sold directly in interstate commerce."[127]

On June 1, 1942, the Supreme Court ordered reargument, limited "to the question whether the Act, insofar as it deals with wheat consumed on the farm of the producer, is within the power of Congress to regulate commerce."[128] Secretary Wickard's brief on reargument recast the Commerce Clause issue in terms more amenable to expansive federal authority: "The question ... is not whether Congress can regulate consumption on the farm, but whether, as a means of regulating the amount of wheat marketed and the interstate price structure, Congress has the power to control the total available supply of wheat, including ... that which is consumed on the farm."[129]

By contrast, counsel for Filburn took refuge in the traditional distinction between production and shipment. The appellee's brief on reargument characterized the government's contention "that feed, seed and food consumed on the farm where it has been raised is a form of competition with commercial products [as] a *reductio ad absurdum* of the theory of competition."[130] Filburn's brief warned that the government's approach to the Commerce Clause "would not only effectually approach a centralized government but could eventually lead to absolutism by successive nullifications of all Constitutional limitations."[131]

---

[125] *Id.* at 41, *reprinted in Landmark Briefs, supra* note 118, at 721.

[126] *See* Brief for Appellee, at 21–23, *reprinted in Landmark Briefs, supra* note 118, at 741, 761–63.

[127] *Id.* at 22, *reprinted in Landmark Briefs, supra* note 118, at 762.

[128] 62 S.Ct. 1289, 1289 (1942).

[129] Brief for the Appellants on Reargument, at 2, *reprinted in Landmark Briefs, supra* note 118, at 765, 770.

[130] Brief for the Appellee on Reargument, at 13, *reprinted in Landmark Briefs, supra* note 118, at 823, 835.

[131] *Id.* at 14, *reprinted in Landmark Briefs, supra* note 118, at 836.

After much maneuvering, the briefs in *Wickard v. Filburn* eventually reached the doctrinal basis on which this case would hang. The
Supreme Court's reargument order minimized the retroactivity and
equity issues that had transfixed the district court. The refocused
dispute squarely presented the New Deal's final unanswered question of
Commerce Clause doctrine.

The Supreme Court Decision

The Supreme Court quickly dispensed with Secretary Wickard's
radio address. Justice Jackson's opinion for a unanimous Court dismissed as "manifest error" the district court's holding "that the Secretary's speech invalidated the referendum."[132] The Court refused to
permit "a speech by a Cabinet officer," even one that might have "failed
to meet judicial ideals of clarity, precision, and exhaustiveness," to
"defeat a policy embodied in an Act of Congress."[133] Indeed, the Court
characterized a complaint based on the speech as "frivolous."[134] The
Supreme Court made comparably short work of the district court's
conclusion that federal law deprived Filburn of due process or otherwise
worked an inequitable result. Insofar as the wheat program lifted prices
above unregulated levels, the Court rejected Filburn's due process
claim:[135] "It is hardly lack of due process for the Government to regulate
that which it subsidizes."[136]

The Court devoted most of its opinion to the Commerce Clause. Yet
the Court intimated that even this issue "would merit little consideration since [its] decision in *United States v. Darby*."[137] The lone difference between *Darby* and *Filburn* lay in "the fact that [the Agricultural
Adjustment] Act extends federal regulation to production not intended in
any part of commerce but wholly for consumption on the farm."[138] And
this factor's significance appeared to have been overstated. The Court
reasoned "that questions of the power of Congress are not to be decided
by reference to any formula which would give controlling force to
nomenclature such as 'production' and 'indirect' and foreclose consider-

---

[132] *Wickard v. Filburn*, 317 U.S. 111, 117 (1942).

[133] *Id.* at 118.

[134] *Id.*

[135] *See id.* at 129–33.

[136] *Id.* at 131; *see also id.* at 133 ("[I]f [Filburn] could get all that the Government
gives and do nothing that the Government asks, he would be better off than this law
allows.").

[137] *Id.* at 118 (citing *United States v. Darby*, 312 U.S. 100 (1941)).

[138] *Id.*

ation of the actual effects of the activity in question upon interstate commerce."[139] Because these terms merely described conclusions without providing useful guidance toward determining which "kinds of intrastate activity [affecting] interstate commerce were ... a proper subject of federal regulation,"[140] the Court rejected "the mechanical application of legal formulas" purporting to "find[] the activity in question to be 'production' " or to call the relevant economic effects " 'indirect.' "[141]

The Court then turned to "the economics of the wheat industry."[142] Its survey of this "problem industry," at home and abroad, was reminiscent of Chief Justice Hughes's description of the breathtaking scale of the Jones & Laughlin Steel Corporation.[143] Although other cases had hinged on the perceived need to maintain "the flow of wheat from the West to the mills and distributing points of the East and Europe,"[144] *Filburn* began but did not stop with "[c]ommerce among the states in wheat."[145] This was no ordinary program for rationalizing domestic distribution of a scarce commodity. The Court's survey of the "large and important" traffic between sixteen wheat-exporting states and their thirty-two wheat-importing counterparts hinted at a crisis of global proportions.[146] The real problem was the "abnormally large supply of wheat" that had "caused congestion in a number of markets; tied up railroad cars; and caused elevators in some instances to turn away grains, and railroads to institute embargoes to prevent further congestion."[147] "Largely as a result of increased foreign production and import restrictions, annual exports of wheat and flour from the United States during the ten-year period ending in 1940 averaged less than 10 per cent of total production, while during the 1920's they averaged more than 25 per cent."[148] The Court's review of market conditions left no doubt that

---

[139] *Id.* at 120.

[140] *Id.* at 122.

[141] *Id.* at 124.

[142] *Id.* at 125.

[143] *See NLRB v. Jones & Laughlin Steel Corp.*, 301 U.S. 1, 25–28 (1937).

[144] *Chicago Board of Trade v. Olsen*, 262 U.S. 1, 36 (1923); *see also Lemke v. Farmers' Grain Co.*, 258 U.S. 50, 53–54 (1922); *Dahnke-Walker Milling Co. v. Bondurant*, 257 U.S. 282, 290–91 (1921); *Munn v. Illinois*, 94 U.S. 113, 131 (1876); *cf. Stafford v. Wallace*, 258 U.S. 495, 516 (1922) (describing "the various stockyards of the country" as "great national public utilities" dominating "the flow of commerce from the ranges and farms of the West to the consumers in the East").

[145] 317 U.S. at 125.

[146] *Id.* at 125.

[147] *Id.*

[148] *Id.*

the appropriate economic baseline was not local, but global. It compared the "average price ... of about $1.16 a bushel," the wheat program's 1941 benchmark, "with the world market price of 40 cents."[149]

Justice Jackson next focused on American farmers. Whereas many farmers in western wheat-exporting states "specializ[ed] in wheat" and sold "the crop for cash," farmers in wheat-importing regions such as New England generally used wheat for multiple purposes, from animal feed to "a nurse crop for grass seeding" and a mere "cover crop to prevent soil erosion and leaching."[150] (So much for the soil conservation law's characterization of wheat as a "soil-depleting" crop.[151]) These regional variations proved dispositive. "[C]onsumption of homegrown wheat," the Court concluded, profoundly affected interstate commerce because "it constitute[d] the most variable factor in the disappearance of the wheat crop."[152] Unlike the "relatively constant" amounts of wheat "consumed as food ... and use[d] as seed," on-farm wheat consumption "appear[ed] to vary in an amount greater than 20 per cent of average production."[153]

This observation about homegrown wheat enabled the Court to make the "aggregation" argument for which *Wickard v. Filburn* is best known today:

> The maintenance by government regulation of a price for wheat undoubtedly can be accomplished as effectively by sustaining or increasing the demand as by limiting the supply. The effect of the statute before us is to restrict the amount which may be produced for market and the extent as well to which one may forestall resort to the market by producing to meet his own needs. That appellee's own contribution to the demand for wheat may be trivial by itself is not enough to remove him from the scope of federal regulation where, as here, his contribution, taken together with that of many others similarly situated, is far from trivial.[154]

This observation brought the Court's Commerce Clause analysis to a swift and decisive conclusion. Plainly the 1938 Act was designed "to increase the market price of wheat and ... to limit the volume thereof."[155] The power of Congress "to regulate the prices [of] ... commodi-

---

[149] *Id.* at 126.

[150] *Id.* at 126–27.

[151] *See supra* text accompanying note 80.

[152] *Filburn*, 317 U.S. at 127.

[153] *Id.*

[154] *Id.* at 127–28.

[155] *Id.* at 128.

ties in [interstate] commerce" could no longer be questioned.[156] The admittedly "substantial influence" of home-consumed wheat left "no doubt that Congress may properly have [swept] wheat consumed on the farm where grown" into the overall marketing quota system, lest unchecked on-farm consumption "defeat[] and obstruct[] [Congress's] purpose to stimulate trade therein at increased prices."[157]

Filburn's *Immediate Impact*

Some of *Filburn*'s earliest critics detected a threat to state sovereignty. At their meekest, commentators demurred that *Filburn* rested "primarily upon a rather extended concept of competition."[158] More audacious critics expressed "wonder as to the limits of [Congress's] tremendous and constantly growing power."[159]

Filburn itself gave no hint of having altered the landscape so dramatically. One of the New Deal's front-line warriors believed that the case contributed relatively little to Commerce Clause jurisprudence: "*Wickard v. Filburn* adds little to the *Darby* case...."[160] In truth, much of the heavy lifting had already been performed. *Darby* and the cases it spawned[161] had all but gutted the shaky distinction between commerce and manufacturing, mining, and agriculture.[162] Not even the "aggregation" argument originated in *Filburn*; a Term earlier, *Darby* had already deployed similar reasoning.[163] In an even earlier case, the Supreme Court

---

[156] *Id.*

[157] *Id.* at 128–29.

[158] Note, *The Supreme Court of the United States During the October Term, 1942: Part I*, 43 Colum. L. Rev. 837, 845 (1943).

[159] John J. Trenam, Note, *Commerce Power Since the* Schechter *Case*, 31 Geo. L.J. 201, 202 (1943).

[160] Stern, *supra* note 58, at 908.

[161] *See United States v. Darby*, 312 U.S. 100 (1941); *Gray v. Powell*, 314 U.S. 402 (1941); *United States v. Wrightwood Dairy Co.*, 315 U.S. 110 (1942); *Cloverleaf Butter Co. v. Patterson*, 315 U.S. 148 (1942); *Kirschbaum v. Walling*, 316 U.S. 517 (1942); *Overnight Motor Transp. Co. v. Missel*, 316 U.S. 572 (1942). All of these cases were cited in *Filburn*, 317 U.S. at 118 & n.12.

[162] *See Carter v. Carter Coal Co.*, 298 U.S. 238, 304 (1936); *A.L.A. Schechter Poultry Corp. v. United States*, 295 U.S. 495, 549–50 (1935); *see also United States v. E.C. Knight Co.*, 156 U.S. 1, 14–16 (1895).

[163] *See* 312 U.S. at 121 ("A familiar ... exercise of power is the regulation of intrastate transactions which are so commingled with or related to interstate commerce that all must be regulated if the interstate commerce is to be effectively controlled."); *id.* at 123 ("[I]n present day industry, competition by a small part may affect the whole and ... the total effect of the competition of many small producers may be great."); *accord, e.g., Filburn v.*

acknowledged that Congress's "plenary" power over interstate commerce "extends to all such commerce be it great or small" and that the Court had never thought such power "to be constitutionally restricted because in any particular case the volume of the commerce affected may be small."[164]

To the extent it relitigated established propositions, *Filburn* seems more analogous to the deservedly obscure *Wrightwood Dairy* case,[165] which revisited the recently vindicated Agricultural Marketing Agreement Act when a federal appeals court "inexplicabl[y]" held "that intrastate milk competing in the same market with interstate was not subject to the commerce power."[166] Indeed, two Terms after *Filburn*, the Supreme Court felt no need to cite *Filburn* for the proposition that the scope of the Commerce Clause "is not to be determined by confining judgment to the quantitative effect of the activities immediately" at issue in a single controversy, but rather in light of the prospect that "the total incidence" of events resembling "the immediate situation," "if left unchecked[,] may well become far-reaching in its harm to commerce."[167] Even *Filburn*'s specific holding–that home-consumed wheat falls within Congress's power over interstate commerce–failed to take firm root in the lower courts. As late as 1966, the Supreme Court summarily reversed a federal circuit court decision exempting, on constitutional grounds, wheat grown at state mental and penal institutions from federal acreage limitations.[168] To be sure, the Supreme Court did acknowledge that *Filburn* had made it impossible to sustain a constitutionally significant distinction between "production" and "commerce."[169] On the whole, *Filburn* helped build the New Deal's Commerce Clause consensus: "If it is interstate commerce that feels the pinch, it does not matter how local the operation which applies the squeeze."[170]

This view of *Filburn* persisted for decades. Despite its reputation for activism, the Warren Court cut little, if any, new ground on federalism.

Helke, 43 F.Supp. 1017, 1022 (S.D. Ohio) (Allen, J., dissenting), *rev'd sub nom. Wickard v. Filburn*, 317 U.S. 111 (1942).

[164] *NLRB v. Fainblatt*, 306 U.S. 601, 606 (1939), *cited in Filburn*, 317 U.S. at 128.

[165] *Wrightwood Dairy*, 315 U.S. at 110.

[166] Robert L. Stern, *The Commerce Clause and the National Economy, 1933–1946 (Part I)*, 59 Harv. L. Rev. 645, 689 (1946).

[167] *Polish Nat'l Alliance v. NLRB*, 322 U.S. 643, 648 (1944).

[168] *United States v. Ohio*, 385 U.S. 9 (1966) (per curiam), *summarily rev'g* 354 F.2d 549 (6th Cir. 1965).

[169] *Mandeville Island Farms v. American Crystal Sugar Co.*, 334 U.S. 219, 228 (1948).

[170] *United States v. Women's Sportswear Mfg. Ass'n*, 336 U.S. 460, 464 (1949); *accord Heart of Atlanta Motel, Inc. v. United States*, 379 U.S. 241, 258 (1964).

The decisions upholding the Civil Rights Act of 1964 as a proper exercise of Congress's commerce power[171] rank among the Warren Court's least innovative–and, consequently, most secure–decisions.[172] *Katzenbach v. McClung*[173] confirmed *Filburn*'s principle that a single actor's impact on interstate commerce, though "trivial by itself," may nevertheless fall within "the scope of federal regulation where ... his contribution, taken together with that of many others similarly situated, is far from trivial."[174] *Heart of Atlanta Motel, Inc. v. United States*[175] reaffirmed an even older Commerce Clause principle. In the early twentieth century, when distinctions between commerce and production and between direct and indirect effects held sway, the Court nonetheless accepted "the authority of Congress to keep the channels of interstate commerce free from immoral and injurious uses."[176] Both *Heart of Atlanta* and *McClung* adopted a rational basis standard of review for challenges to congressional uses of the commerce power.[177] *McClung* also observed that Congress's failure to include "formal findings" is "not fatal."[178]

The Warren Court's most significant Commerce Clause decision, *Maryland v. Wirtz*,[179] upheld the extension of the Fair Labor Standards Act to hospitals, institutions, and schools operated by state and local

---

[171] *See generally* Richard C. Cortner, *Civil Rights and Public Accommodations: The* Heart of Atlanta Motel *and* McClung *Cases* (2001).

[172] *Cf.* Suzanna Sherry, *Too Clever by Half: The Problem with Novelty in Constitutional Law*, 95 Nw. U. L. Rev. 921, 926 (2001) (describing the "perverse incentive[s]" that spur "original, creative, even brilliant" constitutional theories that are also "quite obviously wrong"). *See generally* Daniel A. Farber, *Brilliance Revisited*, 72 Minn. L. Rev. 367 (1987); Daniel A. Farber, *The Case Against Brilliance*, 70 Minn. L. Rev. 917 (1986).

[173] 379 U.S. 294 (1964).

[174] *McClung*, 379 U.S. at 301 (quoting *Wickard v. Filburn*, 317 U.S. 111, 127–28 (1942)).

[175] 379 U.S. at 241.

[176] *Caminetti v. United States*, 242 U.S. 470, 491 (1917); *accord Heart of Atlanta*, 379 U.S. at 256; *see also Champion v. Ames*, 188 U.S. 321 (1903).

[177] *See McClung*, 379 U.S. at 303–04 ("[W]here we find that the legislators ... have a rational basis for finding a chosen regulatory scheme necessary to the protection of commerce, our investigation is at an end."); *Heart of Atlanta*, 379 U.S. at 258 ("The only questions are: (1) whether Congress had a rational basis for finding that racial discrimination by motels affected commerce, and (2) if it had such a basis, whether the means it selected to eliminate that evil are reasonable and appropriate."); *id.* at 252 ("[T]he means chosen by [Congress] must be reasonably adapted to the end permitted by the Constitution....").

[178] *McClung*, 379 U.S. at 304 (citing *United States v. Carolene Prods. Co.*, 304 U.S. 144, 152 (1938)).

[179] 392 U.S. 183 (1968).

governments. In response to the argument that these employers lay beyond the federal power, *Wirtz* invoked *Filburn*'s aggregation principle: "The contention that in Commerce Clause cases the courts have power to excise, as trivial, individual instances falling within a rationally defined class of activities has been put entirely to rest."[180]

As in many other areas of constitutional law,[181] the Burger Court actually outperformed the predecessor Warren Court in extending Commerce Clause jurisprudence. *Perez v. United States*[182] upheld the application of the Consumer Credit Protection Act to a "loan shark" who allegedly engaged in strictly local extortion. Citing *Filburn*, *Darby*, *Heart of Atlanta*, and *McClung*, *Perez* concluded that loan sharks as a class fell "within the reach of federal power," even if individual acts of extortion were " 'trivial' " and local in nature.[183]

Filburn's *Significance Today*

Filburn is regarded today as the high-water mark of the New Deal's constitutional revolution. Even though *Filburn* itself observed that "Chief Justice Marshall," in *Gibbons v. Ogden*,[184] "described the Federal commerce power with a breadth never yet exceeded,"[185] Chief Justice Rehnquist later designated *Filburn* as "perhaps the most far reaching example of Commerce Clause authority over intrastate activity."[186] One commentator has summarized what was once the post-New Deal consensus on the meaning of the Commerce Clause: "In the wake of *Jones & Laughlin* and *Wickard* [v. *Filburn*], it has become clear that ... Congress has authority to regulate virtually all private economic activity."[187]

---

[180] *Id.* at 192–93 (citing *Wickard v. Filburn*, 317 U.S. 111, 127–28 (1942); *Polish Nat'l Alliance v. NLRB*, 322 U.S. 643, 648 (1944); *McClung*, 379 U.S. at 301).

[181] *See, e.g., The Burger Court: The Counter–Revolution That Wasn't* (Vincent Blasi ed., 1983); Henry J. Abraham, *Justices and Presidents: A Political History of Appointments to the Supreme Court* 349 (3d ed. 1992) ("The Burger Court ... was marked by a generally surprising penchant for judicial activism, even in such unexpected areas as civil rights and civil liberties."); Christopher E. Smith & Thomas R. Hensley, *Unfulfilled Aspirations: The Court Packing Efforts of Presidents Reagan and Bush*, 57 Alb. L. Rev. 1111, 1116 (1994) (observing that the Burger Court, "ultimately disappointed conservatives" by moving "in liberal directions" on many issues, "most notably in abortion and affirmative action").

[182] 402 U.S. 146 (1971).

[183] *Id.* at 154 (quoting *Wirtz*, 392 U.S. at 193).

[184] 22 U.S. (9 Wheat.) 1 (1824).

[185] 317 U.S. at 120 (citing *Gibbons*, 22 U.S. at 194–95).

[186] *United States v. Lopez*, 514 U.S. 549, 560 (1995); *accord United States v. Morrison*, 529 U.S. 598, 610 (2000).

[187] Earl M. Maltz, *The Impact of the Constitutional Revolution of 1937 on the Dormant Commerce Clause—A Case Study in the Decline of State Autonomy*, 19 Harv. J.L. & Pub.

Filburn stands for the proposition that "substantial economic effect[s]" outweigh facile distinctions between "direct" and "indirect" effects of economic behavior. Justice Jackson unequivocally declared that "questions of the power of Congress are not to be decided by reference to any formula which would give controlling force to nomenclature such as 'production' and 'indirect' and foreclose consideration of the actual effects of the activity."[188] *Filburn* likewise held that even local, noncommercial activity "may still, whatever its nature, be reached by Congress if it exerts a substantial economic effect on interstate commerce and this irrespective of whether such effect is what might at some earlier time have been defined as 'direct' or 'indirect.' "[189] Later cases have endorsed these propositions, at least superficially.[190] Critically, *Filburn* has added the "aggregation" maneuver to constitutional law's rhetorical arsenal. Thanks to *Filburn*, Congress may reach any economic actor "trivial by itself" as long as its "contribution" to the national economy, "taken together with that of many other[]" actors "similarly situated, is far from trivial."[191] *Filburn's* aggressive stand against willful judicial ignorance of actions "trivial in themselves" influences even *Dormant* Commerce Clause doctrine: the "practical effect" of a state law "must be evaluated not only by considering the consequences of the statute itself, but also by considering how the challenged statute may interact with the legitimate regulatory regimes of the other States and what effect would arise if not one, but many or every, State adopted similar legislation."[192] One critic has lamented *Filburn's* contribution to the erosion of the Supreme Court's respect for state legislative judgments in Dormant Commerce Clause cases.[193]

Pol'y 121, 129 (1995); *see also* Lawrence Lessig, *Translating Federalism:* United States v. Lopez, 1995 Sup. Ct. Rev. 125, 129–30 (observing that "commerce today" reaches "practically every activity of social life" and that "the scope of the powers now exercised by Congress far exceeds that imagined by the framers").

[188] *Filburn*, 317 U.S. at 120.

[189] *Id.* at 125.

[190] *See, e.g., United States v. Morrison*, 529 U.S. 598, 610 (2000); *United States v. Lopez*, 514 U.S. 549, 556 (1995); *New York v. United States*, 505 U.S. 144, 158 (1992); *Garcia v. San Antonio Metro. Transit Auth.*, 469 U.S. 528, 537 (1985); *Hodel v. Virginia Surface Mining Ass'n*, 452 U.S. 264, 308 (1981) (Rehnquist, J., concurring); *Maryland v. Wirtz*, 392 U.S. 183, 196 n.27 (1968).

[191] 317 U.S. at 127–28; *accord, e.g., Lopez*, 514 U.S. at 556; *Perez v. United States*, 402 U.S. 146, 151–52 (1971); *Katzenbach v. McClung*, 379 U.S. 294, 301 (1964); *Heart of Atlanta Motel, Inc. v. United States*, 379 U.S. 241, 275 (1964).

[192] *Healy v. Beer Inst.*, 491 U.S. 324, 336 (1989); *accord Wyoming v. Oklahoma*, 502 U.S. 437, 453–54 (1992); *C & A Carbone, Inc. v. Town of Clarkstown*, 511 U.S. 383, 406 (1994) (O'Connor, J., concurring in the judgment).

[193] *See* Maltz, *supra* note 187, at 129–30.

These criticisms carry greater weight with a Court that pays closer heed to the role of the states within the federal system. Federalism, once thought to have passed into the mists of history,[194] rides again. Still, the scholarly consensus is that the federal "commerce power has swelled to a proportion that would leave the framers 'rubbing their eyes' with amazement."[195] The most strident advocates of decentralized government assert that *Wickard v. Filburn* "cannot pass the 'giggle test.' "[196]

The contemporary revival of the constitutional prerogatives of the states has affected not only *Filburn* but also Commerce Clause jurisprudence at large. In 1995, *United States v. Lopez*[197] invalidated the Gun–Free School Zones Act of 1990, which made it a federal offense "for any individual knowingly to possess a firearm at a place that the individual knows, or has reasonable cause to believe, is a school zone."[198] The Supreme Court held "that the Act exceeds the authority of Congress '[t]o regulate Commerce . . . among the several States.' "[199] Chief Justice Rehnquist acknowledged *Jones & Laughlin*, *Darby*, and *Filburn* as the New Deal cases "that greatly expanded the previously defined authority of Congress under" the Commerce Clause.[200] Among these cases, the Chief Justice singled out *Filburn* as arguably the most nationalistic.[201]

Chief Justice Rehnquist summarized "three broad categories of activity that Congress may regulate under its commerce power":[202]

> First, Congress may regulate the use of the channels of interstate commerce. Second, Congress is empowered to regulate and protect the instrumentalities of interstate commerce, or persons or things in interstate commerce, even though the threat may come only from

---

[194] *See, e.g.*, Larry Kramer, *Understanding Federalism*, 47 Vand. L. Rev. 1485, 1486 (1994) ("[T]o what extent should judges regulate the allocation of power between state and national governments? And the usual answer . . . has been 'hardly at all.' "); William W. Van Alstyne, *The Second Death of Federalism*, 83 Mich. L. Rev. 1709, 1721 (1985) ("[J]udicial enforcement of the constitutional position on federalism is at an end.").

[195] Ann Althouse, *The* Alden *Trilogy: Still Searching for a Way to Enforce Federalism*, 31 Rutgers L.J. 631, 658 (2000) (quoting *Alden v. Maine*, 527 U.S. 706, 807 (1999) (Souter, J., dissenting)).

[196] Richard A. Epstein, *Constitutional Faith and the Commerce Clause*, 71 Notre Dame L. Rev. 167, 173 (1996).

[197] 514 U.S. 549 (1995).

[198] 18 U.S.C. § 922(q)(1)(A) (1988 & Supp. V. 1993).

[199] *Lopez*, 514 U.S. at 551 (quoting U.S. Const. art. I, § 8, cl. 3).

[200] *Id.* at 556.

[201] *See id.* at 560.

[202] *Id.* at 558.

intrastate activities. Finally, Congress' commerce authority includes the power to regulate those activities having a substantial relation to interstate commerce, *i.e.*, those activities that substantially affect interstate commerce.[203]

The gun possession lacked an evident connection "with 'commerce' or any sort of economic enterprise."[204] *Lopez* also faulted the absence of a "jurisdictional element which would ensure, through case-by-case inquiry, that the [proscribed activity] in question affects interstate commerce."[205] Although the Chief Justice putatively affirmed older cases relieving Congress of the need "to make formal findings as to the substantial burdens that an activity has on interstate commerce,"[206] he complained that the absence of findings left "no . . . substantial effect" on commerce "visible to the naked eye."[207] Chief Justice Rehnquist accordingly refused to "authorize a general federal police power" that extended potentially to subjects at the heart of traditional state regulation, "such as family law and direct regulation of education."[208] The Chief Justice declared himself and the Court "unwilling" to erase the "distinction between what is truly national and what is truly local."[209]

In 2000, the Court confirmed that *Lopez* was no fluke. Contrary to commentary treating *Lopez* as an aberration,[210] the Court kept narrowing its interpretation of the Commerce Clause. *United States v. Morrison*[211] invalidated the Violence Against Women Act (VAWA). Chief Justice Rehnquist distilled four "significant considerations" from that case.[212] First, the putatively "economic" nature of the regulated "endeavor" is crucial to judicial approval of "federal regulation of intrastate activity

---

[203] *Id.* at 558–59 (citations omitted).

[204] *Id.* at 561.

[205] *Id.*

[206] *Id.* at 562–63 (citing *Katzenbach v. McClung*, 379 U.S. 294, 304 (1964); *Perez v. United States*, 402 U.S. 146, 156 (1971)).

[207] *Id.* at 563.

[208] *Id.* at 564–65.

[209] *Id.* at 567–568.

[210] *See, e.g.*, David L. Shapiro, *Federalism: A Dialogue* 141 (1995) (predicting that *Lopez* would have a "limited" impact "on broader questions of federal power"); Deborah Jones Merritt, *The Fuzzy Logic of Federalism*, 46 Case W. Res. L. Rev. 685, 693 (1996) ("As a practical matter, *Lopez* has deprived Congress of very little power."); *cf.* John Copeland Nagle, *The Commerce Clause Meets the Delhi Sands Flower–Loving Fly*, 97 Mich. L. Rev. 174, 176 (1998) (pondering whether *Lopez* would be "destined to be a 'but see' citation").

[211] 529 U.S. 598 (2000).

[212] *Id.* at 609.

based upon the activity's substantial effects on interstate commerce."[213] Second, a "jurisdictional element" in the text of a statute "may establish that the enactment is in pursuance of Congress' regulation of interstate commerce."[214] Third, though congressional findings regarding the activity's impact on interstate commerce are not indispensable, *Morrison* reaffirmed *Lopez*'s preference for findings.[215] Finally, the Chief Justice emphasized the "attenuated" nature of "the link between gun possession" and the "effect on interstate commerce" alleged in *Lopez*.[216]

VAWA failed the *Lopez* test. "Gender-motivated crimes of violence," Chief Justice Rehnquist wrote, "are not, in any sense of the phrase, economic activity."[217] Nor did VAWA contain a "jurisdictional element establishing that the federal cause of action is in pursuance of Congress' power to regulate interstate commerce."[218] *Morrison* differed from *Lopez* insofar as Congress made "numerous findings regarding the serious impact that gender-motivated violence has on victims and their families."[219] These findings proved unavailing. Chief Justice Rehnquist refused to treat "the existence of congressional findings . . ., by itself," as "sufficient . . . to sustain the constitutionality of Commerce Clause legislation."[220] *Morrison* considered these findings' connection of sex-based violence with interstate commerce to be so "substantially weakened" that their use as a foundation for federal legislation would "completely obliterate the Constitution's distinction between national and local authority."[221] The Court feared that the extension of "the but-for causal chain from the initial occurrence of violent crime" would permit "Congress to regulate any crime as long as the nationwide, aggregated impact of that crime has substantial effects on employment, production, transit, or consumption."[222] This reasoning curbed *Filburn*'s "aggregation": "We . . . reject the argument that Congress may regulate noneconomic, violent criminal conduct based solely on that conduct's aggregate effect on interstate commerce."[223]

---

[213] *Id.* at 611.

[214] *Id.* at 612.

[215] *See id.*

[216] *Id.*

[217] *Id.* at 613.

[218] *Id.*

[219] *Id.* at 614.

[220] *Id.*

[221] *Id.* at 615.

[222] *Id.*

[223] *Id.* at 617.

Lopez and *Morrison* arguably undervalued "the traditional national interest in the uniform enforcement of civil rights."[224] Some critics believe that *Lopez* and *Morrison* have "single[d] out civil rights laws as being uniquely beyond the scope of Congress's commerce power."[225] Federal environmental law, too, seems shakier.[226] *Lopez* and *Morrison* may transform the traditional rule counseling the interpretation of statutes so as to avoid constitutional doubts[227] into a roving commission to limit statutes that a majority of Justices dislike. Indeed, in subsequent cases involving the federal arson statute[228] and the Clean Water Act,[229] the post-*Morrison* Court appeared to do exactly that.

Wickard v. Filburn's aggregation principle remains valid, but it operates only when the actors or activities at issue are commercial. Gun possession or sex-motivated violence will not qualify, at least when they lack a visible connection to overtly economic activity. This shift restores certain elements of Commerce Clause jurisprudence that prevailed before the New Deal. As Justice Souter observed in his *Lopez* dissent, "[t]he distinction between what is patently commercial and what is not looks much like the old distinction between what directly affects commerce and what touches it only indirectly."[230] Justice Breyer's dissent argued that *Lopez*'s treatment of *Filburn* and its cognate cases "is not consistent" with those cases' actual holdings.[231] To the extent that the *Lopez* majority purported to rely on the New Deal's vision of the Commerce Clause, the decision engaged in "cite and switch," the strate-

---

[224] *See* Julie Goldscheid, United States v. Morrison *and the Civil Rights Remedy of the Violence Against Women Act: A Civil Rights Law Struck Down in the Name of Federalism,* 86 Cornell L. Rev. 109, 131–32 (2000).

[225] Louis J. Virelli III & David S. Leibowitz, *"Federalism Whether They Want It or Not": The New Commerce Clause Doctrine and the Future of Federal Civil Rights Legislation After* United States v. Morrison, 3 U. Pa. J. Const. L. 926, 976 (2001).

[226] *See generally* Christine A. Klein, *The Environmental Commerce Clause,* 27 Harv. Envtl. L. Rev. 1 (2003).

[227] *See, e.g., Edward J. DeBartolo Corp. v. Florida Gulf Coast Bldg. & Constr. Trades Council,* 485 U.S. 568, 575 (1988); *NLRB v. Catholic Bishop,* 440 U.S. 490, 500–01 (1979); *Murray v. The Charming Betsy,* 6 U.S. (2 Cranch) 64, 118 (1804).

[228] *See Jones v. United States,* 529 U.S. 848, 859 (2000) (holding that the arson statute "covers only property currently used in commerce or in an activity affecting commerce" in order to avoid casting doubt on the statute's constitutionality after *Lopez*).

[229] *See Solid Waste Agency v. United States Army Corps of Eng'rs,* 531 U.S. 159, 173–74 (2001) (invalidating the Corps's migratory bird rule in order "to avoid the significant constitutional and federalism questions raised" by the Corps's interpretation of the statutory term "navigable waters").

[230] *United States v. Lopez,* 514 U.S. 549, 608 (1995) (Souter, J., dissenting).

[231] *Id.* at 628 (Breyer, J., dissenting).

gy of paying nominal homage to precedent before ignoring or eviscerating it.[232]

Formally, at least, *Lopez* overruled no precedents. Justice Thomas's concurrence, by contrast, hinted that the Court "must [eventually] modify [its] Commerce Clause jurisprudence,"[233] perhaps by restoring a narrow definition of "commerce" distinct from agriculture, manufacturing, and other activities leading to "the production of goods."[234] Justice Thomas contended that the Court had expanded the Commerce Clause to such an extent that it had rendered "many of Congress' other enumerated powers ... wholly superfluous."[235] In *Morrison*, Justice Thomas again wrote separately to argue "that the very notion of a 'substantial effects' test under the Commerce Clause is inconsistent with the original understanding of Congress' powers."[236] Accepting Justice Thomas's gloss on the Commerce Clause would very tightly constrain congressional power. Realistically, the Court will not adopt a sharp, categorical distinction between commerce and other economic activities such as agriculture, manufacturing, and mining.

The 2005 decision of *Gonzales v. Raich*[237] provides a more realistic view of Commerce Clause jurisprudence. *Raich* involved the application of the federal Controlled Substances Act to marijuana. California exempts limited amounts of medical marijuana from criminal prohibition; federal law does not. Because neither *Lopez* nor *Morrison* had overruled Commerce Clause precedents, a majority of Justices in *Raich* reaffirmed Congress's power to regulate the channels of interstate commerce, to regulate and protect the intrumentalities of interstate commerce (including persons or things), and to regulate activities that substantially affect interstate commerce.[238] *Raich* treated *Wickard v. Filburn* as controlling precedent:

> The similarities between this case and *Wickard* are striking. Like the farmer in *Wickard*, respondents are cultivating, for home consumption, a fungible commodity for which there is an established,

---

[232] *See* Ronald J. Krotoszynski, Jr., *An* Epitaphios *for Neutral Principles in Constitutional Law:* Bush v. Gore *and the Emerging Jurisprudence of* Oprah!, 90 Geo. L.J. 2087, 2093 (2002).

[233] *Lopez*, 514 U.S. at 602 (Thomas, J., concurring).

[234] *Id.* at 587.

[235] *Id.* at 588; *accord* Deborah Jones Merritt, *The Third Translation of the Commerce Clause: Congressional Power to Regulate Social Problems*, 66 Geo. Wash. L. Rev. 1206, 1208–09 (1998).

[236] *United States v. Morrison*, 529 U.S. 598, 627 (2000) (Thomas, J. concurring).

[237] 545 U.S. 1 (2005).

[238] *Id.* at 16–17.

albeit illegal, interstate market.... In *Wickard*, we had no difficulty concluding that Congress had a rational basis for believing that, when viewed in the aggregate, leaving home-consumed wheat outside the regulatory scheme would have a substantial influence on price and market conditions. Here too, Congress had a rational basis for concluding that leaving home-consumed marijuana outside federal control would similarly affect price and market conditions.[239]

Raich distinguished *Lopez* and *Morrison* by characterizing the marijuana trade as "quintessentially economic."[240] Concurring in the judgment, Justice Scalia agreed that marijuana and other controlled substances "are fungible commodities," "never more than an instant from the interstate market" even though "grown at home and possessed for personal use."[241] *Raich*'s ability to analogize home-consumed marijuana to home-consumed wheat overcame three dissenting Justices' objection that "the Court's definition of economic activity ... threatens to sweep all of productive human activity into federal regulatory reach."[242]

 Filburn's legacy today is a mirror image of *Filburn*'s original meaning. Whereas *Filburn* once extended Congress's reach to seemingly trivial activities whose aggregate economic effect reached national or global levels, *Filburn* now marks the extreme boundary of federal power. Distinctions between commerce and production, once a hallmark of formalist Commerce Clause jurisprudence, today hold no sway. Even advocates of a more constrained view of the Commerce Clause concede that the constitutional definition of "commerce" "includes ... the production of ... merchandise through activities such as manufacturing, farming, and mining."[243] With no hint of irony, today's Court has treated the economic character of Roscoe Filburn's farm as a basis for restoring a formal distinction between commercial and noncommercial activities, precisely the distinction that *Wickard v. Filburn* rejected.[244]

---

[239] *Id.* at 18–19.

[240] *Id.* at 25.

[241] *Id.* at 40 (Scalia, J., concurring in the judgment).

[242] *Id.* at 49 (O'Connor, J., dissenting); *see also id.* at 70 (Thomas, J., dissenting) (suggesting that the *Raich* majority was "rewriting" the Commerce Clause to "cover[] the entire web of human activity").

[243] Grant S. Nelson & Robert J. Pushaw, Jr., *Rethinking the Commerce Clause: Applying First Principles to Uphold Federal Commercial Regulations but Preserve State Control over Social Issues*, 85 Iowa L. Rev. 1, 108 (1999).

[244] *See* Jesse H. Choper, *Taming Congress's Power Under the Commerce Clause: What Does the Near Future Portend?*, 55 Ark. L. Rev. 731, 743 (2003) (observing that Chief Justice Rehnquist's attempt to impose a commercial limitation on the aggregation principle is "contradicted by the *Wickard* Court's analysis").

Postscript: The Nature of the Farm

Contemporary Commerce Clause jurisprudence distorts the legacy of *Wickard v. Filburn*. Read in proper historical and economic perspective, *Filburn* cannot fairly be conscripted to support sharp distinctions between the commercial and the noncommercial or between production and traffic. An agriculturally literate understanding of *Filburn* makes it impossible to argue that any economic enterprise is strictly local. Economic, environmental, and political "interconnection" across jurisdictional boundaries "has become too real to ignore"; the "existence of transboundary communities inevitably creates a drive away from localism in all spheres."[245] In a world where virtually every legal endeavor is transforming "from a strictly local undertaking into a global commitment,"[246] no subject is "effectively controlled by a single national sovereign."[247] Today's global reality makes it not only implausible but also unacceptable to credit Roscoe Filburn's complaint that federal regulation invaded an exclusively local sphere of control. In a political system so closely tied to its agrarian roots, the proper cure for constitutional formalism lies in agricultural literacy. A page of economic history is worth volumes of legal logic.[248]

Wickard v. Filburn was at heart a case about wheat.[249] Ah, *"wheat, the king of all grains!"*[250] Earlier agricultural decisions had involved tobacco[251] or milk.[252] Wheat differed in two key respects. First, neither tobacco nor milk can match wheat's global reach. One of the leading plant species in humanity's larder,[253] wheat is grown widely and shipped

---

[245] Daniel A. Farber, *Stretching the Margins: The Geographic Nexus in Environmental Law*, 48 Stan. L. Rev. 1247, 1271 (1996).

[246] Jim Chen, *Fugitives and Agrarians in a World Without Frontiers*, 18 Cardozo L. Rev. 1031, 1051 (1996).

[247] John H. Jackson, *Reflections on International Economic Law*, 17 U. Pa. J. Int'l Econ. L. 17, 25 (1996).

[248] *Cf. New York Trust Co. v. Eisner*, 256 U.S. 345, 349 (1921); *see also* Oliver Wendell Holmes, Jr., *The Common Law* 1 (Little Brown & Co. 1990) (1881) ("The life of the law has not been logic: it has been experience.").

[249] *See* Stern, *supra* note 58, at 901.

[250] O.E. Rölvaag, *Giants in the Earth* 110 (Lincoln Colcord & O.E. Rölvaag trans., 1927).

[251] *See Mulford v. Smith*, 307 U.S. 38 (1939); *Currin v. Wallace*, 306 U.S. 1 (1939).

[252] *See United States v. Wrightwood Dairy Co.*, 315 U.S. 110 (1942); *United States v. Rock Royal Co-op., Inc.*, 307 U.S. 533 (1939).

[253] *See generally* Robert Prescott–Allen & Christine Prescott–Allen, *How Many Plants Feed the World?*, 4 Conservation Biology 365, 366 (1990).

even further.[254] The outbreak of world war magnified the importance of the wheat market. With the rest of the world locked in mortal struggle, the United States did not suffer a wheat shortage. Rather, it complained that a wheat surplus was depressing prices paid to farmers. Second, wheat differed from other commodities in New Deal agricultural controversies–tobacco, milk, cotton–in that wheat can be used as readily by its producer as it can be sold to a processor. Because "[f]armers did not use raw cotton or tobacco themselves," they "brought nearly all to the tobacco warehouse or the cotton gin for marketing."[255] Dairy disputes seem invariably to arise from the economic dependence of relatively numerous producers on relatively few "handlers" of milk.[256] The seemingly "bucolic" and "seren[e]" practice of "milking ... animals in order to make use of their lactic secretions for human food" has "often provok[ed] as much human strife and nastiness as strong alcoholic beverages."[257] A clever regulator (or monopolist) can control these markets by a single bottleneck.

Filburn arose from wheat's exceptional mobility and versatility. At least in Roscoe Filburn's day, many producers could either sell wheat or use it on the farm as animal feed. Whereas a quantitative limit on tobacco reaching warehouses or cotton reaching gins would "reach[] virtually the entire supply" of those commodities,[258] 85 percent of the corn produced during the 1930s moved in commerce as cornfed livestock, poultry, or their milk or egg byproducts.[259] A smaller but comparable portion of the wheat crop was likewise converted into meat, milk, poultry, and eggs. On-farm consumption of wheat "appear[ed] to vary in an amount greater than 20 per cent of average production."[260] Integrated farmers could evade a marketing quota by redirecting wheat to the feed bin.[261] Congress thus decided to treat corn and wheat "alike with respect to the feeding of poultry or livestock for market."[262]

---

[254] *See* Moshe Feldman et al., *Wheats, in Evolution of Crop Plants* 184, 184–92 (J. Smartt & N.W. Simmonds eds., 2d ed. 1995); Jim Longmire & Walter H. Gardiner, Econ. Res. Serv., U.S. Dep't of Agric., *Long-Term Developments in Trade in Feeds and Livestock Products* 2 (1984) (reporting that 90% of wheat traded internationally is used as food).

[255] Stern, *supra* note 58, at 902.

[256] *See Zuber v. Allen*, 396 U.S. 168, 172–74 (1969); Reuben A. Kessel, *Economic Effects of Federal Regulation of Milk Markets*, 10 J.L. & Econ. 51 (1967).

[257] *Queensboro Farms Prods. v. Wickard*, 137 F.2d 969, 972 (2d Cir. 1943) ("[T]he domestication of milk has not been accompanied by a successful domestication of some of the meaner human impulses in all those engaged in the milk industry.").

[258] Stern, *supra* note 58, at 902.

[259] *See* H.R. Rep. No. 75–1645, at 24 (1937); Stern, *supra* note 58, at 902.

[260] *Wickard v. Filburn*, 317 U.S. 111, 127 (1942).

[261] See J.B. Hutson, *Acreage Allotments, Marketing Quotas, and Commodity Loans as Means of Agricultural Adjustment, in* U.S. Dep't of Agric., *Yearbook of Agriculture, 1940: Farmers in a Changing World* 551, 555 (1940); Stern, *supra* note 58, at 903.

[262] S. Rep. No. 76–1668, at 2 (1940), *quoted in* Stern, *supra* note 58, at 902.

A similar strategy governed the New Deal's other agricultural programs. In *Currin v. Wallace*, regulators could not separate tobacco
destined for domestic markets from tobacco earmarked to go abroad.[263]
Nor could milk marketing orders target distinct intrastate and interstate
markets for milk.[264] These problems differed in degree but not in kind
from problems arising from wheat's versatility. *Filburn* assumed that
regulators could not distinguish wheat consumed on the farm from
wheat sold on the open market. The only difference was that the
warehouse in *Currin*, relative to the global wheat market in *Filburn*, is
more obviously "the throat where tobacco enters the stream of commerce."[265]

Contemporary lawyers often believe that Roscoe Filburn converted
his excess wheat into bread.[266] In reality, the notion that "Farmer
Filburn was ... an organic home baker who had decided to raise wheat
for a few loaves of bread" boggles the imagination.[267] To consume 239
excess bushels,[268] the Filburn family would have had to consume nearly
forty-four one-pound loaves of bread *each day* for a year.[269] In Filburn's
time, farmers fed twenty times more wheat to livestock than they
ground into flour for home use.[270]

---

[263] 306 U.S. 1, 11 (1939) ("[T]he transactions on the tobacco market were conducted
indiscriminately at virtually the same time, and in a manner which made it necessary, if
the congressional rule were to be applied, to make it govern all the tobacco thus offered for
sale.").

[264] *See United States v. Wrightwood Dairy Co.*, 315 U.S. 110, 120–21 (1942); *United
States v. Rock Royal Co-op., Inc.*, 307 U.S. 533, 568–69 (1939).

[265] *Mulford v. Smith*, 307 U.S. 38, 47 (1939); *cf. NLRB v. Jones & Laughlin Steel
Corp.*, 301 U.S. 1, 35 (1937) (using a similar "throat" metaphor to describe an impediment
to interstate commerce); *Stafford v. Wallace*, 258 U.S. 495, 516 (1922) (same).

[266] *See, e.g., National Paint & Coatings Ass'n v. City of Chicago*, 45 F.3d 1124, 1130–31
(7th Cir.) (describing *Filburn* as a case involving a "farmer's consumption of bread baked
from [his] own wheat"), *cert. denied*, 515 U.S. 1143 (1995); *Village of Oconomowoc Lake v.
Dayton Hudson Corp.*, 24 F.3d 962, 965 (7th Cir.) (citing *Filburn* for the proposition "that
wheat a farmer bakes into bread and eats at home is part of 'interstate commerce' "), *cert.
denied*, 513 U.S. 930 (1994).

[267] Deborah Jones Merritt, *Commerce!*, 94 Mich. L. Rev. 674, 748–49 & n.316 (1995).

[268] *See Wickard v. Filburn*, 317 U.S. 111, 114 (1942).

[269] One bushel of wheat yields 67 loaves of bread. *See* Tex. Wheat Producers Bd. &
Ass'n, *Fun Facts*, *at* http://www.texaswheat.org/Facts/funfact.htm (visited May 10, 2003).

[270] *See* U.S. Dep't of Agric., *Field and Seed Crops by States, 1949–54*, at 8 (1957)
(reporting wheat consumption statistics for 1944).

Transforming a field crop into grocery staples requires nothing more mysterious than feeding farm animals. This act, and not the tilling of crop fields, may have been the first step in the development of agriculture.[271] By converting excess wheat into milk, meat, poultry, and eggs, the Filburn farm engaged in an age-old practice of regulated firms:[272] manipulating investments between a regulated line of business (wheat) and nonregulated lines (meat, dairy, poultry, and eggs). The Department of Agriculture responded in equally time-honored fashion by treating each farmer's total acreage in wheat as a workable surrogate for the "impossible task" of "computing the actual quantity of wheat marketed by each farmer in the form of wheat or meat."[273] Acreage limitations allowed the wheat program to control prices and supply not only in the regulated market, but also in several derivative product markets.[274] Meanwhile, the Federal Extension Service was exhorting farmers to feed much of their wheat to livestock, ostensibly to beef up America's wartime diet, but not coincidentally also to ease the wheat glut.[275]

Filburn's "aggregation" doctrine reflects economic reality. Simultaneous, uncoordinated acts by vertically integrated, diversified producers take on a significance vastly outstripping that of any single farmer. Like ants, cities, and the Internet, agricultural markets exhibit the "emergent behavior" of a complex adaptive system.[276] Neither Filburn nor any other farmer acting alone exercised enough power to affect global prices merely by deciding either to sell wheat or to integrate wheat production with other farm activities. Filburn had to take the price as he found it; finding the price insufficient, he sought an alternative use. Such "price taking" is the farmer's lot in a world dominated by agribusiness purchasers.[277] But each farmer's seemingly discrete act, multiplied many

---

[271] *See* Constance Holden, *Bringing Home the Bacon*, 264 Sci. 1398, 1398 (1994).

[272] *See, e.g., Colorado Interstate Gas Co. v. Federal Power Comm'n*, 324 U.S. 581 (1945); *Smith v. Illinois Bell Tel. Co.*, 282 U.S. 133 (1930); *City of Houston v. Southwestern Bell Tel. Co.*, 259 U.S. 318 (1922); *Southwestern Bell Corp. v. FCC*, 896 F.2d 1378 (D.C. Cir. 1990).

[273] Stern, *supra* note 58, at 903.

[274] *See, e.g., United States v. Southwestern Cable Co.*, 392 U.S. 157 (1968); *In re Montana–Dakota Utils. Co.*, 278 N.W.2d 189 (S.D. 1979).

[275] *See* U.S. Dep't of Agric., *Annual Report of the Secretary of Agriculture* 69, 80 (1941).

[276] Stephen Johnson, *Emergence: The Connected Lives of Ants, Brains, Cities, and Software* 18 (2001).

[277] *See National Broiler Mktg. Ass'n v. United States*, 436 U.S. 816, 825–26 (1978) (describing the "price taking" that occurs when farmers in an almost perfectly competitive market must sell to concentrated agribusiness purchasers); *id.* at 829 (Brennan, J., concurring) (same); *id.* at 840–41 (White, J., dissenting) (same); *Tigner v. Texas*, 310 U.S. 141, 145 (1940) (same).

times, profoundly affected prices and supplies in the larger market. The relatively inelastic demand for wheat as food and seed[278] transformed on-farm consumption into the legal equivalent of sales on Chicago's Board of Trade, where even the pre-New Deal Court easily discerned that "[s]ales of an article which affect the country-wide price of the article directly affect the country-wide commerce in it."[279] "Untouched, unas-sailable, undefiled, that mighty world-force, that nourisher of nations, wrapped in Nirvanic calm, indifferent to the human swarm, gigantic, resistless, moved onward in its appointed grooves."[280] Congress unques-tionably had power to regulate this market.

Of course, congressional power provides no guarantee that the federal government will achieve its goals.[281] Confronted with the plea that the wheat program was favoring western monocultures over inte-grated operations in the east, *Filburn* pleaded judicial impotence: "[W]ith the wisdom, workability, or fairness, of [this] plan of regulation we have nothing to do."[282] Neither half of the Commerce Clause "pro-tects the particular structure or methods of operation in a ... mar-ket."[283] The wheat program upheld in *Wickard v. Filburn* had distinct (and not altogether desirable) distributional consequences. Wealth trans-fers under the Agricultural Adjustment Act followed the usual practice of "lev[ying] the heaviest taxes against poorer people to subsidize mainly richer farmers."[284] In a nation whose agricultural policy "[h]as [f]ocused on [l]osers,"[285] Roscoe Filburn himself symbolized the most thoroughly

---

[278] *See Wickard v. Filburn*, 317 U.S. 111, 127 (1942) ("The total amount of wheat consumed as food varies but relatively little, and use as seed is relatively constant."); Stern, *supra* note 58, at 904.

[279] *Chicago Bd. of Trade v. Olsen*, 262 U.S. 1, 40 (1923); *cf. Santa Cruz Fruit Packing Co. v. NLRB*, 303 U.S. 453, 464 (1938) (detecting readily "a continuous flow of interstate commerce" in a stream of "fruits and vegetables ... grown in California" and shipped entirely within that state).

[280] Frank Norris, *The Octopus: A Story of California* 360 (Doubleday & Co. rpt. 1947) (1901).

[281] *Cf. CTS Corp. v. Dynamics Corp. of Am.*, 481 U.S. 69, 96–97 (1987) (Scalia, J., concurring in the judgment) ("[A] law can be both economic folly and constitutional.").

[282] *Wickard v. Filburn*, 317 U.S. 111, 129 (1942); *cf. Ferguson v. Skrupa*, 372 U.S. 726, 731 (1963) (consigning arguments over the "social utility" of contested lines of business "to the legislature, not to us").

[283] *Exxon Corp. v. Governor of Md.*, 437 U.S. 117, 127 (1978); *accord* CTS Corp. v. Dynamics Corp. of Am., 481 U.S. 69, 93–94 (1987).

[284] Robert Tempest Masson & Philip M. Eisenstat, *The Pricing Policies and Goals of Federal Milk Order Regulations: Time for Reevaluation*, 23 S.D. L. Rev. 662, 663 (1978); *see also* Jim Chen, *The American Ideology*, 48 Vand. L. Rev. 809, 860–62, 875 (1995) (outlining the distributive case against raising food prices to boost farmers' incomes).

[285] D. Gale Johnson, *U.S. Agricultural Programs as Industrial Policy*, in *Industrial Policy for Agriculture in the Global Economy* 307, 308 (S.R. Johnson & S.A. Martin eds., 1993).

vanquished. Farms like his–farms "maintaining a herd of dairy cattle, selling milk, raising poultry, and selling poultry and eggs" in addition to cultivating "a small acreage of winter wheat"[286]–have become virtually extinct since the Supreme Court last entertained a constitutional challenge to federal regulation of farm prices and incomes.

Filburn drove the final sinker into the pinewood coffin of the American family farm. Only a farm like Filburn's, one integrating grain production with livestock or poultry operations, could switch freely between selling wheat on the open market, storing it to await higher prices, and feeding it to farm animals. As *Filburn* recognized, however, farm organization varied greatly by region. Western wheat-exporting states "specializ[ed] in wheat," such that "the concentration on this crop reache[d] 27 percent of the crop land, and the average harvest r[an] as high as 155 acres."[287] By contrast, some states in New England–a net wheat-importing region and the cradle of the American family farm[288]– devoted "less than one percent of the crop land ... to wheat" and harvested "less than five acres per farm."[289] Thanks to the uneven geographic distribution of wheat specialists versus integrated farmers, the program upheld in *Filburn* systematically shifted wealth from smaller, integrated farms in the east (including Ohio) to larger, specialized farms in the west.[290]

Filburn openly acknowledged the Agricultural Adjustment Act's threat to traditional agriculture. Justice Jackson admitted that wheat which "is never marketed ... supplies a need of the man who grew it which would otherwise be reflected by purchases in the open market."[291] There is no better statement in the *United States Reports* of Ronald Coase's Nobel Prize-winning observation that vertical integration and open-market purchases are flip sides of the same economic phenomenon.[292]

---

[286] *Wickard v. Filburn*, 317 U.S. 111, 114 (1942).

[287] *Id.* at 126–27.

[288] *See* Taylor, *supra* note 60, at 476–80; *cf.* Mark Kramer, *Three Farms: Making Milk, Meat, and Money from the American Soil* 20, 38–42 (2d ed. 1987) (describing the especially tenuous economic position of New England farmers).

[289] *Filburn*, 317 U.S. at 127.

[290] *Cf. McCulloch v. Maryland*, 17 U.S. (4 Wheat.) 316, 408 (1819) ("The exigencies of the nation may require, that the treasure raised in the north should be transported to the south, that raised in the east, conveyed to the west, or that this order should be reversed.").

[291] *Filburn*, 317 U.S. at 128.

[292] *See* R.H. Coase, *The Nature of the Firm*, 4 Economica 386, 388–89, 392 (1937).

Careful parsing of *Wickard v. Filburn* confirms what Coase described in *The Nature of the Firm*. *Filburn* openly admitted that the wheat program "forc[ed] some farmers into the market to buy what they could provide for themselves" and therefore served as "an unfair promotion of the markets and prices of specializing wheat growers."[293] In the three decades after *Wickard v. Filburn*, the proportion of American wheat consumed on the farm where it was grown dwindled from 16 to 5 percent:[294]

Year	Used on farm[†]	Sold[†]	% on-farm use
1944	173,354	886,757	16.35%
1946	161,306	990,812	14.00%
1948	174,541	1,120,370	13.48%
1950	142,536	876,808	13.98%
1952	136,140	1,170,300	10.42%
1954	84,398	884,398	8.58%
1956	84,419	920,978	8.40%
1958	88,025	1,369,410	6.04%
1960	68,061	1,286,648	5.02%
1962	53,023	1,038,935	4.86%
1964	72,620	1,210,751	5.66%
1966	72,188	1,232,701	5.53%
1968	98,852	1,457,783	6.35%
1970	95,300	1,256,258	7.05%
1972	84,964	1,461,245	5.50%
1974	87,534	1,694,384	4.91%
1976	104,755	2,044,025	4.88%
1978	83,151	1,692,373	4.68%

The Department of Agriculture won a Pyrrhic victory, for the statute upheld in *Filburn* accelerated the destruction of farmers like Roscoe Filburn. Shortly after *Filburn*, agricultural analysts began asking Coase's unsettling question: "Why is not all production carried on by one big firm?"[295] By 1957, Harvard economists invented a new word, *agribusiness*, to describe "the sum total of all operations involved in the manufacture and distribution of farm supplies; production operations on the farm; and the storage, processing, and distribution of farm commodi-

---

[293] 317 U.S. at 129.

[294] *See* USDA Econ. & Statistics Sys., *State-Level Wheat Statistics, at* http://usda.mann lib.cornell.edu/usda/ers/89016/whtus.wk1 (current file with data beginning in 1949). All figures marked with a "†" are expressed in thousands of tons.

[295] Coase, *supra* note 292, at 394.

ties and items made from them."[296] Traditional agriculture–"more or less a self-contained industry" characterized by "typical farm famil[ies]" that "produced [their] own food, fuel, shelter, draft animals, feed, tools, and implements and even most of [their] clothing"–was fading.[297] Marginal farms folded, average farm size mushroomed, and industry began performing "virtually all [the] operations relating to growing, processing, storing, and merchandising food and fiber" that had been "a function of the farm."[298] Vertical integration *on* the farm yielded to vertical integration *of* the farm. There is but a vowel's difference between the *firm* and the *farm*; the nature of the firm dictates the destiny of the farm.[299]

In fairness to the New Deal, the traditional farm economy was already doomed. "Whatever the government did or did not do, it seemed certain by the late 1940s and 1950s that the decline in the number of farms and farmers was irreversible."[300] The social, economic, and technological changes wrought by world war ordained as much. Full deployment of mechanical power, fertilizer, and pesticides has sustained the flow of grain ever since.[301] Abundant feed has all but displaced homegrown grain and has shifted a large proportion of American livestock from private pastures and open range to feedlots.[302]

Humans, too, joined the exodus. In the half-century after the war, the farm population of the United States fell from roughly one quarter to less than two percent.[303] America's rise to superpower status all but dictated these demographic shifts. Rural depopulation is a direct consequence of economic growth. Rising urban incomes prompt farmers to abandon farming for city jobs, and the remaining rural landscape hosts fewer, larger farms.[304]

---

[296] John H. Davis & Ray A. Goldberg, *A Concept of Agribusiness* 2 (1957).

[297] *Id.* at 4.

[298] *Id.* at 1.

[299] *See* Douglas W. Allen & Dean Lueck, *The Nature of the Farm*, 41 J.L. & Econ. 343 (1998); Jim Chen & Edward S. Adams, *Feudalism Unmodified: Discourses on Farms and Firms*, 45 Drake L. Rev. 361, 402 (1997).

[300] Fite, *supra* note 54, at 123.

[301] *See* David Goodman & Michael Redclift, *Refashioning Nature: Food, Ecology, and Culture* 109–10 (1991).

[302] *See id.*; James R. Simpson & Donald E. Farris, *The World's Beef Business* 37, 51 (1982).

[303] *See* Chen & Adams, *supra* note 299, at 381 & n.129; *see also* Neil D. Hamilton, *Feeding Our Future: Six Philosophical Issues Shaping Agricultural Law*, 72 Neb. L. Rev. 210, 218–20 (1993).

[304] *See* Yoav Kislev & Willis Peterson, *Prices, Technology, and Farm Size*, 90 J. Pol. Econ. 578, 579 (1982); *cf.* Andrew P. Barkley, *The Determinants of the Migration of Labor*

Filburn and the commodity programs it blessed surely hastened the fading of the agrarian dream.[305] For a program whose "major objectives have been to preserve or restore existing structures or conditions," the agricultural policy of the United States has failed even on its own dubious terms.[306] The New Deal's intended beneficiaries have the bitterest view of its agricultural legacy. Hell has no fury like a duped agrarian: advocates for small American farmers have neither forgotten nor forgiven the federal government for its complicity in the trend toward fewer, larger, more industrialized farms.[307]

The path from barnyard to suburb is the dominant narrative in American history. *Wickard v. Filburn*'s protagonist vividly epitomizes this historical sequence. Roscoe Curtiss Filbrun–he changed the spelling of his family name roughly a decade after losing his Supreme Court case[308]–represented the fifth and final generation of Ohio farmers in his family. In 1966, a quarter-century after initiating his attack on the agricultural New Deal, he persuaded other successors to his grandparents' original 640–acre farmstead to sell their land for development.[309] The Salem Mall in Dayton, Ohio, now occupies much of the land farmed by Filbrun's extended family.[310] Roscoe Filbrun took a leading role in facilitating zoning changes and in developing water and sewage systems for the mall.[311] The ninety-five acres that he farmed became a residential subdivision; the adjoining nine acres of forest became commercial real estate.[312] A street on the land that was his is named Filbrun Lane in his honor.[313] Neither child of Roscoe and Virginia McConnell Filbrun

out of Agriculture in the United States, 1940–84, 72 Am. J. Agric. Econ. 567, 571 (1990) (evaluating the impact of higher nonfarm wages on exodus from farming).

[305] *See* Christopher R. Kelley, *Rethinking the Equities of Federal Farm Programs*, 14 N. Ill. U. L. Rev. 659 (1994).

[306] Johnson, *supra* note 285, at 308.

[307] *See, e.g.*, Marty Strange, *Family Farming: A New Economic Vision* 131–34 (1988); Ingolf Vogeler, *The Myth of the Family Farm: Agribusiness Dominance of U.S. Agriculture* 170–85 (1981); *The New Agrarianism: Land, Culture, and the Community of Life* (Eric T. Freyfogle ed., 2001). For a guide to distinctions between left and right in agricultural policy, see Curtis E. Beus & Riley E. Dunlap, *Conventional Versus Alternative Agriculture: The Paradigmatic Roots of the Debate*, 55 Rural Soc. 590 (1990).

[308] *See supra* note *.

[309] *See Filbrun Family History*, *supra* note 92, at 176; Spurgeon Letter, *supra* note *, at 4–5.

[310] *See Filbrun Family History*, *supra* note 92, at 174, 176.

[311] *See id.* at 176.

[312] *See* Spurgeon Letter, *supra* note *, at 5.

[313] *See Filbrun Family History*, *supra* note 92, at 175, 176; Spurgeon Letter, *supra* note *, at 3.

adopted agriculture as a profession. Their daughter, Mary Lou Filbrun Spurgeon, taught organ.[314] When Mary Lou's husband served overseas in the Army during the 1950s, her father bought the Beverly Shop in nearby Brookville, and Mary Lou joined her mother in managing the business. Roscoe Filbrun, Sr., lifelong farmer, thus became the owner of a ladies' dress shop.[315] Roscoe Jr. (called Tommy) grew up helping his father on the farm, but eventually worked an office job.[316] Tommy's son, John Curtiss Filbrun, carried into a third generation the name of the doctor who saved Martin Filburn's arm.[317]

Roscoe Curtiss Filbrun, Sr., died on October 4, 1987, 85 years old and full of days. His family, like America, "was born in the country and . . . moved to the city":[318]

> [H]ow soon country people forget. When they fall in love with a city, it is forever, and it is like forever. As though there never was a time when they didn't love it. The minute they arrive at the train station or get off the ferry and glimpse the wide streets and the wasteful lamps lighting them, they know they are born for it. There, in a city, they are not so much new as themselves: their stronger, riskier selves.[319]

---

[314] See Filbrun Family History, supra note 92, at 177.

[315] See Background of the Beverly Shop, Ohio Apparel Reg., Jan. 1956, at 15.

[316] See Filbrun Family History, supra note 92, at 177; Spurgeon Letter, supra note *, at 16.

[317] See Filbrun Family History, supra note 92, at 177.

[318] Richard Hofstadter, The Age of Reform: From Bryan to F.D.R. 23 (1955).

[319] Toni Morrison, Jazz 33 (1992).

*

4

Michael J. Gerhardt

The Story of *Bush v. Gore*: The Paradox of Judicial Activism

Several weeks after Election Day, 2000, I appeared as a constitutional law expert on CNN. The topic was a Supreme Court argument scheduled for later that day, the first of two cases arising from the disputed presidential election between then-Governor George W. Bush and Vice–President Al Gore, Jr. The anchor asked me about the significance of the pending argument. When I demurred, he pressed me to explain why I would not acknowledge the obvious—that the case would clearly become one of the most important Supreme Court decisions ever made. I responded I thought that the odds were against that. I suggested it was more likely that the Court would find some basis to avoid reaching the merits of the electoral dispute.

I was wrong, but I was not alone. Few people, at least at that time, foresaw that the Supreme Court would eventually intervene, much less the grounds on which it would intervene, to resolve for the first—and perhaps last—time the winner of a disputed presidential election.

Nearly a decade later, *Bush v. Gore*[1] has become infamous for its anomalies. Both at the time it was decided and since, the case has been widely ridiculed as an affront to the rule of law and judicial activism at its worst. Many people (mostly Democrats) believe that the Court stole the presidential election for George W. Bush and that *Bush v. Gore* was a transparently partisan, unprincipled decision by the conservative justices of the Rehnquist Court to resolve the electoral dispute strictly in accordance with their partisan preferences. Yet, there are many other people who view *Bush v. Gore* as a model of judicial restraint. These

---

[1] 531 U.S. 98 (2000).

people (mostly Republicans) defend the justices in the majority in *Bush v. Gore* for standing firmly on principle, regardless of the political fallout. To be sure, Republicans and Democrats alike appear to be transfixed with the case, so much so that more books have been written about *Bush v. Gore* than any other decision of the Rehnquist Court; and it is one of the few Supreme Court cases that have been made into a movie. But, *Bush v. Gore* is also distinctive for being the only Supreme Court decision that arguably declares that it will have no precedential value. Even so, no case has taught us so much, or demonstrated more extensively, all the ways in which popular elections can go wrong. Consequently, in every major election since 2000, the American people—and the candidates—have braced themselves for the possibility of another *Bush v. Gore*.

These anomalies have made *Bush v. Gore* a hard case to teach. In fact, *Bush v. Gore* was a perfect legal storm; it was the culmination of the convergence of a largely unpredictable mix of legal issues involving federalism, federal and state election law, separation of powers at the state and federal levels, equal protection, due process, and the Court's political question and standing doctrines. But, neither the complex issues nor the unusually tight time constraints on the lawyers fully explain the significance of *Bush v. Gore* in constitutional law. Its importance turns in part on the Court's unprecedented choice to deviate from the path taken on three previous occasions to resolve disputed presidential elections outside the courts. This choice is at the heart of the story of *Bush v. Gore*.[2] For *Bush v. Gore* was the logical extension of the scope of judicial review that the Court had recognized in earlier precedents on voting rights and election law.[3]

The public efforts to characterize *Bush v. Gore* as unprincipled judicial activism or courageous judicial restraint have obscured this significance, though these efforts are telling: whether or not a decision qualifies as judicial activism or restraint is in the eye of the beholder. Judicial activism is a euphemism employed by people to deride judicial decisions with which they disagree, while judicial restraint is how people

---

[2] The present story does not purport to be a comprehensive account of *Bush v. Gore*. It is the story of the *constitutional* issues involved in the dispute over the 2000 presidential election. While the dispute encompassed many non-constitutional issues, this chapter will discuss them only insofar as they are pertinent to, or help to illuminate, the constitutional issues in and ramifications of *Bush v. Gore*. Most of the detailed accounts of the dispute over the 2000 presidential election include extensive discussions of both the constitutional and non-constitutional issues involved. For two excellent accounts relied upon in discussing the factual disputes, legal briefs, and public statements throughout, see Howard Gillman, *The Votes that Counted: How the Court Decided the 2000 Presidential Election* (2001); and Jeffrey Toobin, *Too Close to Call: The Thirty–Six–Day Battle to Decide the 2000 Election* (2002).

[3] *See infra* notes 80–83 and accompanying text.

characterize decisions with which they agree.[4] The characterizations of judicial activism and restraint are made to appeal to particular constituencies and to build, or undermine, popular and political support for controversial Supreme Court decisions; however, these characterizations tend to obscure, rather than illuminate, the significance of a case in constitutional law. *Bush v. Gore* is hardly unique for being criticized as judicial activism or defended as judicial restraint; nor is it unique for being controversial and less than perfect. But, it is unusual in that its stakes are entirely political, and its significance depends on appreciating how such a pervasively political dispute came to be resolved by the Supreme Court. Understanding this significance requires moving beyond the partisan reactions and criticisms of the case to examine the reasons for, and ramifications of, the legal strategies pursued by Bush and Gore to take their conflict into the courts—with Bush preferring to litigate in federal courts and Gore in the state courts. Thus, the ultimate importance of *Bush v. Gore* is what it revealed about the state of judicial review entering the 21st century.

The Initial Path to the Supreme Court

As Election Day, November 7, 2000, neared, the two major party's presidential candidates, George W. Bush and Al Gore, were preparing for a close election, and each was looking to the past for guidance, depending on the outcome. Gore worried that he might lose the popular vote nationally but prevail in the Electoral College, and thus was considering a public appeal to defend that outcome by analogizing it to the last time a president had been elected under similar circumstances—the presidential election of 1888, in which the incumbent president Grover Cleveland conceded to his Republican challenger, Benjamin Harrison, who had lost the popular vote but prevailed in the Electoral College. In anticipation of winning the popular vote but losing in the Electoral College, Bush was considering the possibility of challenging the legitimacy of the Electoral College.

By evening of Election Day, Bush and Gore scrapped their initial expectations, since it had become abundantly clear that the election had come down to the outcome of the popular vote in a single state—Florida. A little before 8 P.M. Eastern Standard Time, the major news networks

---

[4] Judicial activism and judicial restraint are loaded terms. For instance, judicial activism usually has one of two possible pejorative meanings: sometimes, it refers to Supreme Court decisions overturning federal and/or state actions, while at other times it refers to decisions based not on the law but on the justices' personal or political preferences. Similarly, judicial restraint can refer to either the Court's deference or willingness to uphold democratic actions or to judges' or justices' commitment to keeping their personal preferences from influencing their official decisions.

projected, on the basis of exit polls and early counting, that Gore would win Florida. By 10 P.M. that evening, most networks had moved Florida into Gore's win column, and declared that he had won the 2000 presidential election. Bush did not concede, since his own reports pointed to a different, or at least murkier, outcome. Indeed, the networks began retracting their projections of a Gore victory in Florida. At 2:15 A.M. on November 8, the major news networks declared that Bush had in fact won the popular vote in Florida and therefore would receive Florida's electoral votes, which would give him the majority of electoral votes that he would need to prevail in the Electoral College and to win the presidential election. Fifteen minutes later, Gore called Bush to concede the election. But, as Gore prepared to relate this news to his supporters in Nashville, Tennessee, late returns from Florida showed Bush's margin of victory was shrinking. By 3 A.M., it appeared that the final tally in Florida would be so close—less than one half of one percent of the total numbers of votes cast—that it would require a formal re-count of the votes under Florida law. At 3:45 A.M., Gore called Bush back to retract his concession. Thirty minutes later, the networks retracted their projections of a Bush victory in Florida, and declared the election undecided. Although Gore was narrowly leading at that point in the popular vote nationwide, neither candidate could reach 270 electoral votes, the minimum number required for victory in the Electoral College, without winning Florida.

Over the next few weeks, more than a dozen lawsuits were filed with different claims relating to Florida's vote in the presidential election, though only two of these reached the Supreme Court. It is these two lawsuits that are most pertinent to the story of *Bush v. Gore*. In preparing for these two lawsuits (and for their intervention in other lawsuits), Bush and Gore realized that they had to do two things and do them quickly: first, they had to assemble a team of lawyers. They each formed teams with lawyers from their campaigns, local lawyers and (former and present) state officials familiar with Florida election laws, and prominent attorneys from around the country. The leader of Bush's team was James Baker, who had served as his father's Secretary of State. Gore's team leader was Warren Christopher, who had served as Bill Clinton's Secretary of State and whose chief lieutenant was Gore's former chief of staff, Ron Klain.

Second, Bush's and Gore's lawyers had to master federal and Florida election laws. The principal federal statute, the Electoral Count Act of 1887, had been drafted in the aftermath of the disputed 1876 presidential election to provide a procedure for states to follow in order to avoid challenges of their slates of electors in Congress—specifically, by settling disputes over their slates of presidential electors within six days of the scheduled Electoral College vote by "judicial or other methods or procedures" that were based on "laws enacted prior to the day fixed for the appointment of electors."[5] Florida's election statute channeled disputes over election results into two phases, the first of which allowed protests to be filed against the formal certification of the election results. In particular, Section 102.166 of the Florida election statute required that candidates had to decide within 72 hours of midnight of Election Day whether to file any requests for hand recounts of specific counties and that such requests had to be presented to the three-person canvassing boards of the specified counties. The law provided further that the canvassing boards "may authorize a manual recount" of one percent of the ballots, and "shall" correct any "error in vote tabulations which could affect the outcome of the election" through various means, including hand recounts.[6]

Mastering Florida election law further required understanding how the different voting systems used in Florida's 67 counties actually worked and how they could fail. Within 24 hours of election night, the campaigns became aware of problems in four heavily Democratic counties: in Volusia, Miami–Dade, and Broward Counties, there appeared to be large numbers of "undervotes" (punch-card ballots that had not registered a vote for president when they were run through the counting machines). A possible reason for the undervotes was that when voters used the pointed stylus to punch through the paper circle for the candidate of their choice on the ballot, they had not fully detached the perforation, or chad, from the ballot. Democrats believed that a hand recount might reveal voters' intentions depending on the extent of the perforations—punctures or strong indentations in the right place on the ballot might reflect the intention to vote for particular candidates. In Palm Beach, there were larger problems: more than 29,000 ballots had been tossed out because of "undervotes" and "overvotes" (ballots on which more than one preference for president had been registered). Moreover, in Palm Beach County, Independent candidate Pat Buchanan had inexplicably received 3704 votes—more than 2000 votes than he had received in any other Florida county. Democrats and many Palm Beach residents were confounded: Palm Beach County had a large Jewish population, which was not expected to support Buchanan. Many Democrats quickly realized that the surprisingly large support that Buchanan had received in the county was the consequence of the fact that local officials had used a peculiar, butterfly-shaped ballot that placed the punch-hole for Buchanan in between Gore's name and the punch-hole for Gore.

---

[5] 3 U.S.C. § 5 (2000).

[6] Fla. Stat. §§ 102.166(4), (5) (2000).

The first, protest phase appeared to provide more opportunities for Gore than for Bush. Gore favored pursuing it because it entailed actually counting votes, vested major responsibility over the recounts in county canvassing boards that were largely composed of Democrats, and put the onus on Bush to be the first to go to court. Moreover, Gore wanted to block a formal certification of the results of the recount, because he knew that the official required to formally certify the election results was Florida's Secretary of State, Katherine Harris, a co-chair of Bush's campaign in the state. If Gore were to wait for Harris to act, he knew that he could still take advantage of the second phase permitted by Florida law to challenge the election outcome—contesting or challenging the certified results. Bush was wary of a recount because he feared that it would erase the small lead that he still maintained in Florida's popular vote. In fact, Bush was wrong: the automatic machine recount favored Bush, indicating that he had won the popular vote in Florida by less than 300 votes. In response to the automatic recount, Gore promptly asked the canvassing boards of Broward, Volusia, Miami–Dade, and Palm Beach Counties to conduct manual recounts. He asked Harris not to certify the election until the manual recount was completed.

Bush did not wait for Harris' answer, but instead made the first move to enlist the courts on his side. He chose to go to federal court: on Saturday, November 11, his lawyers requested U.S. District Judge Donald Middlebrooks, a Democrat appointed by President Bill Clinton, to issue an injunction to stop the manual recounts that Gore had requested.

The weekend proved to be the calm before the storm of legal activity on Monday, November 13. First, Judge Middlebrooks denied Bush's request, and Bush's lawyers immediately appealed.[7] Second, the State Attorney General, Robert Butterworth, a Democrat who had been one of the co-chairs of Gore's campaign in the state, issued an official opinion defending the lawfulness of the manual recounts in each of the four counties in which Gore had requested them.[8] Third, Gore—and shortly thereafter Bush—intervened in a lawsuit requesting State Circuit Court Judge Terry Lewis, a Democrat, to stop the manual recounts. Fourth, in response to a formal request from the Chairman of the state Republican party, Katherine Harris issued a formal advisory opinion.[9] She minced no words. Harris declared that Florida law required *all* counties within the state to report their vote counts by the close of business the next day, November 14, and that she therefore planned not to accept any recounts,

---

[7] *Siegel v. LePore*, 120 F.Supp.2d 1041 (S.D. Fla. 2000).

[8] Florida Attorney General, Advisory Legal Opinion No. AGO 2000–65, Nov. 14, 2000.

[9] The public statements made by Bush, Gore, Harris and other figures quoted from the protracted contest over the 2000 presidential election can be found in Gillman, *supra* note 2; and Toobin, *supra* note 2.

manual or otherwise, that she received after that date. In her statement, she emphasized the language of the Florida statute that provided that, "if the county returns are not received by the Department of State by 5:00 P.M. of the seventh day following an election, all missing counties shall be ignored, and the results shown by the returns on file shall be certified."[10] She added that she expected that "the presidential election in Florida will be certified by Saturday afternoon [after receipt of all absentee ballots on Friday,] barring judicial intervention." Christopher immediately issued a statement in protest from Gore. Christopher noted that the very next provision of the election code from which Harris had quoted provided that the late results "may be ignored" by the Secretary of State, suggesting (at least to the Gore supporters) that the late returns did not have to be ignored by Harris.[11] Consequently, Christopher called Harris' opinion "arbitrary and unreasonable" and suggested she was motivated by her position as a co-chair of the Bush campaign in Florida. Bush's lawyers responded that Harris' opinion was "an objective decision based on the law of Florida."

The legal activities intensified. First, by the morning of November 13, Gore formally joined the litigation over the 2000 presidential election. He intervened, along with Bush and Palm Beach County, in a case involving the manual recounts that had been ordered in Volusia County. Gore and Volusia County asked the presiding judge, State Circuit Judge Terry Lewis, a Democrat, to force Katherine Harris to extend the deadline for filing the county's recount. After a short hearing held on Monday, Lewis ruled in favor of Harris the next day, November 14.[12] In particular, Judge Lewis ruled that Harris had the authority to refuse to accept any county election results filed after that day. Judge Lewis explained that "the Secretary of State may ignore such late filed returns, but may not do so arbitrarily, rather, only by the proper exercise of discretion after consideration of all appropriate facts and circumstances."[13] So, Judge Lewis concluded, the four counties in which Gore had requested recounts could file late returns but Harris could reject them if she had a reasonable basis for doing so. By 5 P.M. on November 14, Volusia County was the only one of the four counties in which Gore had requested recounts to certify its recount to the Secretary of State. Broward was able only to submit a partial recount by the deadline, and Miami–Dade finished its 1% test recount by 8 P.M. on November 14. Palm Beach County only sent Harris the result of its machine recount and suspended its manual recount until the Florida Supreme Court

---

[10] Fla. Stat. § 102.111(1) (2000).

[11] Fla. Stat. § 102.112 (2000).

[12] *McDermott v. Harris*, 2000 WL 1693713, at *1 (Fla. Circ. Ct. Nov. 14, 2000).

[13] *Id.*

ruled that the recount requested by Gore was legally authorized. After reviewing the counties' submissions, Harris agreed to include the Volusia County recounts but not those of the other counties, leaving Bush with a lead—albeit, a small one of less than 300 votes—in the popular vote for president in Florida. In response to Judge Lewis' ruling, Harris issued a short statement in which she stated that she would require "a written statement of the facts and circumstances that would cause the [three remaining] counties to believe that a change should be made before final certification of the statewide vote." She required the written statement to be submitted to her by 2:00 P.M. the next day, Wednesday, November 15.

Wednesday was frenetic. Early in the morning, Harris petitioned the Florida Supreme Court to stop all the manual recounts and to take control over the election process by consolidating the related proceedings into one state circuit court. But, the Florida Supreme Court rejected the petition and allowed the manual recounts to proceed.[14] It also allowed the Secretary of State and the two campaigns to intervene in a separate case that had been brought by the canvassing board of Palm Beach County to clarify the disagreement between Harris and the State Attorney General on the legality of Gore's requested recounts.[15] By 2 P.M. the canvassing boards submitted their explanations for why they needed more time to complete their recounts, but at 9 P.M. Harris declared that "the reasons given in the requests [for more time to conduct the recounts] are insufficient to warrant waiver of the unambiguous filing deadline imposed by the Florida Legislature." Harris explained that filing late returns was permissible only if there were "proof of voter fraud that affects the outcome of the election," "substantial noncompliance with statutory procedures," and "extenuating circumstances" beyond the control of election officials. Bush relied on the ramifications of Harris' announcement to reject Gore's offer made earlier that day for the two of them to agree to a hand recount in every Florida county.

The next morning, Gore's lawyers returned to Judge Lewis' courtroom to request that he find Harris in contempt of court for refusing to grant extensions of time for Palm Beach, Miami–Dade, and Broward counties to complete their recounts. One day later, November 17, Judge Lewis rejected Gore's request, concluding that Harris had not abused her discretion in refusing to accept late-filed returns from the three counties.[16] The Bush campaign publicly proclaimed that "the rule of law has prevailed." Gore immediately appealed Lewis' ruling to the Florida

---

[14] *Harris v. Circuit Judges*, Emergency Petition for Extraordinary Relief, 2000 WL 1702529 (Fla. Nov. 15, 2000).

[15] This case was to be decided as *Palm Beach County Canvassing Bd. v. Harris*, 772 So.2d 1220 (Fla. 2000).

[16] *McDermott v. Harris*, 2000 WL 1714590 (Fla. Cir. Ct. Nov. 17, 2000).

Supreme Court. The Florida Supreme Court agreed to hear the appeal, consolidated the cases from the counties in which Gore had requested recounts, and set oral argument for Monday, November 20.[17] Moreover, on its own initiative, the Florida Supreme Court unanimously stayed Harris from certifying a winner in the election until "further order from this Court."[18] The Bush campaign immediately denounced the Florida Supreme Court's decision to hear Gore's appeal as purely partisan, pointing to the fact that six of the seven justices had been appointed to six-year terms on the court by Democratic governors.

Meanwhile, the Eleventh Circuit issued a unanimous ruling, *en banc*, upholding Judge Middlebooks' refusal to stop the recounts.[19] The seven Republican and five Democratic judges of the Court of Appeals declared: "Both the Constitution of the United States and [the Electoral Count Act] indicate that states have the primary authority to determine the manner of appointing Presidential Electors and to resolve most controversies concerning the appointment of Electors."[20] Very few people paid attention to, at least at the time, the Bush campaign's statement that "we are free to return to the federal courts to present our constitutional challenges to the selective and subjective manual recount process at an appropriate time in the future."

Harris refused to be stayed. On Saturday, November 18, she declared that she would not wait for the recounts to be submitted by the canvassing boards in Broward, Palm Beach, and Miami–Dade Counties. Based on the recounted votes in Volusia County and the totals of the tallies in Florida's other counties, as well as absentee ballots properly submitted to her office, Harris formally certified that Bush had won the popular vote in the State of Florida by 930 votes.

On November 20, the Florida Supreme Court heard oral arguments in *Palm Beach County Canvassing Bd. v. Harris*. The principal authors of Gore's brief were W. Dexter Douglass, a widely respected Florida attorney, and David Boies, a nationally renowned trial lawyer who had gained notoriety for successfully leading the federal government's antitrust prosecution of Microsoft, and who would handle the oral argument for the Gore campaign. Boies and Douglass made three arguments.[21]

---

[17] *Palm Beach County Canvassing Bd. v. Harris*, 2000 WL 1716481 (Fla. November 17, 2000).

[18] *Palm Beach County Canvassing Bd. v. Harris*, 2000 WL 1716480 (Fla. November 17, 2000).

[19] *Touchston v. McDermott*, 234 F.3d 1130 (11th Cir. 2000).

[20] *Id.* at 1132.

[21] For arguments and quotations, see Joint Brief of Petitioners/Appellants Al Gore Jr. and Florida Democratic Party, *Palm Beach County Canvassing Bd. v. Harris*, 772 So.2d 1220 (Fla. 2000).

First, they emphasized that Florida case law and statutes provided manual recounts to "to determine the voter's intent" so that the election results reflected the views of the populace. Quoting from a much earlier decision of the Florida Supreme Court, *Darby v. State*,[22] Boies and Douglass maintained that canvassing boards "must examine each ballot for *all* evidence of the voter's intent and make its determination on the totality of circumstances." Second, Douglass and Boies chastised Harris for abusing her discretion by choosing "repeatedly . . . to try to stop or delay the lawful manual recount of ballots." They maintained that Florida law did not provide that "she may disregard properly cast votes . . . even if ongoing recounts are in the process of demonstrating that valid ballots were not tabulated and that *the wrong candidate is being certified the winner*" (emphasis in original). Third, they argued that Florida law imposed no "deadline for the submission of corrected, amended, or supplemental returns deemed necessary by the county canvassing board to ensure that the return submitted accurately and completely reflects the votes counted initially and in any recount." They based their construction of Florida law in part on the Florida election statute's definition of "the official return of the election" to include "the return printed by the automatic tabulating equipment" in addition to "write-in, absentee, and manually recounted votes."[23] Gore's lawyers construed this language to mean "that all manually recounted votes be tabulated and that certification be delayed pending the completion of a manual recount that was requested on a timely basis." They concluded that their construction of Florida law was consistent with the Florida Supreme Court's longstanding position to uphold judicial review of election contests to ensure that the people of the state have had the full and fair opportunity to express their will in an election.

The principal authors of Bush's brief were Benjamin Ginsburg, the campaign's general counsel; former Florida Deputy Attorney General Barry Richard; and Michael Carvin, a former Deputy Assistant Attorney General in the Reagan Justice Department and the man who would handle the oral argument in the case. They made four arguments.[24] First, they argued that Gore's reading of Florida's election statute "literally rewrites the Florida code." The law plainly "required county canvassing boards to complete their work, including any recounts, within seven days of an election" and "requires the Commission to certify final election results" even when doing so might "ignore returns from county

---

[22] 75 So. 411 (Fla. 1917).

[23] *See* Fla. Stat. § 101.5614(8) (2000).

[24] For arguments and quotations, see Answer Brief of Intervenor/Respondent George W. Bush, *Palm Beach County Canvassing Bd. v. Harris*, 772 So.2d 1220 (Fla. 2000).

canvassing boards that fail to meet their deadline." Second, they argued that the Electoral Count Act required a state to select its electors "by laws enacted prior to" election day and that "no provision of state law in effect prior to the election ... granted *courts* equitable power to disregard both the deadline and the Secretary's exercise of reasoned discretion." Third, they argued that "all actors at the state level—including judges—are bound to respect the choices made by the Florida legislature as to the process of selecting the state's presidential electors." This obligation arose from the language of Article II, section 1, of the U.S. Constitution, which "provides that the *legislatures* of the States will prescribe the manner in which presidential electors are chosen." Lastly, they suggested that the absence of any uniform standard to guide the canvassing boards in determining the intent of the voter violated the Due Process and Equal Protection Clauses of the Fourteenth Amendment.

In their reply brief, Gore's lawyers proposed a uniform standard to guide the recounts.[25] They asked the Florida Supreme Court to exercise its equitable power and instruct the county canvassing boards to "apply the objective intent standard to determine whether to count a ballot." They suggested that this standard had been first recognized in 1917 in *Darby v. State*[26] and followed ever since by the Florida Supreme Court.

The Florida Supreme Court wasted no time in deciding the case. (Indeed, the court had apparently written its opinion before the oral argument, a fact that Carvin learned just minutes before beginning his oral argument.) In a unanimous *per curiam* opinion issued only a day after oral argument, the justices gave three reasons for ruling in Gore's favor.[27] They began by recognizing two "guiding" principles: the first, derived from precedent and repeatedly reaffirmed,[28] that "the will of the people, not a hyper-technical reliance upon statutory provisions," should be paramount in election cases;[29] the other, "traditional rules of statutory construction."[30] Together, these rules required that "[election] laws

---

[25] For arguments and quotations, see Answer Brief of Petitioners/Appellants Al Gore, Jr. and Florida Democratic Party, *Palm Beach County Canvassing Bd. v. Harris*, 772 So.2d 1220 (Fla. 2000).

[26] *Supra* note 22.

[27] *Palm Beach County Canvassing Bd. v. Harris*, 772 So.2d 1220 (Fla. 2000) (per curiam).

[28] *See Chappell v. Martinez*, 536 S.2d 1007 (Fla. 1988); *Beckstrom v. Volusia County Canvassing Bd.*, 707 So.2d 720 (Fla.1998).

[29] *Palm Beach County Canvassing Bd. v. Harris*, 772 So.2d at 1227 (Fla. 2000) (per curiam).

[30] *Id*. at 1228.

must be liberally construed in favor of the citizens' right to vote," so that courts do "not lose sight of the fundamental purpose of election laws," which is "to facilitate and safeguard the right of each voter to express his or her will in the context of our representative democracy."[31] The court determined that the Secretary of State could refuse to accept late-filed returns only if counting them somehow entailed "precluding a candidate, elector, or taxpayer from contesting the certification of the election" or "precluding Florida voters from participating fully in the federal electoral process."[32] Since the Secretary of State had not determined that either of these conditions were met in the present case, the court concluded she had abused her discretion.[33] The court concluded further "that we must invoke the equitable powers of this Court to fashion a remedy that will allow a fair and expeditious resolution of the questions presented here."[34] The court further ordered not only Palm Beach, Miami–Dade, and Broward Counties to submit the results of their manual recounts to Harris no later than 5:00 P.M. on Sunday evening, November 26, but also Harris to explain her reasons for denying any returns to the Board of Elections.[35]

There were at least two conspicuous gaps in the court's opinion. First, the justices had not specified a uniform standard for the canvassing boards to follow in ascertaining the intent of the voter. Second, the justices had not explained why they had picked November 26 as the deadline by which counties had to submit amended returns to Harris. Apparently, the justices had wanted to give back to the counties the five days they had lost to count amended returns because of Harris' actions. Hence, the Florida Supreme Court set the deadline five days after the day on which it had released its opinion.

None of this made the Bush camp feel any better. Far from it, they were convinced that the justices were helping Gore to steal the election and to rewrite Florida's election laws to accomplish that objective. As James Baker declared, "Two weeks after the election, that court has invented a new system for counting the election results. [It] is simply not fair ... to change the rules, either in the middle of the game, or after the game has been played." In a rare television appearance during the litigation over the election, George W. Bush agreed that "the justices have used the bench to change Florida's election laws and usurp the authority of Florida's election officials." The 24–hour news cycle on

---

[31] *Id.* at 1237.

[32] *Id.*

[33] *Id.* at 1237–39.

[34] *Id.* at 1240.

[35] *Id.* at 1237–38.

cable and radio was flooded with Republican denouncements of the Florida Supreme Court's decision.

The next day, November 23, Bush authorized the filing of a petition for certiorari to the United States Supreme Court. The appellate lawyers, led by Theodore ("Ted") Olson, a former Reagan Justice Department official (and later Solicitor General), largely reiterated the arguments that the campaign's legal team had made to the Florida Supreme Court. Initially, Bush's lawyers, like Gore's, were skeptical that the Court would grant certiorari. They figured that the Court might prefer not only to defer to a state supreme court's interpretations of that court's own state laws but also to avoid appearing to be partisan by interfering in the political dispute in Florida. But over a dozen attorneys who had clerked for the conservative justices on the Rehnquist Court told Olson that the Court would grant certiorari. They were confident that Baker's concerns that Democrats in Florida were trying to steal the presidential election would resonate with the justices. They were right. On November 24, the day after receiving the petition for certiorari, the Supreme Court agreed to hear oral arguments on three questions, the third of which it had raised on its own initiative: (1) whether the Florida Supreme Court had effectively re-written Florida's election statute (and therefore usurped legislative power); (2) whether the Constitution vested the power solely within state legislatures to determine the criteria for selecting presidential electors; and (3) what "the consequences" would be if the Court were to find "that the decision of the Supreme Court of Florida does not comply" with the Electoral Count Act of 1887.[36] The Court did not, however, agree to hear the argument proposed by the Bush lawyers in their cert petition on whether the absence of a uniform recount standard violated the Fourteenth Amendment. The Court gave the parties barely a week to write their briefs, and scheduled oral argument for December 1.

As Bush's and Gore's appellate lawyers scrambled to complete their briefs, the Gore team was the first to move into the second phase of the process authorized in Florida to challenge the election results: it filed a lawsuit on November 27 to formally contest the certification. The case was assigned to State Circuit Judge N. Sanders Sauls, a Republican appointee who had clashed with the Florida Supreme Court on more than one occasion. The Florida Supreme Court had not only frequently reversed his decisions but also had tried unsuccessfully to remove him as the chief judge of the circuit court because of alleged mishandling of his administrative duties. Eventually, the decision out of Sauls' court would eclipse every other legal event related to the disputed presidential election.

---

[36] *Bush v. Palm Beach County Canvassing Bd.*, 531 U.S. 1004 (2000).

On the day before the oral arguments in *Palm Beach County Canvassing Bd. v. Harris*, the Supreme Court announced that it would release an audio recording of the oral arguments immediately afterwards. On the same day, the Florida Supreme Court published a per curiam opinion unanimously dismissing Gore's legal challenge to the butterfly-shaped ballot employed in Palm Beach County.[37] Gore's claim had been that the design of the ballot had been so confusing as to have led Palm Beach County voters to mark their ballots for Pat Buchanan rather than Gore and thus manual recounts were required to vindicate their actual intentions. Gore's lawyers re-focused their energies on the Supreme Court where they were hoping the moderate justices could persuade their colleagues to stay out of the election and allow the recounts to continue.

The Supreme Court, Round I

In the Supreme Court, Ted Olson led the legal team writing Bush's brief and appeared for the campaign before the Supreme Court. The Bush campaign's principal argument was that, in relying on its "equitable powers" to specify a new deadline for filing amended returns, the Florida Supreme Court had exceeded the bounds of its judicial authority and instead exercised state legislative authority in violation of the Electoral Count Act, the U.S. Constitution, and Florida's election statutes.[38] In the campaign's judgment, these three sets of laws clearly vested the state legislature of Florida alone with the authority to dictate the procedures to be followed in determining presidential electors. First, it noted that the Electoral Count Act specified that disputes over electors had to be resolved exclusively by reference to "laws enacted prior" to Election Day. But, the Bush lawyers argued, the Florida Supreme Court had plainly disregarded and re-written those laws. In support of their claim that the dispute did not pose a political question,[39] they cited a

---

[37] *Fladell v. Palm Beach County Canvassing Bd.*, 772 So.2d 1240 (Fla. 2000).

[38] For arguments and quotations, see Brief for Petitioner, *Bush v. Palm Beach County Canvassing Bd.*, 531 U.S. 70 (2000).

[39] The Court has specified that for a legal controversy to qualify as a non-justiciable political question it must involve, among other things, "a textually demonstrable constitutional commitment of the issue to a coordinate political department; or a lack of judicially discoverable and manageable standards for resolving it." *Nixon v. U.S.*, 506 U.S. 224, 228 (1993) (internal citation omitted). While Gore's lawyers (and supporters) pointed out ways in which these criteria were satisfied in *Bush v. Gore*, they failed to recognize the irony that the modern Court's criteria for determining political questions was first announced in *Baker v. Carr*, 369 U.S. 186 (1962) (Chapter 8). Ironically, *Baker* held that a state's apportionment does not constitute a political question. Any contention that *Bush v. Gore* posed a non-justiciable political question was further undermined by two other similar rulings in major voting rights cases. *See infra* notes 80–82 and accompanying text.

largely unnoticed Supreme Court precedent that was more than a century old, *McPherson v. Blacker*.[40] Bush's lawyers read *McPherson* as holding that disputes arising out of the appointment of presidential electors are not political questions but rather raise "a judicial question" for federal courts to decide. Similarly, Bush's lawyers argued that the Florida state legislature's authorization of the Florida Secretary of State to "ignore" returns filed after the seven-day deadline that it specified was perfectly consistent with the requirements of the Electoral Count Act. They argued further that, in "altering Florida's methods and timetables for the determination of controversies regarding the appointment of presidential electors," the Florida Supreme Court had violated the mandate of Article II, section 1, of the Constitution, which "leaves it to the legislature exclusively to define the method of effecting the object of appointing [presidential] electors." The Bush campaign rejected the claim of the Florida Supreme Court that it could rely on the state constitution as a basis for its decision, since that was not a *legislative* enactment.

The primary authors of Gore's brief were Ron Klain, who had been Gore's first Chief of Staff; Peter Rubin, a law professor at Georgetown; and Harvard Law School Professor Laurence Tribe, who would appear before the Court on behalf of Gore. Gore's lawyers made three arguments.[41] First, they defended the Florida Supreme Court's decision as "an ordinary exercise in statutory interpretation" and as grounded in the "traditional rules of statutory construction to resolve [statutory] ambiguities." Second, Gore's lawyers argued that the Florida Supreme Court did not violate the Electoral Count Act. In their judgment, this act imposed no requirements at all on the State of Florida. Instead, they construed the act as merely providing that if a state resolved disputes over its electoral results in accordance with laws that had been in place prior to Election Day then that State's choice of electors was final and could not be challenged in Congress. The law provided, in other words, a "safe harbor" for States—a path they could follow, if they chose, to ensure their determination of presidential electors could not be revised by Congress. Indeed, they argued, the only penalty that would follow from a State's failure to comply with the Electoral Count Act was being forbidden to take advantage of its safe harbor provision. Third, Gore's lawyers argued that *McPherson* required affirming, not reversing, the Florida Supreme Court. They explained that, "in *McPherson* itself, the state Supreme Court below had measured the statute providing for the appointment of electors for conformity with 'the state constitution and

---

[40] 146 U.S. 1 (1892) (upholding judicial review of a claim of abridgement of legislative prerogatives in establishing the mechanism for selecting a state's electors).

[41] For arguments and quotations, see Brief of Respondents, *Bush v. Palm Beach County Canvassing Bd.*, 531 U.S. 70 (2000).

laws,' and this Court concluded that it was not 'authorized to revise the conclusions of the state court on these matters of local law.' " A proper reading of *McPherson* thus required the Court to defer to the Florida Supreme Court's interpretations of Florida's election law.

Whereas the Florida Supreme Court justices had given Carvin the hardest time in the oral argument below, the Supreme Court justices pressed the lawyers for both sides hard.[42] Four of the Court's conservative justices—Chief Justice Rehnquist and Justices O'Connor, Scalia, and Kennedy—indicated, particularly through their questioning of Olson, that they were skeptical that the Electoral Count Act was judicially enforceable. Instead, their questions reflected their possible interest in finding that the Florida Supreme Court had violated the command of Article II of the Constitution that state legislatures, not the state as a whole or its courts, were singularly responsible for establishing the procedures for selecting presidential electors. The Court's more liberal justices—Stevens, Souter, Breyer, and Ginsburg—were clearly trying to steer the lawyers, particularly Tribe, in a different direction—toward recognizing the need for a remand to clarify that the Florida Supreme Court had been doing nothing more than trying to reconcile seemingly conflicting provisions of the Florida election statute enacted by the state legislature.

Since the oral argument had ended on a Friday, it was unclear how long it would take for the justices to decide the case and write an opinion. In fact, it was record time—on Monday morning, December 4, the Supreme Court released a seven-page, unanimous per curiam opinion.[43] After reviewing the facts of the dispute in detail, the Court first addressed the question whether the Florida Supreme Court had violated Article II of the Constitution. The Court acknowledged that, "[a]s a general rule, this Court defers to a state court's interpretation of a state statute. But in the case of a law enacted by a state legislature applicable not only to elections to state offices, but also to the selection of Presidential electors, the legislature is not acting solely under the authority given it by the people of the State, but by virtue of a direct grant of authority under Art. II, section I, cl. 2, of the United States Constitution."[44] This clause provided in pertinent part that, "Each State shall appoint, in such Manner as the Legislature thereof may direct, a Number of Electors, equal to the whole number of Senators and Representatives to which the

---

[42] Two other lawyers participated in the oral argument: Joseph Klock, Jr., for Secretary of State Harris, and Paul Hancock for the Florida Attorney General. Though they were also pressed hard in the oral argument, neither had as much time, or as much apparent impact, as either Olson or Tribe.

[43] *Bush v. Palm Beach County Canvassing Bd.*, 531 U.S. 70 (2000).

[44] *Id.* at 76.

State may be entitled in the Congress."[45] Citing the earlier decision in *McPherson*, the Court said that the clause's reference to the "State" appointing electors "as the Legislature thereof may direct" vested unique authority in state legislatures that could not be limited by other laws or entities in the state. The Court found significant that the clause did not refer to "the people" or "citizens" of the state and was thus troubled by the Florida Supreme Court's references to the importance of vindicating the intentions of the voters. Such references suggested the possibility that the Florida court had construed the Florida Election Code without regard to the extent to which the Florida Constitution could, consistent with Article II, section 1, cl. 2, "circumscribe the legislative power."[46]

Moreover, the Court construed the Electoral Count Act as establishing a "safe harbor" provision that allowed States to insulate their choice of electors from congressional review or revision. Consequently, the Court was concerned with the Florida Supreme Court's failure to address the Electoral Count Act, including the question whether "a legislative wish to take advantage of the 'safe harbor' [set forth in that law] would counsel against any construction of the Election Code that Congress might deem to be a change in the law."[47]

The Court concluded that, "[a]fter reviewing the opinion of the Florida Supreme Court, we find that there is considerable uncertainty as to the precise grounds for the decision," and that this "is sufficient reason for us to decline at this time to review the federal questions asserted to be present."[48] The Court vacated and remanded the case back to the Florida Supreme Court to clarify what it was doing—interpreting or making the law—and, if interpreting the law, on what basis—state or federal law.

Each campaign found a silver-lining in the Court's opinion. Bush's lawyers construed it as a transparent rebuke of the Florida Supreme Court, a shot across the bow, to warn the lower court to change its course or else. Gore's lawyers found it significant that the Court had not ruled that the Florida Supreme Court had violated federal law. They believed that the Court's moderates had shaped the decision, which they read as a plea for the lower court to help the Supreme Court to find a way to avoid further involvement in the case. They were wrong.[49]

---

[45] U.S. Const. art. II, § 2, cl. 2.

[46] *Id.* at 77 (quoting *McPherson v. Blacker*, 146 U.S. 1, 25 (1892)).

[47] *Id.* at 78.

[48] *Id.* (internal citations omitted).

[49] Accounts written after *Bush v. Gore* suggest that the Court's moderates were trying in *Bush v. Palm Beach County Canvassing Bd.* to stave off an effort by the Court's

The Second Path to the Supreme Court

Curiously, the Florida Supreme Court did not immediately respond to the remand, even though the U.S. Supreme Court had given the Florida Supreme Court the chance to show that its decision was grounded in state law and directed by the state legislature (in compliance with the mandate of Article II of the Constitution).[50] Meanwhile, events were rapidly unfolding in other state courts in Florida. A few hours after the Supreme Court had published its opinion in *Palm Beach County Canvassing Bd. v. Bush*, State Circuit Judge Sauls announced his decision in one of Gore's most important (and last) efforts to alter the election results—his request that the court amend, if not toss out, the certification for failing to include votes that had been legally cast for him.[51] Gore's lawyers, led by David Boies, had asserted their right under Florida law to contest the certified election results as long as they could show that there were enough undervotes not counted in the results that could change the outcome of the election. Recognizing that there was insufficient time to conduct manual recounts by December 12 (the last date that would enable the state to take advantage of the safe harbor provision of the Electoral Count Act), Boies asked Judge Sauls to focus on specific ballots that had already been set aside in the two counties as possible "under-votes" – 266 in Miami–Dade and 3800 in Palm Beach. The fact that Miami–Dade and Palm Beach Counties were heavily Democratic obviously gave the Gore campaign hope that counting possible under-votes in each county was likely to help Gore more than Bush.

Responding for Bush, Barry Richards argued that the Miami–Dade and Palm Beach Canvassing Boards each had authority under state law to make the final decisions about the contested ballots and that state courts should not second-guess their decisions unless they were completely unreasonable. But, he suggested, there was nothing unreasonable about the decisions made by the two canvassing boards. Moreover, Richards emphasized, Gore was cherry-picking the under-votes. Richards suggested that Gore was not trying to vindicate a principle of law but

---

conservative justices, even at that early stage, to find that the Florida Supreme Court had violated either the Electoral Count Act or the mandate of Article II.

[50] The remand arguably gave the Florida Supreme Court the chance to insulate its opinion from Supreme Court review altogether. It potentially gave the court the opportunity to show that its decision had an adequate and independent basis in state (legislative) law. Since the Supreme Court has long recognized that it only has the power to review state court decisions that raise questions of federal law, an adequate and independent basis in state law would effectively deprive the Supreme Court of jurisdiction over the Florida Supreme Court decision. *See generally Michigan v. Long*, 463 U.S. 1032 (1983).

[51] *Gore v. Harris*, 2000 WL 1770257 (Fla. Circ. Ct. Dec. 4, 2000).

instead was only looking for the votes that could win the election for him.

Judge Sauls agreed with Bush.[52] Ruling from the bench, his written opinion was only two paragraphs.[53] He made no findings of fact and made no reference to any of the testimony during the two-day hearing in his courtroom. He did, however, conclude that Gore had failed to establish his entitlement to, "a remedy with the attendant burden of proof, a review and recount on all ballots, and all of the counties in this state."[54]

Even before Judge Sauls announced his ruling, Gore had appealed it to the Florida Supreme Court, which agreed to schedule oral arguments for December 7. As the lawyers for each side prepared briefs for this oral argument, other lawyers for the campaigns were reappearing for the second *en banc* argument before the U.S. Court of Appeals for the Eleventh Circuit regarding Bush's request for an injunction against the manual recounts. This appeal was the first in the litigation to focus exclusively on a question of constitutional law—specifically, whether the absence of a uniform standard for determining the voters' intent to guide recounts violated the Equal Protection Clause by making it impossible for Bush to ensure that he received fundamental fairness in the recount and that different standards could not be manipulated on a partisan basis. It only took a day for the 14 full-time judges of the Eleventh Circuit to decide the case, but this time they were not unanimous. Eight of the judges joined a *per curiam* majority opinion.[55] The majority, which included five Democratic and three Republican appointees, concluded that the only question that it had to decide was whether it was reasonable for the trial court to find that continuing the recounts would not irreparably harm Bush. Although the majority determined that the lower court's decision had been reasonable, it noted that the fact that Bush had been certified as the winner of the Florida election precluded a showing of "serious harm, let alone irreparable harm."[56] The majority further held that the plaintiff-voters who had cast their ballots for Bush similarly had failed to show they had suffered irreparable harm. The majority said nothing about the Equal Protection question, although in a separate concurrence, Chief Judge Anderson emphasized that various safeguards were in place in Florida to ensure "that the results of an

---

[52] *Id.*

[53] *See Gore v. Harris*, 2000 WL 1770257.

[54] Transcript of Ruling, *Gore v. Harris*, Case No. 00–2808, Court Proceedings in the Circuit Court of the Second Judicial Circuit, in and for Leon County, Dec. 4, 2000.

[55] *Siegel v. LePore*, 234 F.3d 1163 (11th Cir. 2000).

[56] *Id.* at 1177.

election accurately reflect the intent of its voters."[57] All four of the dissenters were Republican appointees, three of whom wrote separate dissents maintaining that the Florida Supreme Court had re-written Florida's election law in violation of Article II of the Constitution and that the absence of a uniform standard deprived Bush of the assurance the Equal Protection Clause guaranteed of fairly and uniformly conducted manual recounts.[58]

On December 7, Boies and Richards appeared before the Florida Supreme Court in Gore's appeal of Judge Sauls' refusal to count the alleged "under-votes." They largely reiterated the arguments they had made previously to Judge Sauls. The Florida Supreme Court gave both lawyers a hard time. Moreover, several justices clearly felt chastened by the Supreme Court's remand. In particular, they expressed concerns throughout the oral arguments that they might have exceeded their bounds in ordering the recounts and fixing a new deadline rather than allowing the disputes over the appointment of presidential electors to be made exclusively within the framework of laws established by the state legislature prior to Election Day.

The next twenty-four hours reverberated with judicial bombshells. The day began with two state circuit judges jointly releasing their opinions rejecting separate efforts to exclude 25,000 absentee ballots for various improprieties.[59] Only minutes later, the Florida Supreme Court issued its split-decision in *Gore v. Harris*. By a slim 4–3 margin, the Florida Supreme Court reversed Judge Sauls in a *per curiam* opinion and ordered recounts of votes to begin immediately throughout the State.[60] The justices in the majority included three Democratic appointees and the court's only bi-partisan appointee. After acknowledging the importance of both Article II and the Electoral Count Act, the court explained that it was doing nothing more than implementing the state legislature's mandate that no vote shall be ignored "if there is a clear indication of the intent of the voter on the ballot, unless it is impossible to determine the elector's choice."[61] Thus, a legal vote was one in which the voter's "intent may be discerned from the ballot."[62] They emphasized the "clear

---

[57] *Id.* at 1185 (Anderson, C.J., concurring).

[58] *Siegel v. LePore*, 234 F.3d 1163, 1190 (11th Cir. 2000) (Tjoflat, J. dissenting); *Id.* (Birch, J. dissenting); *Id.* at 1193 (Dubina, J. dissenting).

[59] *Taylor v. Martin County Canvassing Bd.*, 2000 WL 1793409 (Fla. Cir. Ct. 2000); *Jacobs v. Seminole County Canvassing Bd.*, 2000 WL 1793429 (Fla. Cir. Ct. 2000).

[60] *Gore v. Harris*, 772 So.2d 1243 (Fla. 2000) (per curiam).

[61] *Id.* at 1254 (internal citations to Florida statutes omitted).

[62] *Id.* at 1256.

message" set forth in Florida's election statute "that every citizen's vote be counted whenever possible . . ."[63] Consequently, the majority remanded the case back to the Circuit Court of Miami–Dade County to commence recounting the ballots, ordered recounts to resume "forthwith" in counties around the state that had not conducted a manual recount or tabulation of the under-votes, and concluded that based on the under-votes already found, 383 votes should be added to Gore's tally, thereby reducing Bush's lead in the state to 154 votes. In the final sentence of its opinion, the majority noted that, "[i]n tabulating the ballots and in making a determination of what is a 'legal' vote, the standard to be employed is that established by the Legislature in our Elections Code which is that the vote shall be counted as a 'legal' vote if there is a 'clear indication of the intent of the voter.' "[64]

The three dissenters in *Gore v. Harris* included Chief Justice Charles Wells. After making "it clear at the outset . . . that I do not question the good faith or honorable intentions of my colleagues in the majority," Chief Justice Wells emphasized that their decision to require new manual recounts "has no foundation in the law of Florida as it existed on November 7, 2000."[65] He expressed his "deep and abiding concern that the prolonging of judicial process in this counting contest propels this country and this state into an unprecedented and unnecessary constitutional crisis,"[66] especially in light of the widespread belief that the lack of clear legislative standards for reviewing ballots creates "equal protection concerns which will eventually cause the election results in Florida to be stricken by the federal courts or Congress."[67]

Although the reaction to the decision tracked party lines, there was no question what the next step would be. Bush's lawyers immediately appealed both the Florida Supreme Court's decision in *Gore v. Harris* and the *en banc* decision of the U.S. Court of Appeals for the Eleventh Circuit in *Siegel v. LePore* to the Supreme Court. Less than 24 hours later, a 5–4 majority of the Supreme Court granted an emergency injunction stopping the recounts, and scheduled oral arguments for December 11.[68] In its brief order granting the stay, the Court adopted the name that Olson had used for the case in his petition for an emergency stay to underscore the stakes—*Bush v. Gore*. It would be the second and last trip to the Supreme Court for the litigants disputing the 2000

---

[63] *Id.* at 1254.

[64] *Id.* at 1262 (citing Fla. Stat. 101.5614(5) (2000)).

[65] *Id.* at 1263 (Wells, C.J., dissenting).

[66] *Id.*

[67] *Id.* at 1267.

[68] *Bush v. Gore*, 531 U.S. 1046 (2000).

presidential election. By this time, Gore's options had narrowed considerably: his chances to keep the recounts going had dwindled to between slim and none given not only the 5–4 vote for the emergency stay but also a concurrence from Justice Antonin Scalia proclaiming that "a majority of the Court ... believe that [Bush had] a substantial probability of success" of showing that continuing the recounts would cause him irreparable harm by "casting a cloud upon what he claims to be the legitimacy of his election."[69]

The Supreme Court, Round II

The Court required the parties to file their briefs by Sunday evening, December 10, and scheduled oral argument for the next day. But, the dynamics of this argument were radically different from those less than 10 days before in *Harris*. Ted Olson re-appeared for Bush, but Gore wanted a change, so he replaced Tribe with David Boies, whom he thought was more familiar with what was happening on the ground in Florida.

Both Olson and Boies understood that this argument was Olson's to lose and that Olson's principal challenge was to avoid making a mistake that would cause any of the justices in the five-member majority to re-think their decision to stop the recount. Olson and Boies understood further that Bush's constitutional arguments had gained credence from the four dissents in the Eleventh Circuit and the three dissents in the Florida Supreme Court. Hence, Olson's argument re-emphasized the points made in these dissents and particularly in Justice Scalia's concurrence in the Court's stay.[70] First, he argued that the Florida election statute had restricted the role of the state courts in election disputes to simply reviewing whether election officials had abused their discretion. Second, he argued that Florida's "arbitrary, selective and standardless manual recounts" violated the Fourteenth Amendment's Equal Protection and Due Process clauses because they gave "the votes of similarly situated voters different effect based on the happenstance of the county or district in which those voters lived." He explained that the problem was that "where there is a partial punch or stray mark on the ballot, that ballot may be counted as a 'vote' in some counties but not others."

Boies figured he did not have to go for broke but instead simply had to persuade one of the justices who voted for the stay to change position. He calculated that the justices whom he had the best chance to persuade to shift positions were Sandra Day O'Connor and Anthony Kennedy and

---

[69] *Id.* at 1046–47 (Scalia, J., concurring).

[70] For arguments and quotations, see Brief for Petitioners, *Bush v. Gore*, 531 U.S. 98 (2000).

that they might be persuaded to follow their usual practice of deferring to state courts' interpretations of their own laws. He thus argued that the Florida Supreme Court's recount order had been based on the state legislature's decision to "expressly grant[] the courts extraordinarily broad remedial authority" whenever the state's judges had reason to believe that certified election results might have announced the wrong winner by missing too many legal votes. In response to the contention that the Florida Supreme Court's standard for guiding the recount was too general and vague, he argued that the Florida Supreme Court's standard of vindicating "the intent of the voter" was a common one throughout the country and was sufficiently clear and fair to preclude any meaningful possibility of mischief on the part of partisan members of canvassing boards. Boies argued further that the Equal Protection Clause did not require that all ballots had to be treated precisely the same under a state-wide, uniform, and mechanical standard for ballot counting. Indeed, such a standard would be impossible given the different voting mechanisms employed throughout Florida. He concluded that, even if the Court were to decide the state court's uniform standard was deficient, the proper remedy was not to throw out all the under-votes but instead to set forth a new standard for the canvassing boards to follow. He urged the Court not to abandon the recount since that would be "vote dilution with a vengeance."

The signs of where the Court was headed were evident in the questions from the bench. While, as one reporter observed, "[m]embers of the Supreme Court's liberal bloc labored visibly ... to fashion a compromise [on the requisite standard] that might resolve the case of *Bush v. Gore* and allow the counting of Florida's presidential votes to resume,"[71] another saw that "none of the conservative justices were lured into a discussion of the standards for recounting ballots."[72] Moreover, Justice O'Connor and particularly Justice Scalia suggested that undervotes were not legal and should not be counted, because Florida law clearly informed voters before casting their votes that they would count only if the chads were fully detached. Since Justice Kennedy seemed interested in the possibility that Article II vested the power in state legislatures alone to select presidential electors, the questioning in the oral argument clearly did not bode well for Boies.

As *Bush v. Gore* was being argued before the Supreme Court, the Florida Supreme Court finally responded to the Court's remand in *Palm Beach County Canvassing Bd. v. Harris*. Six of the seven justices joined a

---

[71] Linda Greenhouse, *Justices' Questions Underline Divide on Whether Hand Recount Can Be Fair*, N. Y. Times, Dec. 11, 2000, at A1.

[72] David G. Savage, *Justices Debate* Bush v. Gore, L.A. Times, Dec. 12, 2000, at A1, A27.

per curiam opinion.[73] While the opinion excluded any reference to the Florida Constitution, it kept virtually all of its original reasoning— repeated word for word—and merely substituted, where appropriate, the points made about Article II and the Electoral Count Act in the Court's remand. The only new clarification that appeared in the Florida Supreme Court's opinion was its explanation of its November 26 deadline. The court stressed that this "was not a new deadline" and that it would have no effect on future elections.[74] Rather, the court explained, it was an attempt to apply "all the provisions of the [Election] Code as a consistent whole" in the circumstances of the dispute before the court.[75] The court explained further that its November 26 deadline was designed to "put the parties in the same position they would have been at the time the Division [of Elections] issued its advisory opinion on Monday, November 13, 2000."[76] The only dissenter was Chief Justice Wells, who criticized his colleagues for rendering a new decision regarding the election dispute, even in response to the remand, "while the United States Supreme Court has under consideration *Bush v. Gore.*"[77]

Few Supreme Court decisions have been more anxiously anticipated than the Court's decision in *Bush v. Gore.* The Supreme Court building was flooded with reporters eager to be among the first to report its decision to the world. By the time the Court released its opinion at 10 P.M. the next day, December 12, the justices and the clerks had already left the building. The first news reports of the decision featured reporters who had skimmed the multiple opinions or were trying to read them while they were reporting their contents. Not surprisingly, the early reports were incomplete and uninformative. It would take at least until the next morning for the nation to better understand the Court's decision to stop manual recounts altogether and declare the 2000 presidential election effectively at an end.

The Court's 13-page *per curiam* opinion, on behalf of the Chief Justice and Justices O'Connor, Scalia, Kennedy, and Thomas, was short and to the point: first, it acknowledged that an "individual citizen has no constitutional right to vote for electors for the President of the United States unless and until the state legislature chooses a statewide election as the means to implement its power to appoint members of the electoral college."[78] The Court explained that state legislatures have plenary authority to prescribe the manner by which electors are chosen.

---

[73] 772 So.2d 1273 (Fla. 2000) (per curiam).

[74] *Id.* at 1290.

[75] *Id.*

[76] *Id.*

[77] *Id.* at 1292 (Wells, C.J., dissenting).

[78] *Bush v. Gore,* 531 U.S. 98, 104 (2000) (per curiam).

Second, the Court found that the recount ordered by the Florida Supreme Court violated the Equal Protection Clause. The majority explained that "the recount mechanisms implemented in response to the decisions of the Florida Supreme Court do not satisfy the minimum requirement for nonarbitrary treatment of voters necessary to secure the fundamental right."[79] The problem in *Bush v. Gore* was that the principle of one person-one vote recognized in three seminal opinions of the Warren Court—*Reynolds v. Sims*,[80] *Wesberry v. Sanders*,[81] and *Baker v. Carr*[82]—required that states may not, "by [...] arbitrary and disparate treatment, value one person's vote over that of another" in a manner that "dilute[s] the weight of a citizen's vote."[83] The majority explained that its one person-one vote decisions required that "the search for" the "intent" of the voter must be "confined by specific rules designed to ensure uniform treatment."[84] The Supreme Court found that the Florida Supreme Court's standard was too general and was easily subject to variation in the treatment of ballots. Thus, its standard was amenable to different applications on the same, as well as different, canvassing boards. For instance, the Court noted that the "more forgiving standard" of Broward County in determining which chads counted as votes produced almost three times as many new votes as had been found in Palm Beach County.[85] The Court concluded that the Florida Supreme Court's standard simply failed to satisfy "minimal procedural safeguards" such as clarifying who was responsible for performing the manual recounts or how much of a recount was required to satisfy the Florida Supreme Court's standard.[86]

Third, the majority held that the only remedy available at this juncture was stopping the recounts. It found that "the Supreme Court of Florida has said that the legislature intended" to take advantage of the federal "safe harbor" provision of the Electoral Count Act, and that the latter federal statute "requires that any controversy or contest that is designed to lead to a conclusive selection of electors be completed by December 12. That date is upon us, and there is no recount procedure in

---

[79] *Id.* at 105.

[80] 377 U.S. 533 (1964).

[81] 376 U.S. 1 (1964).

[82] 369 U.S. 186 (1962).

[83] *Bush v. Gore*, 531 U.S. at 105–06 (quoting *Reynolds v. Sims*, 377 U.S. 533, 555 (1964)).

[84] *Id.* at 106.

[85] *Id.* at 107.

[86] *Id.* at 109.

place under the State Supreme Court's order that comports with minimal constitutional standards. Because it is evident that any recount
seeking to meet the December 12 date will be unconstitutional for the
reasons we have discussed, we reverse the judgment of the Supreme
Court of Florida ordering a recount to proceed."[87]

Fourth, the majority declared that its "consideration is limited to
the present circumstances, for the problem of equal protection in election processes generally presents many complexities."[88] The declaration
was unusual in that in no other major constitutional dispute had the
Court ever declared that its decision would have no force as precedent.
The decision applied only to the instant case and no future ones, or at
least so the Court said.

Although it was clearly the end of Gore's appeal, it was not all the
justices had to say. Three of the justices in the majority—Chief Justice
Rehnquist and Justices Scalia and Thomas—issued a separate concurrence written by the Chief Justice. The concurrence expanded on Justice
Scalia's concurrence in the Court's initial order granting the emergency
stay. Chief Justice Rehnquist began by explaining that, because of the
plenary power vested in state legislatures by Article II to determine the
procedures for selecting presidential electors, any "significant departure
from the legislative scheme for appointing Presidential electors presents
a federal constitutional question."[89] He emphasized that in the special
context of a disputed presidential election, the Court should defer "to
those bodies expressly empowered by the legislature to carry out its
constitutional mandate."[90] This required the Court, in this case, to take
"an independent, if still deferential, analysis of state law" in determining whether the Florida Supreme Court "has infringed upon the legislature's authority."[91] Chief Justice Rehnquist likened the Court's exercise
of judicial review in the case to what the Warren Court had done in
reversing state supreme courts that had stubbornly refused to comply
with either the Court's directives on desegregation or the Equal Protection Clause's prohibition of racial discrimination: "What we would do in
the present case is precisely parallel: hold that the Florida Supreme
Court's interpretation of Florida election laws impermissibly distorted
them beyond what a fair reading required, in violation of Article II."[92]
The Chief Justice then found that, in extending the seven-day deadline

---

[87] *Id.* at 110.

[88] *Id.* at 109.

[89] *Id.* at 113 (Rehnquist, C.J., concurring).

[90] *Id.* at 114.

[91] *Id.*

[92] *Id.* at 115.

for certifying the election results, the Florida Supreme Court had diverged from the implicit statutory time period of seven days to wrap up election contests. The Florida Supreme Court's deadline "empties certification of virtually all legal consequence during the contest."[93] Moreover, Chief Justice Rehnquist found no basis in Florida law on which the Florida Supreme Court could justify its mandated recount of undervotes. He concluded that Section 102.168(8) of Florida's election statute, which vested state courts with authority to grant appropriate relief in election contests, had to be read as implicitly incorporating the safe harbor provision of the Electoral Count Act: "Surely when the Florida legislature empowered the courts of the State to grant 'appropriate' relief, it must have meant relief that would have become final by the cutoff date of [the Electoral Count Act]."[94]

A closer look at the other opinions in the case revealed, however, that seven, not five, justices had found that the Florida Supreme Court's recount standard violated the Equal Protection Clause. Two of the four dissenters—Stephen Breyer and David Souter—agreed with the majority that the Florida Supreme Court's vague standard to guide the recount violated the Equal Protection Clause but maintained that it was not up to the Supreme Court to curtail the recount in Florida. Justice Breyer suggested that the Court should have allowed the Florida Supreme Court to decide if it wanted to follow the December 12 date and Florida's other authorities to respond to any such decision as they saw fit.[95] He argued that the dispute presented a non-justiciable political question that the Court should have refrained from deciding.[96] In his dissent, Justice Souter maintained that there was still enough time left for Florida to conclude its recount.[97]

Justice Ginsburg took issue with the concurrence's efforts to analogize the Florida Supreme Court to the southern state supreme courts that had flagrantly refused to follow the Supreme Court's directives on desegregation.[98] She suggested the Court should instead follow its usual practice of deferring to state courts' interpretations of their own laws. Such deference, she explained, "reflects the core of federalism, on which we all agree.... Were the other members of this Court as mindful as they generally are of our system of dual sovereignty, they would affirm

---

[93] Id. at 118.

[94] Id. at 121.

[95] See id. at 144–58 (Breyer, J., dissenting).

[96] Id.

[97] See id. at 129–35 (Souter, J., dissenting).

[98] See id. at 135–144 (Ginsberg, J., dissenting).

the judgment of the Florida Supreme Court."[99] In a move whose implications were missed by no one, Ginsburg curtly concluded her opinion "I dissent" rather than the customary "I respectfully dissent."[100]

Justice Stevens disagreed fully with the majority and the concurring opinions.[101] First, he argued that "neither [the Electoral Count Act] nor Article II grants federal judges any special authority to substitute their views for those of the state judiciary on matters of state law."[102] He read *McPherson* like the Gore lawyers had read it, as acknowledging that state power under Article II includes that which is "forbidden or required of the legislative power under state constitutions as they exist."[103] Second, Justice Stevens noted that the Court had never previously found that a manual recount had violated the Equal Protection Clause. There was, in other words, no precedent for the Court's decision. Moreover, he suggested that Florida's "intent of the voter" standard was no different, or any more difficult to implement, than many other standards upheld by the Court, including the standard requiring juries in criminal cases to convict only if they agreed "beyond a reasonable doubt."[104] Lastly, he defended the integrity of the Florida Supreme Court. He suggested that Bush's "entire federal assault" rested on "an unstated lack of confidence in the impartiality and capacity of the state judges who would make the critical decisions if the vote count were to proceed. Otherwise, their position is wholly without merit. The endorsement of that position by the majority of this Court can only lend credence to the most cynical appraisal of the work of judges throughout the land."[105] He concluded that, "It is confidence in the men and women who administer the judicial system that is the true backbone of the rule of law. Time will one day heal the wound to that confidence that will be inflicted by today's decision."[106] Even so, he suggested that while "we may never know with complete certainty the identity of the winner of this year's Presidential election, the election of the loser is perfectly clear. It is the Nation's confidence in the judge as an impartial guardian of the rule of the law."[107]

---

[99] *Id.* at 142–43.

[100] *Id.* at 144.

[101] *See id.*, at 123–29 (Stevens, J., dissenting).

[102] *Id.* at 124.

[103] *Id.* at 123 (quoting *McPherson v. Blacker*, 146 U.S. 1, 25 (1892)).

[104] *Id.* at 125.

[105] *Id.* at 128 (Stevens, J., dissenting).

[106] *Id.* at 128.

[107] *Id.* at 128–29 (Stevens, J., dissenting).

The Immediate Aftermath of Bush v. Gore

The Campaigns' Reactions and the End of the 2000 Election

The Bush campaign immediately recognized that the Court's decision had settled the election and secured Bush's status as the President-elect. Purposely avoiding any public gloating, the campaign issued a short statement through James Baker that acknowledged that "[t]his has been a long and arduous process for everyone involved on both sides" but that the Bush camp was "very pleased and gratified that seven justices of the United States Supreme Court agreed that there were constitutional problems with the Florida recount ordered by the Florida Supreme Court."

Gore's team took longer to realize the inevitable. Initially, it responded that it was "reviewing the 5–4 decision issued tonight by the Supreme Court of the United States" and that "it will take time to completely analyze [its] complex and lengthy" decision. By the next morning, the campaign's lawyers concluded that Gore had been left with no choice but to concede the election. Gore quickly did so. In a short, televised address to the country 23 hours after the Court had released its decision in *Bush v. Gore*, Gore announced that, "Just moments ago, I spoke with George W. Bush and congratulated him on becoming the forty-third president of the United States, and I promised him that I wouldn't call him back this time." Gore added that he revered the rule of law as "the source of our democratic liberties" and that he had "tried to make it my guide throughout this contest." He then acknowledged that, "Now the U.S. Supreme Court has spoken. Let there be no doubt, while I strongly disagree with the Court's decision, I accept it." He concluded by quoting Stephen Douglas' statement to Abraham Lincoln immediately after the 1860 presidential election: " 'Partisan feeling must yield to patriotism. I'm with you, Mr. President, and God bless you.' " Within minutes, President-elect Bush appeared on television at a rally with several hundred supporters. He acknowledged that he was the President-elect, and urged Democrats and Republicans alike, in Lincoln's words, to " 'rise above a house divided.' "

Gore's concession and the Supreme Court's decision prompted the Florida legislature and Florida Governor Jeb Bush to stop the efforts that that they each had begun in early December to circumvent the Florida Supreme Court's initial recount order. The legislature dropped a plan to appoint its own slate of electors, while Governor Bush followed the procedures of federal law by sending to the National Archives a formal Certificate of the Final Determination of the Contests Concerning the Appointment of Presidential Electors. The Certificate declared that the conflict over Florida's election results had been "finally determined in favor of Governor George W. Bush and that any further pending contests have been effectively nullified by the United States Supreme Court."

The Florida Supreme Court quickly cleared from its dockets any pending matters relating to the election dispute. In response to the Supreme Court's "remand" in *Bush v. Gore*, the Florida Supreme Court unanimously agreed that no further action was necessary, but only five of the seven justices agreed to say that the recount "standard we directed be employed in the manual recount was the standard established by the Legislature in the Florida Election Code" and that if this was not adequate then "we conclude that the development of a specific, uniform standard necessary to ensure equal application and to secure the fundamental right to vote throughout the State of Florida should be left to the body we believe best equipped to study and address it, the Legislature."[108] In a separate concurrence, Justice Shaw added that the "divisive and confounding" nature of the case "lies not in the partisan nature of the issues but rather in the deeply rooted, and conflicting legal principles that are involved."[109] He disagreed with the Supreme Court that December 12 should have been treated as a firm deadline by which Florida had to select its presidential electors, but acknowledged it would have been impossible for the Florida Supreme Court to "have crafted a remedy under these circumstances that would have met the due process, equal protection, and other concerns of the United States Supreme Court."[110]

The Supreme Court, too, quickly cleared its docket of matters relating to the election dispute. Its final decision was to reject three appeals involving different complaints about the election,[111] including one in *Harris v. Florida Elections Canvassing Commission*[112] on the question of whether it violated Article II of the Constitution for Florida officials to accept overseas ballots that arrived in Florida after the statutory deadline of November 17.

On December 18, 2000, the Electoral College convened. The news media covered the event, which required the 538 electors to meet in the 50 state capitals and the District of Columbia. Since the electors were not technically bound to vote for the people who had won the popular

---

[108] *Gore v. Harris*, 773 So.2d 524, 526 (Fla. 2000).

[109] *Id.* at 527 (Shaw, J., concurring).

[110] *Id.* at 529.

[111] *See Jones v. Bush*, 244 F.3d 134 (5th Cir. 2000), *cert. denied*, 531 U.S. 1062 (2001); *Virginia v. Reno*, 117 F.Supp. 2d 46 (D.D.C. 2000), *cert. denied*, 531 U.S. 1062 (2001).

[112] 235 F.3d 578 (11th Cir. 2000), *cert. denied*, 531 U.S. 1062 (2001).

votes in their respective states, it was possible that some of them might have chosen to vote for Gore, who had won the popular vote by slightly over 500,000 votes. But Gore cut any defections short by asking electors to keep faith with their constituents, and by the end of the day 271 electors had voted for Bush and 266 for Gore. It was the closest margin of victory in the Electoral College since the notorious 1876 presidential election, in which Hayes prevailed over Tilden by a single electoral vote.

The final step required by federal law after the official vote of the Electoral College was the convening of a joint session of Congress to count the electoral votes for president. The man who was constitutionally authorized to preside over the session was the President of the Senate, the outgoing Vice–President of the United States, Al Gore. When the electoral votes from Florida were opened, several members of the Congressional Black Caucus claimed their right under federal law to file an objection to Florida's slate of electors. But, without any senators consenting to sign any objections, they were tabled. Gore proceeded to count the votes, and announced at 2:50 P.M. that George W. Bush had officially received a majority of the electoral votes and thus would become the Forty–Third President of the United States. Two weeks later, Chief Justice Rehnquist, one of the five justices in the majority in *Bush v. Gore*, formally administered the presidential oath of office to George W. Bush.

Reaction of the Media and the American People

If there were any doubt that the media leaned slightly left or toward the Democratic viewpoint before the Court decided *Bush v. Gore*, the decision removed it. Whereas the coverage of the campaign had curiously been harder on Gore than Bush, the reaction to *Bush v. Gore* in the media was overwhelmingly negative. Most of the editorials in the major newspapers and most of the commentary on cable and television news programs around the nation lambasted the decision. However, in the weeks following the Court's decision in *Bush v. Gore*, several newspapers and major news organizations conducted their own recounts of the Florida vote, and based on how they each interpreted the "intent of the voter" standard, reached conflicting results as to whether Bush or Gore would have won had the Court not stopped the recount.[113]

In contrast to the media's reaction to *Bush v. Gore*, the public appeared to be divided over *Bush v. Gore*. Some polls conducted immediately after the Court's decision found that a slight majority of Americans indicated they were "relieved" that the election dispute was over and had confidence in the Court as a non-partisan institution.[114] A Gallup

---

[113] For descriptions of these studies, see Gillman, *supra* note 2, at 166–68.

[114] *See, e.g.*, Janet Elder, *Poll Shows Americans Divided over Election, Indicating that Bush Must Build Public Support*, N.Y. Times, Dec. 18, 2000, at A22; (reporting on CBS

poll released in January 2001 indicated that the Court's approval rating appeared to be roughly the same as it had been in August 2000.[115]

A closer look at the polling reveals approval of the Court among Republicans actually had jumped from 60 percent before to 80 percent after the decision while Democrats' approval of the Court dropped from 70 percent before to 42 percent after the decision. The same polling showed that support from Independents fell from 57 percent approval of the Court before the decision to 54 percent after the decision. On the surface, the polling appeared to reflect no change of opinion about the Court, but it actually reflected sharp splits among voters depending on their partisan preferences.

Criticisms of Bush v. Gore

Bush v. Gore produced a tidal wave of academic commentaries. For the most part, they tracked academicians' political preferences, with most liberals deriding *Bush v. Gore* and most conservatives defending it. Three of the most popular criticisms—and the responses thereto—still resonate in the academic debate over *Bush v. Gore*.

The first, and perhaps most popular, criticism of *Bush v. Gore* is that the Court's five most conservative justices were being transparently partisan and simply voted their political preferences. This was the view of over five hundred law professors who allowed their names to appear in a full-page ad in the New York Times on January 13, 2001, lamenting that the "U.S. Supreme Court used its power to act as political partisans, not judges of a court of law."[116] Support for the belief that the justices were merely being partisan could be found in a widely circulating rumor that on the evening of Election Day Justice O'Connor had been overheard lamenting the possibility that Gore might have won the election.[117] Further support for the belief that the justices in *Bush v. Gore* merely voted their partisan preferences was the fact that the Rehnquist Court otherwise tended to defer to state courts when interpreting their own state laws, coupled with the suspicion that the Rehnquist Court would never have ruled for Gore had the parties' positions been reversed in the case. Moreover, skepticism about the Court's motives in *Bush v. Gore* derived in part from the fact that the Rehnquist

---

poll); Richard Benedetto, *It's Time to Move On, People Say Americans Relieved Fight Is Finally Over*, USA Today, Dec. 18, 2000, at A8.

[115] *See* Wendy Simmons, "Election Controversy Apparently Drove Partisan Wedge into Attitudes towards Supreme Court," Gallup.com, Jan. 16, 2001.

[116] *554 Law Professors Say*, Advertisement, N.Y. Times, Jan. 13, 2001, at A7.

[117] *See, e.g.*, Gillman, *supra* note 2, at 188.

Court had up until then almost invariably held that neutral classifications—those not expressly based on gender or race—do not violate Equal Protection. As Ronald Dworkin complained, "the conservatives' decision to reverse a state supreme court's rulings on matters of state law did not reflect any established conservative position on any general constitutional question. [. . .] [Hence, it is] difficult to find a respectable explanation of why all and only the conservatives voted to end the election in this way ... [raising the concern that] the decision reflected not ideological division, which is inevitable, but professional self-interest."[118] Dworkin was hardly alone: other liberal constitutional commentators criticized the decision in the harshest terms.[119]

Bush v. Gore was not the only decision singled out for being based solely on partisan preferences. Even apart from *Bush v. Gore*, there were the two decisions of the Florida Supreme Court finding Harris had abused her discretion and ordering manual recounts; in the federal district court, Judge Lewis, a Democratic appointee, had initially upheld Gore's request for a recount; and the four dissenters in the Eleventh Circuit's second *en banc* decision to allow the recount were all Republicans and thus arguably disposed to help Bush.

The principal rejoinder to this criticism of *Bush v. Gore* and the other judicial decisions as transparently partisan is that the facts do not support it. In *Bush v. Gore*, seven, not five, of the justices upheld Bush's Equal Protection claim. Justices Souter and Breyer agreed with their five conservative colleagues that Bush had a credible Equal Protection claim, though this seems to conflict with the direction in which many people have supposed that their personal preferences might have led them. In *Palm Beach County Canvassing Bd. v. Harris*, the Supreme Court ruled unanimously; all nine justices—not just the conservative majority—agreed to require the Florida Supreme Court to clarify what it was doing. Moreover, the Florida Supreme Court had rendered five decisions pertaining to the 2000 presidential election, three of which had

---

[118] Ronald Dworkin, *A Badly Flawed Election*, N.Y. Rev. of Books, Jan. 11, 2001, at 53.

[119] See, e.g., David Abel, Bush v. Gore *Case Compels Scholars to Alter Courses at U.S. Law Schools*, Boston Globe, Feb. 3, 2001, at A1 (quoting Margaret Radin as criticizing the decision as a "naked power grab"); Bruce A. Ackerman, *The Court Packs Itself*, The American Prospect, at 48, Feb. 12, 2001 (stating the opinion "betrayed the nation's trust"); Linda Greenhouse, *Another Kind of Bitter Split*, N.Y. Times, at A1, Dec. 13, 2000 (quoting Suzanna Sherry's criticism that "there is very little way to reconcile this opinion other than that they wanted Bush to win"); Neal Kumar Katyal, Op–Ed., *Politics Over Principle*, Wash. Post., Dec. 14, 2000, at A35 (criticizing the decision as "lawless and unprecedented"); Jeffrey Rosen, *Disgrace*, The New Republic, Dec. 25, 2000, at 18 (declaring that the Court's "shabby piece of work ... made it impossible for citizens of the United States to sustain any kind of faith in the rule of law as something larger than the self-interested political preferences" of the conservative justices).

unanimously favored Bush.[120] Only two of the court's decisions actually
favored Gore, and in the second, three Democratic appointees had
vigorously dissented.[121] While it is true that three Republican appointees
on the Eleventh Circuit had dissented in that court's second *en banc*
decision, the majority dismissing Bush's claim in that case had included
five Republican appointees.[122] In addition, the Eleventh Circuit's first *en
banc* ruling on an issue relating to the disputed election was not only
unanimous but also favored Gore, in spite of the fact that most judges on
that court were Republicans.[123] This fact, along with the voting alignments in the other cases, does not support the contention that the judges
throughout the litigation merely voted their personal political preferences.

The second criticism of *Bush v. Gore* is that the decision was poorly
reasoned. Michael McConnell, the widely respected conservative constitutional law scholar (and now a federal appeals court judge), surprisingly
spoke for many liberal critics of the decision, when he derided it as "a
failed attempt at compromise" and for giving Bush "a victory on the
weakest possible ground" because "there is nothing in the Florida court
opinion or the state statutes that expresses a preference for the [safe
harbor deadline of December 12] over completion of a [re]count under
state law."[124] McConnell criticized the five conservative justices for
"their lack of political judgment," particularly their unwillingness to
follow Justices Souter and Breyer in supporting a remand of the case
back to the Florida Supreme Court. McConnell defended following the
latter path on the ground that it had the best chance of any decision by
the Court to "have achieved near-unanimity" and "would [have been]
vastly reassuring to the American people . . . Instead, the Supreme Court
held that there should be a recount, but there [was] not time enough to
do it. That left Bush as president not so much by the will of the
electorate, but by default."[125]

The response to McConnell's complaint is that the justices should
not have been exercising, much less be evaluated for their exercise of,

---

[120] *See Jacobs v. Seminole County Canvassing Bd.*, 773 So.2d 519 (Fla. 2000); *Taylor v.
Martin County Canvassing Bd.*, 773 So.2d 517 (Fla. 2000); *Fladell v. Palm Beach County
Canvassing Bd.*, 772 So.2d 1240 (Fla. 2000).

[121] *See Palm Beach County Canvassing Bd. v. Harris, supra* notes 27–35 and accompanying text; *Gore v. Harris, supra* notes 60–67 and accompanying text.

[122] *See Siegel v. Lepore, supra* notes 55–58 and accompanying text.

[123] *See Touchston v. McDermott, supra* notes 19–20 and accompanying text.

[124] Michael McConnell, *What Now?*, Slate.com, Dec. 13, 2000, http://www.slate.com/id/
93655/entry/95085/.

[125] *Id.*

political judgment. McConnell's complaint seems to be that the Court should have been more activist than it was—that it should have decided the case on whatever basis would have been "vastly reassuring to the American people." Yet, such a decision would not have been grounded on what the law required the Court to do.

One could go further to argue that the Court completely misconstrued the Electoral Count Act. As the dissent (and many other critics) maintained, the Electoral Count Act did not require States to take advantage of its safe harbor provision nor impose a penalty on them for choosing not to do so. Indeed, as Justice Stevens pointed out, "[i]n 1960, Hawaii appointed two slates of electors and Congress chose to count the one appointed on January 4, 1961."[126] There were also several states in the 2000 presidential election that did not experience any adverse consequences as a result of their not reporting their slates of electors to the federal government until after December 12, 2000.[127] Moreover, neither the concurrence in *Bush v. Gore* nor the Bush campaign explained the criteria for determining the point at which a state court's interpretation of its own state's laws lapsed into actual legislating. In addition, it was hardly unreasonable to construe Florida statutes as the Florida Supreme Court had done. While the Florida election statute provided that the Secretary of State "may ignore" late-filed returns and thus plainly had the discretion to reject such returns,[128] other parts of the same statute allowed counties to authorize recounts even if those recounts exceeded the seven days after the election by which the Secretary of State was authorized to certify the election results.[129] As for Bush's equal protection claim, it was apparently so novel, unusual, and weak that Bush's own lawyers had seriously considered not including it in their appellate briefs.[130]

An obvious response to this criticism is that the fact that Gore's lawyers might have had reasonable legal arguments to make does not mean that the Bush lawyers' arguments were unreasonable. Indeed, it was hardly an abuse of discretion for Secretary of State Harris to construe the Florida election statute's directive that she "may ignore"

---

[126] *Bush v. Gore*, 531 U.S. at 127 (Stevens, J., dissenting).

[127] Certificates of Ascertainment for each state can be found at http://www.archives. gov/federal-register/electoral-college/2000/certificates_of_ascertainment.html. California, Iowa, Maryland, and Pennsylvania all missed the December 12 "deadline." In addition, the Oregon certificate is undated and the date on the Vermont certificate is, at least on the version visible over the internet, illegible. All of these states voted for Gore.

[128] See Fla. Stat. § 102.112(3) (2000).

[129] See Fla. Stat. § 102.166(4) (2000).

[130] *See* Gillman, *supra* note 2, at 35–36.

late-filed returns as authorizing her to ignore such returns if she had any reasonable basis for doing so.

The third criticism of *Bush v. Gore* is the point made by Justice Breyer in his dissent that the Court should have dismissed the case as presenting a non-justiciable political question. Justice Breyer had argued that the Electoral Count Act of 1887 set forth a "detailed, comprehensive scheme" by which Congress could work through such disputes.[131] On his view, Congress, in enacting this legislation, had been "fully aware of the danger that would arise should it ask judges, unarmed with appropriate legal standards, to resolve a hotly contested Presidential election contest."[132] Moreover, the dispute in *Bush v. Gore* arguably fit several of the criteria for a non-justiciable political question. For instance, it could be argued that the Constitution in Article II had clearly committed the final decision-making responsibility on appointing presidential electors to state and federal political authorities. Breyer figured that, even if it were not pretty, his solution placed the final responsibility in resolving the election in authorities who could be held politically accountable for their actions.

There are, however, two problems with Breyer's argument. First, the institution that was most empowered as a result of *Bush v. Gore*, other than the Court itself, was Florida's Secretary of State, a politically accountable official. Second, Breyer was the only Supreme Court justice who insisted that the dispute over the 2000 presidential election was a non-justiciable political question. While the other justices did not all agree on whether the Court should have granted certiorari to decide *Bush v. Gore*, they appeared to agree, at least implicitly, that the Court was entitled to exercise judicial review over the merits of the dispute.

Defenses of Bush v. Gore

In the weeks and months following *Bush v. Gore*, the case was defended on at least three other grounds besides the responses above to criticisms of *Bush v. Gore*. First, the Supreme Court's precedents support its exercise of judicial review in both *Palm Beach County Canvassing Bd. v. Harris* and *Bush v. Gore*. As the Chief Justice suggested in his concurrence in *Bush v. Gore*, the decision was arguably analogous to what the Court had done in overturning state courts that had been resistant to desegregation.[133] Moreover, as the Court suggested, its exercise of judicial review in the case followed from its precedents that

---

[131] *Bush v. Gore*, 531 U.S. at 155 (Breyer, J., dissenting).

[132] *Id.* at 156.

[133] *See supra* note 92 and accompanying text.

refused to find political questions in voting rights and election law cases, such as *Baker*, *Reynolds*, and *Wesberry*.[134]

A response to this defense is that it is based on a misreading of the Court's precedents. The Court's voting rights precedents arguably could be read as upholding judicial review to check majoritarian enactments clearly directed at disadvantaging a racial minority. Judicial review was thus necessitated in those cases to combat the primary, if not sole, evil that the Equal Protection Clause was written into the Constitution to guard against—express or longstanding racial discrimination. But in *Bush v. Gore*, the governmental action at issue was not express racial discrimination. Neither the Florida election statute nor the Florida Supreme Court's standard for governing determinations of the "intent of the voter"[135] in recounts was racially discriminatory on its face. Both the statute and the Florida Supreme Court set forth arguably neutral, non-expressly racially discriminatory standards. Hence, consistency with the Supreme Court's precedents might have required subjecting the Florida Supreme Court's recount standard to the rational basis test rather than heightened scrutiny.

The counter-argument to this reading of the Supreme Court's voting rights decisions is that it is not inexorable nor the only plausible construction of them. Bush's lawyers argued that the "one person-one vote" principle is not restricted only to cases involving express discrimination against a racial minority, but rather should be generally applied in all elections. Consequently, the standard set forth by the Florida court to guide the recounts was so vague and easily manipulated that it was bound, in the Court's judgment, to allow different practices in different counties for determining the "intent of the voter" and thus to the dilution of the one person-one-vote principle.

The second major defense of *Bush v. Gore* is that it was needed to avert a constitutional crisis. Perhaps the most sophisticated versions of this defense are made by two prominent scholars who do not always agree with each other, Cass Sunstein and Judge Richard Posner. Sunstein praised the Court for not only refraining from deciding or saying more than it had to in *Bush v. Gore*, but also for imposing "order without law"—imposing order on an otherwise unruly controversy even though the Court had no basis in law for doing so.[136] While Sunstein criticized the Court for not having a basis in state or federal law for the deadline imposed on the recount, he applauded the Court for performing a "service" to the nation by doing two things: it resolved the protracted

---

[134] *See supra* notes 80–82 and accompanying text.

[135] *See* Fla. Stat. § 102.166(7)(b).

[136] *See* Cass R. Sunstein, *Order Without Law*, 68 U. Chi. L. Rev. 757 (2001).

litigation and electoral dispute between Bush and Gore "in a way that carried more simplicity and authority than anything that might have been expected from the United States Congress," and it probably "avoided [the] constitutional crisis" that would have ensued had the Court not intervened.[137] Based on the Constitution and federal statutory law, Sunstein speculated that the recount, once it was done, would have been challenged in Congress, in which the House, with its Republican majority, would have approved Bush's slate of electors from Florida and the Senate would have split 50–50 with Al Gore casting the tie vote in favor of himself. Federal law further provides that if the two Houses of Congress were to disagree on which slate of electors to count then Congress had to accept the slate that was certified by the State's chief executive, who, in this case, was none other than Jeb Bush, George W. Bush's brother.[138] A crisis would then arise because courts might attempt to order Bush to certify an election result with which he disagreed and "the law provides no clear answers" on what should be done under that circumstance.[139]

While Posner foresaw a different crisis than Sunstein did, it still justified the Court's intervention. Posner suggested that the process would likely have degenerated into "a rancorous struggle in Congress when a Gore slate [might be] challenged," followed by further litigation in the Supreme Court and the need to have either the Republican Speaker of the House, Dennis Hastert, or the Republican President Pro Tem of the Senate, Strom Thurmond, become "acting president" until a winner could be determined.[140] Posner could not, however, see the case for "precipitating [such] a political and constitutional crisis merely in order to fuss with a statistical tie [in the Florida popular vote for president] that—given the inherent subjectivity involved in hand counting spoiled ballots—can never be untied."[141] Hence, Posner believed that because "there was a real and disturbing potential for disorder and temporary paralysis" that the Court had to intervene and that its intervention "was greeted with relief" by most of the nation.[142] Posner suggested that the Court opted to do the right thing when it rejected a congressional resolution of the dispute as a viable option, since "it would have poisoned [the winner's] tenure" in office, and instead "took the

---

[137] *Id.* at 758.

[138] *Id.* at 769.

[139] *Id.*

[140] Richard A. Posner, *Breaking the Deadlock* 137–38 (Princeton University Press 2001).

[141] *Id.* at 147.

[142] *Id.* at 143–44.

pragmatic route, cut the Gordian knot, and let Bush get on with the transition and with governing.''[143]

Posner's and Sunstein's defenses of *Bush v. Gore* are, however, arguably based on two flawed premises. First, they presume that the state or federal political process would have broken down and failed to settle the dispute between Bush and Gore. A common complaint is that the vice of judicial activism—unprincipled determinations to strike down democratic action—is that it deprives the American people of the opportunity to have their say on a divisive political subject and thus weakens the electoral process. The same could, however, be said of *Bush v. Gore*—namely, that it demonstrated a profound lack of confidence in the political process to settle the matter and in the American people to hold the responsible political officials accountable for their decisions, good or bad. Like so many of the judicial decisions that conservative scholars condemn—such as *Roe v. Wade*[144]—*Bush v. Gore* could be criticized for providing people with the incentives to go to the courts, rather than the political process, to solve their political disputes. Second, *Bush v. Gore* is arguably based on a belief in judicial supremacy, a belief that the Court is better situated or more competent than Congress, or other political authorities, to settle a sensitive constitutional dispute. Yet, the nation did not collapse even though widely criticized political means had been used to settle the hotly contested presidential elections of 1824 and 1876. Andrew Jackson, who had lost the presidency as a result of the deals made in the House of Representatives to award the election to John Quincy Adams, took his case to the American people, who elected and re-elected him to the presidency by increasingly larger margins in 1828 and 1832. Samuel Tilden, who lost the 1876 presidential election by a straight party-line vote of a special commission established by the House to settle the election, complained about the results for the rest of his life but to no avail. By resolving the 2000 presidential election through judicial rather than political means, the Court arguably demonstrated more trust in itself than Congress or the States.

A final defense of *Bush v. Gore* is that the Florida Supreme Court gave the Supreme Court no other option. While the Court's five most conservative justices were responsible for ending the recount, they could not ignore the insult of the Florida Supreme Court's failure to respond, in a timely fashion, to the remand in *Palm Beach County Canvassing Bd. v. Harris*. There was nothing so pressing on the Florida Supreme Court's docket that it lacked the time or opportunity to answer the Supreme Court's inquiry into the grounds on which it had based its decision ordering the recount. Had it done so, it is possible the justices

---

[143] *Id.* at 141, 150.

[144] 410 U.S. 113 (1973).

might not have felt, as they did in *Bush v. Gore*, the need to slap the Florida Supreme Court down for the disrespect it had shown to the Supreme Court.

Of course, this defense is purely speculative, and it is just as possible, if not more likely, that the Court had set a trap for the Florida Supreme Court that it could not have escaped.[145] One could plausibly argue that, even if the justices of the Florida Supreme Court had responded in a timely (and appropriate) fashion to the remand, the Court would have struck down their decision for violating either the Equal Protection Clause or the mandate of Article II that gives state legislatures the authority to formulate the processes for determining the selection of presidential electors. In short, the state court would have been reversed no matter what it did.

The Continuing and Long–Term Ramifications of Bush v. Gore

The People: Where Are They Now?

It is no secret what became of the two protagonists in *Bush v. Gore*. Within Bush's first year in office, *Bush v. Gore* was eclipsed by the terribly tragic attacks against the United States on September 11, 2001. These attacks—and Bush's response to them, particularly his decision to take the country to war in Iraq—defined the remainder of his presidency. In 2004, he was re-elected President, winning a majority of the popular vote and achieving a slightly larger margin of victory in the Electoral College than he had the first time. However, the continuation of the Iraq war and his Administration's inept response to Hurricane Katrina began to take their toll on Bush's popularity, which plummeted further as a result of the worst downturn in the national economy since the Great Depression. By Election Day, 2008, Bush's popularity was the lowest of any modern president, and helped to pave the way for the historic election of Bush's Democratic successor, Barack Obama. Nevertheless, a lasting legacy of Bush's presidency was the appointment of two new Supreme Court Justices—John Roberts to replace William Rehnquist as Chief Justice and Samuel Alito, Jr., to replace Sandra Day O'Connor. Both at the time he made the appointments and since, Bush emphasized that he had modeled them on Justices Scalia and Thomas, who both had been in the majority in *Bush v. Gore*. Roberts had also advised Bush's legal team on Bush's appeals to the Supreme Court, and was one of the first dozen people whom Bush appointed to the circuit courts of appeal.[146]

---

[145] *See, e.g.*, Michael C. Dorf, Op-ed, *Supreme Court Pulled a Bait and Switch*, L.A. Times, Dec. 14, 2000, at B11.

[146] This group also included Michael McConnell, whom President Bush appointed to the U.S. Court of Appeals for the Tenth Circuit. Although Olson was not in this group, he

After Bush's inauguration, Al Gore largely devoted himself to publicizing the dangers of global warming. In 2007, Gore won an Oscar for the best documentary of the year for the film *An Inconvenient Truth*, which he helped produce on the subject. Later that same year, he won the Nobel Peace Prize for his efforts to mobilize citizens around the world to address the dangers of global warming.[147]

The Electoral College and Election Reform

Bush v. Gore drew the nation's attention to the problems with both the Electoral College and voting technology. Shortly after the decision, there was some renewed interest in rethinking the utility of the Electoral College and doing away with it in favor of a nation-wide popular vote for the presidency. But that interest quickly died, particularly after it became clear that there was no widespread support for amending the Constitution and that a national popular vote would provide incentives for national candidates to spend most of their campaigns in large States and to ignore the smaller States in their quest for the presidency. Meanwhile, Congress authorized a National Commission on National Elections, which former Presidents Jimmy Carter and Gerald Ford co-chaired, to make recommendations on electoral reform in the United States.[148] Although the commission made many recommendations, including using optical scanners instead of paper ballots, almost none of the recommendations were implemented.

Waiting for the Next Bush v. Gore

In each of the major elections after *Bush v. Gore*, the major candidates prepared well before Election Day to handle crises—and legal challenges—arising from election laws and the different mechanisms for casting and counting votes around the country. Nevertheless, in 2004, many Democrats in Ohio were convinced that the election was stolen from the Democratic nominee for president, John Kerry. They complained that Republican state authorities had tried to disqualify more Democrats than Republicans in the run up to, and on, Election Day.

---

served as Bush's first Solicitor General and was reported to be among those being considered for a Supreme Court appointment in 2005. Olson's wife, Barbara, was killed along with everyone else on the plane that terrorists had hijacked and flown into the Pentagon on September 11, 2001. In the immediate aftermath of *Bush v. Gore*, Katherine Harris was elected to the House of Representatives, where she served without distinction for a single term followed by an unsuccessful bid for the U.S. Senate.

[147] Of those on Gore's side, Laurence Tribe remained at Harvard Law School; David Boies returned to private practice at his firm, Boies, Schiller & Flexner in New York City; Peter Rubin became a judge on the intermediate court of appeals in Massachusetts; and Ron Klain returned to private practice but left for a short period to lead an investment firm. On November 12, 2008, Vice–President–Elect Biden appointed Klain to be his Chief of Staff.

[148] *See* Gillman, *supra* note 2, at 168.

They also complained that the voting machines employed for the presidential election that year (which had been designed by a company overseen by a major contributor to Republican campaigns) were defective, and had broken down—and lost many votes—in the State, particularly in Democratic precincts. In 2008, the two major candidates—Barack Obama and John McCain—assembled teams of lawyers in every battleground state to handle legal problems with voter identification and voting arising before and on Election Day.

The Supreme Court

The Supreme Court has not fully escaped from the shadow of *Bush v. Gore*. In answering a question about *Bush v. Gore* after a speech at Princeton University in 2007, Justice Scalia declared, "Get over it, it's eight years ago. I think the vast majority of citizens in the country were glad [that the Supreme Court stopped the ballot recount]."[149] A year later, Justice Ginsburg answered, in response to a question about Justice Scalia's comment, that she continued to maintain a close friendship with Justice Scalia but that *Bush v. Gore* "has never been cited by the Court, and I think it never will be cited."[150] (It is worth noting, however, that the case has been cited in scores of decisions by the lower federal courts.)

Conclusion

Bush v. Gore remains exhibit A in many academics' complaint that the Supreme Court votes its prejudices or manipulates legal materials to maximize the justices' personal preferences. Academics continue to analyze and debate the case, but their own credibility seems to have suffered because of the perception that their reactions to the decision closely tracked their personal political preferences. This was the opinion of Judge Richard Posner, who suggested shortly after *Bush v. Gore* that, if one were to examine "the public comments made by professors of constitutional law during the postelection litigation, it becomes apparent that the academic practice of constitutional law is as political as the judicial practice. Liberal professors who spend their time trying to find a satisfactory rationale for decisions that they like, such as *Roe v. Wade*, made no effort to salvage *Bush v. Gore*, while conservative professors found themselves unaccustomedly supportive of a decision that whatever its merits, which obviously I think not inconsiderable, cannot avoid the label 'activist'."[151]

---

[149] Samantha Pergadia, *Ginsburg: Mutual Respect Unites Nine*, Daily Princetonian, Oct. 24, 2008, at 1.

[150] *Id.*

[151] Gillman, *supra* note 2, at 163 (internal citation omitted).

While *Bush v. Gore* remains an obsession within the legal academy, it is unclear to what extent it continues to shape the public's opinions of the Court. Indeed, shortly after the Supreme Court ruled in *Boumediene v. Bush*[152] that Congress could not indefinitely suspend the writ of habeas corpus for "enemy combatants" detained in the war against terrorism, a poll showed that "60% of voters believe Supreme Court Justices have their own political agendas, while just 23% believe they remain impartial .... [These] sentiments are similar across party lines and among voters of varying ideological beliefs."[153] "When the public is asked, how much confidence do you have in various American institutions, the top one is the military ... The Supreme Court is at 32%; the Presidency is at 26%; Congress is at 12%."[154]

It is hard to say to what extent these figures were shaped by *Boumediene* alone rather than other events, including *Bush v. Gore*. It is harder to imagine that another case will ever capture the nation's attention as much as *Bush v. Gore* did or will come close to approximating its political ramifications or be as closely associated with—if not responsible for—the tenure of a president of the United States. Even if *Bush v. Gore* is never cited by the Supreme Court, it will remain, at the very least, a profound novelty in constitutional law.

---

[152] 128 S.Ct. 2229 (2008).

[153] *60% Believe Supreme Court Justices Have Their Own Political Agendas*, Rasmussen Reports, June 16, 2008, available at http://www.rasmussenreports.com/public_content/politics/mood_of_america/60_believe_supreme_court_justices_have_their_own_political_agendas.

[154] Ronald A. Rotunda, *2008 Supplement to Modern Constitutional Law: Cases and Notes* 40 (8th ed. 2008) (citation omitted in original).

*

5

Christopher L. Eisgruber

The Story of *Dred Scott*: Originalism's Forgotten Past

When the Supreme Court issued its decision in *Dred Scott v. Sandford*,[1] some of the Justices hoped that they had resolved the conflict over slavery and averted a civil war.[2] Instead, they produced what is almost certainly the worst judicial ruling in American constitutional history. Chief Justice Taney's opinion declared, among other things, that African–American descendants of slaves were neither "citizens" nor "persons" under the Constitution; that Congress had no power to prohibit slavery in the territories; and that although the Declaration of Independence had announced that "all men are created equal," it applied only to white men, not "all men." Any one of these conclusions would have sullied the Court's reputation; together, they were a disaster.

After the Civil War, two major constitutional amendments obliterated *Scott*'s basic doctrinal holdings. The Thirteenth Amendment abolished slavery, thereby mooting everything that *Scott* had to say about that topic. The first sentence of the Fourteenth Amendment emphatically reversed *Scott*'s holding with regard to American citizenship. The Amendment provided that every person born or naturalized in the United States was a citizen of the United States, regardless of race or ancestry. One might accordingly assume that *Scott* is of purely historical interest, with few implications for modern jurisprudence.

Yet *Scott* lives on in American law as what Mary Anne Case has called an "anti-precedent," a powerful example of what courts ought not to do.[3] As a result, *Scott* figures prominently in ongoing debates about

---

[1] 60 U.S. (19 How.) 393 (1857).

[2] Don E. Fehrenbacher, *The* Dred Scott *Case: Its Significance in American Law and Politics* 208 (1978).

[3] Mary Anne Case, *"The Very Stereotype the Law Condemns": Constitutional Sex Discrimination Law as a Quest for Perfect Proxies*, 85 Cornell L. Rev. 1447, 1469 n.112 (2000).

the Supreme Court's abortion jurisprudence. Conservative scholars and judges have alleged that decisions such as *Roe v. Wade*[4] and *Planned Parenthood v. Casey*,[5] in which the Court held that the Constitution protects a woman's right to choose whether to terminate a pregnancy, repeated the errors of *Scott*. To these critics, *Roe* and *Casey* were *Dred Scott* all over again, or, put more briefly, "*Dred* Again." Robert Bork's statement of the "*Dred* Again" theory is paradigmatic of the position:

> "[*Scott*] was at least very possibly the first application of substantive due process in the Supreme Court, the original precedent for *Lochner v. New York* and *Roe v. Wade*." . . . *Lochner* and *Roe* have, therefore, a very ugly common ancestor. But once it is conceded that a judge may give the due process clause substantive content, *Dred Scott*, *Lochner*, and *Roe* are equally valid examples of constitutional law. . . . Who says *Roe* must say *Lochner* and *Scott*.[6]

Although most proponents of the "*Dred* Again" theory phrase their claims more modestly than he does, Bork is only one among many scholars and jurists to draw such connections between *Roe* and *Scott*. The first sentence in the quoted passage comes from Professor David Currie.[7] Professor (now Judge) Michael McConnell has made a "*Dred* Again" argument roughly parallel to Bork's.[8] In *Casey* itself, Justice Antonin Scalia claimed in dissent that the majority had repeated *Scott*'s sins and that their reputations would suffer the same ignominious fate as Taney's.[9]

Despite the popularity of the "*Dred* Again" theory, it rests upon a mistaken picture of *Scott v. Sandford*. That picture assumes that the majorities in *Scott*, *Roe*, and *Casey* were united by a "fundamental values/substantive due process" jurisprudence friendly to the recognition of unenumerated rights. It further assumes that the dissenters in all those cases shared an originalist jurisprudence that sought only to follow instructions from the framers. This account of *Scott v. Sandford* contains blunders which should be obvious to anybody who has read the opinion carefully. Few lawyers, however, have even read *Scott*, much less with care. Perhaps that is an excusable omission. The case covers about

---

[4] 410 U.S. 113 (1973).

[5] 505 U.S. 833 (1992).

[6] Robert H. Bork, *The Tempting of America: The Political Seduction of the Law* 32 (1990).

[7] David P. Currie, *The Constitution in the Supreme Court: The First Hundred Years, 1789–1888*, at 271 (1985).

[8] *See* Michael W. McConnell, *A Moral Realist Defense of Constitutional Democracy*, 64 Chi.-Kent L. Rev. 89, 101 (1988).

[9] *Casey*, 505 U.S. at 1001–02 (Scalia, J., dissenting).

250 pages of the United States Reports, and much of it is balderdash—Justice Daniel's concurring opinion, for example, used a pompous discussion of Roman slavery to analyze the relationship between emancipation and slavery in the United States.[10] The case is a snarl of jurisdictional, choice of law, and substantive issues. *Scott v. Sandford* is not only the most unjust decision the Supreme Court has ever rendered; it is also among the longest, the murkiest, and the most obsolete.

This Chapter accordingly explores *Scott*'s textual mysteries and historical context in an effort to correct *"Dred* Again's" persistent distortion of the case. The restored picture does not threaten the reputations of the *Casey* or *Roe* majorities, but instead carries a warning for their critics. What distinguished Taney's jurisprudence from that of the *Scott* dissenters was not its recourse to fundamental values (for Taney made none), nor its rejection of originalism (for Taney embraced it). What separated Taney's jurisprudence from the dissenters' was its explicit and stark indifference to justice.

How the Case Got to the Supreme Court

Dr. John Emerson, an army surgeon, held Dred Scott as a slave in the state of Missouri. Between 1834 and 1838, Emerson traveled to postings at Fort Armstrong, in Illinois, and Fort Snelling, in what is now the state of Minnesota.[11] He took Scott with him to these places. Slavery was unlawful at both Fort Armstrong and Fort Snelling. Illinois was a free state where slavery was prohibited. Minnesota was not yet a state at all; it was instead part of a federal territory governed by the United States Congress. These journeys may have had the legal effect of emancipating Scott. Under a widely accepted nineteenth-century common law doctrine, owners who transported slaves into free territories thereby emancipated them, regardless of whether they had intended to set them free.[12] All that mattered was whether the owner had intended to bring the slave into a free jurisdiction (if the slave went there without the owner's permission, the consequences were quite different: the slave was then a fugitive subject to recapture under the Fugitive Slave Clause of the Constitution and congressional legislation).

---

[10] 60 U.S. at 477–80 (Daniel, J., concurring).

[11] *See* Fehrenbacher, *supra* note 2, at 243–44. This section's summary of the historical background relies heavily on Fehrenbacher's masterful, Pulitzer Prize-winning account of *Scott* and its context. There is also an excellent abridgement, Don E. Fehrenbacher, *Slavery, Law, and Politics: The* Dred Scott *Case in Historical Perspective* (1981). A useful supplementary study, focusing on Harriet Robinson Scott's role in the litigation, is Lea VanderVelde and Sandhya Subramanian, *Mrs. Dred Scott*, 106 Yale L.J. 1033 (1997).

[12] *See* Fehrenbacher, *supra* note 2, at 50–61; *see also* Robert M. Cover, *Justice Accused: Antislavery and the Judicial Process* 83–89 (1975).

There is evidence that Scott exercised the rights of a free man while he was in Minnesota. For example, Scott married Harriet Robinson in a civil ceremony conducted by a government officer. Slaves did not have the right to marry, so this event suggests that Scott regarded himself as free (it also suggests that the government officer, and perhaps Emerson, viewed Scott as free).[13] Later, however, Scott returned with Emerson to Missouri. Why Scott did this is unclear: if indeed he understood himself to have been emancipated, it would have been foolish to return to Missouri. Perhaps Emerson forced him to go, or perhaps Scott did not then know that his trip to Illinois and Minnesota might have made him free.

Emerson claimed the Scotts as his slaves until his death in 1843. Emerson's wife, Eliza Sanford Emerson, then assumed control of Dred Scott, Harriet Robinson Scott, and their two daughters.[14] On April 6, 1846, the Scotts sued Eliza Emerson for their freedom. Their suits alleged state law counts of battery and false imprisonment. That was the typical form taken by freedom suits in Missouri: the physical power that owners wielded against slaves constituted batteries if directed against free persons. Emerson defended on the ground that the Scotts were her slaves, so that she had authority to confine and batter them.[15]

The litigation took ten years to reach the Supreme Court. The Scotts first filed their suits in the Missouri state courts. A young judge named Alexander Hamilton (no relation!) presided.[16] In 1850, after a trial, an appeal, and a second trial, Judge Hamilton ruled in favor of the Scotts. Eliza Emerson appealed to the Missouri Supreme Court. In a two-to-one decision authored by Judge William Scott (no relation!), the court ruled for Emerson. The Missouri Supreme Court had previously endorsed the general doctrine that slaves were emancipated if transported into a free jurisdiction, and that doctrine formed the basis of the Scotts' suits and Judge Hamilton's ruling. Now, however, the Missouri Supreme Court reversed course. It held that Emerson and other owners retained their rights to slaves even after bringing them into free territory.[17]

---

[13] Justice Benjamin Curtis made a related point in his dissenting opinion, where he suggested that if Missouri treated the Scotts as slaves, it would unconstitutionally impair the obligations of their marriage contract. *Scott*, 60 U.S. at 598–601 (Curtis, J., dissenting); *see* Fehrenbacher, *supra* note 2, at 412–13.

[14] *See* Fehrenbacher, *supra* note 2, at 248–49.

[15] *See id.* at 250–53.

[16] *See id.* at 253.

[17] *See id.* at 253–65.

The Missouri Supreme Court ruled on March 22, 1852. Its decision rested principally on Missouri state law, not federal law: it addressed the impact of Emerson's journey upon property rights (in a slave) recognized by Missouri law. As a result, the Scotts did not appeal to the United States Supreme Court.[18] Instead, nineteen months later, Dred Scott filed a new case, again alleging state law battery and false imprisonment claims, but this time in federal court. By that time, in November 1853, Eliza Emerson's brother, John Sanford, had claimed control of the Scotts.[19] He became the defendant in the suit (the Supreme Court reporter misspelled Sanford's name, so the case became known as *Scott v. Sandford*).[20] In a technical, but very important, aspect of the case, Scott claimed that his case fell within the federal court's diversity jurisdiction: Sanford was a resident of New York and Scott was a resident of Missouri, and so, according to Scott, the two parties were citizens of different states.[21]

The move to federal court may at first seem pointless: after all, even aside from the jurisdictional question and concerns about *res judicata*, would not the case turn on the same state law issues as before? And would not the federal court be bound to honor the Missouri Supreme Court's disposition of Missouri state law issues? Not in the nineteenth century. The relevant precedent was *Swift v. Tyson*,[22] not *Erie Railroad Co. v. Tompkins*[23]—meaning that the federal court was free to make an independent judgment about the content of Missouri state law. Scott had a chance of winning since the Missouri Supreme Court's decision in the state court litigation involved an aggressive reinterpretation of state law and a departure from mainstream authorities—indeed the dissenting opinion in the Missouri Supreme Court emphasized the court's failure to

---

[18] In order for the Supreme Court to assert jurisdiction over a case from a state court, it would have had to find that the outcome of the case depended upon resolution of a federal question. Despite the Missouri court's efforts to put the case on a state law ground, the United States Supreme Court might have found a federal question. For example, the Missouri Compromise might have preempted any state laws that purported to address the status of a person who had been transported into territories where the Compromise forbade slavery. Fehrenbacher finds this theory plausible; *see* Fehrenbacher, *supra* note 2, at 268–70. There is, however, little evidence to suggest that such a strategy would have succeeded, and it is not surprising that the Scotts and their lawyers opted for a collateral attack rather than a direct appeal.

[19] It remains unclear how Sanford acquired control over the Scotts, or, indeed, whether he in fact had control. *See* Fehrenbacher, *supra* note 2, at 270–74. For our purposes, it does not matter; Sanford admitted ownership in the suit. *See id.* at 274.

[20] *Id.* at 2 & n.*.

[21] *Id.* at 270–71.

[22] 41 U.S. 1 (1842).

[23] 304 U.S. 64 (1938).

respect Missouri state law precedents.[24] It was also possible (though highly improbable) that the United States Supreme Court would hold that the Missouri Compromise preempted Missouri's state law determinations about slave status.[25]

The case came to trial in May of 1854. Judge Robert Wells of the United States Circuit Court presided. He followed the reasoning of the Missouri Supreme Court and ruled for Sanford on the ground that Scott remained a slave under Missouri law.[26] Scott then sought a writ of error from the United States Supreme Court. The Court heard argument for four days, beginning on February 11, 1856. In May of that year, the Court set the case for reargument, which ran for another four days, beginning on December 15, 1856.[27]

The *Scott* litigation had attracted little notice during its state court and federal trial phases,[28] but upon reaching Washington, it riveted the nation's attention.[29] To defend against Scott's suit, Sanford had claimed, among other things, that Congress had no constitutional authority to ban slavery in the territories. Sanford contended that, for this reason, Emerson's stay at Fort Snelling could not have emancipated Scott; on Sanford's theory, the Missouri Compromise, which made Minnesota free territory, was unconstitutional, and hence there was no valid law prohibiting slavery in the territory. If Sanford's claim were accepted, it would have implications that reached far beyond the *Scott* litigation. The status of slavery in the territories was an explosive political issue in the 1840s and 1850s. If slavery were allowed in the territories, it would be more likely that the territories would eventually enter the Union as pro-slavery states. That in turn would affect the balance of power between anti-slavery and pro-slavery forces.

To many people, it seemed as though the fate of Sanford's argument and Scott's suit could determine how the United States resolved the most durable and violent political conflict it had ever faced. Indeed, on March 4, 1857—two days *before* the *Scott* decision was announced—President James Buchanan declared in his inaugural address that the Court would soon settle the question of slavery in the territories.[30]

---

[24] *See* Fehrenbacher, *supra* note 2, at 265.

[25] As mentioned, *supra* note 18, Fehrenbacher regards this theory as more plausible than do I.

[26] *Id.* at 276–80.

[27] *Id.* at 285–94.

[28] *See id.* at 280, 288–89, 291.

[29] *See id.* at 305 ("By Christmas 1856, Dred Scott's name was probably familiar to most Americans who followed the course of national affairs.").

[30] *See id.* at 313.

Buchanan's prediction was not idle speculation: he had engaged in secret dealings with several Supreme Court justices in order to bring about a pro-slavery decision, and when he gave his inaugural address he knew how the Court was going to rule.[31]

The Court acted on March 6, 1857. Chief Justice Roger Taney announced the decision and read a lengthy opinion from the bench. The two dissenters, John McLean and Benjamin Curtis, also read their opinions, as did two concurring justices, James Wayne and Samuel Nelson. Justices McLean and Curtis immediately released their opinions for publication, but Chief Justice Taney waited several weeks before making his opinion public. He apparently revised it substantially in the interim—Don Fehrenbacher, the leading expert on the case, suggests that Taney probably increased the length of the opinion by fifty percent, or around eighteen pages.[32] This extraordinary procedure gave rise to a bitter dispute between Taney and Curtis, which eventually led Curtis to resign from the Court in September 1857.[33]

The Supreme Court's Opinion

The Supreme Court ruled in Sanford's favor. That much is clear—but little else is. For openers, all nine justices wrote opinions in the case. Although the official reporter captions Taney's opinion as the "opinion of the court," it is maddeningly difficult to count which justices joined which propositions, or to construct a holding for the case.[34] The remainder of this Chapter will follow common convention and focus upon Taney's opinion.

The most infamous portions of Taney's opinion are easily summarized. Taney agreed with Sanford that Congress lacked authority to prohibit slavery in the territories and that the Missouri Compromise was therefore unconstitutional.[35] The Due Process Clause of the Fifth Amendment figured in the portion of Taney's opinion devoted to the Missouri Compromise: Taney implied that by banning slavery, Congress had deprived slaveholders who entered the territories of their property without due process of law.[36]

---

[31] See id. at 307–14.

[32] See id. at 315–20.

[33] See id. at 318–19.

[34] Fehrenbacher's analysis of the problem is characteristically thorough. Id. at 322–34, 404.

[35] Scott, 60 U.S. at 452.

[36] Id. at 450.

These are the elements of Taney's opinion seized upon by the "*Dred Again*" theorists. They are undoubtedly important, but, taken in isolation, they represent Taney's opinion in a way that is not only incomplete but misleading. I will add details as necessary in order to respond to the "*Dred Again*" argument. It is, however, necessary to mention one complication at the outset. Sanford's arguments in the Supreme Court included a challenge to the jurisdiction of the federal courts. He claimed that Scott was not a citizen and hence could not invoke federal diversity jurisdiction. The Supreme Court could rule for Sanford on this jurisdictional ground in either of two ways: by holding that even if Scott were free he could not be a citizen, or else by holding that Scott was not free, and hence was not a citizen (since only free persons could be citizens).

Taney did both. He began his opinion with a lengthy argument upholding Sanford's jurisdictional plea.[37] Taney held that nobody of African descent could ever become a citizen within the meaning of the diversity clause, concluding along the way that African–Americans were not among the "people" referred to by the Constitution.[38] After deciding that the Court lacked jurisdiction, however, Taney went on to consider whether Congress had authority to prohibit slavery in the territories.[39] This combination of rulings generated a long-running debate about whether Taney's pronouncements on the Missouri Compromise were dicta.[40] Some commentators have suggested that Taney's discussion of the Missouri Compromise was an alternative ground for his jurisdictional theory, not an exploration of the merits—as we have already noticed, if Scott was not free, then he could not be a citizen, and so the Court would lack jurisdiction. Insofar as we are concerned with the merits of the "*Dred Again*" argument, we can leave this debate aside; it has no bearing on our topic. Whether or not Taney's analysis of the Missouri Compromise was dicta, his jurisdictional arguments will matter greatly for two reasons: because of their methodology (they are originalist) and because of the relationship between those arguments and his interpretation of the Due Process Clause (the latter depends upon the former).

1. The Property Clause.

We are now in a position to consider the "*Dred Again*" myth in detail. We can begin with a simple, but surprising, textual observation: despite the contrary claims from the "*Dred Again*" theorists, *Scott* and the modern privacy cases (including the abortion cases) depend upon

---

[37] *Id.* at 399–430.

[38] *Id.* at 404–05, 411, 426–27.

[39] *Id.* at 430–54.

[40] For discussion of the debates, see David M. Potter, *The Impending Crisis: 1848–1861*, at 281–86 (1976).

different textual sources. As Justice Stevens pointed out in a 1992 article, the privacy cases were decided under the Liberty Clause: the portion of the Fifth and Fourteenth Amendments guaranteeing that no person will be deprived of *liberty* without due process of law.[41] *Scott v. Sandford* was not decided under this clause. It was decided under the Property Clause of the Fifth Amendment: the portion guaranteeing that no person will be deprived of *property* without due process of law.

For some, this difference will not be enough to sustain a textual distinction. After all, life, liberty and property stand next to one another in a list in the Due Process Clause. The Liberty and Property Clauses share the words preceding ("No person shall ... be deprived of ...," or "nor shall any State deprive any person of ...") and following ("without due process of law") the list. Does the difference matter? There is good reason to think that it does.

Liberty is different from property because the definition of liberty flows from human nature and our ideals, not from historical accidents like thefts, feoffments, and statutes (including, for purposes of *Scott*, the slave laws). Justice Stevens put the point crisply in *Meachum v. Fano*, when he dissented from the majority's claim that a liberty interest must either "originate in the Constitution" or have "its roots in state law."[42] Stevens wrote:

> [Law] is not the source of liberty, and surely not the exclusive source. I had thought it self-evident that all men were endowed by their Creator with liberty as one of the cardinal unalienable rights. It is that basic freedom which the Due Process Clause protects, rather than the particular rights or privileges conferred by specific laws or regulations.[43]

Stevens's argument deliberately echoes the Declaration of Independence, which names "life, liberty, and the pursuit of happiness" as "unalienable rights." The Constitution's Due Process Clause, which (unlike the Declaration) protects both natural and positive rights, substitutes "property" for the "pursuit of happiness." Even during the heyday of natural law thought in American jurisprudence, some theorists recognized that the boundaries of property rights depended largely on positive declaration. Joseph Story, for example, finished a survey of theories about natural law and property rights by declaring:

---

[41] *See* John Paul Stevens, *The Bill of Rights: A Century of Progress*, 59 U. Chi. L. Rev. 13, 20 (1992).

[42] 427 U.S. 215, 230 (1976) (Stevens, J., dissenting) (quoting the majority opinion, *id.* at 226).

[43] *Id.*

> Whatever right a man may have to property, it does not follow, that
> he has a right to transfer that right to another, or to transmit it, at
> his decease, to his children, or heirs. The nature and extent of his
> ownership; the modes in which he may dispose of it; the course of
> descent, and distribution of it upon his death; and the remedies for
> the redress of any violation of it, are in great measure, if not
> altogether, the result of the positive institutions of society.[44]

Story, of course, spoke the now out-moded language of natural law. One
need not resort to natural rights rhetoric, however, to express the basic
point: property depends for its definition upon legislatures in a way that
liberty does not.

The contingent character of property rights is the best reason to
respect the Constitution's distinction between liberty and property when
determining whether the Due Process Clause protects substantive as
well as procedural rights. Even if, however, the *"Dred* Again" theorists
reject this argument, they would have to respond to others. Institutional
considerations, for example, provide another ground for respecting the
distinction between liberty and property. For over seventy years, the
Court has drawn a line between economic regulations and other laws,
holding that the judiciary has little business closely scrutinizing the
former.[45] Insofar as this distinction depends upon the belief that economic rights are relatively unimportant, it has taken some hard knocks in
recent years from critics like Stephen Macedo.[46] Many readers may agree
with Macedo that "[o]ur occupations often shape our identities as deeply
as what we read or take in through the media, as deeply as the intimate
choices we make."[47] Yet even those who share Macedo's views about the
importance of economic liberties might nevertheless believe that considerations of institutional competence leave the Court poorly positioned to
protect economic rights: one might, for example, think that in a complex
market economy it is harder for judges (given their training and resources) to assess the impact of economic regulations on economic
liberties than it is for them to assess the impact of moral regulations on
personal privacy.[48] Those who accept such institutional arguments will

---

[44] Joseph Story, *Natural Law*, *in* 9 Encyclopedia Americana 150, 156 (Francis Lieber
ed., 1836), reprinted in James McClellan, *Joseph Story and the American Constitution: A
Study in Political and Legal Thought* 313–20 (1971).

[45] *See, e.g., Ferguson v. Skrupa*, 372 U.S. 726 (1963), *Williamson v. Lee Optical*, 348
U.S. 483 (1955).

[46] Steven Macedo, *Liberal Virtues: Citizenship, Virtue, and Community in Liberal
Constitutionalism* 183–202 (1990).

[47] *Id.* at 198; *see also* Christopher L. Eisgruber, *Constitutional Self–Government* 162–63
(2001).

[48] Justice Douglas thought that the Court's willingness to protect economic liberties—
not its willingness to give substantive content to the due process clause—was the defining

find in them a reason to read the Due Process Clause in a way that treats liberty and property differently.

In any event, the *"Dred* Again" theorists must offer a reasoned response to Stevens's textual distinction. They cannot dismiss the distinction between liberty and property simply by insisting, as Bork has done, that "[n]either word has any substantive meaning other than what the Court chooses to give it."[49] That position is inconsistent not only with Bork's own professed textualism,[50] but also with the premises of the *"Dred* Again" argument. The argument turns in part upon the claim that *Scott* and *Roe* flow from the same set of words. They do not.

2. Taney's Originalism.

We come now to the most glaring inaccuracy in the *"Dred* Again" theorists' depiction of *Scott*. They assume that Taney might have avoided disaster if only he had embraced originalism. Yet, Taney's opinion in *Scott* was a riot of originalism. The heart of his argument was a lengthy description of racist behavior at the time the Constitution was drafted, all of which he used to argue that African–Americans are neither "people" nor "citizens" under the Constitution.[51] Taney described his interpretive method this way:

> If any of [the Constitution's] provisions are deemed unjust, there is a mode prescribed in the instrument itself by which it may be amended; but while it remains unaltered, it must be construed now as it was understood at the time of its adoption ... it speaks not only in the same words, but with the same meaning and intent with which it spoke when it came from the hands of its framers, and was voted on and adopted by the people of the United States. Any other rule of construction would abrogate the judicial character of this court, and make it the mere reflex of the popular opinion or passion of the day.[52]

---

sin of the *Lochner* era. He accordingly argued that protecting abortion rights did not involve "substantive due process" because abortion rights did not implicate "legislation governing a business enterprise." *Doe v. Bolton*, 410 U.S. 179, 212 n. 4 (1973) (Douglas, J., concurring). By contrast, Douglas expressed concerns that the Court had reinstated the substantive due process doctrine when it used the Equal Protection Clause to scrutinize the empirical foundation for a Florida tax break favoring women. *See Kahn v. Shevin*, 416 U.S. 351, 356 n. 10 (1974); *see also* Eisgruber, *supra* note 47, at 165.

[49] Robert H. Bork, *Again, a Struggle for the Soul of the Court*, N.Y. Times, July 8, 1992, at A19.

[50] *See* Bork, *supra* note 6, at 145 ("[T]he judge is to interpret what is in the text and not something else.").

[51] *Scott*, 60 U.S. at 404–05.

[52] *Id*. at 426.

Here is a credo to warm the hearts of originalists.[53] In service of this ideal, Taney collected a variety of evidence. He traced the export of pro-slavery attitudes from England to the colonies.[54] He surveyed the various state statutes assigning African–Americans to an "inferior and subject condition,"[55] and claimed that "no example . . . can be found of [the] admission [of any free African–American] to all the privileges of citizenship in any State of the Union after these Articles were formed, and while they continued in force."[56] He insisted that the slave states would never have consented to the Constitution if it created the possibility that their slave property might be confused with rights-bearing persons.[57] Most importantly, Taney maintained that the Framers' words should be measured by the Framers' actions, rather than by their aspirations:

> [T]he men who framed [the Declaration of Independence] were great men—high in literary acquirements—high in their sense of honor, and incapable of asserting principles inconsistent with those on which they were acting. They perfectly understood the meaning of the language they used, and how it would be understood by others; and they knew that it would not in any part of the civilized world be supposed to embrace the negro race. . . . They spoke and acted according to the then established doctrines and principles, and in the ordinary language of the day, no one misunderstood them. The unhappy black race were separated from the white by indelible marks, and laws long before established, and were never thought of or spoken of except as property, and when the claims of the owner or the profit of the trader were supposed to need protection.[58]

---

[53] One can, for example, hear echoes of Taney's language in Robert Bork's:

> Statutes, we agree, may be changed by amendment or repeal. The Constitution may be changed by amendment pursuant to the procedures set out in Article V. It is a necessary implication of the prescribed procedures that neither statute nor Constitution should be changed by judges. Though that has been done often enough, it is in no sense proper.
>
> What is the meaning of a rule that judges should not change? It is the meaning understood at the time of the law's enactment. Though I have written of the understanding of the ratifiers of the Constitution, since they enacted it and made it law, that is actually a shorthand formulation, because what the ratifiers understood themselves to be enacting must be taken to be what the public of that time would have understood the words to mean.

Bork, *supra* note 6, at 143–44.

[54] *Scott*, 60 U.S. at 408.

[55] *Id.* at 416; see *id.* at 408–09, 412–16 for Taney's survey of state statutes.

[56] *Id.* at 418.

[57] *Id.* at 416.

[58] *Id.* at 410.

An originalism more contemptuous of fundamental values is scarcely imaginable. Taney found no cause for concern in the possibility that originalist interpretation would render the Constitution unjust.[59] He also refused to assume that the Framers wanted their constitutional principles to transcend the shortcomings of their own conduct. Had Taney adopted such an assumption, it would have favored construing the Framers' intentions, and hence the Constitution, in a way consistent with justice. Instead, Taney made exactly the opposite assumption. He premised his interpretation on the assumption that the Framers could not have intended the Constitution to incorporate a standard of conduct higher than the one they met.

Taney went further. He hinted that the Constitution was founded upon opinions that, in light of new understandings, now appeared unjust: "It is difficult at this day to realize the state of public opinion in relation to that unfortunate race, which prevailed in the civilized and enlightened portions of the world at the time of the Declaration of Independence, and when the Constitution of the United States was framed and adopted."[60] For Taney, in sum, there was no reason to assume that the Framers' intentions were just; some ground to believe that their intentions were in fact unjust; and no cause to interpret their intentions so as to make them just.

To what extent was originalism responsible for Taney's conclusions in *Scott*? Taney's execution of his originalist strategy was clearly deficient by originalism's own standards. For example, Taney's claim that no free blacks were citizens of any State when the Constitution was drafted was flatly wrong, as Justice Curtis pointed out in his dissent.[61] Taney's review of the historical record was replete with such errors.[62] But so what? Originalism does not cease to be originalism when done badly. People who recommend originalism do so knowing that it, like any other approach, will have incompetent as well as competent disciples. Indeed, if originalism is a particularly difficult strategy to carry out (because, for example, the historical record is ambiguous), so that poor originalist arguments dominate good ones, that might be reason to discount originalism's value as an interpretive device. In any event, if Taney was not disingenuous—if, in other words, the result reached actually followed from the reasoning he displayed—then his opinion is compelling evidence of how originalism can contribute to injustice.[63]

---

[59] *See id.* at 426.

[60] *Id.* at 407.

[61] *Id.* at 572–75 (Curtis, J., dissenting).

[62] *See* Fehrenbacher, *supra* note 2, at 340–64.

[63] Of course, Taney might have been lying: he might have invoked originalist arguments, knowing them to be wrong, in order to cover up conclusions reached on other

Moreover, Taney's originalist argument did not depend upon those of his claims that are easily debunked by historical evidence of the kind Curtis offered. All Taney needed was the claim that the Framers formed the United States government on "the white basis"[64] because some of them approved of slavery and the rest either were racist or believed that a permanently racist Union was better than no Union. That claim is not easily refuted. Indeed, even many people who generally admire the Framers nonetheless regard them as racists who sympathized with slavery.[65]

One can, of course, compile evidence that cuts against Taney's view of the Framers. Justice Curtis expressed the conviction that such evidence would prove persuasive.[66] Herbert Storing, among others, carried out the project that Justice Curtis anticipated.[67] The success of any such project may depend, however, upon whether interpreters are willing to adopt the attitude recommended by Justice McLean in dissent. McLean wrote that he preferred "the lights of Madison, Hamilton, and Jay, as a means of construing the Constitution in all its bearings, rather than to look behind that period, into a traffic which is now declared to be piracy, and punished with death by Christian nations."[68] Other interpretations are possible, but McLean's formulation appears to insist that we should construe the Framers' intentions in the way most consistent with justice. McLean recommended an interpretive posture that respected the Framers not by—as Taney would have it—lowering their aspirations to fit their conduct, but by recognizing that the Framers may have had aspirations (and incorporated them into the Constitution) without living up to them.

We may draw two conclusions from our examination of Taney's originalism. First, Taney, unlike either McLean or Curtis, embraced an originalism indifferent to the justice or injustice of the Framers' intentions. Taney may in fact have been the original originalist of this sort.[69]

---

grounds. Yet, characterizing Taney's opinion as a lie would also undercut the *"Dred Again"* myth, for it would excuse substantive due process from blame for *Scott* to exactly the same extent that it excuses originalism.

[64] The quoted phrase belongs to Stephen Douglas, who embraced and defended Taney's vision of the Founding. Paul M. Angle, *The Complete Lincoln–Douglas Debates of 1858* 65 (1958).

[65] See, for example, the discussion of contemporary views in Herbert J. Storing, *Slavery and the Moral Foundations of the American Republic*, in *The Moral Foundations of the American Republic* 313 (Robert H. Horwitz ed., 3d ed. 1986).

[66] *See Scott*, 60 U.S. at 574–75 (Curtis, J., dissenting).

[67] *See* Storing, *supra* note 65, at 313–24.

[68] *Scott*, 60 U.S. at 537 (McLean, J., dissenting).

[69] *See, e.g.*, William E. Nelson, *History and Neutrality in Constitutional Adjudication*, 72 Va. L. Rev. 1237, 1237–38 (1986) (" '[I]ntentionalism' . . . can be traced back at least to

Second, Taney's version of originalism was essential to the result he reached.

3. *Originalism's Role in* Scott's *Logic.*

On the basis of *"Dred* Again's" comparisons between *Scott* and *Roe,* one might expect to find that *Scott,* like *Roe,* centered upon an argument about "due process of law." Not so. Taney's originalism—not his substantive interpretation of the Due Process Clause—was chiefly responsible for *Scott*'s most notorious conclusions. Taney's originalist argument about citizenship and personhood consumed forty-four percent of his opinion.[70] The upshot of Taney's analysis was that the Court had no jurisdiction under the Diversity Clause.[71] That conclusion, predicated on originalist reasoning and independent of the Due Process Clause, would have sufficed as a ground for dismissing Scott's suit.

Taney followed his originalist discussion of citizenship with more originalist argument (equally unconvincing and almost as long) about the Territories Clause.[72] The Due Process Clause rates only a two-sentence mention. It occurs on the fifty-first page of Taney's opinion. Here are the sentences, together with the ones that precede and follow them:

> These powers, and others, in relation to rights of person, which it is not necessary here to enumerate, are, in express and positive terms, denied to the General Government; and the rights of private property have been guarded with equal care. Thus the rights of property are united with the rights of person, and placed on the same ground by the fifth amendment to the Constitution, which provides that no person shall be deprived of life, liberty, and property, without due process of law. And an act of Congress which deprives a citizen of the United States of his liberty or property, merely because he came himself or brought his property into a particular Territory of the

---

the 1857 case of *Scott v. Sandford.*"); *see also* Paul W. Kahn, *Legitimacy and History: Self-Government in American Constitutional Theory* 46 (1986).

[70] I am relying on Fehrenbacher's calculations. Fehrenbacher, *supra* note 2, at 337–40.

[71] *Scott,* 60 U.S. at 427.

[72] Art. IV, § 3, cl. 2 ("The Congress shall have Power to dispose of and make all needful Rules and Regulations respecting the Territory or other Property belonging to the United States."). Taney's argument was bizarre. He first argued that this Clause did not authorize Congress to govern the Northwest Territory. Having deprived Congress of the most natural textual basis for the exercise of legislative authority in the territories, Taney then reversed field, arguing that such a power was conferred by implication in the clause dealing with admission of new states to the Union. Art. IV, § 3, cl. 1 ("New States may be admitted by the Congress into this Union."). For a summary and critique of the argument, see Fehrenbacher, *supra* note 2, at 367–76, 381–82.

United States, and who had committed no offence against the laws, could hardly be dignified with the name of due process of law.

So, too, it will hardly be contended that Congress could by law quarter a soldier in a house in a Territory without the consent of the owner, in time of peace; nor in time of war, but in a manner prescribed by law.[73]

Taney's opinion is thus not in any meaningful sense *about* the Due Process Clause. He did not articulate a theory of the Due Process Clause, in the way that he articulated, and endorsed, an originalist view of constitutional interpretation. There remains, however, an important question: is Taney's substantive interpretation of the Due Process Clause either necessary or sufficient to support his conclusions? If the answer were yes, that would certainly count as a ground for claiming that *Scott* was a "substantive due process" case, whatever else it might be. But the answer is no.

Taney's substantive interpretation of the clause obviously was not necessary to his conclusion that the federal courts could grant Scott no relief. Taney had already reached that conclusion on jurisdictional grounds. The due process argument might nevertheless have been necessary to Taney's conclusions in another respect. Taney's jurisdictional ruling was not principally responsible for the political shockwaves that followed *Scott v. Sandford*.[74] They resulted instead from his conclusion that Congress had no power to prohibit slavery in the territories. Taney's discussion of due process was addressed to that topic: he implied that the Missouri Compromise, because it prohibited slavery in some federal territories, unconstitutionally deprived slaveholders of their property when they entered that territory.[75] If Taney's substantive interpretation of "due process of law" was necessary to his judgment on the

---

[73] *Scott*, 60 U.S. at 450.

[74] "Taney's ruling against Negro citizenship carried nothing like the same emotional charge as his ruling against the Missouri Compromise restriction." Fehrenbacher, *supra* note 2, at 429. The reaction to Taney's opinion reflected, of course, the racist opinions prevalent at the time. Viewed in hindsight, Taney's opinion would still deserve its title as the worst ever produced had he stopped after finishing his Diversity Clause argument, which denied the possibility of African–American citizenship.

[75] I say "implied" because, as Don Fehrenbacher points out, "in spite of a general impression to the contrary, Taney never did specifically declare the Missouri Compromise to be a violation of the Fifth Amendment." Fehrenbacher, *supra* note 2, at 382. Taney said only that Congress could not deprive citizens of property merely because they had brought their property into a federal territory. Taney did not say that the Missouri Compromise displayed this defect, although one may fairly draw that inference from his argument. Fehrenbacher concludes that "Taney's contribution to the development of substantive due process was therefore meager and somewhat obscure." *Id.*

Missouri Compromise, we could at least say that it was necessary to one of his more notorious conclusions.

The Property Clause argument appears, however, to have been no more than one among multiple independent grounds for Taney's conclusion that the Missouri Compromise was unconstitutional. Taney embedded the due process argument in a lengthy discussion about whether the Constitution delegated Congress any power to regulate slavery in the Territories. Although Taney digressed from this argument in order to make his reference to the Due Process Clause, later sentences appear to return to it. Taney's position is anything but clear, but he apparently concluded that the Constitution nowhere enumerated any power that would enable Congress to regulate slavery in the territories.[76] If that is correct, then the argument that the Property Clause precluded Congress from banning slavery was superfluous, because Taney found that the Constitution did not delegate to Congress the power to regulate slavery.

Nevertheless, Taney's argument to the effect that Congress lacked authority to regulate slavery in the territories is muddled. One might accordingly say that he needed the substantive interpretation of the Due Process Clause in order to conclude that Congress could not prohibit slavery in the territories. That is not my view, but reasonable people may differ about the point.

When we turn from the argument's necessity to its sufficiency, we can answer with more confidence. Taney's interpretation of the Due Process Clause as a source of substantive rights is not sufficient to defeat Scott's claim or to invalidate the Missouri compromise. The reason is important: Taney's interpretation of "property" rested upon his originalist denial that African–Americans were persons within the meaning of the Constitution.

Sotirios Barber has made this point clearly:

[One need not be] opposed to the abstract proposition that Congress should respect the property rights of persons who move from one place to another. What is regrettable in *Dred Scott* is the additional proposition that Congress has a duty fully to respect property in human beings. That Congress should respect property is one proposition; that the law either has or can legitimately make human beings ordinary pieces of property is quite another. Everything in *Dred Scott* turns on Taney's affirmative answer to the latter, an answer he pretended to believe was a clear mandate of the American founding.[77]

---

[76] *Scott,* 60 U.S. at 452.

[77] Sotirios A. Barber, *Whither Moral Realism in Constitutional Theory? A Reply to Professor McConnell,* 64 Chi.–Kent L. Rev. 111, 126–27 (1988).

A substantive interpretation of the Due Process Clause, in other words, gets Taney nowhere until coupled with an obnoxious conception of property, which recognizes property in persons. As Barber points out, Taney derived that conception of property from an originalist argument. Indeed, we can readily appreciate how Taney's argument about citizenship provided a foundation for the theory of property he needed: having already decided that the Constitution contemplated African–Americans only as property and not as people, Taney could affirm that the Constitution recognized no reason for treating African–American slaves differently from other property. That is exactly the path he pursued.

Shortly after his two-sentence reference to due process, Taney devoted two paragraphs to defending a positivist theory of property rights.[78] Although he acknowledged that international law distinguished slavery from other forms of property, Taney denied that this distinction was relevant to the Constitution.[79] He referred to "an earlier part" of his opinion, which had concluded that "the right of property in a slave is distinctly and expressly affirmed in the Constitution."[80] Taney was not so kind as to supply a *supra* cite to the passage he had in mind. The only plausible candidate is a discussion of the Importation and Fugitive Slave Clauses, a discussion contained within Taney's interpretation of citizenship.[81] The passage follows immediately after Taney's interpretive axiom, quoted earlier, making the Framers' intentions dependent upon their conduct. Taney's originalism is the crucial basis for his interpretation of these two clauses, and thus also for his assertion that "the right of property in a slave is distinctly and expressly affirmed" by means of two propositions which speak only of persons and never mention slavery or,

---

[78] *Scott*, 60 U.S. at 451.

[79] Taney premised his denial on legal positivism:

[I]t must be borne in mind that there is no law of nations standing between the people of the United States and their Government. . . . The powers of the Government, and the rights of the citizen under it, are positive and practical regulations plainly written down. . . . And if the Constitution recognizes the right of property of the master in a slave, and makes no distinction between that description of property and other property owned by a citizen, no tribunal . . . has a right to draw such a distinction. . . .

Id. at 451.

[80] *Id.*

[81] *See id.* at 410–12. The passage is the only one in which Taney used a textual argument to justify his claim that African–Americans were property. In the course of the passage, Taney said that "[t]he unhappy black race were . . . never thought of or spoken of except as property, and when the claims of the owner or the profit of the trader were supposed to need protection," *id.* at 410; that in the Importation Clause, "the right to purchase and hold this property is directly sanctioned and authorized for twenty years by the people who framed the Constitution," *id.* at 411; and that the Fugitive Slave Clause pledged "to maintain and uphold the right of the master in the manner specified, as long as the Government they then formed should endure." *Id.*

for that matter, property.[82] Taney thus owed his construction of the Property Clause to originalism.

4. *Fundamental Values Jurisprudence & the* Scott *Dissents.*

The *"Dred* Again" school paints the *Scott* dissenters—especially Justice Curtis—as glorious knights of positivism who studiously avoided recourse to moral judgment. Members of the *"Dred* Again" school claim to be the true heirs of these jurists. Once again, their claims rest upon a misrepresentation of *Scott.*

If the *"Dred* Again" school's rendering were a fair one, we would expect the *Scott* dissents to include something like the modern positivist criticism of substantive due process. That criticism maintains either that the Due Process Clause by its terms limits protection only to procedural rights, or that the Framers never intended, as a matter of historical fact, that the Clause would encompass substantive elements. The criticism accepts such textual and historical arguments as dispositive evidence against a substantive reading of either the Property Clause or the Liberty Clause.[83]

Justice Curtis's dissent does indeed contain an argument of this sort. He wrote:

Nor, in my judgment, will the position, that a prohibition to bring slaves into a Territory deprives any one of his property without due process of law, bear examination.

It must be remembered that this restriction of the legislative power is not peculiar to the Constitution of the United States; it was borrowed from *Magna Charta*; was brought to America by our ancestors, as part of their inherited liberties, and has existed in all the States, usually in the very words of the great charter. It existed in every political community in America in 1787, when the ordinance prohibiting slavery north and west of the Ohio was passed.[84]

Curtis then surveyed a variety of state laws depriving slaveholders of their rights over slaves. He pointed out that nobody had ever objected to these laws on the ground that they were inconsistent with Magna Charta.

This form of argument looks somewhat like pure originalism. Curtis adduced evidence that, in the years preceding the Founding, nobody

---

[82] Curtis, in his *Scott* dissent, and Abraham Lincoln, in his debates with Stephen Douglas, both stressed that the Constitution never uses the word "slavery," even in the Fugitive Slave Clause, and everywhere refers to slaves as "persons." Id. at 624 (Curtis, J., dissenting); Angle, *supra* note 64, at 385.

[83] Both arguments appear in quick succession in Bork, *supra* note 6, at 32.

[84] *Scott*, 60 U.S. at 626–27 (Curtis, J., dissenting).

challenged statutes prohibiting slavery on the ground that these statutes were inconsistent with Magna Charta. From this evidence, he inferred that the Framers believed Magna Charta permitted whatever deprivations such statutes effected. His argument maintained that, because the Constitution borrowed the language of the Due Process Clause from Magna Charta, the Framers probably believed that statutes consistent with Magna Charta were likewise consistent with the Due Process Clause. The pure originalist argument would then conclude that these beliefs about the Clause's application were dispositive.

We must, however, distinguish the pure originalist argument from Curtis's. Curtis never quite closed the loop in *Scott*. He did not say, for example, that the Due Process Clause could not have an application different from that of Magna Charta, nor did he say that the constructions the Framers put on Magna Charta were dispositive as to its meaning.[85] Indeed, he expressly skirted the latter question by saying, "I think I may at least say, if the Congress did then violate *Magna Charta* by the ordinance, no one discovered that violation."[86] Curtis thus implicitly demanded that Taney explain why so many reasonable and intelligent people were mistaken about *Magna Charta*'s application. It would, of course, be reasonable to ask that question even if the mistakes made by those people were not in any way binding upon future constitutional interpreters.

Moreover, Curtis did not say that the Due Process Clause protected no substantive rights, nor did he make a favorite argument of positivists today, namely, that the inclusion of the word "process" rules out, as a simple textual matter, the possibility that the Clause protects substantive liberties.[87] Still, if the passage now under discussion were the whole of Curtis's answer to Taney's due process argument, then I would have to concede that "*Dred* Again's" picture renders Curtis more faithfully than it does Taney. While the passage provides at least some basis for designating Curtis a "positivist/originalist/process-means-process" Justice, the reference to Magna Charta is not the whole story.

Here is the way Curtis began his attack on Taney's Property Clause argument:

---

[85] Though Curtis did not claim anything so strong in *Scott*, he arguably did so in an earlier case, *Murray's Lessee v. Hoboken Land and Improvement Co.*, 59 U.S. (18 How.) 272 (1855). There, Curtis said that the "words, 'due process of law,' were undoubtedly intended to convey the same meaning as the words, 'by the law of the land,' in *Magna Charta*." *Id.* at 276.

[86] *Scott*, 60 U.S. at 627 (Curtis, J., dissenting).

[87] A classic statement of the argument, though not by a pure positivist, appears in John Hart Ely, *Democracy and Distrust: A Theory of Judicial Review* 18 (1980).

I will now proceed to examine the question, whether this clause is entitled to the effect thus attributed to it. It is necessary, first, to have a clear view of the nature and incidents of that particular species of property which is now in question.

Slavery, being contrary to natural right, is created only by municipal law. This is not only plain in itself and agreed by all writers on this subject, but is inferable from the Constitution, and has been explicitly declared by this court. The Constitution refers to slaves as "persons held to service in one State, under the laws thereof." Nothing can more clearly describe a *status* created by municipal law. In *Prigg v. Pennsylvania* ... this court said: "The state of slavery is deemed to be a mere municipal regulation, founded on and limited to the range of territorial laws."[88]

Property in slaves is different from other property because slavery is "contrary to natural right." Curtis concluded that, for this reason, it would be unreasonable to construe the Constitution to protect these property rights when the slaveholder allowed the slave to leave the jurisdiction that had created the rights.[89]

In light of the astonishing claims made by *"Dred* Again" theorists, the obvious bears mention: this is an argument about natural rights, not "plain text" or "framers' intent." Curtis claimed that the Fugitive Slave Clause incorporated a distinction between natural and positive rights, and he claimed that one must appreciate that distinction to understand the word "property" in the Due Process Clause. Today the argument would probably be framed in terms of fundamental values or simple justice, but the point would be the same. To understand the constitutional text, one must think about justice.

This is Curtis's first and most extended argument against Taney's substantive reading of the Property Clause. It is also McLean's only argument against that reading.[90] Nevertheless, Curtis's second argument has clear originalist overtones, and it would be silly to claim that his first, natural rights argument was more important simply because he put it first, or because he gave it more text. On the other hand, it would be even sillier to claim that only Curtis's second, originalist argument mattered. For that reason, we can say at least this: fundamental values jurisprudence deserves some credit for the *Scott* dissents (including Justice Curtis's dissent).

---

[88] *Scott*, 60 U.S. at 624 (Curtis, J., dissenting) (quoting *Prigg v. Pennsylvania*, 41 U.S. 539, 611 (1842)).

[89] *Id*. at 625–26.

[90] *Id*. at 547–50 (McClean, J., dissenting).

We must consider one final piece of evidence before we can judge "*Dred* Again's" rendering of Curtis. The "*Dred* Again" theorists are fond of quoting Curtis's summary of his own method, which they take to be a repudiation of all forms of fundamental values jurisprudence. Here is what Curtis wrote:

> To engraft on any instrument a substantive exception not found in it, must be admitted to be a matter attended with great difficulty. And the difficulty increases with the importance of the instrument, and the magnitude and complexity of the interests involved in its construction. To allow this to be done with the Constitution, upon reasons purely political, renders its judicial interpretation impossible—because judicial tribunals, as such, cannot decide on political considerations. Political reasons have not the requisite certainty to afford rules of juridical interpretation. They are different in different men. They are different in the same men at different times. And when a strict interpretation of the Constitution, according to the fixed rules which govern the interpretation of laws, is abandoned, and the theoretical opinions of individuals are allowed to control its meaning, we have no longer a Constitution; we are under the government of individual men, who for the time being have power to declare what the Constitution is, according to their own views of what it ought to mean.[91]

We should not be surprised that positivists would warm to this passage, with its embrace of "strict interpretation" and "fixed rules;" its condemnation of "political reasons" and "theoretical opinions;" and its warning that other modes of interpretation allow wanton judges to hide "what the Constitution is" under "their own views of what it ought to mean." But we should be careful. Before conceding that Curtis was—in the methodology he professed, if not in the method he employed—a precursor to today's "*Dred* Again" theorists, we should examine an ambiguity in his statement. What did Curtis mean when he referred to "the fixed rules which govern the interpretation of laws"?

As G. Edward White has shown, antebellum constitutional theory embraced some rather controversial, and substantive, precepts under the heading, "rules of interpretation."[92] Curtis added the requirement that these rules be "fixed." Nothing in his opinion enables us to be certain

---

[91] *Id.* at 620–21 (Curtis, J., dissenting). Curtis offered this passage after noting that counsel for both sides had neglected the text when arguing the constitutionality of the Missouri Compromise: "No particular clause of the Constitution has been referred to at the bar in support of either of these views." *Id.* at 620.

[92] G. Edward White, *The Marshall Court and Cultural Change: 1815–35*, at 114–19 (abridged ed. 1988) (discussing how Joseph Story could describe nineteen propositions "consistent with an ideological perspective" as "rules of interpretation" that supply a "fixed standard" for judicial review).

about how Curtis understood this phrase.[93] There is, however, an interesting possibility consistent with what Curtis said in *Scott*. Curtis might have considered a rule of interpretation to be fixed if it enjoyed the consent of the legal community. We have already seen him refer to one such rule, a rule which, he said, was "agreed by all writers on the subject." The rule is that "[s]lavery, being contrary to natural right, is created only by municipal law."[94] Taney recognized the existence of a long-standing rule distinguishing between mere municipal regulation and laws consistent with natural right, but he refused, on originalist grounds,[95] to allow this "fixed rule" to govern the interpretation of the Constitution. Curtis's argument about municipal law was a response to Taney's rejection of the distinction. We thus arrive at a hypothesis: in the passage the positivists so admire, Curtis might have meant, *inter alia*, to defend reasonable recourse to natural right against a rampant positivism that rejected any such reference. Indeed, there is a sense in which positivism is a decidedly political doctrine, because it permits a dominant opinion to determine what is law without recourse to any "fixed" standard, such as justice or natural right.

There are a lot of "maybes" in the argument just completed. Moreover, Curtis's statement has a positivist ring to it. We can, however, make two modest claims about what Curtis said. First, the complexion of

---

[93] Curtis made reference to "settled rules" in *Murray's Lessee*, 59 U.S. 272, 283 (1855). The settled rules he adverted to there included, for example, the proposition that "a public agent, who acts pursuant to the command of a legal precept.... cannot be made responsible in a judicial tribunal for obeying the lawful command of the government; and the government itself, which gave the command, cannot be sued without its own consent." *Id.* Although Curtis in *Murray's Lessee* gave two paragraphs' worth of such rules (unaccompanied by citation), it is difficult to infer from the passage the criteria he used to distinguish "settled rules" from other jurisprudential rules.

[94] *Scott*, 60 U.S. at 624 (Curtis, J., dissenting). *See supra* text accompanying note 88. The rule described by Curtis had its most famous articulation in *Somerset's Case*, 20 Howell's State Trials 1, 98 Eng. Rep. 499 (1772), where Lord Mansfield said "[t]he state of slavery is of such a nature, that it is incapable of being introduced on any reasons ... but only [by] positive law ... it's so odious, that nothing can be suffered to support it, but positive law." 20 Howell's State Trials at 82, 98 Eng. Rep. at 510. For discussion, see Cover, *supra* note 2, at 16–17, 29.

The concept of "municipal law" itself reflected a number of legal axioms. Blackstone defined "municipal law" as a "rule of civil conduct prescribed by the supreme power in a state, commanding what is right and prohibiting what is wrong." William Blackstone, 1 *Commentaries on the Laws of England* 44 (1765). He contrasted it with natural law and revealed law, *id.* at 42–43, 54–55, saying that "no human laws should be suffered to contradict these." *Id.* at 42. Joseph Story used the term in a way that was slightly different. He distinguished "municipal regulations" from other laws on the ground that they aimed at "private or local convenience" rather than the "public good." Joseph Story, 1 *Commentaries on the Constitution of the United States* § 421 (1833).

[95] *Scott*, 60 U.S. at 451. *See supra* text accompanying note 79.

Curtis's statement changes when one knows that he issued it in dissent from an originalist opinion. Curtis must have recognized that arguments about original intent, no less than arguments about fundamental values, can be "purely political." Second, Curtis, unlike Taney, never expressed indifference to the possibility that his theory of interpretation would construe the law in a way that made the law unjust. Curtis's theory of constitutional interpretation is thus ambiguous in its positivism. His practice, as we have seen, was unambiguously respectful of fundamental values.

The Immediate Impact of Dred Scott v. Sandford

We have seen that Taney's opinion in *Scott* is originalist in character and devotes very little attention to the Due Process Clause. Perhaps, however, an examination of extra-judicial sources would show that thoughtful antebellum critics of *Scott* regarded Taney's substantive reading of the Due Process Clause as the essence of his decision, and believed, too, that this reading depended upon a rejection of positivism or originalism. If so, that would provide a reason—albeit a rather weak one—for accepting the "*Dred* Again" theory's picture of *Scott*. We could at least say that the public believed Taney had breached judicial duty by improperly construing the phrase "due process of law," even if the pro-slavery effect of his decision proceeded from other errors and even if the *Scott* dissenters did not pursue this point as forcefully as they might have. Does the record allow the "*Dred* Again" theorists to make this claim?

The answer appears to be "no." *Scott* prompted intense public discussion. In the words of the eminent Civil War historian James McPherson, "[I]nstead of removing the issue of slavery in the territories from politics, the Court's ruling became itself a political issue."[96] Many Northern newspapers and anti-slavery politicians criticized the decision harshly.[97] Yet, criticism of *Scott* took a different course from the one that the "*Dred* Again" theory would have us expect. Republicans and abolitionists attacked the decision as political rather than judicial, but they based this charge upon the claim that Taney's assessment of the Missouri Compromise was dicta.[98] These critics argued that once Taney had decided that Scott was not a citizen, and so could not sue, Taney lacked jurisdiction to decide the merits of the case. That is indeed a kind of argument against political judging, but it is not the kind of argument

---

[96] James M. McPherson, *Battle Cry of Freedom: The Civil War Era* 176 (1988).

[97] *See* Fehrenbacher, *supra* note 2, at 417–48.

[98] *See id.* at 417–18; *see also* Potter, *supra* note 40, at 281–83; 3 Charles Warren, *The Supreme Court in United States History 1856–1918*, at 24–40 (1922).

that the *"Dred* Again" theorists wish to make. The *"Dred* Again"
theorists have an argument about the merits of Taney's ruling, not
about his decision to reach the merits.

Of course, the most important antebellum critic of *Scott*, Abraham
Lincoln, did focus upon the merits of Taney's decision. One of Lincoln's
principal complaints about the opinion was that it decided that taking a
slave "into a United States territory where slavery was prohibited by act
of Congress, did not make him free because that act of Congress as they
held was unconstitutional."[99] Taney's substantive reading of the Due
Process Clause is a component (though perhaps not a necessary one) of
his attack on the Missouri Compromise. May we conclude that, at least
for this eminent critic of *Scott*, the interpretation of "due process" was
the core of the decision's turpitude?

Three reasons compel us to say otherwise. First, as we have already
seen, Taney's application of the Due Process Clause to the Missouri
Compromise depends upon his originalist claim that property in persons
is, for constitutional purposes, no different from other kinds of property.

Second, Lincoln singled out Taney's originalist conclusions for special censure. According to Lincoln, *Scott* laid the foundation for national-
izing slavery because it declared that *"[t]he right of property in a slave is
distinctly and expressly affirmed in the Constitution!"*[100] This proposition
is the prerequisite for Taney's application of due process, not a consequence of it. Taney plucked the proposition from his originalist theory of
citizenship. Lincoln took equally vigorous exception to Taney's originalist argument excluding African–Americans from the principles of the
Declaration of Independence.[101]

Third, Lincoln did not object to *Scott* on the ground that it was
inconsistent with a positivist respect for democratic processes. On the
contrary, he excoriated the decision because it corroded moral principles
implicit in the Constitution and explicit in the Declaration of Independence. Lincoln said that "a vast portion of the American people . . . look
upon [slavery] as a vast moral evil."[102] He thought it was important that
Americans could "prove it is such by the writings of those who gave us

---

[99] Angle, *supra* note 64, at 377.

[100] *Id.* at 308 (quoting *Scott*, 60 U.S. at 451). According to Lincoln, the essence of *Scott*
was compressed into the single sentence he quoted. *Id.*

[101] *Id.* at 380 ("[T]hree years ago there never had lived a man who had ventured to . . .
[assert that the Declaration of Independence] did not include the negro. I believe the first
man who ever said it was Chief Justice Taney in the *Dred Scott* case, and the next to him
was our friend Stephen Douglas.").

[102] *Id.* at 35.

the blessings of liberty which we enjoy."[103] The Framers' judgment was evident from the language of the Constitution, which affixed "many clear marks of disapprobation" upon slavery.[104] The most troubling defect in *Scott* was its inconsistency with the principles of the Declaration of Independence.[105] Lincoln urged opposition to *Scott* "because we think it lays the foundation not merely of enlarging and spreading out what we consider an evil, but it lays the foundation for spreading that evil into the states themselves."[106] Lincoln's constitutional interpretation thus was originalist, but his, by contrast to Taney's, was an originalism steeped in justice.[107]

To summarize, insofar as Republicans and abolitionists denounced the decision as political, they did so for reasons irrelevant to the merits of Taney's interpretation of the Due Process Clause. Lincoln's criticism of *Scott* emphasized the importance of construing the Constitution in a way consistent with moral principle. *Scott*'s leading critics accused Taney of injustice, not of infidelity to positivist interpretive methods.

The Continuing Importance of Scott Today

1. Scott's Ironic Legacy.

One might say that Lincoln's argument against *Scott* ensured that the case would have a profound and lasting impact on the American Constitution, though certainly not of the sort that Taney wanted or that any of his brethren envisioned. *Scott* carries none of the precedential authority that Taney hoped it would have. To be sure, one can find occasional post-Civil War opinions that cite *Scott* with approval. For example, in *The Insular Cases*, which dealt with congressional authority over Puerto Rico, some Justices invoked Taney's analysis of congressional power to regulate the territories.[108] But judges and lawyers who rely

---

[103] *Id.*

[104] *Id.* at 386.

[105] *Id.* at 41; *see also* Sotirios A. Barber, *The Ninth Amendment: Inkblot or Another Hard Nut to Crack?*, 64 Chi.–Kent L. Rev. 67, 68–69 (1988) (discussing Lincoln's objections to Taney's reading of the Declaration).

[106] Angle, *supra* note 64, at 333.

[107] *See, e.g., id.* at 100–01 (Americans should heed the Framers because "[t]hey erected a beacon to guide their children and their children's children, and the countless myriads who should inhabit the earth in other ages."); *see also* Eisgruber, *supra* note 47, at 104–05. The classic treatment of Lincoln's response to *Scott* is Harry V. Jaffa, *Crisis of the House Divided: An Interpretation of the Issues in the Lincoln–Douglas Debates* (1959).

[108] *See Downes v. Bidwell*, 182 U.S. 244, 291 (White, J., concurring); 360–61 (Fuller, C.J., dissenting) (1901).

upon the case do so at their peril, and the most common way to use *Scott* is as an illustration of mistakes to avoid.

Yet, while *Scott* lacks precedential authority, it has had a lingering constitutional impact of another kind, for it played a role in the developments that made Lincoln president.[109] Lincoln was arguably responsible for the North's victory in the Civil War, and that victory led to the enactment of the Fourteenth Amendment, which is the fountainhead for much of the Supreme Court's civil liberties jurisprudence. Through this chain of events, modern civil rights law may, oddly enough, be part of *Scott*'s continuing legacy. Explaining *Scott*'s impact on Lincoln's career requires a digression from the *"Dred* Again" theory, but the story of *Scott* would be incomplete without it.

The famous Lincoln–Douglas debates took place in connection with the Illinois senatorial campaign of 1858. Douglas was the incumbent and Lincoln his challenger. Early in the debates, Douglas propounded a series of seven questions designed to embarrass Lincoln. Lincoln deflected these rather easily and then came forward with a series of his own. The most important was a question that Lincoln first posed in the debate at Freeport.[110] He asked whether the people who live in a territory were free to enact laws excluding slavery from it. This question neatly skewered Douglas. Douglas was a moderate Northern politician who had stood up in Congress against pro-slavery forces but enjoyed some Southern support. He had built his position around two principles: first, that the people of each state were free to choose for themselves whether to allow slavery, and, second, that *Scott* and other Supreme Court decisions about slavery deserved the full support of the nation. On their surface, these two principles appeared consistent. *Scott* prohibited Congress from regulating slavery in their territories, which, one might suppose, left the people of the territories free to decide for themselves whether to have it. Yet, as Lincoln reminded Douglas again and again, *Scott* also said that "the right of property in a slave is distinctly and

---

[109] The historian Charles Warren asserted that by his *Scott* opinion, Roger Taney "elected Abraham Lincoln to the Presidency." Warren, *supra* note 98, at 3:79. Fehrenbacher reports that on October 14, 1864, the New York *Times* opined that "the *Dred Scott* decision 'contributed more than all other things combined to the election of President Lincoln.'" Fehrenbacher, *supra* note 2, at 712 n.24. Fehrenbacher is skeptical of such claims. *Id.* at 562–67. On the other hand, James McPherson gives them more credit: "Without the *Dred Scott* decision, it is quite possible that Lincoln would never have become president of the United States." James McPherson, *Politics and Judicial Responsibility*: Dred Scott v. Sanford, *in* Great Cases in Constitutional Law 93 (Robert P. George ed., 2000).

[110] Although Douglas's response to Lincoln became known as "the Freeport Doctrine," Lincoln's question was sensitive but not new. "Douglas had already confronted the issue many times.... Lincoln asked the question anyway; Douglas answered as expected." McPherson, *supra* note 96, at 183–84.

expressly affirmed in the Constitution." A right distinctly and expressly affirmed in the Constitution would seem to trump the right of the people to decide for themselves. Douglas would have to choose between his two principles.

This left Douglas with a politically devastating dilemma. If he said that the Constitution permitted settlers to exclude slavery from the territories, he would have to qualify his unblinking support for *Scott*. He would thereby alienate the South. Alternatively, if Douglas insisted that the Constitution required settlers to permit slavery in the territories, he would have to compromise his commitment to principles of popular sovereignty. He would thereby alienate the North. In response, Douglas articulated a position that came to be known as "the Freeport Doctrine." He said that even though the right to slavery was affirmed in the Constitution, the people of states and territories could refuse to enact any laws supporting it. They would thereby, in practice if not in law, destroy the rights of slaveholders within their jurisdictions.

In effect, Douglas had chosen popular sovereignty over support for *Scott*, the North over the South. The Freeport Doctrine enabled him to defeat Lincoln and win his Senate election. It lost him the support of the South, however, and his presidential ambitions never recovered from the blow. Douglas had been a candidate who might have commanded national support. In the absence of a viable national candidate, the Republicans, a sectional party with no support whatsoever in the South, had a shot at the White House. Lincoln seized the opportunity.[111]

It is, of course, possible that Lincoln would have become president even without *Scott* and the Freeport debate that followed from it. It is also possible that something like the Reconstruction Amendments would have come about without Lincoln's presidency. But it seems clear, at least, that "[i]nstead of crippling the Republican party as Taney had hoped, the *Dred Scott* decision strengthened it by widening the sectional schism among Democrats."[112] Thus, in an ironic twist, Scott may have laid the groundwork for the eventual enactment of the Fourteenth Amendment.

2.   Can Scott *Be Rehabilitated?*

Professor Mark Graber has recently attempted to rehabilitate Taney's opinion in an original and well-researched book, *Dred Scott and the Problem of Constitutional Evil.*[113] Graber's book targets virtually all

---

[111] McPherson, *supra* note 109, at 93.

[112] McPherson, *supra* note 96, at 178.

[113] Mark Graber, Dred Scott *and the Problem of Constitutional Evil* 1 (2006).

present-day critics of Scott, including both Robert Bork and myself.[114] Portions of the book demolish positions that, so far as I can tell, no critic of Scott actually holds. Graber declares, for example, that "[n]o prominent constitutional theory could have ensured perfectly just outcomes during the 1850s."[115] Neither Bork nor I would disagree with this proposition. Bork and I believe that there are better and worse approaches to constitutional interpretation, but we agree with Graber that no approach can guarantee good results or eliminate the possibility of bad ones.

The core of Graber's book, however, is a more interesting claim. He defends Taney's disposition of Scott on the ground that it might have been the most faithful way to preserve the compromises about slavery contained in the original Constitution.[116] In a provocative final chapter, Graber even suggests that constitutionalists should prefer John Bell (one of Abraham Lincoln's rivals in the presidential election of 1860) over Lincoln.[117] Bell's campaign insisted on the importance of preserving the union and avoiding civil war.[118] According to Graber, a principal goal of the Constitution was to preserve peace, and hence Bell may have been more faithful to the Constitution than Lincoln, who (though he said he did not want civil war) was willing to risk war in order to vindicate his view about the immorality of slavery.[119]

Graber's brave book corrects some widespread misconceptions about Scott, and it reminds us that portions of the decision can be defended as legitimate interpretations of a constitution that made unpalatable and ambiguous compromises with slavery. For these reasons, Graber's work now ranks among the books that anyone seriously interested in the case must read. That said, Graber's argument should not lead us to revise the widespread judgment that Scott was a terrible decision.

First, Graber defends a jurisprudential position quite different from the one Taney articulated. Graber concedes that Taney "overreached" when he said that the Constitution explicitly affirmed the right to own slaves; when he said that the Declaration of Independence applied only to the white race; and when he said that free blacks had never been recognized as citizens.[120] On these points, Graber agrees with Lincoln

---

[114] Id. at 24–26 (Bork and other originalists) and 26–28 (myself and other "aspirationalists").

[115] Id. at 85.

[116] Id. at 13–14, 39–45.

[117] Id. at 237–54.

[118] Id. at 240–41.

[119] Id. at 251, 253.

[120] Id. at 68; 56–57; 47–48.

and Taney's modern-day critics. Unlike most of Taney's critics, though, Graber does not seem to think that these mistakes matter very much. For example, Graber's book barely mentions *Scott*'s treatment of the Declaration of Independence. Yet, as we have seen, these passages were crucial to the logic of Taney's opinion, and they were the principal focus of Lincoln's critique. By minimizing the significance of Taney's actual argument, Graber, who likes to accuse *Scott*'s critics of "presentism,"[121] is himself ignoring *Scott*'s historical setting and significance.

Second, Taney's distortions of the constitutional text and history undermine the arguments that Graber constructs in defense of the *Scott* Court. As Graber himself observes, constitutional institutions depend for their success on a commitment to reevaluation and improvement. In Graber's words, "the best justification for constitutional compromises . . . is the belief that human beings are capable of recognizing and abandoning immoral practices when consistently exposed to morally superior ideals and social arrangements."[122] Through its inaccurate descriptions of the Declaration of Independence and the constitutional text, Taney's opinion obscured the principles that (arguably) justified the constitutional compromises about slavery. In particular, Taney implied that the morality or immorality of slavery was irrelevant to the constitutional treatment of it. Taney thereby impaired the capacity of American institutions to cope with the slavery problem. Abraham Lincoln relentlessly attacked Taney's opinion for exactly this reason, and he was correct to do so.

Third, Graber exaggerates the importance of peace and cooperation as constitutional goals. Graber is correct that one purpose of the American Constitution, and of constitutions more generally, is to establish a framework for non-violent political argument about disputed moral questions. Civil war is one form of constitutional failure. But breaches of peace and order are not the only forms of constitutional failure. Constitutions can also have moral goals, and they fail if they cease to serve those goals. That is why most people today believe that Lincoln's position was fully justified: the only way to preserve the Constitution was to insist both on the importance of Union and the immorality of slavery, each of which was indispensible to the Constitution's success.[123]

---

[121] *See, e.g., id.* at 20.

[122] *Id.* at 177–78.

[123] In various places, Graber seems to suggest that Lincoln was simply unfaithful to, or wrong about, basic principles of the antebellum Constitution. *See, e.g., id.* at 13–14, 239. A full answer to this claim is beyond the scope of this short essay. In my view, however, the claim badly underestimates the open-textured and incomplete character of the antebellum Constitution. Indeed, at other points in his argument (when defending Taney rather than

Conclusion

Most people today know *Scott v. Sandford* only through political polemics such as the *"Dred* Again" theory, which—in an effort to impugn the modern Court's privacy jurisprudence—paint *Scott* as dependent upon a substantive construction of the Due Process Clause justified by recourse to (Roger Taney's view of) fundamental values. We can now see that the *"Dred* Again" theory misrepresents *Scott* in at least four ways. First, the crucial question in *Scott* was whether persons can be "property" within the meaning of the Constitution, a question that does not arise in the privacy cases. Second, Taney answered that question by means of a dogmatic originalism that expressly embraced the possibility of unjust results. Taney's originalist reading of the word "property" was the engine that powered *Scott*'s pro-slavery argument. It is therefore wrong to portray Taney's opinion in *Scott* as an example of the risks entailed by fundamental values jurisprudence. Third, both Curtis and McLean opposed Taney's originalism on grounds that implicated natural law. Curtis's methodological credo is consistent with that approach. It is therefore wrong to depict Curtis or McLean as a pure positivist. Fourth, we found no evidence that contemporaneous public condemnation of *Scott* depended upon positivism. On the contrary, the most famous and important critique of the decision, Lincoln's, condemned it in a way that sounds in fundamental values (or simple justice or natural law).

These conclusions may tempt some people to turn the tables on the *"Dred* Again" theorists. Taney's opinion bears the following hallmarks: it is originalist, and it values property no less than liberty. One might seize upon these features of *Scott* to point a finger at originalists who defend property rights. On this view, Robert Bork, Antonin Scalia, and others would be repeating the vices of *Scott*—and so would be guilty of exactly the vice they attribute to their liberal rivals.

That would, however, be a bad argument. Indeed, in spite of all the ink that has been spilled in the battle between originalism and fundamental values, they are, if practiced appropriately, two different jurisprudential paths to the same endpoint.[124] American government aspires to be both democratic and just. To insist that justice and democracy

---

attacking Lincoln), Graber himself insists on the open-textured character of the Constitution. *See, e.g., id.* at 17–18.

[124] In my view, "the Constitution requires Supreme Court justices to construct the people's best judgment about justice; either philosophical argument or historical reflection might aid that task, and which works best is probably a matter of personal style and preference. What matters is not whether judges use historical or philosophical argument, ... but rather that they understand the point of such argument: it should assist judges in their effort to speak about justice on behalf of the people." Eisgruber, *supra* note 47, at 8.

coincide makes heavy but, we may hope, not impossible demands upon
the American people. Until evidence forces us to give up the hope for a
just democracy, the constitutional enterprise compels us to treat that
hope as reasonable. Originalism runs amok when it denies that justice
can teach us about the mind of the people; fundamental values jurisprudence goes awry when it denies that the acts of the people may be a
guide to justice. Taney made originalism's version of that error, not the
fundamental values version of that error, but it does not follow either
that originalism caused the mistake, or that fundamental values jurisprudence could not make a similar mistake. That is not to say that
differences between the paths pursued by originalism and fundamental
values do not matter. The differences matter a great deal when it comes
to selecting the best interpretation of the Constitution.[125] But the distinction between originalism and fundamental values matters very little if
one cares only about avoiding the worst interpretation of the Constitution—about, in other words, avoiding future *Scott v. Sandford*'s.

In the words of the historian David Potter, "the *Dred Scott* decision
was a failure because the justices followed a narrow legalism which led
them into the untenable position of pitting the Constitution against
basic American values, although the Constitution in fact derives its
strength from its embodiment of American values."[126] Taney's sin was
not his embrace of originalism but his indifference to justice. He pledged
himself to a form of originalism that ignored the claims of justice, and he
then used his thoroughly amoral methodology to produce a profoundly
immoral decision.

---

[125] I have argued elsewhere that most forms of originalism are indefensible. Id. at 25–
44.

[126] Potter, *supra* note 40, at 292.

6

Cheryl I. Harris

The Story of *Plessy v. Ferguson*: The Death and Resurrection of Racial Formalism

In 1896 the Supreme Court ruled in *Plessy v. Ferguson* that a Louisiana law mandating segregation of the races on railway cars was constitutionally valid.[1] While some have contended that in its time the decision was an uncontroversial legitimation of the commonplace,[2] *Plessy* is now seen as a landmark decision. As an important if shameful marker of the country's racial past, *Plessy* has achieved the status of an "anticanonical" case,[3] often denounced as a judicial travesty on par with *Dred Scott*.[4] On the prevailing view, *Plessy*'s endorsement of state-imposed

---

[1] 163 U.S. 537 (1896).

[2] According to one account, "the nation's press met the decision mainly with apathy" and the case was largely "invisible," as "within its historical period" it was not "especially controversial." Charles Lofgren, *The* Plessy *Case: A Legal Historical Interpretation* 5 (1987). This view of the case has been criticized: "[Lofgren] overemphasiz[es] the influence of scientific racism at the time and leav[es] the impression that its hegemony was uncontested. Recent overviews of Reconstruction historiography have suggested that we have not fully understood the fate of the egalitarian ideals of Reconstruction." Mark Elliott, *Race, Color Blindness, and the Democratic Public: Albion W. Tourgée's Radical Principles in* Plessy v. Ferguson, 67 J. S. Hist. 287, 291 n.10 (2001).

[3] An anticanonical case "is regularly pointed to as an example of bad constitutional interpretation." Paul Brest & Sanford Levinson, *Processes of Constitutional Decisionmaking* 207 (4th ed. 2000).

[4] *Dred Scott v. Sandford*, 60 U.S. 393 (1857). Indeed, this comparison is invoked in the case itself in Justice Harlan's dissent: "In my opinion, the judgment this day rendered [upholding the Separate Car Act] will, in time, prove to be quite as pernicious as the decision made by this tribunal in the *Dred Scott* case." *Plessy*, 163 U.S. at 559 (Harlan, J.,

racial caste, like *Dred Scott's* rejection of Blacks[5] as citizens of the nation,[6] represents a racial logic long since repudiated.[7]

However, unlike *Dred Scott*, *Plessy* appears to have one saving virtue: Justice Harlan's solitary dissent denounced the majority's endorsement of de jure segregation as a "thin disguise" through which the suppression of Blacks was legitimated and maintained.[8] On one view, the genius of Harlan's dissent was its prescience: Even at a time when Black subordination was viewed as part of the natural order, Harlan condemned state-compelled segregation as a system of racial caste that was inconsistent with the constitutional grant of national citizenship under the Reconstruction Amendments.[9] Thus understood, *Plessy* represents both an egregious endorsement of racial oppression as well as the promise of rectification as prefigured in Harlan's dissent.

Thus, despite universal repudiations of *Plessy's* holding, the case is far from dead: Through Harlan's dissent, the case has become the source of the most salient racial metaphor in contemporary society. Justice Harlan's assertion that "[o]ur constitution is color-blind"[10] is the mantra of current racial politics and discourse, heavily influencing modern day constitutional jurisprudence as well as how we think and talk about race.

---

dissenting); *see* Robert J. Harris, *The Quest for Equality: The Constitution, Congress and the Supreme Court* 101 (1960) (arguing that the decision was "a compound of bad logic, bad history, bad sociology, and bad constitutional law").

[5] *See* Kimberlé W. Crenshaw, *Race, Reform, and Retrenchment: Transformation and Legitimation in Antidiscrimination Law*, 101 Harv. L. Rev. 1331, 1332 n.2 (1988) ("Blacks, like Asians, Latinos, and other 'minorities,' constitute a specific cultural group and, as such, require denotation as a proper noun.").

[6] Specifically the questions were (1) whether Scott could sue in federal court on diversity grounds, and (2) whether Congress had the power to regulate slavery in the territories. According to the Court, the answer to both questions was no. *See Dred Scott*, 60 U.S. at 393, 454.

[7] *Brown v. Board of Education*, 347 U.S. 483 (1954), categorically denounced the notion that with reference to public education, separate could ever be equal under the Constitution. *See id.* at 494–95. Nevertheless, while *Brown* clearly rejected state-imposed segregation in public education, it did not specifically rule on the constitutionality of racial classifications per se. *See* Brook Thomas, *In the Wake of* Plessy, *in* Plessy v. Ferguson: *A Brief History with Documents* 172 (Brook Thomas ed., 1997) ("The Court in *Brown* avoided the question of whether racial classifications were inherently unconstitutional.").

[8] *Plessy*, 163 U.S. at 562 (Harlan, J., dissenting).

[9] After *Brown* was decided in 1954, a *New York Times* editorial stated that "the words [Harlan] used in his lonely dissent ... have become in effect ... a part of the law of the land.... [T]here was not one word in Chief Justice Warren's opinion that was inconsistent with the earlier views of Justice Harlan." Editorial, *Justice Harlan Concurring*, N.Y. Times, May 23, 1954, § 4, at E10, *quoted in* Lofgren, *supra* note 2, at 204.

[10] *Plessy*, 163 U.S. at 559 (Harlan, J., dissenting).

Indeed, under current constitutional doctrine, the general prohibition on governmental consideration of race is grounded in a normative preference for colorblindness; accordingly, any state recognition of racial distinctions is inherently suspect, irrespective of context and purpose.[11] Harlan rejected the blind formalism of *Plessy*'s majority that recast the regime of *de jure* segregation as equal treatment.

Yet, ironically, the colorblind terms on which that formalism was condemned then have become the predicate of a new formalism now embodied in current equal protection doctrine as well as legislative initiatives that seek to ban all considerations of race from public policy, even as part of remedial plans to rectify racial effects.[12] As to constitutional analysis, a majority of the Court has embraced a view of race largely disconnected from history and social meaning. While some mem-

---

[11] This is so even though the Court has allowed that some compelling state interests may justify an exception to the general prohibition against state considerations of race. *See Grutter v. Bollinger*, 123 S.Ct. 2325, 2338 (2003) ("Although all governmental uses of race are subject to strict scrutiny, not all are invalidated by it."). Thus, I do not contend that colorblindness and strict scrutiny are synonymous. Nevertheless, in declaring that all governmental uses of race are suspect and subject to strict scrutiny, current doctrine strongly disfavors even remedial efforts that take account of race. In this sense it embraces colorblindness as a normative ideal even as it allows for narrowly carved exceptions.

[12] Among the examples here would be the so-called California Civil Rights Initiative which barred the state from "discriminat[ing] against, or grant[ing] preferential treatment to, any individual or group on the basis of race, sex, color, ethnicity, or national origin in the operation of public employment, public education, or public contracting." California Civil Rights Initiative, Proposition 209 (adopted Nov. 5, 1996) (codified at Cal. Const. art. I, § 31). Similar measures were adopted in Washington State, Michigan, and most recently in Nebraska. *See* The Washington State Civil Rights Act, Initiative Measure 200 (approved Nov. 3, 1998; effective Dec. 3, 1998) (codified at Wash. Rev. Code § 49.60.400); The Michigan Civil Rights Initiative, Proposal 2 (approved Nov. 7, 2006; effective Dec. 22, 2006) (codified at Mich. Const. art. 1, § 26); The Nebraska Civil Rights Initiative, Proposal 424 (approved Nov. 4, 2008; effective Dec. 10, 2008) (codified at Neb. Const. art. I, § 30). Voters barely rejected an identical proposal in Colorado. The Colorado Civil Rights Initiative, Amendment 46, which would have amended the Colorado Constitution by adding Section 31 of Article II, was defeated by slightly more than one percentage point. *See* Dan Frosch, *Vote Results Are Mixed On a Ban On Preference*, N.Y. Times., Nov. 8, 2008, at A19. Other anti-affirmative action initiatives failed to qualify for the ballot in Missouri, Oklahoma, and Arizona. The Missouri Civil Rights Initiative (also known as Missouri Ballot Measure 009) failed to collect enough signatures on the petition by the deadline. *See* Kavita Kumar, *Missouri Petition Drive Falls Short*, St. Louis Post Dispatch, May 6, 2008, at D1. The Oklahoma State Question 737 or Civil Rights Initiative similarly did not garner sufficient qualifying signatures. *See* Barbara Hoberock, *Affirmative Action Ban Scuttled*, Tulsa World, Apr. 5, 2008, at A13. The Arizona Civil Rights Initiative, Prop. 104, was disqualified from the ballot because of failure to submit enough valid signatures. *See* Matthew Benson and Glen Creno, *Affirmative–Action Initiative Fails to Make Ballot*, Arizona Republic, Aug. 22, 2008, at 1. Efforts to extend the principle of colorblindness further include the California Racial Privacy Initiative, which sought to ban the state from collecting any data based on race. *See* California Racial Privacy Initiative, Proposition 54 (defeated Oct. 7, 2003).

bers of the majority have been unwilling to espouse the more stark expressions of colorblindness staked out by Justices Scalia, Thomas, and now Alito, the general consensus is that strict scrutiny should apply to all uses of race because, absent extraordinary circumstances, race does not and normatively should not matter. Just as *Plessy* reconfigured the asymmetrical relationship between Black and white as equality—there was no constitutional violation because Blacks and whites were equally subject to a rule of exclusion—the current majority treats race as a category devoid of any social significance such that Black and white are once again functionally the same.

This has produced particularly corrosive legal and practical effects. First, equal protection is deemed to require only equal treatment even under conditions of actual inequality.[13] The result is that, as in *Plessy*, most racial inequality is placed outside the reach of law as it is either deemed to be the product of private choices, not public power, or is determined not to constitute a constitutionally cognizable harm. Second, while *Brown* is generally hailed as the cure for the injury inflicted by *Plessy*, the majority's insistence that the remedies adopted to correct the harms of segregation are constitutionally equivalent to segregation itself threatens to eviscerate *Brown* and reinstall the formalist precepts of *Plessy*. In *Parents Involved in Community Schools v. Seattle School District No. 1,* the Supreme Court ruled that local school districts could not undertake voluntary race-conscious school student assignment plans, even where a similar plan had been previously judicially mandated to rectify school segregation.[14] According to the majority, the districts' primary and secondary school desegregation plans were constitutionally infirm because they did not meet the test of strict scrutiny—the plans were neither justified by a compelling governmental interest nor clearly necessary.[15] On this view not only is integration not constitutionally compelled; it is not constitutionally permissible if it takes account of race in assigning students. In effect the opinion treats school desegregation— a remedy implemented under and required by *Brown*—as an "unfair racial preference."[16] While *Parents Involved* does not endorse de jure segregation like *Plessy*, the majority opinion echoes *Plessy*'s logic in finding that the school boards' actions were unjustified because current forms of school segregation were not a constitutionally cognizable

---

[13] *See generally* Cheryl I. Harris, *Equal Treatment and the Reproduction of Inequality*, 69 Fordham L. Rev. 1753 (2001).

[14] *Parents Involved in Comm. Schls. v. Seattle Schl. Dist. No. 1*, 127 S.Ct. 2738 (2007).

[15] *Id.* at 2752–53.

[16] *Id.* at 2767 (querying "What do the racial classifications here at issue do if not accord differential treatment on the basis of race?").

harm.[17] Indeed, the only relevant injury was that suffered by white parents whose preferences were not accommodated in the school boards' imposition of a desegregation plan. In each instance the Court rejected the claim that extant forms of discrimination constituted injuries that warranted any remedy. Indeed, according to Chief Justice Roberts in *Parents Involved*, the answer to systemic patterns of racial disadvantage is tautologically clear: "The way to stop discrimination on the basis of race is to stop discriminating on the basis of race."[18]

Thus, this chapter considers *Plessy* not so much as a sign of what is past but as a window into the present. *Plessy*'s legacy has been little understood beyond the rhetorical gloss of colorblindness. Indeed, *Plessy*'s teachings about the meanings and conception of race are considered gone and buried. In point of fact, the continuities between the racial reasoning of *Plessy* and current debates about race suggest that while the particular form of racial formalism espoused by *Plessy* has been discredited, racial formalism has been resurrected through the template crafted by the case. *Plessy*'s presumptions may be less visible, but they are still with us, with similar corrosive effect.

I begin by exploring what I call *Plessy*'s racial antecedents because part of coming to terms with *Plessy*'s present impact requires confronting the broader historical context out of which the case emerged. *Plessy* is not simply the antecedent to *Brown* nor is it merely a poorly justified decision endorsing a bad law. The story of *Plessy* is the story of race segregation in the United States. This story reveals that segregation was both private and public, political and social, the product of both law and custom. In Southern society, segregation came to be understood as normative and necessary, "what should be and what must be." Even more, segregation's meaning transcended its regional variations. Through *Plessy*, segregation became a nation-building project, an expansion of the modern regulatory state and a means of further consolidating the national identity as white. Understanding segregation in this way helps to disclose what was at stake in the case for the Supreme Court, the litigants, their allies, and the country as a whole. It also sheds some light on the conundrums of the present.

The Relentless Career of Jim Crow

Formal race segregation in the United States has a long history: It was widely practiced, vigorously contested, and imposed both by custom and by law. It is important to see segregation within this matrix of custom, resistance, and law and not as a function of law alone, as

---

[17] *Id.*

[18] *Id.*

"[s]egregation often anticipated and frequently exceeded the law."[19] Segregation functioned at the level of the material and the symbolic: as rationale, as law, as private conduct, as a "natural order" that was constantly under construction and frequently resisted. Segregation both reflected and produced the internal contradictions of a society simultaneously committed to abstract notions of equality and racial hierarchy. Segregation enacted byzantine rituals that regulated the smallest detail of social encounters as well as the most intimate aspects of daily life—where one could sleep, walk, bathe, relieve oneself, live, or die. It also functioned at the level of ideology and political economy, setting the terms of social and political discourse and determining the contours of the nation and the political community bound and protected by the Constitution.

Segregation was not monolithic. Broad historical forces shaped the forms and specifics of segregation such that it differed regionally and over time. Nevertheless, roughly three broad periods can be identified: antebellum segregation, largely an urban phenomenon; Reconstruction, a period of crisis and contestation; and Post–Reconstruction or Redemption, in which segregation was further consolidated as law. The law at issue in *Plessy* was a product of the last period, beginning approximately in 1887, in which de jure segregation in public conveyances and accommodations intensified. Understanding the law's purpose, form, and effect requires some exploration of what preceded it.

Before Emancipation

In the antebellum South, formal segregation was neither possible nor required to maintain racial hierarchy within a functioning slave-based economy.[20] Indeed, the system of slavery "made separation of the races for the most part impracticable,"[21] as constant vigilance over an exploited, recalcitrant, and potentially restive work force was required. Control was direct, immediate, and often violent and coercive. Segregation was especially incongruous for domestic servants, as the very nature of the work required close and intimate contact between the races.

Even during slavery, however, the proximity of the races, and particularly the presence of free Blacks in urban environments,[22] where

---

[19] C. Vann Woodward, *The Strange Career of Jim Crow*, at xiii (3rd ed. 2002) [hereinafter Woodward, *Strange Career*].

[20] *See* W.E.B. Du Bois, *The Souls of Black Folk* 183 (1903).

[21] Woodward, *Strange Career*, *supra* note 19, at 12.

[22] *See* Richard C. Wade, *Slavery in the Cities: The South, 1820–1860* (1964) (noting that "[i]n every city in Dixie, blacks and whites lived side by side, sharing the same

the boundaries of class and race could not be directly policed,[23] heightened anxieties about "amalgamation" and fueled regulation of all forms of social contact and political access: Blacks were excluded from public buildings such as hospitals, from public conveyances, and from public accommodations such as hotels and restaurants.[24] They were further restricted from moving freely or owning weapons, and were excluded from certain trades.[25] At the same time that segregation emerged as an urban phenomenon, residential segregation in Southern cities was relatively unknown through the end of slavery and even for a period shortly thereafter.[26] This stood in marked contrast to entrenched and severe housing segregation in the North.[27]

Antebellum segregation in the South was not without its exceptions. Some light skinned Blacks attained privileged status, although one still inferior to whites. Regional distinctions among different areas of the South were apparent, though virtually all states were consistent in imposing an inferior status on free Blacks relative to whites.[28] Although New Orleans was noted for its fancy balls and other public social spaces reserved for racialized sexual encounters, virtually all Southern cities included a kind of underground "demimonde" where whites engaged in social "play" with Blacks.[29]

Moreover, segregation was deeply entrenched and highly evolved in the North. Not only was "racial prejudice ... all but universal in antebellum northern society," Black men were excluded from the fran-

---

premises if not equal facilities and living constantly in each other's presence"), *quoted in* Woodward, *Strange Career, supra* note 19, at 14. The vast majority of the population, white and Black, lived in rural areas. *See id.* at 16–17. However, by 1860, around 220,000 free Blacks resided in the North and over 260,000 free people of color lived in the south, most in urban areas. *See* John Hope Franklin, *From Slavery to Freedom: A History of American Negroes* 215 (2d ed. 1956).

[23] *See* C. Vann Woodward, *Strange Career Critics: Long May They Preserve*, 75 J. Am. Hist. 857, 858–59 (1988) (arguing that segregation was an impersonal regulatory regime developed to supplement direct control of whites over Blacks).

[24] When Blacks were permitted access, they were assigned to separate facilities. *See* Woodward, *Strange Career, supra* note 19, at 13–14.

[25] Ira Berlin, *Slaves Without Masters: The Free Negro in the Antebellum South* 316–17 (1974).

[26] *See* Woodward, *Strange Career, supra* note 19, at 14.

[27] *Id*. at 19.

[28] *See* Berlin, *supra* note 25, at 317.

[29] *See* Woodward, *Strange Career, supra* note 19, at 15. While sexual relations between the races were often fraught with exploitation, in working class neighborhoods of Southern cities proscriptions on interracial intimacy were frequently violated. *See* Berlin, *supra* note 25, at 265.

chise in all but five New England states and were "confined to menial occupations and subjected to constant discrimination."[30] Racial restrictions on jury service and testimonial bans on Black witnesses were also pervasive. Racial separation was systemic, by custom and by law demarcating racial lines in every field of human existence. Indeed, Blacks "were often educated in segregated schools, punished in segregated prisons, nursed in segregated hospitals, and buried in segregated cemeteries."[31]

Racial exclusion was the practice in the West, as several states not only banned Blacks from public schools but also barred Blacks from entering the boundaries of the state.[32] In states in which slavery had been abolished, virulent racial animus and discrimination were no less evident than in the South and in some respects were more severe.[33] Segregation was sufficiently entrenched that by the late 1830s it had acquired a formal name—Jim Crow.[34]

Segregation in Transportation

Segregated transit was common in both the North and the South. Even before the Civil War, the subordinate status of Blacks was marked by their exclusion from or limited access to modes of public transportation.[35] To the extent that Blacks traveled by public transit, for the most part they were treated as appendages of their masters, permitted access only to the extent that their services were required and then assigned to inferior facilities designated for servants. Free Blacks were in no better position: When they were permitted to ride, they were often forced to quarters such as baggage cars or steamboat decks. This pattern was also

---

[30] Eric Foner, *Free Soil, Free Labor, Free Men: The Ideology of the Republican Party Before the Civil War* 261 (1970) [hereinafter Foner, *Ideology of the Republican Party*].

[31] Leon F. Litwack, *North of Slavery: The Negro in the Free States, 1790–1860*, at 97 (1961).

[32] Foner, *Ideology of the Republican Party*, *supra* note 30, at 261. Where Blacks were not banned outright, they were often required to post bond guaranteeing good behavior. Woodward, *Strange Career*, *supra* note 19, at 20.

[33] Woodward, *Strange Career*, *supra* note 19, at 19 (noting that "the farther west the Negro went in the free states the harsher he found the proscription and segregation").

[34] According to Woodward, the term Jim Crow has its origins in a song and dance performed by Thomas D. Rice in 1832. *Id.* at 7. The lyrics of the song were "Wheel about and turn about and jump Jim Crow." *Jim Crow, in* 8 *The Oxford English Dictionary* 239 (2d ed. 1989).

[35] *See* Barbara Welke, *Recasting American Liberty: Gender, Race, Law, and the Railroad Revolution, 1865–1920*, at 255 (2001) [hereinafter Welke, *Recasting American Liberty*].

true in the North.[36] On occasion, some of the few Blacks who by wealth or privilege of skin color had attained "special" status were allowed access to accommodations reserved for whites, albeit with qualifications. For example, wealthy Black Louisiana planters who were granted access to first-class cabins on steamboats were not allowed to interact with white passengers.[37]

Steamboats were by far the most rigidly segregated form of public conveyances. In part, this reflected the fact that steamboats were also sharply divided by class, with lavish first-class accommodations in the form of staterooms, ladies' parlors, and men's smoking rooms far removed from the deck where cargo and the "lesser" classes were kept.[38] On the deck, not only were there no separate quarters for men and women, no bathing facilities, and no meals, deck passengers were also in close proximity to the boiler and were most at risk of injury from explosions and accidents.[39]

Railway travel did not have the same division of class as in Europe, but as early as the 1840s railroads had designated "ladies' cars" and "smoking cars." Ladies' cars, reserved for ladies and their male companions, were typically at the rear of the train, the safest and the cleanest part, and were fitted like a ladies' parlor complete with water closets and sofas or covered seats. Rude and boisterous conduct was not permitted. While the passengers in both the smokers' car and the ladies' cars paid the same fare, the accommodations in the smoker were markedly different; there were wooden seats and spittoons—in general, bare bones facilities designed to allow men to smoke, drink, chew tobacco, spit, and behave without constraints.[40]

Streetcars "came the closest to being 'classless.' "[41] In part, this is because they functioned as pure conveyances, unlike steamboats and railways where the rituals of everyday life—eating, sleeping, and personal hygiene—were recreated. The threat of intimacy then pervaded the demand for stratification. The carriers catered to the preferences and anxieties of middle and upper class passengers, the majority of travelers on steamboats and railroads, while streetcars, the conveyances for the working class, were not separated by sex or by classes of accommodations. Of course, this did not mean that there was no discrimination:

---

[36] *Id.*

[37] *Id.* at 256.

[38] *Id.* at 252–53.

[39] *Id.*

[40] *Id.* at 255.

[41] *Id.* at 256.

Blacks were often excluded from riding altogether or were not allowed in the interior of the cars.[42]

Even before Emancipation these racial exclusions were vigorously resisted. Frederick Douglass, among others, defied the segregated railway cars on a Massachusetts rail line; Douglass was forcibly removed after refusing to go to the Jim Crow car. In Douglass's view, these "ride-ins" were an important part of a campaign of focusing public attention on segregation and publicly shaming the companies for their practices.[43] By 1843 the railroads in Massachusetts were desegregated.[44]

The Civil War and Reconstruction

By 1865 resistance to streetcar segregation through similar tactics led to the elimination of segregation in Boston, New York, Chicago, and Baltimore.[45] In Washington, D.C., Sojourner Truth repeatedly insisted on riding the horse cars and sitting where she chose. On one occasion Truth was dragged by a streetcar when the conductor picked up her white companion but pulled off as Truth attempted to board; on another, she was assaulted by a conductor when she refused to leave. In both instances, when she reported the incident to the company president, the conductors were dismissed and, in the latter case, she successfully sued the conductor for assault.[46] By these "ride-ins" Truth and a host of other insistent Black residents repeatedly tested the boundaries of racial regulation of the streetcars. As a result, by 1866, segregation on the Washington streetcars had ended.[47]

In the wake of the War and Emancipation, "carriers simply carved a space for Black passengers from the already defined physical space."[48] Steamboats, as the most rigidly segregated public conveyances, reallocated space set aside for second-class passengers or freight, creating the "colored cabin" or the "freedmen's bureau." Some railroads assigned all Blacks—women and men—to the smoking car, the rough equivalent of second-class accommodations. In Virginia, because Blacks were assigned to second-class cars no matter what fare they paid, some Blacks argued

---

[42] *Id*. at 257.

[43] *See* Carleton Mabee, *Sojourner Truth: Slave, Prophet, Legend* 130 (1993).

[44] *See* Woodward, *Strange Career, supra* note 19, at 19.

[45] Mabee, *supra* note 43, at 130.

[46] *Id*. at 133–34. By then Truth was a renowned abolitionist who was known to have influential contacts, and the case attracted a great deal of attention. *Id*.

[47] *Id*. at 133–35.

[48] Welke, *Recasting American Liberty, supra* note 35, at 259.

for the use of separate cars as a way of securing better accommodations.[49] As Booker T. Washington noted, "[I]t is not the separation that
we complain of, but the unequality of accommodations."[50] Some lines
offered the option of separate compartments by partitioning the smoking
car. Other rail carriers solved the problem by offering a second-class
fare—the only ticket the majority of Blacks could afford. Of course, this
meant that Black passengers rode in the company of white men; indeed,
"these practices did not segregate all people of color from all whites; they
segregated most people of color from white ladies."[51]

None of these arrangements offered to Blacks accommodations in
any way equal to those reserved for whites. The conditions were particularly problematic for Black women and children, who were forced to ride
in dirty, smoke-filled cars where all forms of coarse behavior were
customary.[52] Placing Black women in the second-class cars did not simply
expose them to symbolic or dignitary harm; given prevailing social
norms, it put them at risk of sexual assault. While the policy of racial
separation was often justified on the grounds of protecting white women
from Black men's lust, subjecting Black women to encounters with white
men in smoking cars was treated as unproblematic despite the long-
standing practice of white male sexual violation of Black women.[53]

Given the uncertain boundaries between race and gender as reflected in the spatial arrangements on rail carriers, it is unsurprising
that enforcement was uneven and arbitrary, with Black women on
occasion being allowed and then later denied access to ladies' cars on the
same line. These inconsistent practices provided fertile ground for litigation.[54] In response, railways denied that the facilities were inferior and

---

[49] See Lofgren, *supra* note 2, at 13 (noting that a Black legislator introduced legislation
calling for the creation of separate but equal facilities in order to secure improvements).

[50] Booker T. Washington, A Speech Delivered Before the Women's New England Club
(Jan. 27, 1889 [1890]), *in* 3 *The Booker T. Washington Papers* 25, 27–38 (Louis R. Harlan
ed., 1974).

[51] Welke, *Recasting American Liberty, supra* note 35, at 276.

[52] See *id.* at 260–61; *see also* Lofgren, *supra* note 2, at 16.

[53] See Welke, *Recasting American Liberty, supra* note 35, at 319–20.

[54] *Id.* at 261–62. Indeed, the majority of cases challenging this form of segregation were
brought by Black women. *See* Barbara Y. Welke, *When All the Women Were White, and All
the Blacks Were Men: Gender, Class, Race, and the Road to* Plessy, *1855–1914*, 13 Law &
Hist. Rev. 261, 268 (1995) [hereinafter Welke, *Road to* Plessy]. Among the litigants was Ida
B. Wells, renowned journalist and leader of the anti-lynching campaign. *Id.* at 270 n.34,
281. In Louisiana, a sufficient number of challenges were successful that white businesses
became cautious about violating equal accommodations laws. *See* Lofgren, *supra* note 2, at
20.

endeavored to focus attention on the reasonableness of the rules rather than the capricious nature of their enforcement.[55]

These inconsistencies were further exacerbated in the upheaval that attended the Civil War, the formal end of slavery, and Reconstruction; the old racial order was violently disturbed even as continued white control remained the prevailing assumption.[56] The end of slavery clearly triggered deep anxiety about the shifting legal and social status of Blacks. Indeed, it could be said that "the value of white skin dropped when black skin ceased to signify slave status."[57] According to some historians, the radical disruption produced by Emancipation was so severe as to trigger the rapid development of rigid forms of racial separation to take the place of slavery.[58]

Forces committed to enforcing the inferior status of Blacks survived the war; at the same time resistance to subordination intensified in many quarters. On the one hand, by 1866 provisional legislatures in states like Mississippi, Florida, and Texas adopted a series of Black Codes, based on the extensive set of social norms and laws that had been developed to regulate and secure the subordinate position of free Blacks before the Civil War and the end of slavery. These imposed far-reaching restrictions on Black voting, jury service, land ownership and occupancy, and freedom of movement.[59] The end of slavery threatened white hegemony and the control of labor; thus, many statutes required freed Blacks to produce written evidence of employment or license to work upon pain of arrest and fines.[60] Under the guise of protection, the law enacted a form of labor conscription for Black minors through the involuntary apprenticeship of Black children "whose parents have not the means, or who refuse to provide and support said minors."[61] The cumulative effect of these laws was to re-impose slavery in another form, virtually rendering the Thirteenth Amendment a dead letter.

On the other hand, opposition to this repression provided the impetus for congressional reform and prompted the enactment of the 1866 Civil Rights Act guaranteeing to Blacks the right to contract, to own land, and "to full and equal benefit of all laws and proceedings for

---

[55] Welke, *Road to* Plessy, *supra* note 54, at 262.

[56] *See* Woodward, *Strange Career, supra* note 19, at 22–23.

[57] Eva Saks, *Representing Miscegenation Law*, Raritan Rev., Fall 1988, at 39, 47.

[58] *See generally* Joel Williamson, *After Slavery: The Negro in South Carolina During Reconstruction, 1861–1877* (1965). *But see* Woodward, *Strange Career, supra* note 19, at 25.

[59] *See* Theodore Brantner Wilson, *The Black Codes of the South* 41 (1965).

[60] *Id*. at 66.

[61] *Id*. at 67.

the security of the person and property, as is enjoyed by white citizens.''[62] The bill, along with a host of other Reconstruction acts, was vetoed by President Johnson, triggering a move to impeach him. Though Johnson survived impeachment by one vote, under the leadership of the Radical Republicans Congress overrode Johnson's vetoes.[63] The South was placed under military control and federal authority supervised the creation of state constitutional conventions to create new state governments, as well as the registration of Black voters.[64]

Shortly after the adoption of the Civil Rights Act of 1866, the Fourteenth Amendment was proposed and vigorously debated.[65] The open textured language of the amendment prohibiting the states from denying any person "equal protection of the laws" was an invitation for competing interpretations. Some congressmen argued that the amendment did no more than provide the constitutional foundation for the Civil Rights Act. Others claimed that in barring a state from abridging "the privileges and immunities of citizens of the United States" the amendment was dangerously vague, permitting not only school integration but raising the dread specter of "amalgamation."[66] Presaging the distinctions drawn in *Plessy*, Republican stalwarts denied that equality in civil rights for freedmen barred anti-miscegenation laws since such laws imposed equal prohibitions on Blacks and whites.[67]

As additional states came under Republican control, or congressionally authorized governments took office, equal accommodations laws were adopted.[68] Yet, at the same time that Reconstruction governments sought to undo long entrenched patterns of customary segregation, public school segregation was widespread and sanctioned under some of those very governments.[69] The most significant and relevant exception for the purposes of this story is New Orleans, where public schools were integrated until 1877.[70]

---

[62] Civil Rights Act of 1866, ch. 31, § 1, 14 Stat. 27, 27 (codified as amended at 42 U.S.C. § 1981(a) (2000)).

[63] *See* Eric Foner, *Reconstruction: America's Unfinished Revolution, 1863–1877*, at 271–76 (1988) [hereinafter Foner, *Reconstruction*].

[64] *See id.* at 276–77.

[65] *See id.* at 251–61, 267.

[66] *See* Cong. Globe, 39th Cong., 1st Sess. 134 (1866).

[67] *See* Lofgren, *supra* note 2, at 65 (quoting Sen. Lynam Trumbull, sponsor of the Freedmen's Bureau Bill).

[68] See *id.* at 18–19.

[69] Woodward, *Strange Career*, *supra* note 19, at 24–25.

[70] *Id.* at 24.

After Reconstruction: Redemption and Reaction

The formal demise of Reconstruction came in 1877 with the compromise that resolved the deadlock over the presidential election of 1876 in favor of Rutherford B. Hayes, the Republican candidate, over Samuel J. Tilden, the Democratic candidate and apparent winner of the popular vote. Democratic support for Hayes was secured in exchange for a Republican agreement to withdraw federal troops from the South, to permit popularly elected Democratic governors to take office in the three states still under Republican control (the same states in which the returns were disputed), and, most critically, to leave the question of freed Blacks to the Southern states.[71] Redefinition of the status of former slaves became a matter of "states' rights" and "home rule," not federal law.[72] Following the withdrawal of federal troops from the South and the collapse of Republican state legislatures, Black subordination was solidified under newly elected Democratic regimes, through material and symbolic exclusions as well as organized racist violence. Blacks and their dwindling allies vigorously resisted and struggled to retain hard won rights of equal access. Louisiana was a particularly intense battleground on several fronts in which there were temporary victories as well as reversals.

In New Orleans private streetcar companies maintained a system of segregation in which cars for Blacks—fewer than one-fourth of the total—were marked with a star.[73] Black protest was longstanding and by 1865 dissatisfaction with the Star Cars was manifest; as one editorial put it, "our exclusion from the 'white cars' is a brand put upon us, and a relic of slavery that ought not to be tolerated."[74] It was particularly intolerable in the context of the times: Black union officers were unable to ride on streetcars occupied by their own white soldiers.[75] At times, Black passengers refused to board the Star Cars and attempted to board cars occupied by whites, with varying degrees of success.[76] Complaints to the military authorities produced demands on the streetcar company to

---

[71] *See id.* at 6.

[72] *See* Foner, *Reconstruction*, *supra* note 63, at 580–81.

[73] Letter from New Orleans City Railroad Company to Col. C.W. Killborn (Aug. 3, 1864), *in The Thin Disguise: Turning Point in Negro History* 31, 31–32 (Otto H. Olsen ed., 1967).

[74] Editorial, New Orleans Trib., Feb. 28, 1865, *in* Olsen, *supra* note 73, at 33, 33.

[75] *Id.*

[76] An editorial in the local paper denounced such efforts as attempts to provoke a riot. Editorial, New Orleans Times, May 7, 1867, *in* Olsen, *supra* note 73, at 33, 34–35.

explain and justify its policies.[77] The company was forced to admit it "kn[e]w of no fact that justified such regulations except the custom and usage of this City and the prejudices of the people."[78] Despite adverse court rulings, unrelenting opposition to the Star Car system finally resulted in its demise: In May of 1867, General Phil Sheridan issued an order ending it.[79] Segregation on streetcars in New Orleans effectively disappeared until the end of the nineteenth century.[80]

With respect to public schools, the story was less successful. The state constitution of 1868 that provided for the creation of public schools required them to admit students without regard to race.[81] Despite determined resistance, evasion by the local school board and white leaders, and boycotts, the schools in New Orleans were eventually integrated as white parents found private schools too expensive and the price of resistance—the continued presence of federal troops—intolerable.[82] The beginning of the end of this experiment came in 1874 with the rise of violent white resistance under the leadership of the White League, which nearly overthrew the state government and began a campaign of violence and intimidation against students and teachers in the integrated schools. While schools reopened in 1875 on an integrated basis, after the Hayes–Tilden compromise of 1876 and the withdrawal of federal troops from Louisiana, a newly elected Democratic state government actively pursued re-segregation of the schools.[83] These efforts were vehemently resisted by many Blacks, including a delegation led by Aristide Mary, a prominent member of the Creole community, and Paul Trévigne, the editor of a militant bilingual Creole newspaper. Trévigne filed suit alleging in his brief that racial segregation in the public schools "works an irreparable injury to the entire colored population of the city in that it tends to degrade them as citizens by discriminating against them on account of race and color."[84] The suit was dismissed on

---

[77] See Letter from New Orleans City Railroad Company to Col. C.W. Killborn, *supra* note 73, at 31–32.

[78] *Id.* at 32.

[79] Woodward, *Strange Career, supra* note 19, at 27.

[80] Keith Weldon Medley, *Black New Orleans,* Am. Legacy Mag., Summer 2000.

[81] See Liva Baker, *The Second Battle of New Orleans: The Hundred–Year Struggle to Integrate the Schools* 19–20 (1996).

[82] *Id.* at 21–22.

[83] *Id.* at 24–25.

[84] *Id.* at 28.

technical grounds, clearly reflecting the court's unwillingness to intervene.[85]

Despite the fact that the Louisiana Constitution of 1868 provided that all public conveyances and businesses "shall be opened to the accommodation and patronage of all persons, without distinction or discrimination on account of race or color,"[86] by 1890 Louisiana followed the emergent trend towards de jure segregation in railway transportation. Between 1887 and 1892, nine states enacted laws requiring separation of the races on railways and public conveyances.[87] Though they differed in details and requirements, most of the statutes of this period required equal but separate accommodations, and imposed fines and jail terms for railroad employees who failed to comply with the assignment requirement.[88] Of the nine statutes, five imposed criminal fines or imprisonment on non-compliant passengers.[89]

A number of theories have been advanced that seek to explain the proliferation of segregation laws in this period. C. Vann Woodward's highly influential work argued that pervasive legal segregation in the South was not a feature of the immediate post Civil War era.[90] Conceding that there was much segregation that existed by custom and practice, as well as intense racial violence as reflected in the steady increase in the number and frequency of lynchings,[91] Woodward noted that even after the end of Reconstruction in 1877, over ten years passed before the first Jim Crow law was enacted in the South, with similar laws appearing in the older southeastern states more than two decades later.[92] While some

---

[85] *Id.* The Louisiana Supreme Court held that Trévigne's suit to enjoin the New Orleans school district from racially dividing the schools could not be allowed, as the school board had already taken the action sought to be enjoined. *See Trévigne v. School Board*, 31 La. Ann. 105 (1879).

[86] La. Const. of 1868, art. XIII.

[87] For a summary of the provisions of the laws of this period, see Lofgren, *supra* note 2, at 18–23. For example, Florida's law regulated first-class service only and required the sale of first-class tickets to "respectable persons of color" and that they be provided with separate accommodations equal to those for whites. *Id.* at 22. Tennessee, the first state to enact legislation mandating segregation on an equal but separate formula, required the railroads to provide separate cars or partitioned cars in which "all colored passengers who pay first-class passenger rates of fare, may have the privilege to enter and occupy, and such apartments shall be kept in good repair, and with the conveniences, and subject to the same rules governing other first-class cars." *Id.* at 21. The requirement that the separate facilities be equal was generally ignored. *Id.*

[88] *Id.* at 22.

[89] *Id.*

[90] *See* C. Vann Woodward, *American Counterpoint: Slavery and Racism in the North–South Dialogue* 237 (1971).

[91] *Id.* at 43 (noting the dramatic rise in numbers of lynchings).

[92] *Id.* at 34.

have contested Woodward's claim with evidence of widespread customary and legal segregation before the War,[93] it is generally accepted that the period around 1890 marked a significant increase in the turn to legislatively mandated racial segregation.[94]

Woodward argued that systemic de jure segregation did not immediately follow the end of Reconstruction because the rigid segregationist line was but one of several political options for resolving the "place of the Negro" that emerged from the radically changed racial conditions following the Civil War. For example, the elitist conservative camp of the Democratic Party initially opposed de jure segregation even as it firmly held to views of Black inferiority.[95] On the other hand, Populists such as Tom Watson argued that Blacks were potential allies, as Blacks and poor whites shared "the kinship of a common grievance and a common oppressor."[96] Ultimately, both groups abandoned efforts at racial collaboration as political fissures among whites were resolved by scapegoating Blacks as the source of the political and economic crisis of the late 1880s and 1890s.[97]

According to Woodward, concern about the growing political power of small farmers and the possible emergence of a strong independent political party led the Democratic Party to promote Black disenfranchisement as a way of currying favor with the populist movement[98] and furthering the process of "reconciliation of estranged white classes and the reunion of the Solid South."[99] Disturbed by the inability to control the Black vote, and the vulnerability of that vote to manipulation and

---

[93] One important critic of Woodward's thesis is Howard Rabinowitz:

> Instead of simply chronicling the considerable segregation that existed prior to 1890, I asked what it had replaced. I discovered that it was normally exclusion of blacks, rather than integration; ironically, segregation often therefore marked an improvement in the status of blacks, rather than a setback. That view has been widely accepted, most notably and generously by Woodward himself.

Howard N. Rabinowitz, *More Than the Woodward Thesis: Assessing* The Strange Career of Jim Crow, 75 J. Am. Hist. 842, 845–46 (1988).

[94] *See id.* at 849 (noting that "it is now clear that something significant happened in southern race relations during the 1890s").

[95] Woodward, *Strange Career, supra* note 19, at 45, 47–51.

[96] *Id.* at 61.

[97] 1873 marked the beginning of a major economic downturn—the first Great Depression. The panic of 1873 produced severe economic upheaval; by 1876, more than half of the railroads had gone into receivership, and, in 1878 alone, more than 10,000 businesses failed. Foner, *Reconstruction, supra* note 63, at 512. The result was massive unemployment, particularly in the cities. *Id.* at 513–14.

[98] Lofgren, *supra* note 2, at 24–25.

[99] Woodward, *Strange Career, supra* note 19, at 82.

coercion by Democrats, Populists moved towards the disenfranchisement of Blacks as the solution to political instability and the frustration of their political objectives.[100] In many states, nearly concurrently with the proliferation of segregation statutes, the Democratic Party led organized efforts to disenfranchise Black voters.[101] In fact, the franchise was broadened to extend voting rights to propertyless white men at the same time that Blacks were disenfranchised, arguably shifting the property required for voting from land to whiteness.[102] Expansion of democratic rights for whites was accompanied by the contraction of Black rights in a deepening cycle of oppression.[103] Nowhere was this phenomenon more apparent than in the area of the franchise. By 1868 a million Blacks were eligible to vote, and, in 1872, 700,000 voted in the presidential elections. Before 1867, there were no Blacks in public office; by 1870 fifteen percent of all officeholders in the South were Black. By the early 1900s these gains had been completely reversed.[104] In Louisiana, for example, in 1896 there were 130,344 Black voters. By 1904 there were 1,342.[105] While Louisiana had elected a Black governor, and 123 Black legislators served in the state legislature between 1868 and 1877, by 1890 the last Black senator left office, followed by the last Black representatives in 1900. There was not another Black member of the legislature until 1967.[106]

The consolidation of de jure segregation in the South constituted one of the material benefits of racial exclusion and subjugation which functioned to stifle class tensions among whites. Even when the lower class whites did not collect increased pay as a consequence of white privilege, whiteness still yielded what W.E.B. Du Bois called a "public and psychological wage."[107] Black subordination thus was central to the

---

[100] *See* John Hope Franklin, *From Slavery to Freedom: A History of Negro Americans* 270–72 (4th ed. 1974).

[101] *See* Lofgren, *supra* note 2, at 24–25.

[102] Raymond T. Diamond & Robert Cottrol, *Codifying Caste: Louisiana's Racial Classification Scheme and the Fourteenth Amendment*, 29 Loy. L. Rev. 255, 260–61 (1983) (summarizing the disenfranchisement of free Black voters at the same time that property requirements were abolished for white voters).

[103] *See* Woodward, *Strange Career*, *supra* note 19, at 92.

[104] *See* Steven F. Lawson, *Black Ballots: Voting Rights in the South, 1944–1969*, at 1– 16 (1976).

[105] Woodward, *Strange Career*, *supra* note 19, at 83–85.

[106] *See* Charles Vincent, *Black Legislators in Louisiana During Reconstruction* 220 (1976).

[107] W.E.B. Du Bois, *Black Reconstruction in America, 1860–1880*, at 700 (David Levering Lewis ed., 1992) (1935). For a cogent and rigorous exposition of the Du Bois

process of democratization for poor whites. The contradictions between the interests of whites as workers and as the dominant class were blurred by white privilege. The irony, as Woodward put it, was that "[i]t took a lot of ritual and Jim Crow to bolster the creed of white supremacy in the bosom of a white man working for a black man's wages."[108] In the context of the railroads one could even say that "legislation [w]as a means of obtaining segregated cars for poorer whites."[109] Vigorous Black resistance and the emergence of a generation of Blacks not born into slavery and generally unwilling to accede to the traditional demands for deference to whites also heightened the impetus to shore up the tenuous status of white superiority.[110]

Gender also figured crucially in the emerging pattern of legislatively mandated exclusion on common carriers. As Barbara Welke has argued, part of the answer to the question of why things changed in the 1890s lies in "[t]he unwavering goal of white Southerners ... to protect white womanhood, the embodiment of the idea of the South."[111] Historically, railroads and steamboats had separated passengers by sex and class, creating privileged facilities for women. When women of color sought "the privileges of their gender," and "challenged courts to justify a system that would require a woman of color paying first-class fare to accept [inferior] accommodations" that would be unthinkable for a white woman, the law of common carriers responded by permitting carriers to impose race segregation on condition that they provide substantially equal accommodations—equal but separate to all passengers in the same fare class.[112] Reluctant to take on the additional expense imposed by such a requirement, many carriers began to allow "respectable" women of color to have access to first-class ladies' accommodations. The eroding wall of separation "guarding Southern white woman's sacred place—and hence white supremacy" produced the apprehension that legislative action was required to maintain the lines that were otherwise insufficiently safeguarded.[113]

This heightened sense of racialized sexual anxiety fueled the demand for legislatively mandated solutions and was further reflected in

---

thesis, see generally David R. Roediger, *The Wages of Whiteness: Race and the Making of the American Working Class* (1991).

[108] C. Vann Woodward, *Origins of the New South, 1877–1913*, at 211 (1951).

[109] Lofgren, *supra* note 2, at 24.

[110] *See id.* at 25.

[111] Welke, *Road to* Plessy, *supra* note 54, at 266.

[112] *Id.*

[113] *Id.* at 266–67.

the regulation of and prohibitions on interracial marriage. While anti-miscegenation statutes dated back to the 17th century,[114] the "problem" of miscegenation[115] became a particular preoccupation of legislators from 1840 through Reconstruction.[116] While some antebellum miscegenation statutes imposed criminal penalties on both interracial sex and interracial marriage, miscegenous sex, particularly between white men and Black women, was generally accepted and economically beneficial; the progeny of such unions typically, though not always, inherited the slave status of the mother,[117] thereby increasing the property of the father. The existence of a significant population of interracial children was thus testament to the fact of interracial sex on terms that did not threaten white domination.

However, as reflected in the prominence of miscegenation in the debates over the Fourteenth Amendment, the end of slavery and the passage of the Civil Rights Act triggered a complex crisis on multiple levels. The first was a crisis of authority for the Southern states as the expansion of federal power through the Reconstruction Amendments opened up the possibility that interracial sex and interracial marriage might become lawful as a matter of federal law.[118] The result was that anti-miscegenation provisions were included in the post Civil War constitutions of six Southern states, and several states passed laws tightening the restrictions of and penalties for miscegenation during Reconstruction.[119] Control of interracial intimacy was a key test of states' rights. Second, the threat of conferring legal legitimacy on interracial sexual relations related to the crucial issue of restoring the value of property—

---

[114] The first law criminalizing interracial sex was a Virginia statute enacted in 1662. *See* A. Leon Higginbotham, Jr. & Barbara K. Kopytoff, *Racial Purity and Interracial Sex in the Law of Colonial and Antebellum Virginia*, 77 Geo. L.J. 1967, 1967 & n.5 (1989), *reprinted in Interracialism: Black–White Intermarriage in American History, Literature, and Law* 81, 81–82 & n.5 (Werner Sollors ed., 2000).

[115] According to Saks, the term originated in 1864 in a pamphlet authored by David Croly, an editor at a New York paper. The essay was entitled "Miscegenation: The Theory of the Blending of the Races, Applied to the White Man and the Negro." *See* Saks, *supra* note 57, at 42.

[116] *Id.* at 43.

[117] *See* Cheryl I. Harris, *Whiteness as Property*, 106 Harv. L. Rev. 1709, 1719 (1993) (reporting on laws dating from the late 1660s in which children born of white men and African women "shall be bond or free according to the condition of the mother").

[118] Saks noted that Reconstruction and the growth of national power "put state court judges of miscegenous bodies—white men charged with upholding state criminal law against federal constitutional challenges—on the defensive on many levels: sexual, economic, professional, and political." Saks, *supra* note 57, at 44.

[119] *Id.* at 44, 48.

in particular the property in white skin. Anti-miscegenation laws played a crucial role in that project.

The Legal Context

In the courts the question of race segregation was enmeshed in constitutional questions concerning the limits on state regulatory power imposed by the Commerce Clause, the common law of common carriers,[120] and the meaning and scope of the Reconstruction Amendments. While this chapter only addresses the third subject, in many instances doctrine and analysis flowed between each, reinforcing limitations and in the end buttressing the custom and practice of race segregation.

How the Case Got to the Supreme Court

In May of 1890, a law "to promote the comfort of passengers" that required the provision of "equal but separate accommodations for the white, and colored races" on railways in the state was introduced in the Louisiana legislature.[121] According to one daily newspaper in New Orleans, there was "an almost unanimous demand on the part of the white people of the State for the enactment of such a law."[122] At one level, the solid support for legal separation of whites from all "coloreds" would seem to run counter to the image of New Orleans as a cosmopolitan center in which the color line had long been blurred. In addition to the usual demarcation between Blacks and whites, since the 1700s racial classifications in Louisiana had included a third class, *gens de couleur libre*, manumitted descendants of European fathers and African mothers who had long enjoyed unusual autonomy.[123] Indeed, while Louisiana law had prohibited intermarriage between slaves, free people of color, and whites,[124] *gens de couleur* were presumptively free (while the Blacks were

---

[120] Indeed, the doctrine of "equal but separate" was developed in court cases in both state and federal courts three decades before *Plessy* in cases involving common carriers. *See* Lofgren, *supra* note 2, at 116–47.

[121] *See* 1890 La. Acts 111, at 152–54.

[122] Olsen, *supra* note 73, at 9 (quoting the *New Orleans Daily Picayune*).

[123] *See* Roger A. Fischer, *Racial Segregation in Ante Bellum New Orleans*, 74 Am. Hist. Rev. 926, 929–30 (1969). By 1788, the *gens de couleur libre* comprised more than one third of the population of New Orleans. *See* Berlin, *supra* note 25, at 112.

[124] This prohibition dated back to the Spanish administration, although local authorities were given the power to grant special exceptions to the rule. *See* Virginia R. Domínguez, *White By Definition: Social Classification in Creole Louisiana* 24–25 (1986). In the years when Radical Republicans came to power the ban on intermarriage was dropped. *Id.* at 26.

presumed to be slaves),[125] could testify in court against whites,[126] and in some cases had been allowed to inherit the property of their white fathers.[127] Some even became slaveowners themselves.[128] Whites had often relied upon the militia formed from this class for protection against slave rebellions and for securing control over Indians.[129] Indeed, some members of the militia had volunteered to fight for the Confederacy; only after they were refused did they serve in the Union army.[130]

What then explains the turn to the most rigid form of race segregation that restricted all colored persons from associating with whites? In part, the enactment of the Separate Car Act in Louisiana was another indication of the consolidation of the project of national reconciliation through abandonment of the struggle for Black equality. It further represented the rising sense that legislatively mandated segregation was needed to protect white womanhood, and by extension white civilization, from the chaos of Black freedom. Despite its retrogressive effect, segregation was framed within a project and discourse of modernization and of rectification of the error of Reconstruction. Stabilizing the uncertain racial dynamics was cast as key to stabilizing the labor market and reintegrating the South into the national economy.[131]

Immediately upon introduction of the Act, seventeen members of the newly formed American Citizens' Equal Rights Association denounced it as inconsistent with the principle that "Citizenship is national and has no color."[132] The signatories included Louis A. Martinet, an attorney and physician of the Creole community, who in 1889 had founded the militant weekly, the *New Orleans Crusader*. Martinet, also a participant in the founding of the national American Citizens' Equal Rights Association,[133] became the driving force in leading the challenge to the law.

---

[125] *See id.* at 25.

[126] *See* Berlin, *supra* note 25, at 129.

[127] *See* Domínguez, *supra* note 124, at 27–28. As a class they had also accumulated significant property such that "their wealth, social standing and education set them apart from most rural Negroes." Henry P. Dethloff & Robert P. Jones, *Race Relations in Louisiana, 1877–1898*, *in* 9 Louisiana History 301, 322 (1968).

[128] *See* Berlin, *supra* note 25, at 114.

[129] *Id.* at 124.

[130] *See* Olsen, *supra* note 73, at 9.

[131] *See generally* James C. Cobb, *Segregating the New South: The Origins and Legacy of* Plessy v. Ferguson, 12 Ga. St. U. L. Rev. 1017 (1996).

[132] Lofgren, *supra* note 2, at 28.

[133] This multiracial organization was committed to the struggle for racial equality. *See* Letter from Louis A. Martinet to Albion W. Tourgée (Oct. 5, 1891), *in* Olsen, *supra* note 73, at 55, 57–58.

The bill was initially stopped in the state Senate on July 8, 1890, both as a result of the opposition of the railroads based on the economic burden it would impose and classic political horsetrading: Supporters of a bill to recharter the state lottery initially opposed the Separate Car Act in exchange for the votes of the eighteen Black members to override the Governor's veto of the lottery bill. Once the lottery bill passed, however, the segregation law was reconsidered and passed two days after it had been defeated.[134] It was signed into law by Governor Francis T. Nicholls, an ex-Confederate general who had come into office in 1877 as part of the Hayes–Tilden Compromise. As part of the agreement installing Democratic governors in the three contested states entailed a formal commitment to continued support for civil rights, Nicholls's term began with the statement of his opposition to racial bigotry and swearing to "obliterate the color line in politics."[135] That he signed the Separate Car Act reflected the depth of the reversal of the political fate of Blacks in the absence of federal enforcement of civil rights and the concessions to racism deemed expedient in the moment.

Martinet immediately began an assault on the Act, calling for both a boycott of the railroads and a legal challenge. In the pages of the *Crusader*, he exhorted, "We'll make a case, a test case, and bring it before the Federal Court on the grounds of invasion of the right [of] a person to travel through the States unmolested."[136] He was not alone: Albion Tourgée, a former Union soldier, judge, author, and renowned advocate for Black equality, took up the call against the Act in his editorial column, "A Bystander's Notes," published in the *Chicago Inter Ocean*, the city's leading Republican Party newspaper.[137] Tourgée was made aware of Martinet's determination and encouraged it.

Despite their enthusiasm, it was not until a year later, in September of 1891, that the "Citizens Committee to Test the Constitutionality of the Separate Car Law" was formally launched at the urging of Aristide Mary, a leading figure in the Creole community during Reconstruction. In the intervening year, the climate had worsened; new segregation laws had been adopted in six Southern states and lynching was at record highs.[138] Civil rights organizations appeared weak and divided.[139] Never-

---

[134] Olsen, *supra* note 73, at 10.

[135] Keith Medley, *The Sad Story of How "Separate but Equal" Was Born*, Smithsonian, Feb. 1994, at 104, 108.

[136] Olsen, *supra* note 73, at 11.

[137] *See* Elliott, *supra* note 2, at 300, 305.

[138] In 1892 some 255 Black men, women, and children were lynched. *See* Paula Giddings, *When and Where I Enter: The Impact of Black Women on Race and Sex in America* 37 (1984).

[139] *See* Otto H. Olsen, *Carpetbagger's Crusade: The Life of Albion Winegar Tourgée* 310 (1965).

theless, largely as a result of Martinet's efforts, the Citizens' Committee, principally comprised of the Creole elite of the city, raised $3000 "by popular subscription" to fund a lawsuit. Martinet's correspondence with Tourgée led to Tourgée's agreement with the Citizen's Committee to be lead counsel in the case "with control from beginning to end."[140] He agreed to do so without remuneration. Local counsel was more difficult to secure; Martinet's first choice proved somewhat expensive and the second backed out for fear of political retaliation. James Walker was selected in December of 1891 and agreed to take the case for a fee of $1000.[141] Martinet's push to select Tourgée as lead counsel and his decision not to seek the assistance of Black lawyers in part reflected his view that Black lawyers were not competent to raise a constitutional challenge given his view that most of them practiced "almost exclusively in the police courts."[142]

Tourgée and Martinet considered several possible challenges to the Separate Car Act. They could have a Black passenger purchase a ticket out of state and travel into Louisiana in order to raise an interstate commerce challenge or select a fair skinned Black woman who would attempt to enter the ladies' car. According to Martinet, the latter strategy was problematic since she might not be refused admission to the white car, for in New Orleans "people of tolerably fair complexion, even if unmistakably colored, enjoy here a large degree of immunity from the accursed prejudice."[143] Notwithstanding this potential difficulty, Tourgée continued to argue for the selection of a plaintiff "of not more than one eighth colored blood" who phenotypically appeared to be white: the purpose was to expose the ambiguities in the legal definitions of race. As Tourgée explained, "[I]t is a question [the Supreme Court] may as well take up, if for nothing else, to let the court sharpen its wits on."[144] Martinet was also concerned that framing a challenge to a criminal indictment for violating the Act would be impossible if instead of being

---

[140] Letter from Louis A. Martinet to Albion W. Tourgée, *supra* note 133, at 56.

[141] *See* Lofgren, *supra* note 2, at 30–31.

[142] Lofgren, *supra* note 2, at 31, *quoted in* J. Clay Smith, Jr., *Exact Justice and the Spirit of Protest: The Case of* Plessy v. Ferguson *and the Black Lawyer*, 4 How. Scroll 1, 10 (1999). Smith disputes Martinet's assessment, pointing out that there were a number of highly competent Black litigators who both had practiced in federal court and had cases heading to or pending before the Supreme Court. *See* Smith, *supra*, at 10. Smith surmises that the reasons they were overlooked remain a "mystery." *Id.*

[143] Letter from Louis A. Martinet to Albion W. Tourgée, *supra* note 133, at 56–57.

[144] Letter from Albion W. Tourgée to J.C. Walker, Mar. 11, 1892, *quoted in* Elliott, *supra* note 2, at 307.

arrested, the Black passenger were simply denied access as the Act authorized or if, as was not uncommon, the passenger were forcibly and violently ejected. Martinet began talking with officials of the railway in order to arrange their cooperation. At least one railway informed him that it did not enforce the law; another declared its opposition to the Act as too costly, but was loath to publicly oppose it. Finally the Louisville and Nashville Railroad agreed to a test case.[145]

On February 24, 1892, Daniel Desdunes, the twenty-one-year-old son of Rodophe Desdunes, a signatory to the original protest petition and a leading editorial writer for Martinet's *Crusader*, purchased a first-class ticket to Mobile, Alabama, on the Louisville and Nashville Railroad and took a seat in a car reserved for whites. He was arrested and charged with a criminal violation of the Act. On March 14 an information was filed against him and after extensive consultation among the three lawyers—Martinet, Tourgée, and Walker—they filed a "plea of jurisdiction" challenging the authority of the court to hear the case. The major argument asserted was that Desdunes as a passenger in interstate travel had the "right and privilege" to travel "free from any government regulation or control . . . save by the Congress . . . under Art. I Section 8 of the Constitution."[146] Despite the Court's prior ruling that a Mississippi law requiring railways to establish separate cars for the races did not burden interstate commerce,[147] the lawyers believed that it was still an open question whether a law requiring passenger assignment by race would offend the commerce power. Tourgée additionally offered the argument that the determination of race was a complex question of science and law that could not be delegated to a train official to make a summary and essentially standardless judgment. The plea was filed at Desdunes' arraignment and the district attorney demurred to the facts. The lawyers assumed that the plea would be denied, Desdunes would be convicted, and they would promptly appeal. However, the presiding judge, Robert Marr, did not rule immediately and, on April 19, mysteriously vanished.

Meanwhile, on May 25, the Louisiana Supreme Court decided the case of *Lousiana ex rel. Abbott v. Hicks*,[148] involving a prosecution of a train conductor on the Texas and Pacific Railway for admitting a Black passenger into a car reserved for whites. The railway argued that because the passenger was traveling interstate, either the law did not apply, or in the alternative, if it did, it was unconstitutional under the

---

[145] *See* Lofgren, *supra* note 2, at 32.

[146] *Id.* at 34.

[147] *See* Louisville, N.O. & T. Ry. Co. v. Mississippi, 133 U.S. 587 (1890).

[148] 44 La. Ann. 770 (1892).

Commerce Clause. The Louisiana court agreed, holding that such regulations were valid only as to travel within the state; its application to
interstate passengers constituted a regulation of interstate commerce
prohibited by the Constitution.[149] Suddenly, Desdunes was poised to win.
On July 9 the newly appointed judge, John Ferguson, granted the plea of
jurisdiction and the case against Desdunes was dismissed. Martinet was
elated; in the pages of the *Crusader* he asserted, "Reactionists may foam
at the mouth, and Bourbon [redeemer Democrats] organs may squirm,
but Jim Crow is as dead as a door nail."[150]

Having developed in *Desdunes* both the arguments and a solid
working arrangement, the lawyers began a search for a new plaintiff
who would challenge intrastate segregation. They found Homer Plessy, a
friend of Daniel Desdunes' father. He was then a thirty-year-old shoe-
maker, member of the Citizen's Committee, and, like Desdunes, was
phenotypically white. On June 7, 1892, Homer Plessy purchased a first-
class ticket on the East Louisiana Railroad for passage from New
Orleans to the city of Covington, Louisiana, in St. Tammany Parish.
When he entered the train and took the seat in a compartment reserved
for whites, as previously arranged, the conductor of the train ordered
Plessy to leave the car "under penalty of imprisonment" and to go to the
section of the train reserved for "the colored race." When Plessy refused,
a police officer was called and Plessy was forcibly ejected from the train
and imprisoned in the New Orleans parish jail, where he was charged
with violating the 1890 Act. After posting $500 bond Plessy was released.

Louisiana v. Plessy was assigned and an information was filed on
July 20 charging him with violation of the Act. Notably, this information
failed to include any reference to Plessy's race.[151] Arraignment did not
occur until October. As before, on the date of the arraignment Plessy's
lawyers filed a plea to the jurisdiction arguing that the Act was unconstitutional and that therefore the court was without jurisdiction to hear or
determine the facts.

Specifically, Plessy's counsel asserted that the East Louisiana Railway as a common carrier could not be authorized to distinguish between
citizens according to race. As in *Desdunes*, Plessy's lawyers argued that
given the difficulty of making racial classifications, not only was the
conductor not competent to make the decision, the state had no power to
confer the authority on any person "to determine [race] without testimo-

---

[149] *Id.* at 777–78.

[150] Lofgren, *supra* note 2, at 40.

[151] *See* Information, *State of Louisiana v. Homer Plessy* at 14–15, *Plessy v. Ferguson*,
163 U.S. 537 (1896) (No. 15,248). The affidavit of the arresting officer alleged that Plessy
was "a passenger of the colored race." Affidavit of Christopher Cain at 4, *Plessy v.
Ferguson*, 163 U.S. 537 (1896) (No. 15,248).

ny, or to make the rights or privileges of any citizen of the United States
dependent on the fact of race or its determination by such unauthorized
person to compel the citizen to accept such determination, or to make
refusal to comply with the same a penal offence."[152] The Act further
deprived a citizen of a remedy for a wrong since it provided that neither
the railway company nor the conductor would be liable for damages
arising from the placement or removal of passengers. Because the State
was without power to grant exclusive rights and privileges to one race
that are denied to another, the Act established "an insidious destinction
[sic] and discriminates between citizens of the United States based on
race which is obnoxious to the fundamental principles of national citizenship, perpetuates involuntary servitude as regards citizens of the
colored race ... and ... abridges the privileges and immunities of
citizens of the United States and rights secured by the XIIIth and XIVth
amendments...."[153] The plea did not state Plessy's race.

The district attorney filed demurrers to the plea, arguing that it was
insufficient as a matter of law to bar prosecution. The court agreed and
ordered Plessy to answer the information. Plessy filed for a writ of
prohibition in the Supreme Court of the State of Louisiana enjoining
Judge Ferguson from proceeding with the case, because in the absence of
such an order the court would proceed to convict and sentence Plessy
under an unconstitutional statute, and that "there lies no appeal from
such sentence, as the said statute provides."[154] The petition for the writs
of prohibition and *certiorari* alleged all of the same arguments stated in
the plea with one addition: It asserted that "petitioner is of mixed
Caucasian and African descent in the proportion of seven-eighths Caucasian and one-eighth African blood; that the mixture of colored blood is
not discernible in petitioner," and that he was entitled to all the rights
guaranteed to whites under the Constitution.[155]

On November 18 Judge Ferguson overruled the plea and allowed the
prosecution's demurrer. Plessy's lawyers petitioned the state Supreme
Court for a hearing. This effectively stopped Plessy's trial. Francis
Nicholls, Chief Justice of the Louisiana Supreme Court and the former
governor who had signed the Act into law, issued a provisional writ of
prohibition ordering Judge Ferguson to show cause why the writ should
not be permanent. Ferguson answered and the Louisiana Supreme Court
invoked its extraordinary supervisory jurisdiction to consider the case.

---

[152] Defendant's Plea to Jurisdiction at 17, *Plessy v. Ferguson*, 163 U.S. 537 (1896) (No.
15,248).

[153] *Id.* at 18.

[154] Petition for Writs of Prohibition and Certiorari at 3, *Plessy v. Ferguson*, 163 U.S.
537 (1896) (No. 15,248).

[155] *Id.* at 1.

In *Ex parte Plessy*,[156] the court held that the Act did not violate either the Thirteenth or Fourteenth Amendment. Citing the *Civil Rights Cases*, the opinion by Justice Fenner concluded that the case did not implicate rights guaranteed by the Thirteenth Amendment, as segregation in public facilities was not a badge or incident of slavery.[157] The sole question according to the court was whether a statute requiring railways traveling intrastate to provide separate cars for the races and requiring passengers to confine themselves to those cars violated the Fourteenth Amendment. The court concluded that the question of restricting passengers to accommodations separated by race was not difficult in light of numerous decisions establishing the principle "that, in such matters, equality, and not identity or community, of accommodations is the extreme test of conformity to the requirements of the [Fourteenth] Amendment."[158]

Citing *Roberts v. City of Boston*,[159] a pre-Civil War Massachusetts case upholding the legality of race segregation in public schools, the court argued that neither racially separate schools nor racially separate facilities violate the equal protection guarantee even if motivated by some animus, because law had no bearing on sentiment or the social structure of racial hierarchy. As *Roberts* stated, "It is urged that this maintenance of separate schools tends to deepen and perpetuate the odious distinction of caste founded in a deep-rooted prejudice in public opinion. This prejudice, if it exists, is not created by law and can not be changed by law."[160] Thus, the regulation in *Plessy*, like that in *Roberts*, was a reasonable exercise of the police power in which a distinction was drawn on the basis of race. This distinction did not constitute unlawful discrimination. Indeed, "[t]he statute applies to the two races with such perfect fairness and equality that the record brought up for our inspection does not disclose whether the person prosecuted is a white or a colored man. The charge is simply that he 'did then and there unlawfully insist on going into a coach to which by race he did not belong.' Obviously, if the fact be proved, the penalty would be the same whether the accused were white or colored."[161] The court was untroubled by the provision exempting railroad employees from liability for wrongful assignment: it interpreted that clause to be inapplicable to the circum-

---

[156] 45 La. Ann. 80 (1893).

[157] *Id.* at 82–84 (citing *The Civil Rights Cases,* 109 U.S. 3 (1883)).

[158] *Id.* at 85.

[159] 59 Mass. (5 Cush.) 198 (1849).

[160] *Ex parte Plessy*, 45 La. Ann. at 84 (citing *Roberts*, 59 Mass. (5 Cush.) at 209).

[161] *Id.* at 87.

stance of erroneous racial ascription. The exemption extended only to correct assignments of racial identity.[162]

Plessy's lawyers applied for a writ of error before the federal Circuit Court in New Orleans, bond was posted, and trial proceedings were stopped. By February the filings were ready to take the case to the Supreme Court on a writ of error. Tourgée and his colleagues initially were determined to seek an expedited hearing before the Court, but soon changed course. Tourgée assessed that the tenor of the Court was decidedly against them: "Of the whole number of Justices there is but one who is known to favor the view we must stand on.... [Another four would] probably stay where they are until Gabriel blows his horn...."[163] That left four who, while inclined against Plessy, might be persuaded through argument or changing public sentiment. He hoped that the passage of time would improve their prospects, while at the same time recognizing that the stakes were exceedingly high: "The Court has always been the foe of liberty until forced to move on by public opinion.... [In any event it is] of utmost consequence that we should not have a decision *against* us as it is a matter of boast with the Court that it has *never reversed itself* on a *constitutional* question."[164]

However, time did not prove to be an ally. Despite the passage of three years between the filing of the writ in 1893 and the oral argument in April 1896, if anything, the political climate had hardened against the case. In addition to changes in the composition of the Court,[165] the material conditions for Blacks continued to deteriorate and the all-out assault on equality continued unabated. This entailed outright violence, intimidation, and coercion, as well as more subtle forms of domination such as fraud that eroded the gains in income, property ownership, and political power attained through prodigious efforts during Reconstruction. Unlike the previous era, the specter of Black oppression no longer raised concern at the national level and indeed national reconciliation depended upon acceptance of Black subordination as a matter of Southern "home rule." Following the 1896 Presidential campaign, President William McKinley could confidently state that "the north and the south no longer divide on the old [sectional] lines."[166] While there were signs of

---

[162] *Id.* at 88.

[163] Letter from Albion W. Tourgée to Louis A. Martinet, Oct. 31, 1893, *in* Olsen, *supra* note 73, at 78, 78.

[164] Lofgren, *supra* note 2, at 149.

[165] According to Tourgée, "When we started the fight there was a fair show of favor with the Justices of the Supreme Court.... [Now, o]f the whole number of Justices there is but one who is known to favor the view we must stand on." Letter from Albion W. Tourgée to Louis A. Martinet, *supra* note 163, at 78.

[166] Paul H. Buck, *The Road to Reunion, 1865–1900*, at 282 & n.20 (1937).

successful resistance in some quarters,[167] the overall climate was so unrelentingly hostile to the quest for racial equality that some Black leaders adopted the political rhetoric of economic self-sufficiency and self-effacement in an effort to deflect violent white reaction. Booker T. Washington's infamous speech before the Atlanta Exposition in 1895 urged Blacks to "Cast down your bucket where you are," and eschewed "the agitation of questions of social equality [as] the extremest folly."[168] Metaphorically acquiescing to the fact of entrenched racial segregation, he assured whites that, "[i]n all things that are purely social we can be as separate as the fingers, yet one as the hand in all things essential to mutual progress."[169] The acceleration of immigration from Southern and Eastern Europe also increased nativist anxiety that Anglo–Saxon superiority would be diluted, thus drawing many dominant elites, particularly those from New England, towards racialist logics that echoed Southern justifications of white supremacy.[170] Racial hostility against the Chinese had already created restrictive immigration policies including in 1882 the Chinese Exclusion Act.[171] *Plessy* then emerged at a moment of severe crisis.

The Argument and the Decision

Tourgée and S.F. Phillips, local counsel, argued the case before the Supreme Court on April 13, 1896, and, on May 18, the Court issued its opinion. By a vote of 7–1 the Court affirmed the constitutionality of the Act in an opinion written by Justice Henry Billings Brown, of Massachusetts.[172] What follows is a summary of the arguments raised and the Court's response.

The brief filed on Plessy's behalf by Tourgée advanced as its first argument that because the reputation in being regarded as white was of

---

[167] *See* Olsen, *supra* note 73, at 24.

[168] Booker T. Washington, Atlanta Exposition Address (Sept. 18, 1895), *in* Thomas, *supra* note 7, at 119, 121, 124. For reasons that are not entirely clear, Frederick Douglass also initially declined to offer any support to the effort to overturn the law. *See* Letter from Louis A. Martinet to Albion W. Tourgée, July 4, 1892, *in* Olsen, *supra* note 73, at 61, 65. According to Martinet, Douglass was annoyed at the misspelling of his name on a letter sent from the Committee and refused to lend his support. Martinet was deeply disappointed, noting that he had not wanted money as much as moral and political support. *Id.*

[169] *Id.* at 122. The speech earned Washington congratulations from President Grover Cleveland, a known opponent of Black rights. *Id.* at 120.

[170] *See* Michael J. Klarman, *The* Plessy *Era*, 1998 Sup. Ct. Rev. 303, 312–13.

[171] *See generally* Lucy E. Slayer, *Laws Harsh as Tigers: Chinese Immigrants and the Shaping of Modern Immigration Law* (1995).

[172] *See Plessy v. Ferguson*, 163 U.S. 537 (1896). Justice Brewer did not participate in the decision of the case. *Id.* at 552.

undeniable value, empowering a train employee to determine arbitrarily that a passenger who might enjoy the reputation of being regarded as a white man was not in fact white violated constitutional guarantees against the taking of property without due process of law.[173] This property in whiteness was of overwhelming significance and self-evident value:

> How much would it be *worth* to a young man entering upon the practice of law, to be regarded as a *white* man rather than a colored one? Six-sevenths of the population are white. Nineteen-twentieths of the property of the country is owned by white people. Ninety-nine hundredths of the business opportunities are in the control of white people.... Probably most white persons if given a choice, would prefer death to life in the United States *as colored persons.* Under these conditions, is it possible to conclude that *the reputation of being white* is not property? Indeed, is it not the most valuable sort of property, being the master-key that unlocks the golden door of opportunity?[174]

Given that the statute threatened a loss of liberty as well as the deprivation of valuable property, it should rest on the certainty of racial classifications, but in fact, as Tourgée pointed out, such determinations were complex questions of law and fact beyond the competence and authority of any railway employee. Even more, these determinations were anything but scientific, certain, or clear: "[I]n all parts of the country, race-intermixture has proceeded to such an extent that there are great numbers of citizens in whom the preponderance of the blood of one race or another, is impossible of ascertainment, except by careful scrutiny of the pedigree.... [And because of the ban on slave marriages] in a majority of cases even an approximate determination ... is an actual impossibility...."[175]

Moreover, Tourgée noted that, in determining who was white, not only were there no national standards, there were also conflicting rules that, by definition, incorporated white domination:

> It may be said that all those should be classed as colored in whom appears a visible admixture of colored blood. By what law? With what justice? Why not count everyone as white in whom is visible any trace of white blood? There is but one reason to wit, the domination of the white race.[176]

---

[173] Brief for Plaintiff in Error at 8, *Plessy v. Ferguson*, 163 U.S. 537 (1896) (No. 15,248) [hereinafter Brief of Homer Plessy].

[174] *Id.* at 9.

[175] *Id.* at 10.

[176] *Id.* at 11.

The Court attempted to evade this argument by asserting that, although the statute obviously conferred power on the train conductor to make assignments by race, no deprivation of due process had resulted because the issue of Plessy's race did not "properly arise on the record."[177] Because there was nothing to indicate that Plessy had been improperly classified, no claim for a lack of judicial process in reviewing an improper classification would lie. However, the Court was being more than a little disingenuous. While the information filed against Plessy had failed to specify his race, it stated that the conductor had assigned Plessy "to the coach used for the race to which he ... belonged, [and that he] unlawfully did then and there insist on going into a coach to which by race he did not belong."[178] The affidavit of the arresting officer filed before the Recorder's Court and attached to the petition for the writs asserted that Plessy was "a passenger of the colored race."[179] Moreover, the petitions filed for writs of prohibition and *certiorari* had alleged that Plessy was "of mixed Caucasian and African descent in the proportion of seven-eighths Caucasian and one-eighth African blood."[180] Despite the Court's claim that Plessy's race was unknown, there was little doubt that the record contained facts pertaining to Plessy's racial identity, albeit he did not identify himself as "white" or "colored."

Notwithstanding the effort to avoid the claim, the opinion considered whether Plessy had suffered damage to his property in the form of his reputation, a question dependent on the issue of racial classification that the Court had previously declined to address. The Court concluded that, if Plessy were white, any injury to his reputation would be adequately compensated by an action for damages against the company, given that counsel for the state had conceded that the statute's liability exemption for conductors was unconstitutional.[181]

---

[177] *Plessy*, 163 U.S. at 549 (1896). Ferguson argued that the affidavit made before the recorder attached to the petition for a writ of prohibition was not part of the proceedings in the court below. Therefore, Ferguson claimed, "Respondent respectfully represents that, so far as the proceedings in his court are concerned, he does not, cannot, and will not know until the trial of the said Homer A. Plessy ... whether [he] was a white man or a colored man insisting upon going into and remaining in a compartment of a coach to which, by reason of his race or color, he did not belong." Answer of Respondent to Application for Writs of Prohibition and Certiorari at 13, *Plessy v. Ferguson*, 163 U.S. 537 (1896) (No. 15,248).

[178] Information, *State of Louisiana v. Homer Plessy* at 14–15, *Plessy v. Ferguson*, 163 U.S. 537 (1896) (No.15,248).

[179] *Id.* at 2; *see also* Affidavit of Christopher Cain at 4, *Plessy v. Ferguson*, 163 U.S. 537 (1896) (No. 15,248).

[180] Petition for Writs of Prohibition and Certiorari at 1, *Plessy v. Ferguson*, 163 U.S. 537 (1896) (No. 15,248).

[181] *Plessy*, 163 U.S. at 549.

The Court was dismissive of the argument that Plessy's assignment to a railway car for Blacks based on the standardless determination of a railway employee was an arbitrary and unauthorized deprivation of the property in whiteness that offended constitutional requirements of due process. At the same time, however, the Court's decision lent support to the notion of racial reputation as a property interest that required the protection of law through actions for damages. It did not specifically consider or endorse any particular definition of racial categories, but it protected the boundaries of whiteness even as it denied the constitutional relevance of race determinations within a regime of enforced segregation. Notwithstanding the variation among jurisdictions that held that "a preponderance of the blood," as distinct from a rule of three-fourths, conferred white racial status, the Court deferred to state law as the legitimate source of racial definitions, even as it declined to specifically consider Plessy's racial status.[182]

Plessy's lawyers also argued that even if the assignment of access on the basis of race was not a deprivation of due process, it still violated the Fourteenth Amendment's guarantee of national citizenship. That citizenship entailed the "*equality* of personal right and the *free* and secure enjoyment of all public privileges," and barred the "legalization of caste."[183] The police power of the state notwithstanding, the Fourteenth Amendment prohibited discrimination against Blacks as such actions represented an attempt to restore the unequal status that was a mark of slavery. The *Civil Rights Cases* did not address the issue here since, in distinction from that case, the state, not a private actor, imposed the discrimination. And the purpose of the Separate Car Act was clearly discriminatory as revealed by the exemption granted to "nurses attending children of the other race": "The exemption of nurses shows that the real evil lies not in the color of the skin but in the relation the colored person sustains to the white. If he is a dependent it may be endured; if he is not, his presence is insufferable."[184]

The Court flatly rejected this interpretation as inconsistent with the object of the Amendment, which "was undoubtedly to enforce the absolute equality of the two races before the law, but, in the nature of things, it could not have been intended to abolish distinctions based on color, or to enforce social, as distinguished from political, equality, or a commingling of the two races upon terms unsatisfactory to either."[185] Like the Louisiana Supreme Court, the Court pointed to the ubiquitous

---

[182] *See id.* at 552.

[183] Brief of Homer Plessy, *supra* note 173, at 14.

[184] *Id.* at 19.

[185] *Plessy*, 163 U.S. at 544.

practice of school segregation as evidence that these distinctions were non-discriminatory. *Roberts* was cited as evidence that these practices and this interpretation were sound.[186] Against the reading of the *Civil Rights Cases* offered by Plessy's counsel, Justice Brown's opinion asserted that the holding supported the validity of the law: The case established that the Fourteenth Amendment empowered Congress to act only where the state had acted to undermine or subvert "fundamental rights specified in the amendment."[187] Such rights were not implicated in a law commanding the enforced separation of the races in intrastate travel.[188]

The Thirteenth Amendment argument was summarily dismissed. Tourgée's brief argued that the purpose of the Thirteenth Amendment was not simply to abolish "chattelism" but rather to "undo all that slavery had done in establishing race discrimination and collective as well as personal control of the enslaved race."[189] The distinctive feature of American slavery was that it entailed the creation of caste, a "legal condition of subjection to the dominant class" so that the slave was without rights and subject to domination by the entire white race, not simply his owner.[190] The Thirteenth Amendment was designed to eradicate that status and to restore rights of personhood. The Separate Car Act was a mark of caste inconsistent then with the meaning of the Amendment. The Court was utterly unconvinced, stating, "That [the Act] does not conflict with the thirteenth amendment . . . is too clear for argument."[191] While the Court agreed generally that the purpose of the Thirteenth and Fourteenth Amendments was to abolish slavery and to protect the freed slaves from the imposition of "onerous disabilities and burdens," as the *Civil Rights Cases* stated, "[i]t would be running the slavery argument into the ground . . . to make it apply to every act of discrimination. . . ."[192] Ultimately, the Court disaggregated the de jure racial segregation from racial subordination:

> We consider the underlying fallacy of the plaintiff's argument to consist in the assumption that the enforced separation of the two races stamps the colored race with the badge of inferiority. If this be so, it is not by reason of anything found in the act, but solely because the colored race chooses to put that construction upon it.

---

[186] *Id.* at 544–45 (citing *Roberts v. City of Boston*, 59 Mass. (5 Cush.) 198).

[187] *Id.* at 546–47.

[188] *See id.* at 548.

[189] Brief of Homer Plessy, *supra* note 173, at 33.

[190] *Id.* at 32.

[191] *Plessy*, 163 U.S. at 542.

[192] *Id.* at 542–43 (citing The Civil Rights Cases, 109 U.S. 3 (1883)).

The argument necessarily assumes that if, as has been more than once the case, the colored race should become the dominant power in the state legislature, and should act in precisely similar terms, it would thereby relegate the white race to an inferior position. We imagine that the white race, at least, would not acquiesce in this assumption. The argument also assumes that social prejudices may be overcome by legislation.... [But] [l]egislation is powerless to eradicate racial instincts, or to abolish distinctions based on physical differences....[193]

The Dissent

Justice Harlan's dissent began by noting that the civil rights guaranteed by the Constitution were not dependent upon race; indeed, "the Constitution," he asserted, "does not ... permit any public authority to know the race of those entitled to be protected...."[194] He noted that the purpose of the Thirteenth Amendment was to prevent the imposition of burdens that constituted badges or incidents of slavery. Taken as a whole the Reconstruction Amendments "removed the race line from our governmental systems."[195] Against the argument that the statute imposed a mere distinction based on race, Harlan bluntly asserted the reality: "Every one knows that the statute in question had its origin in the purpose, not so much to exclude white persons from railroad cars occupied by blacks, as to exclude colored people from coaches occupied by or assigned to white persons."[196] Under the "guise of giving equal accommodations," Blacks were to be kept to themselves. This act then was in direct conflict with the personal liberty guaranteed to all citizens and offended the rights of both Blacks and whites to sit where they chose. The state could not defend the law on the ground that it was reasonable for if that were so, then by a reductio ad absurdum, it could compel Blacks and whites to walk on different sides of the street, force them to sit on different sides of the courtroom,[197] separate them in the legislative chambers, and even segregate "native and naturalized citizens ... or Protestants and Roman Catholics."[198] Harlan assumed that such

---

[193] *Id.* at 551.

[194] *Id.* at 554 (Harlan, J., dissenting).

[195] *Id.* at 555 (Harlan, J., dissenting).

[196] *Id.* at 557 (Harlan, J., dissenting).

[197] It is ironic of course that the hypothetical rules that Harlan assumed would be found unreasonable and unsound in fact became public policy in many states: Not only were Blacks assigned to different places in the courthouse, a separate Bible was assigned for Black witnesses to be sworn in. *See* Woodward, *Strange Career, supra* note 19, at 68–69.

[198] *Plessy*, 163 U.S. at 558 (Harlan, J., dissenting).

regulations would be unreasonable as unsound public policy; however, he conceded, to invalidate a rule as inconsistent with public policy was not a judgment for the court.

Harlan then turned to the larger issue at stake:

> The white race deems itself to be the dominant race in this country. And so it is, in prestige, in achievements, in education, in wealth, and in power. So, I doubt not, it will continue to be for all time, if it remains true to its great heritage, and holds fast to the principles of constitutional liberty. But in the view of the constitution, in the eye of the law, there is in this country no superior, dominant, ruling class of citizens. There is no caste here. Our constitution is color-blind, and neither knows nor tolerates classes among citizens. In respect of civil rights, all citizens are equal before the law.[199]

Looking to the future, Harlan assessed the corrosive impact of the decision:

> In my opinion, the judgment this day rendered will, in time, prove to be quite as pernicious as the decision made by this tribunal in the *Dred Scott* case.... The present decision, it may well be apprehended, will not only stimulate aggressions, more or less brutal and irritating, upon the admitted rights of colored citizens, but will encourage the belief that it is possible, by means of state enactments, to defeat the beneficent purposes which the people of the United States had in view when they adopted the recent amendments.... Sixty millions of whites are in no danger from the presence here of eight millions of blacks. The destinies of the two races, in this country, are indissolubly linked together, and the interests of both require that the common government of all shall not permit the seeds of race hate to be planted under the sanction of law.[200]

This was not, as Harlan argued, a question of seeking social equality, but rather a matter of civil rights, as the separation of the races on a public highway was a "badge of servitude wholly inconsistent with the civil freedom and the equality before the law established by the constitution."[201]

Finally, to illustrate the absurdity of the law Harlan pointed to yet another anomaly:

> There is a race of men so different from our own that we do not permit those belonging to it to become citizens of the United States.

---

[199] *Id.* at 559 (Harlan, J., dissenting).

[200] *Id.* at 559–60 (Harlan, J., dissenting).

[201] *Id.* at 562 (Harlan, J., dissenting).

Persons belonging to it are, with few exceptions, absolutely excluded from our country. I allude to the Chinese race. But, by the statute in question, a Chinaman can ride in the same passenger coach with white citizens of the United States, while citizens of the black race ... who have all the legal rights that belong to white citizens ... are yet declared to be criminals ... if they ride in a public coach occupied by citizens of the white race.[202]

Harlan further dismissed the precedents asserted by the majority, as the most important of them (such as *Roberts*) were rendered prior to the adoption of the Reconstruction Amendments and others were part of the era of slavery. As such they could not provide guidance in this case. Ultimately, Harlan scorned "the thin disguise of 'equal' accommodations," as it "will not mislead any one, nor atone for the wrong this day done."[203]

Impact and Implications

Following the decision in *Plessy*, the order affirming the judgment of the state court in *Ex parte Plessy* was issued. On January 11, 1897, Plessy entered a plea of guilty in the Criminal District Court and paid a fine of $25. The balance of the funds raised to prosecute the case by the Citizens Committee—approximately $220—was distributed to local charities in New Orleans, and $60 was used for a testimonial for Tourgée, who had worked on the case for nearly five years without fees. The *Crusader*, Martinet's paper, had ceased publication. The final report of the Citizen's Committee stated, "In passing laws which discriminate between its citizens ... the State was wrong.... Notwithstanding this decision we, as freeman, still believe that we were right, and our cause is sacred."[204] Martinet asserted, "In defending the cause of liberty, we met with defeat, but not with ignominy."[205]

The Black press vigorously denounced the decision and, at least in the Northern press, the decision was opposed as well. Booker T. Washington even declared that while separation "may be good law, ... it is not good common sense."[206] However, the consensus assessment is that the response to *Plessy* was muted.[207] Indeed, from the time of the

---

[202] *Id.* at 561 (Harlan, J., dissenting).

[203] *Id.* at 562 (Harlan, J., dissenting).

[204] Medley, *supra* note 135, at 117.

[205] Lofgren, *supra* note 2, at 208.

[206] Booker T. Washington, *Who is Permanently Hurt?*, Boston Our Day, June 1896, *quoted in* Thomas, *supra* note 7, at 135.

[207] *See* Lofgren, *supra* note 2, at 5 (asserting that the decision was met "mainly with apathy").

decision up to the 1940s, the case did not appear in, or was cited only in footnotes of, major textbooks of constitutional history and treatises.[208] In that respect *Plessy* was utterly successful in appearing routine—a mere ratification of the pre-existing racial logic.

Indeed, assessing *Plessy*'s impact is complicated by the fact that at one level the decision affirmed an entrenched practice and legitimated accepted doctrine. What followed *Plessy* then looked considerably like what preceded it: The law at issue in *Plessy* was part of a trend towards legislated segregation in transportation beginning in 1887. For this reason, some have concluded that the case made little difference, either doctrinally or in the broader political landscape.[209]

It is true that if one looks to the entrenched belief in Black inferiority, *Plessy* did not represent any radical restructuring of the common racial understanding. Yet, it would be an error to conclude that *Plessy* was insignificant. The legislation at issue in *Plessy* "represented not so much an initial resort to law, but a change in the place of segregation within the legal matrix."[210] That change placed law more squarely in the forefront of ratifying what had been common practice but now took on increased importance in disciplining the potential for Black freedom, restoring racial and economic order, and reuniting the nation.

At one level, the effect of the decision was to calcify the practice of race segregation and to buttress the logic of racial subordination. In Louisiana, the decision arguably gave encouragement to the delegates to the 1898 state constitutional convention who made racially integrated schools illegal, established a pension fund for the relatives of confederate soldiers, made the Democratic party an organization for whites only, and declared that "Our mission was to establish the supremacy of the white race."[211] By 1900 the state legislature had no Black representatives; it was 1967 before any were elected again.[212] Segregation by law extended to schools with little judicial interference and with little concern for the question of whether equal facilities attended the mandated separation.[213]

---

[208] *Id.*

[209] *See id.* at 203–04; *see also* Klarman, *supra* note 170, at 392–94.

[210] Lofgren, *supra* note 2, at 201.

[211] Medley, *supra* note 135, at 106.

[212] *Id.*

[213] A particularly significant decision was *Cumming v. Richmond County Board of Education*, 175 U.S. 528 (1899), which, in an opinion by Justice Harlan, upheld the taxation of Black parents in Richmond County, Georgia, notwithstanding the school board's decision to close the Black high school for "purely economic reasons in the education of the negro race" and open other schools in the facility formerly occupied by the school. Subsequently, in *Berea College v. Kentucky*, 211 U.S. 45 (1908), the Court upheld

Plaintiffs who sought relief for wrongful assignment to cars reserved for "colored persons" faced the difficult burden of establishing their racial status, since the burden of proof remained on the plaintiff and was "to be determined not only by evidence of the admixture of negro blood, but by evidence of reputation, of social reception, and of the exercise of the privileges of a white man."[214]

More specifically, *Plessy* arguably consolidated the national identity as white in the post-Reconstruction period. The consignment of Blacks to second-class cars was the daily and public re-instantiation of their status as second-class citizens, who, while formally included in the nation, could not in any way stand for the nation. In affirming the legitimacy of that status, *Plessy* inaugurated a new formalist account of race and equality that facilitated the continuation of racial subordination even within a revised constitutional framework. Certainly, *Plessy* alone did not achieve this result, but it made crucial contributions to the project in at least three significant ways.

First, *Plessy* solidified a particular interpretation of the Fourteenth Amendment under which equal treatment came to stand for and constitute the whole of the equal protection guarantee. Second, *Plessy* revised and updated the conception of race in ways that cohered with and sustained the racial status quo. Finally, *Plessy* not only installed colorblindness as the dominant metaphor animating understandings of equal protection, it encrypted racial hierarchy within the framework of colorblind analysis. In this regard, *Plessy* established the principle that the only equality that is constitutionally relevant is that which depends upon a colorblind conception of race—the idea that race has no social meaning.

Plessy upheld equal treatment as the principle that defines equal protection in its entirety. Underpinning the holding in *Plessy* was the assumption-indeed the assertion-that racial exclusion meant the same thing for Blacks and whites; because the law extended equal treatment to different racial groups, there was no equal protection violation. The majority's holding that Plessy had no viable constitutional claim because the law barred Blacks from cars reserved for whites, and barred whites from cars reserved for Blacks, embodied the racial formalism roundly rejected by Harlan's dissent.

---

the indictment and conviction of Berea College, a private school, for violating a state law prohibiting racially integrated schools. *Gong Lum v. Rice*, 275 U.S. 78 (1927), completed the extension of the segregationist logic to Chinese children who, like other "colored children," were excluded from high schools reserved for whites. *Plessy* and *Cumming* featured prominently in the Court's reasoning.

[214] *Lee v. New Orleans Great N. R. Co.*, 51 So. 182 (1910) (refusing to award judgments to plaintiff's minor children who had been assigned to a "colored" car despite evidence that their father was white because of questions about the mother's racial ancestry).

Of course, rules of equal prohibition like those in *Plessy* are no longer seen as consistent with the constitutional mandate of the Fourteenth Amendment, but the notion of equal treatment as equal protection did not die. Equal treatment as equal protection is now the core of both the doctrinal rules for the treatment of race and public policy initiatives that seek to enact a regime of colorblindness.[215] The current Court's insistence on the extension of strict scrutiny to all uses of race, even when deployed to remediate long-standing patterns of racial inequality,[216] repackages *Plessy*'s essential precepts. Actual racial differences are beyond the reach of the law unless there is evidence that they were intentionally or maliciously produced, or, the argument runs, they are not legally relevant differences. The absurdity of *Plessy* and the basic reason its holding has been repudiated is that, as Harlan argued, it ignored the obvious and conclusive evidence that segregation was the product of the intent to subordinate—to impose a system of racial caste. However, *Plessy*'s basic conception of equality remains intact: As long as massive racial inequality cannot be traced to unequal treatment, such inequality is treated as residual and outside the purview of law—a matter of social equality, or private power, but not of juridical concern. Under *Plessy*'s principle of equal treatment, current racial subordination remains deeply entrenched. As the Supreme Court stated in *Jenness v. Fortson*, "Sometimes the grossest discrimination can lie in treating things that are different as though they were exactly alike...."[217] That caution has frequently gone unheeded by the Court itself.[218]

---

[215] One primary example is the former Proposition 209, which amended the California Constitution to ban any "preference based on race." The object was to eliminate affirmative action on the grounds that this violated the principle of equal treatment of all people regardless of race. *See* California Civil Rights Initiative, Proposition 209 (adopted Nov. 5, 1996) (codified at Cal. Const. art. I, § 31).

[216] *See, e.g., Adarand Constructors, Inc. v. Pena*, 515 U.S. 200, 223–24 (1995) (rationalizing the extension of strict scrutiny to government affirmative action program despite history in which minority-owned businesses had very little participation in government contracts); *Rice v. Cayetano*, 528 U.S. 495 (2000) (extending application of strict scrutiny to review of election procedures for state trust created to turn over to statutorily-defined Native Hawaiians the administration of lands previously taken from native Hawaiians).

[217] 403 U.S. 431, 442 (1971).

[218] The Court's insistence on proof of specific intent to discriminate in cases where facially neutral laws have produced even gross racially disparate impact severely limits the reach of the Constitution in addressing racial and other forms of inequality. *See, e.g., McCleskey v. Kemp*, 481 U.S. 279 (1987) (rejecting evidence of racially disparate impact of the death penalty); *Washington v. Davis*, 426 U.S. 229 (1976) (rejecting an equal protection challenge to a screening test brought by unsuccessful Black applicants for police department positions because a discriminatory intent on the part of the department was not shown); *Milliken v. Bradley*, 418 U.S. 717 (1974) (rejecting a desegregation plan for suburban Detroit school districts on the ground that there was no direct evidence of intentional discrimination by the districts, despite evidence of racially discriminatory

Equally as significant as *Plessy*'s influence on equality discourse is *Plessy*'s impact on current understandings of race. The conception of race as a natural biological category was contested by Plessy's lawyers: Because Plessy was only "one-eighth African blood ... [and] the mixture of colored blood [was] not discernible" in him, his lawyers argued that the conductor's assignment of Plessy to the "colored" car was an arbitrary determination of race, a complex question of fact and law, and a deprivation of the reputation of being regarded as white. While there has been some debate about whether a favorable ruling on this claim would have ended segregation or simply expanded white privilege to include those who could pass for white,[219] by exposing the arbitrary character of racial determinations and, hence, the constructed and *un*natural character of race, Plessy's lawyers sought to render segregation laws unenforceable as the line between Black and white would be impossible to maintain.[220] Under Louisiana's tripartite racial structure, Plessy was classified as a "colored"—*gens de couleur*—as distinct from "negro."[221] Further, he was phenotypically indistinguishable from a white man. Plessy's indeterminate racial phenotype highlighted the imprecision of rules of racial assignment as well as the unstable foundation of the edifice of legalized segregation and the broader project of white dominance. Yet, notwithstanding Tourgée's anti-racist motivation, Tourgée's insistence in the brief that Plessy was seven-eighths white, and that it was therefore absurd to classify him as colored, functioned to reinforce existing intra-racial distinctions within the Black community around color caste.

Ultimately, the argument had little effect on the outcome of the case as the Court gave cursory treatment to the claim, asserting that the remedy for wrongful racial classification was a matter of state, not federal, law. The Court seemed to equivocate on Plessy's claim that the

---

policies in the Detroit school district and of public collaboration in creating residential segregation).

[219] Some argue that it would have brought down the structure of segregation. *See, e.g.,* Olsen, *supra* note 73, at 20. Others argue that it would merely have extended the category of those considered entitled to white privilege. *See, e.g.,* Eric Sundquist, *Mark Twain and Homer Plessy*, 24 Representations 102, 114 (1988).

[220] *See* Olsen, *supra* note 73, at 12; *see also* Elliott, *supra* note 2, at 307 & n.48. Despite Plessy's lawyers' intentions, however, their argument was fraught with inherent tensions and ambivalence that reflect the uncertain trajectory of strategies grounded in destabilizing racial categories. *Plessy* could be read as reflective of the strengths and vulnerabilities of such strategies.

[221] Louisiana decisions and statutory law long made distinctions between *gens de couleur* and "negros," the principal one being that colored persons were presumptively free while Blacks were not. Domínguez, *supra* note 124, at 25–26; *see also supra* note 125 and accompanying text.

reputation in whiteness was a form of property,[222] but in fact the Court protected the property interest in whiteness by acknowledging that the reputation of being white could be safeguarded through a suit for damages. In effect this legitimized state rules defining race that were grounded in the fiction of blood and white exclusivity. Of particular interest is that at the same time the Court affirmed state power to maintain racial determinations that were arbitrary, conflicting, and grounded in white superiority, the Court shifted the meaning of race from a biological category reflecting the hierarchy of white over Black to a formal social category deemed irrelevant as a matter of constitutional law. In a sense race, like commerce, was federalized, a domain in which power was divided between state and national authority. In *Plessy*, the Court abandoned the conception of race as a natural hierarchy—what Neil Gotanda calls status race—and embraced formal race, in which race is seen as a "neutral, apolitical description[], reflecting merely 'skin color' or country of ancestral origin . . . unrelated to ability, disadvantage, or moral culpability."[223] Under *Plessy*'s logic, race became a formal identity category disconnected from history and from subordination, past and present. As Gotanda has argued, *Plessy*'s shift to a formalist account of race was a major contribution to sustaining racial hegemony.[224] Indeed, *Plessy* initiated an alternate construction of race that has proven highly durable and adaptable to changing conditions: Whatever race is (a matter of biology, a question of state law, a set of social customs), all racial identities are the same and all racial distinctions are prohibited.

What is less apparent is that current equality doctrine has its antecedents in Harlan's ambivalent invocation of colorblindness in the dissent; colorblindness is actually juxtaposed to and situated as consonant with racial hierarchy. Harlan's famous declaration that "Our constitution is color-blind," is immediately preceded by an assertion of white dominance: "The white race deems itself to be the dominant race in this country. And so it is, in prestige, in achievements, in education, in wealth, and in power. So, I doubt not, it will continue to be for all time."[225] Even assuming that this phrase was more rhetorical assurance than actual commitment, note that even as Harlan denounced state imposition of racial caste, he simultaneously re-marked the distinction between equality under law—that which is constitutionally guaranteed— and social and economic equality—that which is outside the bounds of constitutional concern. Moreover, to bolster his conclusion that the

---

[222] *See Plessy v. Ferguson*, 163 U.S. 537, 549 (1896).

[223] Neil Gotanda, *A Critique of "Our Constitution is Color-Blind"*, 44 Stan. L. Rev. 1, 4 (1991).

[224] *See id.* at 38.

[225] *Plessy*, 163 U.S. at 558 (Harlan, J., dissenting).

Louisiana law was unreasonable, Harlan argued that the law had produced an unthinkable irony: a Black citizen could be barred from railway
cars reserved for whites, while a Chinese person, a member of "a race so
different from our own that we do not permit those belonging to it to
become citizens," would have been permitted to sit next to a white
man.[226] Harlan's opinion thus legitimated distinctions among true citizenship, subordinate racial citizens, and subordinate racial non-citizens
or outsiders. Although Harlan refused to accept the fictive equality of
Jim Crow's racial prohibitions, in effect he echoed the majority's assertion that equal protection could be satisfied by ignoring race even in the
face of material racial inequality. Harlan lifted the metaphor of colorblindness from Albion Tourgée,[227] but in effect rendered its meaning
ambiguous by reaffirming the distinctions between formal equality and
social equality, and further endorsing the power of the state to define
citizenship in racial terms. As constitutional principle then, colorblindness was encoded from the outset with deeply racialized assumptions
and hierarchies. As such it offered a qualified assault on segregation that
mapped the distinction between de jure and de facto segregation, between intentional discrimination and disparate impact, that remains
doctrinally salient today.

Conclusion

Plessy's demise as formal doctrine took over five decades, a protracted legal battle, and something of a social revolution. Yet *Plessy*'s racial
formalism arguably never died. Colorblind equality, like "separate but
equal," renders racial inequality virtually irremediable. Under strict

---

[226] This was not a momentary or singular lapse:

> [Harlan] was a faithful opponent of the constitutional rights of Chinese for much of his
> career on the Court.... Concededly, Harlan was ahead of his colleagues on the *Plessy*
> Court in recognizing that "separate but equal" was categorically flawed.... Harlan's
> vision of a Constitution which protected some non-whites, yet approved of discrimina-
> tion against other non-whites on the basis of race, was ultimately as unprincipled and
> unstable as the particular form of race hierarchy he rejected.

Gabriel J. Chin, *The* Plessy *Myth: Justice Harlan and the Chinese Cases*, 82 Iowa L. Rev.
151, 156–57 (1996).

[227] This contrasts with the different meaning of colorblindness as conceived by Tourgée. In his novel, *Bricks Without Straw*, Tourgée used the phrase as a critique of legal
formalist analysis that effectively refused to address the actual conditions of inequality and
subordination. The narrator argued, "Rights [the freedman] had in the abstract: in the
concrete, none. Justice would not hear his voice. The law was still colorblinded by the
past." Albion W. Tourgée, *Bricks Without Straw* 35 (1880). *See generally* Elliott, *supra* note
2 (arguing that Tourgée invoked colorblindness in a dual sense, at times as an affirmative
goal and at times as a critique of the failure to recognize the concrete reality of racial
oppression, reflecting his rejection of the view that race should never be taken into
account).

scrutiny all racial identities are the same, and all racial distinctions, irrespective of intent, are generally prohibited except when justified by extraordinary interests. This rule in effect treats all identities as symmetrical and similarly situated, as the Court did in *Plessy*. Modern political and racial discourse marks progress by its presumed distance from *Plessy*. The deep irony may be that while the terms of the debate have evolved, that distance is in fact more imagined than real.

7

Neil Gotanda

The Story of *Korematsu*: The Japanese–American Cases

Introduction

Korematsu v. United States refuses to join history. *Korematsu*'s stories—and many narratives surround the decision—begin with the Japanese attack on Pearl Harbor. Within four months, 120,000 Japanese Americans, including immigrants, citizens, men, women, children and infants, were detained by the FBI and Army and sent to a chain of prisons and detention camps. The constitutionality of singling out Japanese–American citizens was litigated in four intertwined cases: *Yasui v. United States*, *Hirabayashi v. United States*, *Korematsu v. United States*, and *Ex parte Endo*.[1] After a period of quiet, activists of the 1970s brought back the original parties—Yasui, Hirabayashi and Korematsu—for a constitutional encore, four decades after their original hearings. And in a tragic coda, another violent attack—September 11—refocuses attention on the original questions of emergency war powers, race, and the place of judicial review. This chapter provides short surveys of four *Korematsu* episodes.

(1) We begin with the opinion and the sharp confrontations among the Justices. As a question of constitutional war powers, the majority and dissenters divide over whether the actions taken against Japanese Americans had crossed into what Justice Murphy called "the ugly abyss of racism."[2] Justices Hugo Black and Owen Roberts debate whether detention of American citizens without hearings violates basic due pro-

---

[1] *Yasui v. United States*, 320 U.S. 115 (1943); *Hirabayashi v. United States*, 320 U.S. 81 (1943); *Korematsu v. United States*, 323 U.S. 214 (1944); *Ex parte Endo*, 323 U.S. 283 (1944).

[2] *Korematsu*, 323 U.S. at 233 (Murphy, J., dissenting).

cess rights. And in a concurring opinion, Justice Frankfurter criticizes Justice Jackson's conception of how the Court should review emergency military actions.

(2) After examining those legal questions, we look to the most human story within *Korematsu*. *Korematsu* ratified the harsh and summary removal of the small Japanese–American population from cities and farms throughout the Pacific Coast to scattered and isolated concentration camps. Through a look at the litigants—four Nisei, second-generation American citizens—we can glimpse the interrupted lives of the Japanese–American community.

(3) The first half of the story of Japanese exclusion was tragic—detention, imprisonment and disruption of peaceful communities. After the war, most Japanese returned quietly to the West Coast and successfully reestablished themselves. Many felt deeply wronged by the government actions, but for personal and social reasons were constrained from speaking out about their experiences. A small minority, however, felt the injustice of the Japanese camps should be publicized, discussed and if possible, challenged.

The activist minority among Japanese Americans eventually mobilized the community on several fronts: seeking monetary redress in Congress, suing the federal government for damages, and reopening the all but forgotten trial court convictions that were the basis for the Supreme Court opinions. These campaigns, loosely grouped together as the "Japanese–American Redress Movement," were remarkably successful. By 1990, the second half of the story of Japanese–American internment had become a story of redemption. Four decades after the end of the Japanese internment, American justice was redeemed with apologies from the President and Congress, a grant of $20,000 for each survivor of the internment, and in the courtroom, reversal of the criminal convictions of Yasui, Hirabayashi and Korematsu. This narrative, with its happy ending, could have marked closure for the Japanese–American cases.

(4) But more recently, and especially in the wake of the terrorist attacks of 9–11, prominent jurists attempted to rehabilitate *Korematsu*, at least in part.[3] This renewed academic debate has sparked a reexamination of the fundamental issues confronted in *Korematsu*: When faced with a clear threat to our national security, what actions by the military

---

[3] *See* WILLIAM REHNQUIST, ALL THE LAWS BUT ONE, CIVIL LIBERTIES IN WARTIME 207–211 (1998). *See also* Alfred C. Yen, *Introduction: Praising with Faint Damnation—The Troubling Rehabilitation of* Korematsu, 40 B.C. L. REV. 1 (1998); Pamela Karlan & Richard Posner, *The Triumph of Expedience*, HARPER'S MAG., May 2001, at 31, 39. Posner's comments were part of his debate with Professor Karlan, who refers to *Korematsu* as "disastrous law." *Id.* at 37.

and our government are permissible under the constitutional justification of "war powers"? Can crude classifications of religion, appearance, citizenship, or race be the basis for aggressive and invasive efforts to locate, deter and prosecute persons deemed terrorists? Is the charge that these classifications are racist justified? And once the immediate crisis has subsided, what is the role and responsibility of the courts to review those actions in "the calm perspective of hindsight?"[4] After a half-century, we find ourselves once again facing the issues posed in *Korematsu v. United States.*[5]

The Opinions: The Justices Debate Racism, Due Process, and Judicial Review

The three important opinions that comprise the Japanese–American cases—*Hirabayashi v. United States, Korematsu v. United States* and *Ex parte Endo*—segment the internment into discrete issues. This separation was by no means a natural division and was debated by the Court. As parsed in these opinions, there were four separate legal questions: curfew, exclusion, detention, and indefinite incarceration.[6] The Court issued three opinions.

Gordon Hirabayashi was charged and convicted on two different counts. One was for violating a curfew applicable only to Japanese; the other was for violating an order to report to an assembly center for detention. Chief Justice Stone's *Hirabayashi* opinion chose to address only the curfew issue and left unresolved the issue of the order to report to a military assembly center. In *Korematsu*, the Court reviewed Fred Korematsu's conviction for failure to leave his home in California. His conviction, according to Justice Black's opinion, was for violating the exclusion order (the order to leave the Coastal Military Zones), not for his failure to report to be detained in an assembly center. Because exclusion and reporting for detention were part of a coordinated Army program, the dissenters objected to the use of this formal distinction to avoid reviewing the constitutionality of detaining an American citizen.

The last decision, *Ex parte Endo*, was announced the same day as *Korematsu*. *Endo* held that Mitsuye Endo, conceded by the government to be a loyal American citizen, could not continue to be held indefinitely

---

[4] *Korematsu*, 323 U.S. at 224.

[5] *See* ERIC K. YAMAMOTO ET AL., RACE, RIGHTS, AND REPARATION: THE LAW AND THE JAPANESE AMERICAN INTERNMENT (2001) for a comprehensive collection of materials on these episodes.

[6] *See* Jerry Kang, *Denying Prejudice: Internment, Redress, and Denial* 9 (2003) (unpublished manuscript, on file with author). Kang calls this parsing "segmentation" and argues that this allowed the Court to avoid responsibility for the larger internment process.

in a concentration camp. The Court thus avoided a discussion of how
Mitsuye Endo came to be imprisoned in the camp. In this fashion, the
Stone Court evaded the most difficult issue—summary imprisonment of
American citizens without a hearing.

Unlike many Court opinions addressing a complicated set of facts,
the *Korematsu* opinion simply continues the discussion begun in the
earlier opinion, *Hirabayashi v. United States*. After a brief period of
relative public quiet following the attack on Pearl Harbor, there quickly
came loud public demands by politicians and various special interest
groups for removal of Japanese from the West Coast.[7] After intense
internal debate among officials in Washington and the West Coast
military command, President Roosevelt issued Executive Order 9066 on
February 19, 1942. Within a month, Congress had passed supporting
legislation. Together, they authorized the Secretary of War to establish
military areas and to exercise complete authority over the presence,
movement and exclusion of any person or persons from the military
areas. General John L. DeWitt of the Western Defense Command issued
the required orders establishing military areas covering the entire Pacific Coast and major parts of Washington, Oregon, California, and Arizona. DeWitt followed with orders establishing curfew and exclusion, and
requiring Japanese to report to assembly centers.[8]

Gordon Hirabayashi was convicted both for violating curfew and for
failing to report to an assembly center. In the Supreme Court proceedings, Chief Justice Stone chose to approach the decision in as narrow a
fashion as appropriate. After argument, during the Court's initial vote in
chambers, Justices Douglas, Rutledge and especially Murphy, expressed
serious reservations and indicated they intended to vote against the
government. Stone was nonetheless able to persuade all of the Justices
to join him.[9] In the end, even Justice Murphy changed his dissent into a
concurrence in which he complained that the government action "goes to
the very brink of constitutional power."[10] Stone did acknowledge the
charge of racial discrimination by noting in passing: "Distinctions between citizens solely because of their ancestry are by their very nature
odious to a free people whose institutions are founded upon the doctrine
of equality. For that reason, legislative classification or discrimination

---

[7] *See, e.g.*, Greg Robinson, By Order of the President: FDR and the Internment of
Japanese Americans 87–88 (2001).

[8] *See* Hirabayashi v. United States, 320 U.S. 81, 83–89 (1943).

[9] *See* Peter Irons, Justice at War: The Story of Japanese-American Internment Cases 227–
250 (1983).

[10] *Hirabayashi*, 320 U.S. at 111 (Murphy, J., concurring).

based on race alone has often been held to be a denial of equal protection."[11]

Three Debates: Racism, Due Process for Citizens, and Judicial Review of the Army

In *Korematsu*, the Justices went directly to the core issues, but this time Chief Justice Stone was unable to persuade all of his brethren to join in support of the government. The Court divided sharply, producing five separate opinions, including three dissents: Hugo Black's majority opinion for the Court; Felix Frankfurter's short concurrence; Owen Roberts' due process dissent; Frank Murphy's extraordinary denunciation of the internment as racist; and Robert Jackson's eloquent but unsatisfying examination of judicial review of emergency military actions.

Upon a close reading, these opinions engage three distinct debates. Justice Black's opinion replies first to Justice Murphy, then to Justice Roberts, and concludes with a paragraph once again emphatically disavowing racial prejudice by the government. The first debate is therefore between Justices Murphy and Black. They carry on a heated exchange over the charge that the program of Japanese internment was racist. Second, Justices Roberts and Black argue over whether the removal and imprisonment of citizens without individual factfinding or review violates due process rights. Justice Roberts' emphasis is less on race than on the fact that U.S. citizens were imprisoned en masse, without individual hearings. Finally, Justice Frankfurter challenges Justice Jackson on the role of the courts in judicial review of emergency military actions.

At the Court's initial discussion of *Korematsu v. United States* on Monday, October 16, 1944, five days after oral argument, the Justices split 5–4 in favor of the government. Besides the three ultimate dissenters, Justice William O. Douglas initially voted in favor of Korematsu. And Justice Wiley Rutledge, who in *Hirabayashi* had been a reluctant supporter of Stone, once again voted with the Chief Justice in favor of the government, albeit with great reluctance. Stone assigned Hugo Black to write the opinion.

Was The Internment Racist?

Justice Murphy Charges Racism

Justice Frank Murphy was President Roosevelt's fifth appointment. In his ten years on the Court, he acquired a reputation as deeply committed to individual rights and social justice. One of the opinions

---

[11] *Id.* at 100.

that contributed to his reputation was the blunt charge of racism in his *Korematsu* dissent:

> This exclusion of "all persons of Japanese ancestry, both alien and non-alien," from the Pacific Coast area on a plea of military necessity in the absence of martial law ought not to be approved. Such exclusion goes over "the very brink of constitutional power" and falls into the ugly abyss of racism.[12]

He acknowledged the need to defer to the military in wartime. In the Court's review of wartime emergency actions, Justice Murphy first suggests a test: "In adjudging the military action taken in light of the then apparent dangers, we must not erect too high or too meticulous standards; it is necessary only that the action have some reasonable relation to the removal of the dangers of invasion, sabotage and espionage."[13]

Yet for Murphy, the military failed even this deferential standard.

> But the exclusion, either temporarily or permanently, of all persons with Japanese blood in their veins has no such reasonable relation. And that relation is lacking because the exclusion order necessarily must rely for its reasonableness upon the assumption that *all* persons of Japanese ancestry may have a dangerous tendency to commit sabotage and espionage and to aid our Japanese enemy in other ways. It is difficult to believe that reason, logic or experience could be marshalled in support of such an assumption.[14]

Justice Black's Response

Justice Black's opinion for the Court in *Korematsu* begins by addressing the charge of racism. In language that has become part of the constitutional law canon as the strict scrutiny standard of review, Black states, in very strong terms, the proper constitutional response to real racial prejudice, including a test for when such legal restrictions upon a single group are permissible:

> It should be noted, to begin with, that all legal restrictions which curtail the civil rights of a single racial group are immediately suspect. That is not to say that all such restrictions are unconstitutional. It is to say that courts must subject them to the most rigid scrutiny. Pressing public necessity may sometimes justify the existence of such restrictions; racial antagonism never can.[15]

---

[12] Korematsu v. United States, 323 U.S. 214, 233 (1944) (Murphy, J., dissenting).

[13] *Id.* at 235 (Murphy, J., dissenting).

[14] *Id.* (Murphy, J., dissenting).

[15] *Id.* at 216.

Justice Black then goes on to discuss the actions taken against the Japanese. He draws upon *Hirabayashi*'s finding that the military's actions were reasonable, given the threat.[16] Black concludes his opinion by reiterating that the Army actions were not based on racial antagonism or prejudice:

> To cast this case into outlines of racial prejudice, without reference to the real military dangers which were presented, merely confuses the issue. Korematsu was not excluded from the Military Area because of hostility to him or his race. He was excluded because we are at war with the Japanese Empire....[17]

The exact meaning of Black's distinction between "racial prejudice" and "excluded because we are at war with the Japanese Empire" remains unclear. His language, however, suggests at least two possibilities. The first is that it was *logical* to expect acts of sabotage and espionage from people who share a racial and national bond with the population of Japan, a nation at war with the United States. In this view, the Army's suspicion of Japanese and Japanese Americans was based on a fair and honest assessment of national character and human nature rather than racial prejudice in the sense of an irrational ascription of character traits to a racial group. The second and related possibility is that Black was making an *evidentiary* statement—the charge of racial prejudice is not supported by sufficient evidence of subjective ill will towards the Japanese on the part of Army officials. In either approach, the likelihood of disloyalty—espionage and sabotage by Japanese Americans to aid the "Japanese Empire"—was the key concept to be understood and analyzed.

Justice Murphy recognized clearly that prejudgment of Japanese–American loyalty was the fundamental issue. But for Murphy, the question of loyalty was a factual issue to be examined to see whether the military acted reasonably. In his dissent, Murphy outlined his theories of the constitutional violations, beginning with racial discrimination.[18] Murphy then acknowledged the gravity of the military emergency and the constitutional necessity of deferring to reasonable military determinations and actions. But, as noted above, in Murphy's review of the military actions actually taken by General DeWitt and the Western

---

[16] *Id.* at 217.

[17] *Id.* at 223.

[18] Murphy outlines three theories: discrimination in violation of equal protection; deprivation of the right to work and live as one chooses; and "excommunication" without hearing in violation of procedural due process. Murphy asserts as accepted doctrine that the Fifth Amendment encompasses equal protection. *See Korematsu*, 323 U.S. at 234–35 (Murphy, J., dissenting). However, this is a position that is not formally adopted by the Court until *Bolling v. Sharpe*, 347 U.S. 497 (1954).

Defense Command, he found "no such reasonable relation."[19] For further support, Murphy reviewed General DeWitt's *Final Report, Japanese Evacuation from the West Coast, 1942*:

> That this forced exclusion was the result in good measure of this erroneous assumption of racial guilt rather than bona fide military necessity is evidenced by the Commanding General's Final Report on the evacuation from the Pacific Coast area. In it he refers to all individuals of Japanese descent as "subversive," as belonging to "an enemy race" whose "racial strains are undiluted," and as constituting "over 112,000 potential enemies ... at large today" along the Pacific Coast.[20]

Justice Black's reply on the debate over the adequacy of facts comes in his closing comments. Black suggests that the military did meet its minimum evidentiary requirements:

> There was evidence of disloyalty on the part of some, the military authorities considered that the need for action was great, and time was short. We cannot—by availing ourselves of the calm perspective of hindsight—now say that at that time these actions were unjustified.[21]

Justice Murphy appears to have won the debate over the factual support for the Army's evacuation of Japanese. The historical consensus has been that these actions were racist and based upon erroneous assumptions—a consensus vindicated by the reversal and vacation of the three convictions in the 1980s *coram nobis* hearings.

The Summary Imprisonment of Citizens—Justice Black vs. Justice Roberts

Justice Roberts' dissent focuses on the "imprisonment" of American citizens rather than on the question of race or ancestry. He explains:

> This is not a case of keeping people off the streets at night as was *Hirabayashi v. United States*, nor a case of temporary exclusion of a citizen from an area for his own safety or that of the community, nor a case of offering him an opportunity to go temporarily out of an area where his presence might cause danger to himself or to his fellows. On the contrary, it is the case of convicting a citizen as a punishment for not submitting to imprisonment in a concentration camp, based on his ancestry, and solely because of his ancestry, without evidence or inquiry concerning his loyalty and good disposi-

---

[19] *Id.* at 235.

[20] *Id.* at 235–36 (footnotes omitted) (citing John L. DeWitt, *Final Report, Japanese Evacuation from the West Coast, 1942* (June 5, 1943)).

[21] *Id.* at 223–24.

tion towards the United States. If this be a correct statement of the facts disclosed by this record, and facts of which we take judicial notice, I need hardly labor the conclusion that Constitutional rights have been violated.[22]

The reference to ancestry makes clear Roberts' belief that racial prejudice against the Japanese was part of the decision. A good part of Roberts' discussion addresses technical aspects of the orders issued by the Army Command. Roberts' real concerns, however, are seen in his ironic tone in the sidebar skirmish with Hugo Black over the rhetoric of the evacuation. In discussing the Army order that Korematsu report to an Assembly Center located in the proscribed zone, Roberts adds: "General DeWitt's report to the Secretary of War concerning the programme of evacuation and relocation of Japanese makes it entirely clear . . . that an Assembly Center was a euphemism for a prison. No person within such a center was permitted to leave except by Military Order."[23]

Roberts' choice of the terms "imprisonment" and "prison" over "detention" and "assembly center" is carried forward in even stronger terms in his discussion of the transportation of Japanese to permanent military camps: "[O]n March 18, 1942, the President had promulgated Executive Order No. 9102 establishing the War Relocation Authority under which so-called Relocation Centers, a euphemism for concentration camps, were established pursuant to cooperation between the military authorities of the Western Defense Command and the Relocation Authority. . . ."[24] Roberts and the Court were well aware of the reports from Europe of the treatment of Jews by the German government and military. His choice of the politically charged term "concentration camps" reflected his sentiments.

Justice Black does not respond directly to the charge of imprisonment. Part of his defense is the highly technical claim that the only issue before the Court is the exclusion order that Korematsu move outside of the proscribed area.[25] Discussion of his forced transfer to, and incarceration in, a permanent camp was supposedly outside the scope of this decision. Yet by the time the case reached the Court, all Japanese had already been removed from the Pacific Coast. Black must have been aware that the Court was not simply forestalling but entirely evading the question that would be presented by a case about "conviction for failure to report to an assembly or relocation center."

---

[22] *Id.* at 225–26 (Roberts, J., dissenting) (citation omitted).

[23] *Id.* at 230.

[24] *Id.* (footnote omitted).

[25] *Id.* at 221–22.

Roberts was dismissive of Black's technical, quasi-jurisdictional response to the charge of unconstitutional imprisonment:

> The only course by which the petitioner could avoid arrest and prosecution was to go to that camp according to instructions to be given him when he reported at a Civil Control Center. We know that is the fact. Why should we set up a figmentary and artificial situation instead of addressing ourselves to the actualities of the case?[26]

Roberts concluded by charging that the Court was, in effect, creating a new constitutional doctrine that, in the face of an illegal imprisonment, Korematsu could not directly challenge the constitutionality of the imprisonment, but had to obey the order, consent to imprisonment, and only from within prison file a petition for habeas corpus.[27]

Since Justice Black chose not to engage directly with Justice Roberts, it is difficult to determine who prevailed. In support of Justice Black, we can point to the constitutional law hornbooks and textbooks that cite *Korematsu* as standing for the principle that national security can be a "compelling interest" under equal protection strict scrutiny review which justifies the exclusion and imprisonment of a racial minority.[28] Those interpretations of *Korematsu* suggest summary group imprisonment of American citizens may, under certain circumstances, be permissible.

We should probably place the late Chief Justice Rehnquist in support of Justice Roberts. In his 1998 book, discussed below, Rehnquist expressed serious misgivings about the treatment of U.S. citizens, as opposed to aliens. Opposing Rehnquist among current jurists would be Judge Posner, who contends that *Korematsu* was properly decided. In 2004, eight Justices (all except Clarence Thomas) thought that the Constitution entitled a U.S. citizen held in military detention as an enemy combatant to *some* individualized process to support that determination.[29] Yet the Supreme Court has still not ruled on exactly what the government must show in such cases. (Chapter 15).

Judicial Review—Justice Frankfurter vs. Justice Jackson

The final issue debated by the Justices within *Korematsu* is between Justices Frankfurter and Jackson. Like his fellow dissenters, Justice

---

[26] *Id.* at 232 (Roberts, J., dissenting).

[27] *Id.* at 233.

[28] *See, e.g.,* Erwin Chemerinsky, *Constitutional Law: Principles and Policies* 698 (3rd ed. 2006); John E. Nowak & Ronald D. Rotunda, *Constitutional Law* 385–386 (7th ed. 2004).

[29] *See* Hamdi v. Rumsfeld, 542 U.S. 507 (2004).

Jackson is convinced there is a racial component to the exclusion orders. He contrasts Korematsu's harsh treatment with treatment of "a German alien enemy, an Italian alien enemy, and a citizen of American-born ancestors, convicted of treason but out on parole," none of whom would be subject to the exclusion order,[30] and suggests the Court has approved a "Corruption of Blood."[31]

Justice Jackson's main concern, however, is how the Court should address controversial and questionable actions of the military. Jackson's approach is cautious and pragmatic. He is well aware of the need to defer to the military in wartime.[32] But in expressing his caution, he makes a controversial suggestion:

> When an area is so beset that it must be put under military control at all, the paramount consideration is that its measures be successful, rather than legal. The armed services must protect a society, not merely its Constitution.... [A] commander in temporarily focusing the life of a community on defense is carrying out a military program; he is not making law in the sense the courts know the term. He issues orders, and they may have a certain authority as military commands, although they may be very bad as constitutional law.[33]

The separation of military authority from constitutional law is the proposal that drew Justice Frankfurter's response.

In effect, Justice Jackson says the Constitution should be held in suspension during a wartime emergency. The military cannot realistically be expected to act in the same manner or be held to the same standard as civilian lawmakers and judges. Jackson continues:

> But if we cannot confine military expedients by the Constitution, neither would I distort the Constitution to approve all that the military may deem expedient. That is what the Court appears to be doing, whether consciously or not. I cannot say, from any evidence before me, that the orders of General DeWitt were not reasonably expedient military precautions, nor could I say that they were. But even if they were permissible military procedures, I deny that it follows that they are constitutional. If, as the Court holds, it does follow, then we may as well say that any military order will be constitutional and have done with it.[34]

---

[30] *Korematsu*, 323 U.S. at 243 (Jackson, J., dissenting).

[31] *Id.* (quoting U.S. CONST. art. III, § 3).

[32] *See Korematsu*, 323 U.S. at 244.

[33] *Id.*

[34] *Id.* at 244–45.

For Justice Jackson, the question is one of timing. Though the courts may be powerless to enjoin some military actions prospectively, that fact need not entail after-the-fact approval. A judicial decision, unlike a military incident, Jackson says, "has a generative power of its own."[35]

Justice Frankfurter was deeply troubled by Jackson's suggestion that reasonable actions of the military carried out within the scope of the Constitution's war powers might be found to violate the Constitution. He observes that "[t]he provisions of the Constitution which confer on the Congress and the President powers to enable this country to wage war are as much part of the Constitution as provisions looking to a nation at peace."[36] He quotes Chief Justice Hughes for the proposition "that the war power of the Government is 'the power to wage war successfully.' "[37]

Emphasizing that courts and military authorities exist within separate spheres of authority, Frankfurter pointedly criticizes Jackson's suggestion that actions of the military could be permissible yet still ultimately be found unconstitutional. Such "dialectic subtleties," Frankfurter contends, could not have been intended by the Constitution's "hard-headed Framers, of whom a majority had had actual participation in war."[38]

Frankfurter's approach—under which a military order cannot be simultaneously within the military's authority and unconstitutional—reflects the current standard for judicial review of military actions. Yet Justice Jackson's final warning is better remembered:

> Much is said of the danger to liberty from the Army program for deporting and detaining these citizens of Japanese extraction. But a judicial construction of the due process clause that will sustain this order is a far more subtle blow to liberty than the promulgation of the order itself. A military order, however unconstitutional, is not apt to last longer than the military emergency. Even during that period a succeeding commander may revoke it all. But once a judicial opinion rationalizes such an order to show that it conforms to the Constitution, or rather rationalizes the Constitution to show that the Constitution sanctions such an order, the Court for all time has validated the principle of racial discrimination in criminal procedure and of transplanting American citizens. The principle then lies about like a loaded weapon ready for the hand of any authority that can bring forward a plausible claim of an urgent need. Every

---

[35] *Id.* at 246.

[36] *Id.* at 224 (Frankfurter, J., concurring).

[37] *Id.* (citing Hirabayashi v. United States, 320 U.S. 81, 93 (1943) (Frankfurter, J., concurring), and Home Bldg. & Loan Ass'n v. Blaisdell, 290 U.S. 398, 426 (1934)).

[38] *Korematsu*, 323 U.S. at 225 (Frankfurter, J., concurring).

repetition imbeds that principle more deeply in our law and thinking and expands it to new purposes.[39]

Jackson's memorable image of a "loaded weapon" has been cited frequently.

Nonetheless, on the issue of judicial review, Justice Frankfurter appears to have prevailed.[40] Even though Justice Jackson's eloquence is more quotable, the standard of judicial review of the exercise of war powers appears to be reasonableness.

Excluded and Imprisoned Japanese Americans

The *Korematsu* decision was only one piece of a large picture. Over a year before the attack on Pearl Harbor, government agencies began in earnest their preparations for possible war with Japan. They compiled and collated various lists of potentially dangerous and subversive aliens. The lists were not bureaucratic busywork. The day after Pearl Harbor, the *Los Angeles Times* reported a "great man hunt was underway ... in Southern California." Federal agents "sought 300 alien Japanese suspected of subversive activities." That evening, 736 Japanese, along with a smaller number of Germans and Italians, were arrested.[41] In this initial drive against suspect aliens, over two thousand Japanese on the mainland and nearly nine hundred in Hawai'i were detained. The numbers involved a substantial percentage of adult Japanese men, since most of the adult Japanese population were immigrants barred by race from becoming naturalized citizens. Since the focus of the lists was immigrants in important positions in community organizations, many of which had ties to Japan, those arrested comprised virtually the entire community leadership.

These arrests came amidst inflammatory and erroneous claims of fifth column sabotage in Hawai'i and signals to enemy submarines in California. Notwithstanding these lurid reports, actual incidents of espionage among Japanese–American residents on the West Coast were nonexistent after Pearl Harbor.[42] Many of those arrested in the roundup, however, spent the war years in camps and detention centers.[43] For

---

[39] *Id.* at 245–46 (Jackson, J., dissenting).

[40] It is possible that the military might engage in unconstitutional action that cannot be judicially reviewed because it raises a nonjusticiable political question. But even then, courts would not take Justice Jackson's approach of after-the-fact condemnation; they would simply decline to adjudicate the issue.

[41] *See* Irons, *supra* note 9, at 19.

[42] *See id.* at 21–24.

[43] *See* WENDY NG, JAPANESE AMERICAN INTERNMENT DURING WORLD WAR II: A HISTORY AND REFERENCE GUIDE 49–51 (2002).

many, their principal offense was being a person of influence in the community. The top list of suspects included fishermen, produce distributors, Shinto and Buddhist priests, farmers, influential businessmen, and, not surprisingly, members of the Japanese Consulate. Other aliens suspected of pro-Japanese sentiments included Japanese-language teachers, martial arts instructors, travel agents and newspaper editors.[44] All together, some eight thousand Japanese immigrants were arrested by the FBI and military.[45]

In 2002, a poignant account of such an enemy alien was published in the *Los Angeles Times*. Teresa Watanabe, a staff writer for the *Times*, stumbled onto the story of her grandfather, imprisoned for over two years during the war.[46] Watanabe's sister had sought to hire a Japanese–American carpenter whose hobby and private passion was researching the stories of Japanese immigrants detained and jailed in the first wave of arrests. Two months after the conversation, the carpenter had located the grandfather's file—132 pages—through Freedom of Information requests and had forwarded the file to the Watanabe family. The file, complete with mug shots and fingerprints, begins with the FBI report.

Yoshitaka Watanabe, Teresa's grandfather, had been a fruit and vegetable dealer at the Pike Place Market on Seattle's waterfront when he was arrested on March 7, 1942, and separated from his invalid wife and five children. The report reveals that Yoshitaka Watanabe was arrested because of his membership in Sokokukai, demonstrated by his subscription to the *Sokoku* magazine during 1940 and 1941. The organization had been deemed subversive by the Justice Department. At his hearing before the three-man alien enemy board in April, Watanabe denied allegiance to the Emperor of Japan, expressed a desire for peace between the U.S. and Japan, and expressed support for America to win the war. He stated that he had only subscribed to *Sokoku* to help out a friend and that he barely read the magazine. His general statements, however, were insufficient to overcome the presumption that members of Sokokukai should be imprisoned. After the hearing, Watanabe was transferred from an INS facility in Montana to one of the special U.S. Army centers for enemy alien internees in Louisiana.

Teresa Watanabe was startled by the suggestion that her grandfather had been a member of a subversive organization and sought more

---

[44] *See* Irons, *supra* note 9, at 22.

[45] *See* Teresa Watanabe, *Deja Vu; After Pearl Harbor, About 8,000 Japanese Immigrants Were Arrested and Detained in the U.S. as Enemy Aliens—Among Them Yoshitaka Watanabe. Sixty Years Later, Amid a Similar Climate of Suspicion, His Family Finally Knows Why*, L.A. TIMES, June 8, 2003, Part 9 (Magazine), at 16.

[46] Yoshitaka Watanabe's biographical information has been taken from Teresa Watanabe's article. *See id.*

information about the group. She inquired of American historians and Japanese experts, and none had ever heard of Sokokukai. The Seattle FBI records had been destroyed. She was finally able, through connections with the *Los Angeles Times* Tokyo bureau, to locate copies of the magazine and make contact with Kenichi Matsumoto, a prominent commentator on modern Japanese politics. Matsumoto suggested the FBI may have mistakenly suspected the Sokokukai of ties to a notorious right-wing organization, but he denied any such links or that the leader of Sokokukai had ever advocated hatred or violence against the U.S. He speculated that the FBI might have been alarmed by the translation of the journal's name "Sokoku": *Motherland*. This suspicion was reinforced for Teresa Watanabe when she learned the FBI had no Japanese translators at the outbreak of the war.

Yoshitaka Watanabe was paroled from military prison after petitions on his behalf, organized by Reverend Emery Andrews, who was white, of Seattle's Japanese Baptist Church. Andrews had moved voluntarily to the Idaho plains to minister to his Japanese congregation in the Minidoka interment camp. The actions of Yoshitaka Watanabe's children supported his claim of loyalty to the United States. Two of his sons, his son-in-law, and his youngest daughter's fiancée all entered the military from the Minidoka internment camp. Only the youngest son, still in school, did not join the Army. Yoshitaka Watanabe's son Mas returned a decorated veteran of the segregated, all-Japanese 442nd Regimental Combat Team, which fought in Europe. His son-in-law Ned fought in the same unit and was killed in battle. Teresa's father was assigned to the Army's Military Intelligence Service, translating Japanese documents.

With the favorable recommendation, Yoshitaka Watanabe was sent from the Army prison to join his family in the civilian War Relocation Authority camp at Minidoka, Idaho. He did not leave Minidoka until September 18, 1945, a month after the end of the war.

Citizen Litigants—Minoru Yasui

Minoru Yasui was born in Hood River, Oregon to immigrant Japanese apple orchard farmers.[47] He was raised a Methodist, attended local public schools, and the University of Oregon. His college years included reserve officer training, and he received his commission as Second Lieutenant in the Army Infantry Reserve in 1937. He then attended the University of Oregon Law School. After graduation in 1939, he had difficulty finding a legal position, so through family contacts, he took a job with the Japanese Consulate in Chicago. As a U.S. citizen working

---

[47] Yasui's biographical information has been taken from Irons, *supra* note 9, at 81–87 and also from JOHN TATEISHI, AND JUSTICE FOR ALL: AN ORAL HISTORY OF THE JAPANESE AMERICAN DETENTION CAMPS 62–93 (1984).

for a foreign government, he registered with the State Department as a foreign agent. The day after Pearl Harbor, Yasui received a telegram from his father urging him to enlist in the Army immediately. Yasui took the advice, resigned from the Consulate and, even though the railroads initially refused to sell tickets to the West Coast to a Japanese, he reported to Fort Vancouver near Portland, Oregon. Before his induction as an officer, however, he was ordered off the base. Despite his eight attempts, the military refused to allow him to enlist.

In the meantime, his father had been arrested by the FBI as a suspect alien and sent to a Justice Department detention center in Missoula, Montana. Yasui attempted to represent his father as an attorney, but was only permitted to watch as a member of the family. After a summary hearing, his father was classified as disloyal and remained imprisoned until 1945. Minoru Yasui, angry at the unfounded charge of disloyalty against his father and the continuing harassment of Japanese–American citizens, returned to Portland. Executive Order 9066 was issued two weeks later. Rumors were rampant about what might happen, and Yasui sought a means to challenge any government action singling out Japanese–American citizens. After consulting with a local lawyer friend and a former law school classmate who was an FBI agent, he first tried to recruit one of his acquaintances to step forward as a test case. Finding none, he soon decided to issue his own challenge.

The curfew order aimed only at Japanese was to go into effect at midnight, March 28, 1942. That evening—a Saturday—he had his secretary call the police and tell them there was a Japanese on the streets in violation of the curfew. Yasui had a difficult time getting arrested. Even after showing the police a copy of the curfew order and his birth certificate showing he was Japanese, they kept telling him to go home and stay out of trouble. Finally, he went to a police station where a desk sergeant agreed to arrest him. Forgetting that there was no bail over the weekend, he ended up in the drunk tank and was not released on bail until Monday morning.

At a trial held without a jury, the district court judge issued a lengthy opinion reviewing the relation between civil courts and military authority, as well as the application of martial law and military necessity. The district court concluded that at least as to citizens, the curfew order discriminated on the basis of race or color and was therefore unconstitutional. However, the court went on to say the regulations were permissible when applied to aliens. The court then found that Yasui, through his actions while working for the Japanese Consulate, had elected to renounce his American citizenship and choose Japanese citizenship. On that basis, the district court convicted Yasui.[48]

---

[48] United States v. Yasui, 48 F.Supp. 40 (D. Or. 1942).

Yasui's appeal to the Supreme Court was heard along with Gordon Hirabayashi's. In his brief opinion in Yasui's case, Chief Justice Stone noted that the curfew order had been upheld as to a citizen in *Hirabayashi*, but because the government did not controvert Yasui's claim of U.S. citizenship, the case was remanded for resentencing and striking of the findings as to Yasui's loss of citizenship.[49]

Citizen Litigants—Gordon Hirabayashi

Gordon Hirabayashi was a college senior at the outbreak of war. Like Yasui, Hirabayashi chose to make himself a test case.[50] Hirabayashi was born in 1918 in Auburn, Washington, a small farming town twenty miles south of Seattle. His family belonged to a pacifist group with ties and beliefs similar to the Quakers. The group worshiped without ministers and rejected military service and war. He attended the University of Washington and was active in Japanese–American groups, the YMCA and the University Quaker Meeting. After Pearl Harbor, he initially remained in school but then dropped out, disturbed by the initial March 28, 1942 curfew order and his experience helping the first group of excluded Japanese—those from nearby Bainbridge Island. Hirabayashi obeyed the curfew order for the first month but then decided not to let the curfew direct his life and began to ignore it. He kept a diary of these violations. The record created by his diary would later be the basis for his conviction of curfew violations.

After further conversations with friends and lawyers, Hirabayashi decided to object to the evacuation. Word of his intentions reached members of the local American Civil Liberties Union, which had decided to help any Japanese who chose to resist the evacuation order. When approached by the ACLU, Hirabayashi welcomed their offer of assistance and a small support committee was established.

On the morning of May 16, 1942, accompanied by his lawyer, Hirabayashi turned himself in to the Seattle FBI office. He brought a four-page typed statement entitled, "Why I refused to register for evacuation." The statement reflected Hirabayashi's pacifist background and registered his strong personal conviction that "this order for the mass evacuation of all persons of Japanese descent denies them the right to live." Hirabayashi carried with him his briefcase, which contained his personal diary. When the FBI reviewed the diary, it added the curfew violation charge to the charge of refusing to report for evacuation.

---

[49] Yasui v. United States, 320 U.S. 115 (1943).

[50] Hirabayashi's biographical material has been taken from Irons, *supra* note 9, at 87–93.

Hirabayashi was convicted at trial on both charges and both counts were appealed to the Supreme Court.[51] The decision by Chief Justice Stone to address only the curfew violation and not review the evacuation order was part of a conscious choice to defer the more controversial issue. The year-long delay between the *Hirabayashi* decision and the *Korematsu* opinion gave the Court additional time to consider its final course of action as events in the field developed. The delay meant, of course, that the Japanese remained interned in the camps.

Citizen Litigants—Fred Korematsu

Unlike Minoru Yasui and Gordon Hirabayashi, Fred Korematsu never decided to resist the evacuation order to test the constitutionality of the government actions.[52] His goals were deeply personal and did not initially involve legal notions of civil liberties or an ideology of social justice. Fred Korematsu was born and raised in Oakland, California. After graduation from Oakland High School in 1938, he enrolled briefly in Los Angeles City College but was forced to drop out for financial reasons. After returning to Oakland, he attended a welding school and then found work as a shipyard welder. In June of 1941, he sought to enlist in the Navy but was turned down.

After Pearl Harbor, Korematsu's Boiler Makers Union expelled all Japanese members. Korematsu lost his shipyard position and worked at a series of short-term welding jobs. When the evacuation order was issued, his family all reported to Tanforan Race Track Assembly Center. The horse stalls were hastily converted into barracks for the Japanese. Fred Korematsu chose to stay in Oakland so he could remain with his fiancée—Ida Boitano. He hoped to earn enough money so they could move together to the Midwest. Korematsu underwent plastic surgery from a disreputable physician so he would look less Oriental and not embarrass his wife when they left California. Despite his efforts, he was arrested on May 30, 1942, in San Leandro, California. After claiming to be of Spanish–Hawai'ian origin from Las Vegas, his story soon fell apart and he confessed his true identity.

Fred Korematsu was not the only Japanese American arrested outside of an assembly center. There were at least nine others in the San Francisco area and six in Sacramento. Ernest Besig, the director of the San Francisco ACLU office, visited a number of these Japanese–Ameri-

---

[51] United States v. Hirabayashi, 46 F.Supp. 657 (W.D. Wash. 1942), *aff'd*, 320 U.S. 81 (1943).

[52] Korematsu's biographical information has been taken from Thomas Y. Fujita–Rony, *Korematsu's Civil Rights Challenges: Plaintiffs' Personal Understandings of Constitutionally Guaranteed Freedoms, the Defense of Civil Liberties, and Historical Context*, 13 Temp. Pol. & Civ. Rts. L. Rev. 51 (2003) and Irons, *supra* note 9, at 93–99.

can arrestees seeking a volunteer who would challenge the evacuation orders. Only Korematsu agreed to join with the ACLU. Korematsu had almost no community support or outside assistance other than ACLU representation. He went forward on the basis of his own conviction. He indicated in a short, heartfelt statement to Besig, "In order to be imprisoned, these people should have been given a fair trial in order that they may defend their loyalty at court in a democratic way, but they were placed in imprisonment without any fair trial!"[53]

Ernest Besig then recruited Wayne Collins—a young, radical San Francisco attorney—to represent Korematsu. Collins continued to represent Korematsu throughout the Supreme Court proceedings. In addition, Collins took up some of the most difficult and controversial issues on behalf of Japanese Americans.[54]

Citizen Litigants—Mitsuye Endo

Mitsuye Endo's challenge followed a different legal strategy. Her case did not challenge the curfew, evacuation, or internment directly. Rather, she sought a writ of habeas corpus to effectuate her release from incarceration.[55] Endo was recruited through the Japanese American Citizens League. Her name had been obtained after lawyers investigated an effort in Sacramento by the State Personnel Board to purge all Japanese from civil service positions with the State. San Francisco attorney James Purcell's Personnel Board efforts were sidetracked by the exclusion order, but the contacts remained. Purcell surveyed the interned state employees and selected Mitsuye Endo as a likely petitioner for a habeas corpus action. Born in Sacramento in 1920, her father operated a grocery store. She attended public schools and a local Methodist Church. After graduation from high school, she went to work for the State of California as a typist. She later noted that "[b]ecause there was so much discrimination against the Japanese Americans, the only position we could get was with the state, unless we worked for a Japanese firm."[56] Her brother was drafted into the army in 1941 before the attack on Pearl Harbor.

Endo's entire case was carried out by correspondence. She initially reported to the Walerga Assembly Center, constructed on a migrant

---

[53] Irons, *supra* note 9, at 99.

[54] *See generally* DONALD E. COLLINS, NATIVE AMERICAN ALIENS: DISLOYALTY AND THE RENUNCIATION OF CITIZENSHIP BY JAPANESE AMERICANS DURING WORLD WAR II (1985); Neil Gotanda, *Race, Citizenship, and the Search for Political Community Among "We the People"*, 76 OR. L. REV. 233 (1997).

[55] Endo's biographical information has been taken from Irons, *supra* note 9, at 99–103 and TATEISHI, *supra* note 47, at 60–61.

[56] TATEISHI, *supra* note 47, at 60.

workers' camp near Sacramento. She was then sent to the Tule Lake camp on the northern edge of California next to Oregon. Mitsuye Endo, based upon Purcell's survey of Japanese–American state employees, was recruited from Tule Lake to participate in the habeas petition. She never met her attorney Purcell and made no court appearances. In her own words, she was selected because "[t]hey felt that I represented a symbolic, 'loyal' American."[57] Endo made important sacrifices to further the litigation. Many of her friends were transferred or released from camp before the end of 1944. She qualified for early release and apparently was even offered early freedom by a government attorney. That would have mooted her habeas corpus petition, however, and so, at the request of her attorneys, she stayed in the camp until the Supreme Court ruled.[58]

The case was delayed several times in the lower courts before being argued before the Supreme Court on October 11, 1944, the same day as *Korematsu*. The opinion was also issued the same day as *Korematsu*, though the exact timing has raised a number of questions. There were rumors that the opinion was being held back by Chief Justice Stone. Justice Douglas, the author of *Endo*, complained in a memo on November 28, 1944, to Stone that although the opinion had already been approved and distributed on November 8, 1944, it was being delayed because "officers of the government have indicated that some change in detention plans are [sic] under consideration."[59] Circumstantial evidence that the opinions were leaked to the administration can be seen in the highly unusual Sunday War Department Press Release on December 17, 1944. The head of the Western Defense Command announced that "persons of Japanese ancestry whose records have stood the test of Army scrutiny during the past two years" would be released from the camps after January 2, 1945.[60] The Supreme Court issued its opinions in *Korematsu* and *Endo* the very next day, on Monday, December 18.

Justice Douglas, writing for the Court, ordered Mitsuye Endo's release. While the opinion lacks clarity, Douglas purported to avoid the constitutional issues and held that the War Relocation Authority—a congressionally created civilian agency and not a part of the military—lacked authority to detain citizens conceded by the government to be loyal.[61] As a nominally statutory rather than constitutional case on an

---

[57] *Id*. at 61.

[58] *See id.*; Irons, *supra* note 9, at 102–103.

[59] Patrick O. Gudridge, *Remember Endo?*, 116 HARV. L. REV. 1933, 1935 n.11 (2003).

[60] Irons, *supra* note 9, at 345.

[61] *See Ex parte Endo*, 323 U.S. 283, 297 (1944).

issue that was, due to the Army's preemptive action, largely moot, *Endo* has been remembered largely as a footnote to *Korematsu*.[62]

Meanwhile, and ironically, in constitutional doctrine *Korematsu* itself came to serve as a precedent for heightened judicial review—strict scrutiny. The first clear use of *Korematsu* as a citation for strict scrutiny was in 1954 in *Bolling v. Sharpe*,[63] the federal Fifth Amendment companion case to *Brown v. Board of Education*.[64] In *Bolling*, Chief Justice Warren noted that "[c]lassifications based solely upon race must be scrutinized with particular care."[65] How did *Korematsu*—a war powers case upholding discrimination—get turned around into a doctrinal tool for attacking prejudice? Part of the answer can be found in the modest coalition between Japanese–American civil rights attorneys and the well-known civil rights lawyers attacking Jim Crow segregation.[66] But more broadly, we may speculate that over time, the Supreme Court came to regret *Korematsu*, and used the later cases as an opportunity to repudiate by redeeming it.

The Japanese American Redress Movement: Korematsu *and 1960s Activism*

Comment and interest in *Korematsu* and the Japanese internment waned in the 1950s and 1960s. Among Nisei, after the immediate postwar traumas of resettlement and reintegration into society, there was little discussion in public or even within families of the evacuation and years in the camps. One touching story is told about Fred Korematsu. During the 1960s, his daughter heard a student report at school about *Korematsu v. United States*. Curious, when she returned home, she asked if they were related to those Korematsus. Only then did Fred Korematsu tell his daughter, "Well, that was me."[67]

---

[62] *See* Gudridge, *supra* note 59, at 1959 (exploring why *Endo* has been largely forgotten and arguing that the case was not "in any central sense ... about statutory interpretation").

[63] 347 U.S. 497 (1954).

[64] 347 U.S. 483 (1954). *See also* Hernandez v. Texas, 347 U.S. 475, 478 n.4 (1954), a case decided just two weeks before *Brown* that found racial discrimination against persons of Mexican descent in jury selection violated equal protection. The Court's opinion in *Hernandez* cited *Hirabayashi* but not *Korematsu*.

[65] *Bolling*, 347 U.S. at 499.

[66] *See* Greg Robinson and Toni Robinson, *Korematsu and Beyond: Japanese Americans and the Origins of Strict Scrutiny*, 68 LAW & CONTEMP. PROB. 29 (2005).

[67] Fujita-Rony, *supra* note 52, at 62 (citing Peter Irons, *Justice Long Overdue*, NEW PERSPECTIVES, Winter/Spring 1986, at 5).

The urge to forget began to weaken with the broad wave of social concern and activism of the 1960s and 1970s. That activism was most notable among college students. During student strikes for ethnic studies, especially at San Francisco State, U.C. Berkeley and U.C.L.A., Asian students participated and described themselves for the first time as "Asian Americans."

Consistent with the era, activism among Sansei—third-generation Japanese Americans—varied widely across many different issues. There also developed a desire among some second-generation Nisei to publicize their wartime experiences. There remained among most Japanese a profound sense that they had suffered an injustice. The desire to raise the issue to a broader American audience and seek some public redress slowly took shape in various venues. These strands of social concern eventually coalesced around three legal movements: (i) the petitions for writs of error *coram nobis* to reverse the trial convictions of Gordon Hirabayashi, Minoru Yasui and Fred Korematsu; (ii) monetary reparations legislation in Congress; and (iii) direct federal claims for monetary damages. As with all social movements, many interesting figures participated, some highly trained and others with modest backgrounds.

One extraordinary individual, Aiko Herzig–Yoshinaga, participated directly in all three efforts. She played a key role as the unofficial "movement" archivist of the internment records stored in Washington, D.C., in the National Archives, and she was a member of the official commission that held hearings which led directly to the reparations legislation. She and her husband were activists who joined the class action lawsuit. And as archivist, not only was she virtually the only person with knowledge and understanding of the content of the vast National Archives materials on the internment, she also found the sole remaining copy of the unexpurgated version of General DeWitt's *Final Report, Japanese Evacuation from the West Coast, 1942*. The document—withheld in 1944 from the Supreme Court—became a crucial piece of evidence in the *coram nobis* hearings.

In 1941, Aiko Yoshinaga was an honors high school student in Los Angeles who was set to graduate in June and planning to attend secretarial school in the fall. Pearl Harbor and then Executive Order 9066 cast their shadows over the lives of Japanese in Los Angeles. Yoshinaga, instead of going with her family to one of the camps in Arkansas, decided to go with her fiancée to Manzanar in the California high desert on the eastern slopes of the Sierra Nevada Mountains. In Manzanar she married, gave birth to a child, and was able to travel to the Arkansas camp to see her father once before he died, though without her husband, who was barred from the trip. After she was released from the camp, Yoshinaga first moved back to California, but later joined other family members in New York City.[68]

As part of New York City's Japanese–American community, Yoshinaga made the acquaintance of a loose group of community-oriented activists. Divorced and remarried, she continued her contact with such individuals as artist Miné Okubo, who wrote *Citizen 13660*,[69] and Michi Nishiura Weglyn, author of *Years of Infamy: The Untold Story of America's Concentration Camps*.[70] Published in 1976, the latter was the first important study of the camps authored by a Nisei since the 1950s. Herzig–Yoshinaga worked during those New York years as a secretary and office manager.

On the West Coast, energetic Nisei pressed harder for awareness of the camps. In Los Angeles in 1969, Sue Kunitomi Embrey led a small caravan in the first pilgrimage visit to the Manzanar camp. In 1970, at the annual meeting of the Japanese American Citizens League, Ray Okamura and Edison Uno, longtime JACL inside critics, sponsored a general resolution calling for the JACL to take action on Japanese–American redress. Such early efforts led to modest success in 1976 when President Gerald Ford issued a presidential proclamation rescinding Executive Order 9066. This was, of course, a legal formality since the original order had been suspended by President Truman in 1946. But Ford's proclamation was accompanied by a statement that the evacuation was wrong and Japanese Americans were "loyal Americans." By the late 1970s, the efforts that had produced the Ford proclamation had grown into a movement—the redress movement—which was focused on monetary redress for individual Japanese Americans interned during World War II.

Aiko Herzig–Yoshinaga and her husband Jack Herzig had moved in 1978 to Washington, D.C., the year before the formation of the National Council for Japanese American Redress. In Washington, Herzig–Yoshinaga decided she could satisfy her personal curiosity and interest by examining the materials on internment in the National Archives. Her interest soon blossomed into a major project. Though she had no professional training as a librarian or archivist, she began to sort and index the large collection of materials. Working as a volunteer, she transformed her years of office secretarial experience into archival expertise. She soon became the resident expert on the Japanese–American materials in the National Archives.

---

[68] *See* Josh Getlin, *WWII Internees; Redress: One Made a Difference*, L.A. TIMES, June 2, 1988, at 1.

[69] MINÉ OKUBO, CITIZEN 13660 (1983).

[70] MICHI WEGLYN, YEARS OF INFAMY: THE UNTOLD STORY OF AMERICA'S CONCENTRATION CAMPS (1976).

The redress movement, with its loose national coalition of individuals and community organizations, gained the attention of the four Japanese–American members of Congress. Moderate elements within the redress movement allied with the congressional delegation and developed a less aggressive proposal. They supported establishing a congressional commission that would hold hearings across the country but would defer the demand for monetary reparations. The hearings of the Commission on Wartime Relocation and Internment of Civilians along with its final report recommending reparations ultimately proved crucial to the success of the congressional reparations bill.

When proposed, however, the Commission precipitated a split in the redress movement. Opponents argued that the Commission's go-slow approach was a "sell-out." They felt that at the end of the hearings, the prestigious national figures on the Commission would never recommend monetary reparations. One opposition group, headed by Chicago activist William Hohri and joined by Aiko and Jack Herzig, sought a more direct route. Reorganized as the National Council for Japanese American Redress—NCJAR—they secured the services of a small but established Washington, D.C. law firm. In 1983 they filed a set of federal class action claims on behalf of the 125,000 interned Japanese Americans. The action sought $10,000 for each of twenty-two causes of action with a total demand of $27 billion.[71] Though ultimately unsuccessful, the suit is credited as being an important part of the overall campaign for Japanese–American redress.[72]

With the support of the Japanese–American congressional delegation, the Commission on Wartime Relocation and Internment of Civilians was established in 1980. Because the Commission needed a staff resource person, Aiko Herzig–Yoshinaga's self-taught expertise launched her on a new career. She was hired in 1981. As a staff member, she continued her research in the archives and participated in the Commission's work of holding hearings in nine cities. The nine-member Commission included a number of national figures: Arthur Flemming, former Eisenhower cabinet member and Chairman of the U.S. Commission on Civil Rights; former senator Edward Brooke; former Supreme Court Justice Arthur Goldberg; and Reverend Robert F. Drinan, Jesuit priest

---

[71] *See* William Minoru Hohri, Repairing America: An Account of the Movement for Japanese-American Redress 38–50, 191 (1988); Mitchell T. Maki et al., Achieving the Impossible Dream: How Japanese Americans Achieved Redress 125 (1999).

[72] That action, *United States v. Hohri*, followed a tortuous history, with a Supreme Court decision in 1987 on a jurisdictional question. On remand, the Court of Appeals for the Federal Circuit ruled against the plaintiffs, and the second petition for *certiorari* to the Supreme Court was not dismissed until three months after Congress had passed and President Reagan had signed the redress legislation. *See* 482 U.S. 64 (1987), *remanded to* 847 F.2d 779 (Fed. Cir. 1988), *cert. denied*, 488 U.S. 925 (1988).

and former congressman from Massachusetts. Over 750 witnesses testified, including ordinary Japanese Americans whose pre-war lives had been shattered by the internment as well as a number of surviving government officials who had participated in the Roosevelt Administration's decision. The Commission's work was successful in several ways. For the many individuals who testified, and for Japanese Americans as a community, the hearings were a painful and cathartic experience. They broke a decades-long community silence. For the government officials who testified, it was an opportunity for some to apologize and for others to maintain steadfastly that they had acted properly.

The Commission's first report, *Personal Justice Denied: Report of the Commission on Wartime Relocation and Internment of Civilians*, was issued in December 1982 with the unanimous backing of all Commission members. The 480–page report gave an account of Japanese–American history in the United States, the decision-making process in Washington, and a conclusion that the internment decision was shaped by "race prejudice, war hysteria and a failure of political leadership."[73] Besides suggesting a national apology in the form of a congressional resolution signed by the President, the Commission recommended, with one dissent, $20,000 individual monetary compensation for each surviving Japanese who had been subjected to exclusion or detention, payable from a $1.5 billion fund. That legislation was passed and funded by Congress.[74]

Aiko Herzig–Yoshinaga had not yet finished participating in these events. During her research and work at the National Archives, she encountered Peter Irons, then a political science professor at the University of Massachusetts, Amherst, who was doing research for a book on the Japanese–American cases. Irons, however, was not simply an accomplished political scientist with published works on the New Deal and the Supreme Court, but an attorney as well. Furthermore, he had been a draft resister during the Vietnam War and had spent one and a half years in federal prison.[75] As he gathered material, he began to realize that besides the opportunity to tell the important and until then untold story in the memos and reports of decades-old conversations, there was also the possibility of legally revisiting the original convictions of Hiraba-

---

[73] Commission on Wartime Relocation and Internment of Civilians, 97th Cong., *Personal Justice Denied: Report of the Commission on Wartime Relocation and Internment of Civilians* 18 (1982). *See also* Commission on Wartime Relocation and Internment of Civilians, 97th Cong., *Personal Justice Denied, Part 2: Recommendations* (1983).

[74] *See generally* LESLIE T. HATAMIYA, RIGHTING A WRONG: JAPANESE AMERICANS AND THE PASSAGE OF THE CIVIL LIBERTIES ACT OF 1988 (1993).

[75] *See* Tony Perry, *Curbs on Use of High Court Tapes Lifted; Law: UC San Diego Professor's Battle Opens the Door to the Distribution and Broadcast of Recordings of U.S. Justices' Sessions*, L.A. TIMES, Nov. 3, 1993, at A36.

yashi, Yasui and Korematsu. Irons and Herzig–Yoshinaga agreed to cooperate and share materials.

Irons and Herzig–Yoshinaga had uncovered clear evidence of disputes between the different government lawyers and hints of a missing document—the original version of General DeWitt's *Final Report*.[76] Prepared by DeWitt after the Japanese had been evacuated, the report had been submitted to the Court and used by the government in its *Korematsu* oral argument. Aiko Herzig–Yoshinaga made the key discovery. During her regular work she noticed an unfamiliar document on an archivist's desk. Thumbing through it, she realized it was a different version of DeWitt's *Final Report*—the suppressed first draft. General DeWitt's original language stated that the evacuation was necessary because it was impossible to distinguish the loyal Japanese from the disloyal Japanese. Insufficient time was not the question. DeWitt wrote that "it was simply a matter of facing the realities that a positive determination could not be made, that an exact separation of the 'sheep from the goats' was unfeasible."[77] In other words, for DeWitt, there was simply no way to tell Japanese apart. Upon receipt of the report in Washington, the Under Secretary of War, John J. McCloy, recognized that the language was at odds with the government position that wartime exigencies necessitated the evacuation. DeWitt's stated reason was a bare racial assertion that loyal and disloyal Japanese could never be distinguished. To be sure, this was a position DeWitt held openly and publicly, most famously saying in public that a "Jap's a Jap. It makes no difference whether he is an American citizen or not."[78] But DeWitt's racist view was not supposed to have been the official position of the Government.

DeWitt, it turned out, had resisted changing his report, but McCloy had finally prevailed. After removing the damaging language, War Department lawyers and officers certified to the "burning of the galley proofs, galley pages, drafts and memorandums of the original report of the Japanese Evacuation."[79] Furthermore, DeWitt's *Final Report*, originally scheduled for release to the general public, was released only to War Department lawyers. The contents of the corrected version were not only withheld from Fred Korematsu's attorneys, they were also not given

---

[76] *See* Irons, *supra* note 9, at 206–12 (citing U.S. War Department, *Final Report, Japanese Evacuation from the West Coast, 1942* (Washington, D.C., 1943)).

[77] Irons, *supra* note 9, at 208.

[78] *See* David Cole, *Enemy Aliens*, 54 Stan. L. Rev. 953, 990 (2002) (citing Brief of Japanese American Citizens League, Amicus Curiae at 198, *Korematsu v. United States*, 323 U.S. 214 (1944) (No. 22), reprinted in 42 Landmark Briefs and Arguments of the Supreme Court of the United States: Constitutional Law 309–530 (Philip B. Kurland & Gerhard Casper eds., 1975)).

[79] Irons, *supra* note 9, at 211.

directly to Justice Department lawyers preparing briefs and oral arguments before the Supreme Court.[80] McCloy, who later went on to a very distinguished career in government and business, always defended both the evacuation and his role, including in his testimony before the Commission on Wartime Relocation in 1981.[81]

The evidence of manipulation and withholding of evidence suggested to Peter Irons that reopening the criminal cases might be possible. Others had made similar suggestions, but the materials Irons and Herzig–Yoshinaga had located in the archives provided, for the first time, a solid evidentiary basis for reexamination. Irons testified before the Commission on Wartime Relocation and was encouraged by Commissioner William Marutani, a judge and the only Japanese American on the panel, to pursue possible *coram nobis* actions. Irons visited all of the former defendants and secured their permission to explore the cases. To proceed further, Irons understood there would have to be a substantial team of volunteer attorneys to represent the three defendants. Defendant Minoru Yasui, a non-practicing attorney, had extensive Japanese community contacts and provided Irons with a list of possible lawyers, but only one was living in any of the cities in which the defendants were tried.[82] That lawyer, Dale Minami, was not an ordinary lawyer.

Dale Minami, son of internees at a camp near Rohwer, Arkansas, was a 1971 graduate of U.C. Berkeley's Boalt Hall during the tumultuous years of demonstrations against the Vietnam War and student strikes for ethnic studies. Minami had begun his practice on a shoestring. He worked out of his Volkswagen minibus, traveling between the Oakland storefront office of the fledgling Asian Law Caucus, the Asian–American Studies Department at U.C. Berkeley, and courtroom appearances in San Francisco and Oakland. A decade later, Minami was a partner in a small, respected firm and was recognized as a leader in Asian–American affairs, having served as the first president of the Asian Pacific Bar Association of California. He was a strong supporter of the redress movement.

Minami responded enthusiastically to Irons' inquiries. After a series of meetings, discussions and draft petitions, Minami and local supporters had organized three teams of attorneys in Portland to work with Minoru Yasui, in Seattle to work with Gordon Hirabayashi, and in the San Francisco Bay Area as counsel to Fred Korematsu. The efforts were

---

[80] *See id.* at 212.

[81] *See id.* at 351.

[82] *See* Peter Irons, *Introduction*, in JUSTICE DELAYED: THE RECORD OF THE JAPANESE-AMERICAN INTERNMENT CASES 9 (Peter Irons ed., 1989).

marked by extraordinary enthusiasm and energy. Irons captures some of the spirit of their work when he describes one visit to the Bay Area:

> One group of Berkeley undergraduates, students in a course on Asian American legal issues taught by Dale Minami and Don Tamaki, prepared a giant chart, some ten feet long, that matched all the important statements in the government documents, court briefs, and Supreme Court opinions, tracing their origins and connections. Despite the intense pace, a note of healthy irreverence marked the work; one lawyer addressed his memos to "Maximal Leader Minami" and signed them "Batty, Bilious Backroom Boy." The legal team began calling itself the "Western Defense Commandos," a play on the Army unit headed by General DeWitt.[83]

Behind the scenes, Aiko Herzig–Yoshinaga continued her quiet work supporting these legal preparations. After leaving the Commission, she and her husband Jack continued their research, turning their Washington apartment into a redress archive of internment files. As much as any individual, her mastery of these materials provided the expertise for the factual allegations at the core of the *coram nobis* petitions.[84] It was reported that during the hearings, one frustrated government attorney described Herzig–Yoshinaga as a "destructive force."[85]

The *Korematsu* petition was filed on January 19, 1983, in the Northern District of California, with the *Hirabayashi* and *Yasui* petitions filed two weeks later. The three defendants had never met as a group until they gathered in Oakland on the eve of the *Korematsu* petition. The filing received national publicity and marked a major legal step in the redress movement. Over the next five years, the three cases went through numerous hearings and appeals. By the end of the proceedings, all three underlying convictions had been vacated.

Two Decades of the Redress Movement

By 1990, the redress movement was essentially over and had achieved stunning successes. On the congressional legislative front, Japanese Americans had received government apologies at the very highest level. The national hearings of the Commission on Wartime Relocation had provided an opportunity for long-suppressed testimonials by those interned in the camps. And in an amazing legislative victory, Congress had enacted and President Reagan had signed the Civil Liber-

---

[83] *Id.* at 13.

[84] *See id.* at 12. *See generally* Thomas Fujita–Rony, *"Destructive Force": Aiko Herzig–Yoshinaga's Gendered Labor in the Japanese American Redress Movement*, 24 FRONTIERS 38 (2003) [hereinafter *Destructive Force*].

[85] *Destructive Force, supra* note 84, at 52.

ties Act of 1988, providing for individual payments of $20,000 to each internee from a trust fund with an authorization of over a billion dollars.[86]

The *coram nobis* petitions were equally successful. Forty years after their convictions, the named defendants in the three wartime Supreme Court opinions had their convictions vacated. While the notoriety of the cases had fueled media attention, the hard work of the teams of volunteers along the length of the Pacific Coast had provided the basis for the courtroom victories.

Even the unsuccessful class action for damages could count itself as contributing to the redress victories. The Supreme Court in its June 1987 decision did not dismiss the action but rather remanded the case for further consideration. That decision came while the redress legislation was still pending in Congress. Several commentators have noted that the Supreme Court kept the litigation alive, in what could have been interpreted as a quiet signal to Congress to take some action on the redress legislation. The ultimate dismissal of the final petition for *certiorari* came just two months after the Civil Liberties Act of 1988 had been signed into law.[87]

Conceptions of Race and Critical Race Theory

Conceptions of Race among the Justices

In 1944, when Justice Murphy sparred with Justice Black over the charge of racism, Murphy's understanding of race and racism drew upon the racial practices of the day. In his *Korematsu* dissent, he points out that the military and General DeWitt in particular used the metaphors of blood, descent, and biology to describe the Japanese race and Japanese racial traits. Murphy further notes that the exclusion applied to all persons with "Japanese blood in their veins," and that in DeWitt's *Final Report*, DeWitt "refers to all individuals of Japanese descent as belonging to 'an enemy race' whose 'racial strains are undiluted.' "[88]

Murphy emphasizes that DeWitt's racial understanding is key to DeWitt's support for the evacuation: "[T]he exclusion order necessarily must rely for its reasonableness upon the assumption that *all* persons of Japanese ancestry may have a dangerous tendency to commit sabotage

---

[86] 50 U.S.C. §§ 1989b–3, 1989b–4 (1988).

[87] *See* Hohri v. United States, 488 U.S. 925 (1988) (denying petition for writ of *certiorari*).

[88] Korematsu v. United States, 323 U.S. 214, 236 (1944) (Murphy, J., dissenting) (quoting from John L. DeWitt, *Final Report, Japanese Evacuation from the West Coast*, 1942).

and espionage.... "[89] In a footnote, Murphy quotes DeWitt's earlier 1943 House testimony:

> I don't want any of them ... here. They are a dangerous element. There is no way to determine their loyalty.... The danger of the Japanese was, and is now—if they are permitted to come back— espionage and sabotage. It makes no difference whether he is an American citizen, he is still a Japanese. American citizenship does not necessarily determine loyalty....[90]

Murphy deems this attribution of the likelihood of disloyalty an assumption of "racial guilt."[91]

In his own analysis and critique of the Army, Justice Murphy avoids DeWitt's crude notions of "Japanese blood" or "racial strains."[92] Murphy carefully separates the social category of Japanese Americans from any particular trait. Thus, he criticizes the Army's justifications as being based upon "questionable racial and sociological grounds not ordinarily within the realm of expert military judgment."[93] He concludes, "[t]he main reasons relied upon by those responsible for the forced evacuation, therefore, do not prove a reasonable relation between the group characteristics of Japanese Americans and the dangers of invasion, sabotage and espionage."[94] Murphy here uses a three-part analysis: (i) the category of Japanese Americans; (ii) their group characteristics—which for Murphy are not necessarily linked to ancestral blood lines; and (iii) the dangerous traits of invasion, sabotage and espionage. Justice Murphy's conclusion is that the group characteristics of the Japanese–American category and the traits of invasion, sabotage and espionage have no demonstrable relationship to each other. The military's inclination to link them together is based on an "accumulation of ... misinformation, half-truths and insinuations."[95] Justice Murphy's analysis is strikingly contemporary. He analyzes whether there is an appropriate nexus between the racial profile and the racial classification. Finding none, he condemns the exclusion and internment of Japanese Americans.

Justice Black's support for the Army in response to Murphy is consistent with the racial understandings of 1944. Black emphasizes the idea of "racial prejudice." He uses the term twice, the second time to

---

[89] *Id.* at 235 (Murphy, J., dissenting).

[90] *Id.* at 236 n.2.

[91] *Id.* at 235.

[92] *Id.* at 235–36.

[93] *Id.* at 236–37.

[94] *Id.* at 239.

[95] *Id.*

distinguish military actions from prejudice: "To cast this case into the outlines of racial prejudice, without reference to the real military dangers which were presented, merely confuses the issue. Korematsu was not excluded from the Military Area because of hostility to him or his race."[96] Black thus strongly suggests that attributions of disloyalty are distinct from notions of "racial prejudice." He offers no clarification as to why the attributions of disloyalty have nothing to do with the West Coast history of hostility to Japanese. He concludes by deferring to the military. The military's actions and its characterizations and conclusions as to "all citizens of Japanese ancestry" should not, in "the calm perspective of hindsight," be deemed "unjustified."[97] For Black, it appears that racial prejudice means *unfounded* racial generalizations, and because he is unwilling to think of himself as holding racial prejudices, he assumes that the stereotypical views he holds of Japanese Americans (not to mention African Americans) are well-founded.

The three dissenters, in contrast, are more cautious in their use of race. Justices Roberts and Jackson emphasize ancestry and citizenship. Justice Roberts refers to "Japanese ancestry" but focuses on whether "it is lawful to compel an American citizen to submit to illegal imprisonment."[98] Justice Jackson uses the terms "citizens of Japanese extraction" and "citizen of Japanese ancestry."[99] As noted above, Justice Murphy's racial usages are also very carefully crafted.

In looking at the language of Justices Black and Murphy in their debate over whether the Army's actions against Japanese were racist, we can now see variations in the way they analyze the concept of race. Justice Black seems at ease with traditional understandings. Racial categories are straightforward and unproblematic, and racism is primarily a question of racial prejudice in the sense of irrational hatred. Justice Murphy's analysis appears more consistent with our current framework of racial profiling. He explicitly discusses the category of Japanese–American citizen, rather than making a common-sense presumption of Japanese as a racial category. On the question of disloyalty of Japanese Americans, Murphy rejects the Army's racially-based presumptions of blood lines and instead demands proof of disloyalty. He seeks evidence to support a conclusion that will be applicable to the entire racial category of Japanese–American citizens and will justify their wholesale incarceration.

---

[96] *Id*. at 223 (Opinion of Black, J.).

[97] *Id*. at 223–24.

[98] *Id*. at 226, 233 (Roberts, J., dissenting).

[99] *Id*. at 245, 246 (Jackson, J., dissenting).

Korematsu and Critical Race Theory

Korematsu v. United States was debated and decided in an America of Southern Jim Crow segregation, legal racial and sex discrimination, widespread prohibition of interracial sex and marriage, racial barriers to the naturalization of immigrants from Asia, and alien land laws, which were state bars to ownership of real property by those immigrants barred from becoming citizens. The end of segregation, the civil rights movement, and the significant population growth of "other non-whites" has meant that American racial practices and our understandings of those racial practices have changed. Equal protection theory, civil rights analysis, and critical race theory have all contributed to a much different terrain for investigations of race and racialization.

A developing focus within critical race theory has been the examination of the distinct legal conditions affecting Asian Americans. Within the writings on Asian Americans in the critical race theory tradition, two intertwined themes relate to these *Korematsu* stories: the *model minority* and *foreignness*. The idea of the *model minority* is that Asians are a successful racial minority within American society and serve as a social "model" for other racial minorities. *Foreignness* ascribes to every Asian the status of immigrant along with a possibility or likelihood of disloyalty to America. Especially since 1965, these two understandings have been applicable to any Asian American. Critical scholars do not claim these conceptions are always present, but rather that they are part of our American tendency to create and impose racialized understandings of people and communities.

Model Minority

In the context of *Korematsu*, the story of the redress movement has evolved into a model minority narrative. A racial minority—Japanese Americans—who have overcome the injustice and racial prejudice of the wartime internment and come to occupy a successful position in American society, can serve as a model for other racial minorities. Most of the books and commentaries on the redress movement participate in this broad narrative of redemptive justice: the wartime internment was the product of "race prejudice, war hysteria and a failure of political leadership."[100] The *coram nobis* cases and the Civil Liberties Act of 1988 complete this story of America's collective redemption for that past injustice. Critique of this model minority narrative was an important theme in several presentations at a 1998 Boston College Symposium:

---

[100] Commission on Wartime Relocation and Internment of Civilians, *supra* note 73, at 18.

The Long Shadow of Korematsu.[101] To vastly over-simplify a large and nuanced literature, the critical race perspective highlights how a seemingly benign characterization such as "model minority" is nonetheless highly problematic: it essentializes Asian Americans; it is inextricably linked with other, less benign characterizations; and it absolves the larger society from responsibility for racial injustice generally by suggesting that a work ethic alone suffices to undo generations of oppression.

Foreignness

In legal journals, the idea of foreignnness as racial was first explored in *"Other Non–Whites" in American Legal History: A Review of Justice at War*, a book review of Peter Irons' treatise.[102] That 1985 essay places the *Korematsu* opinion in the context of some of the landmark Supreme Court opinions that have affected Asian Americans—notably the many decisions on Chinese exclusion and the 1920s decisions upholding the racial barrier to Asians becoming naturalized American citizens. Within this legal history, foreignness can be seen as more than a stereotype or product of misunderstanding. By the end of the nineteenth century, foreignness was an established part of the racial identity of Asian Americans. The emergence of foreignness as applied to Chinese can be seen in the Court's review of Congress' efforts to stop Chinese immigration.

In 1884, Justice Field dissented in the first Supreme Court opinion reviewing the Chinese Restriction Act.[103] Field later came to speak for a majority of the Court on Chinese exclusion:

> [The Chinese] have remained among us a separate people, retaining their original peculiarities of dress, manners, habits, and modes of living, which are as marked as their complexion and language. They live by themselves; they constitute a distinct organization with the laws and customs which they brought from China. Our institutions have made no impression on them during the more than thirty years they have been in the country. They have their own tribunals to which they voluntarily submit, and seek to live in a manner similar to that of China. They do not and will not assimilate with our

---

[101] *See* Sumi Cho, *Redeeming Whiteness in the Shadow of Internment: Earl Warren, Brown, and a Theory of Racial Redemption*, 19 B.C. THIRD WORLD L.J. 73 (1998); Chris K. Iijima, *Reparations and the "Model Minority" Ideology of Acquiescence: The Necessity to Refuse the Return to Original Humiliation*, 19 B.C. THIRD WORLD L. J. 385 (1998); *see also* Natsu Taylor Saito, *Symbolism Under Siege: Japanese American Redress and the "Racing" of Arab Americans as "Terrorists,"* 8 ASIAN L.J. 1 (2001). On the model minority generally, see FRANK H. WU, YELLOW: RACE IN AMERICA BEYOND BLACK AND WHITE (2002).

[102] Neil Gotanda, *"Other Non–Whites" in American Legal History: A Review of* Justice at War, 85 COLUM. L. REV. 1186 (1985).

[103] Chew Heong v. United States, 112 U.S. 536 (1884).

people; and their dying wish is that their bodies may be taken to China for burial.[104]

The argument of the Asian–American critical race theorists has been that foreignness and its variations, including inassimilability and disloyalty, emerged as part of the racialized understandings of Chinese, Japanese and other Asian Americans. These notions were clearly at work, if just below the surface, in *Korematsu*.

Korematsu *Rehabilitated*

The modern rehabilitation of *Korematsu* begins with Chief Justice Rehnquist's discussion in *All The Laws But One*.[105] Rehnquist's defense is not unequivocal and he is less than precise in his analysis of Black's opinion. But in his second of two chapters on these opinions, he focuses on the distinction between citizens and non-citizens. He strongly defends the government actions as to aliens, though he seems troubled by the difference in treatment between Japanese aliens versus German and Italian resident aliens. Ultimately, he gives credence to the military claims that the proximity and concentration of Japanese near militarily sensitive locations created security concerns. He concludes: "These distinctions seem insufficient to justify such a sharp difference of treatment between Japanese and German and Italian aliens in peacetime. But they do seem legally adequate to support the difference in treatment between the two classes of enemy aliens in time of war."[106]

Presaging his joinder of Justice O'Connor's plurality opinion in the *Hamdi* case, in his book, Rehnquist is more troubled by the treatment of Japanese–American citizens. He faults the military for its speedy judgment of the possible disloyalty of the Nisei. The available information, he writes,

> might have justified exclusion of Nisei, as opposed to other citizens, from work in aircraft factories without strict security clearance, but it falls considerably short of justifying the dislodging of thousands of citizens from their homes on the basis of ancestry. The submissions by the military showed no particular factual inquiry into the likelihood of espionage or sabotage by Nisei, only generalized conclusions that they were "different" from other Americans. But the military has no special expertise in this field, and it should have taken far

---

[104] *Id*. at 566–67 (Field, J., dissenting). Justice Field's description of Chinese is similar in spirit in subsequent Chinese exclusion cases.

[105] Rehnquist, *supra* note 3.

[106] *Id*. at 211.

more substantial findings to justify this sort of discrimination, even in wartime.[107]

How then does Rehnquist defend Black's majority opinion? He observes that constitutional doctrine had not yet matured, either as to the Fifth Amendment equal protection considerations or as to the question of racial discrimination itself. He points to the 1954 decisions in *Brown v. Board of Education* and its companion case, *Bolling v. Sharpe*, as establishing necessary precedent. Rehnquist concludes, "Had this doctrine been the law ten years earlier, the Supreme Court might have found it easier to reach a different result in *Hirabayashi* and *Korematsu*."[108]

Chief Justice Rehnquist implicitly disagrees with the three dissenters as to whether it was appropriate in 1944 to overrule the actions of the government. But he is at least sympathetic to the Japanese, both citizen and non-citizen, in his examination of those events.

Judge Posner's defense of *Korematsu* is far less measured and much broader in scope. For Posner, the *Korematsu* case was correctly decided. In his usual outspoken fashion, he made the following statement in a 2001 Chicago forum, later published in *Harper's Magazine*:

> Although the majority opinion, written by Justice Hugo Black is very poor, the decision itself is defensible. The court could have said: We interpret the Constitution to allow racial discrimination by the government when there are urgent reasons for it, and if the military in the middle of a world war says we have to do this, then we're going to defer, because the Constitution is not a suicide pact.[109]

Judge Posner's argument is also presented in *Breaking the Deadlock: The 2000 Election, the Constitution and the Courts*, his book on the 2000 presidential election.[110] There he links the question to an argument against "liberals" who support affirmative action. His criticism, however, is polemical rather than analytic, so it is unclear as to his own exact standard of review. His language from *Harper's Magazine* suggests that when the military acts under its emergency war powers, even if the actions constitute racial discrimination that would otherwise violate equal protection, the proper standard of review for the courts is to defer to the military. His view appears to be quite close to the one expressed in Justice Frankfurter's *Korematsu* concurrence.

---

[107] *Id*. at 209.

[108] *Id*. at 208.

[109] Pamela Karlan & Richard Posner, *The Triumph of Expedience*, HARPER'S MAG., May 2001, at 39.

[110] RICHARD A. POSNER, BREAKING THE DEADLOCK: THE 2000 ELECTION, THE CONSTITUTION, AND THE COURTS 170–73 (2001).

Posner disparages Justice Jackson's *Korematsu* dissent as an "elo-quent but strange opinion." Posner doubts that "because a court is in no position to determine the reasonableness of a military order, the order's reasonableness cannot be a defense to a charge of racial discrimina-tion."[111] For Posner, so long as the military actions are reasonable, they are constitutional—even if the crisis has subsided and regardless of whether the case involves an examination of war powers alone or a particular application of Fifth Amendment equal protection principles.

Neither Chief Justice Rehnquist nor Judge Posner was writing in reaction to the attacks of September 11. Their comments were responses to the broad range of issues facing America at the end of the century. Large-scale violence had already visited the United States in the 1990s in the form of the Oklahoma City and the first World Trade Center bombings. The Supreme Court had issued its opinion in *Reno v. Ameri-can–Arab Anti–Discrimination Committee* holding the Court lacked juris-diction to consider a selective-enforcement suit based on the deportation of eight non-citizens, initially targeted because of their association with an "international terrorist and communist organization."[112] It is not surprising, therefore, that the *Korematsu* opinion would reemerge as the basis for a new examination of civil liberties in wartime.

And if *Korematsu* was once again relevant before September 11, 2001, the aftermath of that tragic day only heightens its contemporary importance. Accordingly, let us examine some of the anti-terrorist ac-tions taken by our government in light of the three issues originally debated in *Korematsu*: Is the action racist? Do the actions involve detention and incarceration in violation of due process? And what is the role of the courts in reviewing measures taken in the name of national security?

Is Ethnic Profiling of "Arab–Looking Men" Racist? Revisiting Hugo Black

David Cole discussed the use of "ethnic profiling" in his critique of government actions in the War on Terrorism. In the wake of the September 11 attacks, he reports both anecdotes and opinion surveys supporting closer security scrutiny of "Arab-looking men" boarding airplanes.[113] To ask whether this is a racist practice is to revisit the assertion Hugo Black made about the exclusion of Japanese Americans. Black stated: "Korematsu was not excluded . . . because of hostility to him or his race. He was excluded because we are at war with the

---

[111] *Id.*

[112] 525 U.S. 471, 473 (1999).

[113] Cole, *supra* note 78, at 974.

Japanese Empire. . . . ''[114] To paraphrase Black's assertion in the current context would be to claim "ethnic profiling" of Arab Americans is not a question of racial prejudice—i.e., it is not racist—but rather, it is done because we are at war with Arab (or somewhat more precisely, radical Islamic) terrorists.

Justice Black's assertion about the potential for disloyalty of Japanese Americans was supported by the history and currency of applying the presumptions of "foreignness" to Japanese Americans. Today, the assertion that racial profiling is not racial prejudice turns upon the idea that greater security measures against Arab Americans and Muslim Americans are simply a common-sense application of the idea that Arabs and Muslims are more likely to be disloyal terrorists. In other words, the presumption of foreignness applies to Arabs and Muslims—they are more likely to be disloyal in wartime. The follow-up conclusion is that we should defer to the government for emergency assessment of the need for profiling.

Having placed the issue in the context of Black's *Korematsu* opinion, we continue to face the questions of race and racism. We must question these conceptions both as a society and as a matter of constitutional law. While the critical race theorists and Asian–American studies scholars argue that acting upon the presumption of foreignness amounts to racial prejudice, this is not a universally held conclusion. At the popular level, the opinion surveys that Cole cites in his article suggest strongly that we do not have a popular consensus that ascribing foreignness to different groups—most saliently of late, Arab Americans and (to a lesser extent) Chinese Americans—is really racial prejudice and therefore racist.[115]

Moreover, even if we do conclude that the attribution of foreignness is a form of prejudice, we could treat the "inconvenience" of such security measures as more intrusive airport checks as simply the price citizens must pay in wartime. Just as a unanimous Supreme Court in *Hirabayashi* upheld the imposition of a curfew applicable only to Japanese Americans, so we might say that profiling of Arab Americans for security purposes is a troublesome but permissible practice.

To put the best face on the argument for profiling, we might accept that the risk that any particular Arab American intends to bring about catastrophic harm is exceedingly small, but also think there nonetheless really are a small number of people who do intend such harm, and that these people are disproportionately or even overwhelmingly Arab and/or Muslim. If the factual predicate is correct, does this justify profiling

---

[114] Korematsu v. United States, 323 U.S. 214, 223 (1944).

[115] On racial profiling of Arab Americans, see generally Saito, *supra* note 101. On racial profiling of Chinese Americans, see generally Neil Gotanda, *Comparative Racialization: Racial Profiling and the Case of Wen Ho Lee*, 47 UCLA L. REV. 1689 (2000).

Arabs and Muslims? Does the answer depend upon the scale of the harm likely to be inflicted? Given the difficulty of quantifying both the size of the harm and the risk, is it possible to distinguish between sober cost-benefit analysis and racial prejudice?

Korematsu is clearly relevant but does not provide clear answers to these questions. In World War II, many people who later came to be regarded as civil libertarians were prepared to credit the military's unsupported assumptions about Japanese Americans. Those who support profiling Arabs and Muslims today no doubt think their judgments based on facts rather than prejudice, but that was true of those who supported the Japanese curfew, exclusion, and detention as well. The fact that the supporters of racial profiling were wrong then does not necessarily mean today's supporters of the practice will be proven wrong by history, of course. But *Korematsu* should at least give us pause.

Do Government Actions Against Citizens Violate Due Process?

In his book, Chief Justice Rehnquist drew a sharp distinction between citizens and non-citizens, while Judge Posner's support for *Korematsu* does not depend on the distinction.[116] The Supreme Court itself later held in *Hamdi* that a citizen cannot simply be detained in military custody as dangerous on the say-so of the President.[117] As Justice O'Connor memorably wrote: "a state of war is not a blank check for the President when it comes to the rights of the Nation's citizens."[118] A concurrence in *Hamdi* by Justice Souter (joined by Justice Ginsburg) would have invalidated the detention on statutory grounds, repeatedly noting that the nation's laws had been amended precisely to avoid "another *Korematsu*."[119] Even the Bush Administration recognized the citizen versus non-citizen distinction, while unsuccessfully arguing for substantial authority over citizens as well.

The *Hamdi* Court measured the due process rights of citizens by a balancing test.[120] War-on-terror cases involving non-citizens confirm a judicial role in reviewing military authority, although by the end of the Bush Administration, the courts still had not spelled out the substantive rights of detainees. (Chapter 15 addresses these cases in detail.) Whether President Obama's decision to close the detention facility at Guantanamo Bay—with its uncomfortable echoes of *Korematsu*—moots the question of substantive rights remains to be seen.

---

[116] *See* Rehnquist, *supra* note 3, at 205; Posner, *supra* note 110, at 170–73.

[117] Hamdi v. Rumsfeld, 542 U.S. 507 (2004).

[118] *Id.* at 536.

[119] *Id.* at 543 (Souter, J., concurring).

[120] *Id.* at 532–33.

Judicial Review

Since *Korematsu*, there has been little support for Justice Jackson's suggestion that the courts should not attempt to stop reasonable military actions, but apply constitutional standards after the crisis has passed. Indeed, Justice O'Connor's *Hamdi* plurality cited Justice Murphy's *Korematsu* dissent for the proposition that the Court retains power to review the reasonableness of military claims of authority, even during wartime.

By contrast, Jackson's assertion of the ultimate authority of the Court and the proper application of constitutional standards against "racial discrimination in criminal procedure and of transplanting American citizens" has taken root.[121] And his metaphor of the alternative approach leaving a dangerous principle that "lies about like a loaded weapon ready for the hand of any authority that can bring forward a plausible claim of an urgent need,"[122] has been frequently quoted in defense of civil liberties.

The War on Terrorism has created an additional dimension of uncertainty to Jackson's formulations. Exactly when did the War on Terrorism start? On September 11, 2001, when the attacks occurred? On September 14, 2001, when Congress authorized the President to use force against those who participated or aided in the attacks?[123] Is a congressional declaration of war necessary to trigger deferential review of government actions, and if so, has Congress issued such a declaration or its equivalent? And what will mark the end of the War on Terrorism?

Justice Jackson's comments were made in an era when wars were usually declared and a cease-fire or surrender marked an end to war. We are now in an era of continuing conflict and ongoing military actions. Does this imply indefinite deference? Although the Supreme Court has made clear that it can exercise judicial review over military actions, it has barely begun to specify the substance of that review. The legacy of *Korematsu* remains uncertain.

---

[121] Korematsu v. United States, 323 U.S. 214, 246 (1944) (Jackson, J., dissenting).

[122] *Id.*

[123] *See Authorization for Use of Military Forces*, H.J. Res. 64, 107th Cong. (2001).

*

8

Stephen Ansolabehere and Samuel Issacha-roff*

The Story of *Baker v. Carr*

Occasionally in all walks of life, law included, there are break-throughs that have the quality of truth revealed. Not only do such ideas have overwhelming force, but they alter the world in which they operate. In the wake of such breakthroughs, it is difficult to imagine what existed before. Such is the American conception of constitutional democracy before and after the "reapportionment revolution" of the 1960s.

Although legislative redistricting today is not without its riddle of problems, it is difficult to imagine so bizarre an apportionment scheme as the way legislative power was rationed out in Tennessee, the setting for *Baker v. Carr*. Tennessee apportioned power through, in Justice Clark's words, "a crazy quilt without rational basis."[1] Indeed, nearly half a century after *Baker*, with "one person, one vote" a fundamental principle of our democracy, it may be hard to imagine what all the constitutional fuss was about. Yet the decision in *Baker*, which had striking immediate impact, marked a profound transformation in American democracy. The man who presided over this transformation, Chief Justice Earl Warren, called *Baker* "the most important case of [his] tenure on the Court."[2]

Perhaps the simplest way to understand the problem is to imagine the role of the legislator faced with the command to reapportion legislative districts after each decennial census. Shifts in population mean that

* The authors wish to thank Maclin Davis, Harrison Gilbert, and John Seigenthaler for their time and support for this project, and to thank Daniel Suleiman for his research assistance. Ansolabehere gratefully acknowledges the support of the Carnegie Foundation for this research.

[1] *Baker v. Carr*, 369 U.S. 186, 254 (1962) (Clark, J., concurring).

[2] Earl Warren, *The Memoirs of Earl Warren* 306 (1977), *quoted in* Lucas A. Powe, Jr., *The Warren Court and American Politics* 200 (2000).

new areas of a state are likely to emerge as the dominant forces of a legislature. But what if the power to stem the tide were as simple as refusing to reapportion? It happened at the national level when Congress, realizing that the swelling tide of immigrant and industrial workers had moved power to the Northeast and the Midwest, simply refused to reapportion after the 1920 census. And it happened throughout the U.S. for much of the twentieth century as rural power blocs in state legislatures realized that reapportioning would yield power to the urban and suburban voters and remove incumbent politicians from their clubby sinecure.

When the original complaint in *Baker* was filed in 1959, the Tennessee Legislature had been refusing for nearly fifty years to apportion the state legislative districts. This was despite the express requirement of the Tennessee Constitution that each legislative district have the same number of qualified voters.[3] As a result, there existed an enormous disparity in the voting strength of individual voters. For example, south-central Moore County, with 2,340 voters, had one seat in each house of the state legislature, while Shelby County, covering the city of Memphis, had only seven seats for its 312,345 voters.[4] "Districts with 40 percent of the state's voters could elect sixty-three of the ninety-nine members of the house, and districts with 37 percent of the voters could elect twenty of the thirty-three members of the senate."[5]

This pattern of maldistribution of representatives, which existed across the country, resulted from the increasingly urban nature of American life during the twentieth century. As urban areas grew, the malapportionment of representatives increased. Between 1900 and 1960, the voting population of Tennessee grew from 487,380 to 2,092,891.[6] Accompanying this growth was a massive migration from the rural areas of the state to the cities of Memphis, Nashville, Knoxville, and Chattanooga. And, while the Tennessee Constitution provided for legislative reapportionment on the basis of each decennial census, there was no way for the people of Tennessee to compel the legislature to reapportion. The state courts were unresponsive to the cause,[7] and Tennessee lacked any procedure of popular referendum or initiative. Because rural Tennessee legislators, like those in Georgia, Alabama, Florida, California, and many other states, had everything to lose by reapportioning their legislative

---

[3] For the relevant provisions of the Tennessee Constitution, see *Baker*, 369 U.S. at 188–89.

[4] Powe, *supra* note 2, at 200.

[5] *Id.*

[6] *Baker*, 369 U.S. at 192.

[7] *See Kidd v. McCanless*, 292 S.W.2d 40 (Tenn. 1956), *cert. denied*, 352 U.S. 920 (1956).

districts according to the population shift, they stood firm, decade after decade defying the mandate of their state constitution. And "when the movement toward [the cities] began, then swelled to floods at the end of World War II, the political power stayed behind on the cotton flats, the hills and the ridgeland farms."[8] The only remedy for this profoundly lopsided version of democracy lay in the hands of the very legislators whose political lives depended upon its continued existence. In short, the majority of voters in Tennessee were "caught up in a legislative strait jacket."[9]

Yet it was not until 1962, when the Supreme Court announced in *Baker* that challenging the constitutionality of a legislative apportionment "presents no nonjusticiable 'political question,' "[10] that a cure for the disproportionate concentration of power in the hands of rural legislators was finally found. Why were the obstacles to judicial correction of legislative misapportionment so difficult to overcome?

Before Baker

Tennessee was not alone in the first half of the twentieth century in its unwillingness to reapportion.[11] "[R]ural control of mid-century state legislatures was a political fact of life,"[12] as were disparities in voter strength in national congressional districts. The reason, in large part, was that, pre-*Baker*, the leading Supreme Court case on the subject declared the federal judiciary powerless to intervene in reapportionment controversies.[13]

A. Colegrove v. Green *and Frankfurter's "political thicket"*

The dispute in *Colegrove v. Green*[14] arose over Illinois's failure to equitably apportion the state's congressional districts. After establishing election districts in 1901, the Illinois Legislature refused to reapportion according to the huge urban population growth, as documented in the censuses of 1910, 1920, 1930, and 1940; this failure to reapportion led in

---

[8] Gene Graham, *One Man, One Vote:* Baker v. Carr *and the American Levellers* 15 (1972).

[9] *Baker*, 369 U.S. at 259 (Clark, J., concurring).

[10] *Id.* at 209.

[11] For a list of congressionally-maldistricted states as of 1958 population figures, see Anthony Lewis, *Legislative Apportionment and the Federal Courts*, 71 Harv. L. Rev. 1057, 1062 n.26 (1958).

[12] Powe, *supra* note 2, at 200.

[13] *Colegrove v. Green*, 328 U.S. 549 (1946).

[14] *Id.*

turn to election districts ranging in population from 112,000 to more than 900,000.[15] As alleged in the complaint, "in one district, a voter ha[d] the voting strength of eight voters in another district."[16]

At the time *Colegrove* was decided, the injustice of the situation in Illinois was well recognized. The district court, dismissing the complaint in a per curiam decision, called it "disgraceful,"[17] finding that Supreme Court precedent "has resulted in our reaching a conclusion contrary to that which we would have reached but for that decision."[18] The court continued: "We are an inferior court. We are bound by the decision of the Supreme Court, even though we do not agree with the decision or the reasons which support it."[19] Justice Black, writing for three of the seven Justices who participated in the decision, dissented from the Supreme Court's subsequent rejection of the challenge on the grounds that the Illinois Apportionment Act of 1901 violated the Equal Protection Clause and Article I of the Constitution.[20] Even Justice Rutledge, who in a special concurrence cast the deciding vote in favor of dismissing the complaint, agreed that "the case made by the complaint is strong."[21]

The opinion of Justice Frankfurter, however, which he wrote on behalf of three Justices (including himself), took a different view, and it is that view which became controlling for the next sixteen years. In spite of the seeming unfairness of rural legislators' refusal to reapportion in Illinois and, by extension, across the country, Frankfurter believed that the Court had no role to play in solving the problem. First, he believed that for the Court to intervene would be to enter a sphere of power reserved to the legislative branch, that to do so would "cut very deep into the very being of Congress."[22] Second, he had concerns about the institutional competence of the Court in redressing apportionment wrongs, the resolution of which "this Court has traditionally held aloof."[23] Third, Frankfurter thought the Court poorly positioned to fashion a remedy. "At best we could only declare the existing electoral system invalid,"[24] he wrote. "The result would be to leave Illinois

---

[15] *Id.* at 569 (Black, J., dissenting).

[16] *Colegrove v. Green*, 64 F.Supp. 632, 633 (N.D. Ill. 1946) (per curiam).

[17] *Id.* at 633.

[18] *Id.* at 634 (relying on *Wood v. Broom*, 287 U.S. 1, 6 (1932)).

[19] *Id.*

[20] *Colegrove*, 328 U.S. at 569–70 (Black, J., dissenting).

[21] *Id.* at 565 (Rutledge, J., concurring).

[22] *Id.* at 556 (Opinion of Frankfurter, J.).

[23] *Id.* at 553 (Opinion of Frankfurter, J.).

[24] *Id.*

undistricted and to bring into operation, if the Illinois legislature chose not to act, the choice of members for the House of Representatives on a state-wide ticket. The last stage may be worse than the first."[25] This view was echoed by Justice Rutledge, who voted to dismiss the complaint "for want of equity," because "the cure sought may be worse than the disease."[26]

Finally, and at the heart of Frankfurter's opinion, was the firm belief that the judiciary simply did not belong in the "peculiarly political" battles over reapportionment: "[D]ue regard for the effective working of our Government [has] revealed this issue to be of a peculiarly political nature and therefore not meet for judicial determination."[27] This application of the so-called "political question" doctrine reflected Frankfurter's concerns, and those of Justices Reed and Burton, who joined the opinion, about the prudential limitations on the Court's jurisdiction. In what is perhaps the most oft-quoted passage from the decision, Frankfurter declared: "Courts ought not to enter this political thicket."[28]

And so they didn't. Legislative reapportionment was left to the ordinary political process, which was effectively to doom it to failure. As Anthony Lewis recognized in 1958:

> If [Frankfurter's argument] is not a cynical resolution of the problem—and it surely is not so intended—its premise must be that there is a reasonable chance of action in the legislative branches. But the historical evidence indicates that there is no basis whatsoever for this premise.
>
> Legislative fairness in districting is inhibited by factors built into our political structure. Once a group has the dominant position—as the rural legislators generally have—its overriding interest is to maintain that position. The motives of most individual legislators are just as selfish. Any substantial change in districts means that the members must face new constituents and deal with uncertainties—in short, undergo risks that few politicians would voluntarily put upon themselves. Voting for a fair apportionment bill would in many cases mean voting oneself out of office. That is too much to ask of most politicians. The result is that the state legislatures do not reapportion fairly or, more commonly, do not reapportion at all.[29]

---

[25] *Id.* (Opinion of Frankfurter, J.).

[26] *Id.* at 565–66 (Rutledge, J., concurring).

[27] *Id.* at 552 (Opinion of Frankfurter, J.).

[28] *Id.* at 556 (Opinion of Frankfurter, J.).

[29] Lewis, *supra* note 11, at 1091–92 (footnote omitted).

Not surprisingly, following the Supreme Court's decision in *Colegrove*, legislative malapportionment remained "a political fact of life."[30] With little incentive to reapportion, and no threat from the judiciary, rural state legislators were free to continue disregarding state constitutional requirements, thereby denying city-dwellers adequate representation in state legislatures and Congress. The result for the country's rapidly growing cities was devastating. John F. Kennedy described the problem in a *New York Times Magazine* article he wrote while still a Senator. Calling unrepresentative state legislatures "the shame of the states," Kennedy wrote:

> [T]he urban majority is, politically, a minority and the rural minority dominates the polls. Of all the discriminations against urban areas, the most fundamental and the most blatant is political: the apportionment of representation in our Legislatures and (to a lesser extent) in Congress has been either deliberately rigged or shamefully ignored so as to deny the cities and their voters that full and proportionate voice in government to which they are entitled. The failure of our governments to respond to the problems of the cities reflects this basic political discrimination.[31]

Yet as the Supreme Court confirmed in several cases after *Colegrove*,[32] the courts were powerless, or just unwilling, to intervene.

B.   *A Crack in the Plaster*: Gomillion v. Lightfoot

The 1960 case of *Gomillion v. Lightfoot*,[33] however, cast a pall over the logic of *Colegrove*—in spite of Frankfurter's having written the *Gomillion* opinion for a unanimous Court.

The challenge in *Gomillion* arose over Local Act No. 140 of the Alabama State Legislature, passed in 1957, which redefined the boundaries of the City of Tuskegee in such a way as to exclude 99 percent of Tuskegee's black voters from the municipality:

> Prior to the passage of Act No. 140, the boundaries of the municipality ... formed a square, and, according to the complaint ... contained approximately 5,397 Negroes, of whom approximately 400 were qualified as voters in Tuskegee, and contained 1,310 white persons, of whom approximately 600 were qualified voters in said municipality. As the boundaries are redefined by said Act No. 140,

---

[30] Powe, *supra* note 2, at 200.

[31] John F. Kennedy, '*The Shame of the States*', N.Y. Times Mag., May 18, 1958, at 12, 37.

[32] *See, e.g., Kidd v. McCanless*, 352 U.S. 920 (1956); *South v. Peters*, 339 U.S. 276 (1950); *MacDougall v. Green*, 335 U.S. 281 (1948).

[33] 364 U.S. 339 (1960).

the municipality of Tuskegee resembles a "sea dragon." The effect of the Act is to remove from the municipality of Tuskegee all but four or five of the qualified Negro voters and none of the qualified white voters.[34]

The *Gomillion* plaintiffs, black citizens of Alabama who were residents of Tuskegee at the time of the redistricting, claimed that the Act redrawing the shape of their municipality so as to exclude them from it discriminated against them in violation of the Due Process and Equal Protection Clauses of the Fourteenth Amendment and denied them the right to vote in violation of the Fifteenth Amendment.[35] While the district and circuit courts sustained the defendants' motion to dismiss, the Supreme Court unanimously reversed, holding that "if the allegations are established, the inescapable human effect of this essay in geometry and geography is to despoil colored citizens, and only colored citizens, of their theretofore enjoyed voting rights,"[36] in violation of the Fifteenth Amendment.

Frankfurter, as the author of the principal opinion in *Colegrove*, took pains to distinguish that case, arguing that because the Alabama Legislature was singling out a racial minority for special discriminatory treatment, in violation of the Fifteenth Amendment, the case was "wholly different" from *Colegrove*:[37] "Apart from all else," he wrote, "these considerations lift this controversy out of the so-called 'political' arena and into the conventional sphere of constitutional litigation."[38]

But as one commentator noted:

> [T]he Tuskegee case had put [Frankfurter] in a most distressing philosophical quandary. As a case involving districting by a state legislature in a voting situation, it ran across the grain of ... labeling ... such cases as political and beyond judicial remedy. But to deny remedy in this instance was to permit blatant racial discrimination of the sort that Frankfurter had never been willing to tolerate.[39]

While the Fifteenth Amendment claim made in *Gomillion*, that the Alabama Legislature had denied plaintiffs the right to vote on the basis of race, did effectively distinguish the case from the situation in *Colegrove*, which involved the dilution of the urban vote, Frankfurter's

---

[34] *Gomillion v. Lightfoot*, 167 F.Supp. 405, 407 (M.D. Ala. 1958).

[35] *Gomillion*, 364 U.S. at 340.

[36] *Id.* at 347.

[37] *Id.* at 346.

[38] *Id.* at 346–47.

[39] Graham, *supra* note 8, at 223.

argument that the "peculiarly political nature" of districting removed it from the province of the courts was at least called into question. Frankfurter himself was compelled to note in *Gomillion* that to exalt the states' political power "to establish, destroy, or reorganize . . . its political subdivisions . . . into an absolute is to misconceive the reach and rule of this Court's decisions."[40] He remarked further that "[w]hen a State exercises power wholly within the domain of state interest, it is insulated from federal judicial review. But such insulation is not carried over when state power is used as an instrument for circumventing a federally protected right."[41]

After *Gomillion*, the logic of *Colegrove* that the remedy for unfair legislative districting lay exclusively in the hands of the legislature seemed considerably less compelling; less than two years later, it came undone.

The Politics of Constitutional Litigation

Constitutional law's traditional focus on the courts as the only relevant actors misses the dynamics of constitutional litigation. Particularly in the domain of the apportionment of political power, constitutional litigation is inevitably infused with a large dose of political struggle. The path to *Baker v. Carr* not only was no exception; it was almost the embodiment of this principle.

With continued urban population growth following World War II, malapportionment in state legislatures only worsened.[42] As a result, political pressures to change the districting process in the states intensified. The National Municipal League, the United States Conference of Mayors, and other organizations interested in stronger urban legislative representation sought to change state legislative apportionment through the ballot, legislation, and legal action.[43] Occasionally these efforts yielded significant state court cases, but the state courts, citing Frankfurter's opinion in *Colegrove*, chose to stay out of the legislative process.[44] But even had state courts been willing to hear these challenges on the merits, judicially-mandated reapportionment would not necessarily have resulted. There were other obstacles to equal population representation.

---

[40] *Gomillion*, 364 U.S. at 342.

[41] *Id.* at 347.

[42] Paul T. David and Ralph Eisenberg, *Devaluation of the Urban and Suburban Vote: A Statistical Investigation of Long–Term Trends in State Legislative Representation* 7–16 (1961).

[43] Ward E.Y. Elliott, *The Rise of Guardian Democracy* 13–16 (1974).

[44] *See Reynolds v. Sims*, 377 U.S. 533, 613–14 (1964) (Harlan, J., dissenting) (providing history of post-*Colegrove* litigation, including summary affirmances by Supreme Court).

Three political obstacles proved nearly insurmountable during the 1950s. First, most states required constitutional revision to eliminate malapportionment. In 1962, thirty-five state constitutions contained provisions that inevitably produced unequal district populations.[45] The most common such requirement was a guarantee that every county or, in the New England states, town receive at least one seat in the legislature. The Connecticut Constitution, written in 1818, guaranteed all towns at least one state representative and no town more than two. Nothing short of a constitutional convention could have changed this arrangement. Holding a constitutional convention, however, may not have produced population-based districting. In 1902, Connecticut called a constitutional convention to address, among other matters, the basis of representation, but the compromise produced by that body was not acceptable to the electorate.[46] In other states, more recent conventions actually created the unequal representation, such as New York in 1894 and Ohio in 1903.[47]

Second, in many states, the electorate supported malapportionment. Between the *Colegrove* and *Baker* decisions, at least ten states voted on measures that sought to change the apportionment of legislative seats or to force the legislature to abide by existing requirements.[48] In some of these states, such as California and Florida, reapportionment was brought before the electorate several times between 1946 and 1962. In all but Washington State, initiatives to make representation in both chambers based on population failed. Initiatives in Arkansas and Michigan put new, permanent boundaries in place in the 1950s. Indeed, it was the initiative process that produced the most inequitable representation. For example, the California electorate approved a "federal plan" in 1926 that replaced population-based representation in the Senate with an apportionment that gave each county at most one seat in the Senate.[49]

Third, state legislatures often failed to reapportion in line with population, even when it was their constitutional duty. In 1956, the voters of Washington State approved through initiative a new state

---

[45] Gordon E. Baker, *State Constitutions: Reapportionment* 1–23, 63–70 (1960); Robert B. McKay, *Reapportionment: The Law and Politics of Equal Representation* 459–75 (1965).

[46] *See* Wesley W. Horton, *Connecticut Constitutional History, 1776–1988*, at 22–24, *in Connecticut's Four Constitutions* (1988), *available at* http://www.cslib.org/cts4ch.htm (last modified Dec. 1, 2008).

[47] *See* McKay, *supra* note 45, at 380–90, 397–401.

[48] These are Arkansas, California, Colorado, Florida, Illinois, Michigan, Missouri, Oregon, Texas, and Washington.

[49] Stephen Ansolabehere et al., *Why Did a Majority of Californians Choose to Limit Their Own Power?*, Paper Presented at the Annual Meeting of the American Political Science Association (Sept. 1999).

legislative district map that would have created equal population representation. The state legislature promptly amended the initiative to keep the boundaries substantially the same as before the initiative.[50] Twelve state legislatures in 1962 had significant malapportionment solely because they had failed or refused to comply with constitutional requirements of equal district populations at each decennial census.[51]

Such was the case in Tennessee. The 1890 Tennessee Constitution required representation on the basis of population in both the Senate and the House, but by 1962 neither chamber had been reapportioned since 1901.

A. *Kidd v. McCanless*

The Tennessee legislature's refusal to reapportion in fifty years was symptomatic of broader sociological factors that affected all states and specific political factors at work in the state. As in many other states, the rapid growth of Tennessee's urban population at the end of the nineteenth century prompted those in power to keep their positions by not reapportioning.[52]

Paradoxically, state politics in Tennessee were dominated not just by a rural faction, but also by a powerful urban machine that was led by a single individual. From 1932 to 1954, Edward Hull Crump controlled the sizable Memphis vote through political control of city and county jobs and by managing the African–American vote. He was then able to leverage that vote into the controlling share within the statewide Democratic primaries.[53] Within the legislature, Crump forged an alliance with eastern Tennessee Republicans and rural Democrats to block his rivals within the legislature from the other cities, Chattanooga, Knoxville, and, especially, Nashville. East Tennessee Republicans gained safe U.S. House seats in exchange for their support of this arrangement, and rural Democrats were given disproportionate power within the state legislature. Even though it was underrepresented, Memphis in this way was able to broker power within the legislature.

---

[50] McKay, *supra* note 45, at 444.

[51] Alabama, Indiana, Kansas, Kentucky, Michigan, Minnesota, Nebraska, Oklahoma, Tennessee, Washington, Wisconsin, and Wyoming were noted by Robert McKay, *id.* at 460–75, for their failures to reapportion in line with state constitutional requirements. Minnesota had slight reapportionment in 1959 under court order, but not enough to create districts with equal populations.

[52] The phenomenon occurred in many other democracies as well, most notably England. *See* Charles Seymour, *Electoral Reform in England and Wales: The Development and Operation of the Parliamentary Franchise, 1832–1885*, at 489–518 (1915). On California, see Ansolabehere et al., *supra* note 49.

[53] *See* V. O. Key, Jr., *Southern Politics in State and Nation* 58–81 (1949).

Legal challenges to malapportionment occurred as political reformers began to mobilize in the aftermath of the Memphis machine suffering twin setbacks in statewide elections. In 1948, Estes Kefauver defeated U.S. Senator Tom Stewart; then, four years later, Albert Gore, Sr., defeated U.S. Senator K.D. McKellar. Although Kefauver and Gore by no means controlled the state's politics, they served as prominent critics of the state's Democratic establishment. While the Crump organization still brokered power within the state, it now had prominent rivals who held a different vision of civil and political rights. More than that, Kefauver and Gore were the inspiration for a new generation of reformers. That generational change accelerated, along with the disintegration of the political alignments within the state, when, in October 1954, Boss Crump died.

Reapportionment politics took a decided turn that year as well. In the fall of 1954, Haynes and Mayne Miller, brothers and partners in their own law firm in Johnson City, Tennessee, decided to raise a legal challenge to the state's legislative apportionment. Mayne Miller had recently returned home from Nashville, where he had been employed as a lobbyist at the state legislature. Mayne had his sights set on a run for the U.S. House, but as a Democrat in East Tennessee, he found the path effectively blocked by Republican dominance of East Tennessee House elections.[54] At his brother's suggestion, Haynes Miller had set upon the reapportionment of the state legislature as a new "project" for their law practice, and, with Ella V. Ross, the Dean of Women at East Tennessee State University (then College), they formed an organization to bring suit against the state.[55]

Mayne Miller brought on board Tom Osborn, a personal friend and trial lawyer in Nashville. Osborn's participation in the case brought strong ties to the city of Nashville, as well as a talented lawyer. Miller and Osborn had met in law school in the summer of 1948 when they became fast friends. Osborn was a gifted orator and a rising star among trial lawyers in Nashville.[56] After two years as an Assistant U.S. Attorney, Osborn joined the firm of Armisted, Waller, Davis, and Lansden, which was closely tied to Senator McKellar and where Osborn developed a professional tie to the state's political establishment. His next position, though, would transform him. In 1953, Osborn left Armisted, Waller, Davis, and Lansden to become an attorney for the city of Nashville and its new mayor, Ben West.

---

[54] Graham, *supra* note 8, at 42.

[55] *Id.* at 44.

[56] Interview with Harris Gilbert (Apr. 29, 2002) [hereinafter *Interview with Gilbert*].

Tom Osborn brought to his partnership with the Miller brothers and Ross a hard-nosed understanding of the effects of malapportionment, an understanding that shaped not only the present challenge, but the subsequent effort in *Baker v. Carr*. Speaking to Gene Graham, who wrote the definitive history of the *Baker* case, Osborn recounted:

> Now, I knew of the existence of the problem prior to that [his service as city attorney], but I did not personally have any genuine interest until I had been exposed firsthand to the way in which the legislature divided the tax money. I realized there was inequitable apportionment but it meant nothing. As a matter of fact, prior to going to City Hall, if anything I approved it. I was more or less *status quo*. And it was not until I went over to City Hall and actually saw the abuse to which city dwellers were being subjected, money-wise, that I changed my feelings about it.[57]

With Osborn's ties to Nashville, the group now spanned Eastern and Central Tennessee. The organization fell short of a truly statewide effort, however. Memphis was notably absent. Ella Ross and the Millers cultivated support from one of the state's most prominent political leaders, Memphis Congressman and former mayor Walter Chandler. They invited Chandler to bring the suit forward in February of 1955. Chandler courteously declined the honor.[58]

Shortly before the Millers began their crusade, another member of the new generation in Tennessee politics began his career and was to join the push for reapportionment, but this time in the legislature. Maclin Paschall Davis, Jr., a young attorney from a prominent legal family in Nashville, ran for one of six seats for state representatives from Davidson County. Winning the Democratic primary at that time was tantamount to winning the election, and out of forty-six candidates on the Democratic party ballot in August 1954, Maclin Davis came in sixth.

As a freshman legislator in January 1955, Davis received advice from many colleagues, especially the leaders of his party, that he "should be careful not to rock any boats" and, above all, "should be loyal to the Democratic party."[59] But the freshman from Nashville was driven by more than the instinct to "go along." Davidson County deserved nine seats in the Tennessee House of Representatives, not six, and the county deserved three seats in the state Senate, not two:

> In spite of all of that advice, I knew it was my duty to represent the people of Davidson County and to do what I could to obtain for them the equal representation in the Legislature that they were guaran-

---

[57] Graham, *supra* note 8, at 48–49.

[58] *Id.* at 51–53.

[59] Letter from Maclin Davis 3 (Oct. 20, 2001) [hereinafter *Letter from Davis*].

teed by the Constitution. Therefore, I devised a plan that I thought
would result in increasing the representation of the under-represented counties and eventually result in the equal representation in
the Legislature guaranteed by the Constitution. My plan was to
introduce a bill to reapportion the House of Representatives by
increasing the representation in the most under-represented counties by approximately one-third of the increase that would have
given them equal representation and to apportion the House seats
among the 99 new House districts in such a way that, if the
Representatives from districts that would gain representation and
the Representatives that would not be affected would all vote for my
reapportionment bill, the bill would receive affirmative votes of
approximately 60% of the members of the House and Senate.[60]

Davis's confidence in the political self-interest of the affected areas
proved misplaced. Not only did the proposed reapportionment fail, but
the entire Shelby County delegation, the county that stood to gain the
most, fell in line with the entrenched party bosses. By March of 1955,
the legislative process for reapportioning the state legislature once again
ended without bringing the districts in line with the state's constitution.

Although his bill had died in the legislature, Davis found that his
efforts had new life in the courts. Tom Osborn, Maclin Davis's friend
from their years together at Armistead, Waller, Davis, and Lansden,
invited Davis to join the legal challenge to the state's reapportionment.
The death of Davis's bill proved a very important legal point—the state
legislature refused to abide by the state constitution. Given this fact, it
was important to act against the current legislature, but, by March 1955,
time was running out on the legislative session.

Unable to entice Walter Chandler to join the suit, the Millers chose
Gates Kidd, an automobile dealer from Washington County and chair of
their organization's Finance Committee, to lead the list of plaintiffs.[61]
They struck out widely against the state establishment. They sued the
state Attorney General George F. McCanless, the secretary of state,
three members of the state elections board, thirty-seven members of the
state Republican Primary Election Commission, thirty-six members of
the state Democratic Primary Election Commission, and county election
commissioners in Washington, Carter, and Davidson counties. On March
8, 1955, the Millers filed *Kidd v. McCanless* in Davidson County Chancery Court.[62]

---

[60] *Id.* at 4.

[61] Graham, *supra* note 8, at 53–54.

[62] *Id.* at 54; Letter from Davis, *supra* note 59.

The case seemed star-crossed from the beginning. First, one of the defendants from the list of Republican primary committee members, Hobart Atkins, persuaded his party to sue Governor Frank G. Clement and the state legislature in a cross-action.[63] This added a clear partisan dimension to the suit and placed the state legislature on both sides of the case. Atkins, though, would prove an invaluable part of the legal team that championed the cause of equal population representation in *Kidd* and later *Baker*. Second, the plaintiffs had chosen Davidson County Chancery Court as a venue on the belief that veteran Chancellor Thomas A. Shriver, Sr., might be a receptive judge. But three months before the case was to be heard, Shriver was elevated to the Tennessee Court of Appeals. Governor Frank Clement chose his replacement, 33–year-old Thomas Wardlaw Steele. This looked like a particularly bad turn of events. Not only had Governor Clement selected Steele after the case was filed, but Steele had served as a loyal member of the Tennessee House of Representatives in 1949 and 1950, representing a district that encompassed two agricultural counties, Tipton and Lauderdale.[64]

Surprisingly, however, Chancellor Steele ruled in favor of the plaintiffs. In a tightly reasoned, fifty-three-page opinion, Steele disagreed with the Attorney General's contention that the court could not declare a legislative apportionment act void because it was unconstitutional. He dismissed the applicability of Frankfurter's opinion in *Colegrove* as just one opinion in a divided court, rather than a majority ruling. He challenged the justice of the existing apportionment. And he declared that any future elections held under the existing apportionment would be "without any legal authority whatever."[65] The victory, though, was short-lived. Upon appeal, the Tennessee Supreme Court reversed the Chancellor's ruling, holding that the court did not have jurisdiction over legislative apportionment, and the U.S. Supreme Court denied the petition for a writ of *certiorari*.[66]

In the months that followed, the plaintiffs, their lawyers, and other supporters of the legal action considered filing a federal lawsuit, but in the end decided that their chances of success were poor. As strong states' rights advocates, Mayne Miller and Maclin Davis further objected to an end run around the state Supreme Court on principle. Indeed, only Tom Osborn and Hobart Atkins stuck with *Kidd v. McCanless* through its appeal to the U.S. Supreme Court. Despite their defeat in the appeals process, Steele's decision and the expertise that the Millers assembled

---

[63] Graham, *supra* note 8, at 57–58; Letter from Davis, *supra* note 59, at 5.

[64] Graham, *supra* note 8, at 60.

[65] *Id.* at 73–75; Letter from Davis, *supra* note 59, at 6.

[66] *Kidd v. McCanless*, 292 S.W.2d 40 (Tenn. 1956), *cert. denied*, 352 U.S. 920 (1956).

provided the foundation for a nearly identical, but ultimately successful, legal challenge two years later: *Baker v. Carr*.

B.   *Baker v. Carr*

Given the political history of Tennessee, it is significant that *Baker* originated not in Nashville or East Tennessee, but in Memphis. Two things had changed since 1954. First, following Crump's death, the political organization and alliances that he had constructed unraveled completely, and, without them, Shelby County's political influence within the state declined. Memphis now found itself in the same political position as its rival Nashville, and that meant that Memphis also found that it now received nowhere near its fair share of state funds.

Second, Frankfurter's opinion in *Colegrove* had begun to lose its air of invincibility and had suffered its first setback, this time in federal court. Dan Magraw and Frank Farrell, residents of the sprawling 42nd House District in St. Paul, Minnesota, brought suit against Minnesota to reapportion the state legislature. Plaintiffs in *Magraw v. Donovan* attacked the political question doctrine directly with a mix of legal arguments based on the Fourteenth Amendment and an analysis of the demographics of the state legislature developed by two political scientists. On July 10, 1958, a federal panel ruled that the courts did have jurisdiction over the apportionment of the Minnesota state legislature "because of the federal constitutional issue asserted."[67]

David Harsh, chairman of the Shelby County Commission, had followed the Minnesota case closely. He saw in it the prospect of relief for Memphis. Since *Brown v. Board of Education*, the Court had embraced a broader interpretation of the Fourteenth Amendment than that expressed in *Colegrove*, and the Minnesota litigation invited a revisiting of the constitutional challenge. Though *Kidd v. McCanless* was just two years past, the time seemed ripe to challenge the state's apportionment again.

The most significant change, however, was not so much legal as political. The telling indicator of the change in the state's politics was the change of heart of one of its leading citizens: Walter Chandler. When Harsh initiated legal action late in 1958, he retained Chandler to represent Shelby County in its challenge to the state legislative apportionment, and, in May 1959, it was Walter Chandler who filed *Baker v. Carr*.

While the facts of *Baker* were not appreciably different from *Kidd*, the legal strategy was. From the beginning, the goal was to win a federal appeal. Given the *Magraw* and *Kidd* decisions, Walter Chandler realized

---

[67] *Magraw v. Donovan*, 163 F.Supp. 184, 187 (D. Minn. 1958), *vacated as moot*, 177 F.Supp. 803 (D. Minn. 1959).

that any lower court decision would produce a conflict with existing legal rulings, which would virtually require a ruling by the federal appeals courts, perhaps even the U.S. Supreme Court.[68] Chandler decided to construct the *Baker* case around the same group that brought *Kidd*. He invited the Millers, Maclin Davis, Tom Osborn, and Hobart Atkins to join the case. Osborn and Atkins jumped at the opportunity. With Chandler, Osborn and Atkins set out to build the constitutional case around the framework that Thomas Steele had laid out in his opinion.

They had to establish, first, that the state legislature refused to craft districts in compliance with the state constitution. Chandler persuaded the Shelby delegation in the state legislature to introduce an apportionment bill, strikingly similar to that of Maclin Davis, in 1955 and again in 1957. That bill and another apportionment bill were defeated in the Senate in 1959; the House never bothered to take them up.[69]

Chandler also brought in legal expertise for making the appeal. He retained noted lawyer Charles Rhyne to aid in the construction of the case and to take over the case once it reached the federal level. The choice of Rhyne had a political dimension. Rhyne was a close friend of Lee Rankin, Eisenhower's Solicitor General. Rhyne's ties to the administration, it was hoped, would improve the chances that the U.S. Attorney General would side with the plaintiffs.

The legal team took a page from the Minnesota case, too. Magraw and Farrell enlisted two political science professors, one from the University of Minnesota and the other from North Dakota State University (then Agricultural College), to provide statistical and historical data regarding the discrepancies in district populations. Osborn enlisted the City of Nashville. Mayor Ben West had assigned the City Auditor and a young attorney, Harrison Gilbert, to compile a report on the discrepancies in district populations in the state.[70] The audit went much further and documented the corresponding discrepancies in the distribution of state money to county and local governments, especially for schools and highways. Harris Gilbert also assembled an analysis by the state historian showing a pattern of discrimination and speeches by James Cummings showing the intention to discriminate against urban areas.[71] Finally, West provided one other resource lacking in *Kidd*: money. At his request, the City Council authorized $25,000 for the legal challenge, enough to defray most of the costs. With this commitment, Chattanooga and Knoxville joined the case as well.

---

[68] Interview with Gilbert, *supra* note 56.

[69] Graham, *supra* note 8, at 136.

[70] Interview with Gilbert, *supra* note 56.

[71] *Id.*

The case proceeded quickly. In December 1959, the U.S. District Court unsurprisingly held for the defendants in *Baker v. Carr*. An appeal to the U.S. Supreme Court was now set. Although the legal strategy in setting up the case fell into place in 1959, the case faced three political setbacks that served to undermine much of what the plaintiffs sought.

First, the state legislature of Minnesota agreed to draw new district boundaries that would accommodate in part the ruling in *Magraw v. Donovan*. That the legislature was willing to reapportion appeared to underscore Frankfurter's contention that these matters could be addressed in the legislatures.[72] Second, the morass of school integration cases following on *Brown v. Board of Education* also buttressed Frankfurter's view that the courts were ill equipped to deal with social problems. School integration throughout the country required extensive intervention and management by the courts. It was not a political thicket, but a thicket nonetheless. Chandler's team realized that, for their case to be successful, they would have to show that equal representation of population could be interpreted and enforced easily, and with a minimum of court oversight.[73] Third, Richard Nixon lost the presidential election in 1960, thus rendering Rhyne's ties to the Solicitor General of no value. Further, it was unclear how the new Kennedy administration would view the case, but the prospects looked dim, considering that *Baker* was widely viewed as a matter of states' rights and was, thus, opposed in principle by many within the Democratic party.

Nonetheless, the Kennedy administration proved to be one of the case's strongest allies. Coming out of the 1960 campaign, the reform wing of the Tennessee Democratic party had two important voices in the office of Attorney General Robert F. Kennedy—John J. Hooker, Jr., and John Seigenthaler. Seigenthaler had met Robert Kennedy in 1957. Seigenthaler had been investigating a series of violent crimes against Teamsters for his paper, and he brought these to the attention of the chief counsel for the subcommittee headed by Senator John McClellan: Robert Kennedy. Slowly the two established a close and enduring friendship and, in 1961, John Seigenthaler left the *Nashville Tennesseean* to become Robert Kennedy's scheduler and press officer.[74]

On February 3, 1961, Tom Osborn, Harris Gilbert, and John J. Hooker came to the Justice Department to make their case to the administration, with the hope that the administration would join their suit. Seigenthaler arranged a meeting with Robert Kennedy and further

---

[72] *Id.*

[73] *Id.*

[74] Interview with John Seigenthaler (Apr. 30, 2002) [hereinafter *Interview with Seigenthaler*].

arranged for the Tennessee lawyers to see the new Solicitor General, Archibald Cox, whom he had befriended during the 1960 presidential campaign. Although the meeting with the Attorney General did not occur, the meeting with Cox proved critical. As Harris Gilbert later recalled: "Cox really amazed us. He denied that he had any prior knowledge of our case, but he started immediately with questions that cut right to the core of the matter." The meeting went on late into the afternoon as Cox plumbed many of the angles of the case with Osborn and Gilbert. After the meeting, the lawyers were unsure if the adminis- tration would support them, but they were satisfied that they had been given a full hearing.[75] Soon after that meeting, Cox met with Robert Kennedy about the case. Cox recalled that meeting:

> I was in the Attorney General's office and remarked to him that his friend John Jay Hooker had been in and sent his regards. The Attorney General asked what he wanted, and I told him that he wanted us to file a brief in *Baker-Carr*. The Attorney General asked whether I was going to do it, and I said, well, I thought I would unless he saw some strong objection. The Attorney General said, "Well, are you going to win?" I said, "No, I don't think so, but it would be a lot of fun anyway."[76]

C. *Before the Court*

By custom, the U.S. Solicitor General would each year designate a case for his personal attention before the Court. Archibald Cox chose *Baker* and divided the argument time with the state lawyers. Cox's role was to address the constitutional issues directly, while Charles Rhyne and Tom Osborn were to take on matters concerning state law and the actions of the state legislature. Two issues dominated the argument before the Court.

First, there was no apparent way in which the Court could rule for the Tennessee plaintiffs without repudiating *Colegrove*. Since *Colegrove* was a relatively recent case, and since the author of the opinion, Justice Frankfurter, was still on the Court, this was no small sticking point. As an institution, the Court is leery about reversing its own pronounce- ments, and Cox had the experience of the anguish surrounding the ultimate rejection of *Plessy v. Ferguson*[77] in *Brown v. Board of Edu- cation*.[78] Cox's approach was to confront directly the continued vitality of *Colegrove* after *Gomillion*. While *Gomillion* had carefully relied only on

---

[75] Interview with Gilbert, *supra* note 56.

[76] Graham, *supra* note 8, at 216–17.

[77] 163 U.S. 537 (1896).

[78] 347 U.S. 483 (1954).

the Fifteeenth Amendment, it had nonetheless pierced the political question doctrine that apparently shielded all political arrangements from judicial review. Using Frankfurter's own words from the majority opinion in *Gomillion*, Cox argued that the Court could not at once sustain the particular application of constitutional protections of the value of the franchise to one group, as in *Gomillion*, while denying an equivalent guarantee of the franchise to the broader group, the population as a whole.

Second, Cox believed, rightly, that *Gomillion* paved the way for overcoming the question of justiciability, but not that of remedy. The composition of the Court had changed substantially since *Colegrove*, but there remained important advocates of the line drawn in *Colegrove*, most notably Justices Frankfurter and Harlan. Because of the experience with school integration, there was great reluctance to embrace a legal ruling and standard that would embroil the courts in the details of the districting process. Nor was the legal team prepared to propose a remedy. The lawyers were themselves split on the matter. Harris Gilbert, representing the City of Nashville, would have personally preferred a "federal plan," like that in California, in which one house represented population and the other area.[79] Even still, the plaintiffs' lawyers and Cox saw that they needed to convince the Justices that some remedy was needed and that the remedy would not embroil the courts in a political battle on par with desegregation.

They began by arguing that the cities received less than their fair share of government expenditures because of rural domination of the legislature. The City Auditor's report and the new 1960 Census figures were provided to each Justice during the argumentation—a highly unusual development, then as now. The Justices leafed through the data as the arguments proceeded, even though it was not introduced as evidence. Frankfurter jumped on the implication of the data for the decision. Surely, he demanded, the plaintiffs were not arguing that the courts must guarantee equality. Cox dodged, artfully. They had reached, he sensed, the boundary of what the Court would accept. Cox interpreted the public finance data as evidence not of the need for an egalitarian remedy but of the reason why the state legislature would not provide relief.[80] In the absence of an initiative process and facing a legislature that had strong incentives not to reapportion and a history of discrimination against urban areas, only the courts could provide relief, whatever form that might take.

Frankfurter and Osborn tangled over the same issue in the final rebuttal, and Frankfurter lit into Osborn:

---

[79] Interview with Gilbert, *supra* note 56.

[80] *Id.*; Graham, *supra* note 8, at 250–54.

You're telling us that 33 per cent of the Tennessee electorate elects 66 2/3 of the legislature and we should agree with your position that some way or another—with a magic wand probably—there will be some remedy worked out. So the court will agree to some alleviation. And the next year 40 per cent will be electing 60 per cent of the legislature. You'll be right back up here complaining about that, won't you?[81]

And Osborn, with a twist of humor and a presage of things to come, replied: "Yessir. For a fee."[82]

Thus, the principle of "one-man, one-vote" was vital for the success of the case even if it was still unstated. Unlike "integration," population equality of legislative districts is a simple idea to grasp, both as an abstract principle and as a practical administrative matter. Equality itself was not stressed overly in the argument before the Court. Instead, Cox kept the argument focused on the fact that the plaintiffs lacked any mechanism for relief in their own state because of the reluctance of the state court to enter the issue, because of the absence of an initiative process, and because the legislature had no incentive to act—the very arguments that Justice Clark would take up in his concurrence. But one-man, one-vote (or, one-person, one-vote, as we now term it) lurked in the background. Had population equality not been an easy concept to define in practical, as well as abstract, terms, the case may not have succeeded.[83]

The Supreme Court Decision

The Supreme Court noted probable jurisdiction in *Baker* in November 1960. There remained so much disagreement after oral argument in April 1961, however, that the Court took the extraordinary step of ordering reargument for the following October. Then, in a 6–2 decision issued in March 1962, the Court "startled the nation,"[84] and issued what was perhaps the most profoundly destabilizing opinion in Supreme Court history. The majority opinion, written by Justice Brennan, was accompanied by three concurrences, from Justices Douglas, Clark, and Stewart, and two dissents, one from Justice Frankfurter, the other from Justice Harlan. Justice Clark was, according to Harris Gilbert, the biggest surprise. Until *Baker*, he had consistently voted with Frankfurter on

---

[81] Graham, *supra* note 8, at 254.

[82] *Id.*

[83] Interview with Harris Gilbert (Jan. 23, 2002).

[84] Robert G. McCloskey, *The Supreme Court 1961 Term—Foreword: The Reapportionment Case*, 76 Harv. L. Rev. 54, 54 (1962).

matters like this, but the other Justices voted as the legal team had hoped.[85] Brennan's opinion, coolly shattering decades of precedent, offered little guidance to the lower court for how to fashion its remedy, but it firmly established the court's entry into the political thicket, paving the way for the "reapportionment revolution."[86]

Justice Stewart emphasized in his concurrence that the Court in *Baker* held three things "and no more": (1) that the Court possessed jurisdiction over the subject matter; (2) that appellants had standing to challenge the Tennessee apportionment statutes; and (3) that a justiciable cause of action was stated upon which relief could be granted.[87] Let us address each in turn.

A. *Jurisdiction of the Subject Matter and Standing*

In the first part of his opinion, Justice Brennan disposed of the possible claims that the Court lacked subject matter jurisdiction and that the plaintiffs lacked standing to sue. First separating the issue of subject matter jurisdiction from that of justiciability, Brennan maintained that, pursuant to Article III, Section 2 of the Constitution, "[i]t is clear that the cause of action is one which 'arises under' the Federal Constitution," and that, as such, the district court "should not have dismissed the complaint for want of jurisdiction of the subject matter."[88] Further, he disposed of the defendants' claim that *Colegrove* supported the contrary position by arguing that a majority of the *Colegrove* Court believed the requirement for subject matter jurisdiction to be satisfied.[89]

As to the issue of standing, the Court held on the basis of precedent, including *Colegrove*, that because plaintiffs "seek relief in order to protect or vindicate an interest of their own, and of those similarly situated," they had standing to sue.[90]

B. *Justiciability*

The heart of the majority opinion, and the piece that generated the most controversy, was the section on justiciability, or the "political question" doctrine. Because *Colegrove* and a number of subsequent per

---

[85] Interview with Gilbert, *supra* note 56.

[86] For a fuller discussion of the "reapportionment revolution," see Samuel Issacharoff et al., *The Law of Democracy: Legal Structure of the Political Process* 141–216 (rev. 2d ed. 2002).

[87] *Baker v. Carr*, 369 U.S. 186, 265 (1962) (Stewart, J., concurring).

[88] *Baker*, 369 U.S. at 199.

[89] *Id.* at 202 ("Two of the opinions expressing the views of four of the Justices, a majority, flatly held that there was jurisdiction of the subject matter.").

[90] *Id.* at 206–08.

curiam cases appeared to foreclose the possibility that the Court could adjudicate constitutional claims surrounding legislative reapportionment, Justice Brennan set out in *Baker* to distinguish that line of cases without explicitly overruling any precedents.[91] While the effect of the majority decision was of course to render these decisions obsolete, Brennan's method was to cast them as cases that had not conclusively ruled against judicial review of legislative apportionment.[92]

In so doing, Justice Brennan undertook what amounted to a wholesale redefinition of the political question doctrine[93] by deriving a set of standards from an examination of the various fields in which the Court had traditionally declined to involve itself: (a) foreign relations; (b) dates or duration of hostilities; (c) validity of enactments; (d) the status of Indian tribes; and (e) Guaranty Clause[94] claims. Having already established that political questions involve separation-of-powers-based disputes rather than federalism-based ones,[95] Brennan announced the political question "test" in the following famous passage:

> Prominent on the surface of any case held to involve a political question is found a textually demonstrable constitutional commitment of the issue to a coordinate political department; or a lack of judicially discoverable and manageable standards for resolving it; or the impossibility of deciding without an initial policy determination of a kind clearly for nonjudicial discretion; or the impossibility of a

---

[91] Brennan wrote:

We understand the District Court to have read the cited cases as compelling the conclusion that since the appellants sought to have a legislative apportionment held unconstitutional, their suit presented a "political question" and was therefore nonjusticiable. We hold that this challenge to an apportionment presents no nonjusticiable "political question." The cited cases do not hold the contrary.

Id. at 209.

[92] *Id.* at 234 ("[O]ur decisions in favor of justiciability ... afford no support for the District Court's conclusion that the subject matter of this controversy presents a political question. Indeed, the refusal to award relief in *Colegrove* resulted only from the controlling view of a want of equity. Nor is anything contrary to be found in those *per curiams* that came after *Colegrove*.").

[93] It is important to note that all Brennan purported to do in this section of the opinion was to "consider the contours" of the doctrine, *id.* at 210, as though the standards he ultimately derived had existed all along.

[94] U.S. Const. art. IV, § 4 ("The United States shall guarantee to every State in this Union a Republican Form of Government, and shall protect each of them against Invasion....").

[95] *Baker*, 369 U.S. at 210 ("[I]t is the relationship between the judiciary and the coordinate branches of the Federal Government, and not the federal judiciary's relationship to the States, which gives rise to the 'political question.' "); *id.* ("The nonjusticiability of a political question is primarily a function of the separation of powers.").

court's undertaking independent resolution without expressing lack of the respect due coordinate branches of government; or an unusual need for unquestioning adherence to a political decision already made; or the potentiality of embarrassment from multifarious pronouncements by various departments on one question.[96]

By recasting the many and various political question cases as those meeting one or more of these criteria, the majority dispensed with the notion that any single category of cases is necessarily nonjusticiable.[97] In the context of *Baker*, this conclusion had most force with respect to the Guaranty Clause issue, particularly because Justice Frankfurter argued in dissent that the Fourteenth Amendment claim made by the plaintiffs "[wa]s, in effect, a Guarantee Clause claim masquerading under a different label."[98] Historically, the Court had refused to hear cases based on the Guaranty Clause,[99] but, under the majority's theory, the reason such claims were nonjusticiable was solely that they "involve those elements which define a 'political question.' "[100] In other words, "the nonjusticiability of such claims has nothing to do with their touching upon matters of state governmental organization."[101]

From here, the majority's remaining moves were few, though no less controversial. Applying the political question test to the facts of *Baker*, Brennan concluded that "none" of the characteristics typically associated with political question cases were present,[102] and that the historical nonjusticiability of Guaranty Clause claims had no effect on the actual Fourteenth Amendment claim made by the plaintiffs.[103] Next, the Court invoked *Gomillion* to support the conclusion that "[w]hen challenges to

---

[96] *Id.* at 217.

[97] Note, for example, the qualifying statements made in the discussions of each of the so-called "political question" categories. *See id.* at 211–15, 218–29. Consider three examples. On foreign relations: "Yet it is error to suppose that every case or controversy which touches foreign relations lies beyond judicial cognizance." *Id.* at 211. On the validity of enactments: "But it is not true that courts will never delve into a legislature's records upon such a quest [to inquire whether the legislature has complied with all requisite formalities].... The political question doctrine, a tool for maintenance of governmental order, will not be so applied as to promote only disorder." *Id.* at 214–15. On the status of Indian tribes: "Yet, here too, there is no blanket rule." *Id.* at 215.

[98] *Id.* at 297 (Frankfurter, J., dissenting).

[99] The primary example offered by both the majority and Frankfurter is *Luther v. Borden*, 48 U.S. (7 How.) 1 (1849).

[100] *Baker*, 369 U.S. at 218.

[101] *Id.*

[102] *Id.* at 226.

[103] *Id.* at 227.

state action respecting matters of 'the administration of the affairs of the State and the officers through whom they are conducted' have rested on claims of constitutional deprivation which are amenable to judicial correction, this Court has acted upon its view of the merits of the claim."[104] Finally, the Court distinguished *Colegrove* and the subsequent per curiam decisions, concluding that "the complaint's allegations of a denial of equal protection present a justiciable constitutional cause of action upon which appellants are entitled to a trial and a decision."[105]

After Baker

Justice Frankfurter argued in dissent that the majority's opinion in *Baker v. Carr* amounted to "a massive repudiation of the experience of our whole past,"[106] worrying, among other things, that the Equal Protection Clause provided no clear guide for judicial examination of apportionment methods and that, as a result, the courts were unable to fashion a reasonable remedy.[107] To some extent, this worry was reflected in the majority's opinion, precisely because the Court provided no guidance to the lower courts as to what a proper remedy might look like, concluding merely that "[j]udicial standards under the Equal Protection Clause are well developed and familiar"[108] and that, as a result, "it is improper now to consider what remedy would be most appropriate if appellants prevail at the trial."[109]

Yet whoever had the better argument on this point, the immediate reaction to the decision in *Baker* made one thing very clear: In 1962, the time was right for a "massive repudiation" of legislative misapportionment. Within nine months of the Court's decision, litigation was underway in thirty-four states challenging the constitutionality of state legislative apportionment schemes.[110] Calling the short-term response "nothing short of astonishing," Robert McCloskey wrote in the *Harvard Law Review* six months after *Baker*:

> It has been as if the decision catalyzed a new political synthesis that was already straining, so to speak, to come into being. Not only

---

[104] *Id.* at 229 (citing Boyd v. Nebraska *ex rel.* Thayer, 143 U.S. 135, 183 (1892) (Field, J., dissenting)).

[105] *Id.* at 237.

[106] *Id.* at 267 (Frankfurter, J., dissenting).

[107] *Id.* at 269–70, 323 (Frankfurter, J., dissenting).

[108] *Id.* at 226.

[109] *Id.* at 198.

[110] *Reynolds v. Sims*, 377 U.S. 533, 556 n.30 (1964).

federal judges, but state judges as well, have taken the inch or so of encouragement offered by the Supreme Court and stretched it out to a mile. . . .

When a decision fails to strike a responsive cord in the public breast, the tendency is at best to abide by its minimum compulsions grudgingly interpreted. The tendency suggested by early reactions to the reapportionment decision seems very different from this, and it may warrant the conjecture that the Court here happened to hit upon what the students of public opinion might call a latent consensus.[111]

Driven by this consensus, the Court in the years following *Baker* greatly expanded the scope of the decision, first articulating the principle of "one person, one vote" in the context of primary vote counting[112] and federal congressional elections,[113] then setting the actual standard for state legislative reapportionment,[114] which the Court had declined to do in *Baker*.

Reynolds v. Sims was the most sweeping of the post-*Baker* decisions, holding, among other things, that "the Equal Protection Clause requires that the seats in both houses of a bicameral state legislature must be apportioned on a population basis,"[115] by which the Court meant that a state must "make an honest and good faith effort to construct districts, in both houses of its legislature, as nearly of equal population as is practicable."[116]

What Frankfurter feared the Court was doing in *Baker*, "choos[ing] . . . among competing theories of political philosophy,"[117] it seemed undeniably to do in *Reynolds*. "Logically," wrote Chief Justice Warren:

---

[111] McCloskey, *supra* note 84, at 57–59 (footnotes omitted).

[112] *Gray v. Sanders*, 372 U.S. 368, 381 (1963) (striking down Georgia's "county-unit" system of counting votes and holding that "[t]he conception of political equality from the Declaration of Independence, to Lincoln's Gettysburg Address, to the Fifteenth, Seventeenth, and Nineteenth Amendments can mean only one thing—one person, one vote"); *id.* at 379 ("Once the geographical unit for which a representative is to be chosen is designated, all who participate in the election are to have an equal vote—whatever their race, whatever their sex, whatever their occupation, whatever their income, and wherever their home may be in that geographical unit.").

[113] *Wesberry v. Sanders*, 376 U.S. 1, 7–8 (1964) (concluding that "construed in its historical context, the command of [Article 1, Section 2 of the Constitution], that Representatives be chosen 'by the People of the several States' means that as nearly as is practicable one man's vote in a congressional election is to be worth as much as another's" (footnotes omitted)).

[114] *Reynolds v. Sims*, 377 U.S. 533, 568, 577 (1964).

[115] *Id.* at 568.

[116] *Id.* at 577.

[117] *Baker v. Carr*, 369 U.S. 186, 300 (1962) (Frankfurter, J., dissenting).

[I]n a society ostensibly grounded on representative government, it would seem reasonable that a majority of the people of a State could elect a majority of that State's legislators.... Since legislatures are responsible for enacting laws by which all citizens are to be governed, they should be bodies which are collectively responsive to the popular will....

To the extent that a citizen's right to vote is debased, he is that much less a citizen. The fact that an individual lives here or there is not a legitimate reason for overweighting or diluting the efficacy of his vote. The complexions of societies and civilizations change, often with amazing rapidity. A nation once primarily rural in character becomes predominantly urban. Representation schemes once fair and equitable become archaic and outdated. But the basic principle of representative government remains, and must remain, unchanged—the weight of a citizen's vote cannot be made to depend on where he lives.[118]

Reynolds, along with its companion case *Wesberry v. Sanders*,[119] was an earth-shattering decision, going well beyond what anyone could have anticipated from the Court's holding in *Baker v. Carr*.[120] *Wesberry* called into question 90 percent of the districts in the House of Representatives, and *Reynolds* did the same for nearly every seat in the upper houses of state legislatures and most of the seats in the lower houses.[121] And while the "reapportionment revolution" continued well beyond the decision in *Reynolds*, it is perhaps that decision more than any other after *Baker* that signaled that the apportionment battle begun in that case had been won by the reformers. It was a less popular decision than *Baker*, but "as states came rapidly into compliance with *Reynolds*, there was neither a public outcry to return to the past nor a desire of the newly elected to return to private life.... *Reynolds* went from debatable in 1964 to unquestionable in 1968."[122]

Coda

Mayne and Haynes Miller left Tennessee not long after the *Kidd* decision. Following the state Supreme Court decision in 1955, Haynes

---

[118] *Reynolds*, 377 U.S. at 565–67 (footnotes omitted).

[119] 376 U.S. 1 (1964).

[120] For an illuminating discussion of *Reynolds* and its impact, see Powe, *supra* note 2, at 245–55.

[121] *Id.* at 252.

[122] *Id.* at 255.

set off on a new project, working for the State Department in Laos. He died in a traffic accident in Paris in 1967 at age 41.[123] Mayne Miller ran for a congressional seat from East Tennessee in 1958. He won the primary handily, but found himself an outcast within the Democratic Party in the state. Unable to raise funds, he lost the November 1958 general election. He moved to Wyoming not long thereafter.[124]

Tom Osborn returned to Nashville in 1962 a hero. Now widely recognized as one of the leading trial lawyers in the state, he had his pick of cases. He took on the defense of James Hoffa in the investigation of the Teamsters, which had originated with John Seigenthaler's investigative reporting for the *Nashville Tennesseean*. As the trial proceeded, however, Osborn was caught attempting to tamper with the jury. He was indicted in 1963 and sentenced to two years in prison. He was permanently disbarred in mid-January 1970. Ruined, he committed suicide two weeks later.[125]

Hobart Atkins ran for the state Senate following the *Kidd* decision and found himself embroiled in the politics of redistricting. After losing a bid for the state Senate in 1958, he won the state Senate seat in 1960 and represented Knoxville from 1961 to 1965.[126] After *Baker v. Carr*, he spearheaded the efforts to force the state legislature to comply with the law. In 1965, two weeks before his death, Hobart Atkins and Walter Chandler filed *Baker v. Clement*, the first of a series of cases implementing the one-person, one-vote standard in Tennessee.[127]

Harris Gilbert took on the role that Osborn and Atkins had served in the original *Baker* case, serving as lead counsel in the series of cases in Tennessee that were needed to force the legislature to implement the one-person, one-vote standard. After these victories, though, he left election law and politics behind and established his own law firm in Nashville, which subsequently merged with Wyatt, Tarrant, and Combs.[128]

Maclin Davis's struggles within the Democratic Party did not end with *Kidd v. McCanless*. Eventually, in 1964, he broke with his party completely and became a Republican. He has since represented the

---

[123] Graham, *supra* note 8, at 307–15.

[124] *Id.* at 303–06.

[125] Interview with Seigenthaler, *supra* note 74; Graham, *supra* note 8, at 322.

[126] Tenn. Dep't of State, *Tennessee Blue Book* 22 (1966).

[127] Graham, *supra* note 8, at 326.

[128] Interview with Gilbert, *supra* note 56.

Republican Party in its legal struggles to get a fair redistricting plan out of a Democratic-dominated legislature.[129]

---

[129] Interview with Maclin Davis (Aug. 15, 2002).

9

David E. Bernstein

The Story of *Lochner v. New York:* Impediment to the Growth of the Regulatory State

In *Lochner v. New York*,[1] the Supreme Court invalidated a ten-hour day law for bakers, ushering in the so-called "*Lochner* era" that lasted from approximately 1905 to 1937. According to the prevailing myth propagated by Progressives and New Dealers—and widely, and uncritically, accepted even today—*Lochner* era Supreme Court Justices, influenced by pernicious Social Darwinist ideology, sought to impose their laissez-faire views on the American polity through a tendentious interpretation of the Due Process Clause of the Fourteenth Amendment.[2] The *Lochner* era Justices, infected with class bias, knew that their decisions favored large corporations and harmed workers.[3] Because of their "survival of the fittest" mentality that is exactly what they intended.[4] Only a

---

[1] 198 U.S. 45 (1905).

[2] *See, e.g.*, Frank R. Strong, *Substantive Due Process of Law: A Dichotomy of Sense and Nonsense* 95 (1986) ("The Justices of the [*Lochner* Court], steeped in the economics of Adam Smith and the sociology of Herbert Spencer, unabashedly read their philosophy into the Constitution.").

[3] *See generally* James W. Ely, Jr., *Economic Due Process Revisited*, 44 Vand. L. Rev. 213, 213 (1991) (reviewing Paul Kens, *Judicial Power and Reform Politics: The Anatomy of* Lochner v. New York (1990)) ("In many constitutional histories the presentation of economic issues between 1880 and 1937 resembles a Victorian melodrama. A dastardly Supreme Court is pictured as frustrating noble reformers who sought to impose beneficent regulations on giant business enterprises.").

[4] *E.g.*, Archibald Cox, *The Court and the Constitution* 135 (1987) (claiming the Supreme Court engaged in a "willful defense of wealth and power"); Alfred H. Kelly & Winfred A. Harbison, *The American Constitution: Its Origins and Development* 498 (4th ed.

few prophetic dissenters, notably Justices Oliver Wendell Holmes and Louis Brandeis, protested against this abuse of judicial power. These dauntless Justices' views emerged triumphant when the heroic Franklin Roosevelt stood up to the Nine Old Men and, over time, remade the Court in his image.[5]

This morality tale bore only a modest relation to reality.[6] However, it suited the political needs of the Progressive and New Deal era advocates of constitutional change who initially wove it. It also played to, and to some extent confirmed, the political and ideological prejudices in favor of the modern regulatory state held by post-World War II constitutional scholars. These scholars used the *Lochner* decision as the symbol of everything they despised about the pre-New Deal Court's constitutional jurisprudence, especially the Court's willingness to engage in substantive review of economic regulations.

Lochner thus became the leading case in the "anti-canon," the group of wrongly decided cases that help frame what the proper principles of constitutional interpretation should be.[7] Indeed, a century after it was decided, "avoiding '*Lochner*'s error' remains the central obsession . . . of contemporary constitutional law."[8] Supreme Court Justices are at pains to deny that their opinions declaring laws unconstitutional are *Lochner*ian,[9] while dissenting Justices use *Lochner* as an epithet to

---

1970) (arguing that *Lochner* era judges were "concerned primarily with protecting the property rights and vested interests of big business," which manifested itself in the doctrine of freedom of contract).

[5] *See, e.g.*, Melvin I. Urofsky, *Myth and Reality: The Supreme Court and Protective Legislation in the Progressive Era*, 1983 Sup. Ct. Hist. Soc'y Y.B. 53, 58 (stating that Justice Holmes's dissent in *Lochner* "raised the spirits of the faithful and kept them hoping for a better day and a Court more attuned to contemporary realities").

[6] *See* David E. Bernstein, Lochner *Era Revisionism, Revised:* Lochner *and the Origins of Fundamental Rights Constitutionalism*, 92 Geo. L.J. 1, 4 (2003) [hereinafter Bernstein, Lochner *Era Revisionism, Revised*].

[7] *See* David E. Bernstein, Lochner*'s Legacy's Legacy*, 82 Tex. L. Rev. 1, 63 (2003) [hereinafter Bernstein, Lochner*'s Legacy's Legacy*].

[8] Gary D. Rowe, Lochner *Revisionism Revisited*, 24 Law & Soc. Inquiry 221, 223 (1999) (reviewing Owen M. Fiss, *History of the Supreme Court of the United States: Troubled Beginnings of the Modern State* (1993), Howard Gillman, *The Constitution Beseiged: The Rise and Demise of* Lochner *Era Police Powers Jurisprudence* (1993), and Morton J. Horowitz, *The Transformation of American Law, 1870–1960: The Crisis of Legal Orthodoxy* (1992)).

[9] *See, e.g.*, *College Sav. Bank v. Florida Prepaid Postsecondary Educ. Expense Bd.*, 527 U.S. 666, 690 (1999); *United States v. Lopez*, 514 U.S. 549, 601 n.9 (1995) (Thomas, J., concurring); *TXO Prod. Corp. v. Alliance Res. Corp.*, 509 U.S. 443, 455 (1993) (plurality opinion) (Stevens, J.).

criticize their colleagues.[10] Along with *Dred Scott v. Sandford*[11] and *Plessy v. Ferguson*,[12] *Lochner* is one of the most reviled Supreme Court cases of all time.

However, over the last two decades or so, a combination of factors has encouraged many scholars to reassess the traditional *Lochner* morality tale. First, temporal distance from the controversy over the New Deal has allowed scholars to take a more objective look at the *Lochner* era. Second, while prior generations of constitutional scholars tended to practice "law office history"—historical scholarship intended to support a preconceived thesis—over the last few decades constitutional history has matured into a legitimate academic field able to accept complexity and nuance regarding the origins and effects of *Lochner*. Third, the increased popularity and visibility of libertarian economic thought[13] has made the *Lochner* line of decisions seem less evil and less daft. It remains to be seen whether the perception that lax regulation of financial markets led to the severe economic downturn of late 2008, will in turn revive the hoary myth.

Contemporary historical scholarship on the *Lochner* era focuses on the continuity between *Lochner*ian jurisprudence and legal and political philosophies that had informed American public discourse since the nation's founding. Virtually no serious scholar of the *Lochner* era believes any longer that the *Lochner* Court simply tried to impose laissez-faire or was influenced much by Social Darwinism. Rather, contemporary historians and legal scholars have noted that the Supreme Court's *Lochner*ian decisions, including *Lochner* itself, were based on what were then mainstream (and longstanding) jurisprudential ideas; that, with some anomalous exceptions, the *Lochner* era Court upheld the vast majority of regulatory legislation that came before it through the early 1920s, and that even during the Court's most activist period it upheld most regulatory legislation that came before it; that the *Lochner* era Court's invalidation of economic regulation often aided groups that lacked the power to protect themselves in the political process; and that the *Lochner* era Court did not limit strict review to economic issues, but also issued several civil liberties decisions that became the basis for

---

[10] *See, e.g., Alden v. Maine*, 527 U.S. 706, 814 (1999) (Souter, J., dissenting); *Dolan v. City of Tigard*, 512 U.S. 374, 406–09 (1994) (Stevens, J., dissenting); *Planned Parenthood of S.E. Pa. v. Casey*, 505 U.S. 833, 959–61 (1992) (Rehnquist, C.J., concurring in the judgment in part and dissenting in part).

[11] 60 U.S. (19 How.) 393 (1857).

[12] 163 U.S. 537 (1896).

[13] The manifestation of this in the legal academic realm has been the tremendous influence of Chicago School law and economics.

modern constitutional protection of unenumerated fundamental rights
against hostile state action.

Historical Background

For such an important decision, the *Lochner* case had inauspicious
origins. The story of *Lochner* begins in the late nineteenth century with
agitation by unionized New York bread bakers who sought to limit their
working hours to ten hours per day and sixty hours per week. Bakers
favored shorter hours because they wanted more leisure time, and
because they were typically paid by the day. If bakers were paid two
dollars a day for twelve hours of work, they expected to get paid the
same two dollars for ten hours a day of work (though employers would
obviously try to switch to hourly pay schedules). Also, many bakers
apparently believed that shorter hours would eventually lead to *higher*
wages, though it is not clear by what mechanism they thought this
would occur.[14] Bakers' demands for a ten-hour day increased in periods
of economic hardship, when many bakers could not find work. It was
thought that by limiting the hours of labor, jobs would be spread among
more bakers, thereby reducing unemployment and want among them.[15]

Bakers also sought shorter hours because baking was an unpleasant
and, many believed, an unhealthful profession. Bakers were exposed to
flour dust, gas fumes, dampness, and extremes of hot and cold. On the
other hand, unlike many other workers bakers faced almost no risk of
sudden death or catastrophic injury.[16] The bakers' primary health complaint was that they believed themselves to be at increased risk of
developing "consumption," an ill-defined catch-all for lung diseases.[17]
The most common form of consumption was tuberculosis. Even though
late nineteenth century scientists knew that tuberculosis was caused by
contagious bacteria and not by lifestyle and environment, many bakers
and their reformist allies insisted that long hours of exposure to various
airborne particles caused the disease.[18]

---

[14] *Unconstitutional*, Bakers' J., May 6, 1905, at 1 ("Those who know their economics,
and those who are acquainted with the history of wages in this state, are aware that the
shorter work day eventually results in increased wages. . . .").

[15] *Now for the Ten–Hour Day*, Bakers' J., Apr. 20, 1895, at 1; *see also* Matthew S.
Bewig, Lochner v. The Journeymen Bakers of New York: *The Journeymen Bakers, Their
Hours of Labor, and the Constitution—A Case Study in the Social History of Legal
Thought*, 38 Am. J. Leg. Hist. 413, 440 (1994) (stating that this was the "primary
argument" advanced by bakers for shorter hours).

[16] Paul Kens, *Judicial Power and Reform Politics: The Anatomy of* Lochner v. New
York 9 (1990).

[17] *Id.*

[18] *Id.* at 9–11.

By 1887 unionized New York bakers had grown frustrated with efforts to obtain a uniform ten-hour day through negotiation, and therefore drafted a bill for submission to the legislature limiting bakers' hours to ten per day. The bill was defeated in the state Assembly by a vote of fifty-six to forty-five.[19] The free labor market, however, began to address the hours issue. As American living standards improved because of economic growth and increases in productivity, working conditions gradually improved for bakers. Modern, sanitary, and efficient bread bakeries increased their market share at the expense of traditional smaller bakeries. The larger bakeries tended to be unionized, and were staffed by bakers of German descent, who came to dominate the Bakery and Confectionery Workers' International Union ("the bakers' union").[20] The smaller bakeries employed a hodgepodge of ethnic groups, primarily French, Germans, Italians, and Jews, usually segregated by bakery and generally working for employers of the same ethnic group. Employees of smaller bakeries were generally not unionized, especially among the non-Germans.

By the mid–1890s, bakers in large bakeries rarely worked more than ten hours per day, sixty hours per week.[21] However, these bakers were concerned that their improved situation was endangered by competition from small, old-fashioned bakeries, especially those that employed Italian, French, and Jewish immigrants. These old-fashioned bakeries were often located in the basement of tenement buildings to take advantage of cheap rents and floors sturdy enough to withstand the weight of heavy baking ovens.[22] Unlike the more modern "factory" bakeries, which operated in shifts, the basement bakeries often demanded that workers be on call twenty-four hours a day, with the bakers sleeping in or near

---

[19] *The Demonstrations of the Bakers of New York and Brooklyn*, Bakers' J., Apr. 27, 1895, at 1.

[20] Given that the baker's union later called for a complete ban on small, less modern basement bakeries, it seems safe to assume that most of their members did not work in such bakeries. *See infra* text accompanying notes 54–55.

[21] *Tenth Annual Report of the Factory Inspectors of the State of New York* 42 (1896) [hereinafter, *Factory Inspectors' Report*].

[22] Kens, *supra* note 16, at 8; Paul Brenner, *The Formative Years of the Hebrew Bakers' Unions, 1881–1914*, 18 Yivo Ann. of Jewish Soc. Sci. 39, 41 (1983). Jewish bakers did not compete directly with German bakers because the Jewish-owned bakeries supplied the kosher market, which the German bakers could not supply. However, while observant Jews could not eat non-kosher bread, non-Jews could eat kosher bread, so there was a danger that Jewish bakers would come to dominate the general New York bread market. *See* Brenner, *supra*, at 55–56 ("Faced with the prospect of having its overwhelmingly German membership literally driven out of the New York labor market, the Union had a substantial incentive to reduce existing wage-and-hour disparities by lifting the standards of Jewish workers.").

the bakery during down times. Workers in such bakeries often worked far more than ten hours per day.[23]

Competition from basement bakery workers was also thought to drive down other bakers' wages.[24] An article in the bakers' union's weekly newspaper, the *Bakers' Journal*,[25] reflected common sentiment among unionized bakers in condemning "the cheap labor of the green hand [a euphemism for recent immigrants] from foreign shores" that, along with long hours and competition from underpaid apprentices, "has driven countless numbers of journeymen [bakers] into other walks of life, into the streets, the hospitals, alms houses, insane asylums, penitentiaries and finally death through poverty and desperation."[26] Union members believed that a ten-hour day law would not only aid those unionized bakers who had not successfully demanded their hours be reduced, but would also help reduce competition from nonunionized workers.[27]

Immigrant bakers who were not part of the established German group, especially the French, were notoriously difficult to unionize, and remained largely oblivious to pleas from the bakers' union.[28] Evidently,

---

[23] Dennis Hanlon, *Inspection of Bake-Shops, in Ninth Annual Convention of the International Association of Factory Inspectors of North America* 1415 (1895) (stating that bakers' lodging often involved sleeping in bakeries, sometimes in bakerooms); Brenner, *supra* note 22, at 42 (noting that for Jewish bakers on the day before the Sabbath "[r]est was available only while the batches of dough were rising" and that bakers "were usually required to board and lodge with their employers"); *Complaints of the Bakers*, N.Y. Times, Nov. 21, 1895, at 9 ("The majority of the men board with the 'bosses' and sleep in the bakeshop. They work fifteen or sixteen hours a day . . . ." (quoting Charles Iffland, manager of the bakers' union)).

[24] *Factory Inspectors' Report*, *supra* note 21, at 42–43.

[25] The bakers' union's primary publication was the German-language *Baecher–Zeitung*. The English-language *Bakers' Journal* was smaller and intended as a propaganda tool for organizing English-speaking bakers. Brenner, *supra* note 22, at 110 n.65.

[26] *Now for the Ten-Hour Day*, *supra* note 15; *see also For the Abolition of Saturday-Night and Sunday Work*, Bakers' J., Oct. 15, 1897, at 102 (discussing the reluctance of French bakers to unionize, and the negative effect this has had on the movement to abolish work on Saturday nights and Sundays); *The Jewish Bakers' Strike in New York*, Bakers' J., Sept. 23, 1905, at 1 (stating that Jewish bakers were mostly unorganized, but did organize for a strike in 1905); *Non-Union Bakeries*, Baker's J., Aug. 19, 1905, at 1 ("We also wish to call your attention to the fact that all French and Italian bread is non-union. All of your efforts to unionize their bakers have been so far in vain, having met with the severest opposition by both employers and employees.").

For a discussion of the on-again off-again unionization of Jewish bakers, see generally Brenner, *supra* note 22. Unionization did not take strong hold among the Jewish bakers until 1909. *Id.* at 97–101.

[27] *See Now for the Ten-Hour Day*, *supra* note 15.

[28] *For the Abolition of Saturday-Night and Sunday Work*, *supra* note 26.

other bakers believed that the union primarily served the interests of their German rivals. The bakers' union, for example, organized a Jewish section in New York City in 1893, but it attracted almost exclusively "German-speaking Jews, who would probably have joined the unions even if separate Jewish sections had not existed."[29] Yiddish-speaking Jews, the overwhelming majority of Jewish bakers, were not interested. Even native-born English-speaking bakers, who had once been active in the defunct bakers' union associated with the Knights of Labor, were reluctant to join the newly-powerful and German-dominated Bakery and Confectionery Workers' International Union.[30]

The bakers' union's political fortunes grew under the leadership of Henry Weismann, a German immigrant who came to the United States as a young adult. He initially settled in California, where he was active in the union-sponsored Anti–Coolie League of California, which was violently opposed to the presence of Chinese workers in the U.S. After a jail term for possession of explosives, Weismann became involved in organizing for the bakers' union. He moved to New York in 1890 to become editor of the *Bakers' Journal*. By 1894 he was the union's unofficial leader and spokesperson and led a new campaign for a ten-hour law in New York.[31]

While the bakers' union focused on lobbying for a ten-hour law, others grew concerned with the sanitary conditions in basement bakeries, and the effects those conditions could have on both the public health and the health of bakers. In 1894, a dying Jewish baker was carried from a cellar bakery on the Lower East Side. Weissman publicized the incident, and demanded an investigation into the health and sanitary conditions in cellar bakeries in Brooklyn and Manhattan.[32] Weismann persuaded the *New York Press* to send a team of reporters—accompanied by union bakers who were familiar with the worst bakeries—to investigate.[33] The result was an exposé by muckraking reporter Edward Marshall detailing unsanitary conditions in bakeries, as well as poor working conditions, and calling for legislative intervention.[34]

As with Upton Sinclair's *The Jungle*, a famous muckraking work on the meatpacking industry, the public was more interested in the sanitary

---

[29] Brenner, *supra* note 22, at 63.

[30] *See The English Speaking Bakers*, N.Y. Times, July 15, 1893, at 1.

[31] Kens, *supra* note 16, at 47–48.

[32] Brenner, *supra* note 22, at 64–65.

[33] Edward Marshall, *Bread and Filth Cooked Together*, N.Y. Press, Sept. 30 1894, § 4, at 1.

[34] Kens, *supra* note 16, at 50–51.

conditions that could impact their health than in working conditions. Marshall's story included tales of cockroaches on the walls and on baking utensils, flour mixed in a tub that had been used to wash a sick child's clothes, and graphic illustrations of other unsanitary conditions. The specifics of Marshall's reporting—or at least how representative his findings were of cellar bakeries in general—are a bit suspect, because he was known for his reformist sympathies, his article was researched at the urging and with the cooperation of Weismann, and the piece was timed to coincide with the bakers' union's campaign for a ten-hour law.[35]

Nevertheless, the gist of Marshall's article is supported by a state factory inspectors' report issued two years later, based on inspections conducted in 1895.[36] The inspectors found "[l]eaky pipes, open sewers, filthy closets and untrapped sinks." They ordered the removal of hundreds of water closets, often in disgusting condition, from their locations in bake rooms or rooms contiguous to bake rooms.[37] The worst conditions for bakers were found in the stuffy and unventilated tenement basement bakeries in Manhattan and Brooklyn.[38] Moreover, the sanitary conditions in those bakeries threatened the public health:

> Cockroaches and other insects, some of them the peculiar development of foul bakeries and never seen elsewhere, abounded, and as chance willed became part of the salable products. Rats, which seemed not to fear the human denizens of these catacombs, ran back and forth between the piled up bread and their holes.[39]

The inspectors added that the bakers who lived in their bakeries "hardly ever get out of their baking clothes, that they, as well as their bedding, are in a nauseatingly filthy condition, totally unfitted to serve as chief factors in the production of the staff of life."[40]

The attention garnered by Marshall's article led to calls for a bakery reform law. A proposed act consisting of a series of sanitary reforms for "biscuit, bread, and cake factories" was introduced in the legislature, and gathered the support of many leading reformers, including American Federation of Labor president Samuel Gompers, philanthropist and

---

[35] The union's primary interest was in limiting working hours, a provision that could be piggybacked on to a sanitary law. But the union also supported the regulation or closure of basement bakeries. *See The English Speaking Bakers*, *supra* note 30; *The Movement for Sanitary Bakeshops*, Bakers' J., Mar. 23, 1895, at 1.

[36] For a contemporaneous report on the ongoing inspections, see *Inspecting Bakeries in the State*, N.Y. Times, July 25, 1895, at 6.

[37] *Factory Inspectors' Report*, *supra* note 21, at 45.

[38] *Id.* at 46.

[39] *Id.*

[40] *Id.* at 56.

founder of the Ethical Culture Society Felix Adler, prominent Episcopal pastor Rev. William Rainsford, and Civil War hero and prominent German–American General Franz Sigel.[41]

The Bakeshop Act, as it came to be known, was modeled on England's Bakehouse Regulation Act of 1863.[42] The sanitary provisions in the proposed New York law were similar to those in the English law, but the New York proposal included a maximum hours provision—tacked on at the urging of the bakers' union—that limited biscuit, cake, and bread bakers' hours to ten per day and sixty per week.[43] The hours provision received an important endorsement from state Health Commissioner Cyrus Edson, who wrote, "The provision limiting the hours of worktime of the men is especially good from a sanitary standpoint. There is unmistakable evidence that these men are overworked, and that, in consequence of this, they are sickly and unfit to handle an article of food."[44]

Not surprisingly, the Bakeshop Act also received the strong support of the bakers' union. The union's official rationale for supporting the Act was that it was "a sanitary measure solely" and therefore "will stand the closest scrutiny of constitutional lawyers and the courts."[45] However, the union also believed that the Act, especially its hours provision, would benefit its members for reasons beyond improved sanitary conditions. An editorial in the same issue of the *Bakers' Journal* promised that the ten-hour workday would solve all of the problems faced by (unionized) bakers, including "[t]he lack of work, increased numbers of apprentices, cheap labor, insane competition among employers, [and] the era of 3-cents loaves of bread."[46] "The weapon of a timely and popular law is about to be placed into our hands," the editorial continued, "Will the journeymen bakers of New York use it?"[47]

As submitted to the New York legislature, the first section of the Bakeshop Act contained the hours provision. The next three sections contained various sanitary regulations, such as prohibiting domestic animals in bakeries and prohibiting workers from sleeping in a bake room. The final two provisions provided for enforcement by the state

---

[41] *The Bakers' Bill Progressing*, Bakers' J., Mar. 30, 1895, at 1.

[42] *See People v. Lochner*, 69 N.E. 373, 382 (N.Y. 1904).

[43] *Id.*; *see also* Kens, *supra* note 16, at 44–59.

[44] *The Bakers' Bill Progressing, supra* note 41.

[45] *The Bakers' Bill to be Signed by Governor Morton*, Bakers' J., Apr. 20, 1895, at 2.

[46] *Now for the Ten-Hour Day, supra* note 15.

[47] *Id.*

factory inspector.[48] The Bakeshop Act passed unanimously in both houses of the legislature.[49] At the last minute, the bill was amended to
prohibit only employees from working more than ten hours a day;
employers were permitted to work as many hours as they saw fit. This
change was made to aid owners of small bakeries, some of whom were
sole proprietors. It was supported by the bakers' union because, as
Weismann wrote, "our aim [is] principally to protect the employee."[50]
That change was approved unanimously by both houses, and Governor
Levi P. Morton signed the Act into law on May 2, 1895. Weismann wrote
in the *Bakers' Journal* that this day "will stand forth as one of the most
memorable days in the history of the great struggle of American bakers
for better and more humane conditions."[51]

Progress in enforcing the Bakeshop Act was slow.[52] State factory
inspectors found that many small tenement basement bakeries ignored
both the sanitary provisions and the hours provisions of the law. The
inspectors received many anonymous complaints about working hours in
basement bakeries, but few workers were willing to sign affidavits that
they had been asked to work more hours than the law allowed. Because
the bakery was not only their workplace, but also where they lived, a
vengeful employer might not only fire them, but evict them as well.[53] The
inspectors recommended that the Bakeshop Act be amended to abolish
basement bakeries entirely, as that was the only way that the abuses
targeted by the Bakeshop Act would ever be ended.[54] The bakers' union
also called for a ban on basement bakeries.[55] Attempts to pass such
legislation failed, as did attempts by a coalition of bakery owners,
tenement house landlords, and flour dealers to weaken the original law.[56]

Meanwhile, the executive committee of the bakers' union, pleased by
Weismann's success in promoting the Bakeshop Act, had elected him to
the union's highest office, international secretary.[57] Weismann, however,

---

[48] N.Y. Laws ch. 415 (1897).

[49] Paul Kens, Lochner v. New York: *Rehabilitated and Revised, But Still Reviled*, 1995
J. Sup. Ct. Hist. 31, 34; *see also* Kens, supra note 16, at 59.

[50] *The Baker's Bill to be Signed by Governor Morton, supra* note 45.

[51] Bakers' J., May 11, 1895, at 11.

[52] *See* Brenner, *supra* note 22, at 68 (noting that only eight arrests were made in all of
New York City in 1896, despite widespread flouting of the law).

[53] *Factory Inspectors' Report, supra* note 21, at 43, 46.

[54] *Id*. at 47.

[55] *Complaints of the Bakers, supra* note 23.

[56] Kens, *supra* note 16, at 60–61.

[57] *Id*. at 98.

resigned in 1897 amid allegations that he had received kickbacks from the company that printed the *Bakers' Journal* and had skimmed off advertising money. Weismann soon opened a bakery of his own, while studying law and passing the New York bar exam. He also became active in the New York Association of Master Bakers, the bitter enemy of the ten-hour law. He later wrote that as a master baker, he underwent "an intellectual revolution, saw where the law which I had succeeded in having passed was unjust to the employers."[58]

There things stood until Utica bakery owner Joseph Lochner was arrested during the second week of April in 1902 for violating the hours provision of the Bakeshop Act. He had allegedly employed a worker named Aman Schmitter for more than sixty hours in one week. Lochner had a longstanding dispute with the bakers' union, and it appears that the union persuaded the factory inspectors to file a complaint against him.[59] This was Lochner's second arrest for violating the ten-hour law. The first time, he had been convicted and fined twenty-five dollars.[60] A grand jury indicted Lochner in October. At a pretrial hearing, his attorney, William S. Mackie, of local law firm Lindsley & Mackie, unsuccessfully requested dismissal on technicalities. At trial in February 1903, Lochner refused to plead guilt or innocence, and offered no defense. The court found Lochner guilty, and he was sentenced to pay a fifty dollar fine or spend fifty days in jail.[61]

The Legal Background

The fact that Lochner offered no defense suggests that the New York Association of Master Bakers had persuaded Lochner to allow this prosecution to become a test case regarding the constitutionality of the hours provision of the Bakeshop Act. The Association had some reason to hope for a positive outcome. The New York Court of Appeals (New York's highest court) had taken a leading role in limiting through constitutional interpretation the scope of government regulatory power, especially the power to regulate labor contracts.

State courts had invalidated labor legislation under two theories. First, courts closely scrutinized legislative classifications to ensure that

---

[58] *Henry Weismann*, Bakers' J., May 27, 1905, at 1.

[59] Kens, *supra* note 16, at 79.

[60] *Decision Given in Labor Case*, Utica Herald Dispatch, Apr. 17, 1905, at 2; Morris Hillquit, *The Decision of the United States Supreme Court on the Ten-Hour Law for Employees of Bakeries—The Passage and Provisions of the Law*, Bakers' J., May 13, 1905, at 1.

[61] Kens, *supra* note 16, at 80–81.

they were reasonable, that they had a valid public purpose. If the Court found that a classification was unreasonable or arbitrary, the underlying legislation constituted "class legislation," legislation that illegitimately favored or disfavored particular groups. Opposition to class legislation had been a constant in American politics since at least the Jacksonian era, and arguably since the Founding.[62] After the Civil War, courts gradually concluded that class legislation was unconstitutional under the Fourteenth Amendment's Equal Protection Clause and state equivalents.

Regulatory laws that applied only to certain industries, like the hours provision of the Bakeshop Act, were especially vulnerable to the charge of class legislation,[63] although the outcome of challenges to various regulations very much depended on the jurisdiction in which the challenges were brought. The many state decisions invalidating laws on class legislation grounds led treatise writer Ernst Freund to conclude in 1904 that the ban on unequal laws is "one of the most effectual limitations upon the exercise of the police power," the states' power to regulate on behalf of the health, safety, and welfare of the public.[64] The impact on protective labor legislation was particularly stark—the prohibition on class legislation was seen as the greatest constitutional barrier to regulation of the labor market.

Another strand of state constitutional case law suggested that any regulation of contractual relations that lacked a valid police power rationale was arbitrary and unreasonable, and therefore unconstitutional. The right to be free from arbitrary or unreasonable regulation had deep roots in Anglo–American natural rights thinking. The only question was whether judges had the constitutional authority to enforce this right. While constitutional objections to class legislation were mainly addressed under the Fourteenth Amendment's Equal Protection Clause, postbellum judges located the constitutional source of the more general right to be free from arbitrary or unreasonable regulations in the Due Process clauses of the Fourteenth Amendment and state constitutions. Courts were especially vigilant in their review of labor regulations, which they saw as potentially violating the fundamental right to "free labor," a right that had been an explicit ideological basis of the Civil War. Several courts consistently rejected state claims that novel labor regulations had valid police power purposes, but other courts were more willing to defer to the legislature.

---

[62] *See generally* Gillman, *supra* note 8.

[63] *See* Bernstein, Lochner *Era Revisionism, Revised, supra* note 6.

[64] Ernst Freund, *The Police Power: Public Policy and Constitutional Rights* § 682, at 705 (1904).

The New York Court of Appeals had issued some of the leading opinions invalidating regulations, especially regulations that the court saw as interfering with the right to pursue an occupation. Most famously in 1885 the court invalidated a law banning cigar manufacturing in tenement apartments as a violation of due process rights.[65] Even more propitious for Lochner was a 1901 decision invalidating a requirement that state contractors pay their workers the "prevailing wage." In that case, the Court of Appeals explicitly endorsed a wide range of state court decisions invalidating various types of "paternal" labor regulations that were found to have no valid health or safety rationale.[66] On the other hand, the Court of Appeals had also issued several opinions upholding regulations, including labor regulations, as within New York's police power.[67]

Armed with at least some favorable class legislation and due process precedents, Lochner appealed to a New York Appellate Division court. The court split 3–2 in favor of upholding the hours law.[68] Judge John M. Davy wrote the rather cryptic majority opinion. Davy stated that the hours law was a valid police power measure, with the goal of improving public health. He found that the law was not class legislation because it was "directed to all persons engaged in the bakery business" and "neither confers special privileges, nor makes unjust discrimination."[69] Davy added that the hours law did not infringe on the fundamental right to pursue an occupation because it was not prohibitory, but merely regulatory.[70]

Lochner appealed the Appellate Division's decision to the Court of Appeals.[71] He lost once again, this time in a 4–3 decision. Chief Judge Alton B. Parker wrote the majority opinion. Parker stated that it was "beyond question" that the public had an interest in having clean bakeries.[72] Therefore, it was within the power of the legislature to regulate the conduct of business so as to provide for and protect the health of people. Parker added that the Bakeshop Act as a whole was clearly intended to promote public health, with the hours provision a

---

[65] *See In re Jacobs*, 98 N.Y. 98 (1885).

[66] People *ex rel. Rodgers v. Coler*, 59 N.E. 716 (N.Y. 1901).

[67] *See generally* Felice Batlan, *A Reevaluation of the New York Court of Appeals: The Home, the Market, and Labor, 1885–1905*, 27 Law & Soc. Inquiry 489 (2002).

[68] *People v. Lochner*, 76 N.Y.S. 396 (N.Y.A.D. 1902).

[69] *Id*. at 401–02.

[70] *Id*. at 401.

[71] *See People v. Lochner*, 69 N.E. 373 (N.Y. 1904).

[72] *Id*. at 379.

part of the overall plan to improve bakery sanitation. After all, Parker contended, a worker would be more likely to be careful and clean when not overworked than when exhausted with fatigue. Even assuming *arguendo* that the statute was not meant to protect public health, Parker continued, the law still operated to protect the health of bakers and was therefore within the police power.[73]

Judge John Clinton Gray wrote a concurring opinion. While Gray believed that the sixty-hour workweek restriction might be invalid as an infringement of liberty of contract if considered alone, when read *in pari materia* with the rest of the Bakeshop Act its connection to health regulation was plain. Gray emphasized that the only appropriate rationale for upholding the law was that it protected *public* health and not just the health of bakers.[74]

Judge Irving Vann also concurred. He stated that the hours law could be upheld only if "from common knowledge" the court could say that working in a bakery was unhealthful.[75] Vann stated that in resolving that factual issue, the court "may resort to such sources of information as were open to the legislature."[76] He then quoted books and articles discussing the negative effect of flour and sugar particles and excess heat on bakers, which purportedly left bakers vulnerable to consumption. He also cited statistics showing a higher mortality rate for bakers than for other industrial workers. Exactly where Vann came across these data is not clear; none of the studies he cites were mentioned in either party's brief. Vann found that the evidence "leads to the conclusion that the occupation of a baker or confectioner is unhealth[ful], and tends to result in disease of the respiratory organs."[77]

Judge Denis O'Brien dissented. He argued that the hours provision was unduly paternalistic, and therefore illicitly infringed on the liberty and property rights of citizens. O'Brien also contended that the hours provision was class legislation that discriminated in favor of one person against another, as it applied only to a very small class of bakeries and confectioners, but not other occupations.[78] O'Brien conceded that the hours provision would still be valid if it were a legitimate exercise of police power, but he contended that the hours provision could not be so

---

[73] *Id.* at 379–81.

[74] *Id.* at 381 (Gray, J., concurring).

[75] *Id.* at 382 (Vann, J., concurring).

[76] *Id.*

[77] *Id.* at 382–84 (Vann, J., concurring).

[78] *Id.* at 385–87 (O'Brien, J., dissenting).

construed because it was "quite impossible to conceive" its relation to the production of healthful bread.[79]

Moreover, O'Brien claimed the hours provision could not be justified as a measure aimed at protecting the health of bakers. Baking was not known to be unhealthful, O'Brien wrote, and the law allowed self-employed bakers to work as many hours as they wished, providing further evidence that the hours provision was a "labor law," not a health law.[80] O'Brien also pointed out the hours provision was codified in the Labor section and not the Health section of the New York Code.[81] Dissenting judge Edward Bartlett echoed O'Brien's contention that there was no evidence that baking was unhealthful. He found the hours provision to be "paternal[istic]" and argued that it should be invalidated.[82]

Union supporters were pleased with the victory, but were unhappy with how close and difficult the case was. For example, the *South Dakota Herald* proclaimed, "What a Victory! This has become the richest country on earth, and we boast of being the most civilized, and yet with all our wealth, with all our civilization, ten hours is now hailed by the toilers as a shortened workday. Why, eighteen years ago the organized workers of this country were agitating for an *eight* hour work day."[83]

Meanwhile, the New York Association of Master Bakers met in February 1904 and decided to levy an assessment of one dollar on each member to pay for an appeal of the case to the Supreme Court.[84] At some point, the Association decided to replace Mackie as Lochner's attorney with the team of prominent Brooklyn attorney Frank Harvey Field and Henry Weismann.[85] Weismann told the *New York Times* that while he understood opposition to a system that required bakers to be on call at all hours for a daily salary, the hours provision unreasonably prohibited bakers from working a standard ten-hour day and then being paid a double wage for overtime.[86]

The *Bakers' Journal*, in contrast, stated that:

---

[79] *Id.* at 387 (O'Brien, J., dissenting).

[80] *Id.* at 388 (O'Brien, J., dissenting).

[81] *Id.* at 387–89 (O'Brien, J., dissenting).

[82] *Id.* at 389 (Bartlett, J., dissenting).

[83] *Opinion of Others*, Bakers' J., Feb. 27, 1904, at 1 (quoting the *South Dakota Herald*).

[84] *Down With Ten-Hour-Law! Is the War-Cry of the Boss Bakers*, Bakers' J., Feb. 27, 1904, at 1.

[85] *Made the 10-Hour Law, Then Had it Unmade*, N.Y. Times, Apr. 19, 1905, at 1.

[86] *Master Bakers Keep Up Fight*, N.Y. Times, Feb. 27, 1904, at 5.

Every time the boss bakers appeal to have the ten-hour law declared unconstitutional, they show themselves in a stronger light as the most bitter and irreconcilable enemies of every improvement of the condition of the worker, they show themselves as brutal exploiters without conscience, who do not care a continental for the existence of a happy life of the families of their employees. They show themselves in their true light as men who would sooner sacrifice the health and life of thousands of workingmen than to comply at least with the smallest demands of the workers.[87]

With regard to the master bakers' appeal to the Supreme Court, the *Journal* stated: "[W]e have no reason at all to become excited on account of an eventual appeal to the Supreme Court of the United States." The opinion of Judge Parker, the *Journal* editorialized, "provides indelible evidence that conditions exist in the bakery trade which undermine the health of the bakery workers and absorb their intellectual and physical powers."[88]

The Supreme Court Case

The prospects for Lochner's appeal did not seem promising. The Supreme Court had acknowledged that illicit class legislation violated the Fourteenth Amendment's Equal Protection Clause, but had a very narrow conception of what constituted illicit class legislation.[89] While the Court had recently invalidated several laws as blatant class legislation,[90] the Court had consistently upheld laws regulating labor relations, most prominently in *Holden v. Hardy*,[91] in which the Court upheld an hours law that applied only to underground miners. Over the next several years, the Court upheld three additional labor statutes challenged as class legislation, with the dissenters never getting more than three votes.[92]

A class legislation/equal protection claim was thus a longshot, as was the other possible ground for Lochner's appeal—that the hours provision of the Bakeshop Act violated the right of Lochner and his workers to "liberty of contract." The Court had recently recognized in dicta that

---

[87] *Boss Bakers Will Appeal Again*, Bakers' J., Feb. 20, 1904, at 1.

[88] *Id.*

[89] *See* Bernstein, Lochner *Era Revisionism, Revised, supra* note 6.

[90] *E.g., Connolly v. Union Sewer Pipe Co.*, 184 U.S. 540 (1902).

[91] 169 U.S. 366 (1898).

[92] *Atkin v. Kansas*, 191 U.S. 207 (1903); *Consolidated Coal Co. of St. Louis v. Illinois*, 185 U.S. 203, 207 (1902); *Knoxville Iron Co. v. Harbison*, 183 U.S. 13, 22 (1901).

liberty of contract was a fundamental right protected by the Due Process Clause of the Fourteenth Amendment.[93] However, by the time of Lochner's appeal, the Court had consistently refused to invalidate purported police power regulations of labor as violations of liberty of contract.[94]

Faced with limited and unattractive options, Lochner attorneys Field and Weismann apparently decided that their strongest argument was that the hours provision was illicit class legislation, and they focused on this point in their brief. First, they argued that the hours provision was class legislation because it applied to some bakers and not to others.[95] According to Lochner's brief, the hours provision did not cover at least one-third to one-half of people in the baking business because they worked not in the biscuit, bread, or cake bakeries covered by the law, but in pie bakeries, hotels, restaurants, clubs, boarding houses, or for private families. The brief alleged that working conditions for these bakers were actually less sanitary and healthful than those of the modern bakery.[96]

What most of the unregulated workers had in common was that their work was seasonal and often involved long hours in season. The legislature exempted these workers not because the health risks to them were small compared to the health risks to other bakers, but because the legislature chose to exempt one class of workers for the benefit of their employers.[97] The hours provision, moreover, allowed bakery owners to work as many hours as they chose. This meant that the more than one-half of all bakeries in New York that were owner or family operated were not covered by the law.[98] The meager and inconsistent coverage of the hours provision, the brief argued, showed that the law was unconstitutional class legislation.

The next part of the brief argued that the hours law was not within the police power because there was no reason to single out bakers for special regulation. The brief argued that unlike mining, the subject of *Holden v. Hardy*, baking was a generally healthful occupation. Allowing

---

[93] *Northern Securities Co. v. U.S.*, 193 U.S. 197, 351 (1904); *Patterson v. Bark Eudora*, 190 U.S. 169, 173–75 (1903); *United States v. Joint-Traffic Ass'n*, 171 U.S. 505, 572–73 (1898); *Allgeyer v. Louisiana*, 165 U.S. 578, 589 (1897).

[94] *Atkin*, 191 U.S. at 220–24; *Knoxville Iron Co.*, 183 U.S. at 18–22; *Holden v. Hardy*, 169 U.S. 366, 388–98 (1898).

[95] Brief for Plaintiff in Error at 78, *Lochner v. New York*, 198 U.S. 45 (1905) (No. 292), *reprinted in* 14 *Landmark Briefs and Arguments of the Supreme Court of the United States: Constitutional Law* 653 (Philip B. Kurland Gerhard Casper eds., 1975).

[96] *Id.* at 10–11.

[97] *Id.* at 10, 12.

[98] *Id.* at 8, 15.

baking to be subject to the police power "would mean that all trades will eventually be held within the police power."[99] The brief included an appendix compiling further evidence of the relative healthfulness of baking.[100]

After a thorough (but not always convincing) discussion of relevant precedents, the brief tried to show that the hours provision of the Bakeshop Act was not within the state's police power because it was not a health measure. The brief noted that the law at issue seemed modeled on England's Bakehouse Regulation Act of 1863, except that the English law did not regulate adult working hours.[101] Meanwhile, the demand from the bakers' union for shorter hours was independent of health considerations. The brief explained that the first ten-hour day bill for bakers, introduced in 1887, contained no sanitary provisions. Moreover, in 1897, when the New York legislature consolidated the laws of the state into various categories, it put the hours provision of the Bakeshop Act into the Labor Law category, while the rest of the Act was placed in the Health Law category.[102]

The most interesting and influential part of the brief was the appendix, referred to by one scholar as "an incipient 'Brandeis Brief.' "[103] Perhaps inspired by Judge Vann's opinion below alleging that baking was unhealthful, the appendix provided statistics about the health of bakers. According to mortality figures from England from 1890 through 1892, bakers had a mortality rate of 920, somewhat below the average of 1,000 for all occupations. The appendix next cited articles from various medical journals that recommended sanitary and ventilation reforms to aid the health of bakers, but did not advocate shorter hours. Indeed, one article in the British medical journal *The Lancet* mentioned that shorter hours had not solved the underlying problem.[104] The appendix also cited the *Reference Handbook of Medical Sciences*, which stated that out of twenty-one occupations, bakers had the eleventh-highest mortality rate, very similar to those of cabinet makers, mason and brick layers, blacksmiths, clerks, and other mundane occupations. An expert at the British Home Office, meanwhile, found that

---

[99] *Id.* at 37.

[100] *See infra* text accompanying notes 103–105.

[101] Brief for the Plaintiff in Error, *supra* note 95; *see also People v. Lochner*, 69 N.E. 373, 383 (N.Y. 1904).

[102] Brief for the Plaintiff in Error, *supra* note 95, at 41.

[103] Stephen A. Siegel, Lochner *Era Jurisprudence and the American Constitutional Tradition*, 70 N.C. L. Rev. 1, 19 n.77 (1991).

[104] Brief for the Plaintiff in Error, *supra* note 95, at 57–58.

bakers ranked eighteenth out of twenty-two occupations for mortality, and they had the lowest rates of pulmonary disease.[105]

In contrast to Lochner's lengthy and reasonably thorough brief, New York's brief was only nineteen pages long, and contained very few citations of precedents. Perhaps New York's Attorney General thought *Lochner* was an easy case governed by *Holden*, and therefore was not worth wasting resources on. Or perhaps he was distracted by the more pressing—and at the time more controversial—*Franchise Tax Cases*, another Supreme Court appeal he was working on that would determine the constitutionality of New York's special franchise tax on streetcar lines, gas works, and other public utilities.[106] Regardless, New York's brief made three points: first, that the burden was on Lochner to show that the law was unconstitutional; second, that the Bakeshop Act's purpose was to safeguard both the public health and the health of bakers; and third, that the law was within the police power because it was a health law.

The Supreme Court heard oral arguments on February 23, 1905, and issued its ruling on April 17, 1905. Much to almost everyone's surprise, Lochner won, in a 5–4 ruling.[107] As expected, Justices David Brewer and Rufus Peckham, who rarely saw a labor law they thought was constitutional, voted in Lochner's favor. So did Chief Justice Melville Fuller, who had dissented with Brewer and Peckham in the Court's most recent major labor regulation case.[108] The majority also managed to pick up the votes of Justices Henry Brown and Joseph McKenna, neither of whom had previously voted to invalidate a state labor regulation for infringing Fourteenth Amendment rights.

Lochner's victory may have been a very close call, as some evidence suggests that Justice Peckham's majority opinion was originally written as a dissent, and that Justice John Marshall Harlan's dissenting opinion was originally the opinion of the Court.[109] Whether one of the Justices indeed switched his vote at the last minute, and if so why, remains a mystery. As for the unusual votes of Brown and McKenna, they can most

---

[105] *Id.* at 60.

[106] Kens, *supra* note 16, at 113.

[107] *Lochner v. New York*, 198 U.S. 45 (1905).

[108] *See Atkin v. Kansas*, 191 U.S. 207 (1903).

[109] *See* Charles Henry Butler, *A Century at the Bar of the Supreme Court of the United States* 172 (1942) (claiming that John Maynard Harlan, the Justice's son, stated that his father told him that Harlan's opinion was originally the majority opinion); John E. Semonche, *Charting the Future: The Supreme Court Responds to a Changing Society, 1890–1920*, at 181–82 (1978) (arguing that the internal construction and style of the dissent arguably indicates it was intended to be a majority opinion).

plausibly be attributed to the creativity of Lochner's brief in presenting a statistics-filled appendix showing that baking was not an especially unhealthful profession, combined with the singularly ineffective brief filed by New York.

Also surprising, given the Lochner brief's focus on class legislation, Peckham's majority opinion ignored that issue in favor of a fundamental rights/due process analysis.[110] Peckham began by finding that the hours provision of the Bakeshop Act statute clearly interfered with the right of contract, a right the Court had recognized in *Allgeyer v. Louisiana* as part of the liberty guaranteed by the Due Process Clause of the Fourteenth Amendment.[111]

Under *Holden v. Hardy*, liberty of contract could be infringed to protect necessitous workers or to preserve the health of either bakers or the public at large. The presumption was in favor of liberty of contract. This presumption could be overcome if the law was a "labor law" and was needed to redress some deficiency in the bakers' ability to negotiate their contracts, or if the law was a "health law." Either way, the law would be within the state's police power. Peckham rejected out of hand the idea that public health was an adequate rationale for the law, stating that "[c]lean and wholesome bread does not depend upon whether the baker works but ten hours per day or only sixty hours per week."[112]

Peckham also concluded that bakers did not need special aid from the state in negotiating their contracts. Peckham argued that unlike women, children, and to some extent "necessitous" miners, bakers are "in no sense wards of the state."[113] Thus, unless the hours provision, which "interfer[ed with bakers'] independence of judgment and of action," was intended to redress particular health effects of baking, it was unconstitutional as a violation of the fundamental right to liberty of contract protected by the Due Process Clause.[114]

To determine whether the hours provision was indeed a health law, Peckham first ascertained whether baking was known to be an unhealthful profession. He concluded that baking was an ordinary trade, not generally known to be unhealthful.[115] Next, Peckham found that the

---

[110] For further discussion of this point, see Bernstein, Lochner *Era Revisionism, Revised*, *supra* note 6.

[111] *Lochner*, 198 U.S. at 53 (citing *Allgeyer v. Louisiana*, 165 U.S. 578, 589 (1897)).

[112] *Id.*

[113] *Id.* at 57.

[114] *Id.*

[115] *Id.* at 58 ("To the common understanding the trade of a baker has never been regarded as an unhealthy one."); *cf. id.* at 63 (criticizing increased legislative interference with the "ordinary trades").

available scientific evidence suggested that baking was not an especially unhealthful profession.[116] For this conclusion, he clearly relied on—but, to the detriment of his reputation, did not explicitly cite—the studies discussed in the appendix to Lochner's brief showing bakers had similar mortality rates to many ordinary professions that the legislature did not regulate.[117] Given, in Peckham's view, the absence of any sound reason to believe that the maximum hours law was in fact a health law, it was not a valid police power measure, but a "mere meddlesome interference[] with the rights of the individual,"[118] and an unconstitutional violation of liberty of contract.

Peckham concluded that "[t]he act is not, within any fair meaning of the term, a health law, but is an illegal interference with the rights of individuals, both employers and employees, to make contracts regarding labor upon such terms as they may think best, or which they may agree upon with the other parties to such contracts."[119] Peckham noted that the other provisions of the act, which related to sanitary concerns, might be valid, but the sixty-hour workweek was not.[120]

Finally, Peckham noted that the incidences of legislative interference in the workplace under the guise of health regulation had been increasing. In examining purported health laws, "[t]he purpose of a statute must be determined from the natural and legal effect of the language employed; and whether it is or is not repugnant to the Constitution of the United States must be determined from the natural effect of such statutes when put into operation, and not from their proclaimed purpose."[121]

Justice John Marshall Harlan, joined by Justices Edward White and William Day, wrote the main dissent. Harlan argued that the state police power extends at least "to the protection of the lives, the health, and the safety of the public against the injurious exercise by any citizen of his own rights," and that the Fourteenth Amendment was not intended to interfere with this police power.[122] Thus, Harlan said, while there exists a

---

[116] *Id.* (finding "no reasonable foundation for holding this to be necessary or appropriate as a health law to safeguard the public health or the health of [bakers]").

[117] *Id.* at 59–61 (comparing bakers to a wide range of other occupations, shown by Lochner's brief to be approximately as healthful as baking, that could also be regulated if the bakers' law was upheld, but never noting any reliance on data from the brief).

[118] *Id.* at 61.

[119] *Id.*

[120] *Id.* at 61–62.

[121] *Id.* at 64.

[122] *Id.* at 65 (Harlan, J., dissenting).

clear right to liberty of contract, it may be subordinated to a lawful exercise of police power.[123] According to Harlan, the Court should only invalidate a purported health or safety law if the law had "no real or substantial relation to those objects, or is, beyond all question, a plain, palpable invasion of rights secured by the fundamental law."[124] Any doubts should be resolved in favor of the statute.

Harlan then asserted that the purpose of the hours provision of the Bakeshop Act was at least in part to protect bakers' health. Harlan quoted medical treatises and statistics that supported the claim that work done by bakers was unhealthful.[125] Where he came across these data is unclear, because they do not appear in New York's brief. Harlan argued that it was reasonable for New York to presume that labor in excess of ten hours per day in a bakery "may endanger the health and shorten the lives of the workmen, thereby diminishing their physical and mental capacity to serve the state and to provide for those dependent upon them."[126] Because the statute was not "plainly and palpably" inconsistent with the Fourteenth Amendment, it should be upheld.[127]

Justice Oliver Wendell Holmes, Jr. filed a lone dissent, one of the most celebrated dissenting opinions in American constitutional history. Holmes asserted that the majority's opinion was based on "an economic theory which a large part of the country does not entertain."[128] He contended that the state's power to interfere with the right to contract in ways that could not easily be distinguished from the bakers' hours law, including such ancient laws as those against usury and work on Sundays, was well established.[129] "[A] Constitution," Holmes wrote, "is not intended to embody a particular economic theory, whether of paternalism and the organic relation of the citizen to the state or of *laissez faire*."[130] "The Fourteenth Amendment," he added, "does not enact Mr. Herbert Spencer's *Social Statics*," a famous pro-laissez-faire work.[131]

---

123 *Id.* at 65–66 (Harlan, J., dissenting).

124 *Id.*

125 *Id.* at 70–71 (Harlan, J., dissenting).

126 *Id.* at 72 (Harlan, J., dissenting).

127 *Id.* at 73 (Harlan, J., dissenting).

128 *Id.* at 75 (Holmes, J., dissenting)

129 *Id.*

130 *Id.*

131 *Id.* This remark by Holmes seems to be the basis for the decades-old claim that the *Lochner* majority was motivated by Social Darwinism, as many people consider Spencer to have been a leading Social Darwinist. However, in context it is clear that Holmes is using Spencer as an example of a believer in extreme laissez-faire libertarianism, and is not

According to Holmes, the term "liberty" is perverted whenever it is "held to prevent the natural outcome of a dominant opinion," save when everyone could agree that a challenged statute "would infringe fundamental principles as they have been understood by the traditions of our people and our law."[132] He argued that a reasonable person could find the hours provision to be a valid health measure, and therefore the law should be upheld.

The Reaction to Lochner

The initial reaction of the *Bakers' Journal* to the *Lochner* decision was surprisingly muted. The *Journal* editorialized on April 22, 1905, that the decision just showed that "under the present conditions [bakers'] rights and their interest will only be preserved and defended by their own organization and power."[133] As the decision sank in, however, the *Journal*'s editorials grew far harsher. A May 20, 1905, *Journal* column stated that *Lochner* was the "hardest blow ever dealt by the courts of this country to organized labor."[134] A week later, the *Journal* editor wrote that "[t]he bakery workers die like flies, of consumption, rheumatism and other physical punishments for the breaking of nature's laws. But what do the *learned* justices care for the laws of nature? Capitalist laws are alone sacred to them! What are wage workers for but to be exploited!"[135]

Ultimately, however, the bakers' union had little reason to complain about the *Lochner* ruling. In the ten years since the Bakeshop Act had become law, productivity and working conditions had improved throughout the United States as the nation grew richer. Shorter hours were becoming the norm nationwide, including in the baking industry. By 1909, less than nine percent of bakers nationwide worked more than ten hours a day, and, by 1919, eighty-seven percent of bakers worked nine hours a day or less and only three percent of bakers worked more than

---

accusing the majority of Social Darwinism. Holmes may have chosen Spencer because Holmes was a master of the flip aphorism, and *Spencer's Social Statics* is a memorable alliteration.

[132] *Id.* at 75–76.

[133] *Bake Shop Law of the State of New York Prescribing Ten Hours a Day and Sixty Hours Week for Labor in Bakeries Declared Unconstitutional by United States Supreme Court*, Bakers' J., Apr. 22, 1905, at 1.

[134] *The Decision of the United States Supreme Court on the Ten-Hour Law for Employees of Bakeries—The Passage and Provisions of the Law*, Bakers' J., May 20, 1905, at 1.

[135] *The Decision of the Supreme Court*, Bakers' J., May 27, 1905, at 2.

ten hours a day.[136] The practical effect of *Lochner* on bakers' hours was very small.

Of course, interested observers understood that the ramifications of the *Lochner* decision could reach well beyond the issue of bakers' hours, and the decision provoked strong reactions from various commentators. The few libertarian periodicals of the day hailed *Lochner*, seeing it as a blow against labor union tyranny. *The Nation* editorialized that the main effect of the decision "will be to stop the subterfuge by which, under the pretext of conserving the public health, the unionists have sought to delimit the competition of non-unionists, and so to establish a quasi-monopoly of many important kinds of labor."[137] *The New York Times* praised the Supreme Court for refusing to enforce "any contracts which may have been made between the demagogues in the Legislature and the ignoramuses among the labor leaders in bringing to naught their combined machinations."[138]

In contrast, the *Lochner* ruling met with immediate condemnation in Progressive and labor union circles. According to one historian, "[n]ot since the debacle of 1895 [when the Supreme Court invalidated the federal income tax] had a case stirred as much protest in the popular press and professional journals. What was at issue was not simply the law in the case but a nationwide movement to use government to redress imbalances in the industrial society."[139] Progressives and labor activists had railed for years against "reactionary" state court decisions invalidating labor regulations, but had taken comfort in the fact that the United States Supreme Court had consistently voted to uphold labor reforms. Now, however, the Supreme Court, in issuing its first decision holding a state labor law void, had seemingly gone over to the dark side.[140]

Progressive legal scholars joined the chorus of condemnation. Somehow overlooking both the appendix to Lochner's brief and Justice Peckham's blunt statement that his view of the relative healthfulness of baking was informed by "looking through statistics regarding all trades and occupations,"[141] legal scholars such as Roscoe Pound, Ernst Freund, and Learned Hand accused the *Lochner* majority of engaging in "mechanical jurisprudence," or abstract reasoning, instead of relying on

---

[136] Hazel Kyrk Joseph Stancliffe Davis, *The American Baking Industry* 60–61, 108 (1925).

[137] Editorial, *A Check to Union Tyranny*, 80 Nation 346, 347 (1905).

[138] *Fussy Legislation*, Editorial, N.Y. Times, Apr. 19, 1905, at 10.

[139] Semonche, *supra* note 109, at 184.

[140] Ernst Freund, *Limitation of Hours of Labor and the Federal Supreme Court*, 17 Green Bag 411, 413 (1905).

[141] *Lochner v. New York*, 198 U.S. 45, 58 (1905).

modern scientific knowledge about the health effects of long hours on bakers.[142] Hostility to *Lochner*'s purported formalism directly led to the development of what became known as sociological jurisprudence. Sociological jurisprudence held that the purpose of law is to achieve social aims, and that legal rules, including constitutional rules, cannot be deduced from first principles.[143] Accordingly, abstract notions of rights should not bind judges.[144] Instead, judges should consider the public interest and modern social conditions or "social facts" when interpreting the Constitution. Sociological jurisprudence came to dominate the leading law schools and had significant impact on one of the most important innovations in legal thought in the twentieth century, legal realism.

Many believers in sociological jurisprudence saw attorney, and future Supreme Court Justice, Louis Brandeis's Supreme Court brief in *Muller v. Oregon*[145] in 1908 as a successful attempt to put principles into practice. The brief contained only a short legal argument, but it provided the Court with many pages of sociological reports and data supporting maximum hours laws for women. Brandeis's brief was less radical than it seemed; he knew that Oregon was filing a traditional brief in the case so he did not need to reiterate the state's arguments. Moreover, the idea of presenting relevant data to the Court was actually pioneered not by Brandeis but by Field and Weismann in the appendix to their *Lochner* brief,[146] and Brandeis was likely motivated to write a "sociological" brief by Peckham's assertion in *Lochner* that he had relied on statistics demonstrating the relative healthfulness of baking. Nevertheless, the brief received a mention in the Court's opinion upholding the law at issue (although, many have failed to notice, only for reinforcing what the Justices said they already knew from "common sense"), and the so-called "Brandeis Brief" became a staple of constitutional argument over Progressive reforms.

Lochner's *Long Term Impact*

Despite all this ferment, *Lochner* turned out to be neither the stuff of libertarian dreams nor of Progressive nightmares; rather, for almost two decades *Lochner* turned out to be an aberration. Not that the Court

---

[142] *See, e.g.*, Freund, *supra* note 140; Learned Hand, *Due Process of Law and the Eight-Hour Day*, 21 Harv. L. Rev. 495, 501–08 (1908); Roscoe Pound, *Mechanical Jurisprudence*, 8 Colum. L. Rev. 605, 615–16 (1908).

[143] *See* Roscoe Pound, *Liberty of Contract*, 18 Yale L.J. 454, 464 (1908).

[144] *See* Louis D. Brandeis, *The Living Law*, 10 Ill. L. Rev. 461, 467 (1916).

[145] 208 U.S. 412 (1908).

[146] *See supra* text accompanying note 103.

always upheld challenged regulations. Indeed, a few of its rulings invalidating state laws had significant impacts on American life. Following
Lochner, the Court invalidated as violations of liberty and property
rights protected by the Due Process Clauses of the Fifth and Fourteenth
Amendments laws that prohibited employers from forbidding their employees to join labor unions.[147] These rulings likely inhibited the growth
of labor unions. The Court also invalidated a Louisville law requiring
residential segregation, a decision that helped prevent the spread of
South African-style apartheid in the American South and, by preventing
rigid racial zoning, allowed hundreds of thousands of African Americans
to leave impoverished rural plantations for a better life in cities.[148]

At least through the early 1920s, however, the Court rarely interfered with regulations claimed to be within the states' police power. In
the decade after *Lochner*, the Court upheld almost every state labor
reform law that came before it, including laws banning child labor,[149]
regulating the hours of labor of women,[150] making mining companies
liable for their willful failure to furnish a reasonably safe place for
workers,[151] and mandating an eight-hour day for federal workers or
employees of federal contractors,[152] as well as many others. Congress
altered the Supreme Court's jurisdiction in 1914 to allow the Court to
review judgments from state courts invalidating state statutes as violations of federal constitutional rights.[153] Congress did so because it saw
the Court, with its consistent willingness to uphold reformist legislation,
as a check on state courts that were invalidating Progressive legislation,
especially labor legislation.

By 1917, *Lochner* seemed to be dead and buried for good. In that
year the Court upheld four very controversial labor reforms: workers'
compensation laws,[154] a federal law that not only limited railroad workers

---

[147] *Muller v. Oregon*; *Adair v. United States*, 208 U.S. 161, 180 (1908).

[148] *Buchanan v. Warley*, 245 U.S. 60 (1917); *see generally* David E. Bernstein, *Philip Sober Controlling Philip Drunk:* Buchanan v. Warley *in Historical Perspective*, 51 Vand. L. Rev. 797 (1998). For a discussion of the more subtle benefits African Americans received from *Lochner*ian decisions protecting liberty of contract, see David E. Bernstein, *Only One Place of Redress: African Americans, Labor Regulations, and the Courts from Reconstruc-tion to the New Deal* (2001).

[149] *Sturges & Burn Mfg. Co. v. Beauchamp*, 231 U.S. 320, 325–26 (1913).

[150] *Bosley v. McLaughlin*, 236 U.S. 385, 392–95 (1915); *Miller v. Wilson*, 236 U.S. 373, 380–82 (1915); *Riley v. Massachusetts*, 232 U.S. 671, 679–81 (1914); *Muller v. Oregon*, 208 U.S. 412, 418–23 (1908).

[151] *Wilmington Star Mining Co. v. Fulton*, 205 U.S. 60, 70–74 (1907).

[152] *Ellis v. United States*, 206 U.S. 246, 254–56 (1907).

[153] Act of Dec. 23, 1914, Pub. L. No. 632–24, 38 Stat. 790 (1914).

[154] *Mountain Timber Co. v. Washington*, 243 U.S. 219 (1917); *Hawkins v. Bleakly*, 243 U.S. 210 (1917); *N.Y. Cent. R.R. v. White*, 243 U.S. 188 (1917).

to an eight-hour day but also fixed wages at the level the workers had received when working longer hours,[155] a minimum wage law for women,[156] and a maximum hours law for all industrial workers.[157] The latter ruling seemed to directly contradict *Lochner* and therefore overruled its specific holding *sub silentio*.[158]

Lochner, however, underwent a surprising renaissance in the 1920s when the more aggressively *Lochner*ian wing of the Court, bolstered by four appointments by President Warren Harding, took firm control. With a strong *Lochner*ian majority in place, led by Chief Justice (and former president) William Howard Taft, the Court both reviewed economic regulation much more aggressively than it had in the past and also applied *Lochner*ian jurisprudence outside the economic realm.

The Court froze and formalized various doctrinal exceptions to the liberty of contract, such as the government's virtual carte blanche to regulate businesses "affected with a public interest." In *Charles Wolff Packing Co. v. Court of Industrial Relations*,[159] the Court unanimously held that states could not require industrial disputes to be settled by government-imposed mandatory arbitration. The state claimed that the industries in question were "clothed with a public interest," which led the Court, in an opinion by Chief Justice Taft, to spell out the various categories of businesses affected with a public interest.[160] By doing so,

---

[155] *Wilson v. New*, 243 U.S. 332 (1917).

[156] *Simpson v. O'Hara*, 243 U.S. 629 (1917). This was actually a 4–4 decision. Justice Brandeis recused himself because he had worked on the case before being appointed to the Supreme Court, but he clearly would have cast the fifth vote for upholding such laws.

[157] *Bunting v. Oregon*, 243 U.S. 426 (1917).

[158] *See, e.g., Adkins v. Children's Hosp.*, 261 U.S. 525, 564 (1923) (Taft, C.J., dissenting) ("It is impossible for me to reconcile the *Bunting* Case and the *Lochner* Case, and I have always supposed that the *Lochner* Case was thus overruled *sub silentio*."); Edward S. Corwin, *Social Insurance and Constitutional Limitations*, 26 Yale L.J. 431, 443 (1917) (concluding that *Lochner's* "constitutional 'rigorism' is at an end").

[159] 262 U.S. 522 (1923).

[160] *Id.* at 535. The Court stated that the following businesses were "affected with a public interest":

(1) Those which are carried on under the authority of a public grant of privileges which either expressly or impliedly imposes the affirmative duty of rendering a public service demanded by any member of the public. Such are the railroads, other common carriers and public utilities. (2) Certain occupations, regarded as exceptional, the public interest attaching to which, recognized from earliest times, has survived the period of arbitrary laws by Parliament or colonial Legislatures for regulating all trades and callings. Such are those of the keepers of inns, cabs, and gristmills. (3) Businesses which, though not public at their inception, may be fairly said to have risen to be such and have become subject in consequence to some government regulation. They have come to hold such a peculiar relation to the public that this is superimposed upon

Taft ensured that the "affected with a public interest" doctrine would be limited to those categories, and would no longer be expanded on a case-by-case basis.

In *Adkins v. Children's Hospital*, a 5–4 majority of the Court explicitly revived *Lochner* while invalidating a minimum wage law for women.[161] The *Adkins* Court announced that "freedom of contract is . . . the general rule and restraint the exception, and the exercise of legislative authority to abridge it can be justified only by the existence of exceptional circumstances."[162] The Court acknowledged that government regulation could be used for traditional police power purposes. Beyond that, the Court asserted that precedent limited interference with liberty of contract to cases involving the following issues: (1) "[t]hose dealing with statutes fixing rates and charges to be exacted by businesses impressed with a public interest," (2) "[s]tatutes relating to contracts for the performance of public work," (3) "[s]tatutes prescribing the character, methods, and time for payment of wages," and (4) "[s]tatutes fixing hours of labor" to preserve the health and safety for workers or the public at large.[163] Thus, during the Taft Court era the exceptions to liberty of contract created by prior Court decisions were retained, but they were categorized and applied narrowly to prevent what the Court saw as further erosion of individual liberty.

It was only after *Adkins* that *Lochner* was no longer an anomaly, but the governing precedent of the Supreme Court when considering constitutional challenges to police power regulations. The next decade or so was the only time in Supreme Court history in which the Court did not apply a strong presumption of constitutionality to economic regulation. Even so, the Taft Court upheld most of the laws that came before it, including such far-reaching regulatory innovations as exclusionary zoning. Meanwhile, *Lochner* came to symbolize for Progressives the worst excesses of conservative judicial activism on behalf of business interests and against workers. By contrast, *Lochner*'s supporters, although relatively few and far between in the 1920s, believed that the

---

them. In the language of the cases, the owner by devoting his business to the public use, in effect grants the public an interest in that use and subjects himself to public regulation to the extent of that interest although the property continues to belong to its private owner and to be entitled to protection accordingly.

Id. (citations omitted).

[161] 261 U.S. 525 (1923).

[162] *Id.* at 546. For more on *Lochner* and protective laws for women, see David E. Bernstein, Lochner's *Feminist Legacy*, 101 Mich. L. Rev. 1960 (2003) (reviewing Julie Novkov, *Constituting Workers, Protecting Women* (2001)).

[163] *Id.* at 546–48.

Court was appropriately protecting traditional American libertarian values against encroachment by the government.

Often overlooked in histories of the Supreme Court in the 1920s is that the Court not only revived *Lochner*'s protection of liberty of contract, but also began to protect what today we call civil liberties. In doing so, the Court resolved the ongoing ambiguity over whether the Due Process Clause protected non-economic rights. In the wake of abuses by the Wilson Administration during and after World War I and by state governments dominated by nativist hysteria after the War— abuses that included Palmer Raids, imprisonment of antiwar dissidents, and Ku Klux Klan-inspired laws intended to shut down Catholic schools—the Court broadly expanded protection under the Due Process Clause beyond economic liberties to civil liberties.

The expansion of *Lochner*ian due process jurisprudence to civil liberties began with *Meyer v. Nebraska*,[164] in which the Court invalidated a Nebraska law that banned the teaching of German in private schools or by private tutors. Arch–*Lochner*ian Justice James McReynolds wrote a sweeping opinion holding that the Due Process Clause protects a wide range of freedoms, including not only the "right of the individual to contract," and "to engage in any of the common occupations of life," but also "to acquire useful knowledge, to marry, establish a home and bring up children, [and] to worship God according to the dictates of his own conscience,"[165] along with other "privileges long recognized at common law as essential to the orderly pursuit of happiness by free men."[166]

Two years later in *Gitlow v. New York*,[167] the Court assumed, and later held, that freedom of expression was protected against the states by the Fourteenth Amendment. Decisions that followed invalidated laws banning private schools,[168] forbidding private Japanese language schools,[169] and banning display of the Communist flag.[170] All of these

---

[164] 262 U.S. 390 (1923).

[165] *Id.* at 399–400 (citations omitted).

[166] *Id.*

[167] 268 U.S. 652, 666 (1925) ("For present purposes we may and do assume that freedom of speech and of the press—which are protected by the First Amendment from abridgment by Congress—are among the fundamental personal rights and 'liberties' protected by the due process clause of the Fourteenth Amendment from impairment by the States."); *see also Stromberg v. California*, 283 U.S. 359, 368 (1931) ("It has been determined that the conception of liberty under the due process clause of the Fourteenth Amendment embraces the right of free speech.").

[168] *Pierce v. Society of Sisters*, 268 U.S. 510 (1925).

[169] *Farrington v. Tokushige*, 273 U.S. 284 (1927).

[170] *Stromberg v. California*, 283 U.S. 359 (1931).

cases were decided on the ground that they involved fundamental liberties protected by the Due Process Clause.

As it turned out, however, the 1920s and the Taft Court represented the last gasp of classical liberal principles in American public life for decades to come. By the 1920s, libertarian views, especially on economics, had already been marginalized among American intellectuals, but they retained a tenuous foothold in elite legal circles despite the onslaught of sociological jurisprudence and legal realism. The classical liberal foundations of *Lochner*ian jurisprudence, however, could not survive the strains of the Great Depression. With almost no support among the intellectual class, with the unemployed and underemployed clamoring for government intervention, and with statism ascendant across the globe in the forms of fascism, communism, and social democracy—each of which had its share of admirers in the United States—the Court's commitment to limited government seemed outlandishly reactionary to much of the public. The Court's *Lochner*ian position that libertarian presumptions were fundamental to Anglo–American liberty became untenable as the Depression wore on, with many Americans blaming the purported laissez-faire policies of previous administrations for the continuing economic crisis.

Given the lack of intellectual and public support for *Lochner*ism, its demise was inevitable, but still required a change of personnel on the Court. President Hoover, a Progressive Republican, put the first nails into *Lochner*'s coffin by appointing to the Court Justices Charles Evan Hughes, Owen Roberts, and Benjamin Cardozo, each of whom had views well to the left of the conservatives who dominated the Court in the 1920s. By 1934, a majority had formed willing to broadly expand the "affected with a public interest" doctrine to the point where just about any regulation of prices was constitutional.[171] After a short period of resistance to the more extreme aspects of the New Deal, the end of the *Lochner* era was signaled when, in 1937, the Court reversed *Adkins* and upheld a minimum wage law for women.[172] President Franklin Roosevelt sealed *Lochner*'s fate by appointing a series of New Dealers and other political allies to the Court.

Lochner's *Significance Today*

*Lochner*ian fundamental rights analysis, however, lived on. The Court, while largely abandoning review of economic regulations under the Due Process Clause, gradually incorporated most of the Bill of Rights

---

[171] *See Nebbia v. New York*, 291 U.S. 502, 533 (1934) (defining "affected with a public interest" as "subject to the exercise of the police power").

[172] *See West Coast Hotel Co. v. Parrish*, 300 U.S. 379 (1937).

into the Fourteenth Amendment, thereby continuing to enforce fundamental rights against the states. The incorporation doctrine both limited
and expanded the scope of fundamental rights by associating them with
the text of the Bill of Rights, rather than basing them simply on the
Justices' own understanding of fundamental rights.[173]

The post-*Lochner* reincarnation of fundamental rights began in 1938
in the famous Footnote 4 of *Carolene Products*,[174] which expressed the
Court's reluctance to entirely abandon judicial review of purported police
power regulations. The Court suggested that "[t]here may be narrower
scope for operation of the presumption of constitutionality when legislation appears on its face to be within a specific prohibition of the
Constitution, such as those of the first ten Amendments, which are
deemed equally specific when held to be embraced within the Fourteenth."[175]

Footnote 4 also suggested that the Court was willing to preserve the
*Lochner*ian civil liberties decisions of the 1920s and 1930s by reinterpret-
ing them as decisions protecting "discrete and insular minorities."[176]
Cases cited by the Court in Footnote 4, including the civil liberties
decisions of the 1920s, were reinterpreted as decisions invalidating
statutes because the (facially-neutral) laws in question were directed at
"particular religious, or national, or racial minorities."[177] Laws that
threaten such groups "may call for a correspondingly more searching
judicial inquiry."[178] Protection of discrete and insular minorities from
hostile legislation by an equal protection analysis is a limited, modern
liberal version of the older prohibition against class legislation, with the
caveat that the modern version allows and in some cases requires the
Court to inquire into the legislative intent of facially-neutral laws.[179]

Protection of non-textual rights under the Due Process Clause
largely disappeared for a couple of decades. In the 1960s, however,
Griswold v. Connecticut relied in part on *Lochner*ian civil liberties
decisions from the 1920s for the proposition that the Due Process Clause
protects a fundamental unenumerated right to privacy.[180] By resurrecting

---

[173] *See* Kurt T. Lash, *The Constitutional Convention of 1937: The Original Meaning of
the New Jurisprudential Deal*, 70 Fordham L. Rev. 459, 459–66 (2001).

[174] *United States v. Carolene Prods Co.*, 304 U.S. 144, 152 n.4 (1938).

[175] *Id.*

[176] *Id.*

[177] *Id.*

[178] *Id.*

[179] *See Washington v. Davis*, 426 U.S. 229, 239 (1976).

[180] 381 U.S. 479 (1965).

the *Lochner*ian notion that due process protects fundamental unenumerated rights, the *Griswold* Court ensured that many of the great constitutional issues of the last forty years would be decided as Due Process
cases, rather than being decided based on notions of equality under the
Equal Protection Clause or even left to the political branches to sort out.

Critics frequently charged the Warren and Burger Courts with
*Lochner*ian judicial activism.[181] With liberals in the majority, however,
the Court and its defenders brushed off such criticism. By the late 1980s,
many constitutional law scholars grew unhappy with the traditional
critique of *Lochner*. With the ascendancy of a conservative majority on
the Supreme Court, they recognized that some of their most cherished
Warren and Burger Courts decisions—not least, *Roe v. Wade*[182]—were
vulnerable to being overruled as *Lochner*ian.[183]

For example, Professor Robert Post, reflecting mainstream liberal
sentiment, wrote that *Lochner* is a problem "because we do not have a
convincing account of the criteria by which our own aspirations to
preserve constitutional rights should be compared to, and therefore
distinguished from, what has become a paradigmatic example of judicial
failure."[184] Discomfort with the traditional critique of *Lochner* led to
something of a cottage industry of *Lochner* reinterpretation among
constitutional law scholars. While conservatives argue that the current
Court should reassess its endorsement of *Griswold*, *Roe*, and other cases
recognizing implicit fundamental rights under the Due Process Clause
because they are in the same tradition as *Lochner*, many liberal constitutional law scholars demur.

Some scholars have argued that *Lochner* and *Roe* are not really in
the same tradition,[185] but their claims are not persuasive. Indeed, the
recognition that *Lochner* and *Roe* are in the same fundamental rights
tradition has caused other contemporary liberal scholars to reassess
their understanding of *Lochner*. The *Lochner* era Court, they argue,
chose an appropriate role for the Court—defender of last resort of

---

[181] *See* Fiss, *supra* note 8, at 10 ("[C]omparisons with *Lochner* were frequently made to
reproach the Warren Court.").

[182] 410 U.S. 113 (1973).

[183] *E.g.*, Robert H. Bork, *The Tempting of America: The Political Seduction of the Law*
31–32 (1990).

[184] Robert C. Post, *Defending the Lifeworld: Substantive Due Process in the Taft Court
Era*, 78 B.U. L. Rev. 1489, 1494 (1998).

[185] *E.g.*, Gillman, *supra* note 8, 1–18 (attributing *Lochner* to opposition to class
legislation); Cass R. Sunstein, Lochner's Legacy, 87 Colum. L. Rev. 873, 873–75 (1987)
(attributing *Lochner* to the Court's desire to constitutionalize common law rules and
entitlements). For rebuttals, see Bernstein, Lochner's *Legacy's Legacy*, *supra* note 7, and
Bernstein, Lochner *Era Revisionism, Revised*, *supra* note 6, respectively.

fundamental rights—but simply chose the wrong rights to emphasize; the Court focused on liberty of contract, a right that had become anachronistic in a modern industrial economy. Instead, the Court should have focused on the civil liberties necessary for a properly-functioning modern liberal democracy.[186] These liberal scholars argue that the Court eventually got it right, and *Lochner*, perhaps, should be recognized as a misstep on an otherwise sound path, not an irredeemable mistake.

Lochner's reputation has been sufficiently polished that some leading legal scholars, albeit from the libertarian minority, forcefully argue that *Griswold* and *Lochner* were *both* correctly decided,[187] that the mistake of the modern Court has been that it has not applied the logic of *Lochner* to the economic sphere and has instead left important economic rights vulnerable to government overreaching.[188] But even if *Lochner* seems to be gradually losing its anti-canonical status, *Lochner*'s important role in the debate over American constitutionalism is likely to continue for some time.

---

[186] A position along these lines is advocated by Ackerman and Fiss. *See* 2 Bruce Ackerman, *We the People: Transformations* 255–78 (1998); Fiss, *supra* note 8, at 9–21.

[187] *See, e.g.*, Richard A. Epstein, *Liberty, Equality, and Privacy: Choosing a Legal Foundation for Gay Rights*, 2002 U. Chi. Legal F. 73, 84–93 ("[T]he traditional *Lochner* framework supports *Griswold*'s outcome without its messy resort to penumbras in the desperate effort to distance itself from *Lochner*."); *see also* Randy E. Barnett, *Justice Kennedy's Libertarian Revolution:* Lawrence v. Texas, 2003 Cato Sup. Ct. Rev. 21 (defending *Lochner* and praising Justice Kennedy's extension of *Griswold* in *Lawrence v. Texas*, 123 S.Ct. 2472 (2003)).

[188] *See, e.g.*, Hadley Arkes, *The Return of George Sutherland: Restoring a Jurisprudence of Natural Rights* (1995); Alan J. Meese, *Will, Judgment, and Economic Liberty: Mr. Justice Souter and the Mistranslation of the Due Process Clause*, 41 Wm. Mary L. Rev. 3, 3–11 (1999) (suggesting that the Court was wrong to abandon *Lochner* completely); Michael J. Phillips, *Entry Restrictions in the* Lochner *Court*, 4 Geo. Mason L. Rev. 405, 40506 (1996) (contending that *Lochner*ian decisions prohibiting monopolization of certain occupations were correct); Roger Pilon, *How Constitutional Corruption Has Led to Ideological Litmus Tests for Judicial Nominees* 7 Cato Policy Analysis No. 446 (Aug. 8, 2002); Note, *Resurrecting Economic Rights: The Doctrine of Economic Due Process Reconsidered*, 103 Harv. L. Rev. 1363, 1363–64 (1990) (calling for a revival of *Lochner*ian jurisprudence); *see generally* James W. Ely, Jr., *Melville W. Fuller Reconsidered*, 1998 J. Sup. Ct. Hist. 35 (defending *Lochner* and other controversial Fuller Court decisions as forward-looking and consistent with contemporary public opinion and political economy). David Strauss has argued that the Lochner Court was correct to protect liberty of contract, but that it interpreted the doctrine too broadly. David A. Strauss, *Why Was* Lochner *Wrong?*, 70 U. Chi. L. Rev. 373, 375 (2003).

*

10

Lucinda M. Finley

Contested Ground: The Story of *Roe v. Wade* and its Impact on American Society

Introduction

Sarah Weddington, the lawyer who initiated *Roe v. Wade* in March, 1970, when she was barely two years out of law school, and successfully argued it in the United States Supreme Court a year and a half later, has written that this landmark case "started at a garage sale, amid paltry castoffs."[1] In the fall of 1969, Weddington and her friends from their Austin, Texas women's liberation consciousness raising group were holding a garage sale to raise money for their various cause-oriented activities. Two of the women helping Weddington with the garage sale, Judy Smith and Bea Durden, were actively involved in an underground abortion referral service, which gave women information about skilled and safe, albeit illegal, abortion providers in Texas and Mexico. Worried that they could be prosecuted as accomplices under a Texas law that made performing an abortion a crime, Smith and Durden asked their friend Sarah, who had recently graduated from the University of Texas Law School, for advice. While demurring that she knew nothing about abortion law, which certainly was never mentioned during her legal education, Weddington promised her friends that she would do some legal research for them.

Weddington's commitment to the issue of legalizing abortion was rooted in her own unplanned pregnancy while still in law school. She and her then boyfriend, and eventual husband Ron Weddington, who was about to start law school himself, decided that there was no way

---

[1] Sarah Weddington, *A Question of Choice* 35 (1992).

they could both stay in school and support a child. They learned of a willing doctor in Mexico, and when she emerged alive and healthy, she began to question why women were forced to risk their lives in Mexican border towns to avoid a pregnancy that could permanently ruin their educational and economic prospects.

Weddington's legal research uncovered some legal developments that she thought could provide precedential support for challenging the Texas law. When she shared her findings with Judy Smith, Smith decided that they should file a lawsuit. Smith eventually persuaded Weddington that, despite her youth and inexperience, she was the lawyer who should do it.

Notwithstanding Weddington's homey account of *Roe*'s almost accidental origins,[2] the case was but one of numerous legal efforts in the late 1960s and early 1970s to liberalize or overturn state laws that made abortion a crime. The origins of all these efforts, including *Roe*, can just as well be anchored in many other instances of tragic personal experiences, frustrated legislative reform efforts, path-breaking legal decisions, innovative legal thinking, and women's emboldened activism. These formative instances include: the personal experience of hospital doctors who grieved over the mounting carnage of women dying from attempts at self-induced abortion or from sloppy and unsanitary illegal abortions, frustrated that they had the medical skills to perform abortions safely and thus prevent these needless deaths while questioning the wisdom of laws that prohibited them from doing so; the personal experience of many other women who, like Weddington, endured the danger and humiliation of illegal abortions, and who vowed, when they were among the lucky who survived, that they would work tirelessly to change the laws that had forced them into a preventable life-and-death situation; the opportunity provided by newly formed women's liberation movement consciousness-raising groups, like the one in Austin, Texas, for women to share these experiences with each other and to start leafleting, letter writing, and planning demonstrations; the personal experiences of women's rights activists and male state legislators who had lost friends to illegal abortion, and were motivated to prevent such future tragedies by trying to change their state's laws; the experience of N.Y.U. law student Roy Lucas, who helped his girlfriend travel to Puerto Rico for a safe legal abortion, then wrote his third-year paper on the implications for abortion laws of the recently decided case of *Griswold v. Connecticut*,[3] which struck down a law prohibiting contraceptive use by married couples, and upon graduation started putting his theories into practice through litigation; the frustration of abortion reform advocates with the tenuous-

---

[2] For a longer version of the foregoing account, *see id.* at 35–38, 41–47.

[3] 381 U.S. 479 (1965).

ness of the legislative process, as they watched their initial successes in a few states run into increasingly strong opposition and defeat in others; the frustration of women's rights activists with some of the initial abortion reform laws that did pass in the late 1960s, because these laws simply gave doctors more control over the decision whether to perform an abortion, while leaving women in the untenable situation of having to convince a hospital committee that they would kill themselves if they could not have an abortion, or of being told they must continue an unwanted pregnancy by this group of strange men; and the frustration of physicians who performed what they thought were legal medically indicated abortions, but nonetheless risked the ire of prosecutors responsive to local anti-abortion sentiment. All of these factors coalesced to persuade advocates for decriminalizing abortion that federal lawsuits to declare state abortion laws unconstitutional were the most promising vehicle for taking the abortion issue out of the purview of state legislators and prosecutors, and placing it in the hands of women, their families, and physicians.

Far from coming out of the blue, *Roe v. Wade* built on these experiences and was one of several federal suits filed in the early 1970s, all with the hope of reaching the Supreme Court for a definitive nationally binding ruling. The Texas suit made it to the Court through the happenstance of litigation timing. But it was historically appropriate that the case that won the race to Washington emanated from a women's lib group and was filed by two young women lawyers, given the crucial impetus the women's rights movement gave to abortion law reform efforts.

To fully appreciate the personal, societal, and legal developments that led to a garage sale conversation about abortion that prompted a young lawyer first to the law library, and eventually to the United States Supreme Court in a case that has profoundly altered American women's lives and American electoral politics, it is necessary to understand the social and legal context of the hundred-year period when abortion was a crime.

Historical Background of Abortion Regulation in the United States

Prior to 1860, abortion was widely practiced and largely outside the purview of the law. Although it was estimated that one in five pregnancies ended in abortion,[4] no official statistics were kept and abortion practice was a private matter between pregnant women and midwives.

---

[4] David J. Garrow, *Liberty and Sexuality: The Right to Privacy and the Making of Roe v. Wade* 271 (1994).

Only New York had a criminal statute against all abortion,[5] and even the Catholic Church condoned the English common law doctrine that abortion was acceptable before "quickening," the time when a woman first felt fetal movement, until Pope Pius IX condemned non-therapeutic abortions in 1869.[6] In the middle of the nineteenth century, an unlikely alliance targeted abortion. "Anti-vice" crusaders who railed against both contraception and abortion as contributing to male sexual licentiousness, prostitution, and the undermining of women's traditional moral role as progenitor and nurturer of children, joined doctors, who were attempting to professionally organize and solidify their stature and expertise. As part of their efforts, doctors sought to supplant midwives, and in addition to claiming that only physicians could safely deliver babies, they argued that abortion was unsafe and immoral.[7] Physician groups, including the newly formed American Medical Association ("AMA") became quite politically active in lobbying against abortion, and found the most success in influencing public sentiment and legislation when they coupled health and safety arguments with claims about women's natural roles. If women used contraception or abortion to avoid their predestined maternal role, physicians argued, it would have disastrous consequences for their physical and mental health, and would undermine social morality.[8]

In 1860 Connecticut passed an anti-abortion law eliminating the "quickening" doctrine, and made abortion a crime for both those who performed it and the women who obtained it.[9] The Connecticut law became a model for other states, and by the 1890s every state had succumbed to the doctors' and anti-vice campaign and passed criminal abortion laws. Most of these laws made abortion a crime at any stage of pregnancy, but allowed "therapeutic" legal abortion if a woman's life was at risk from the pregnancy. To comply with this aspect of the law, hospitals established abortion review committees empowered to approve

---

[5] New York passed a law in 1828 making abortion at any stage of pregnancy a felony, although this law was rarely enforced. *Id.* For a complete history of abortion law in the nineteenth century, see generally James C. Mohr, *Abortion in America: The Origins and Evolution of National Policy, 1800–1900* (1978).

[6] Leslie J. Reagan, *When Abortion Was a Crime: Women, Medicine, and Law in the United States, 1867–1973*, at 7 (1997); Gerald N. Rosenberg, *The Hollow Hope: Can Courts Bring About Social Change?* 353 (1991).

[7] *See* Mohr, *supra* note 5, at 147–70; Reva Siegel, *Reasoning from the Body: A Historical Perspective on Abortion Regulation and Questions of Equal Protection*, 44 Stan. L. Rev. 261, 300–01 (1992).

[8] *See* Siegel, *supra* note 7, at 294; Cyril C. Means Jr., *The Law of New York Concerning Abortion and the Status of the Foetus, 1664–1968: A Case of Cessation of Constitutionality*, 14 N.Y.L.F. 441 (1968).

[9] Conn. Pub. Acts, c. 71, § 1 (1860).

or disapprove physician requests for therapeutic abortions. Four states, Louisiana, Massachusetts, New Jersey, and Pennsylvania, had no exceptions in their laws, thus presumably prohibiting abortion even when necessary to save a woman's life.[10] These nineteenth century laws remained on the books with little change until countervailing liberalizing legislative reform efforts began in the 1960s.

During the approximately one hundred year period when abortion was illegal, law enforcement vigor and thus the availability and safety of abortion varied from decade to decade. In response to publicity about the newly enacted criminal laws, police and prosecutorial crackdowns on abortion providers, especially midwives, were vigorous from the 1880s until the 1920s, particularly when a death or injury resulted from an illegal abortion. Police accosted women in the hospital and threatened them with prosecution unless they divulged the name of the abortion provider and agreed to testify against her or him. The enforcement focus on midwives created the greatest hardships for black women, since relatively few white physicians were willing to serve poor minority populations.[11]

Sexual attitudes started to liberalize in the United States in the 1920s, with a corresponding loosening of enforcement of laws against contraception and abortion. The stock market crash of 1929, and the ensuing economic depression in the 1930s had a dramatic impact on public attitudes about abortion. Massive unemployment, poverty, and the resulting inability of many families to feed their existing children fostered increased public acceptance of abortion even for married women. In urban and rural areas alike, police often deliberately ignored abortion providers, or accepted bribes to protect them. Some doctors, emboldened by the tolerant law enforcement attitudes and moved by the economic desperation of the times, openly advertised and operated abortion clinics.[12] Experts studying abortion trends estimated that somewhere between 600,000 and 800,000 illegal abortions occurred each year during the Depression.[13] As more skilled physicians became willing to perform illegal abortions, the rate of death and injury to women from illegal abortion declined during the 1930s, though it remained unacceptably high in the view of many physicians. Estimates of deaths from

---

[10] See Mohr, *supra* note 5, at 200–25; Roy Lucas, *Federal Constitutional Limitations on the Enforcement and Administration of State Abortion Statutes*, 46 N.C. L. Rev. 730, 733 (1968).

[11] See Reagan, *supra* note 6, at 90–112.

[12] See *id.* at 132–159.

[13] See Garrow, *supra* note 4, at 272 (800,000); Frederick J. Taussig, *Abortion, Spontaneous and Induced, Medical and Social Aspects* 338 (1936) (600,000 based on questionable methodology).

illegal abortions in this period range from 8,000 to 17,000 women per year.[14]

The growing demand for and number of abortions during the 1930s, coupled with doctors' realization that they had the medical skills to drastically reduce the death and injury rate if they could legally practice these skills, led to the first calls for reform of the criminal laws. In 1933, two books written by doctors calling for legal change were published; by the early 1940s articles appeared in medical journals arguing that the criminalization of abortion only encouraged "butchering quacks," and that the laws should be changed to give skilled doctors more discretion and flexibility.[15]

This period of open tolerance and improved relative safety of illegal abortion started to end in the mid–1940s. As World War II ended, the United States was seized with a pro-natalist "baby boom" enthusiasm. Women were exhorted to leave the jobs they had occupied during the war and return to their natural roles within the home to help replenish the species. As public sentiment coalesced around the idea that it was women's natural and patriotic duty to marry and have babies, political pressure increased to enforce the laws against abortion. Police now raided the clinics where only a few years before they had steered their wives, girlfriends, daughters or friends.[16] The crackdown on abortion intensified in the 1950s, as a general social conservatism, especially around sex, family, and women's roles gripped the country. Support for abortion was linked with support for communism when the Soviet Union legalized abortion in the mid–1950s.[17]

The renewed intensity of police and prosecutorial action focused on physicians. For example, in 1950 the Baltimore police conducted a highly publicized raid of the medical office of Dr. George Timanus, detaining the doctor, his staff, and the woman who was on the operating table.[18] Dr. Timanus was a highly regarded physician connected to the city's medical establishment at Johns Hopkins University Hospital, and he had been specializing in abortion, accepting referrals from physicians throughout the east coast, for over twenty-five years. By all accounts, he had provided safe, skilled care, including follow-up.[19] Dr. Timanus sought

---

[14] *See* Garrow, *supra* note 4, at 272 (larger figure); Taussig, *supra* note 13, at 361 (smaller figure).

[15] *See* Garrow, *supra* note 4, at 273–74.

[16] *See* Reagan, *supra* note 6, at 160–64.

[17] *See id.* at 172–73.

[18] *Id.* at 181.

[19] *See id.* at 158.

to use his criminal trial to raise public consciousness about changing the abortion laws; he also argued that the abortions he had performed were medically necessary, either for physical or mental health, and that they were based on physician referral, and thus legal. But he found himself abandoned by his medical colleagues who did not want to jeopardize their own professional standing by testifying in his defense. The prosecution also successfully argued that the therapeutic exception in the law should apply only to physical health risks, not to pregnancies that impaired a woman's mental health or general social and economic well-being. Timanus was convicted, fined heavily, served four and half months in prison, and then announced his retirement.[20]

The prosecution and conviction of physicians drove most skilled medical practitioners away from performing abortions, and led hospital therapeutic review committees to deny a greater proportion of requests to authorize an abortion. It did not, however, do anything to reduce women's demand for abortion. Indeed, demand intensified in the 1950s and 1960s, as more women were attending college and entering the workplace even if married. Although women's educational and economic opportunities were expanding, in this era they were still likely to lose their jobs or be removed from school if they became pregnant. With contraception still largely illegal or unavailable for unmarried women, many saw abortion as a crucial way to control reproduction.

The rising demand from women, coupled with the reduction in willing physicians, ushered in the proverbial era of the "back alley." Unskilled or disreputable people filled the supply vacuum to meet the demand. Those entering the abortion trade included "motorcycle mechanics, bartenders, and real-estate agents, who knew little more than that women needed abortions and that inducing them was profitable."[21] As a result of the legal repression, abortion in the 1950s and 1960s became more dangerous, expensive, and cloaked in secrecy. As historian Leslie Reagan has noted, it was not until this period, "quite late in the history of illegal abortion, that women's descriptions of illegal abortions included meeting intermediaries, being blindfolded, and being driven to a secret and unknown place where an unseen and unknown person performed the abortion."[22] The number of abortions remained at around one million per year,[23] but the number of women's deaths or serious injury grew, despite advances in antibiotics, medical technique and safety over the Depression era. Abortion complications were listed as the

---

[20] See id. at 188.

[21] Id. at 200.

[22] Id. at 197.

[23] Rosenberg, supra note 6, at 354.

official cause of death for 2,700 U.S. women in 1930,[24] and accounted for
approximately fourteen percent of maternal mortality.[25] In 1950, abortion was estimated to account for twenty-five percent of maternal
deaths, and had climbed to approximately forty-five percent of maternal
deaths by 1960.[26] In New York City alone, both the absolute number of
abortion deaths and the number of abortion deaths per thousand live
births doubled from 1951 to 1962. A resident who worked at New York
City hospitals in the 1960s described the "Monday morning abortion
line-up": Women used their Friday paychecks to obtain illegal abortions
over the weekend, and by Monday morning they would be lined up,
stretcher to stretcher, outside the operating room, hemorrhaging or in
septic shock.[27] Consider three snapshots of one busy urban hospital: In
1930, approximately 800 abortion-related medical cases were admitted to
Cook County Hospital in Chicago; in 1950 approximately 1600; and by
1960 the number of abortion-related cases of death or serious injury had
soared to around 4,500.[28] Hospitals around the country reported similar
experiences.

Class and race disparities also intensified during this era of legal
repression. While wealthy white women were more likely to be able to
afford to travel to another country or to find a doctor or hospital willing
to perform an abortion quietly, poor and minority women had no option
but the dangerous back alley, and disproportionately suffered the increasingly deadly consequences. Women who did survive back alley
abortions reported humiliating instances of sexual abuse or harassment
by their abortionist, or demeaning treatment in filthy rooms by dirty
men reeking of alcohol. These degrading and dangerous experiences and
social inequities fueled the passion of the incipient women's liberation
movement to change the laws that created this set of choices between, on
the one hand, sexual intimacy, career and, education, and on the other
hand, life, health and dignity.

The growing carnage in hospital emergency rooms also energized
doctors to seek legal change. Doctors were frustrated that while they
possessed medical skills and improved techniques that made abortions
far safer than childbirth, the law prevented them from using their
training to help women. Doctors came to understand that no law could
stop women from having abortions; all law did, in their view, was force

---

[24] *Id.* at 353

[25] *See* Reagan, *supra* note 6, at 213–14 & fig.7.

[26] *See id.*

[27] Carole Joffe, *Doctors of Conscience: The Struggle to Provide Abortion Before and After* Roe v. Wade 60 (1995).

[28] *See* Reagan, *supra* note 6, at 210 & fig.4.

women to have unsafe abortions. In addition to seeing the legal situation as an easily preventable public health travesty, many physicians were also motivated by awareness of the hypocrisy and unfairness in the system. Hospital therapeutic abortion committees often had unwritten quotas on the number of abortions they would approve as medically necessary and thus legal, out of fear that authorizing too many would bring scrutiny from prosecutors. Doctors noted that approval frequently turned on the applicant's wealth and connections rather than her medical need. One medical resident in the late 1960s observed that "as long as you were the banker's daughter, the doctor's daughter, the golf buddy's daughter, it was always taken care of."[29] Other residents recounted instances of doctors who publicly decried abortion and voted against every abortion request, but privately arranged for an abortion for their wife or daughter.[30] Doctors who presented cases to committees resented the hostile grilling from colleagues who questioned their medical judgment; they felt an ethical dilemma in counseling patients how to claim convincingly that they would commit suicide if they could not have an abortion. As women's false claims of suicidal feelings became so common that many hospital review committees routinely ignored them, some women in fact did attempt or commit suicide when their abortion requests were turned down.[31]

Two highly publicized incidents in the 1960s further stimulated the consciousness of the public and the medical profession about the need for abortion law reform. In 1962, Sherri Finkbine, happily married and pregnant, learned that the drug thalidomide—which her husband had brought from Europe to help her sleep and alleviate morning sickness—was linked with severe birth defects. Finkbine was the local host of her Phoenix television station's edition of the nationally popular children's show Romper Room, the Sesame Street of its day. The Finkbines' doctor counseled them to have a therapeutic abortion, and successfully shepherded the request through the hospital committee. Comfortable with the media, Finkbine contacted the local press to publicize her plight, anxious to alert other women who might have taken thalidomide. The national media picked up the story, and the Finkbines were thrust into a media circus, and were inundated with letters both supportive and hostile. Romper Room promptly fired her. Nervous about the publicity and possible interest from the local prosecutor, the hospital canceled the scheduled abortion. Because they had the resources, the Finkbines quickly arranged to travel to Sweden, where Sherri had a safe, legal abortion of a fetus too deformed to have lived. Their trip received daily

---

[29] Joffe, *supra* note 27, at 64.

[30] *See id.*

[31] Reagan, *supra* note 6, at 202.

coverage in national newspapers, and upon their return the Finkbines gave press conferences defending their traumatic decision as best for that pregnancy and for their other children.[32]

The Finkbine story changed media coverage of abortion from something dirty and criminal to a compelling human story that affected real families faced with difficult decisions. It also increased public sympathy for changing the law. A Gallup poll conducted a month after her return from Sweden reported that fifty-two percent of respondents said Finkbine had done the right thing, with thirty-two percent labeling her choice wrong. Even a third of Catholics were willing to say she had done the right thing.[33]

Around the same time as the Finkbine controversy was increasing sympathetic attention to abortion, an epidemic of rubella, or German measles, swept the country. It was now medically established that a pregnant woman who contracted rubella faced a high risk of birth defects. Between 1962 and 1965, approximately 15,000 babies in the United States were born with birth defects linked to rubella.[34] Although most doctors and hospital abortion review committees supported abortions for women with rubella, in 1966 a strongly anti-abortion member of the California Board of Medical Examiners prodded San Francisco authorities to prosecute nine eminent obstetricians because they had been performing hospital abortions on women with rubella.[35] Again, the national media gave prominent attention to the story, and it provoked protests from many physicians around the country, including the deans of over one hundred medical schools. The attention forced the prosecutor to drop the charges, but the case played an important role in increasing support for legal change among the public and medical professionals. Increasingly, doctors concluded that even though most state laws permitted "therapeutic" or medically necessary exceptions, the legal regime left their medical judgment vulnerable to prosecutorial override.

The Initial Legislative Reform Movement

The first serious stirrings of legal reform came in 1955, when the national medical director for Planned Parenthood organized a conference on "Abortion in the United States." The conference organizers felt they had to avoid publicity, but they nonetheless published the conference

---

[32] *See* Garrow, *supra* note 4, at 285–89; Joffe, *supra* note 27, at 32; Sherri Finkbine, *The Baby We Didn't Have to Have*, Redbook, Jan. 1963, at 50, 99–104.

[33] *See* Garrow, *supra* note 4, at 289.

[34] *See* Joffe, *supra* note 27, at 33.

[35] *See id.*

proceedings, which attracted favorable reviews in scientific journals and from Yale law and medical professors.[36] Only four years later, in 1959, the American Law Institute ("ALI"), an elite organization of prominent lawyers, judges, and law professors that drafted model laws, including the Model Penal Code, held a meeting to endorse a proposal that the penal code's abortion restriction be liberalized. The ALI largely adopted the physician proposals that were developed at the Planned Parenthood conference, to clarify and expand the acceptable legal therapeutic justifications for abortion to include mental health reasons, fetal defects, or pregnancy resulting from rape and incest.[37]

Although some speakers at the ALI conference suggested that abortion should be allowed whenever a woman wanted one, that suggestion was quickly dismissed as politically infeasible. It also did not fit with what most physicians saw as the problem with existing criminal laws— their intolerable ambiguity as to what constituted a legal therapeutic abortion, thus leaving their medical judgment subject to the vagaries of prosecutorial discretion.

The ALI endorsement of liberalized laws received front page press attention, led to increased numbers of national magazine articles sympathetically describing the horror stories of women who had illegal abortions, and sparked supportive law review and medical journal articles and even articles in practitioner-oriented bar journals from prosecutors supporting legal change.[38] It also prompted some state legislators to draft reform bills along the lines suggested by the ALI.[39]

The first legislative hearings on a reform bill were held in California in late 1962, a few months after the Finkbine saga. Several prominent physicians testified in support, noting that the bill would essentially codify and thus legitimate what doctors were, in fact, doing. A women's group presented a petition with hundreds of signatures favoring liberalization. The bill also stirred the opposition, and a representative of the Catholic Conference of Hospitals testified against it. Although the bill died in 1962, it was reintroduced in each of the following legislative sessions by Assemblyman, later Congressman, Beilenson, who continued to push for it until its eventual passage in 1967. Supporters named the rubella epidemic and the publicity over the attempted San Francisco prosecution as crucial factors in garnering enough support finally to pass the bill.[40] But in the intervening years between 1962 and 1967, there was

---

[36] See Garrow, supra note 4, at 275–76.

[37] See id. at 277.

[38] See id. at 280–81.

[39] See id. at 282–83.

[40] See id. at 301.

also a sustained social movement: growing numbers of speeches and articles in favor of liberalization by prominent doctors and lawyers; even more popular media attention sympathetic to women who wanted abortions and the health dangers of illegality;[41] and national societies and committees formed for the purpose of advocating for change in the abortion laws.[42] Even the AMA, which had been so instrumental in pushing for criminal abortion laws in the nineteenth century, in 1965 officially endorsed the ALI reform law.[43] In 1968 the American College of Obstetricians and Gynecologists endorsed very liberal reform—arguing that social or economic factors should count as legally sufficient grounds for obtaining an abortion—and surveys of obstetricians, gynecologists, and general practitioners reported that eighty-five percent supported reform.[44] Major religious groups ranging from the American Baptist Convention to the Unitarians to the American Jewish Committee also started to endorse reform.[45] During the 1960s, abortion went from being treated as a dirty secret issue to a matter of serious medical, legal, media, and political debate and attention.

The period 1967 through 1969 proved to be the highpoint for legislative reform activity. Reform bills modeled on the ALI proposal were introduced in thirty state legislatures.[46] Colorado was the first state to pass reform, in the spring of 1967; North Carolina followed in May, and California in June. While there was little public attention or opposition in North Carolina, in California and Colorado, which had far greater Catholic populations, and where bills had been pending longer, there was organized and intense opposition. In Colorado, a crowd organized by the Catholic Lawyers Guild turned out for a Senate hearing and, presaging a tactic that marked the anti-abortion movement in the 1980s and '90s, brandished bottled medical specimens of fetuses in the face of startled legislators. Between 1968 and 1969, seven states—Arkansas, Delaware, Georgia, Kansas, Maryland, New Mexico, and Oregon—passed ALI-style

---

[41] Sympathetic media accounts included a CBS documentary, and articles in Redbook, Look Magazine, Time, and the Sunday New York Times Magazine. *See* Garrow, *supra* note 4, at 299–301.

[42] In the mid–1960's, California activist Patricia Maginnis formed the Society for Humane Abortion (SHA), advocating repeal of all criminal restrictions and New York journalist Larry Lader and prominent physician Dr. Robert Hall formed the Association for the Study of Abortion (ASA). *See* Garrow, *supra* note 4, at 297–304.

[43] *See* Rosenberg, *supra* note 6, at 184; Garrow, *supra* note 4, at 333.

[44] Reagan, *supra* note 6, at 234.

[45] *See* Garrow, *supra* note 4, at 291–92, 333; Rosenberg, *supra* note 6, at 184.

[46] *See* Rosenberg, *supra* note 6, at 262. For a detailed discussion of legislative activity in New York and California, see Lawrence Lader, *Abortion II: Making the Revolution* 56–71 (1973).

reform laws that expanded and clarified the legal therapeutic reasons for abortion. However, the other states refused to pass reform laws. The degree of opposition varied from state to state, often depending on how organized and active the Catholic church was in the geographical area, but each legislative victory for abortion reform stimulated abortion opponents to become more active and organized.[47]

Meanwhile, another sort of opposition to the ALI-style reform legislation was also growing: those who felt that outright repeal of the criminal laws, leaving the abortion decision a private matter between a woman and her health care provider, was the appropriate action. Some activists criticized the reform legislation as too modest, because it would legitimize only five percent of women's demand for abortions, leaving far too many women to negotiate the potentially deadly back alley. Advocates of outright repeal also worried that ALI-style reform bills would blunt and delay legislative impetus for broader change. Activists who had placed great hope in reform legislation also became disillusioned when hospitals in Colorado, California, and Georgia—which had enacted reform laws—nonetheless retained quotas; indeed, some hospital committees became even more conservative in approving abortion requests, because of concerns that the more specific legislative criteria and increased attention to abortion would bring greater prosecutorial scrutiny.[48] Some of the leading voices for repeal came from legislators, such as Dick Lamm, who had sponsored the Colorado reform bill, and from doctors, including Alan Guttmacher, who had been president of Planned Parenthood Federation, and Robert Hall, who had co-founded a national group, the Association for the Study of Abortion (ASA), that had initially advocated only ALI-style reform. The American Public Health Association also endorsed repeal late in 1968, issuing a statement that women had a personal right to choose abortion.[49] Also in 1968, some of the leading professional repeal advocates—physicians such as Hall and Chicago anesthesiologist Lonnie Myers, and journalist Larry Lader—formed NARAL, (which at the time stood for) the National Association for Repeal of Abortion Laws.

But by far the most significant impetus for the move from modest legislative reform to efforts to decriminalize abortion entirely came from women's rights activists. The growing voice and organization of the women's rights movement in the late 1960s was a crucial factor in shaping the direction of abortion law and public opinion. Pat Maginnis, who had become active in California in 1962, when the first reform bill was introduced, had long been calling for repeal, through her organiza-

---

[47] See generally Garrow, supra note 4, at 335–88; Lader, supra note 46, at 56–71.

[48] Garrow, supra note 4, at 36, 341–42.

[49] See Garrow, supra note 4, at 357.

tion Society for Humane Abortion. Maginnis and her group argued that women should not have to bare their difficult personal situations to a group of male strangers on hospital review committees. The group took the position that the decision to terminate a pregnancy was one "which the person or family involved should be free to make as their own religious beliefs, values, emotions, and circumstances may dictate."[50] Women's rights activists found the whole system of abortion regulation degrading and inconsistent with the proposition that women were equal human beings fully entitled to make personal decisions that greatly affected their health, liberty, and life. As more women entered the movement through small localized consciousness raising groups and organized speak-outs on abortion, they shared abortion stories and learned both how prevalent the procedure was and how humiliating and scary so many women's experiences were. They also emboldened each other as they critiqued the male-dominated, social, political and health care systems that left them feeling a disempowering lack of control over their own reproduction. Sexual freedom and reproductive control became central to the feminist analysis of the necessary conditions to alleviate women's oppression. Women's groups also radically challenged the central reform philosophy of doctor's groups; women, they argued, and not physicians, should be viewed as the experts and most trusted decision makers on abortion.

While the media initially treated the women's movement as a subject for satire or derision, by 1969 the positions and organizations were being taken seriously. Also by 1969, "abortion [had] been transformed from a taboo topic to daily newspaper copy."[51] Mainstream general interest publications such as Reader's Digest, Redbook, Time, and the New York Times Magazine gave prominent and sympathetic attention to abortion, women's experiences and women's rights claims, the ineffectiveness of reform laws, and the growing call for outright decriminalization. Time Magazine reported a Harris poll that found that sixty-four percent of Americans, including sixty percent of Catholics, now felt that abortion should not be a legal question, but a private decision between family and doctor.[52]

Repeal advocates first looked to state legislatures, just as their predecessors had with respect to reform. In 1969 repeal bills fell just a few votes shy of passage in the Illinois and Michigan Senates. Hearings on a repeal bill in New York received extensive media attention when a

---

[50] Reagan, *supra* note 6, at 223–24.

[51] Judith Blake, *Abortion and Public Opinion in the 1960–70 Decade,* 171 Science 540 (1971)

[52] Garrow, *supra* note 4, at 376; Time, June 6, 1969, at 26–27.

radical feminist group disrupted them because, with the exception of a Catholic nun, the witnesses were all men.[53]

The repeal movement achieved its greatest legislative successes in 1970. Hawaii repealed its criminal abortion laws in February, and the bill drew support from groups ranging from the state medical association to labor unions to the Chamber of Commerce. The Catholic Church actively lobbied against repeal, and brought heavy veto pressure on the Catholic Governor, who let the bill become law without signing it, issuing a statement that he had to make a decision best for the health of all state citizens, and not a personal religious decision. But the Hawaii law was limited to state residents, and required that all abortions be performed in hospitals. The Alaska and Washington legislatures also passed repeal laws, and Washington voters ratified the legislative decision in a November statewide referendum.[54]

The most publicized and dramatic battle was in New York. The Catholic Church lobbied hard, and after the initial vote it appeared that the repeal measure had fallen one vote short in the Assembly. Then, his voice shaking, legislator George Michaels asked to change his vote to "yes." He acknowledged that due to the Church's influence in his district, he was probably voting to end his political career, but that he could not in good conscience cast the vote that killed a bill so important to women's health.[55] The New York Senate passed the bill the next day, despite the majority leader reading the gruesome "autobiography" of a fetus about to be aborted, and Gov. Rockefeller signed the law in April.

The New York law was a true repeal of the criminal penalties for all abortions prior to twenty-four weeks of pregnancy; it was not restricted to state residents, and it contained no hospital requirement. Planned Parenthood immediately set up telephone banks to field calls from around the country from women seeking legal abortions, and doctors quickly opened clinics in the major cities. An administrator from one of those first clinics in the months after New York repealed its abortion law tells harrowing tales of having to play God on the phone, as she made triage decisions about which desperate begging women to schedule for the limited appointments available. When staff showed up for work each morning, they would find women who had traveled from other states camped on their doorstep, refusing to leave until they got an abortion.[56]

---

[53] Garrow, *supra* note 4, at 367.

[54] *See* Garrow, *supra* note 4, at 411–14, 431–32, 466.

[55] Garrow, *supra* note 4, at 420. Documentary filmmaker Dorothy Faidman's video "From Danger to Dignity" shows moving footage of the actual legislative debate and the Michaels speech. Dorothy Faidman et al., *From Danger to Dignity: The Fight for Safe Abortion* (Concentric Media 1995).

[56] Interview with M. Buckham.

Despite these four legislative successes for the repeal movement in 1970, repeal bills were blocked that year in other states, and several states, notably Massachusetts, rejected even modest reform bills. In 1971, the legislative repeal movement came perilously close to losing its great victory in New York. Galvanized by the 1970 repeal law, the Catholic Church became even more politically active. It organized large right-to-life rallies, released a strong anti-abortion letter that President Nixon had written to the Cardinal, and put heavy pressure, including bitter personal attacks, on legislators. At a session replete with displays of fetuses in jars, several legislators changed their votes and a bill to rescind the previous year's repeal passed both chambers, despite public opinion polls showing consistent sixty percent support for the initial repeal law.[57] Governor Rockefeller vetoed it, so the initial repeal law remained on the books.

Nonetheless, the close call in liberal New York persuaded many advocates for changing abortion law that they could not rely on legislatures alone. The strategy of legal change through legislation was questioned as taking too long, requiring vast human and financial resources, and fraught with vulnerable indeterminacy because everything could be brought up repeatedly, so that a victory one year might turn into a defeat the next. It would also, at best, achieve geographically spotty change, leaving women in many states without meaningful access to safe legal abortion. Although sixteen states did pass liberalized abortion laws, efforts stalled in other states, and the increasingly vocal and well-organized opposition appeared to have halted legislative progress. A growing number of activists realized that if their primary goal was recognition of a secure right to choose safe abortion for all women, regardless of where they lived in the United States, then a nationally binding court ruling based on the Constitution was the best way to achieve it.

From Legislatures to Courts

An early proponent of test-case litigation as the best strategy for changing the nation's criminal abortion laws was Spurgeon LeRoy Lucas, known as Roy. Raised in the South and inspired by the civil rights movement, Lucas entered NYU Law School in the fall of 1963. During his second year, when his girlfriend told him she was pregnant, careful inquiries about abortion to certain faculty members led him to Dr. Alan Guttmacher, the noted Planned Parenthood abortion reform advocate. Dr. Guttmacher advised Lucas that he and his girlfriend needed to take a "vacation" to Puerto Rico, where Guttmacher arranged an appoint-

---

[57] *See* Garrow, *supra* note 4, at 546.

ment with a doctor. This experience of having to travel clandestinely to a strange place piqued Lucas' interest in studying U.S. abortion laws, and he received approval to do his third year research paper on the topic. The Supreme Court had just decided *Griswold*, striking down Connecticut's ban on the use of birth control by married couples as violating a right of privacy found in the "penumbras" of several provisions of the Bill of Rights. Yale Law Professor Tom Emerson, who had argued *Griswold*, wrote in a law journal symposium on the case that the decision might support a challenge to many aspects of the abortion laws.[58] Stimulated by this provocative suggestion, Lucas determined to develop it further in his paper.

Showing far more bravado than most law students, Lucas circulated drafts of his paper to Harriet Pilpel, counsel to Planned Parenthood, NARAL co-founder Larry Lader, and other legal experts on abortion. These readers thought he had developed a persuasive argument, and his supervising professor gave him an A+ and encouraged him to publish the paper, which he did.[59] Lader and Pilpel began to discuss with Lucas the idea of using his legal analysis as the basis for test case litigation challenging state abortion laws.

The Lucas paper located a right to abortion in the same set of constitutional provisions and doctrines that the Court had articulated in *Griswold*.[60] Analyzing the cases in which the Supreme Court had found individual liberty rights in family or other important personal matters or privacy rights protected against state intrusion, Lucas argued that for a woman, the decision whether to terminate a pregnancy was a more important liberty and privacy consideration than any of these previous matters:

> The right to terminate her pregnancy shortly after conception may seem to a woman to be much more fundamental and of greater day-to-day importance in her life than the right to send her children to a private school, to associate with others for the advocacy of ideas, or to be free from racial discrimination in seeking an education. To secure an abortion may seem to her an infrequent, but necessary step when the exercise of her fundamental right to contraception has not been successful. It is an anomaly that a woman has absolute control over her personal reproductive capacities so long as she can

---

[58] *See* Thomas I. Emerson, *Nine Justices in Search of a Doctrine*, 64 Mich. L. Rev. 219 (1965).

[59] *See* Roy Lucas, *Federal Constitutional Limitations on the Enforcement and Administration of State Abortion Statutes*, 46 N.C. L. Rev. 730 (1968).

[60] *See id.* at 755–56.

successfully utilize contraceptives but that she forfeits this right when contraception fails.[61]

Lucas then addressed the argument that a fetus is a legal human being with its own due process right to life, and rejected it based on historical treatment by law, religion, and biology. He argued that the legitimate state interest in health and safety warranted some regulation of abortion, such as limiting its practice to licensed physicians, but was actually undermined by criminal abortion laws. Finally, he suggested that state laws that allowed abortions only when necessary to preserve a woman's life could be challenged as too vague to satisfy due process standards, and as leading to arbitrary and capricious decisions by hospital review committees and prosecutors. He concluded with a call for constitutional litigation, proposing "a frontal attack on the very assumptions of abortion legislation ... through judicial enforcement of the guarantees of human rights found in the amendments to the United States Constitution."[62]

This call inspired Sarah Weddington when she came across it in her library research for her friend Judy Smith, as it inspired several other lawyers. Lucas prepared a model legal brief based on his article, and his research and arguments provided the blueprint for all of the subsequent legal efforts. In that regard the importance of his contributions to *Roe v. Wade* cannot be overstated.

Although Lucas' article eloquently addressed women's liberty interests, his preferred litigation strategy was to sue on behalf of doctors, asserting that abortion laws impermissibly interfered in "physician-patient decisions concerning the termination of pregnancy."[63] He assumed it would be easier to find doctors willing to endure the publicity of a challenge to the abortion law than to find a woman who wanted an abortion and was willing to thrust herself into the harsh glare of public scrutiny. He also thought courts would be more receptive to an argument based on physician's rights to exercise medical judgment than to a woman's rights appeal. Other lawyers argued that the best test case strategy was to wait for a doctor who was facing actual prosecution, because that would avoid standing and ripeness concerns.[64]

Such an opportunity presented itself in California in 1967, when Dr. Leon Belous was convicted for referring a patient who wanted an

---

[61] *Id.* at 759.

[62] *Id.* at 777.

[63] Garrow, *supra* note 4, at 338.

[64] That concern was based on the experience of the challenge to the Connecticut contraception law, which was dismissed on such grounds in *Poe v. Ullman*, 367 U.S. 497 (1961), before it was accepted in *Griswold*.

abortion to a Mexican doctor who performed unlicensed abortions in southern California. Lawyers who had been active in the California legislative reform battle offered their services for Dr. Belous' appeal to the California Supreme Court, and they prepared an amicus brief setting forth the constitutional arguments. The brief was signed by many nationally prominent doctors and medical school deans. The California Supreme Court vacated Dr. Belous' conviction, and declared the precursor statute to California's reform law unconstitutional, because terms under which abortions were permitted if "necessary" to "preserve life" were too vague. But, in dicta, the court gave great hope to proponents of a broader challenge based on *Griswold*. Relying heavily on the doctors' amicus brief, the court opined that it would be fruitless for the legislature to try to tighten the definition of permissible life-saving abortions, because "a definition requiring certainty of death would work an invalid abridgment of the woman's constitutional rights. The rights involved in the instant case are the woman's rights to life and to choose whether to bear children."[65] The court went on to reject the argument that the state had a compelling interest in protecting fetuses, noting all the instances in the law in which fetuses were treated differently from born children. Moreover, the court concluded, the pregnant woman's interest in life would take precedence over any fetal interest.[66]

This endorsement by a prestigious state Supreme Court of the proposition that the liberty and privacy rights articulated in *Griswold* applied to the abortion decision convinced Lucas and other attorneys that the litigation strategy to declare state abortion laws unconstitutional was likely to be successful. Lucas, who by now had formed a public interest legal institute in New York City for the purpose of challenging abortion laws, working with Harriett Pilpel, Mel Wulf from the ACLU, and NYU Law Professor Norman Dorsen, filed a federal court case in the fall of 1969 challenging New York's criminal abortion law. The named plaintiffs were Dr. Hall, Dr. Guttmacher, and other eminent gynecologists. Lucas had plotted a timetable for this case, *Hall v. Lefkowitz*,[67] that would have it arriving at the U.S. Supreme Court in 1971. It was Lucas' consuming ambition to be the attorney that brought, briefed, argued and won the case in the Supreme Court declaring criminal prohibitions of abortion unconstitutional. Although he assumed his New York case would be that vehicle, Lucas and attorneys from his James Madison Institute were also busy working with lawyers and ACLU affiliates in several other states to lay the groundwork for cases challenging those

---

[65] *People v. Belous*, 458 P.2d 194, 199 (1969) (citing, *inter alia*, *Griswold*).

[66] *See id.* at 963.

[67] 305 F.Supp. 1030 (S.D.N.Y. 1969) (granting motion for a three judge panel, finding constitutional questions substantial).

laws. But the young women in Texas were not plugged into Lucas'
networks, and they were working independently.

Shortly after the New York complaint was filed in *Hall*, another
court decision endorsed the extension of *Griswold* to abortion. A Washington, D.C. doctor, Milan Vuitch, had been performing abortions
throughout the Maryland, Virginia, and D.C. area for several years, and
he was frequently arrested. Although only one jury had been willing to
convict him, when he was arrested again in D.C. he and his attorneys
moved to dismiss his indictment by challenging the constitutionality of
the D.C. abortion law, even though it was one of the most liberal pre-
reform laws in the country, since it allowed abortions necessary to
preserve "health" as well as "life." In November 1969, U.S. District
Judge Gerhard Gesell, who would later issue important rulings arising
out of Watergate and the Iran-contra affair, struck down the D.C. law.[68]
Like the *Belous* ruling, the *Vuitch* opinion stressed that the "health"
and "life" exceptions were too vague to enable doctors to know when
they might be risking criminal penalties. But, also like the California
court, Judge Gesell wrote:

> There has been ... an increasing indication in decisions of the
> Supreme Court of the United States that as a secular matter a
> woman's liberty and right of privacy extends to family, marriage and
> sex matters and may well include the right to remove an unwanted
> child at least in the early stages of pregnancy.[69]

Then, presaging the Supreme Court opinion in *Roe*, he concluded
that the privacy right has limitations, and that Congress could regulate
abortion practice, "perhaps even establishing different standards at
various phases of pregnancy, if informed legislative findings were made
after a modern review of the medical, social, and constitutional problems
presented."[70]

The federal government appealed to the United States Supreme
Court, and though Lucas managed to insinuate himself into Dr. Vuitch's
legal team, internal disagreements kept him from presenting the oral
argument. The Court then reversed Judge Gesell, ruling that the health
exception in the D.C. law was not so vague as to violate due process.[71]
The majority did not believe that the question whether the law violated a
Griswold-style right of privacy was properly before the Court, as it was
not the basis of Judge Gesell's ruling.[72] However, two dissenters indicat-

---

[68] *See United States v. Vuitch*, 305 F.Supp. 1032 (D.D.C. 1969).

[69] *Id.* at 1035 (citing *Griswold* and *Loving v. Virginia*, 388 U.S. 1 (1967)).

[70] *Vuitch*, 305 F.Supp. at 1035.

[71] *See United States v. Vuitch*, 402 U.S. 62 (1971).

[72] *See id.* at 72–73.

ed that they were inclined to hold that the right to privacy and intimate family and sexual relations encompassed abortion.[73]

With the main event temporarily forestalled, other abortion cases continued to work their way through the lower courts. Lucas's New York *Hall* litigation was rendered moot when the New York legislature repealed the state's criminal abortion law. To ensure himself of a Supreme Court argument, he remained active in other cases. He filed a constitutional challenge to New Jersey's abortion law, and was involved in or aware of court challenges brought in 1970 or 1971 to the abortion laws in Wisconsin, Ohio, California, Colorado, Connecticut, Georgia, Kentucky, Arizona, Illinois, Indiana, Florida, Michigan, Minnesota, Missouri, Louisiana, South Dakota, Kansas, and Texas.[74]

But some of these cases, notably the ones in Connecticut, Georgia, and Texas, were started by women's rights groups with women attorneys, and featured women rather than doctors as their lead plaintiffs. These cases more prominently emphasized women's rights than a doctor's right to practice medicine without state interference. Beyond these strategic and philosophical differences were personal ones. Lucas came to learn that young women attorneys like Sarah Weddington in Texas and Margie Hames in Georgia were not about to take a back seat to a man in a case they regarded as central to women's rights.

Roe v. Wade—*The Case that Won the Race to the Supreme Court*

When Sarah Weddington went to the University of Texas law library to research for her friend Judy Smith, she found the Supreme Court decision in *Griswold*, and Roy Lucas's compelling analysis extending it to abortion. She also found the California Supreme Court decision in *Belous*, and Judge Gesell's decision in *Vuitch*, lending judicial support to Lucas's law review argument. She learned about suits filed in New York, Illinois, and Wisconsin.

When she reported all this to Smith and her law student husband Ron, the conversation quickly turned to bringing a suit to challenge the Texas law. Judy expressed exasperation with the legislative process in Texas, where modest reform bills were being buried. Weddington remembers Smith arguing and asking: "It will take forever to change the laws against abortion in a state-by-state legislative process. But if we

---

[73] *See id.* at 78 (Douglas, J., dissenting); *id.* at 96–97 (Stewart, J., dissenting).

[74] *See YWCA of Princeton, N.J. v. Kugler*, 342 F.Supp. 1048 (D.N.J. 1972); Garrow, *supra* note 4, at 383, 416, 432–33, 459–60, 465–467, 540–41.

could overturn the laws through the federal courts, that would apply nationwide. Is that a possibility?"[75]

Smith and other members of her women's lib group felt strongly that a woman lawyer should bring the case and eventually persuaded Weddington that, despite her inexperience, she was the right woman for the job. Weddington herself assumed that the Texas legal effort would be supplemental to the litigation already pending in federal court, and could ride on the momentum of the other cases. She enlisted help from her law school classmate Linda Coffee, who was with a Dallas law firm and had invaluable federal litigation experience from her post-law school judicial clerkship with one of the few female federal judges, Sarah Hughes in Dallas.[76]

Weddington and Coffee started to draft a federal court complaint, but they lacked a plaintiff. Test-case litigation designed to challenge and change the law often grows out of group advocacy efforts and legal planning without direct involvement or impetus from injured or otherwise affected would-be plaintiffs. This aspect of test-case litigation carries with it seeds of conflicts between the lawyers and cause-oriented groups and the individuals who eventually become plaintiffs. What may be best for the individuals in the short term may not be best for the long-term cause. These tensions were present in *Roe* from the beginning.

Weddington and Coffee first thought they could use an organized women's group or Smith's abortion referral service as plaintiffs, but they concluded that the laws of standing and the publicity risks to the referral service made this strategy too risky. They needed to find women who would be directly affected by the law prohibiting abortion, and were willing to be lead plaintiffs in a suit. They could give the plaintiffs pseudonyms to protect their privacy.

The lawyers found their first plaintiff, Marsha King, when Linda Coffee spoke about the planned lawsuit to the Women's Alliance of Dallas' First Unitarian Church, a group that had been active in Texas abortion law reform efforts. King was interested in trying to change the abortion laws because she and her husband had a traumatic experience with an abortion in Mexico. While Marsha was experiencing some significant health problems from a neurochemical disorder, she became pregnant, and her doctor advised against continuing the pregnancy. But the health problems, while seriously debilitating, were not life threatening, and thus she did not qualify for a legal therapeutic abortion under Texas law. She had an abortion in Mexico City, but it was very painful, and she almost lost consciousness on the flight home, requiring oxygen from the flight attendants. King's doctor advised her to avoid pregnancy

---

[75] Weddington, *supra* note 1, at 45.

[76] *Id.* at 48–49.

until her health improved, but he also advised that because of her neurochemical imbalance, she should avoid taking birth control pills. Realizing the relatively high failure rate of condoms, foam, or diaphragms, Marsha and David King felt that the unavailability of safe abortion as a back-up for contraception severely impaired their marital intimacy. This harm to them as a married couple formed the basis of the complaint on their behalf. Coffee and Weddington called them John and Mary Doe in the court complaint.[77]

The Kings were not ideal plaintiffs, however, because Marsha was not pregnant, and accordingly, not in immediate need of an abortion. A court might therefore find that the Kings lacked standing to challenge the law. To avoid this possible procedural hurdle, the lawyers asked women's groups and acquaintances to help them find a pregnant woman who wanted an abortion. Henry McCluskey, a Dallas lawyer who handled adoptions and was friends with Linda Coffee, found their second plaintiff, Norma McCorvey, whom the complaint called Jane Roe.[78]

McCorvey came to McCluskey's office to discuss arranging an adoption for the unwanted pregnancy she was carrying. She was broke, unemployed, unhappily almost four months pregnant and wanting an abortion, but unable to find a doctor in Texas who would perform one and unable to afford the trip to New York or Mexico for a relatively expensive late abortion. When she told McCluskey that what she really wanted was an abortion, and adoption was a poor last resort, he told her about Coffee and Weddington and their lawsuit. McCorvey agreed to meet them in a Dallas pizza parlor.[79]

Although only twenty-two, Norma McCorvey had already lived a long and hard life. She was a ninth-grade drop-out whose parents had divorced when she was thirteen. She had a tempestuous relationship with her mother and subsequent stepfathers. She often rebelled against her mother, who had her confined in a reform school. At sixteen, while working as a car-hop at a Dallas hamburger take-out joint, she met the twenty-four year old Woody McCorvey, a charming, itinerant unemployed sheet metal worker from Buffalo, New York. He quickly seduced her, and a few months into a sexual relationship, Norma told Woody that she wanted to get married. After she withheld sex for a few days, Woody agreed to marry her, and they had a hasty courthouse ceremony.[80]

---

[77] *Id.* at 50; Garrow, *supra* note 4, at 400–01.

[78] Weddington, *supra* note 1, at 51–52; Garrow, *supra* note 4, at 402–04.

[79] Weddington, *supra* note 1, at 51–52; Garrow, *supra* note 4, at 403–04; Norma McCorvey & Andy Meisler, *I Am Roe: My Life,* Roe v. Wade, *and Freedom of Choice* 112–115 (1994).

[80] *See* McCorvey & Meisler, *supra* note 79, at 35–47.

Woody then moved the couple to California, where he hoped to have better work prospects. There he became abusive, and was absent for increasing stretches of time. When Norma told Woody that she was pregnant, he beat her so badly that she resolved to leave him. She borrowed money from a friend and made her way back to her mother in Texas. After Norma gave birth to a daughter, her mother gained custody of the baby.[81]

Norma started working in gay bars, using drugs and drinking heavily, and realized she was a lesbian. She moved in with a woman, and seemed to be finding some stability in her life. But she still occasionally had flings with men. She met a man she calls Carl[82] in a bar, and started accompanying him to pool tournaments. She regarded him solely as a friend, but had sex with him anyway. In her autobiography, McCorvey recounts how she was still fundamentally ignorant about her body and birth control; ruefully, she calls herself a lesbian who got pregnant each of the few times she slept with men. A few months after splitting from Carl, while working at a seasonal carnival, McCorvey realized she was pregnant. The carnival would soon close, leaving her unemployed. Her mother refused to take her in, and she tracked down her father who offered her his couch. To try to blot out the pregnancy, she spent her days and nights drinking at bars and abusing drugs. When a woman she met told her there was a way to get rid of a pregnancy, especially if she was willing to claim she had been raped, she went to the doctor who had delivered her daughter. Although she made the necessary rape allegation, the doctor refused to perform an abortion anyway, instead referring her to the adoption attorney McCluskey.[83]

When McCorvey met with Coffee and Weddington in the pizza parlor, they explained the proposed lawsuit to her, and what would be expected of her as a plaintiff. McCorvey agreed to participate and also asked whether it would help the case if she had been raped, implying that she had been. The lawyers said it would not make any difference, and they decided to omit from the complaint any reference to how McCorvey might have become pregnant. They were not interested in winning a right to abortion only for rape victims. Nonetheless, news accounts of the case stated that McCorvey had been raped.[84] Later, when McCorvey first went public as Jane Roe, she told the media elaborate tales of her rape. Then, a few years after that, she revealed that the rape story was false; the media and anti-abortion activists harshly criticized

---

[81] *See id.* at 51–56.

[82] *See id.* at 92. His actual name may have been Bill. *See* Garrow, *supra* note 4, at 403.

[83] *See* McCorvey & Meisler, *supra* note 79, at 93–109.

[84] Weddington, *supra* note 1, at 52–53, 256.

Weddington and pro-choice groups, accusing them of perpetrating a fraud on the Supreme Court. When Weddington defended by showing that the complaint and legal briefs had made no allegation of rape, the brief media firestorm abated.[85]

McCorvey recalls that when she met with the lawyers she got the impression that the lawsuit would get her an abortion, and that she kept stressing to the lawyers that an abortion was what she really wanted. Weddington and Coffee recall that they explained she was probably too far along in her pregnancy to get an abortion, and that it was unlikely that the suit could be completed in time for her to have an abortion, but that the suit would help her and other women in the future. Apparently, the lawyers never considered putting McCorvey in touch with Judy Smith's referral service, because what they needed to ensure standing in court was a plaintiff who remained pregnant and unable to get an abortion. Weddington candidly admitted that they "considered the individuals who would be involved in the cases as ancillary to the primary focus on all women who, if pregnant, would want to have access to all options, including legal abortion."[86] Roe and the Does were, in her view, only vehicles for presenting the larger issues. This conflict between the client and cause created lasting tension between client and attorneys. McCorvey had little active involvement in her case. She did not attend any of the court hearings, and only spoke with Weddington and Coffee occasionally when they contacted her to keep her apprised of developments. While the suit was pending, she gave birth to a boy whom she immediately surrendered for adoption. McCorvey later expressed feelings of having being been exploited by the lawyers, whom she perceived as caring more about helping other women than her.

Weddington and Coffee stayed much more involved with the Kings. It was clear that they felt more comfortable with this educated, professional middle class couple than with the uneducated, lesbian, down and out, substance-abusing McCorvey. The Kings attended court arguments, including the two momentous Supreme Court arguments, and remained active in the abortion rights cause.[87] Yet because it was Jane Roe's— Norma McCorvey's—name which was first on the court caption, the Kings' role as plaintiffs has been largely overlooked by history.

With their plaintiffs set, Weddington and Coffee finished the complaint and supporting affidavits and a motion seeking an injunction to halt enforcement of the Texas law. Their legal causes of action tracked

---

[85] See id. at 256–57.

[86] Id. at 61.

[87] McCorvey & Meisler, supra note 79, at 117–21, 127–28, 198–99; Garrow, supra note 4, at 515–17, 523, 572, 601.

the Lucas blueprint derived from *Griswold*. They asserted that the Texas law violated a right to privacy found in the First, Fourth, Fifth, Eighth, Ninth, and Fourteenth Amendments to the Constitution. They also asserted that the Texas law violated due process because of vagueness. The named defendant, Henry Wade, was the district attorney for Dallas County. He was a thirty-five year veteran of law enforcement, and had become nationally prominent when he successfully prosecuted Jack Ruby for shooting Lee Harvey Oswald, the accused assassin of President Kennedy.

The lawyers filed in federal court in Dallas in the hope of drawing Judge Sarah Hughes, who Coffee knew would be sympathetic to their legal arguments. On March 3, 1970, Coffee filed the complaint and personally paid the filing fee out of her own pocket. To their delight, they did draw Judge Hughes.

Coffee and Weddington had also filed a request to have the case referred to a special three-judge panel comprised of district and appellate judges. Then, as now, most federal court cases were heard by a single federal district judge, with a right of appeal to a three judge panel of the Court of Appeals, followed by discretionary review by the Supreme Court. When *Roe* was initiated, however, federal law also authorized an initial hearing by three judges in cases challenging the constitutionality of statutes and seeking to enjoin them; an appeal then went directly to the Supreme Court.

Hughes granted the request, and district court judge William Taylor and Fifth Circuit Court of Appeals Judge Irving Goldberg were also assigned to the case. Weddington and Coffee considered this about as favorable a panel as they possibly could have obtained. Goldberg had issued several brave and pioneering decisions on civil rights, and was also considered brilliant and legally innovative. Taylor had a reputation as quite fair and open-minded.[88]

The hearing on *Roe v. Wade* was held on May 22, 1970. Rather than a trial with witness testimony, the case proceeded on the basis of factual affidavits and lawyers' legal briefs, with lawyers' legal arguments and judges' questions. In addition to pseudonymous affidavits from McCorvey and the Kings, Weddington and Coffee presented an affidavit from the medical director of the University of Texas Health Center, which addressed the safety of legal abortion, the demand from women for abortion, the reasons why women sought abortions—including contraception failure and health risks as well as educational, economic, and social factors—and the difficulties and dangers women faced trying to obtain abortions.

Linda Coffee handled most of the oral argument for the plaintiffs. Much of her time was consumed with addressing procedural issues.

---

[88] *See* Weddington, *supra* note 1, at 58.

When she started to address all the constitutional amendments that could support a right to privacy, Judge Goldberg asked her to focus on the Ninth Amendment, which states: "The enumeration in the Constitution, of certain rights, shall not be construed to deny or disparage others retained by the people." Sarah Weddington then presented one issue, whether the state had any compelling interest in restricting abortion. Goldberg asked her to assume a Ninth Amendment right, and to focus on what types of regulations a state might still be permitted, such as a hospital requirement or a requirement for approval by multiple physicians. Weddington and Coffee felt from the tenor of the questioning that the court would definitely find a constitutional right, and was only interested in exploring the limits of a constrained regulatory role for the state.[89]

Jay Floyd of the Texas Attorney General's office defended the statute. He argued first that the Does and Roe lacked standing, contending that they did not face prosecution, and also argued that the case was moot because Roe had already given birth. On the merits, Floyd had difficulty responding to the court's invitation to distinguish the Texas statute from the California one found vague in *Belous*. John Tolle from the Dallas District Attorney's office also defended the law. He strongly asserted that the state had a right to protect fetal life, and that a fetus' right to life was superior to a woman's right to privacy.

Less than a month later, the court issued a unanimous *per curiam* decision finding the Texas statute unconstitutional.[90] Although no judge signed as primary author, Hughes had written the initial draft and made several changes in response to a lengthy memo from Goldberg.[91] First, the decision declared the statute too vague to be enforced.[92] But the court went on to address the broader issue, and found that "the Texas abortion laws infringe upon plaintiffs' fundamental right to choose whether to have children."[93] The panel relied on Justice Goldberg's concurring opinion in *Griswold*, which articulated the Ninth Amendment basis for privacy, and also cited *Belous*, *Vuitch*, and court decisions striking down the Wisconsin and South Dakota abortion statutes.[94] However, the judges refused to enjoin enforcement of the Texas law,

---

[89] *See* Weddington, *supra* note 1, at 62–67; Garrow, *supra* note 4, at 440–44.

[90] *See Roe v. Wade*, 314 F.Supp. 1217 (N.D. Tex. 1970).

[91] *See* Garrow, *supra* note 4, at 451–53.

[92] 314 F.Supp. at 1223.

[93] *Id.* at 1222.

[94] *See id.* at 1222 (citing *Babbitz v. McCann*, 310 F.Supp. 293 (E.D Wis. 1970); *State v. Munson* (S.D. Cir. Ct. Pennington Cty., Apr. 6, 1970)).

because they assumed that the District Attorney in good faith would not institute prosecutions.[95] The failure to issue an injunction was a disappointment to the plaintiffs' attorneys because most doctors would be unwilling to risk their freedom and livelihoods on prosecutors' good faith, but it also meant the case could go directly to the Supreme Court, bypassing the Fifth Circuit Court of Appeals.

The decision was front page news all over Texas, and received some notice in other areas, including in the New York Times. Wade immediately announced that the state would appeal to the Supreme Court, and that he would not dismiss any pending prosecutions of doctors unless there was a definitive ruling from that court. The Kings, speaking to the press as the Does, hailed the decision. Even the president of the Catholic Women of the Dallas Diocese told the press the ruling was the only one the court could have made, because she agreed the law was too vague to sustain prosecutions.[96] She expressed hope that the legislature would pass a law with more carefully crafted exceptions. Major hospitals in Dallas and the University of Texas Health Center, after conferring with the District Attorney's office, concluded that the decision would not lead to a change in their policies of very limited approvals of life-saving therapeutic abortions, because the risk of prosecution still remained. Frustrated by the lack of any apparent change in the availability of abortions, the Austin Women's Liberation Group, from which Smith and Durden's initial inquiries to Weddington had originated, issued a statement that the ruling actually meant "very little."[97]

Weddington and Coffee cross-appealed the denial of the injunction because they believed that without a ban on prosecutions, doctors would not regard abortion as completely legal. At the time they started working on their petition to the Court, several other abortion cases were also making their way to Washington. The Wisconsin case of *Babbitz v. McCann*,[98] was the first to arrive, but the Supreme Court declined jurisdiction.[99] An appeal was docketed in a case striking down the Illinois law, and in a case striking down Georgia's law. Lawyers awaiting decision in the lower courts in New Jersey, Minnesota and other states also announced that they would file appeals as soon as decisions were

---

[95] 314 F.Supp. at 1224.

[96] Garrow, *supra* note 4, at 454–55.

[97] *Id.* at 454.

[98] 310 F.Supp. 293 (E.D. Wis. 1970).

[99] 400 U.S. 1 (1970).

entered.[100] The Minnesota case, *Doe v. Randall*,[101] was particularly compelling. The lead plaintiff, Nancy Widmyer, was a married mother of three who had contracted rubella during her fourth pregnancy. Her physician, prominent abortion reform advocate Dr. Jane Hodgson, recommended an abortion, and obtained several other medical opinions that a therapeutic abortion was justified. Because Minnesota's statute allowed exceptions only to save a woman's life, and not for fatal fetal defects, the federal case was filed seeking an affirmative injunction permitting an immediate abortion. The district judge thought the case might not be ripe until Hodgson first tried to perform an abortion and was prosecuted, so Hodgson went ahead with the procedure. She was promptly arrested and indicted, marking the first time in American history that a physician was prosecuted for performing a hospital-approved therapeutic abortion.[102]

With so many abortion cases involving right-to-privacy challenges to state laws soon to inundate the Supreme Court, it appeared inevitable that the Justices could no longer duck the issue they had avoided in their *Vuitch* ruling. Although critics have contended that the Supreme Court should have waited for more development of the issue in the lower courts, there were at least twenty cases progressing in lower federal or state courts, with the decisions about equally split as to whether abortion laws were constitutional.[103] Whether there was a constitutional right

---

[100] *See Doe v. Scott*, 321 F.Supp. 1385 (N.D. Ill. 1971), *vacated and remanded sub nom. Hanrahan v. Doe*, 410 U.S. 950 (1973); *Doe v. Bolton*, 319 F.Supp. 1048 (N.D. Ga. 1970), *prob. jurisdiction noted*, 402 U.S. 941 (1971), *aff'd* 410 U.S. 179 (1973); *YWCA of Princeton, N.J. v. Kugler*, 342 F.Supp. 1048 (D.N.J. 1972). *See also* Garrow at 416, 471 (Lucas hoped that New Jersey case would be his vehicle for getting to the Supreme Court).

[101] 314 F.Supp. 32 (D. Minn. 1970).

[102] *See id.* at 35–37; Garrow at 428–30, 466–68.

[103] Cases striking down abortion laws, in addition to *Roe v. Wade* from Texas, included: *Babbitz v. McCann*, 310 F.Supp. 293 (E.D. Wis. 1970), *app. dismissed*, 400 U.S. 1 (1970); *Doe v. Bolton*, 319 F.Supp. 1048 (N.D. Ga. 1970), *prob. jurisdiction noted,* 402 U.S. 941 (1971); *Doe v. Scott*, 321 F.Supp. 1385 (N.D. Ill. 1971), *appeal docketed sub nom. Hanrahan v. Doe*, 410 U.S. 950 (1973); *YMCA of Princeton, N.J. v. Kugler*, 342 F.Supp. 1048 (D.N.J. 1972); *People v. Belous*, 458 P.2d 194 (1969), *cert. denied*, 397 U.S. 915 (1970); *Abele v. Markle*, 342 F.Supp. 800 (D. Conn. 1972); *State v. Barquet*, 262 So.2d 431 (Fla. 1972); *Poe v. Menghini*, 339 F.Supp. 986 (D. Kan. 1972); *State v. Nixon*, 201 N.W.2d 635 (Mich. 1972). In addition, in unreported criminal cases against doctors, trial courts in South Dakota, and Pennsylvania struck down state laws. *See Abele v. Markle*, 342 F.Supp. at 803, n.14. A lower court in Arizona struck down that state's law, but the decision was reversed in *Nelson v. Planned Parenthood*, 505 P.2d 580 (Ariz. App. 1973).

Cases upholding abortion laws as constitutional included: *Steinberg v. Brown*, 321 F.Supp. 741 (N.D. Ohio 1970); *Rosen v. La. St. Bd. of Med. Exam'rs*, 318 F.Supp. 1217 (E.D. La. 1970); *Corkey v. Edwards*, 322 F.Supp. 1248 (W.D.N.C. 1971), *vacated and remanded* 410 U.S. 950 (1973); *Crossen v. Attorney General of Kentucky*, 344 F.Supp. 587 (E.D. Ky. 1972); *State v. Abodeely*, 179 N.W.2d 347 (Iowa 1970); *Spears v. State*, 257 So.2d 876 (Miss. 1972); *State v. Munson*, 201 N.W.2d 123 (S.D. 1972); *Rogers v. Danforth*, 486 S.W.2d 258 (Mo. 1972); *Cheaney v. State*, 285 N.E.2d 265 (Ind. 1972); *Nelson v. Planned Parenthood*, 505 P.2d 580 (Ariz. App. 1973).

to choose abortion had become such a hot legal issue with so many conflicting legal rulings and continued prosecutorial defiance such as that displayed by Henry Wade, and so much media and public attention, that it would have been irresponsible of the Supreme Court to decline to answer the question posed in these cases.

Weddington, Coffee, and the lead lawyer in the Georgia case, Margie Hames, assisted each other with their respective appeals. The Georgia case, *Doe v. Bolton*,[104] was noteworthy because it challenged the constitutionality of the reform statute that had been passed with such fanfare only in 1968. It required all abortions to be performed in hospitals, required the approval of two physicians, and limited the reasons for performing an abortion. Advocates who had come to realize the limitations of the reform strategy had unsuccessfully sought passage of a repeal bill by the Georgia legislature in 1969. But the rationale of *Griswold* could apply to invalidate a limited reform law as well as a nineteenth century "life exception only" law, because the former sort of law also interfered with a woman's private decision based on her own situation and reasons for seeking an abortion. Accordingly, women's movement lawyers saw a court challenge as potentially much more fruitful than continued legislative struggle. Judith Bourne, an activist who had been leading the legislative efforts, called the director of the Georgia ACLU to help find a woman lawyer. She immediately thought of Margie Hames, who had left a major law firm to raise her young children, but was still one of the most experienced and respected woman litigators in Atlanta. Although eight months pregnant with her second child, Hames eagerly accepted the case.[105] Young women lawyers from Legal Aid and Emory Legal Services were recruited to help, and they filed their complaint and request for a three-judge court around the same time that Coffee filed *Roe*. Several prominent doctors, nurses, ministers, and social workers joined as plaintiffs. Still, Hames thought the lead plaintiff should be a woman who had been turned down for an abortion under the quota system that hospitals continued to use even after the enactment of the reform law. The cooperating doctor and nurse plaintiffs from Grady Memorial Hospital put such a woman, Sandra Bensing, in touch with Hames. Initially Hames and the doctors tried to help Bensing win approval at another hospital, and raise the money for the abortion. However, by this time Bensing was trying to reconcile with her abusive husband, and nearing five months pregnant. When she felt fetal movement, Bensing changed her mind about having an abortion, but agreed to be the lead plaintiff as Jane Doe.[106]

---

[104] 319 F.Supp. 1048 (N.D. Ga. 1970).

[105] *See* Garrow, *supra* note 4, at 422–24.

[106] *Id.* at 425–28.

Bensing's life story bears remarkable similarities to Norma McCorvey's. She too was a ninth grade drop-out, who married a drifter from Oklahoma at seventeen, and quickly had two children. Her husband worked only sporadically, and was arrested for child abuse. Consequently, the state removed the children and placed them in foster care. When Bensing became pregnant again at twenty-two, during a particularly conflict-ridden time in the marriage, she decided to try to leave her husband and sought an abortion. Like McCorvey, she ultimately put the child up for adoption.[107]

While working with Hames on their respective appeal papers to the Supreme Court, Weddington heard from Roy Lucas. This was his first effort to become involved in the Texas case. Lucas presented himself as the nation's leading abortion law expert, and offered to write the jurisdictional statement to convince the Court to accept the case. Because Linda Coffee was inundated with law firm work, and Sarah and Ron Weddington were preparing to move to Fort Worth to start new full time law jobs, Weddington accepted Lucas's offer. But she naively failed to define and reduce to writing the terms of the agreement, a decision she came to regret as Lucas tried to wrest the entire case away from her.

On May 21, 1971, the Supreme Court announced that it would hear both *Roe v. Wade* and *Doe v. Bolton*,[108] with briefs due over the summer and argument in the fall. Sarah Weddington's new boss, the city attorney for Fort Worth, refused to grant her leave to work on the Supreme Court case, so she and Ron made the financially wrenching decision that she would quit her job and devote herself full time to the unpaid work of taking her case to the Supreme Court. Lucas offered her part-time paid work at his Institute in Manhattan, so she moved to New York for the summer to work on the *Roe* brief.[109]

Lucas had said he would take the lead on the brief, but he always seemed to be busy on other abortion cases, including Dr. Hodgson's Minnesota case, an appeal to the Supreme Court in a North Carolina case, and an amicus brief in *Doe v. Bolton*. As the deadline approached with no draft from Lucas, Weddington decided that despite her inexperience she would have to write the brief. Ron came up from Texas to help her, and she also enlisted a law student working for the Institute for the summer. Sarah and Ron, sleeping in a hot small room with only a mattress on the floor, worked madly researching and writing. Several University of Texas law students also helped out, producing lengthy research memos on various points, and the head of the Obstetrics and

---

[107] *Id.* at 426–27, 444–45, 465.

[108] *See* 402 U.S. 941 (1971) (noting probable jurisdiction).

[109] Weddington, *supra* note 1, at 83–84.

Gynecology department at the medical school compiled medical information for the team.[110]

They produced a 150–page brief that did not even address the constitutional claims until page 91. The brief first presented the plaintiffs. It described Jane Roe as an unmarried pregnant woman who sought an abortion "because of the economic hardship which pregnancy entailed and because of the social stigma attached" to bearing an illegitimate child, who did not have a job or the funds to travel to a jurisdiction where she could undergo a legal safe abortion.[111] Mary Doe was presented as embodying the "frequent case of a married woman whose health, but not life, would be seriously affected by unwanted pregnancy."[112] The brief then quoted extensively from medical texts and journals to describe the progression of pregnancy as well as the number that result in spontaneous miscarriage or induced abortion, and presented the historical progression in medicine from the dangers of abortion in the nineteenth century to the safe abortion techniques available in the twentieth. It stressed the vastly different safety records of legal and illegal abortion, and the extremely limited number of therapeutic abortions approved under the existing legal regime. This part of the brief was designed to convince the Court that any asserted state health justifications for maintaining criminal abortion laws were at best counterproductive and at worst a ludicrous sham.

The brief then surveyed the history of abortion laws, including the growing pace of legislative reform. It also presented the numerous medical groups, including the Texas Medical Society and the AMA, that now endorsed legal abortion. In this regard, the brief sought to assure the Court that it would merely be following legislative trends and prevailing professional standards, rather than breaking radical new ground. The brief also presented information about the failure rates and dangers of available contraceptive methods, to dispel the impression that women who sought abortions were simply irresponsible.[113]

After addressing jurisdictional issues such as standing and mootness, the core constitutional argument was presented in steps: the right to privacy is a fundamental human and constitutional right; the right to seek and receive medical care for general well-being is a fundamental liberty recognized by courts in the United States and around the world; the Court had long recognized in many decisions, culminating in *Griswold*, that the fundamental privacy right included marital and intimate

---

[110] *See id.* at 85–95.

[111] Brief for Appellant at 9, *Roe v. Wade*, 410 U.S. 113 (1973) (No. 70–18).

[112] *Id.* at 10.

[113] *See id.* at 34–37.

personal relations and important aspects of family life; the right to possess and control one's own physical person is also a core part of the privacy and liberty right; and the right of a woman to terminate an unwanted pregnancy is an integral part of these privacy and liberty rights.[114]

The brief next argued that the state had no compelling interest in restricting abortion. After disparaging any asserted interest in promoting health or regulating sexual conduct, the brief boldly asserted that the state's supposed interest in protecting the fetus was belied by its disregard for fetal interests outside the abortion context. It pointed out all the ways that Texas law, and the law of other states, did not recognize fetuses as persons. For example, state laws did not treat the killing of a fetus as homicide, including when pregnant women were assaulted. Similarly, tort and property rights depended on live birth. The brief also asserted that science could not answer the question of when life or potential life begins, and that that issue should ultimately be one for personal moral resolution. "It is obvious," Weddington argued, "that the legislative decision forbidding abortion also destroys potential life— that of the pregnant woman—just as a legislative decision to permit abortions destroys potential life. The question then becomes not one of destroying or preserving potential, but one of who shall make the decision."[115] The legislative decision-making process had led to chaos and thousands of dead women. Thus, the state must yield to the individual woman's rights and choice.[116] Finally, just in case the Court was more inclined to take the narrow road adopted by the California court in *Belous*, the brief presented the vagueness argument.

The Texas brief, principally authored by Jay Floyd, was less than half the length, and only mentioned *Griswold* in passing, stating that its marital privacy right to have sexual relations was not implicated by a statute restricting abortions.[117] In only a single page with few citations, the state argued that the right to privacy was limited and relative, and could always be conditioned on the health and well-being of others, as in mandatory vaccinations.[118] Twenty-four of the brief's fifty-seven pages were devoted to fetal development, complete with numerous enlarged pictures of thumb-sucking fetuses that appeared quite developed. As the brief concluded, this survey of fetal development led to the inescapable conclusion that the fetus is fully human from the very earliest stages of

---

[114] *See id.* at 91–109.

[115] *Id.* at 123–24.

[116] *See id.* at 124.

[117] Brief for Appellee at 26, *Roe v. Wade*, 410 U.S. 113 (1973) (No. 70–18).

[118] *See id.* at 28.

its development, and that the state had a compelling interest in protect-ing it. Whatever limited relative privacy right a pregnant woman may have must give way to the right of the unborn child to life.[119] The state's brief, which was far less legal than Weddington's, seemed to be based on the assumption that fetal pictures would be worth more than thousands of words.

Margie Hames's brief in *Doe v. Bolton* was also much shorter and tighter than Weddington's. She succinctly presented the marital privacy and vagueness arguments, and focused her challenge on the arbitrari-ness of abortion review committee decisions and the lack of due process afforded women who were given no reasons for denials and had no recourse. She also argued that in practice far more poor and black women were turned down, so that the statutory scheme violated their rights to equal protection of the laws.[120]

Some commentators have criticized the attorneys in *Roe* and *Doe* for relying on privacy, and for failing instead to make an argument based on women's right to equality. This critique resonates with the women's movement arguments for a right to abortion, which were premised on reproductive control as fundamental to a woman's ability to be an equal, unoppressed citizen. But a lawyer has to make considered strategic judgments about what arguments are most likely to be successful, and have the strongest precedential support. At the time *Roe* was briefed, the Supreme Court had rejected all claims that the equal protection clause applied to sex discrimination.[121] An equality-based argument would have been far more radical and unprecedented than the *Griswold*-based privacy and liberty arguments.

Nonetheless, some of the amicus briefs filed in support of the plaintiffs in *Roe* did present a gender equality argument to the Court, including a brief prepared by feminist attorney Nancy Stearns on behalf of women's rights organizations.[122] The fact that the Justices were alerted to the equality argument but chose to ignore it appears to

---

[119] *See id.* at 55.

[120] *See* Brief for Appellant at 22–41, 46–50, *Doe v. Bolton*, 410 U.S. 179 (1973) (No. 70–40).

[121] The first case in which the Court used the Equal Protection Clause to strike down a gender classification in a state statute was decided three months after Weddington submitted her brief in *Roe*. *See Reed v. Reed*, 404 U.S. 71 (1971) (striking down a preference for males as estate administrators). Given that *Reed* dealt with an explicit gender preference for a legal benefit, it was a larger precedential leap from that case to abortion than from the right-to-birth-control context of *Griswold*.

[122] *See* Elizabeth M. Schneider, *The Synergy of Equality and Privacy in Women's Rights*, 2002 U. Chi. Legal F. 137, 139–40 & nn.11–12 (2002).

vindicate the principal lawyers' decision to concentrate on the priva-cy/liberty argument.

As attention turned to the oral argument, Lucas was presenting himself as lead counsel and the brief's primary author. Unbeknownst to Weddington, Lucas also wrote to the Supreme Court Clerk's office that he would be presenting the oral argument. Lucas sent Weddington a long letter arguing that he should do the argument, trumpeting his greater experience and knowledge. He also denigrated Margie Hames's abilities, and snidely said that since *Doe* was in less than capable hands, at least *Roe* should be argued by the best possible attorney. Lucas and Hames had a particularly bitter relationship since she had rebuffed his efforts to take over *Doe v. Bolton*. But Weddington was also being lobbied by Marsha King, Linda Coffee, and women's groups who argued that she should present the argument, and that only a woman could convey the grave issues at stake for women. In an attempt to make peace, Weddington asked the Supreme Court if she and Lucas could split the argument. When this request was denied, she decided she had to force the issue. The Kings preferred her; she tracked down her other client, Norma McCorvey, with whom she had not communicated in a while, and McCorvey decided that despite her bitter feelings toward Coffee and Weddington, she wanted a woman she knew to argue her case, rather than an unfamiliar man. The clients were consulted to a greater extent about who should argue before the Supreme Court than about any other issue in the *Roe* litigation.[123]

The oral argument occurred on December 13, 1971, but there were only seven Justices on the Court because of vacancies President Nixon was having difficulty filling. Sarah Weddington graciously invited Lucas to sit with her and Linda Coffee at counsel table, with Ron Weddington sitting in a chair behind them. Marsha and David King were there, but McCorvey was in Texas, barely aware that the argument was occurring. Henry Wade also chose not to attend. Hames and Weddington wished each other good luck, while Hames tried to avoid Lucas.[124]

Weddington went first, for her allotted thirty minutes. Although she has written of her utter nervousness, in the audio recording of the oral argument her voice sounds strong and confident.[125] Immediately, the Justices started asking questions about all the jurisdictional issues, and these topics consumed most of the argument, which no doubt left the audience frustrated. Weddington did, however, manage to get in an

---

[123] *See* Garrow, *supra* note 4, at 462–64, 503–04, 515–17; Weddington, *supra* note 1, at 100–02; McCorvey & Meisler, *supra* note 79, at 148–49.

[124] *See* Garrow, *supra* note 4, at 523; Weddington, *supra* note 1, at 113–14.

[125] The audio of the complete oral argument and reargument in *Roe* is at http://www.oyez.org/cases/1970–1979/1971/1971_70_18.

eloquent articulation of why the abortion right was so crucial to women's lives: A pregnancy is perhaps the most determinative aspect of a woman's life, she argued. "It disrupts her body, it disrupts her education, it disrupts her employment, and it often disrupts her entire family life."[126] She also touched on the health risks of childbirth compared to the safety of legal abortion, and asserted that because of pregnancy's impact on a woman, it was of such fundamental concern "that she should be allowed to make the choice whether to continue or terminate her pregnancy."[127]

Weddington was then asked whether the privacy right should be based in the Ninth Amendment or the Fourteenth Amendment, and she was pressed on whether she would admit to any state interest in protecting fetal life during the period of the pregnancy. She stood her ground that birth should be the determining point for granting legal rights.

Jay Floyd, arguing for Texas, started off with a clumsy attempt at sexist humor. "[W]hen a man argues against two beautiful ladies like this, they're going to have the last word."[128] He seemed unnerved when, instead of the expected laughter, a stony silence filled the room, and Chief Justice Burger glared at him. Floyd fumbled around for a while. He maintained that a woman only had a choice before she got pregnant, which prompted Justice Stewart to quip that "maybe she makes her choice when she decides to live in Texas."[129] Floyd stuck to his brief's position that a fetus was a human entitled to legal protection from the moment of conception, but admitted under questioning that he could provide no scientific data to support a single moment as the beginning of life.[130]

Hames then argued in *Doe v. Bolton*. She asserted that any state interest in protecting fetal life was fatally undermined by the state's decision to allow some abortions, but not others. As in her brief, she concentrated her remarks on the cumbersome, expensive, and arbitrary nature of all the procedural hoops women had to jump through to receive hospital approval for an abortion. The practical effect of the limited reform law was to deny women their due process liberty right just as much as an outright ban on abortion.[131]

---

[126] Weddington, *supra* note 1, at 116.

[127] *Id.*; Garrow, *supra* note 4, at 524.

[128] Weddington, *supra* note 1, at 119; Garrow, *supra* note 4, at 525.

[129] Garrow, *supra* note 4, at 526.

[130] Weddington, *supra* note 1, at 120.

[131] Garrow, *supra* note 4, at 527.

Dorothy Beasley, arguing for Georgia, focused on the fetus, its humanness and right to life, and the state's interest in valuing and protecting it. She contended that the privacy right had to be limited when another human being was involved.[132]

A few days later, the Justices met in private conference to consider the case. Chief Justice Burger expressed reluctance to find any constitutional infirmity with the Texas law, but Justices Douglas, Brennan and Stewart all argued that the statute was unconstitutional. Stewart and Marshall indicated willingness to permit greater state regulation as pregnancy progressed. Justice White expressed strong views in support of fetal life and against an abortion right. Justice Blackmun said he did not think a woman had an absolute right to do anything she wanted with her body, but that women did have a Fourteenth Amendment right that was implicated by the abortion laws; he also thought the statute infringed on doctors' rights to practice medicine.[133] The straw vote on *Roe* was 5–2, but there was no clear majority in *Doe*.

Justice Blackmun, at that time the most junior member of the Court, was assigned to write the opinion. But Douglas and Brennan also started exchanging proposed drafts and long memos. When President Nixon's latest nominees, William Rehnquist and Lewis Powell, were finally confirmed by the Senate, Chief Justice Burger asked his colleagues which cases they thought were important enough to re-argue before the full complement of nine Justices. Blackmun promptly nominated *Roe* and *Doe*. Douglas strongly objected, arguing that the cases had been thoroughly worked over, and there was a solid majority. But he was outvoted, and in June 1972, Weddington received a terse notice from the Court that the case was restored to the calendar for reargument.[134]

Weddington, who was by now busy campaigning for a seat in the Texas legislature, and Coffee, quickly wrote a short supplemental brief, which pointed out that Wade was still threatening prosecution, Texas doctors were still afraid to perform abortions, and over 1,600 Texas women had had to travel to New York in 1971 to obtain safe legal abortions. It also updated some important legal developments, including more court decisions invalidating state abortion laws, and the Supreme Court's ruling early in 1972, in *Eisenstadt v. Baird*,[135] sustaining a challenge to a birth control activist's prosecution for distributing contraceptive devices to unmarried college students. The Court said in *Eisen-*

---

[132] *See id.* at 527.

[133] *Id.* at 529–32.

[134] *Id.* at 534–38, 552–60.

[135] 405 U.S. 438 (1972).

stadt that there was a fundamental constitutional right of the married and unmarried to decide whether to "bear or beget a child."[136]

Lucas made an ardent written plea to Weddington that he should present the reargument. His letter alternated between claiming that he could do a better job, and self-pitying whining that he was the one who had convinced the Court to hear the case, and had devoted four years of his life to the issue only to be thanklessly shoved aside. Weddington did not dignify his missive with a response.[137]

The reargument was on October 11, 1972. Justice White quickly pounced on Weddington and asked whether her case hinged on finding that the fetus was not a person. She acknowledged that if the fetus were a person, then the state would have a compelling interest in protecting its life, but that interest would still have to be balanced against the woman's interest. She reiterated, however, that the fetus had never been treated as a legal person. Robert Flowers, from the state attorney general's office in replacement of Jay Floyd, argued that the fetus was a human being, but he stumbled under sharp questioning from Justice Stewart about whether this was a medical question, a religious question, or a legal question. When Flowers replied that it was a legal issue, he was forced to acknowledge that Weddington was correct that neither Texas law nor the Fourteenth Amendment included fetuses in the definition of persons.[138]

After the reargument, Weddington returned to Texas to finish her campaign, and in November she was elected to the Texas House of Representatives by a huge margin. Now, she felt, even if she lost the case perhaps she could help the legislature change Texas' abortion law.

The Court decisions in *Roe* and *Doe* were announced on January 22, 1973. Despite their momentousness, they were supplanted as the major news headline by former President Lyndon Johnson's death on the same day. By 7–2 votes, the Court, with Justice Blackmun writing the majority opinions, struck down both the Texas law and Georgia's reform law as unconstitutional violations of a fundamental right of privacy. The Court held that a woman's right to decide whether to terminate a pregnancy had to be balanced against state interests in safeguarding women's health, maintaining medical standards, and protecting potential life. The Court divided pregnancy into trimesters; during the first three months of pregnancy, the woman's interests overrode all state interests; during the second trimester, the state could adopt reasonable regulations to protect health and medical standards; the state's interest in protecting

---

[136] *Id.* at 454.

[137] Garrow, *supra* note 4, at 563–64.

[138] Garrow, *supra* note 4, at 568–70; Weddington, *supra* note 1, at 137–40.

potential life did not become compelling until the last three months of gestation, but even at that stage the state had to permit abortions necessary to preserve the health or the life of the woman.[139] This trimester framework was suggested in none of the briefs; it appears to have been Justice Blackmun's innovation.

Weddington learned the news from a New York Times reporter's phone call. In between fielding press and congratulatory calls, she managed to reach Marsha and David King, Judy Smith, and Dr. Jane Hodgson, whose prosecution would now be voided. But Weddington and Coffee were unable to locate Norma McCorvey to give her the news.

McCorvey later wrote that she learned of the decision from reading the newspaper, while her lover Connie was taking a shower. When Connie emerged, Norma told her the Supreme Court had legalized abortion, and when she replied "[t]hat's good," asked her whether she wanted to meet Jane Roe. Then, Jane Roe came out of the closet.[140]

Women's groups were stunned and elated at the seemingly sweeping nature of the Court's decision. At the time, they seemed little troubled by the aspect of the decision that divided pregnancy into trimesters, and invited various kinds of state regulation of abortion, especially later in pregnancy.

With the notable exception of the Dallas Morning News, the editorial pages of the nations' newspapers reacted largely with praise, labeling the decision compassionate, humane, wisely affirming the traditional right of privacy, and based on common sense.[141] The Catholic Church and other anti-abortion groups reacted with dismay.

Although the *Doe* decision was lost in the sweeping nature of *Roe*'s pronouncement of a fundamental right, in many ways it turned out to be the more practically significant of the two. In striking down the 1968 reform law as also violating a woman's fundamental right, the Court demonstrated how the right announced in *Roe* constrained the options available to legislatures. In striking down the Georgia requirement that abortions had to be performed in hospitals as too great an infringement on women's and physicians' rights, unsupported by sufficient health interests, the Court paved the way for the rise of freestanding abortion clinics. The woman's health movement quickly pushed for clinics devoted to abortion as more woman-centered, less costly, and more accessible alternatives to overcome the continued reluctance of many hospitals to perform abortions.

[139] 410 U.S. 113, 153–54, 163–64.

[140] McCorvey & Meisler, *supra* note 79, at 150–51.

[141] Garrow, *supra* note 4, at 606.

The Aftermath of Roe

1.   The People in the Case

Sarah Weddington became a champion for women's rights during three terms in the Texas legislature. She helped enact an Equal Rights Amendment to the state constitution, and a state equal access to credit law. She became national President of NARAL, which, after its repeal goal was realized through *Roe*, changed its name to the National Abortion Rights Action League, and she continues actively to speak on the importance of preserving abortion rights, especially to young women on college campuses who have no memory of the pre-*Roe* days. Her marriage fell apart not long after the *Roe* decision, unable to withstand the strain of her professional prominence and busy campaign and legislative life, but she and Ron continued to practice law together and remain friends. In 1977, President Carter offered her a high level appointment in his administration, as a special assistant focusing on women. Ironically, her last act in the Texas legislature was to argue to her House colleagues that they should defeat a bill to recriminalize most abortions in Texas. She failed to persuade enough of her colleagues, many of whom may have voted in favor of recriminalization as an empty gesture designed to placate growing anti-abortion lobbying, assuming that the courts would strike down the law in any event. One of Weddington's first tasks in Washington was to try to persuade President Carter to drop his opposition to Medicaid funding for poor women's abortions.[142] Weddington currently serves as adjunct professor in the Government Department of the University of Texas at Austin.

Linda Coffee retreated from the abortion limelight, concentrating on her law practice in the bankruptcy area, and many have forgotten her key role in *Roe v. Wade*. Roy Lucas suffered from ongoing bouts with cancer. He would drop out of sight for long periods of time, resurfacing for a while as an artist living on a ranch in Montana. Occasionally, he offered his legal services to abortion providers, and contacted abortion rights groups seeking to write amicus briefs in Supreme Court cases. However, his offers of assistance were marked by his tendency to proclaim himself the only qualified lawyer who really understood the issues involved in abortion law, while denigrating the efforts of other lawyers.[143] While Lucas largely disappeared again in 1998, apparently to

---

[142] Weddington, *supra* note 1, at 181–93.

[143] For example, when the United States Supreme Court was considering *Hill v. Colorado*, 530 U.S. 703 (2000), a case concerning the first amendment validity of a statute limiting the location of anti-abortion protests, Lucas wrote to the National Abortion

undergo more cancer treatment, there were rumors of occasional sightings of him in the Supreme Court library in Washington, where he was reported to be working on his memoirs. He died of a heart attack in November 2003 while conducting research in Prague, his memoirs incomplete.[144]

Margie Hames had a long and distinguished legal career up to her death from old age, remaining active in women's rights cases, including helping Sandra Bensing, the *Doe* plaintiff, regain visitation rights with her children. She received many awards for her civil liberties work, and for her important contributions to securing abortion rights.[145]

Sandra Bensing, now known as Sandra Cano, became a born-again Christian who came to regret her role in *Doe v. Bolton*, and she affiliated with the militantly anti-abortion group Operation Rescue in the late 1980s. Declaring her role in the case a huge mistake resulting from mental instability, she filed a legal petition seeking to reopen *Doe v. Bolton* and have its result nullified. Although this effort to undo a final decision was rebuffed, resulting media attention helped the then eighteen-year old Doe baby girl she had given up for adoption to find her.[146] Cano has remained actively involved with an anti-abortion project known as "Operation Outcry" organized by the Justice Foundation. This project collects affidavits from women asserting that they have been psychologically traumatized and physically harmed by abortion, as part of a new effort by anti-abortion activists to persuade legislatures and courts that banning abortion is necessary to protect women.[147] In furtherance of this work, Cano submitted an *amicus* brief, with hundreds of these affidavits excerpted, to the Supreme Court in *Gonzales v. Carhart*, a 2007 decision upholding a federal law banning a method of performing late-term abortions that had been labeled "partial birth abortion."[148]

Federation and offered to pen an amicus brief, contending that lawyers in previous abortion protest cases, including the author of this chapter, did not understand the issues.

[144] *See* Ian Urbina, *Roy Lucas, 61, Legal Theorist Who Helped Shape Roe Suit, Dies*, N.Y. Times, Nov. 7, 2003, at C10.

[145] Garrow, *supra* note 4, at 602; the author of this chapter attended some of these awards ceremonies.

[146] *Id.* at 603. Cano tried again in 2003 to re-open *Doe v. Bolton*, again unsuccessfully, in a suit alleging that abortion harms women. Cano v. Bolton, 2005 WL 3881370 (N.D. Ga. 2005); Bill Rankin, *Unintentional Plaintiff Fights to Overturn Abortion Rulings*, Hous. Chron., Oct. 5, 2003, at A12.

[147] *See* Reva B. Siegel, *Dignity and the Politics of Protection: Abortion Restrictions Under Casey/Carhart,* 117 Yale L. J. 1694, 1727 (2008); Reva B. Siegel, *The New Politics of Abortion: An Equality Analysis of Woman–Protective Abortion Restrictions*, 2007 U. Ill. L. Rev. 993, 1026 (2007).

[148] 550 U.S. 124 (2007); *See* Brief for Sandra Cano and 180 Women Injured by Abortion as *Amici Curiae* Supporting Petitioner, *Gonzales v. Carhart* (No. 05–380).

Norma McCorvey's life also took odd turns. After revealing herself to be Jane Roe, McCorvey cultivated press attention, but gave varying accounts of her life and whether or not she had been raped. She received enough money for selling her story rights to a made-for-television movie about *Roe* to enable her and Connie to live more comfortably and afford health insurance. She briefly worked at an abortion clinic in Dallas, and was an honored VIP guest at a massive pro-choice march on Washington in 1989, when it appeared that the Supreme Court might reverse *Roe v. Wade* in the pending *Webster* case.[149] She started to engage in public speaking on behalf of abortion rights, and in 1994 published a ghost-written autobiography in which she was still strongly and unapologetically pro-choice. By 1995, however, McCorvey had grown to feel unappreciated and exploited by the pro-choice movement. She, like Sandra Cano, became involved with Operation Rescue, and had a highly publicized "born-again" baptism by its Dallas based leader Flip Benham, whom she had previously shouted at when he picketed the abortion clinic where she worked. McCorvey declared that while she still thought women should have the right to choose abortion in the first trimester, she thought later abortions were wrong.[150] Although she struggled with her new friends when they tried to convince her lesbianism was sinful and to renounce her relationship with Connie, she eventually drifted back into their fold. She occasionally appears as an anti-abortion speaker, and, like Cano, she tried unsuccessfully to re-open *Roe v. Wade* when the case was thirty years old.[151]

Marsha and David King, the other *Roe* plaintiffs, remain strongly pro-choice, and continue their social activism. They both became lawyers, and eventually had two healthy children when Marsha's health improved.[152]

2. *Roe*'s Impact on Abortion

Those who blame *Roe* for causing a tragedy of abortion in the United States are largely mistaken: *Roe v. Wade* did not create demand for abortion and did not lead vastly increased numbers of women to have

---

[149] The Court's opinion in *Webster v. Reproductive Health Services*, 492 U.S. 490 (1989), hinted that there were five Justices prepared to overturn *Roe*, although when the Court was given that opportunity three years later in *Planned Parenthood v. Casey*, 505 U.S. 833 (1992), the Justices instead cut back on *Roe*, by changing the legal standard for assessing state abortion regulations, but retaining its "central holding." *Id.* at 846.

[150] *See Jane Roe Joins Anti–Abortion Group*, N.Y. Times, Aug. 1, 1995, at A12; Laurie Goodstein, *'Jane Roe' Renounces Abortion Movement*, Wash. Post, Aug. 11, 1995, at F1.

[151] *See McCorvey v. Hill*, 2003 WL 21448388 (N.D.Tex. 2003), *aff'd* 385 F.3d 846 (5th Cir. 2004); *New Challenge to Roe v. Wade: Ex–Plaintiff Tries to Topple Ruling*, N.Y. Newsday, June 18, 2003, at A2.

[152] Weddington, *supra* note 1, at 296.

abortions. Estimates of the numbers of illegal abortions in years prior to *Roe*, while inevitably imprecise, are close to the more reliable statistics about the number of abortions performed after *Roe*.[153] The number of legal abortions, both in absolute terms and percentage, increased most dramatically in the two years prior to *Roe*, growing from 193,500 in 1970 to 586,800 in 1972.[154] This may be attributable to the profound impact of the four states that repealed their abortion laws in 1970, and the thousands of women who streamed to New York and Seattle. Statistics about the pregnancy rate and the birth rate did not show dramatic change after *Roe*, which suggests that a similar number of pregnancies were terminating in abortion prior to *Roe* as after.

The principal practical consequence of *Roe* was to dramatically increase the safety of abortion. With abortion legal, physicians and other health care providers could openly receive training and conduct research into improved methods and safety, and share experiences at medical conferences. The invasive surgical method of dilation and curettage—scraping the uterus with sharp instruments—that prevailed in the early 1970's has now been supplanted for early abortions by much safer gentle suction or tissue aspiration techniques, or by abortions induced with drugs. Abortion quickly moved from being one of the leading causes of maternal death in the 1960s, to being one of the safest of all medical procedures, with a complication rate, especially in the first trimester, on a par with tooth extraction.[155] In this regard, *Roe* can be hailed as preventing numerous women's deaths each year, and this factor alone makes it a significant source of important social change. Indeed, it is hard to think of any other Supreme Court decision that has come close to preventing so much death and injury.

The movement of abortion out of hospitals and into specialized clinics has proven a mixed blessing. While it has kept the cost down and made abortion much more accessible for women, it has also left free-standing clinics more vulnerable to picketing and vandalism. Far fewer anti-abortion activists are willing to blockade or bomb a community

---

[153] Rosenberg, *supra* note 6, at 353–55.

[154] *Id.* at 180.

[155] The federal Center for Disease Control tracks abortion statistics from 47 states plus the District of Columbia (all states but California, Louisiana, and New Hampshire in the most recent data). In 2005, the participating jurisdictions reported 820,151 abortions, of which 88 percent were performed in the first trimester. There were seven maternal deaths from legal abortion in 2004 (the last year for which mortality data were available). Assuming the total number of abortions in 2004 was roughly the same as in 2005, this represents a fatality rate of less than one per 100,000 legal abortions. In 1972, there were 65 deaths associated with (legal plus illegal) abortions, for a fatality rate of 4.1 per 100,000. *See* Sonya B. Gamble et al., CDC, *Abortion Surveillance—United States,* Morbidity and Mortality Weekly Rep., Nov. 28, 2008.

hospital than are willing to take such actions at a clinic that primarily performs abortions, and police are much more likely vigorously to respond to any attempted disruption of a hospital. Moreover, the movement of abortion into clinics has contributed to its marginalization within medicine. Rather than being regarded by most physicians as an essential and integral part of women's health care, many doctors and hospitals still hold a pre-*Roe* view: glad that some doctors are willing and able to do it so they can quietly refer their patients, but also glad they don't have to wade into the controversy or risk attack.[156]

Changes in the law have also truncated *Roe*'s initial promise of easily available low-cost abortion care for any woman who wanted one. Beginning four years after *Roe*, the Supreme Court started upholding various legislative restrictions, commencing with limitations on using Medicaid to fund poor women's abortions, then requirements that minors notify or get the consent of their parents, and culminating in laws that require clinics to give women certain largely anti-abortion information several days before they can have the operation.[157] As a result, for many women, especially the poor, the young, and those living in rural areas, it may be almost as difficult in 2009 to find and get to an affordable abortion provider as it was in 1972. But, the crucial difference remains that when a woman now can overcome the hurdles to get to a clinic, she is able to have a safe, legal procedure in a supportive atmosphere with highly trained staff and counselors.

Apart from its practical impact in making abortion safe, *Roe* has had a profound symbolic impact. Sex and reproduction are of defining importance in many women's lives, and the inability to control reproduction can be a central cause of women's social and economic subordination. To have this most crucial aspect of women's lives recognized as a constitutional right signals, more than any other development in the history of constitutional law, women's inclusion as self-determining equal citizens. To many women, a legal regime that condoned a choice between forced pregnancy or possible death was one in which women would always remain an oppressed group. Indeed, the Supreme Court eventually came to recognize *Roe's* place in securing women's right to equal citizenship. In *Planned Parenthood v. Casey* in 1992,[158] the Justices overcame "the reservations" some of them apparently had about "reaffirming the central holding of *Roe*" because of the abortion right's larger social significance. As the majority explained, "[t]he ability of women to

---

[156] Joffe, *supra* note 27, at 2–6, 27–52.

[157] *See Maher v. Roe*, 432 U.S. 464 (1977); *Harris v. McRae*, 448 U.S. 297 (1980); *Hodgson v. Minnesota*, 497 U.S. 417 (1990); *Planned Parenthood v. Casey*, 505 U.S. 833 (1992).

[158] 505 U.S. 833 (1992).

participate equally in the economic and social life of the nation has been facilitated by their ability to control their reproductive lives."[159]

Casey, however, profoundly altered Roe's legal framework. While its fundamental-privacy-right principle enjoys new vitality in legal areas such as the expansion of gay rights,[160] Roe has little contemporary legal relevance to abortion regulation. Although affirming "the essence" of Roe, Casey completely altered its doctrine. A woman's right to choose to have a pre-viability abortion is no longer a fundamental right that can only be curtailed to further a "compelling" state interest. It is now merely a right that is protected from "undue interference" by the government. As applied by the Court in Casey and subsequent cases, "undue interference" seems to amount to a legislative restriction that actually or in practical effect bans access to most safe abortion methods.[161] Additionally, Casey strengthened and elevated the state's interest in protecting potential fetal life to apply throughout pregnancy, rather than to the post-viability period set forth in Roe. This governmental interest includes not only protecting the potential life of the fetus, but also extends to the state's expression of its preference for childbirth over abortion as well as a general moral commitment to the dignity of life.[162] The legal framework established by Casey has led to judicial approval of a far greater range of legislative restrictions, such as state-mandated "informed consent" requirements that adopt anti-abortion arguments of dubious scientific validity,[163] than would have been upheld under an undiluted Roe.

The full extent of the Supreme Court's abandonment of the doctrinal framework of Roe became evident in the 2007 decision in Gonzales v. Carhart.[164] The case involved a federal law banning "partial-birth" abortion, defined as an abortion procedure in which most of the fetus is delivered intact into the birth canal before it is terminated. Justice Kennedy, who had joined the Casey opinion, including the portion with the stirring rhetoric about the importance of the ability to control reproduction to women's equality and dignity, now switched sides to join the Justices who had long been ardent opponents of finding any constitutional right to access to abortion. Kennedy's shift had been presaged seven years earlier, in a dissent from a decision striking down the same

---

[159] Id. at 856.

[160] See, e.g., Lawrence v. Texas, 539 U.S. 558, 573–74 (2003).

[161] See Caitlin Borgmann, Taking Stock of Abortion Rights After Casey and Carhart, 31 Fordham Urb. L. J. 675 (2004).

[162] See Siegel, Dignity and the Politics of Protection, supra note 147.

[163] Id. at 1719–20.

[164] 550 U.S. 124 (2007).

type of restriction the Court now upheld,[165] and seemed prompted by visceral disgust with the details of this controversial method of abortion, which he concluded blurred the line between abortion and infanticide. Kennedy was now able to elevate many aspects of his earlier dissent into the majority opinion in *Carhart*, as the Court, by a 5–4 margin, upheld a complete ban on a method of performing abortion without any exception for instances when a physician deemed the banned procedure necessary to protect a woman's health. The deference to medical judgment that had permeated *Roe* was now explicitly discarded.[166] Instead, the Court deferred to Congress's medical findings, although they were based on legislative testimony by anti-abortion professionals that was largely deemed scientifically unreliable by the trial courts.[167]

The *Carhart* opinion also adopted other rhetoric of the anti-abortion movement. The fetus is referred to throughout as an "unborn child" or a "baby," and women who are seeking abortions are called "mothers." [168] In a sharp departure from the recognition of the need for women's reproductive automony in *Casey*, the majority opined that "[r]espect for human life finds an ultimate expression in the bond of love the mother has for her child."[169] The Court then cited Sandra Cano's *amicus* brief to conclude that while there is no reliable data supporting any supposed post-abortion psychological difficulties, nonetheless "some women come to regret their choice to abort the infant life they once created and sustained."[170] Notably, the opinion ignored a competing *amicus* brief submitted on behalf of women who had faced situations necessitating the procedure at issue, chronicling their successful medical and psychological outcomes.[171] Nor did Kennedy's opinion explain why the reaction of some women might be at all relevant to banning a method of performing abortion.

Many in the anti-abortion movement were strongly encouraged by both the result and the rhetoric in *Carhart*. Bans on "partial-birth" abortion were the culmination of a strategy to focus public attention on

---

[165] Stenberg v. Carhart, 530 U.S. 914 (2000). *Stenberg* involved "partial-birth" abortion bans enacted by several states, and the Court struck them down both because the definitions of the banned procedures were so broad as to encompass virtually all safe methods of performing second-trimester abortions, and because the bans lacked an exception to preserve women's health.

[166] 550 U.S. at 163.

[167] *See Carhart*, 550 U.S. at 174–179 (Ginsburg, J., dissenting).

[168] *Id.* at 134, 138–39, 143, 153, 158–60.

[169] *Id.* at 159.

[170] *Id.*

[171] Siegel, *Dignity and the Politics of Protection*, supra note 147, at 1732 n. 110.

the blow-by-blow reality of what the abortion procedure does to fetuses, in the hope of eroding public support for abortion.[172] If one method can be banned because it offends human dignity, then other much more common methods may be banned on the same rationale. In addition, starting in the 1990's many anti-abortion activists turned to advancing woman-protective arguments against abortion, such as the notion of post-abortion psychological harm, in the hope of blunting the accusation of abortion rights supporters that they were more concerned about fetuses than women.[173]

Whether the apparent shift in attitude by Justice Kennedy and his adoption of some anti-abortion movement rhetoric in *Carhart* portends an abandonment by the Court of even the faint "essence" of *Roe* that still survives remains to be seen. The *Carhart* decision will, however, energize continued efforts to persuade some state legislatures to ban most abortions, in the hope of creating a test case that begs the Court to overrule *Roe's* holding that the Constitution protects a woman's right to decide whether to have an abortion. This will no doubt sharpen the long-running debate over whether abortion is a topic that can be better settled by legislatures and public referenda, rather than courts.

3.   *Roe's* Impact on American Politics and Society.

Just as some have blamed *Roe* for the phenomenon of abortion, others have castigated the Supreme Court decision for plunging the nation into political turmoil and creating the right-to-life movement. Critics contend that the Supreme Court acted precipitously, well ahead of public opinion and with shaky precedential grounds, to pluck the issue away from state legislatures; if abortion regulation had been left to the deliberative political process in state legislatures, they argue, then the nation gradually would have achieved consensus around abortion.[174]

These critics have unrealistic ideas about the state legislative process, and overlook significant aspects of the history of *Roe* and abortion legislation. Although public opinion polls in the early 1970s showed growing majority support for leaving the abortion decision to women, legislative reform efforts were becoming increasingly contentious well before the Supreme Court opinion. The introduction of each bill, especially repeal laws, energized anti-abortion activists, and tactics such as

---

[172] *Id.* at 1707–08.

[173] Id. at 1714–19.

[174] *See* Ruth Bader Ginsburg, *Speaking in a Judicial Voice*, 67 N.Y.U. L. Rev. 1185, 1208 (1992); Mary Ann Glendon, *Abortion and Divorce in Western Law* 42–43 (1987); Elizabeth Mensch & Alan Freeman, *The Politics of Virtue: Is Abortion Debatable?* 126–27 (1993).

fetus displays and threats to or picketing of repeal supporters appeared before *Roe*.

Abortion is a topic about which people have either strong or deeply conflicted and contextual feelings; this was true before *Roe*, and is likely to remain true no matter what happens in the Supreme Court. *Roe* certainly did not create anti-abortion activism; it did, however, energize it, shape it and channel it, just as it led to complacency on the part of many pro-choice activists, who mistakenly thought their struggles were over. *Roe* has become an important symbol for both anti-abortion and pro-choice activists, but it is not the cause of activism on either side. Deeply held world views about women's roles and religion are far more important motivators than a Supreme Court decision.[175]

Roe also did not remove abortion regulation from legislatures. In fact, since *Roe*, far more bills regarding abortion are introduced in any single year in the state and federal legislatures than before *Roe*. Abortion is such a prevalent topic of legislative attention that bills on subjects ranging from bankruptcy reform, to United Nations funding, to military appropriations become bogged down in abortion debates.[176] *Roe* removed only the most restrictive legislative options from the table. *Roe*'s legislative impact, then, is in refocusing anti-abortion energy from efforts to ban abortion to proposals to regulate it to the point of practical unavailability for many women. The array of abortion regulations that have been passed or proposed is vast. It includes: Funding restrictions; parental consent for minors; laws mandating waiting periods before a woman can have an abortion; laws banning particular methods of performing abortions; laws specifying the dimensions of clinic facilities and the extent of their equipment; bills to punish people who help minors cross state lines to get an abortion to avoid parental consent; and restrictions on public or military hospitals performing abortions. The Supreme Court has been engaged in an ongoing dialogue with legislatures, approving some of these restrictions and rejecting others. All this legislative ferment has done little to achieve consensus; it has instead kept abortion as a hot

---

[175] *See* Kristin Luker, *Abortion and the Politics of Motherhood* 158–91 (1984); Faye D. Ginsburg, *Contested Lives: The Abortion Debate in an American Community* 133–97 (1989).

[176] In the immediate aftermath of *Roe*, 260 abortion-related bills were introduced in state legislatures, and in 1974 189 bills were introduced. Legislative activity continued unabated into the late 1970s. Rosenberg, *supra* note 6, at 187. The proliferation of abortion related bills continues into the twenty-first century. In annual reports tracking state and federal legislation introduced and enacted, NARAL reports 502 restrictive state abortion bills were considered in 2008, with 24 enacted, while noting that during the two-term Presidency of George W. Bush, state legislatures considered over 4,200 measures restricting abortion, and enacted 317 of them. NARAL Pro–Choice America, *Who Decides? A State by State Review of Abortion and Reproductive Rights* 4 (18th ed. 2009), http://www.pro choiceamerica.org/choice-action-center/in_your_state/who-decides/introduction/whodecides 2009.pdf.

button issue that keeps activists busy and can affect elections. If *Roe* were to be overturned, returning even the criminal ban option to the legislature, it is likely the debate would escalate, rather than abate, because the pro-choice movement would become re-energized to counter the already-energized anti-abortion movement. This is borne out by recent experience in South Dakota, where abortion bans were put to the test of public referenda in 2006 and again in 2008, but were defeated by larger than expected margins due to extensive pro-choice organizing.[177]

It is also unfair and inaccurate to blame the Supreme Court decision in *Roe* for the most extreme form of the abortion controversy in U.S. society—the turn to violent attacks on clinics and abortion providers. For eleven years after the decision, anti-abortion opposition was largely peaceful, if sometimes vociferously so. It was not until 1984 that clinic bombings started, and the first large scale blockades organized by Operation Rescue did not occur until 1988. The turn to violence in the anti-abortion movement was inspired far more by the rise of a radical strand of Protestant evangelism with a theology of direct action than by any decision of the U.S. Supreme Court.[178] Violence might well have occurred in any state that had legalized abortion, even if the Supreme Court had never entered the abortion debate.

It is unlikely that quiescent consensus on abortion will emerge in American society so long as it is a public topic for debate in any legal arena, whether judicial or legislative. Even during the century of criminalization, there was hardly consensus on abortion, even though it was driven underground and out of public debate. Women continued to seek abortions in large number; doctors and others risked prosecution in providing them; some police and prosecutors turned a blind eye or protected abortionists, while others cracked down. Abortion laws were among the most disregarded laws on the books, with too often fatal consequences for women. The only lasting impact of *Roe* that can be asserted with any confidence is that by giving women the constitutional right to control their own reproduction, it has brought an end to the Monday morning emergency room line-ups and wasted lives of hundreds of thousands of women.

It also endures as a symbol and rallying cry: for women's rights groups as the cornerstone of full constitutional equality, and for anti-abortion groups as the death knell for pre-born humans and the family structure. Abortion is controversial because what divides people who feel strongly about it are fundamentally different conceptions of women's

---

[177] *See Voting for Reproductive Freedom*, N.Y. Times, Nov. 12, 2008, at WK8.

[178] *See* James Risen & Judy L. Thomas, *Wrath of Angels: The American Abortion War* 57–66, 121–30, 138–39 (1998).

nature and proper societal role, of sexuality, faith and family.[179] As both
the 19th century arguments against abortion and the new 21st century
woman-protective anti-abortion arguments that started to take hold in
Carhart illustrate, the anti-abortion position rests on a notion that
women are primarily destined to be mothers, that no woman could
voluntarily choose abortion if she really understood its implications, and
that abortion therefore does equal violence to unborn children and the
bodies and psyches of women. As Justice Ginsburg's passionate dissent
in *Carhart* illustrates, the pro-choice position rests on a recognition that
many women can quite reasonably choose not to be mothers, and that
full reproductive rights, including unfettered access to contraception and
abortion, are essential in order to ensure that each woman can shape her
own destiny based "on her own conception of her spiritual imperatives
and her place in society."[180] Thus, for many, a reversal of *Roe* would
signal a return to the days when women were relegated to the status of
dependent, second-class citizens, with a Constitution callously indifferent
to their most central needs and concerns.

Women are the ultimate contested ground of the abortion debate.

---

[179] *See* Siegel, *Dignity and the Politics of Protection*, supra note 147, at 1797–98.

[180] 550 U.S. at 185 (Ginsburg, J., dissenting) (quoting *Casey,* 505 U.S. at 852) (internal
quotation marks omitted).

11

Ashutosh A. Bhagwat

The Story of *Whitney v. California*: The Power of Ideas

The opinion of Justice Louis Brandeis in *Whitney v. California*[1] has been variously described as "arguably the most important essay ever written, on or off the bench, on the meaning of the first amendment,"[2] as providing "the dominant theoretical underpinnings of the Court's free speech jurisprudence,"[3] as "probably the most effective judicial interpretation of the First Amendment ever written,"[4] as "the first impressive appearance of the self-governance rationale in First Amendment theory,"[5] and as the source of the entire modern "project of bifurcated constitutional review."[6] Over eighty years after its publication, *Whitney* remains a mainstay of constitutional casebooks and among the most cited cases ever decided by the Supreme Court.[7] When the decision is examined closely, however, its prominence is revealed as something of a puzzle. Justice Sanford's majority opinion did not create any new law,

---

[1] 274 U.S. 357 (1927).

[2] Vincent Blasi, *The First Amendment and the Ideal of Civic Courage: The Brandeis Opinion in* Whitney v. California, 29 Wm. and Mary L. Rev. 653, 668 (1988).

[3] Bradley C. Bobertz, *The Brandeis Gambit: The Making of America's "First Freedom," 1909–1931*, 40 Wm. and Mary L. Rev. 557, 645 (1999) (citing Gerald Gunther, *Individual Rights in Constitutional Law* 644 (4th ed. 1986)).

[4] David M. Rabban, *Free Speech in its Forgotten Years* 369 (1997).

[5] G. Edward White, *The First Amendment Comes of Age: The Emergence of Free Speech in Twentieth–Century America*, 95 Mich. L. Rev. 299, 325 (1996).

[6] *Id.* at 326.

[7] Bobertz, *supra* note 3, at 645 & n.594.

but rather treated the case as a rather unexceptional application of the Court's earlier decision in *Gitlow v. New York*, which itself was viewed by the Court's majority as applying well established principles of judicial deference to legislative policymaking so as to limit the scope of First Amendment claims.[8] And even Justice Brandeis's separate opinion— which was in fact a concurrence rather than a dissent—did not purport to offer any new legal standard, but rather to apply (and perhaps slightly clarify) the "clear and present danger" test developed in previous First Amendment opinions written by Justice Oliver Wendell Holmes, Jr., both for the Court and in dissent.[9] What then explains the extraordinary influence and lasting power of the case?

The answer is simple, but surprising. *Whitney* exemplifies the enduring power of *ideas* in constitutional jurisprudence, and in law generally. The story of *Whitney* is not a story of doctrine; it is a story of theory and principles, and a demonstration of the ability of ideas to shape the course of the law. In *Whitney*, Justice Brandeis articulated a complex, carefully calibrated, and heartfelt *theory* of free speech and the First Amendment. That theory, since embraced by generations of justices and scholars, has had a profound effect on modern First Amendment law. For that reason alone, *Whitney* is a case that is well worth closer examination. In addition, the story behind the *Whitney* decision, including the life of Anita Whitney, the defendant in the case, and the circumstances that led to her prosecution for Criminal Syndicalism, provides a fascinating glimpse into the age of American Radicalism and the reaction against it during, and immediately after, World War I. As we live through another era in which the claims of order press hard against those of liberty, we may learn from the experience of our early twentieth century forebears.

How The Case Got to the Supreme Court

Charlotte Anita Whitney was born on July 7, 1867 in San Francisco, California. Among her ancestors were five members of the Mayflower complement, an early governor of Massachusetts Colony, and several veterans of the Revolutionary War. Her father was a successful attorney who later served as a State Senator in California. On her mother's side of the family, one of her uncles (by marriage) was Stephen J. Field, Associate Justice of the United States Supreme Court. Whitney attended Wellesley College and graduated in 1889 with a Bachelor of Science

---

[8] *See Whitney*, 274 U.S. at 371 (citing *Gitlow v. New York*, 268 U.S. 652, 666–68 (1925)).

[9] *See, e.g., Schenck v. United States*, 249 U.S. 47, 52 (1919); *Abrams v. United States*, 250 U.S. 616, 627–28 (1919) (Holmes, J., dissenting); *Gitlow*, 268 U.S. at 672–73 (Holmes, J., dissenting).

degree. After graduation, she undertook a six month tour of Europe, before returning to her hometown of Oakland, California. In short, Anita Whitney was very much a member of the cultural and economic elite of the late-nineteenth century United States, seemingly destined for the typical life of women of that stratum.[10] As it turned out, however, Whitney's life took quite a different course, culminating in her appearance before the United States Supreme Court as a criminal defendant.

Whitney's transformation from a life of upper-class privilege to that of a social activist appears to have begun during a trip to the east coast in 1893, when she first seriously took up charitable work. Upon returning to Oakland, Whitney became actively involved in local charitable endeavors, and in 1901 was named the secretary of the Associated Charities of Alameda County. In 1903 she was appointed the first (unpaid) juvenile probation officer for Alameda County. And in 1906 Whitney participated in relief efforts in Oakland following the San Francisco earthquake and fire, assisting in the care of thousands of refugees who fled San Francisco for Oakland. After the crisis created by the great earthquake had eased, Whitney spent several years working with charitable organizations in Boston and New York City, until in 1911, worn out and disillusioned, she returned once again to Oakland.

In the following years, Whitney's interests gradually evolved from social work to politics. Contemporary press accounts of her trial and conviction describe Whitney as a "club woman," a member of the sorts of women's social clubs that were frequented by the upper middle class, educated elite, and which during this period were transforming into vehicles for women's involvement in politics.[11] Whitney began her own political career by joining the Prohibition movement, and then the Women's Suffrage movement. She served as a leader of the effort to extend the right to vote to women in California, which end was accomplished in 1911, and then as the first president of the California Civic League (while simultaneously assisting with suffrage movements in Oregon and Nevada). During this period (the early to mid nineteen-teens), Whitney was for the first time brought into contact with the workers' movement in the United States. The growing power of, and attacks against one part of that movement, the Industrial Workers of the

---

[10] The details of Anita Whitney's early life provided here and later are taken from Al Richmond, *Native Daughter: The Story of Anita Whitney* 17–89 (1942), a hagiography published on the occasion of Whitney's seventy-fifth birthday. Another valuable source is Lisa Rubens, *The Patrician Radical: Charlotte Anita Whitney*, 65 California History 158–171 (1986).

[11] For a discussion of the growth of women's social clubs during the nineteenth century, and their role in incubating political activism by women during the early twentieth century, see Jason Mazzone, *Freedom's Associations*, 77 Wash. L. Rev. 639, 642–44 (2002).

World ("IWW"), had a profound influence on Whitney's own developing radicalism.

The IWW, better known as the "Wobblies," was founded in 1905.[12] The stated aim of the organization, which exists to this day, albeit with less influence, was, and is, to create "One Big Union," and its statement of purpose begins with the declaration that "[t]he working class and the employing class have nothing in common." The form of radicalism represented by the Wobblies was new and unusual in the United States, and the IWW was, rightly or wrongly, accused of fomenting violence during strikes. As a consequence, the Wobblies were unsurprisingly met by great hostility from "the employing class." During the first decade of the Wobblies' existence, their organizers, leaders, and members faced constant harassment and violence from the authorities, but also developed substantial support among workers, especially in the western United States. Public opinion was divided regarding the IWW's treatment by the authorities. Interestingly (and in retrospect ironically), the Wobblies played a pivotal role during this period in the development of a true, modern free speech movement, though their interest in free speech was more as a tool to fight for workers' causes than as a general right.[13]

The Wobblies' activities during the first two decades of the twentieth century, particularly their "free speech fights" and their militant organizing of destitute and socially powerless workers (among them migrant workers) elicited a great deal of support and admiration in progressive circles, including from Anita Whitney. With the entry of the United States into World War I in the spring of 1917, however, the tide of public opinion turned decisively against the IWW and other left-wing organizations. The IWW and other leftist organizations such as the Socialist Party were firmly opposed to America's entry into the war, which they viewed as being waged on behalf of capitalist and colonialist interests at the expense of workers. Such opposition, however, was widely viewed as treasonous in the highly patriotic atmosphere of 1917 to 1919. In addition, the Bolshevik Revolution in November of 1917 fed widespread fears of a violent, workers' revolution in the United States and western Europe. The immediate product of wartime hysteria and the post-war Red Scare was the enactment of a series of laws essentially outlawing opposition to the war or support of violent revolution. The most important of these laws was the federal Espionage Act of 1917, which was used to initiate a wave of prosecutions against opponents of the war, including most famously the prosecution and imprisonment of

---

[12] Much of the background information about the IWW is taken from the IWW's official website: http://www.iww.org. I also draw upon Blasi, *supra* note 2, at 653–56, and Bobertz, *supra* note 3, at 566–86.

[13] *See* Rabban, *supra* note 4, at 77–128; Bobertz, *supra* note 3, at 566–72.

Eugene Debs, the leader of the Socialist Party.[14] In addition, many states adopted "criminal syndicalism" statutes forbidding the advocacy of criminal or violent action as a means of industrial reform. These state statutes were directed specifically at the Wobblies, and were used to imprison much of the IWW leadership. California's Criminal Syndicalism statute, which came into effect on April 30, 1919, was typical, inasmuch as it was wielded primarily against the Wobblies. In late 1919, however, the statute ensnared a most unusual and unexpected victim: Anita Whitney.

During the years following Whitney's successful work in the women's suffrage movement, she was exposed to radical activists in the workers' rights movement. By 1914, observing the brutal treatment accorded IWW organizers and increasingly convinced that changes in industrial organization were essential if any serious progress was to be made in addressing poverty and its related ills, Whitney joined the Socialist Party of Eugene Debs.[15] Her radicalism increased over the next several years. This process culminated in the summer of 1919, when as a result of the Bolshevik Revolution in Russia, the Socialist Party split over the question of whether it should join the Communist International. At a convention in Chicago, the more radical elements (who supported the Soviet Union) were expelled from the Socialist Party, and formed the rival Communist Labor Party. While Whitney was not present in Chicago, upon hearing of the split she helped to organize the Communist Labor Party of California, leading the local Oakland chapter of the Socialist Party into the newly organized party and serving on the credentials and resolutions committee at the Communist Labor Party's organizing convention. At the convention Whitney personally supported a relatively moderate platform advocating only an electoral strategy; but her position was defeated, and the California party adopted the national party's more radical platform, which among other things, explicitly endorsed the activities and "example" of the IWW. Whitney made no protest against this result, and remained active in the party, serving as a member of the party's state executive committee. During this same period, though she never joined the IWW, Whitney provided substantial support to the IWW defense committee and committed most of her personal fortune to providing bail for jailed Wobblies. Whitney's support of the Wobblies, along with her membership in the Communist Labor Party, led to her criminal prosecution and ultimately the Supreme Court's decision in *Whitney v. California*.

---

[14] *See Debs v. United States*, 249 U.S. 211 (1919) (Holmes, J.) (affirming conviction of Debs under Espionage Act of 1917). While serving his prison term Debs ran for President on the Socialist Party ticket in 1920, and won over a million votes. He was subsequently pardoned by President Harding.

[15] Rubens, *supra* note 10, at 161–63.

In late November of 1919, Anita Whitney delivered a speech in Oakland to the California Civic League (of which she had been a founding member) on the subject of "The Negro Problem," speaking out against recent lynchings and race riots. Because of Whitney's political activities the talk was controversial, but the membership of the organization voted to proceed nonetheless. At the end of her address, Whitney was placed under arrest by Inspector Fenton Thompson of the Oakland police department, an active red-baiter. In arresting Whitney, Thompson acted against the wishes of his immediate superior, Oakland chief of police Walter Peterson (who later supported a pardon for Whitney), but with the support of other, more senior officers.

Three months later, Whitney's trial began.[16] Whitney was represented at trial by Thomas H. O'Connor, a well-respected criminal defense attorney. O'Connor, however, only became involved in the case on the eve of trial, and was refused a continuance to better prepare by the trial judge, James G. Quinn of the Superior Court, even though O'Connor's daughter was suffering from influenza at the time. Despite the defense's best efforts, the beliefs and actions of Whitney herself received little attention during the trial. In the prosecution's view (which was favorably received by the judge), such matters were irrelevant because the California Criminal Syndicalism statute forbade not only syndicalism itself (defined as "advocating . . . the commission of crime, sabotage . . . , or unlawful acts of force and violence or unlawful methods of terrorism as a means of accomplishing a change in industrial ownership"), but also mere *membership* in any organization "organized or assembled to advocate, teach or aid and abet criminal syndicalism."[17] Because of this expansive definition of the offense, the prosecution was able to enter into evidence sensational and damaging (and occasionally perjured) testimony regarding the credo and positions of the Communist Labor Party, and by extension of the Communist International and the IWW. As a consequence, Whitney's trial devolved into another part of the larger national campaign during the Red Scare to eviscerate these organizations, notwithstanding the reality that Anita Whitney herself had never engaged in, nor even directly advocated, the use of violence.

Two days into the trial, O'Connor contracted influenza. Once again, however, Judge Quinn refused a continuance, requiring O'Connor to proceed despite his fever. A few days later O'Connor fell into a delirium, and died soon after. Once again, a continuance was denied, and Whitney had to proceed with new, unprepared counsel (one Nathan C. Coghlan).

---

[16] A detailed description of the trial is provided in Woodrow C. Whitten, *The Trial of Charlotte Anita Whitney*, 15 Pacific Historical Review 286 (1946). The description provided here is derived largely from that source.

[17] *Whitney*, 274 U.S. at 359–60.

After several more weeks of testimony, Whitney was convicted on one count of criminal syndicalism based on her membership in the Communist Labor Party, and sentenced to serve one to fourteen years in the San Quentin penitentiary.

Reaction to Whitney's conviction was mixed. There was predictable criticism from the Left—*The Nation*, for example, published a scathing description of her arrest and trial[18]—but prosecutions under state syndicalism acts continued across the country with wide public support. Whitney seemed headed for prison when her request for bail was denied, and did in fact serve several days in the county jail before the judge relented and granted bail pending appeal because of concerns about the effects of imprisonment upon her health (Whitney was already fifty-two years old at the time of her conviction). Whitney did not have the funds to cover her bail because most of her fortune was tied up in providing bail for convicted Wobblies; as a result, friends raised the necessary funds on her behalf and Whitney remained a free woman.

Whitney first appealed her conviction to the California District Court of Appeal. On April 25, 1922, that court issued a very brief opinion roundly denying Whitney's claims.[19] The primary arguments Whitney presented to the appellate court were that her indictment suffered from a technical flaw because it failed to specify the allegedly syndicalist organization to which Whitney belonged, and that the evidence presented at trial was insufficient to establish that the Communist Labor Party fell within the prohibition of California's syndicalism statute. The Court of Appeals summarily denied both claims, relying on a recent decision of the California Supreme Court, *People v. Taylor*,[20] which had considered and rejected precisely those arguments. The tone of the appeals court opinion is well illustrated by the portion rejecting Whitney's argument that the evidence failed to demonstrate her knowledge of the relevant activities of the Communist Labor Party of California:

> That this defendant did not realize that she was giving herself over to forms and expressions of disloyalty and was, to say the least of it, lending her presence and the influence of her character and position as a woman of refinement and culture to an organization whose purposes and sympathies savored of treason, is not only past belief but is a matter with which this court can have no concern, since it is

---

[18] Clare Shipman, *The Conviction of Anita Whitney*, 110 The Nation No. 2855, March 20, 1920, at 365–67; *see also* Anna Porter, *The Case of Anita Whitney*, The New Republic, July 6, 1921, at 165–66.

[19] *People v. Whitney*, 57 Cal.App. 449, 207 P. 698 (1922), *aff'd* 274 U.S. 357 (1927).

[20] 187 Cal. 378, 203 P. 85 (1921).

one of the conclusive presumptions of our law that a guilty intent is presumed from the deliberate commission of an unlawful act.[21]

Clearly Whitney was not going to secure relief from the California Court of Appeal.

Whitney then sought discretionary review in the California Supreme Court, which was denied with two justices dissenting. Finally, having exhausted her options in state court, Whitney filed for review of her conviction in the United States Supreme Court.

The Supreme Court Decision

Whitney obtained new lawyers for her appeal to the Supreme Court: Walter H. Pollak and Walter Nelles, whom Professor Vincent Blasi describes as "two of the ablest and most prominent civil liberties lawyers of the day."[22] In their brief to the Supreme Court, Whitney's lawyers raised a host of constitutional issues, including a number of claimed violations of the Due Process and Equal Protection Clauses of the Fourteenth Amendment, as well as a handful of claims based on the speech and association rights protected by the First Amendment.[23] Interestingly, by far the greatest focus of the brief was on five Due Process claims, which took up the first thirty-nine pages of the brief's argument section (out of a total of fifty-eight). The primary Due Process arguments advanced were that Whitney's indictment, and the Syndicalism statute itself, failed to provide Whitney with proper notice of the offense with which she was charged (there were also attacks on the sufficiency of the evidence on various points, and on the prejudicial effect of admitting certain kinds of evidence). Whitney's First Amendment claims were squeezed into fourteen pages of her brief, and those arguments ranged over a wide area, invoking everything from the prior restraint doctrine to the right of association.[24] The crucial argument regarding the protections the First Amendment accords to subversive speech—the point for which the case has subsequently been remembered, and which was the subject of Justice Brandeis's separate opinion—was summarized in a mere *five pages* out of an eighty-four page brief. Reading the brief makes

---

[21] *Whitney*, 57 Cal.App. at 452, 207 P. at 699.

[22] Blasi, *supra* note 2, at 661. Among other things, Walter Pollak was the father of Louis Pollak, later dean of the Yale and University of Pennsylvania law schools, and now a federal district court judge.

[23] Whitney's brief is reprinted in 25 Philip B. Kurland and Gerhard Casper, eds., *Landmark Briefs and Arguments of the Supreme Court of the Untied States*: Constitutional Law 565–655 (1975).

[24] The final five pages of the brief were devoted to an Equal Protection argument that the Syndicalism statute improperly discriminated between different opinions.

clear that Whitney's lawyers did not place much hope in her First Amendment arguments.

The brief for the State of California[25] similarly (and unsurprisingly) focused the great bulk of its attention on Whitney's Due Process claims, devoting twenty of twenty-eight pages of argument to those issues. Indeed, the State dedicated only three pages to the free speech issues; and those pages consisted almost entirely of lengthy quotations from previous state court opinions. There was no mention of the Clear and Present Danger test, no serious discussion of previous Supreme Court decisions, and indeed little in the way of reasoned analysis. It is thus quite clear from their brief that the attorneys for the State did not regard Whitney's free speech claims as a serious threat to her conviction.

Lest there be surprise about the parties' off-hand treatment of the First Amendment issues raised by Whitney's conviction, it should be remembered that at the time that Whitney's case was finally argued in the Supreme Court in late 1925, there existed an unbroken line of precedent in the Supreme Court, beginning with the *Schenck v. United States* decision in 1919[26] and continuing through the very recent decision in *Gitlow v. New York*,[27] soundly rejecting any First Amendment protection for subversive speech. The early decisions in this line of cases had all been unanimous, and some of them—notably the *Debs* case[28]—had rejected First Amendment claims in circumstances which were even more problematic than those surrounding Whitney's arrest. The more recent decisions (beginning with the 1919 *Abrams* case[29]) had included powerful dissents from Justices Holmes and Brandeis; but while we today—and even some of their contemporaries—might recognize Holmes and Brandeis as visionaries, from the point of view of Whitney's lawyers they represented only two of nine votes.

Moreover, not only had the Court uniformly rejected free speech claims in the prior cases, but the most recent decision, *Gitlow*, had unambiguously *weakened* the First Amendment protection available in situations like Whitney's, holding that when a statute specifically targets subversive speech, the relevant constitutional test is an extremely deferential one, permitting a statute to be struck down only if a reviewing court concludes it is "arbitrary or unreasonable"[30]; Holmes' "clear and

---

[25] Kurland & Casper, *supra* note 23, at 657–702.

[26] 249 U.S. 47 (1919).

[27] 268 U.S. 652 (1925).

[28] *Debs v. United States*, 249 U.S. 211 (1919); *see supra* note 14 & accompanying text.

[29] *Abrams v. United States*, 250 U.S. 616 (1919).

[30] *Gitlow*, 268 U.S. at 668, 670. It should be noted that *Gitlow* was decided after the original briefing on Whitney's appeal was completed; but it was decided before oral argument, and before the supplemental briefing on rehearing (which is discussed below).

present danger" test was limited to situations where a statute which by
its terms regulated conduct was, in a particular case, being applied to
speech.[31] There was thus very good reason for Whitney's lawyers to lack
faith in her First Amendment arguments.

Finally, Whitney's focus on the Due Process Clause in her appeal
made some sense in the historical context, which was after all the
Lochner era, when Due Process was king. Indeed, the very day that
Whitney's appeal was finally resolved, and rejected, by the Supreme
Court, the Court decided *Fiske v. Kansas*[32] in which the Court for the
first time reversed a criminal conviction based on subversive speech.
That case involved the Syndicalism conviction of a Wobblie, and the
textual basis for the Court's decision was the Due Process Clause, *not*
the First Amendment.

Oral argument was held in Whitney's case on October 6, 1925. Two
weeks later the Supreme Court issued a bombshell—it dismissed Whitney's appeal for want of jurisdiction, on the grounds that the federal
issues in the case had not been properly raised and decided by the state
courts below.[33] Her legal options seemingly at an end, prison now looked
inevitable for Anita Whitney. Press accounts of the decision and Whitney's looming jail term were largely negative, and a massive nationwide
campaign was launched—supported by, among others, the novelist Upton Sinclair, the Dean of the Columbia Law School, and the Presidents of
Wellesley, Smith, Vassar and Swarthmore Colleges—to seek a gubernato-
rial pardon for Whitney.[34] The willingness of such mainstream figures to
support Whitney showed that the peak of the Red Scare had clearly
passed. Interestingly, Whitney herself did not especially support this
campaign, suggesting that given the large number of men behind bars
for Syndicalism, she should not receive any special favors on account of
her sex or social status.[35] In any event, Governor Friend W. Richardson
refused to grant the pardon, explaining (in an open letter to Upton
Sinclair) that he believed Whitney had avoided prison because of her
wealth and influence, and should now be forced to serve her time.[36]

Then, once again, lightning struck in the Supreme Court. On
December 14, 1925 the Court granted the Petition for Rehearing filed by
Whitney's lawyers on November 27. Whitney's Petition had pointed out

---

[31] *Id.* at 670–71.

[32] 274 U.S. 380 (1927).

[33] *Whitney v. California*, 269 U.S. 530 (1925).

[34] *See* Blasi, *supra* note 2, at 661–62.

[35] *Id.* at 662–63.

[36] *Pardon for Miss Whitney is Refused*, Oakland Tribune, November 2, 1925, at 1–2.

that in December of 1924, over two years after its decision and after the Supreme Court had taken up the case, the California Court of Appeals had issued an order, stipulated by the parties, indicating that the Court of Appeals *had* in fact resolved the constitutionality of the California Syndicalism Act even though it did not mention the federal Constitution in its official opinion (the Petition also cited portions of Whitney's briefs to the Court of Appeals demonstrating that she had raised her constitutional claims). On this basis the Supreme Court granted rehearing and ordered supplemental briefing. The supplemental briefs were promptly filed, and on the merits they largely repeated the parties' original arguments (though the State added a citation of the *Gitlow* opinion decided since the original briefing, in support of its argument on the First Amendment issue). Finally, on March 18, 1926, the case was reargued.

After reargument, Whitney's appeal lingered in the Supreme Court for over a year, the opinion in the case not being issued until May 16, 1927.[37] The majority opinion was authored by Justice Sanford, the author of *Gitlow*—clearly not a good portent for Whitney (though it should be noted that Sanford also authored *Fiske*). The opinion begins by considering the jurisdictional question, concluding that the Court of Appeals' stipulated judgment, while "not to be commended," did vest the Supreme Court with jurisdiction.[38] The opinion then proceeds to the merits, starting with a brief recounting of the facts of the case and then turning to the Due Process issues. The Court summarily rejected Whitney's sufficiency-of-the-evidence claims, finding that those were issues for the jury, and also easily denied the claim that the Syndicalism Act was void for vagueness.[39] Next the Court considered Whitney's claim that the Act violated the Equal Protection Clause of the Fourteenth Amendment because it discriminated between people who advocate the use of violence to *change* industrial and political conditions, as opposed to those who advocate violence to maintain those conditions (if this seems a peculiar argument, it should be remembered that this was a time when anti-union employers were infamous for their use of hired thugs). The Court rejected the argument on the grounds that "[t]he Syndicalism Act is not class legislation; it affects all alike" and that there were no grounds to believe "that those desiring to maintain existing industrial and political conditions did or would advocate" violence.[40] Finally, turning to the First Amendment issues, the Court quickly rebuffed the claim that Whitney's prosecution violated free speech rights, citing *Gitlow* for

---

[37] *Whitney v. California*, 274 U.S. 357 (1927).

[38] *Id.* at 361.

[39] *Id.* at 366–69.

[40] *Id.* at 370.

the proposition that "a State in the exercise of its police power may
punish those who abuse this freedom [of speech] by utterances inimical
to the public welfare, tending to incite to crime, disturb the public peace,
or endanger the foundations of organized government and threaten its
overthrow by unlawful means."[41] Indeed, the Court viewed Whitney's
case as *easier* than Gitlow's because Whitney had, by joining an organization, entered into a criminal conspiracy, which "involves even greater
danger to the public peace and security than the isolated utterances and
acts of individuals."[42] With that, Whitney's conviction was affirmed.

Justice Brandeis, joined by Justice Holmes, filed a separate opinion,
and it is this opinion for which *Whitney* is of course remembered. The
opinion is styled a concurrence because ultimately Brandeis agreed with
the Court that Whitney's conviction should be affirmed; but his reasoning was flatly inconsistent with the majority's—the basis for his vote to
affirm was his view that Whitney had not properly invoked the clear and
present danger test in the courts below.[43] Unlike the majority, however,
Brandeis had no doubt that that was the correct test, and that there
were grave doubts if it could be met by the prosecution in this case.[44]

Brandeis's concurring opinion begins by noting that the offense for
which Whitney had been convicted was different from, and much broader than, the traditional conspiracy offense. The opinion then reiterates
that the relevant constitutional test in a case such as this one is whether
the defendant's conduct "constitutes a clear and present danger of
substantive evil," and that the courts should not defer to a legislative
judgment on this central question. At this point Brandeis added a coy
"compare" citation to *Gitlow*, but otherwise failed to acknowledge that a
solid majority of the Court had already rejected his views on this
question.[45]

A pause is in order here. It should be noted that at this point, eight
years after the Court's original Espionage Act decisions and two years
after *Gitlow*, the continued refusal of Justices Holmes and Brandeis to

---

[41] *Id.* at 371 (*citing Gitlow*, 268 U.S. at 666–68).

[42] *Id.* at 372.

[43] *Id.* at 378–79 (Brandeis, J., concurring).

[44] Professor Bradley Bobertz recounts that apparently the heart of Brandeis's opinion
in *Whitney* had originally been prepared as a dissent in another case involving the
conviction of a leading American Communist, Charles Ruthenberg. Ruthenburg's case was
mooted by his death, however, and so Brandeis incorporated his dissent into the *Whitney*
opinion. Bobertz, *supra* note 3, at 640–41. Any thought that Brandeis chose to concur
rather than dissent in *Whitney* out of political considerations is clearly dispelled by this
background, since a dissent in the Ruthenberg case would surely have been more controversial than in *Whitney*.

[45] *Whitney*, 274 U.S. at 374 (Brandeis, J., concurring).

acquiesce in the majority's view of the proper scope of the First Amendment was nothing short of extraordinary (especially in that day and age), and indeed might be called lawless or at least disrespectful. Brandeis compounded that disregard by failing to even acknowledge the gap between himself and the majority. How can one defend this sort of judicial behavior? There is no clear answer to this question, except perhaps to note that after all, Brandeis was right.

In any event, having reaffirmed his commitment to the clear and present danger test, the central part of the opinion then begins. Brandeis noted that to date, the Court had "not yet fixed the standard by which to determine" how to apply that test (again contrary to the truth), and in resolving those questions it was useful to "bear in mind why a State is, ordinarily, denied the power to prohibit dissemination of social, economic and political doctrine which a vast majority of its citizens believes to be false and fraught with evil consequences."[46] Then follow several paragraphs in which Brandeis set forth his theory of the First Amendment, and which are the basis for the hortatory comments which began this chapter. The first paragraph commences with an invocation of history, purporting to set forth the views of "[t]hose who won our independence." The core of those beliefs, according to Brandeis, was that in government "deliberative forces should prevail over the arbitrary," that free speech was an essential component of political liberty, that "discussion affords ordinarily adequate protection against the dissemination of noxious doctrine," and that—in perhaps the most memorable passage in the opinion—"the greatest menace to freedom is an inert people" and thus "public discussion is a political duty."[47] In this paragraph Brandeis thus explained the critical thought underlying his view of the purposes of the First Amendment, which is the connection between the constitutional guarantee of free speech on the one hand, and popular participation in a democratic government on the other. Later in the paragraph Brandeis also suggested a second, related function of free speech in a free society, which was that of a safety valve, since "repression breeds hate [and] hate menaces stable government."[48] By the end of this paragraph, the core of Brandeis's political philosophy has been made plain.

In the next paragraph, Brandeis turned to more specific issues. He began by opining that fear alone cannot justify suppression of speech. "Men feared witches and burnt women."[49] From this Brandeis concluded that to justify limiting speech a danger must be both *serious* and

---

[46] *Whitney*, 274 U.S. at 374 (Brandeis, J., concurring).

[47] *Id*. at 375.

[48] *Id*.

[49] *Id*. at 376.

imminent, not merely possible. In this respect Brandeis seems to be adding something to the clear and present danger test as enunciated by Holmes, albeit in the way of elaboration rather than an overhaul.

Brandeis then turned back to history, but this time with a somewhat different focus. Where before he was invoking democracy, in this paragraph he invoked civic courage: "Those who won our independence by revolution were not cowards. They did not fear political change. They did not exalt order at the cost of liberty."[50] As a consequence, Brandeis argued, the Constitution that they created did not fear speech, and permitted its suppression only in an emergency. And furthermore, not any emergency (or "imminent danger") would do; the danger to be averted must be serious, or else the State might use the excuse of the most trivial harms (trespass is the example Brandeis used—a prophetic comment in light of the later Civil Rights movement sit-ins) to repress speech. Thus did Brandeis connect his historical and philosophical view of the First Amendment with his strict interpretation of the clear and present danger test.

Finally, Brandeis concluded by applying his views to the facts of Whitney's prosecution. Here, however, Brandeis's analysis faltered. He noted that Whitney might have raised serious questions about whether there truly existed in California in late 1919 conditions which created a sufficiently immediate and serious danger as to justify the State's repression of her speech. But he also noted that Whitney failed to raise these arguments, and that therefore the Court lacked the power to reverse her conviction. And so like the majority, he concluded that her conviction must be affirmed.

The Immediate Impact of Whitney v. California

On a legal level, the immediate impact of the Supreme Court's decision in *Whitney v. California* was relatively limited. As the above discussion indicates, the majority opinion in *Whitney* made no new law but rather treated the case as an unproblematic application of the principles announced in *Gitlow*. Even Justice Brandeis's separate opinion—which of course could not alter the law—did little more than restate the speech-protective version of the clear and present danger test announced in previous dissenting opinions, most notably Justice Holmes's opinions in *Abrams v. United States*[51] and *Gitlow v. New York*.[52] It is not quite fair to say that Brandeis's opinion adds nothing to the doctrine

---

[50] *Id.* at 377.

[51] 250 U.S. 616, 627 (1919) (Holmes, J., dissenting).

[52] 268 U.S. 652, 672–73 (1925) (Holmes, J., dissenting).

advocated by Holmes. The Brandeis opinion clarifies several points: first, that in application of the test courts owe no deference to legislative judgments; second, that a clear and present danger must be *immediate* to the point of emergency; and third, that the danger to be averted must be a *serious* one. But these are minor elaborations, perhaps even implicit in Holmes's previous opinions; and in any event, they were not the law.

The immediate significance *Whitney* did have is that it confirmed the constitutionality of California's Syndicalism statute, and by implication the constitutionality of the many other existing state Syndicalism statutes. In addition, the broad language of the majority opinion largely precluded even as-applied challenges to Syndicalism convictions on First Amendment grounds (though as noted above, the Court's decision in *Fiske v. Kansas* on the same day opened up the possibility of Due Process challenges to such convictions). For the dozens of people in California, and the hundreds around the country, who were in jail because of Syndicalism convictions, therefore, *Whitney* largely ended their hope of a successful constitutional challenge based on the First Amendment.

Finally, for Anita Whitney herself the Supreme Court's decision appeared to have ended her seven-year reprieve from prison. On hearing the news of the Supreme Court's decision Whitney announced she would not request a pardon from the Governor because she "had done nothing to be pardoned for," and that she was ready to serve her sentence.[53] It was not, however, to be. Immediately after Whitney's conviction was finally affirmed, her lawyers requested a pardon on her behalf from the new Governor of California, C. C. Young, and a massive new state-wide writing campaign on her behalf was initiated, as a result of which thousands of letters and telegrams were sent to the Governor's office. Whitney's supporters at this stage included prominent businessmen, clergymen, the legislator who originally drafted the California Syndicalism statute, and the Mayor of Oakland.[54] On June 20, Governor Young issued a lengthy statement granting Whitney a full pardon. The Governor explained that the Syndicalism Act had never been intended to apply to people like Whitney, but was instead targeted at the violent Wobblies, that her conviction was a product of post-war hysteria and of a deeply

---

[53] *Anita Whitney Must Go to Prison As U.S. Court Denied Her Final Appeal: Syndicalism Act of State Held Valid,* Oakland Tribune, May 16, 1927, at 1. The affirmance of Whitney's conviction elicited a banner headline in the Oakland paper and her subsequent pardon garnered national attention, demonstrating the continued public interest in her fate.

[54] *Will C. Wood and Ray Benjamin Send Pleas to Young in Whitney Pardon,* Oakland Post–Enquirer, June 10, 1927; *Executive Clemency for Anita Whitney Asked By Dr. Lowther of First M.E.,* Oakland Post–Enquirer, June 13, 1927; *Syndicalism Act Raked in New Whitney Pardon Plea,* San Francisco Chronicle, June 13, 1927.

flawed trial, and that to send Whitney to prison given the circumstances was "an action absolutely unthinkable."[55] So Anita Whitney went free to fight more battles.

The Importance of Whitney v. California *Today*

If the immediate impact of the *Whitney* decision on the legal land-scape was relatively moderate, its long-term impact has been immeasurable. The impact of Justice Brandeis's opinion in *Whitney* has been felt at two very different levels—one immediate and doctrinal, and the other in its influence on the very shape and fabric of modern First Amendment law.

The impact on First Amendment law of Justice Brandeis's opinion began to manifest itself just four years (almost to the day) after the decision in *Whitney* was announced, in the Supreme Court's opinion in *Stromberg v. California.*[56] *Stromberg* involved a challenge, brought by a nineteen-year-old camp counselor at a Young Communist youth camp in the San Bernadino mountains, to a California statute which forbade the display of red flags under certain circumstances. The Court held, by a seven to two vote, that the statute violated the First Amendment because it permitted prosecution solely because a red flag had been displayed " 'as a sign, symbol or emblem of opposition to organized government.' "[57] The opinion was a narrow one, going out of its way to reaffirm the majority decisions in *Gitlow* and *Whitney* and noting that even under those cases this statute went too far. But in the opinion is language discussing the central role of "free political discussion" in assuring a responsive government and maintaining our constitutional system, which might have been taken verbatim from the Brandeis opinion in *Whitney*. The influence of Brandeis's ideas was beginning to be felt.

More significantly than its narrow holding, *Stromberg* represented the first step in a revolution in First Amendment law. In the ten years following *Stromberg* the Supreme Court, its membership increasingly composed of Roosevelt appointees, turned its back on the speech-restric-tive decisions of the post-World War I era. In a series of decisions

---

[55] *Miss Whitney Gets Pardon from Young*, Oakland Tribune, June 21, 1927; *Gov. Young Gives Liberty to S.F. Bay Club Woman*, San Francisco Chronicle, June 21, 1927; *Gov. Young Grants Plea for Pardon*, Oakland Post–Enquirer, June 21, 1927; *see also* Blasi, *supra* note 2, at 696–97 & nn. 148–149 (*citing The Pardon of Anita Whitney*, The New Republic, Aug. 10, 1927, at 310–12).

[56] 283 U.S. 359 (1931).

[57] *Id.* at 535 (*quoting* Cal. Penal Code § 403(a)).

including *Near v. Minnesota*,[58] *De Jonge v. Oregon*,[59] *Herndon v. Lowry*,[60] *Schneider v. State*,[61] and *Cantwell v. Connecticut*,[62] the Court extended substantial First Amendment protection to unpopular, dissident and subversive speech, drawing ever more clearly on the principles championed by Holmes and Brandeis along the way. This process culminated in 1941 with the Court's decision in *Bridges v. California*,[63] a case involving contempt prosecutions of speakers who commented on pending litigation. In *Bridges* a majority of the Court (in an opinion by Justice Black) expressly adopted the clear and present danger test as the relevant constitutional standard when speech is suppressed because of its alleged potential to cause social harm. Indeed, the Court suggested that clear and present danger had long been the standard, and proceeded to cite Justices Brandeis's opinion in *Whitney* (including its language requiring that the feared evil must be "serious" and "imminent") as if it were binding precedent.[64] After *Bridges* the doctrinal ascent of the Holmes/Brandeis approach to the First Amendment proceeded rapidly.[65]

In 1954 the Court finally explicitly confronted the continuing vitality of the majority opinions in *Gitlow* and *Whitney* in a case actually involving prosecution for subversive speech—the McCarthy era prosecutions under the Smith Act of the leaders of the Communist Party. In *Dennis v. United States*[66] a clear majority of the Court took the view that the relevant test in such cases was the clear and present danger test as formulated by Holmes and Brandeis, and that the majority approach in cases such as *Gitlow* and *Whitney* had been abandoned.[67] Admittedly, the Court then proceeded to affirm the convictions, and in the process almost certainly watered down the test as enunciated by Brandeis by adding a balancing element; but at least in form Brandeis's doctrinal views had become law.

---

[58] 283 U.S. 697 (1931).

[59] 299 U.S. 353 (1937).

[60] 301 U.S. 242 (1937).

[61] 308 U.S. 147 (1939).

[62] 310 U.S. 296 (1940).

[63] 314 U.S. 252 (1941).

[64] *Id.* at 262–63.

[65] *See, e.g., Terminiello v. Chicago*, 337 U.S. 1 (1949); *Feiner v. New York*, 340 U.S. 315 (1951).

[66] 341 U.S. 494 (1951).

[67] *Id.* at 507 (plurality opinion); *id.* at 527 (Frankfurter, J., concurring); *id.* at 588 (Douglas, J., dissenting).

It took another fifteen years before the spirit, as opposed to the letter, of the Brandeis approach was adopted by the Court, in *Brandenburg v. Ohio*.[68] *Brandenburg* involved the prosecution for criminal syndicalism of a leader of the Ku Klux Klan (an ironic contrast to the facts of *Whitney*, certainly). In *Brandenburg* the Court adopted the most speech-protective standard for subversive speech yet, holding that a State may not "forbid or proscribe advocacy of the use of force or of law violation except where such advocacy is directed to inciting or producing imminent lawless action and is likely to incite or produce such action."[69] In so holding, the Court once and for all overruled the majority opinion in *Whitney*. Interestingly, the *Brandenburg* majority never actually uses the language of "clear and present danger," and indeed the two concurring opinions explicitly repudiate that test (or at least the watered down version adopted by the *Dennis* plurality).[70] Moreover, most commentators agree that the *Brandenburg* standard, which of course remains the extant constitutional standard governing the protection of speech inciting unlawful action, is in fact not identical to the Holmes/Brandeis test but is rather *more* speech protective. Thus in some sense *Brandenburg* represents the beginning of the end of the ascendancy of the constitutional test shaped by Holmes and Brandeis. But in truth, especially given the distortion of that test by the *Dennis* Court, there seems little doubt that *Brandenburg* represents the doctrinal triumph of Brandeis's views as expressed in *Whitney*.

For all of its significance, however, focusing on the ascent of the clear and present danger test substantially understates the influence on First Amendment law of Brandeis's opinion in *Whitney*—especially because the clear and present danger test was, after all, originally and primarily the creation of Justice Holmes, not Brandeis. Where Brandeis's influence can truly and uniquely be felt is in the realm of ideas. The Brandeis concurrence in *Whitney* represents the first judicial enunciation of a comprehensive theoretical justification for why speech warrants protection, a justification which has become almost universally accepted, and which has had a profound influence on the development of modern First Amendment jurisprudence, and indeed on constitutional law more broadly.

It is today an axiom of constitutional jurisprudence that the separate opinions of Justices Holmes and Brandeis during the 1920s essentially created modern free speech law—an axiom which has been made into a truism by the fact that constitutional law casebooks typically begin their study of the First Amendment with the Holmes and Brandeis

---

[68] 395 U.S. 444 (1969) (per curiam).

[69] *Id.* at 447.

[70] *Id.* at 449–50 (Black, J., concurring); *id.* at 454 (Douglas, J., concurring).

opinions. In any event, there is no reason to doubt the enormous influence of Holmes and Brandeis. Moreover, the influence of the Holmes/Brandeis opinions has been felt at two levels: first, at the doctrinal level in the evolution of the clear and present danger test; but additionally, in the articulation (for essentially the first time in the judiciary) of a rationale—actually, rationales—for the constitutional protection of free speech. The statement and acceptance of these rationales has had at least as great, and probably a greater, influence on the development of free speech law as has the clear and present danger test. And in this area, Brandeis's influence has been enormous, and quite distinct from Holmes's.

The first, and to this day probably most famous judicial statement of a *theory* of the First Amendment was provided by Justice Holmes in his dissent in *Abrams v. United States*, where he seized upon the metaphor of the "marketplace of ideas."[71] Holmes argued (in typically eloquent fashion) that given the uncertainty inherent in political truth ("when men have realized that time has upset many fighting faiths"), the wisest course is to permit all viewpoints to be aired and to jockey for approval since "the best test of truth is the power of the thought to get itself accepted in the competition of the market." Only in the most grave emergencies does the Constitution permit that competitive process to be impeded by the suppression of speech. In *Abrams* Holmes thus provided an appealing and seemingly powerful explanation for *why* we should protect speech from state censorship, and therefore why the Supreme Court's failure to provide such protection ran contrary to the spirit of the Constitution.

Upon closer examination, however, Holmes's free speech theory turns out to be highly problematic, and not well calibrated to the actual shape of First Amendment law, or for that matter to history. For one thing, it is well accepted that despite the broad language of the First Amendment, not all speech is entitled to equally stringent constitutional protection, and in particular that *political* speech is entitled to special constitutional solicitude. Yet the concept of the marketplace of ideas does not seem to provide any particular reason why this should be so—after all, the search for truth is hardly peculiar to the political sphere. To the contrary, it might be argued that political ideas are especially ill-suited to being sorted in a competitive process. Competition among political ideologies tends to be sporadic, and most listeners approach political speech with sufficient pre-formed prejudices and emotional attachments that mere exposure to differing ideas is unlikely to change their hearts and minds. Thus even if one believes that in general (say, in the scientific arena) the airing and clash of ideas is likely to ultimately

---

[71] 250 U.S. 616, 630 (1919) (Holmes, J., dissenting). It should be noted that Holmes himself never used the specific language of a "marketplace of ideas," but the views he expressed in *Abrams* have since been (accurately) described as endorsing that concept.

expose the truth, one might doubt the validity of that assumption with respect to political ideas. Indeed, and this criticism goes to the very heart of the Holmes rationale, one might question whether the concept of political "truth" is in any sense a meaningful one. The conflicting ideologies at the heart of the cases Holmes was considering—pacifism versus patriotism, socialism versus capitalism—do not seem to lend themselves to a determination of "truth" at all. Rather, they seem to exist in the sphere of belief, and often quasi-religious belief at that. Even in the post-Cold War era it would be difficult to pronounce that capitalism is "true;" one could only insist that history has shown it to be more effective than communism at securing prosperity. Thus while Holmes's discussion might explain why constitutional protection is accorded to scientific speech, and perhaps commercial speech (though such speech did not secure constitutional protection until the 1970s), it provides very weak support for the protection of political speech, the very area in which the Holmes/Brandeis tradition was forged.

In addition to its internal flaws, a final, potentially serious criticism of Holmes stems from the fact that the marketplace of ideas has no clear historical provenance. There is little evidence that protecting the search for truth was the main goal of those who drafted and ratified the First Amendment. True, the framers were broadly familiar with John Milton's critique of press licensing, including Milton's argument that censorship operates "primely to the discouragement of all learning, and the stop of truth, not only by disexercising and blunting our abilities in what we know already, but by hindering and cropping the discovery that might be yet further made both in religious and civil wisdom."[72] Yet the free speech clause, like the rest of the Bill of Rights, was considered at the time of its drafting to be very much a political document involving political rights. Holmes's focus on competition was thus very much a reflection of his time and place. Holmes, it must be remembered, was a Boston Brahmin, born in 1841, who served in the Union Army during the Civil War. His was the generation most deeply influenced by Darwinism and evolutionary theory, as exemplified by the Social Darwinism which provided the basis for the dominant political and economic philosophy of that time. It is true that Holmes famously rejected the idea that the Constitution "enact[ed] Mr. Herbert Spencer's *Social Statics*,"[73] but his thinking, his First Amendment theory included, was nonetheless deeply, and inevitably, influenced by the intellectual climate in which he came of age.[74]

---

[72] John Milton, *Aeropagitica* 48 (J.C. Suffolk ed., Univ. Tutorial Press, Ltd. 1968) (1644).

[73] *Lochner v. New York*, 198 U.S. 45, 75 (1905) (Holmes, J., dissenting).

[74] *See generally* Louis Menand, *The Metaphysical Club* (2001); Rabban, *supra* note 4, at 356.

It is here that the differences between Holmes and Brandeis become critical. While the two men were colleagues and ideological allies on the Court, and often voted together, Brandeis's intellectual roots and political sympathies were very different, and decidedly more *modern*, than those of Holmes, although he was only fifteen years younger than Holmes. Brandeis was the child of German Jewish immigrants, and the first Jewish member of the Supreme Court. As a leading lawyer in the Progressive movement and a pioneer in developing what came to be called the "Brandeis brief" (as well as a close advisor to President Wilson), politically Brandeis, unlike Holmes, was both active and very much an activist. At bottom, the contrast between Holmes and Brandeis might be stated as that between a pessimistic intellectual and an optimistic believer. Unsurprisingly, Holmes and Brandeis's First Amendment theories reflect these differences.

As noted above, for Brandeis the importance of free speech centered on democracy and history. It was, however, an idealized and romanticized version of both. Brandeis's vision of democracy is not the battle of warring interest groups which so dominates modern thinking, nor is it the cynicism of Holmes. Rather, it is a heartfelt belief in populism and popular participation in the governmental process as the path to a free and stable society, and public *deliberation* as a critical component of that participation. Moreover, the justification for public participation and deliberation was not merely instrumental. It flowed from Brandeis's commitment as a Progressive to the idea that the People, not elected politicians, rule in our system of government. (It should be remembered that among the political reforms championed by the Progressives were direct democracy in the form of citizen initiatives and the direct election of Senators.) Free speech was an essential element of Brandeis's vision: how can the People rule if they cannot meaningfully deliberate amongst themselves? In short, in *Whitney v. California*, Brandeis reintroduced into constitutional law the concept of popular sovereignty,[75] the principle that the American Revolution 150 years before had made central to American political ideology.[76] The commitment to popular sovereignty that pervades Brandeis's philosophy of free speech is a Romantic commitment, far removed from the dirty details of daily politics, but it is a commitment that resonates deeply with the modern psyche, in a way that the cold rationality of Social Darwinism does not. It is for that reason that Brandeis's understanding of why free speech matters, and is worthy of special constitutional protection, has become so widely accept-

---

[75] *See* White, *supra* note 5, at 324–25 (Brandeis's *Whitney* opinion marked "the first impressive appearance of the self-governance rationale in First Amendment theory.").

[76] *See generally* Gordon S. Wood, *The Creation of the American Republic*, 1776–1787 (1969).

ed in the decades since *Whitney*, and why it has had such a profound impact on constitutional law.

Like his democratic theory, Brandeis's view of history as expressed in *Whitney* is undoubtedly, in the words of Robert Bork, "highly romanticized."[77] It must be understood, however, that Brandeis did not attempt in the *Whitney* opinion to recreate any specific "Intent of the Framers" of the First Amendment, nor indeed did he suggest that such a narrowly defined intent, even in the unlikely event that it could be identified, was relevant to constitutional interpretation. Rather, Brandeis was expounding a political theory, and arguing that this theory was both a product of the views of the revolutionary generation, and the proper cornerstone of modern First Amendment law. Bork's famous extended attack on Brandeis (and to a lesser degree on Holmes), through a bit of selective quotation—including notably excluding from the quoted portions of Brandeis's opinion the discussion of the dangers of an inert people[78]—ignores this point entirely. Instead, Bork mistakes theory for "rhetorical flourishes" and attributes to Brandeis a theory of free speech which has little to do with the democratic core of Brandeis's reasoning.[79] Bork then criticizes Brandeis for adopting an approach to the First Amendment which intrudes on the proper prerogatives of elected legislatures. In fact, however, Brandeis's faith in popular sovereignty and participatory democracy, as well as the connection he draws between these ideas and free speech, provide a convincing account of why legislative majorities—who are after all mere agents of the sovereign people—must be denied the power to control popular discourse about government and its purposes. Moreover, Bork's insistence that the *Gitlow* and *Whitney* majorities were correct to exclude advocating the forcible overthrow of the government from First Amendment protection[80] misses the point that this was *precisely* the form of speech in which the revolutionary generation engaged. Indeed, the right to engage in such speech seems to follow inevitably from the premise that the *People* (not the established government) enjoy ultimate sovereignty, and that all governmental forms gain their legitimacy only from the continued assent of the governed. To deny this truth is to close one's eyes to the full implications of the American Revolution.

It is precisely for the reasons that Bork's critique of Brandeis fails that Brandeis's views have so profoundly affected development of mod-

---

[77] Robert H. Bork, *Neutral Principles and Some First Amendment Problems*, 47 Ind. L.J. 1, 24 (1971).

[78] *Id.*

[79] *Id.* at 24–25 (identifying four benefits that Brandeis allegedly claims derive from free speech, none of which are related to free speech's contribution to self government).

[80] *Id.* at 29–32.

ern First Amendment law. Professor Vincent Blasi has traced the impact of Brandeis's *ideas* on crucial First Amendment opinions from Justice Douglas's dissent in the *Dennis* case to Justice Brennan's majority opinion in *New York Times v. Sullivan* to Justice Harlan's opinion for the Court in *Cohen v. California*.[81] In *Sullivan* and *Cohen*, in particular, the Court drew explicitly on the Brandeisian faith in self-governance in striking down governmental suppression (whether through the creation of civil liability or through criminal prosecution) of political speech which might otherwise have been thought to be socially harmful. Other examples of Brandeis's influence abound, including several decisions which, like *Dennis*, date from the McCarthy era. For example, in *Wilkinson v. United States*, Justice Black, dissenting from yet another prosecution of an alleged Communist, cited Brandeis in making the point that political persecution of the sort practiced under McCarthyism is inconsistent with democratic self-government.[82] In addition, Justice Douglas, concurring in *Gibson v. Florida Legislative Investigation Committee*, cited Brandeis in explaining why the State of Florida's investigation (during the Civil Rights era) of possible Communist infiltration of the NAACP violated the First Amendment because it intruded on the power of citizens to associate and disseminate ideas.[83]

More recently, in its leading case involving campaign finance legislation, *Buckley v. Valeo*, the Court cited Brandeis for the proposition that the First Amendment above all protects public discussion of political issues, and therefore restrictions on political candidates' speech must be viewed with extreme suspicion.[84] Similarly, both a concurring and a dissenting opinion in the Court's decision in *Nixon v. Shrink Missouri Government PAC*, in which the Court upheld a state statute limiting campaign contributions to political candidates, cite Brandeis's *Whitney* opinion for the proposition that the First Amendment protects speech in order to safeguard and cultivate the political process—though of course they reach polar opposite conclusions regarding the implications of that insight for regulations of the political process.[85]

Nor has the *Whitney* concurrence been cited only in cases with directly political stakes. For example, in *Turner Broadcasting System v. FCC*, a case arising in the modern context of the electronic mass media,

---

[81] Blasi, *supra* note 2, at 683 (discussing *Dennis*; *New York Times v. Sullivan*, 376 U.S. 254 (1964); and *Cohen v. California*, 403 U.S. 15 (1971)).

[82] 365 U.S. 399, 421–23 & n.11 (1961) (Black, J., dissenting).

[83] 372 U.S. 539, 575–76 & n.12 (1963) (Douglas, J., concurring).

[84] 424 U.S. 1, 53 (1976).

[85] 528 U.S. 377, 401 (2000) (Breyer, J., concurring); *id.* at 410–11 (Thomas, J., dissenting).

Justice Breyer defended a regulation of cable television operators which was designed to increase the diversity of voices heard on the media by again citing Brandeis to make the point that diverse speech better enhances the democratic-participation values undergirding the First Amendment than does a *laissez faire* regulatory philosophy which turns a blind eye to media concentration.[86] In *Bartnicki v. Vopper*, Justice Stevens invoked Brandeis and *Whitney* to support a ruling that the press may not be punished for disseminating information on matters "of public concern," even if that information had been illegally obtained by a third party.[87] And dissenting in *Morse v. Frederick*, Justice Stevens again relied on *Whitney* to object to the majority's conclusion that there was a sufficiently serious state interest in discouraging "pro-drug" speech to warrant disciplining a public high school student who displayed the somewhat Delphic banner proclaiming "BONG HiTS 4 JESUS" at a school event celebrating the Olympic Torch Relay, because the impact of such actions would be to stifle public debate on an important political issue.[88]

In short, it is impossible to imagine modern First Amendment law possessing the breadth and shape that it does without the influence of the ideas expressed in Justice Brandeis's concurring opinion in *Whitney v. California*. The modern focus on political speech as the central component of the First Amendment; the strong protection accorded by the modern Court to the speech of political dissenters; and the nearly universal acceptance in this country of the desirability of granting broad protection for speech all owe their existence to the association first drawn by Brandeis between speech and democracy, in a way that the marketplace-of-ideas rationale could not have matched. The practical impact of these developments is also immense. Without the influence of Brandeis on modern First Amendment jurisprudence, for example, the free speech cases of the Civil Rights and the Vietnam War era might well have turned out quite differently. Would the result in the Pentagon Papers case,[89] for example, have been reached without a free speech jurisprudence rooted in a theory of democratic self-governance? Similarly, would the civil rights protestors in *Edwards v. South Carolina*[90] have escaped prosecution without the protection of a Brandeisian First Amendment? Could the modern ballot access cases such as *Anderson v.*

---

[86] 520 U.S. 180, 226–27 (1997) (Breyer, J., concurring).

[87] 532 U.S. 514, 535 (2001).

[88] 127 S.Ct. 2618, 2445–46, 2651 (2007) (Stevens, J., dissenting).

[89] *New York Times v. United States*, 403 U.S. 713 (1971).

[90] 372 U.S. 229 (1963).

Celebrezze[91] have existed without a tie between popular democracy and free speech? There can of course be no definitive response to these questions, but one suspects that at least in some instances the most reasonable answer is "no." And if that is so, then Justice Brandeis's opinion in *Whitney* did not merely reshape First Amendment law; it helped mold the very society in which we live.

Aftermath: Whitney *and Radicalism*

Anita Whitney's collision with the California Syndicalism Act by no means ended her brushes with the law or her political activism. She experienced several legal difficulties during the decade following her pardon, including a conviction in the 1930s for allegedly falsifying attesting signatures to an election petition on behalf of the Communist Party, for which she avoided jail time only because her nephew chose to pay her $600 fine.[92] In 1934 Whitney ran for State Treasurer on the Communist Party ticket and earned 100,000 votes—a sufficient number to secure the party's position on the ballot.[93] She repeated that performance running for State Comptroller in 1938, and then for the United States Senate in 1940. Whitney also served as state chair of the Communist Party from 1936 to 1944, and during the later years of this period served as a member of the party's national committee.[94] In addition to her electoral activities, throughout the period from the late 1920s through the 1940s Whitney also supported various organizations (including the famous Brotherhood of Sleeping Car Porters) active in anti-segregation/civil rights causes and worked on behalf of farm workers in central California, many of whom were racial minorities—all at a time when civil rights issues were almost entirely ignored by the mainstream of American politics.[95] Whitney's life remained to its end an exemplar of the sort of active, participatory citizen of a democracy which Justice Brandeis extolled in the Supreme Court case bearing her name.

When Whitney ran for the Senate in 1940, she was already seventy-three years old. Yet by all reports she remained extremely active in the Communist Party, and willing to fight for her beliefs through activities such as picketing, leafletting, and public speaking, for many years afterward. Anita Whitney finally died in February of 1955, at the age of

---

[91] 460 U.S. 780 (1983).

[92] *Nephew Saves Anita Whitney from Jail Cell: Pays $600 Fine After She Elects to Serve 300–Day Term*, San Francisco Chronicle, Dec. 6, 1935.

[93] *See* Richmond, *supra* note 10, at 167–68.

[94] *Id.* at 171–72; *see also* Rubens, *supra* note 10, at 166–67.

[95] Rubens, *supra* note 10, at 165–66, 170; Richmond, *supra* note 10, at 142–45.

87.[96] By the time of her death the United States was living through another, even more virulent, period of persecution of Communists and other radicals, now under the aegis of McCarthyism. For her part, Whitney probably escaped prosecution only because of her advanced age. As during the Red Scare, once again the Supreme Court spectacularly failed to enforce the First Amendment to stem this tide—most notably, ironically, in the *Dennis* case in which the Court purportedly overruled *Whitney v. California* and adopted the approach of the Brandeis concurrence.[97] Today, of course, the *Dennis* Court's "balancing" version of the clear and present danger test has been replaced by the even more speech-protective rule of *Brandenburg v. Ohio*. One wonders nonetheless if Anita Whitney would have felt that she and her political kin were finally safe from political pogroms.

---

[96] *Anita Whitney, Socialite Red, Dead*, San Francisco Chronicle, February 5, 1955.

[97] *See supra* nn. 66–67 and accompanying text.

12

Vincent Blasi and Seana V. Shiffrin*

The Story of *West Virginia State Board of Education v. Barnette*: The Pledge of Allegiance and the Freedom of Thought

"The case is made difficult not because the principles of its decision are obscure but because the flag involved is our own." With this confident declaration, the Supreme Court in *West Virginia State Board of Education v. Barnette* ruled that "no official, high or petty" possesses the authority to require any student to pledge allegiance to the flag of the United States.[1] That judgment, handed down in June of 1943 as American troops were engaged in combat in North Africa and the South Pacific, overruled a Court decision rendered only three years before. *Minersville School District v. Gobitis* had held that a student's religious scruples against flag worship did not furnish the basis for a constitutional right to be exempted from a requirement to recite the pledge of allegiance.[2]

The Court's odyssey from *Gobitis* to *Barnette* rewards study on several levels. Seldom in its history has a constitutional controversy generated such antipathy within the Court, such widespread civic violence directly attributable to a judicial decision, such anticipatory public recanting by individual justices, such a daring switch of rationale, such

* The authors are grateful to Benjamin P. Liu and Gabriel Shapiro for extraordinary research assistance, and to Robert Amdur, Barbara Herman, Kenneth Karst, Subha Narasimhan, and Steven Shiffrin for excellent advice.

[1] *West Va. State Bd. of Educ. v. Barnette*, 319 U.S. 624, 641–42 (1943).

[2] *Minersville Sch. Dist. v. Gobitis*, 310 U.S. 586 (1940).

memorable and pointed prose in a majority opinion, and such persistent uncertainty regarding the grounds and limits of decision. Seldom has a case outcome seemed so obviously correct as that in *Barnette* and yet so difficult to justify.

History

The controversy over the pledge of allegiance represented a clash between two relatively small but intense segments of the American public: the Jehovah's Witnesses and a congeries of private patriotic groups including the American Legion, the Veterans of Foreign Wars, and the Daughters of the American Revolution. The strength and fervor of their respective beliefs regarding the flag and the requirements of allegiance generated a bitter conflict of enduring constitutional significance.

The pledge of allegiance was written in two hours[3] by Francis Bellamy in 1892, a man variously described as a children's author, a socialist trade unionist, a nationalist, a minister, a muckraker, and a huckster.[4] Bellamy wrote it for the *Youth's Companion* as part of a national effort to celebrate the quadricentennial of Columbus's voyage. In part, Bellamy hoped to evoke the sense of an "indivisible" union that had survived the Civil War.[5]

The first state statute providing for a flag salute ceremony in the public schools was passed in New York in 1898, the day after the

---

[3] Cecilia Elizabeth O'Leary, *To Die For: The Paradox of American Patriotism* 161–62 (1999).

[4] *See e.g.*, *id.* at 157–8; John W. Baer, *The Pledge of Allegiance: A Centennial History, 1892–1992* (1992), *available at* http://history.vineyard.net/pledge.htm. The last, unflattering characterization derives from the recent description of his descendant who claims that the pledge was written as part of an extended advertising campaign to increase flag sales. *See* Michael Bellamy, *The Last Page*, Dissent, Summer 2002, at 112.

[5] O'Leary, *supra* note 3, at 161. Bellamy flirted with including references to equality and fraternity in the pledge but decided these ideas were too progressive for the American public. "Liberty and justice for all" had ecumenical appeal and could serve both socialists and individualists. *Id. See also* Baer, *supra* note 4, *passim.*

During the Civil Rights Era, efforts were made to alter the pledge to include references to equality. In 1959, Rep. Charles Diggs of Michigan, a Legionnaire and the founder of the Congressional Black Caucus, introduced a joint resolution to amend the pledge so that the final clause read "liberty, equality, and justice for all." *See* H.R.J. Res. 400, 86th Cong. (1959); *see also* H.R.J. Res. 351, 87th Cong. (1961); H.R.J. Res. 386, 88th Cong. (1963). Similar resolutions were introduced by Representative Fulton of Pennsylvania. H.R.J. Res. 532, 86th Cong. (1959); H.R.J. Res. 835, 87th Cong. (1962); H.R.J. Res. 668, 88th Cong. (1963) (suggesting the language: "liberty, equality of opportunity and equal justice under law for all.").

commencement of the Spanish–American War.[6] In the aftermath of World War I, newly created veterans' organizations such as the American Legion and the Veterans of Foreign Wars took up the cause of promoting respect for the flag.[7] The Legion lobbied for state laws requiring that the flag be flown over public buildings, including schools, and that teachers devote at least ten minutes of each school day to patriotic exercises to foster "one hundred percent Americanism." It established a National Americanism Commission, which drafted a flag code in 1923 that was distributed to schoolchildren nationwide.[8] By 1940, the year of the *Gobitis* decision, nine states had laws requiring that flag salute exercises be held in the public schools and another eighteen had statutory provisions for teaching about the flag. Even in states without specific flag laws, the practice of having students pledge allegiance to the flag was widespread.[9]

Although federal officials had long encouraged its recitation, the pledge of allegiance was not officially adopted by the federal government until 1942, well after the *Barnette* litigation was underway. The federal statute of that year in essence enacted into law the American Legion's flag code. The law was unusual in that it deliberately lacked an enforcement mechanism.[10] It aimed to codify and establish national customs of respect for the flag.[11] No federal law directs that students must recite the pledge of allegiance in school, nor for that matter does any federal law require the recitation of the pledge by any civilian at any other venue.[12]

---

[6] David R. Manwaring, *Render Unto Caesar: The Flag Salute Controversy* 3 (1962).

[7] Peter Irons, *The Courage of Their Convictions* 16 (1988). The Ku Klux Klan was also active in flag-respect campaigns, using its involvement, in part, to represent itself as a mainstream organization. Manwaring, *supra* note 6, at 7.

[8] *Id*. at 6.

[9] *Id*. at 4–5.

[10] For one discussion of this feature, see *To Codify Rules on the Use of the Flag of the United States of America: Hearings on H.J. Res. 288 Before the Subcomm. Of the Comm. On the Judiciary*, 77th Cong. 7–9 (1942) (remarks of Representative Hobbs, Representative Hancock, Representative McLaughlin, and Francis Sullivan, Acting Director of the National Legislative Commission of the American Legion). The Representatives emphasize that the statute is "recommendatory material," and that codification serves citizens by providing a clear guideline for those who wish to show respect for the flag in a standard, customary way. The Legionnaire remarks that penalties are unnecessary, but that the intent is that "if the average person reads that it is an enactment of Congress, he will realize then that it is an official rule and that it should be obeyed...."

[11] It was also unusual in that its literal terms empowered the President (in his capacity as Commander in Chief of the armed forces) to alter, unilaterally and without Congressional approval, the terms of the custom as necessary. Joint Resolution of June 22, 1942, Pub. L. No. 623, § 8, 56 Stat. 377, 380 (current version at 4 U.S.C. § 10 (2000)).

[12] To become a naturalized citizen, a person must take an oath to, among other things, "bear true faith and allegiance" to the Constitution and laws of the United States. 8 U.S.C.

Legal requirements that school children recite the pledge arise entirely from state and local law.[13]

The pledge of allegiance at issue in *Barnette* and *Gobitis* differed from the pledge's contemporary format in that it made no explicit reference to God.[14] Nonetheless, the primary grievance of the Gobitases,[15]

---

§ 1448(a)(4). In the case of *In re* Petition of Battle, 379 F.Supp. 334 (E.D. N.Y. 1974), a Jehovah's Witness who was prepared to swear true faith and allegiance but with the caveat that he could not vote, serve on a jury, or salute the flag was held nevertheless to satisfy this requirement. Other decisions have ruled, with one exception, that Witnesses who refused as a matter of principle to exercise the franchise or discharge jury duty could not be denied naturalization on that account. *Compare In re Pisciattano*, 308 F.Supp. 818 (D. Conn. 1970); *In re Naturalization of Del Olmo*, 682 F.Supp. 489 (D. Or. 1988) *with In re Petition for Naturalization of Matz*, 296 F.Supp. 927 (E.D. Cal. 1969).

[13] Nearly every state has a provision in its code for patriotic exercises in the classroom that includes the opportunity or a requirement to recite the pledge of allegiance. *But see* Colo. Rev. Stat. § 22–1–106 (1989) (merely directing that teachers may teach students how to salute the flag when passing in parade, proper respect of the flag, and proper use of the flag in decoration and display); Ohio Rev. Code Ann. § 3313.602 (West 1997) (directing school boards to adopt a policy specifying whether or not the pledge will be part of the school program). Some states also have their own, often colorful, pledges of allegiance to the state flag. Michigan's rhymes: "I pledge allegiance to the flag of Michigan, and to the state for which it stands, 2 beautiful peninsulas united by a bridge of steel, where equal opportunity and justice to all is our ideal." Mich. Comp. Laws § 2.29 (1967). South Dakota's is aspirational: "I pledge loyalty and support to the flag and state of South Dakota, land of sunshine, land of infinite variety." S.D. Codified Laws § 1–6–4.1 (Michie 1992). New Mexico's is officially bilingual: "Saludo la bandera del estado de Nuevo Mejico, el simbolo zia de amistad perfecta, entre culturas unidas"; "I salute the flag of the state of New Mexico, the Zia symbol of perfect friendship among united cultures." N.M. Stat. Ann. §§ 12–3–7, 12–3–3 (Michie 1978). South Carolina's requires more than allegiance: "I salute the flag of South Carolina and pledge to the Palmetto State love, loyalty and faith." S.C. Code Ann. § 1–1–670 (Law. Co-op. 1977). Others refer, directly or indirectly, to God. *See e.g.* Kentucky's salute: K.R.S. § 2.035 "I pledge allegiance to the Kentucky flag, and to the Sovereign State for which it stands, one Commonwealth, blessed with diversity, natural wealth, beauty, and grace from on High,"; *See also* Lousiana, LA. Rev.Stat. 49.1 167; Mississippi, Miss. Code Ann. § 37–13–7.

[14] In 1942, the pledge of allegiance read "I pledge allegiance to the flag of the United States of America, and to the Republic for which it stands, one Nation indivisible, with liberty and justice for all." Joint Resolution of Dec. 22, 1942, Pub. L. No. 829, § 7, 56 Stat. 1074, 1077. The 1942 version also differs from the original wording. The original version pledged allegiance to "my flag." Concerns about the referent of this phrase when uttered by aliens prompted the substitution of "the flag of the United States of America." During the *Gobitis* litigation and at the start of the *Barnette* litigation, when reciting the pledge, one began with one's right hand over one's heart but then at "my flag" extended one's arm out toward the flag, palm turned up, for the remainder of the pledge. This too closely resembled the posture of the Nazi salute and was altered in December 1942. *Compare* § 7, 56 Stat. at 380 with § 7, 56 Stat. at 1077. The addition of "under God" after "one nation" did not happen until 1954. *See infra* text accompanying notes 153–62.

[15] Due to a clerk's error, although the family name is Gobitas, the parties' name in the case came to be known as "Gobitis." Shawn Francis Peters, *Judging Jehovah's Witnesses:*

the Barnetts, and the Jehovah's Witnesses generally was that the requirement to recite the pledge impaired their free exercise of religion. They objected that the salute represented a pledge of loyalty to a flag. In their view, were they to make such a pledge, even under legal compulsion, they would contravene the biblical requirement against serving other gods or graven images and violate their duty of supreme loyalty to God. They were willing instead to utter a pledge of allegiance that asserted ultimate loyalty to God, allegiance to all U.S. laws consistent with biblical law, and respect for the flag as a symbol of universal freedom and justice.[16]

Protests against flag salute requirements did not originate with the Jehovah's Witnesses. In 1916, in an episode that became famous in Chicago, an eleven-year-old African–American student named Hubert Eaves refused to salute the flag because of its association with racial discrimination and lynching.[17] Members of other sects, beginning with the Mennonites in 1918, refused to salute the flag for religious reasons.[18] Only when the issue became salient to the Jehovah's Witnesses, however, did this act of conscience evolve into a full-scale protest movement supported by constitutional litigation.

The Jehovah's Witnesses were established in 1870 in Pennsylvania. By 1938 the sect had over 28,000 active members within the United States and 72,000 internationally. Over the next five years, domestic membership tripled and international membership doubled. The Witnesses read the Bible as forecasting the imminent destruction of our world in a battle between Christ and Satan in which Christ will save only true, observant believers. While they do not believe in hell, they do believe that the faithful will be saved from annihilation and will enjoy resurrection and "everlasting life." Around 1914, Witness leaders began to advocate proselytizing by each and every member to convert sinners into true believers in preparation for the coming Armageddon. All Jehovah's Witnesses are regarded as ordained ministers with a duty to present every person with the choice to side with God or against him. This duty propelled members of the sect to engage en masse in boisterous forms of public address and dogged person-to-person and door-to-door efforts to deliver their message. At the time of the flag salute

---

Religious Persecution and the Dawn of the Rights Revolution 38 (2000). Apparently, the Barnett name was also victim to clerical error and became "Barnette" in court documents. Manwaring, *supra* note 6, at 303 n.14.

[16] Brief for Appellees at 8–9, *West Va. State Bd. of Educ. v. Barnette*, 319 U.S. 624 (1943) (No. 591).

[17] Eaves was arrested but the charges were dismissed at trial. O'Leary, *supra* note 3, at 231.

[18] *See* Manwaring, *supra* note 6, at 11–15.

controversy, their teachings included the view that all worldly organizations, including the United States government, were instruments of Satan.[19] Witnesses were instructed to obey the law so long as it did not conflict with their religious duties, but to regard the state as a temporary and spiritually corrupt entity of human design. Although the Witnesses had contempt for all other religious organizations, their leader described the Catholic Church as "the chief visible enemy of God, and therefore the greatest and worst public enemy."[20] These unusual beliefs, along with their proselytizing, gave this small group a high and controversial profile.

The leader of the group from 1916 to 1942, "Judge" Joseph Rutherford, had practiced law for sixteen years, including serving as counsel to the sect's founder, Charles Taze Russell. Rutherford was an energetic and confrontational leader who transformed the Witnesses into a sect given to relentless and sometimes intrusive mass proselytizing. During World War I, he served prison time under the Espionage Act for criticizing American entry into the war and urging all Witnesses to claim draft exemptions both as conscientious objectors and ordained ministers.[21] Rutherford was a pioneer in using the radio to organize religious proselytizing and protest.

Witness resistance to the pledge of allegiance first emerged at the grass roots level, possibly sparked by sympathy for the plight of co-religionists in Germany who were being persecuted for refusing to deliver the Nazi salute.[22] On September 30, 1935, Carleton Nicholls, a Jehovah's Witness, remained seated and refused to salute the flag during the opening exercises of his third grade class in Lynn, Massachusetts, announcing that he would not pay tribute "to the Devil's emblem." As a result, he was expelled from school.[23] Rutherford praised the boy in his weekly radio address and encouraged all Witnesses to follow Nicholls's example. In response, Jehovah's Witnesses all over the nation began refusing to salute the flag. Within one year of Rutherford's October 6,

---

[19] Manwaring, *supra* note 6, at 29; M. James Penton, *Apocalypse Delayed: The Story of Jehovah's Witnesses* 138–39 (2d ed. 1997).

[20] Manwaring, *supra* note 6, at 24 (quoting Joseph F. Rutherford, Enemies 328 (1937)).

[21] Thousands of Jehovah's Witnesses were incarcerated for resisting the draft and constituted a hefty proportion of those jailed for draft resistance from World War I through the Vietnam War. Penton, *supra* note 19, at 142.

[22] *See infra* note 47.

[23] Nicholls's father and a friend, who had accompanied the boy to school that day to support his protest, were arrested for disturbing a public meeting. The friend was Edward H. James, a nephew of the novelist Henry James and philosopher William James. *See* Peters, *supra* note 15, at 165–66.

1935 radio address, some 120 Witnesses were expelled from school for not participating in flag ceremonies.

Gobitis

The week after Rutherford's radio address, two Witnesses, twelve-year-old Lillian Gobitas and her ten-year-old brother William, stopped saluting the flag, prompting their expulsion from the Minersville, Pennsylvania school system. After fruitless efforts to achieve an administrative resolution, the students and their parents, supported by lawyers supplied by Rutherford as well as the American Civil Liberties Union, sued to enjoin the school board.

In the interim, the Gobitas children participated in home schooling. They were warned, however, that unless they attended a "qualified school" they would be sent to a reformatory. By removing the wall between their living and dining rooms, Witnesses Paul and Verna Jones created a cramped classroom in their home for all the Witness children in the region who faced a similar predicament. Two hour bus rides in a converted delivery truck were necessary for some of these students to reach their makeshift school.[24]

The federal district court[25] enjoined the Minersville School District from expelling the students or requiring them to participate in the flag ceremony and the Third Circuit Court of Appeals affirmed the decision.[26] With the financial backing of the American Legion and other patriotic societies, the school district appealed the case to the United States Supreme Court.[27] Both parties litigated the case with emphasis on the question whether the flag ceremony has religious significance. The school district contended that "[t]he act of saluting the flag has no bearing on what a pupil may think of his Creator or what are his relations to his Creator.... Like the study of history or civics ... the salute has no religious implications."[28] On this point, the Gobitas brief joined issue with gusto: "The saluting of the flag of any earthly govern-

---

[24] See Irons, *supra* note 7, at 27–28.

[25] *Gobitis v. Minersville Sch. Dist.*, 24 F.Supp. 271 (E.D. Pa. 1938).

[26] *Minersville Sch. Dist. v. Gobitis*, 108 F.2d 683 (3d. Cir. 1939).

[27] See Manwaring, *supra* note 6, at 116. The Gobitases' legal position was supported by amicus briefs from both the ACLU and the newly established Committee on the Bill of Rights of the American Bar Association. Irving Dilliard, *The Flag–Salute Cases*, in John A. Garraty, ed., *Quarrels that Have Shaped the Constitution* 285, 291–93 (rev. ed. 1987).

[28] *Minersville Sch. Dist. v. Gobitis*, 310 U.S. 586, 588 (1940) (argument for petitioners).

ment by a person who has covenanted to do the will of God is a form of religion and constitutes idolatry."[29]

In an opinion by then-recently-appointed Justice Felix Frankfurter, the Supreme Court reversed the courts below and vacated the injunction. In holding that the Witnesses could be compelled to salute the flag on pain of expulsion from school, the majority declined to decide whether the duty to pledge allegiance to a secular symbol amounts to a religious burden of First Amendment import. Instead, Justice Frankfurter seized the occasion to write into law two basic principles with resonance far beyond the immediate controversy.

The first principle was that general laws passed for secular purposes and enforced evenhandedly are never unconstitutional for failure to provide religious exemptions. Far from acknowledging a need to spare children from conflicts between school requirements and their religious duties as perceived by their parents, Frankfurter suggested that the schools might properly attempt to "awaken in the child's mind considerations as to the significance of the flag contrary to those implanted by the parent."[30]

The second principle underlying the *Gobitis* holding was that disputes over the meaning of religious liberty or the freedom of speech do not provide exceptions to the obligation of courts in constitutional cases to uphold the laws and practices of politically accountable branches of government "[e]xcept where the transgression of constitutional liberty is too plain for argument."[31] This principle received the most elaboration in Justice Frankfurter's opinion.

Justice Frankfurter explicitly sought to reject and refute the argument for a form of robust judicial review in cases involving civil liberties that had been introduced the previous term by Justice Harlan Fiske Stone in the now-famous footnote four of his majority opinion in *United States v. Carolene Products*.[32] An amicus brief filed in *Gobitis* by the Committee on the Bill of Rights of the American Bar Association had urged the Court to apply Justice Stone's *Carolene Products* theory to the case at hand.[33] It is noteworthy that among the several distinguished

---

[29] *Id.* at 590 (argument for respondents).

[30] *Gobitis,* 310 U.S. at 599.

[31] *Id.*

[32] 304 U.S. 144, 152 n.4 (1938). There, while articulating a general posture of deference to legislative judgment, Justice Stone suggested the propriety of "a more exacting judicial inquiry" in cases "when legislation appears on its face to be within a specific prohibition of the Constitution," or "restricts those political processes which can ordinarily be expected to bring about repeal of undesirable legislation," or involves such "prejudice against discrete and insular minorities" that the full and fair access of those groups to remedial political processes is questionable. *Id.*

[33] 1940 WL 47062. See also Manwaring, *supra* note 6, at 128; Donald L. Smith, *Zechariah Chafee, Jr.: Defender of Liberty and Law* 203–04 (1986).

lawyers who worked on that brief were Harvard law professor Zechariah Chafee, Jr.,[34] the legendary scholar of free speech, and Louis Lusky, subsequently a Columbia law professor, who had served as a law clerk for Justice Stone during the year he wrote his *Carolene Products* opinion.[35] Interestingly, despite Professor Chafee's prominent hand in the project,[36] the ABA brief contained no contention that the Freedom of Speech Clause of the First Amendment provided a basis for immunizing the Witness children from the obligation to recite the pledge; the brief advanced only claims grounded in the free exercise of religion and substantive due process.[37]

In private correspondence with Justice Stone, Justice Frankfurter characterized the *Gobitis* case as tragic. It represented, he thought, a foolish effort to extract respect for a symbol from religious recalcitrants. Frankfurter emphasized, however, that the responsibility to correct the folly lay with the legislature. Upholding the constitutionality of the requirement and leaving the issue to state legislatures would, he believed, put into practice the "true democratic faith of not relying on the Court for the impossible task of assuring a vigorous, mature, self-protecting and tolerant democracy."[38]

What is most striking about the *Gobitis* decision is the level of generality at which the Court engaged the issues presented. The majority opinion made little effort to assess either the Witnesses' burden or the government's efficiency interest in avoiding exemptions. For Justice Frankfurter, who emigrated from Austria to the United States when he was twelve years old and unable to speak English, the case was all about national identity and patriotic assimilation, matters so fundamental as to dwarf considerations of distinctive injury or incremental efficacy:

> The ultimate foundation of a free society is the binding tie of cohesive sentiment. Such a sentiment is fostered by all those agencies of the mind and spirit which may serve to gather up the traditions of a people, transmit them from generation to generation, and thereby create that continuity of a treasured common life which

---

[34] Smith, *supra* note 33, at 202–03.

[35] *Id.* at 202; Manwaring, *supra* note 6, at 126.

[36] Smith, *supra* note 33, at 202–04.

[37] Manwaring, *supra* note 6, at 126–31. Professor Chafee's brief did, however, cite some free speech cases in support of its *Carolene Products* contention that robust judicial review for the Witnesses' free exercise claims was warranted due to the structural barriers that made political relief most unlikely. 1940 WL 47062 at *20 (citing *Stromberg v. California*, 283 U.S. 359, 369–370 (1931) and *Lowell v. Griffin* 303 U.S. 444, 452 (1938)).

[38] Dilliard, *supra* note 27, at 295 (quoting Letter from Justice Frankfurter to Justice Stone (May 27, 1940), *in* Alpheus Thomas Mason, *Security Through Freedom: American Political Thought And Practice* 217 (1955)).

constitutes a civilization. "We live by symbols." The flag is the symbol of our national unity, transcending all internal differences, however large, within the framework of the Constitution.[39]

The decision in *Gobitis* was by a vote of eight to one. Justices Black and Douglas joined the Frankfurter majority opinion.[40] Justice Stone was the lone dissenter.[41]

Stone's dissenting opinion is best considered an extension of his effort the year before in the *Carolene Products* case to mark out a sphere of constitutional controversy in which an independent judiciary has a major role to play. Stone was obviously troubled by what he took to be the Minersville School District's categorical disregard for the Witnesses' religious sensibilities. "[W]here governmental functions . . . conflict with specific constitutional restrictions, there must . . . be reasonable accommodation between them so as to preserve the essentials of both. . . . [C]ompelling the pupil to affirm that which he does not believe," was not a reasonable accommodation given the pedagogic alternatives available to the state "to inspire patriotism and love of country."[42] "The Constitution expresses more than the conviction of the people that democratic processes must be preserved at all costs."[43] Majoritarian institutions cannot always be counted on to respect the "freedom of mind and

---

[39] 310 U.S. at 596.

[40] Roger K. Newman, author of the most detailed biography of Justice Black, offers the following explanation for Black's surprising vote:

> Stone circulated a powerful dissent on the day before the conference at which Frankfurter's opinion was approved. Black did not know about Stone's plans. A majority of the Court, he later said, might have bolted from Frankfurter's opinion after reading Stone's dissent—the rush of work at the term's close prevented the justices' looking at the dissent until after the opinion came down—but Black, Douglas, and Murphy found Frankfurter's argument so moving they had assured him they would support him and were loath to break their word. Immediately, "we knew we were wrong," Black told an obituary writer in 1967, but "we didn't have time to change our opinions. We met around the swimming pool at Murphy's hotel and decided to do so as soon as we could." At once they notified Stone that they would stand with him at the first opportunity. Over a half century later, Black's excuse still sounds lame. . . . Unmentioned in all his (and Douglas's) rationalizations are the forcefulness of [Chief Justice] Hughes's statement at conference and that no justice wished to change his position to vote against Hughes.

Roger K. Newman, *Hugo Black: A Biography* 284–85 (1994).

[41] Justice Frank Murphy drafted a dissenting opinion but eventually scrapped it and joined the majority. Murphy's leading biographer concludes: "What seems to have occurred is that an indecisive freshman justice who had served on the Court only a few months discussed his proposed dissent with the chief justice [Hughes], who persuaded him to go along with the Court." Sidney Fine, *Frank Murphy: The Washington Years* 185–86 (1984).

[42] 310 U.S. at 603–4 (Stone, J., dissenting).

[43] *Id.* at 606.

spirit."[44] And contrary to Justice Frankfurter, Stone declared that "it is the function of the courts to determine whether such accommodation is reasonably possible."[45] In the present case, "we have such a small minority entertaining in good faith a religious belief, which is such a departure from the usual course of human conduct, that most persons are disposed to regard it with little toleration or concern."[46]

The Court's ruling upholding the power of the school board to require all children, including the Witnesses, to salute the flag was handed down June 3, 1940, as routed French and British troops were desperately being evacuated from Dunkirk. Many Americans regarded the Witnesses' refusal to recite the pledge as evidence of disloyalty and of their sympathy and even collaboration with the Nazi regime.[47] Fears at the time ran high about a "fifth column," a largely imagined network of domestic spies and enemies.[48] The Witnesses were suspected by some of involvement in such a network. These misguided suspicions were only reinforced as the Witnesses persisted in their refusal to recite the pledge even after *Gobitis* was handed down.[49]

In the weeks following the Supreme Court's decision, there were hundreds of violent attacks against Witnesses and their property, some abetted by local law enforcement officials.[50] In Richwood, West Virginia,

---

[44] *Id.*

[45] *Id.* at 603.

[46] *Id.* at 606.

[47] Manwaring, *supra* note 6, at 30. Ironically, the Witnesses viewed the required pledge as an imported mechanism of Nazi oppression aimed particularly at them. Although they misperceived the impetus and historical origins of the pledge, the Witnesses' fears of the Nazis were well grounded. The Nazis outlawed the movement's activities in 1933, and in response the Witnesses refused to deliver the Nazi salute. Approximately 10,000 Jehovah's Witnesses in Germany were sent to concentration camps. *Id; see also* J.S. Conway, *The Nazi Persecution of the Churches, 1933–45,* at 196 (1968) ("Foremost among the opponents of Nazism were the Jehovah's Witnesses, of whom a higher proportion (97 per cent) suffered some form of persecution than any of the other churches. No less than a third of the whole following were to lose their lives as a result of their refusal to conform or compromise.") The Witness movement was also banned in Canada and Australia for a short period of years in the 1940s. Witnesses have suffered a variety of forms of persecution in a number of other countries as well, among them Spain, Italy, Greece, Argentina, Egypt and Indonesia. Penton, *supra* note 19, at 133, 135.

[48] For a study of how this "largely chimerical" threat "gripped the American public mind in the period preceding the Pearl Harbor attack and continuing through the first year of United States intervention in the Second World War," *see* Francis MacDonnell, *Insidious Foes: The Axis Fifth Column and the American Home Front* vii (1995).

[49] Peters, *supra* note 15, at 72–3. "Fifth column" fears were also frequently cited as the reasons for the forced internment of Japanese immigrants and Japanese–American citizens from the West Coast. *See* MacDonnell, *supra* note 48, at 82–90.

[50] Victor W. Rotnem and F.G. Folsom, Jr., *Recent Restrictions Upon Religious Liberty,* 36 Am. Pol. Sci. Rev. 1053, 1061 (1942).

a group of American Legion vigilantes, led by a sheriff's deputy, forced several Witnesses to drink large quantities of castor oil, roped them together, then paraded them through the town. Over five hundred taunting citizens followed the procession, which at one point was halted for an impromptu flag salute ceremony and a reading of the American Legion constitution. Finally, the Witnesses were marched to the edge of town, where they found their automobiles painted with swastikas and graffiti accusing them of being "Hitler's spies" and a "Fifth Column."[51] A Rawlins, Wyoming mob beat up five Witnesses, three men and two women, and burned their cars; in another Wyoming community, a member of the sect was literally tarred and feathered.[52] Two months after the *Gobitis* decision, in August 1940, Albert Walkenhorst was lured from his home in Norfolk, Nebraska, by a group of vigilantes posing as fellow Witnesses and castrated.[53] A month later, near Little Rock, Arkansas, a Jehovah's Witnesses convention ground was assaulted by workers from a federal pipeline project wielding as weapons screwdrivers, pipes, and firearms; two Witnesses were shot and four others were hospitalized.[54]

Although vigilante activity against the Witnesses increased dramatically following the Court's flag salute ruling, there had been disturbing incidents earlier that year. In April of 1940, Walter Chaplinsky, a vociferous Jehovah's Witness preaching in Rochester, New Hampshire, was surrounded by a group of men who scornfully invited him to salute the flag. While one veteran attempted to pummel Chaplinsky, the town marshal looked on, warned the Witness that things were turning ugly, but refused to arrest the assailant. After the marshal left, the assailant returned with a flag and attempted to impale Chaplinsky on the flagpole, eventually pinning him onto a car while other members of the crowd began to beat him. A police officer then arrived, not to detain or disperse members of the mob but to escort Chaplinsky to the police station. En route, the officer and others who joined the escort directed epithets at the hapless Witness. When Chaplinsky responded in kind, calling the marshal who had reappeared "a damn fascist and a racketeer," he was arrested for, and later convicted of, using offensive language in public.[55]

---

[51] Peters, *supra* note 15, at 89–92.

[52] Manwaring, *supra* note 6, at 165.

[53] Peters, *supra* note 15, at 95.

[54] Manwaring, *supra* note 6, at 165–66.

[55] Peters, *supra* note 15, at 211–15. The conviction was upheld unanimously on appeal to the Supreme Court. The decision gave rise to the "fighting words" doctrine, a principle holding that speech that by its "very utterance inflict[s] injury or tend[s] to incite an immediate breach of the peace" is not subject to First Amendment protection. *Chaplinsky v. New Hampshire*, 315 U.S. 568, 572 (1942). The Court's opinion included no mention of

The American Civil Liberties Union collected reports of these assaults. Its records, which were forwarded to the Justice Department, indicated that in 1940 attacks were mounted against nearly 1500 Jehovah's Witnesses in 335 separate incidents in 44 states.[56] After reviewing the files, Justice Department attorneys Victor W. Rotnem and F. G. Folsom, Jr., observed: "Almost without exception, the flag and the flag salute can be found as the percussion cap that sets off these acts."[57] In Litchfield, Illinois, vigilantes pulled Witness Bob Fischer from his car, draped a flag over the hood, and when he refused their demand that he salute the flag, slammed his head against the hood for nearly thirty minutes as the chief of police looked on. One participant later bragged, "We almost beat one guy to death to make him kiss the flag."[58] A Connorsville, Indiana mob went on the attack after the rancorous trial of Witnesses Grace Trent and Lucy McKee for flag desecration, sedition, and riotous conspiracy. The attorney for the defendants, his wife, and several other Witnesses who attended the proceedings were beaten and chased out of town. The behavior of the defendants that provoked the prosecution and the vigilantes' wrath consisted of distributing literature opposing the compulsory pledge of allegiance and refusing to salute a Legionnaire's flag lapel pin.[59] The Boston Globe reported that after the Witnesses' Kingdom Hall in Kennebunk, Maine was burned, "someone affixed a small American flag to the charred front of the hall."[60] Reporter Beulah Amidon observed a crowd "in an unnamed hamlet in the Deep South" throwing pieces of wood and rubble at a procession of seven Jehovah's Witnesses. When she asked the local sheriff, who was enjoying the spectacle, what had caused the disturbance, he explained that the Witnesses were being run out of town: "They're traitors—the Supreme Court says so. Ain't you heard?"[61]

---

the incident with the flag, the crowd's attack on Chaplinsky, or the acquiescence of town officials.

[56] Peters, *supra* note 15, at 100.

[57] Rotnem and Folsom, *supra* note 50, at 1062. In the World War I period, the nation had endured somewhat similar episodes of "patriotic" vigilantism and state persecution for what was considered inadequate respect for the flag by German–Americans, Germans, African–Americans, ministers, socialists, unionists, and peace activists. O'Leary, *supra* note 3, at 234–35.

[58] Peters, *supra* note 15, at 85–87.

[59] *Id.* at 125, 130–36. For these transgressions the two Witnesses were convicted and sentenced to 2 to 10 years in prison. Trent and McKee eventually prevailed on appeal but not before enduring a year and a half of incarceration and efforts by local officials to deny them legal representation as well as access to a court transcript. *Id.* at 130–38; Manwaring, *supra* note 6, at 166.

[60] Peters, *supra* note 15, at 79 (quoting Boston Globe, June 10, 1940).

[61] *Id.* at 83–84 (quoting Beulah Amidon, *"Can We Afford Martyrs?"*, Survey Graphic 457 (Sept. 1940)).

The impact of *Gobitis* on schoolchildren was also widespread and severe, if less gruesome. In early 1940, before the Court's decision, school expulsions of Witnesses had occurred or were in process in fifteen states.[62] According to the Witnesses' records, in the wake of *Gobitis* over two thousand children of their faith were expelled from school for refusal to pledge allegiance to the flag, with such expulsions occurring in each of the forty-eight states.[63]

There can be no doubt that the enmity the Witnesses aroused stemmed in large part from their scruples against saluting the flag. Their resistance to military service also contributed to the climate of hostility and violence they encountered. Moreover, throughout the 1930s and 1940s, the sect adopted unusually aggressive mass proselytizing tactics. During that period, thousands of Witnesses were arrested in connection with their often intrusive preaching and pamphleteering in streets and parks, on public sidewalks, and in the doorways of private residences.[64] In those street campaigns, they gave persistent voice to their leader Joseph Rutherford's contemptuous attitude toward other religions, especially the Roman Catholic Church. In their literature, they ridiculed the veterans' organizations that promoted flag worship, labeling their principal nemesis "the un-American Legion."[65] Zechariah Chafee, co-author of an amicus brief in *Gobitis* in support of the Witnesses,[66] characterized the group on another occasion as "a sect distinguished by great religious zeal and astonishing powers of annoyance."[67]

Barnette

Against this background, the Supreme Court decided to revisit the constitutional issues in 1943 in *West Virginia State Board of Education v. Barnette*. Much had changed in the three years since *Gobitis*. The nation was fully engaged in war, rather than simply apprehensive about its near prospect. Fears of a Nazi fifth column, though, had abated.[68] The personnel of the Supreme Court had also changed, with two members of

---

[62] *See* Manwaring, *supra* note 6, at 187.

[63] *Id.*

[64] *See* Peters, *supra* note 15, at 125.

[65] *Id.* at 73.

[66] *See* Smith, *supra* note 33, at 202–04.

[67] Zechariah Chafee, Jr., *Free Speech in the United States* 399 (1941).

[68] *See* MacDonnell, *supra* note 48, at 8: "In the autumn of 1942, fears about the Axis Fifth Column declined precipitously. The Allies' move to the offensive, the failure of any effective domestic spy threat to emerge, and the reduced intensity of government warnings to the public calmed home-front anxieties."

the *Gobitis* majority, Chief Justice Charles Evans Hughes and Justice James McReynolds, having retired—replaced by Roosevelt appointees Robert Jackson and Wiley Rutledge. Equally important, as it turned out, three members of the *Gobitis* majority, Justices Black, Douglas, and Murphy, had changed their minds about the constitutional questions presented by compulsory flag ceremonies in public schools, and had said so in a dissent in a case involving a different issue of religious liberty.[69] This signal encouraged Witness attorney Hayden Covington to search for a case through which to overturn *Gobitis*.[70]

Shortly after the *Gobitis* decision was announced, the West Virginia legislature passed a statute requiring all schools in the state, public and private, to offer regular courses in history and civics " 'for the purpose of teaching, fostering and perpetuating the ideals, principles and spirit of Americanism.' "[71] A little over a year later, the state Board of Education adopted a resolution requiring all public school teachers and students to participate in "the salute honoring the Nation represented by the Flag." The resolution included extended verbatim passages from Justice Frank-furter's majority opinion in *Gobitis*, and provided that "refusal to salute the Flag be regarded as an act of insubordination, and shall be dealt with accordingly."[72] The sanction specified by state law for such insubordina-tion was expulsion from school with readmission to be denied "until such requirements and regulations be complied with."[73] Parents and legal guardians of children who were absent from school were subject to prosecution; the eligible penalties included imprisonment.

Many Witness children continued to refuse to say the pledge and were expelled from West Virginia schools. The McClures, the Stulls, and the Barnetts were related to one another and to a family whose members had been victimized in the Richwood incident. They all had children expelled for failure to say the pledge and two of the parents were convicted for their children's failure to attend school (though the state then dropped the parents' case on appeal). Attorneys for the Jehovah's Witnesses brought a class action on their behalf and on behalf of others similarly situated to enjoin enforcement of the flag salute requirement.[74]

---

[69] *See Jones v. Opelika*, 316 U.S. 584, 623–24 (1942) (Black, Douglas, and Murphy, J.J., dissenting).

[70] Peters, *supra* note 15, at 245.

[71] *West Va. State Bd. of Educ. v. Barnette*, 319 U.S. 624, 625 (1943) (quoting W. Va. Code § 1734 (Supp. 1941)).

[72] *Id.* at 626 (quoting *W. Va. State Bd. of Educ.*, Resolution (Jan. 9, 1942)).

[73] *Id.* at 629 (quoting W. Va. Code § 1851 (Supp. 1941)).

[74] Manwaring, *supra* note 6, at 210–11. Three separate state actions had been brought for injunctive relief, all of which had been denied without hearing. *Id.*

As in *Gobitis*, they prevailed in federal district court.[75] The opinion for a special three-judge panel was written by Fourth Circuit Judge John J. Parker. Twelve years earlier, Judge Parker had been nominated by President Hoover to the United States Supreme Court but was denied Senate confirmation by two votes, apparently on account of his conservative rulings in labor cases and because of a speech he gave while running for governor in North Carolina in which he defended the disfranchisement of black citizens.[76] The court's judgment in favor of the Witnesses was extraordinary in light of the recent *Gobitis* precedent from the Supreme Court. Judge Parker surmounted that obstacle by noting that "[o]f the seven justices now members of the Supreme Court who participated in that decision, four have given public expression to the view that it is unsound."[77] Finding the flag salute "violative of religious liberty when required of persons holding the religious views of plaintiffs," the opinion stated "we feel that we would be recreant to our duty as judges, if through a blind following of a decision which the Supreme Court itself has thus impaired as an authority, we should deny protection to rights which we regard as among the most sacred of those protected by constitutional guaranties."[78] The case was then appealed by the state directly to the United States Supreme Court.

By a vote of six to three, the Court affirmed the district court's injunction against compelling any student to participate in the flag ceremony. Justice Robert Jackson's majority opinion is among the most eloquent to be found in the whole of the U. S. Reports.[79]

"[T]he issue as we see it," said Justice Jackson "does [not] turn on one's possession of particular religious views or the sincerity with which they are held."[80] For "[i]t is not necessary to inquire whether nonconformist beliefs will exempt from the duty to salute unless we first find power to make the salute a legal duty."[81] Justice Frankfurter's opinion in *Gobitis* had skipped over this preliminary step with nary a misgiving. "That the flag-salute is an allowable portion of a school program for those who do not invoke conscientious scruples is surely not

---

[75] *Barnette v. West Va. State Bd. of Educ.*, 47 F.Supp. 251 (S.D. W. Va. 1942).

[76] *See* Richard L. Watson, Jr., *The Defeat of Judge Parker: A Study in Pressure Groups and Politics*, 50 Miss. Valley Hist. Rev. 213 (1963).

[77] 47 F.Supp. at 253.

[78] *Id.*

[79] For a study of the rhetorical qualities of the various opinions in *Gobitis* and *Barnette,* see Robert A. Ferguson, *The Judicial Opinion as Literary Genre*, 2 Yale J. L. & Humanities 201 (1990).

[80] *West Va. State Bd. of Educ. v. Barnette*, 319 U.S. 624, 634 (1943).

[81] *Id.* at 635.

debatable,"[82] Frankfurter had said. Three years later, however, Jackson and the majority in *Barnette* found just such a debate to be of the essence: "We examine rather than assume existence of this power and, against this broader definition of issues in this case, reexamine specific grounds assigned for the *Gobitis* decision."[83] In questioning the general power of government to compel participation in a flag salute, the Court transformed the case from a dispute over special religious exemptions to one that implicated the freedom of speech of all students, including those whose objections to participation derived from moral or political rather than religious scruples. This re-conception of the central constitutional issues at stake came largely at the Court's own initiative. The briefs of the Witnesses and their amici had focused almost exclusively on freedom of religion, as had the briefs in *Gobitis*.[84]

One of the "specific grounds" that Justice Jackson reexamined concerned the high level of generality at which the *Gobitis* Court addressed the flag salute issue. Justice Frankfurter had perceived in the controversy "the problem which Lincoln cast in memorable dilemma: 'Must a government of necessity be too *strong* for the liberties of its people, or too *weak* to maintain its own existence?' "[85] Justice Jackson would have none of this hyperbole: "It may be doubted whether Mr. Lincoln would have thought that the strength of government to maintain itself would be impressively vindicated by our confirming power of the State to expel a handful of children from school."[86] Jackson followed this left jab at Frankfurter with a right hook that must have stung the self-appointed guardian of the judicial craft: "Such oversimplification, so handy in political debate, often lacks the precision necessary to postulates of judicial reasoning."[87]

In *Gobitis,* Justice Frankfurter had expressed concern that a judicial intervention on behalf of the Witnesses "would in effect make us the school board for the country."[88] In *Barnette*, Justice Jackson answered

---

[82] *Minersville Sch. Dist. v. Gobitis*, 310 U.S. 586, 599 (1940).

[83] 319 U.S. at 636.

[84] *See* Manwaring, *supra* note 6, at 65, 89–90, 217–24. The brief filed by Hayden Covington, attorney for the Witnesses, had included the contention that the compulsory flag salute violates the freedom of speech on analogy to the right, established in *Stromberg v. California*, 283 U.S. 359 (1931), not to be punished for displaying a flag associated with disfavored ideas or regimes. This argument was dwarfed in Covington's brief, however, by the arguments based on the Religion Clauses. Manwaring, *supra* note 6, at 217–20.

[85] 310 U.S. at 596 (quoting President's Message to Congress in Special Session (July 4, 1861)).

[86] 319 U.S. at 636.

[87] *Id.*

[88] 310 U.S. at 598.

this point with an argument that could have come straight out of Madison's Federalist No. 10. School boards, said Jackson, "have, of course, important, delicate, and highly discretionary functions, but none that they may not perform within the limits of the Bill of Rights." In fact, "small and local authority may feel less sense of responsibility to the Constitution, and agencies of publicity may be less vigilant in calling it to account." He contrasted Congress's respect for minority scruples "in making flag observance voluntary" and providing for conscientious objection "in a matter so vital as raising the Army."[89] Justice Frankfurter's trust in local school officials in a matter touching the rights of reviled minorities seemed to Jackson quite misplaced: "There are village tyrants as well as village Hampdens, but none who acts under color of law is beyond reach of the Constitution."[90]

The majority opinion in *Gobitis* had called for judicial deference not only to local officials but also to the state political processes that might serve as a remedy for the transgressions of village tyrants. The Witnesses remained free, in this view, to "fight out the wise use of legislative authority in the forum of public opinion and before legislative assemblies rather than to transfer such a contest to the judicial arena."[91] In *Barnette* Justice Jackson confronted this argument directly with an unabashed defense of the judicial role:

> The very purpose of a Bill of Rights was to withdraw certain subjects from the vicissitudes of political controversy, to place them beyond the reach of majorities and officials and to establish them as legal principles to be applied by the courts. One's right to life, liberty, and property, to free speech, a free press, freedom of worship and assembly, and other fundamental rights may not be submitted to vote; they depend on the outcome of no elections.[92]

In response to Justice Frankfurter's assertion in *Gobitis* that courts possess "no marked and certainly no controlling competence"[93] to resolve the flag salute controversy, Justice Jackson stated: "[W]e act in these matters not by authority of our competence but by force of our commissions. . . . [H]istory authenticates . . . the function of this Court when liberty is infringed."[94]

---

[89] 319 U.S. at 637–38.

[90] *Id.* at 638.

[91] 310 U.S. at 600.

[92] 319 U.S. at 638.

[93] 310 U.S. at 597–98.

[94] 319 U.S. at 640.

Finally, Justice Jackson considered the extended argument in the *Gobitis* majority opinion that national security rests on a form of national unity symbolized by the common gesture of pledging allegiance to the premier symbol of the nation. Justice Frankfurter had said in *Gobitis*: "The ultimate foundation of a free society is the binding tie of cohesive sentiment."[95] Jackson did not question the legitimacy or the importance of national unity as a goal of governmental policy. "The problem," he said, "is whether under our Constitution compulsion as here employed is a permissible means for its achievement."[96] He concluded that it is not.

This question of the respective roles of governmental persuasion and coercion activated in Jackson's mind a theme to which he would return in later cases involving the interpretation of the First Amendment: how best to preserve what Madison once termed "that moderation and harmony" on which stable government depends, particularly in a democracy.[97] "Struggles to coerce uniformity of sentiment" have a rich historical pedigree, Jackson observed. "Nationalism is a relatively recent phenomenon but at other times and places the ends have been racial or territorial security, support of a dynasty or regime, and particular plans for saving souls."[98] Whatever the objective, the destructive dynamic is the same:

> As first and moderate methods to attain unity have failed, those bent on its accomplishment must resort to an ever-increasing severity. As governmental pressure toward unity becomes greater, so strife becomes more bitter as to whose unity it shall be. Probably no deeper division of our people could proceed from any provocation than from finding it necessary to choose what doctrine and whose program public educational officials shall compel youth to unite in embracing.[99]

The opinion canvassed various programs through the ages to coerce unity, from the Roman drive to stamp out Christianity to the persecution of religious dissenters by the Inquisition to the Russian extermina-

---

[95] 310 U.S. at 596.

[96] 319 U.S. at 640.

[97] James Madison, *A Memorial and Remonstrance Against Religious Assessments*, ¶ 11, *reprinted in* Writings 29 (Jack N. Rakove ed., 1999). Subsequent cases in which Justice Jackson explored the challenge of maintaining the spirit of moderation in a regime of freedom of speech include *Beauharnais v. Illinois*, 343 U.S. 250, 287 (1952) (Jackson, J. dissenting); *Terminiello v. City of Chicago*, 337 U.S. 1, 13 (1949) (same); and *Kunz v. New York*, 340 U.S. 290, 295 (1951) (same).

[98] 319 U.S. at 640.

[99] *Id.* at 640–41.

tion of Siberian exiles to "the fast failing efforts of our present totalitarian enemies."[100]

These horror stories, it must be said, seem rather more severe than the school suspensions and expulsions explicitly at issue in the case at bar. One might have expected Justice Jackson to acknowledge the wave of vigilante violence in response to *Gobitis* as well as the degree of state acquiescence in this perverted form of patriotic fervor. He refrained, however, on the advice of Chief Justice Stone, who hoped to forestall the perception that the overruling of *Gobitis* stemmed from political or humanitarian rather than strictly legal considerations.[101] Instead, Jackson resorted to the slippery slope: "the First Amendment to our Constitution was designed to avoid these ends by avoiding these beginnings."[102]

A key step in Justice Frankfurter's *Gobitis* argument had been that the governmental interest in national unity is of a different order, more fundamental than the interests at stake in the ordinary run of constitutional controversies. In *Barnette,* Jackson rejected the implication that a diminution of liberty follows from any such scaling of state interests: "[F]reedom to differ is not limited to things that do not matter much. That would be a mere shadow of freedom. The test of its substance is the right to differ as to things that touch the heart of the existing order."[103] Indeed, if the issue is to be joined at the level of constitutional first principles, Justice Jackson indicated, it is the Witnesses who must prevail:

> If there is any fixed star in our constitutional constellation, it is that no official, high or petty, can prescribe what shall be orthodox in politics, nationalism, religion, or other matters of opinion or force citizens to confess by word or act their faith therein. If there are any circumstances which permit an exception, they do not now occur to us.[104]

In a finishing flourish, the majority opinion in *Barnette* explicitly overruled *Gobitis.*

Justices Black and Douglas wrote a joint concurring opinion in *Barnette* in order to explain their voting to overrule a decision they had joined. Their concurrence introduced a supplementary rationale for the

---

[100] *Id.* at 641.

[101] As the draft opinion was circulated within the Court, Chief Justice Stone repeatedly urged Justice Jackson to eliminate references to the violence against the Witnesses. *See* Peters, *supra* note 15, at 251.

[102] 319 U.S. at 641.

[103] *Id.* at 642.

[104] *Id.*

Court's decision. Although Black and Douglas joined Justice Jackson's majority opinion, and not just its result,[105] the reasons they gave for their change of position from *Gobitis* sounded exclusively in *religious* liberty, not the freedom of speech that Justice Jackson invoked. A strictly religious rationale would have narrower scope because a free speech rationale would apply to all students, even those whose objections were not religiously grounded. Justices Black and Douglas characterized the West Virginia requirement as "a form of test oath" that, like all such loyalty oaths, is ultimately self-defeating in its invitation to insincere attestation.[106] As such, the compelled recitation served no genuine state interest. Rather, "[t]he ceremonial, when enforced against conscientious objectors, more likely to defeat than to serve its high purpose, is a handy implement for disguised religious persecution."[107] Their conclusion that the compulsory dimension of the flag salute ceremony served no legitimate state interest perhaps explains how Black and Douglas could have joined Justice Jackson's majority opinion, with its exclusive reliance on the freedom of speech, even as they articulated the problem solely in terms of religious persecution.[108]

Justices Reed and Roberts, who also had been members of the *Gobitis* majority, reaffirmed their adherence to "the views expressed by the Court" in that decision and to the position that a school board can require all students to salute the flag. Their one-sentence dissenting opinion did not address Justice Jackson's new free speech rationale.[109]

Justice Frankfurter submitted a dissenting opinion that reads as a combined jeremiad and lamentation from a constitutional prophet wounded by the jurisprudential heresies of his colleagues on the bench.[110]

---

[105] We know this because the Jackson opinion is labeled in the Reports the "Opinion of the Court." Without Black and Douglas there would have been no such Court majority, only a plurality.

[106] 319 U.S. at 643–44 (Black and Douglas, J.J., concurring).

[107] *Id.*

[108] Justice Murphy contributed a separate concurrence explaining his change of view since *Gobitis*. He sidestepped the issue of whether freedom of expression or religious freedom in particular was at issue by defining the right in dispute as "the freedom of the individual to be vocal or silent according to his conscience or personal inclination." *Id.* at 646 (Murphy, J., concurring).

[109] 319 U.S. at 642.

[110] One of his biographers found the *Barnette* decision to be a pivotal moment in Justice Frankfurter's judicial career:

Psychologically, the period marked off by *Barnette* and the end of the 1942 term produced in Frankfurter a sense of being under siege. Unexpectedly, he found himself in a position of opposition; his leadership had been rejected. He would react in a manner that had become a familiar part of this psychological makeup. The reaction

The opening sentence reveals how thoroughly he personalized the issue: "One who belongs to the most vilified and persecuted minority in history is not likely to be insensible to the freedoms guaranteed by our Constitution."[111]

There followed fully twenty-five pages of heartfelt advocacy of his trademark philosophy of judicial deference to the constitutional understanding and responsibility of the electorally accountable institutions of governance in *all* cases, not excluding those involving small, unpopular— and, some would assert, politically defenseless—minorities. "It can never be emphasized too much," Frankfurter admonished his brethren, "that one's own opinion about the wisdom or evil of a law should be excluded altogether when one is doing one's duty on the bench."[112] His preferred standard for identifying a constitutional violation under the First Amendment was not different from the deferential standard the majority had come to embrace for cases of economic regulation challenged under the Due Process Clause: "whether legislators could in reason have enacted such a law."[113]

Justice Frankfurter took umbrage not only at the majority's expansive conception of the judicial role in cases touching the individual conscience but also its promiscuous use of history:

> The flag salute exercise has no kinship whatever to the oath tests so odious in history. For the oath test was one of the instruments for suppressing heretical beliefs. Saluting the flag suppresses no belief nor curbs it. Children and their parents may believe what they please, avow their belief and practice it. It is not even remotely suggested that the requirement for saluting the flag involves the

---

would be particularly bitter, for this time his opponents were former allies; the challenge was in a domain where he had every reason to anticipate complete success; and he had no choice but to remain where he was and fight it out.

H.N. Hirsch, *The Enigma of Felix Frankfurter* 176 (1981). *See also* James F. Simon, *The Antagonists: Hugo Black, Felix Frankfurter and Civil Liberties in Modern America* 118–19 (1989).

[111] 319 U.S. at 646 (Frankfurter, J., dissenting). Apparently, Justices Jackson and Frankfurter had a tense personal history regarding matters of patriotism and war preparation, including the flag salute question. Secretary of the Interior Harold Ickes reported in his diary that the night before the *Gobitis* decision was announced, Jackson (then Attorney General) and Frankfurter had argued long into the night, exchanging sharp words regarding "the European situation." 3 *The Secret Diary of Harold L. Ickes: The Lowering Clouds, 1939–1947.* at 199 (1954). Ten days later, "Bob Jackson told [a Cabinet meeting] about the hysteria that is sweeping the country against aliens and fifth columnists. He is particularly bitter about the decision recently handed down by the Supreme Court in the Jehovah's Witness case." *Id.* at 211.

[112] 319 U.S. at 647.

[113] *Id.*

slightest restriction against the fullest opportunity on the part both
of the children and of their parents to disavow as publicly as they
choose to do so the meaning that others attach to the gesture of
salute. All channels of affirmative free expression are open to both
children and parents.[114]

Thus, Justice Frankfurter forthrightly denied the incongruity that the
Court majority had posited in defense of its holding. "To sustain the
compulsory flag salute," Justice Jackson had stated, "we are required to
say that a Bill of Rights which guards the individual's right to speak his
own mind ... left it open to public authorities to compel him to utter
what is not in his mind."[115]

Justifying the Decision

The more intuitive ways to explain *Barnette* and the opinion's most
eloquent passages do not, on their own, provide a solid foundation for
the Court's decision. In fact, *Barnette* turns out to be surprisingly
difficult to defend. Take, for example, Justice Jackson's stirring declaration that no orthodoxies of word or act in politics, nationalism, or
religion may be prescribed by the state. Although the passage is inspiring and has been quoted in many prominent opinions,[116] the Court's
maxim threatens to be overbroad. At the least, it fails to provide
guidance as to its own limit.

If the assertion is that the state itself cannot take strong, even
unequivocal, positions on matters of politics and nationalism, then it
seems unsustainable.[117] Surely the state may design and execute a
curriculum that takes firm stands such as these: that democracy is a
superior form of government to tyranny or aristocracy; that the Constitution is legitimate and worthy of fidelity; and that public and private
racial, religious, and gender discrimination are wrong. It seems perfectly

---

[114] *Id*. at 663–64.

[115] 319 U.S. at 634.

[116] *See, e.g., Texas v. Johnson*, 491 U.S. 397, 415 (1989); *Wallace v. Jaffree*, 472 U.S. 38,
55 (1985); *Board of Educ. v. Pico*, 457 U.S. 853, 870 (1982); *Branti v. Finkel*, 445 U.S. 507,
513 n.9 (1980); *Abood v. Detroit Bd. Of Educ.*, 431 U.S. 209, 232 n.28, 235 (1977); *Elrod v.
Burns*, 427 U.S. 347, 356 (1976) (Brennan, J., plurality opinion); *Street v. New York*, 394
U.S. 576, 593 (1969); *Schware v. Bd. of Bar Exam.*, 353 U.S. 232, 244 n.15 (1957); *see also,
e.g., Webster v. Reproductive Health Services*, 492 U.S. 490, 572 n.17 (1989) (Stevens, J.,
concurring in part and dissenting in part); *Connell v. Higginbotham*, 403 U.S. 207, 209–10
(1971) (Marshall, J., concurring in the result); *Scales v. United States*, 367 U.S. 203, 267–68
(1961) (Douglas, J., dissenting); *Barenblatt v. U.S.*, 360 U.S. 109, 148 (1959) (Black, J.,
dissenting); *First Unitarian Church of L.A. v. County of Los Angeles*, 357 U.S. 545, 548
(1958) (Douglas, J., concurring).

[117] *See* Steven Shiffrin, *Government Speech*, 27 U.C.L.A. L. Rev. 565, 567–68 (1980).

proper for the state to require students to take courses that expose them to the state's positions on these matters.

Though it is more plausible to declare that the state must maintain a posture of neutrality when it comes to religious matters, that obligation does not supply a stable foundation for *Barnette* either. The wording of the pledge at issue in *Barnette* did not include any reference to God and took no explicit stance on any religious question. And, Justice Jackson's opinion represented itself as relying on the Free Speech Clause of the First Amendment, not the Religion Clauses. For the "no religious orthodoxy" principle to justify the outcome in *Barnette*, the decision would have to be interpreted as allowing individual citizens to define what, for them, counts as an illicit establishment or interference with free exercise. While the holding of *Barnette* may be justifiable on establishment or free exercise grounds, the principle cannot be that any citizen who considers a law to be a form of establishment or an illicit interference with her free exercise rights is ipso facto correct. Such a view would create a limitless exception for those who claim religious exemptions from otherwise valid laws.

So what is it about the case of compelled speech that differentiates it from curriculum requirements? One might be tempted to say that compelled speech violates a basic right not just to speak but to choose whether to speak at all. On this view, for the right of freedom of speech to be meaningful, one must be able to remain silent. Yet surely it is not always true that for the right to particular treatment or to engage in a specific activity to be meaningful one must have the option to elect different treatment or to refuse to so act. For example, the right to be free from torture retains its value even in environments in which people have no opportunity to waive the protection against torture. The right to life may have great importance even if there is no corresponding right to die.

But there is more to the idea that the right to speak entails a right *not* to speak than there is to the general claim that a right to particular treatment or to engage in specific activity implies a right to reject that treatment or to refuse that activity. For the right of free speech to be fully meaningful, the conditions for sincere, deliberate communication should be satisfied. People should have the opportunity to express what they mean at the times, places, and discursive junctures they find appropriate. To have to speak prematurely may interfere with a person's deliberative process and force him to speak before his thoughts are adequately settled. Or it may impede strategically timed interventions. The right not to speak also protects both the First Amendment and privacy interests individuals have in controlling how they represent and express themselves to others. Further, in a hostile atmosphere, the right to be silent or to remain anonymous may provide social cover for dissenters.

Nonetheless, though this argument for a right not to speak has powerful application in some contexts, it does not clearly pertain to the right at issue in *Barnette*. For the mandatory recitation of the pledge did not require any individual to speak her mind or to make any statement that even appeared to represent her thoughts as an individual. Quite the contrary! If a student participated in the mandatory pledge, no observer who knew the conditions of the exercise could reasonably conclude that the recitation represented the speaker's viewpoint. If one were interested in remaining silent or anonymous, in functional terms, then one should participate. Abstention or exemption from the practice, not participation, causes self-exposure.

Much the same may be said in reply to the suggestion that the mandatory pledge interferes with a right to express oneself to others. There is really scant risk here that a participant will be understood or misunderstood as communicating her personal patriotism or her authentic pledge of allegiance. A reasonable observer would not take communication to be going on at all. Or, rather, a reasonable observer would take any communication to be emanating from the state.

Those who claim that the problem with compelled speech of this sort is that the state is forcing false, inauthentic, or misleading communication must also grapple with Justice Frankfurter's point that there was no penalty attached to later disavowing the contents of the pledge.[118] Those who deplored its content or the requirement that one say the pledge could clarify their stance on the forced conditions of the recitation. For that matter, those who endorsed the pledge sincerely could always clarify the authenticity of the sentiments they recited. While the risks of miscommunication may be present when a compulsory speech requirement is unknown by the audience or when speakers are constrained from clarifying their position, these were not the conditions disputed in *Barnette*.

What then explains *Barnette* if standard appeals to neutrality, anonymity, and the constitutional interest in unrestricted and undistorted communication fail? As we have argued, efforts to explain *Barnette* that focus on the direct effect the recitation requirement has on the speaker-audience relationship are strained at best. Speakers are not really at risk of being misunderstood or involuntarily exposed. The focus of constitutional concern should be turned inwards towards speakers, not outwards towards their audiences. We suggest that what underpins *Barnette* is the First Amendment interest in the speaker's freedom of thought and

---

[118] Justice Rehnquist echoes this point in his dissent in *Wooley v. Maynard*, 430 U.S 705, 722 (1977) (Rehnquist, J., dissenting).

freedom of conscience. The main constitutional defects with the mandatory pledge lie in the attitude and the message the recitation requirement conveys toward the speaker and the risks that such a requirement
will exert an untoward and inappropriate influence on the speaker's
freedom of thought.

These themes were prominent in Justice Jackson's opinion but have
often been submerged or underemphasized in subsequent reconstruc-
tions of the meaning of *Barnette*. Noting that in the United States "[w]e
set up government by the consent of the governed," the opinion stated
that "the Bill of Rights denies those in power any legal opportunity to
coerce that consent."[119] And Jackson concluded the majority opinion with
the declaration that the compulsory flag salute "invades the sphere of
intellect and spirit which it is the purpose of the First Amendment to
our Constitution to reserve from all official control."[120] What was constitutionally offensive about the mandatory pledge scheme at issue in
Barnette and *Gobitis* was not that the government had a substantive
view about obedience to the law and the meaning of America. Rather,
what was wrong was the means used to try to elicit the public's
agreement.

There is, we believe, a fundamental difference between the state
voicing the view that patriotic people would pledge allegiance to a flag
and would regard the flag and the country as standing for liberty and
justice, and the state requiring that individuals attest and enact this
view in their own voice, however insincerely. Requiring potentially
insincere recitation, and especially rote and periodic recitation, poses
constitutional problems because it utilizes disrespectful methods of communication and persuasion. These methods constitute efforts forcibly to
inculcate and to instill rather than to persuade through direct, transparent arguments, reasons, or even direct, transparent emotional appeals.
By employing such disrespectful methods, the government contradicts
presuppositions about moral character that underlie the First Amendment.

There are two basic difficulties with required recitations of substantive views. First, such methods explicitly manifest indifference to the
actual thoughts and judgments of the person required to speak. It is of
no importance whether the speaker agrees or disagrees, is sincere or
insincere. This implicit attitude, latent in the requirement, is already at
odds with an underlying constitutional respect for individuals' First
Amendment right to develop, voice, and exercise independent opinions
and commitments. It is hard to articulate a rationale that makes sense of

---

[119] 319 U.S. at 624.

[120] *Id*. at 642.

compelled recitation that is consistent with an attitude of respect for sincere statement and independent judgment.

For what is the point of such a requirement given that, as was previously discussed, the recitation should not be taken by an audience as an authentic expression of the reciter's beliefs and attitudes? Perhaps the reciter is being used as a means for broadcasting the government's message. Or the point may be, as some defenders of the mandatory pledge freely advertise, to "instill" in the reluctant student the government's view about patriotism—to engender sincere belief by requiring repeated, possibly insincere, recitation.

Using the speaker merely as a means for disseminating and saturating the environment with the government's message fails to exhibit respect for individual dignity and intellectual independence. Compelled speech differs importantly from legitimate efforts to teach or persuade students of such things as the contents of the pledge, its vision of America, and the worthiness of allegiance. Presenting to students information, ideals, visions, reasons, and arguments for their evaluation, deliberation, and assessment manifests a clear division between the proponent of the views (the state) and the intended audience (the students). This separation intrinsically recognizes the distinctness of the audience in a way that compelled speech requirements do not. The latter literally conflate the speaker and the intended audience and mark no explicit recognition of the separation between them.

Moreover, educational efforts keyed to persuasion go further and show more nuanced attention to the beliefs of students. A teacher who employs the pedagogy of persuasion engages with the questions and doubts of her students. Such a teacher actively nurtures the evaluative and deliberative capacities of students to help them arrive at conclusions that are truly their own. Such interactions show respect for the judgments and attitudes of students, in contrast to the indifference manifest in recitation requirements.

Finally, addressing students as an audience, instead of corralling them into speaking, recognizes a virtue that contributes in a comprehensive way to the various purposes served by the freedom of speech. Many different values of the First Amendment depend upon or are enhanced by sincerity on the part of individual citizens. Justice Jackson invoked the importance of sincerity when he scathingly described the compulsory flag salute as designed either to produce "unwilling converts" or assent simulated "by words without belief and by a gesture barren of meaning."[121] If some part of the value and justification of the First Amendment rests upon an interest in approaching and appreciating the truth, this effort is vastly facilitated by speakers giving voice to what they

---

[121] 319 U.S. at 633.

actually believe has merit (or may have merit, or is at least worth grappling with). The same may be said of the connection between sincerity and views of freedom of speech that emphasize the importance of speakers' interests in expressing themselves. An ethic of sincere belief in the truth of one's professions helps to focus the collective attention of the populace on the ideas that hold the most promise of meeting the various human needs, whether practical or intellectual. An ethic of sincere belief also focuses citizens' interest and attention on truth, whereas state measures that flaunt an indifference to sincerity encourage cynicism and ambivalence about the value of truth.

The same may be said even more forcefully of the importance of sincerity in arguments for freedom of speech that stress its role in facilitating mutual understanding among citizens who appreciate each others' needs and concerns and who strive to forge political accommodations on the basis of this appreciation. Genuine understanding and accommodation depend upon citizens' voicing their needs sincerely and abstaining, so far as possible, from grandstanding, manipulation, and other forms of cynical gamesmanship.[122] A serious defect of substantive recitation requirements is that, at best, they manifest indifference to a character virtue that should be encouraged and supported if the values of the First Amendment are to be well realized.

A related, perhaps more important, concern is that a recitation requirement places a person who strives to be sincere, but who does not believe the contents of the recitation, in a dilemma: either disobey the law or fail to practice the character virtue, a virtue that supports and is presupposed by the constitutional structure. Citizens who read the pledge to assert that the nation is in fact providing liberty and justice for all but who doubt that this claim is true must fail to satisfy either the

---

[122] Meir Dan–Cohen has illuminatingly discussed contexts in which sincerity is not expected from a speaker. We are not troubled by the employer requirement that the telephone operator thanks us for using that company's service, although that gratitude is unlikely to be a sincere, heart-felt expression on the part of the employee; we might well be troubled and disconcerted if he really did care (though, perhaps it is a worthy aspiration that the workplace be that inspiring). Meir Dan–Cohen, *Harmful Thoughts: Essays on Law, Self, and Morality* 246–49 (2002). Dan–Cohen's point is partly that there are contexts in which it is ordinary and reasonable for speech to be required of a person that fits a role she is asked to perform but with which she is not identified. *Id.* Insincere utterances may even have a place in school. They may reasonably be elicited in language instruction courses, for instance. We may ask Johnny to announce his intention to learn the salsa so as to teach him how to pronounce the relevant words. We need not dispute this. For at the least, utterances *qua* citizen are not a context in which insincerity is reasonably expected and transparently associated with a role with which one is not supposed to identify. There is no well-defined role with clear, discrete boundaries comparable to the employee or to the language learner that the pledge reciter is to occupy that justifies the indifference to sincerity. The state's defense of its practice cannot rely on the idea that it is reasonable to expect disassociation on the part of the citizen from the role of the citizen.

duty of obedience or the duty of sincerity. The functioning of a free republic depends on the widespread honoring of both duties.

We do not suggest that the First Amendment should be interpreted so as to enhance the character virtues that we have identified simply because those virtues are intrinsically worth promoting. Nor do we claim that the First Amendment presupposes a character ideal that judicial interpretation should strive to promote as part of an effort to approximate or approach an ideal society. Instead, our argument is that the successful operation of an ongoing, stable freedom of speech culture in our actual, non-ideal society presupposes that, by and large, citizens exhibit and practice concern for the truth, sincerity, and minimal forms of intellectual independence. Given the commitment represented by the First Amendment, it is inconsistent for the state to implement laws that undermine these character traits. Likewise, it is inconsistent for the state to show significant forms of disrespect for the requisite character traits or otherwise to cast profound doubt upon the state's commitment to protecting the conditions necessary for the successful operation of a vital freedom of speech culture.[123]

These issues about character connect to a second major problem with compelled speech requirements of the sort at issue in *Barnette*. Recitation requirements threaten to interfere with freedom of thought. They may represent illicit efforts to influence the speakers' thoughts in a covert, opaque way that circumvents critical reflection and exploits speakers' character virtues.

---

[123] For two quite different elaborations of the claim that a concern for character constitutes a major justification for the freedom of speech, see Vincent Blasi, *Free Speech and Good Character: From Milton to Brandeis to the Present*, in *Eternally Vigilant: Free Speech in the Modern Era* 61 (Lee C. Bollinger & Geoffrey R. Stone eds., 2002), and Lee C. Bollinger, *The Tolerant Society: Freedom of Speech and Extremist Speech in America* (1986). In an interesting article that addresses many of the problems that we discuss, Abner S. Greene maintains that the right to be excused from a patriotic recitation requirement cannot be derived from the freedom of speech but rather must rest upon an unenumerated, generalized right of autonomy, which he finds to be of constitutional pedigree. *See* Abner S. Greene, *The Pledge of Allegiance Problem*, 64 Fordham L. Rev. 451, 473–75, 480–82 (1995). We believe that our argument from character properly connects the freedom from forced recitation to the freedom of speech, thereby supplying a rationale for the *Barnette* majority's invocation of the First Amendment.

One of the implications of this emphasis on character is that the *Barnette* principle does not extend to claims by corporate entities to be free from compelled speech or forum access requirements. *See, e.g., Pacific Gas & Electric Co. v. Public Utilities Comm'n*, 475 U.S. 1 (1986); *PruneYard Shopping Center v. Robins*, 447 U.S. 74 (1980); *Glickman v. Wileman Bros. & Elliott, Inc.*, 521 U.S. 457 (1997). The character-based rationale is applicable only to natural persons. In some contexts, there might be instrumental reasons, or reasons deriving from notions of institutional autonomy, for protecting non-natural actors from certain compelled speech requirements. *See, e.g., Miami Herald Publishing Co. v. Tornillo*, 418 U.S. 241 (1974). They are reasons, however, that gain no support from *Barnette* as we understand the decision.

As we have argued, there is a central First Amendment interest in preserving the integrity of the process of thought and speech production. The speaker, as well as the community of which she is a part, has an interest in her thinking and reasoning about subjects sincerely and authentically. Compelled speech may threaten to interfere with the achievement of this interest. For reasons unrelated to whether the contents have inspired her appreciation or assent, having to repeat a message over and over again may influence what and how a person thinks. The things a person finds herself regularly doing and saying will have an understandable impact on what subjects she thinks about: their regular presence may predictably have an influence on what topics seem salient. The message will become familiar to her. Its regularity may become a comfort and an internal source of authority for consultation. Commonly heard sentiments may become comfortable sentiments. Commonly *voiced* sentiments have an even more intimate relation to the self and may have a greater influence on a person's thoughts.

This worry is open to an obvious objection. Since the speaker (as well as her audience) knows that the speech is compelled, won't this knowledge have an impact on how great is the influence of her compelled recitation on what she thinks? Is it not less likely that these spoken words will become a source of intuitive reliance than in cases in which the element of compelled recitation is absent? Won't the recited sentiments be segregated in the speaker's mind as having a compelled, special origin?

The brief reply to this objection is that it seems reasonable to posit that speakers have an interest in avoiding an analog to cognitive dissonance. They have an interest in avoiding what might be termed performative dissonance: a state of conflict or tension between what a person says or appears to say and what a person thinks. Speakers have an interest in the opportunity to develop forthright practices, habits, and character traits of thought and assertion. In particular, those who strive to be sincere aim to develop the habit of saying what they believe to be true, especially about topics of importance; they strive to avoid such performative dissonance. This interest provides some subtle internal pressure to conform their thoughts to their utterances and vice versa. Where the utterances cannot be altered, because they are compelled, the impulse to avoid performative dissonance may exert subtle, perhaps unconscious pressure to alter one's thoughts to conform to the content of one's utterances.[124] This form of influence takes advantage of speakers'

---

[124] Some results in cognitive psychological research may lend support. *See, e.g.*, Robert W. Levenson et al., *Voluntary Facial Action Generates Emotion–Specific Autonomic Nervous System Activity*, 27 Psychophysiology 363, 364, 368, 376, 382 (1990) (exercises directing actors and non-actors to configure their faces as though they were experiencing emotion as well as those directing subjects to relive a past emotional experience significant-

efforts and impulses to be sincere in order, as many proponents of the pledge advertise, to "inculcate" patriotic sentiments. This is an insidious way to attempt to instill a message or attitude in the public. While it may often be perfectly legitimate for the government to take a substantive position and attempt to persuade citizens of its merits, it is illegitimate to try to do so indirectly by bypassing their critical capacities and attempting to exploit a character virtue, sincerity, that is integral to the value of free expression.

To defend the recitation requirement on the ground that speakers could internally exempt themselves from efforts at sincerity in this context may be overdemanding of speakers. It requires them sometimes to evince sincerity when speaking about public matters and at other times to adopt a posture of pretense. It would be reasonable for speakers to resist developing such flexibility. Such compartmentalization may be psychologically costly and difficult to achieve. Certain kinds of utterances reasonably have special gravity for speakers: e.g., oaths, promises, attestations—even the occasional informal but solemn affirmation. Their significance to speakers and audiences may be reduced if these utterances are issued insincerely or if usage becomes such that their linguistic context does not unequivocally convey the speaker's (contextual) meaning. It is important to some religious persons, for example, not to "take the Lord's name in vain," even when a swearing utterance is understood by the speaker and the audience not to be serious.[125] Significant civic

---

ly influenced subjects' current mental and emotional states); Paul Ekman and Richard J. Davidson, *Voluntary Smiling Changes Regional Brain Activity*, 4 Psychological Science 342, 345 (1993) (distinguishing between the presentation of voluntary and involuntary smiles but finding that deliberately produced smiles generate some of the brain activity associated with positive emotions); Robin Damrad–Frye and James D. Laird, *The Experience of Boredom: The Role of the Self–Perception of Attention*, 57 J. Personality and Social Psychology 315, 315 (July–Dec. 1989) (reporting "[m]uch research" that "people . . . induced to act as if they held particular emotions, attitudes, motives, or beliefs" report later having these mental states). The studies tend to confirm the view that actions can influence feelings and beliefs, not just reflect them. Some of these studies conflate more behaviorist views (that the relevant mental states are identical to a set of activities) and epistemological views (that one's mental states are known by observing one's behavior) with the causal thesis we are interested in (that the relevant mental states may be caused by and not only causes of the relevant activities). *See, e.g.*, *id.* One might believe the causal thesis without agreeing about its underlying mechanism and without subscribing to one of the tenets of self-perception theory: that agents infer their mental states from their activities and these inferences either constitute their mental states or cause these mental states to happen.

[125] Analogously, there may be practices it is important not to *pretend* to engage in. Some parents object to their children playing with toy guns because they think it may be important to our resistance to killing not to pretend to kill. In an editorial written just after the inclusion of "under God" in the Pledge of Allegiance, an actively religious, Christian academic voiced his general objections to public pressure to attest to religious belief. Arguing that "the only respectable reason for professing a religion is the conviction

performances may be cheapened if people engage in them insincerely or pretend at them.

Children & The First Amendment

It might be objected that the fact that the affirmation requirement involved children poses a problem for this analysis of *Barnette*. Perhaps adults should not be compelled to affirm messages they may not believe. But the best reasons for that prohibition do not apply to children, at least not obviously. Adults have reached the age of majority and crossed a threshold of informed independence such that their judgments and preferences deserve respect. Children, however, must mature, gain experience, and acquire a minimum of knowledge before they can be said to have the full set of cognitive and emotional resources necessary for the meaningful exercise of intellectual autonomy. We are not required to treat them as though they have already reached that stage. To the contrary, we have a responsibility to educate them as well as possible. Evidence still suggests that rote learning can be highly effective.[126] Thus, it might be argued that children are legitimate subjects of forced civic inculcation and compulsory training in patriotism.[127]

---

that it is true," he expressed concern that efforts to inculcate religious practice or belief through "non-spiritual pressures" dilute or otherwise have a corrupting influence on religion and religious belief. Hoxie N. Fairchild, *Religious Faith and Loyalty,* The New Republic, October 11, 1954, at 11, 12.

[126] *See, e.g.,* Carol Muske–Dukes, *A Lost Eloquence,* 27 Am. Educ. 42, 42–3 (2003) (discussing advantages of rote memorization of poetry); Florence Myles et al., *Rote or Rule? Exploring the Role of Formulaic Language in Classroom Foreign Language Learning,* 48 Language Learning 323, 359 (1998) (study showing rote learning facilitated early stages of foreign language acquisition); Marilee Rist, *Learning by Heart,* 14 Exec. Educ. 12, 12–19 (1992) (discussing controversy over and success rates of rote methods).

[127] For a strong expression of this position see Joseph Tussman, *Government and the Mind* 51–85 (1977):

There is no society which does not recognize the distinction or mark by some right of passage, the movement from one condition to the other—the achievement, as we would say, of the age of consent. No single set of principles can adequately govern both minor and adult; we need both caterpillar principles and butterfly principles. *Republic* is a discussion of the raising of children; *On Liberty* is a discussion of the governing of adults. They are complementary works about different generations. John Stuart Mill would have been horrified by the application of the principles of *On Liberty* to children. . . .

The natural right of self-preservation lies behind not only the traditionally asserted powers of war or defense, but also the universally claimed right of the community to shape its children. More fundamental and inalienable than even the war power stands the tutelary power of the state, or, as I shall call it, the teaching power. *Id.* at 53–54.

In response to this argument, we contend that there is an important constitutional distinction to be drawn between compulsory education and compulsory inculcation. Educational methods convey information, arguments, ideas, and views to children, often by means of required exercises. But they do so in ways that explicitly and implicitly treat the child as a distinct, independent mind whose genuine understanding is the objective. The child's agreement may well be sought and usually does follow, but methods that are educational in the fullest sense elicit agreement through developing understanding and earning assent. Education methods, as we conceive them, often require a student to demonstrate comprehension, even mastery, of a position. They do not, however, require her to agree with the position or represent herself as sincerely embracing it. Moreover, education methods do not attempt to produce agreement by bypassing the student's critical understanding. To accept this distinction between education and compulsory inculcation, one need not condemn rote learning as such. But rote learning involving normative judgments or commitments is indeed problematic, especially when it involves declarations of belief or affirmation by students.[128]

Furthermore, transmitting the central ideals of citizenship by inculcation rather than education is likely to be counter-productive. The obedience and patriotism that inculcation produces may be rigid and brittle if they are not encouraged to develop on the basis of understanding and tolerant persuasion.[129] Views that are the product of indoctrina-

---

[128] Do these arguments suggest that mandatory exercises in which "The Star–Spangled Banner" is sung are constitutionally vulnerable? It seems a borderline case. It is, we think, worth being sensitive to the fact that that song, as do many other patriotic songs, makes implicit normative claims about the achievements and genuine aspirations of the country that some, in good faith, might dispute, e.g., that this really is a land of, or that genuinely aspires to, freedom. Melodies also serve as powerful mnemonic devices and so may nest deeply in singers' minds. Songs represent a more complex case than recitations, however, because, except in the charming fiction of musicals, people rarely burst out in song to communicate their own views and thoughts. Songs are usually sung "in role" and in this way differ from standard forms of discursive communication. *See supra* note 122. In that respect, the concerns about the difficulties and frailties of self-imposed compartmentalization may be more attenuated in this case.

What about teaching the Pledge of Allegiance by rote in order to study its poetic meter? Is this ruled out by our argument? The context and purposes in which rote learning happens matter enormously, we believe, and make a difference as to whether the character traits associated with sincerity are implicated. Nonetheless, in this case, it seems highly unlikely that the Pledge of Allegiance would merit study for its poetic achievements. Such a claim should be scrutinized quite carefully as very likely to be pretextual. Requiring students to memorize Lincoln's Gettysburg Address would be quite a different matter.

[129] One international study found a strong correlation between "extensive" use of patriotic ritual in the classroom and a cluster of attitudes showing strong support for the government, a high level of civic participation, but a low level of support for democratic values. The United States was an example of a nation whose students tended to fit this

tion can degenerate into reflexive reactions. When that occurs, such views escape the ongoing scrutiny that yields a deeper and stronger form of sincere affirmation. As Justices Black and Douglas observed in *Barnette,* "[w]ords uttered under coercion are proof of loyalty to nothing but self-interest. Love of country must spring from willing hearts and free minds...."[130]

But does this view, that civic education is constitutionally permissible but civic inculcation is not, wrongly attribute to children the capacities of adults? We think not. The requirement that loyalty be a product of education does not presuppose that children have the full panoply of capacities and virtues of adult citizens. Recall that our interpretation and defense of *Barnette* is not a conventional argument from autonomy. Rather, it derives from the assumption that a person's youth and schooling are the primary time and place at which the moral, civic, and intellectual virtues, virtues essential to the functioning of a democratic society, are developed. Sincerity, authenticity, tolerance, responsibility for one's beliefs, and intellectual independence cannot emerge and flourish in a context of inculcation and are not easily or reliably acquired later in life. Hence the importance of the developmental years to the realization of a culture that sustains and celebrates the freedom of speech.[131]

Extending Barnette

Because the school setting is so crucial to the development of civic and personal character, teachers play a special role in nurturing the First Amendment virtues. Accordingly, it is important that teachers exemplify and practice that which they aim to produce by means of

---

pattern, more than many other industrialized, democratic nations. Judith V. Torney et al., *Civic Education in Ten Countries* 230–33 (1975).

[130] *West Va. State Bd. of Educ. v. Barnette,* 319 U.S. 624, 644 (1943) (Black and Douglas, J.J., concurring).

[131] Louis Michael Seidman criticizes our argument on the grounds that it implausibly assumes that absent the pressures exerted by mandatory recitation, children will engage rationally with the arguments for the propositions and attitudes manifested and implied by the pledge. To the contrary, Seidman claims, children are subject and responsive to all forms of social and parental pressure that attempts to evade their rational processes; the pledge is a legitimate form of counter-pressure. Louis Michael Seidman, *Silence and Freedom* 158–9 (2007). Although Seidman is surely right to emphasize that the state is not the only entity to attempt to influence children through means that circumvent and bias their judgment, it is not clear that this warrants the state's adopting "similar tactics" given its tremendous power and its commitment to the values propelling the First Amendment. The Constitution may require the state to act as an exemplar with respect to the conditions supporting free speech and the character traits that support it, even if many of its citizens do not.

education. This is one of the reasons why we believe that *Barnette,* correctly applied, protects teachers from being compelled to lead or recite the pledge. Several lower court cases since *Barnette* have considered whether a public school teacher can be required to lead his students in pledging allegiance to the flag. Most courts have recognized a teacher's right not to be so compelled as a condition of employment, at least when the school has alternative means of conducting the ceremony for willing students.[132] The pedagogic spectacle of insincere recitation that such an obligation entails is deeply antithetical to the character ideal that informs the *Barnette* decision.

Adults, of course, typically are less impressionable than children. That does not render compelled affirmations by adults entirely innocuous, however. Although they have greater resources to resist efforts to bypass their deliberative faculties, adults are not immune to efforts at subconscious influence and the cognitive pressures associated with what we have labeled performative dissonance. A duty of public affirmation, with a desired job hanging in the balance, asks a teacher to embody the virtues necessary for a successful free speech culture by conducting a war within himself. Enforcing such obligations also sends a confusing message to children about the real level of tolerance for conscientious abstention. Mandating affirmations that may be ambivalent or equivocal undermines the First Amendment's character ideal by placing in doubt whether sincerity and independence are, in fact, honored by the state.

These concerns are not alleviated by the fact that persons with scruples against reciting the pledge of allegiance are not required to accept employment as public schoolteachers. Even if public employment is not a right, it cannot be conditioned on the waiver of a free speech opportunity or immunity absent some reason to consider the assertion of the free speech prerogative to be antithetical to the demands of the job. To find such a conflict in a teacher's unwillingness to lead a flag salute would imply that dissenters with scruples are not fit role models but rather persons of questionable civic status who cannot discharge the high office of teaching children. *Barnette* precludes such a crude and cruel characterization. Nor can the demands of administrative efficiency

---

[132] *See Russo v. Central Sch. Dist.,* 469 F.2d 623 (2d Cir. 1972); *Hanover v. Northrup,* 325 F.Supp. 170 (D. Conn. 1970); *State v. Lundquist,* 278 A.2d 263 (Md. 1971); *Opinion of the Justices to the Governor,* 363 N.E.2d 251 (Mass. 1977). In *Russo,* the court noted that the complainant was a probationary teacher who co-taught a class with a regular member of the faculty who did not object to leading the pledge. 469 F.2d at 625. In *Palmer v. Board of Education,* 603 F.2d 1271 (7th Cir. 1979), the court upheld the firing of a kindergarten teacher for refusing both to lead the pledge and other acts of patriotism, as well as to teach patriotic lessons including why Lincoln's birthday is celebrated. In a subsequent dictum the *Palmer* holding was described by the Seventh Circuit to stand for the proposition that as a general matter teachers can be required to lead the pledge. *See Sherman v. Community Consol. Dist. 21,* 980 F.2d 437, 439 (7th Cir. 1992) (Easterbrook, J.).

justify the requirement that all teachers pledge allegiance to the flag. Means can be found to facilitate the holding of the flag salute even if for reasons of conscience the regular teacher is unavailable to lead it.

* * *

One case that has troubled some observers as a possibly implausible extension of *Barnette* is *Wooley v. Maynard*.[133] The state of New Hampshire issued license plates whose border featured the state motto: "Live Free or Die." The Maynards, also Jehovah's Witnesses, objected to having to display the slogan because their religious understanding of the conditions of life's value was significantly more encompassing. Mr. Maynard covered the slogan with tape, was fined, and then jailed for failure to pay the fines. In litigation, the Maynards claimed a right not to speak and the state claimed a right to voice its own commitments through its own property. The Maynards prevailed on the ground that *Barnette* guaranteed them a constitutional right not to speak.

Does this outcome make sense on the rationale for *Barnette* that we have articulated? A license plate, after all, does not implicate or involve the driver to the degree that the recitation requirement at issue in *Barnette* did. The driver need never articulate the words of the motto, much less repeat them by rote. These differences, we agree, make *Wooley* a harder case. But *Barnette*'s rationale still has substantial traction here.

As in *Barnette*, the state's imposition of the speech and the forced association with the individual betrays complete indifference to the attitudes and beliefs of those made to become the courier for the state's ideological message. Drivers are being used as a means to convey the state ideal and the state is explicitly uninterested in whether its bearers agree with it or not. The *Wooley* Court explained:

> Here, as in *Barnette*, we are faced with a state measure which forces an individual, as part of his daily life—indeed constantly while his automobile is in public view—to be an instrument for fostering public adherence to an ideological point of view he finds unacceptable. In doing so, the State "invades the sphere of intellect and spirit which it is the purpose of the First Amendment to our Constitution to reserve from all official control."[134]

True, New Hampshire drivers were not made to utter the words of the motto. But as the Court noted, they were forced to display those words on belongings that are commonly identified with them as individuals, as distinguished from currency and coins. The latter are objects that are exchanged and not identified with the person, whereas one's words,

---

[133] 430 U.S. 705 (1977).

[134] *Id.* at 715 (quoting *Barnette*, 319 U.S. at 642).

clothes, and cars usually are.[135] This sort of association may not have the same causal influence on one's beliefs as repetition does, but there still is reason to worry that some persons will subtly adapt their beliefs to fit those ideas with which they are publicly identified, even if the identification results from legal compulsion. Surely the rationale of *Barnette* would be violated if a state or municipality were to require all its citizens to wear a pin depicting the American flag.

There is a further consideration at play in *Wooley*. Along with the t-shirt, the back of one's car is one of the very few places in which, in our culture, average people regularly engage in speech directed at the general public.[136] The license plate motto not only is inserted into what for many persons is their principal forum for political advocacy, but unlike in *Barnette*, the state's compelled affirmation rides alongside an individual's actual speech constantly and simultaneously. It thus threatens, in a way that a recitation requirement often may not, to distract, dilute, and possibly even contradict a driver's own sincere speech. Imagine the mixed message of a New Hampshire motorist who, prior to the Court's ruling in *Wooley*, displayed both a peace symbol on his bumper and the mandatory state motto on his license plate.

Aftermath

In contrast to the well-documented surge in violence following *Gobitis,* the impact of the *Barnette* decision on vigilante violence directed against the Jehovah's Witnesses is not easily assessed. In quantitative terms, the violence had subsided considerably by the end of 1942, several months prior to the Court's ruling, owing in part to the diminution of fifth column anxieties.[137] By no means, however, did the Witnesses gain the freedom to enjoy their First Amendment rights in peace. Writing in 1962, David R. Manwaring, author of the most detailed study of the flag salute controversy, observed that although "1943 seems to have seen the last of the special *concentrations* of persecution," intermittent physical

---

[135] In an interesting discussion of forms of ownership that implicate identity, Meir Dan–Cohen cites the relationship to one's car as exemplary. Dan–Cohen, *supra* note 122, at 268–71. We differ, somewhat, between us about how significant is the degree of connection and identification between the individual and her car. One of us is an Angelena; the other resides in Manhattan.

[136] James W. Endersby & Michael J. Towle, *Tailgate Partisanship: Political and Social Expression Through Bumper Stickers*, 33 The Social Science Journal 308, 308 (1996) (discussing bumper stickers as a common form of individual political expression); *see also* John E. Newhagen & Michael Ancell, *The Expression of Emotion and Social Status in the Language of Bumper Stickers*, 14 Journal of Language and Social Psychology 312 (1995).

[137] *See* Manwaring, *supra* note 6, at 169–73; MacDonnell, *supra* note 48, at 8.

violence continued to form a backdrop to the Witnesses's proselytizing.[138] The proselytizing itself appears to have been fairly effective. Estimates of active membership in the Jehovah's Witnesses in the United States place their growth from slightly over 72,000 in 1943 to over 187,000 by 1955,[139] reaching five million by 1996.[140]

Neither the sobering episodes of brutal attacks against the Witnesses nor the resolution of the recitation controversy in *Barnette* dampened official or cultural flag fervor.[141] Ironically, the flag code has introduced more orthodoxies in the years since *Barnette*. For example, the 1942 federal statute declared explicitly that citizens could show adequate respect to the flag even if they did not say the pledge but stood in silence while the pledge was recited.[142] In 1976, the declaration that standing evinces adequate respect was removed from the flag statute without discussion or explanation.[143] The statute was also amended that

---

[138] Manwaring, *supra* note 6, at 240. Efforts to regulate and restrict their proselytizing methods, and litigation in response, continue to this day. *See, e.g., Watchtower Bible and Tract Soc'y of N.Y., Inc. v. Village of Stratton*, 536 U.S. 150 (2002) (invalidating, under the First Amendment, a requirement that a permit be obtained before engaging in door-to-door advocacy).

[139] Manwaring, *supra* note 6, at 20. International figures put them at over 700,000 in 1957 and well over 2 million by 1977. Penton, *supra* note 19, at 84.

[140] Jerry Bergman, *Jehovah's Witnesses: A Comprehensive and Selectively Annotated Bibliography* 1 (1999).

[141] More recently, in the wake of September 11, some Arab–Americans felt pressure to display flags as a self-protection measure. *See, e.g.,* Nahal Toosi, *Civic Duty, Civil Rights*, Milwaukee Journal Sentinel, Dec. 2, 2001, at 1A (Arab and Arab–American owned businesses hang flags to express patriotism and to fend off attack); Michael Luo, *For One Arab–American Family, the Flag is Both a Symbol and a Shield*, Associated Press, Oct. 7, 2001, *available at* DIALOG, File no. 258; *Behind the Flags, Feelings of All Stripes*, Portland Press Herald (Me.), Oct. 1, 2001, at 1A (reporting an episode in Detroit in which a group of white residents confronted Arab–Americans and ordered them to "go home" while waving flags and in which the Arab–Americans responded by waving flags back as a response); Elizabeth W. Crowley, *Shafts of Hate Strike Aimlessly on South Shore*, The Patriot Ledger (Quincy, Mass.), Sept. 19, 2001, at 9 (reporting on violence and boycotts against Arab–Americans and the use of flag displays as defensive protection). *See also* Robert Snell, *We the People*, Lansing State Journal, July 4, 2002, at 1A (Chinese Americans and immigrants encouraged to fly the flag to dispel suspicion and to improve their image).

[142] During the 1970s, the question whether a student can be required to stand in silent attention while classmates recite the pledge was litigated in three federal circuits. All ruled that under *Barnette* an objecting student cannot be required to stand, or even to choose between standing or leaving the room, so long as her conduct while remaining in the room is not disruptive. *See Goetz v. Ansell*, 477 F.2d 636 (2d Cir. 1973); *Lipp v. Morris*, 579 F.2d 834 (3d Cir. 1978); *Banks v. Bd. Of Pub. Instruction*, 314 F.Supp. 285 (S.D. Fla. 1970), aff'd 450 F.2d 1103 (5th Cir. 1971).

[143] *Compare* Joint Resolution of Dec. 22, 1942, Pub. L. No. 829, § 7, 56 Stat. 1074, 1077 ("citizens will always show full respect to the flag when the pledge is given by merely standing at attention") *with* 4 U.S.C.A. § 4 (2000).

year to include the astonishing declaration that "[t]he flag represents a living country and is itself considered a living thing."[144] One might have thought that the assertion that the flag is itself a living creature would have given some pause both for metaphysical reasons and from heightened concern about the reservation some religious people might have about pledging allegiance to a living thing that is not God. Strangely, this clause received no comment or explanation in the Senate hearings devoted to the proposed amendments.[145]

Controversies over homage to the flag have continued to play a prominent role in national politics and in Supreme Court jurisprudence. The issue figured prominently in the 1988 presidential campaign when candidate Michael Dukakis was criticized for his decision as governor of Massachusetts to veto a bill requiring teachers to lead the pledge. He cited in his defense an advisory opinion by the Supreme Judicial Court of Massachusetts holding that a state statute imposing that obligation on public school teachers would violate the First Amendment.[146] But Dukakis's successful opponent, George H. W. Bush, made much of the issue on the campaign trail, pointedly leading his audiences in mass recitals of the Pledge of Allegiance. Bush asked about Dukakis, "What is it about the American flag which upsets this man so much?"[147] Twenty years later, Barack Obama proved more adroit. Obama had earlier chosen not to don a flag lapel pin because he thought the gesture would substitute

---

[144] Joint Resolution of July 7, 1976, Pub L. No. 94–344, 90 Stat. 810, 812 (current version at 4 U.S.C. § 8 (2000)). Odder still, this ontological declaration is quietly nested within a paragraph discussing the use of the flag motif as or adorning apparel. *See also Smith v. Goguen*, 415 U.S. 566, 603 (1974) (Rehnquist, J., dissenting) (noting that the flag is a unique physical object, "[it] is not just another 'thing,' and it is not just another 'idea' ").

[145] However, pages of the hearings focus on the next sentence of the statute concerning the placement of flag lapel pins and discuss whether a lapel pin may be respectfully worn in places other than the left lapel, such as one's tie. *See Flag Code Revision: Hearing Before the Subcomm. on Fed. Charters, Holidays, and Celebrations of the Comm. on the Judiciary*, 93rd Cong. 17–18 (June 7, 1974) (Testimony of Allen W. Finger, Executive Secretary, U.S. Flag Found., and Mrs. William D. Leetch, Honorary Vice Pres., Am. Coalition of Patriotic Soc., Inc.).

The peculiar statutory assertion that the flag is itself alive may derive from a typically hyperbolic remark of flag enthusiast Gridley Adams, former chair of the National Flag Code Committee and founder of the United States Flag Foundation. He declared "[t]he National Flag represents the living country and is itself considered a living thing ... every star a tongue, every stripe articulate." E.J. Kahn, Jr., *Profiles: Three Cheers for the Blue, White and Red*, The New Yorker, July 5, 1952, at 29, 29 (quoting an unspecified publication of Adams') (ellipsis in original).

[146] *See Opinion of the Justices to the Governor*, 363 N.E. 2d 251 (Mass. 1977); Robert Justin Goldstein, *Flag Burning & Free Speech: The Case of* Texas v. Johnson 88–89 (2000).

[147] Goldstein, *supra* note 146, at 88–89.

empty symbolism for true patriotism. After that choice became a campaign issue, he wore the pin.[148]

In 1989, in a five to four decision with a most unusual division among the Justices, the Supreme Court upheld the First Amendment right of Gregory Lee Johnson to burn a flag as part of a political protest at the 1984 Republican National Convention.[149] Justice Brennan's majority opinion frequently invoked *Barnette*. His most stirring line paralleled the rhetorical structure of Justice Jackson's famous remarks about constitutional astronomy, declaring "[i]f there is a bedrock principle underlying the First Amendment, it is that the government may not prohibit the expression of an idea simply because society finds the idea itself offensive or disagreeable. We have not recognized an exception to this principle even where our flag has been involved."[150] The decision sparked a firestorm of protests and congressional activity. In response to the Court's decision, Congress quickly passed a federal statute to protect the flag against deliberate mutilation or defacement. The next year, a divided Court invalidated that statute. The Justices once again disputed whether the government has a valid interest in preserving the symbolic value of the flag and whether that interest could outweigh the free speech interests of those who would deface the flag for expressive purposes.[151] Although *United States v. Eichman* decisively settled the constitutionality of efforts to protect the flag from expressive destruction, it did not settle the political issue. Repeatedly, proposed amendments to the Constitution have been introduced that would grant to Congress the power to prohibit flag desecration. The House of Representatives has approved the proposals by the required two-thirds supermajority on four occasions, but the amendment has never passed the Senate.[152]

Perhaps the most important development in the flag salute controversy in the years since *Barnette* was the insertion in 1954 of the words "under God" in the wording of the pledge of allegiance. The Knights of Columbus, a Catholic fraternal organization, achieved its goal of adding the reference to a deity after campaigning for only two years. In the Congressional hearings, discussion of the change was again surprisingly

---

[148] *See* Jim Rutenberg & Jeff Zeleny, *The Politics of the Lapel, When It Comes to Obama*, N.Y. Times, May 15, 2008, at A27.

[149] *Texas v. Johnson*, 491 U.S. 397 (1989). Justice Brennan's opinion for the Court was joined by Justices Marshall, Blackmun, Scalia, and Kennedy. Chief Justice Rehnquist and Justices White, O'Connor, and Stevens dissented.

[150] *Id.* at 414 (citations omitted).

[151] *See United States v. Eichman*, 496 U.S. 310 (1990).

[152] *Flag–Burning Debate Again Raises Hackles on the Hill*, Chicago Tribune, July 18, 2001, at 15.

brief. The inclusion of "under God" was thought necessary to distinguish the American system of government from communism and to underscore the commitment to inalienable, individual rights guaranteed by God.[153]

This revision of the pledge added a major doctrinal complication to the question whether it is sufficient for a school district to excuse objecting students from the obligation to pledge allegiance while continuing to conduct the flag ceremony for students who prefer to participate or choose not to assert their right to be excused. For the addition of the phrase "under God" raises an Establishment Clause issue, especially after the Supreme Court's landmark school prayer decision, which occurred eight years after the revision of the pledge. In *Engel v. Vitale*[154] the Justices ruled, with only one dissenting vote, that even if objecting students are excused from participating, a public school may not conduct a daily classroom ceremony in which a state-authored prayer is recited.

The *Engel* precedent raises two questions about the constitutional status of the pledge in the post-*Barnette* era. First, with "under God" now a part of the pledge, might *Engel* support the transformation of the *Barnette* principle from a student's right to be excused into a denial of the power of public schools to conduct the pledge of allegiance ceremony even for students who do not object to participating? The Court was at pains in *Engel* to deny that implication: "patriotic or ceremonial occasions bear no true resemblance to the unquestioned religious exercise that the State of New York has sponsored in this instance." Although Justice Black's majority opinion did not mention the flag ceremony specifically, it did observe that "there are many manifestations in our public life of belief in God," not all of them problematic under the Establishment Clause.[155] Subsequent challenges to public school ceremonies that excused objecting students but employed the post–1954 "under God" version of the pledge produced a division among the federal circuits and, in 2002, a groundswell of patriotic indignation.[156]

---

[153] *H. J. Res. 243 and Other Bills on Pledge of Allegiance: Hearing Before the Subcomm. No. 5 of the Comm. on the Judiciary*, 83rd Cong. 7, 13, 37 (1954) (statement of Rep. Louis C. Rabaut, Rep. Charles G. Oakman, and Rep. Peter W. Rodino). *See also* the cited excerpts of Reverend Doeherty's influential sermon on the subject at 99 Cong. Rec. 7763 (1954).

[154] 370 U.S. 421 (1962).

[155] *Id.* at 435 n.21.

[156] *Compare Sherman v. Community Consol. Dist. 21*, 980 F.2d 437 (7th Cir. 1992) *with Newdow v. United States Congress*, 292 F.3d 597, 608 (9th Cir. 2002). *Newdow*'s holding, that the "under God" passage of the contemporary pledge violated the Establishment Clause, was overturned on grounds that Newdow, the non-custodial parent who brought the case on behalf of his daughter, lacked standing. *Elk Grove Unified School Dist. v. Newdow*, 542 U.S. 1 (2004). The controversy over *Newdow* prompted the introduction of

Justice Jackson's majority opinion in *Barnette* cannot help one to decide whether the inclusion of a passing reference to a deity gives the pledge ceremony theological import for purposes of the constitutional prohibition on the establishment of religion. Much of the doctrinal importance of *Barnette* lies in the fact that the Court rested its decision on the Freedom of Speech and not the Religion Clauses of the First Amendment. In our judgment, the Court's holding and opinion in *Barnette* does not (and does not aim to) provide guidance regarding what sorts of reference to religion raise questions of improper endorsement. The emphasis on character that we take to be at the heart of Justice Jackson's rationale is consistent with an accommodating approach to "ceremonial deism" but also with the competing view that an impermissible endorsement occurs whenever the official words of the nation affirm a particular religious understanding, even if that understanding is widely shared and expressed in purportedly ecumenical terms.

Second, whether or not the pledge refers to God, might the *Engel* approach be the sounder one? Even without compulsion to participate, might it be contrary to the First Amendment's character ideal to expose students in the authoritative context of the school environment to a ritual aimed to win over their hearts without appealing to their judgment? On that issue, the justification for the *Barnette* decision that we have identified has implications.

One might disapprove of all forms of rote patriotic recitation, at least when conducted on a daily basis in an educational environment, on the ground that such ceremonies undermine the First Amendment character ideal of a citizenry given to independent judgment, particularly regarding matters of political loyalty and consent. That objecting students are not required to participate does not fully address the problem, in this view. For the political independence of students who voluntarily pledge allegiance to the flag day after day matters just as much, and possibly is more at risk, as that of students who assert their right to be excused. Moreover, we might worry that some students who object to participating in a collective, school-sponsored flag salute will fail to assert their constitutional right to be excused for fear of incurring the displeasure or worse of their teachers and classmates.[157]

---

many resolutions in Congress, all aimed to reaffirm the inclusion of "under God" within the pledge. On November 13, 2002, one such reaffirmation was signed into law. Among other things, the statute included a criticism of *Newdow* and the assurance that the nation's motto continues to be "In God We Trust." Reaffirmation—Reference to One Nation Under God in the Pledge of Allegiance, Pub. L. No. 107–293, §§ 1, 3, 116 Stat 2057, 2060 (2002).

[157] Peer pressure of this sort was a major consideration in the Court's ruling that the inclusion of a religious invocation and benediction in a graduation ceremony violates the Establishment Clause. *See Lee v. Weisman*, 505 U.S. 577, 592–4 (1992). Indeed, in a

These concerns are not trivial. There is something profoundly troubling about a ceremony that, particularly when conducted in the lower grades, has the aim or effect of programming impressionable children to hold, if not a set of specific beliefs, at least a set of specific attitudes toward their country.[158] That students collectively voice their allegiance before they fully understand its meaning only enhances the risk that patriotic sentiments will become default—and ultimately shallow—attachments that are seated before they are comprehended, appreciated, and freely adopted. This form of inculcation is rather different from the use of rote or drill to instill knowledge of the multiplication tables or to provide the foundation for lasting appreciation of a poem.

We question the constitutionality of routine, ostensibly voluntary pledge exercises for the very young. Our misgivings are not nearly so strong, however, regarding flag ceremonies for students who have reached the minimal level of sophistication necessary to understand both the pledge and their right to exempt themselves from participation. We conclude that the better reading of *Barnette* is that it protects such

---

probing discussion of *Barnette*, Louis Michael Seidman observes that the *Barnette* protection may disrupt individual students' privacy and their freedom to be silent. Once the protection is in place, it becomes reasonable for observers to infer that students who recite the pledge agree with it, because dissenters would decline to participate. Whereas the mandatory pledge impedes observers from drawing reasonable inferences about students' beliefs and thereby creates cover for dissenters who do not wish to be identified, if the *Barnette* protection is in place, dissenters must either reveal themselves or risk being misunderstood. Seidman, *supra* note 131, at 155–7.

Seidman's argument, taken at face value, does not so much suggest that the right not to recite the pledge disrupts individual freedom. Rather, it calls into question *Barnette*'s compromise that a required pledge is constitutional so long as it has an opt-out provision. The argument he makes closely resembles the argument in *Lee* against allowing prayer in schools with an opt-out provision; just as the flaws of the opt-out system do not really themselves provide sustenance for the claim that mandatory prayer is constitutional, so too this argument at best shows that *Barnette*'s protection may not sweep far enough. This connects to a further response: the bite of Seidman's argument and the concern it evokes for dissenters turns on the fact that a required pledge with an opt-out provision still puts substantial pressure on all students to participate. Given the content of the pledge and the official and social pressures associated with a required pledge, some students are likely to feel so exposed and vulnerable if they opt out that feigned or insincere recitation will seem the lesser evil. These pressures may cast doubt on the claim that observers of students reciting the pledge would have warrant to conclude that the students agreed with its contents.

[158] *See e.g.*, Robert Hess and Judith Torney, *The Development of Political Attitudes in Children*, 16, 26, 29–30, 105–8 (1967) (While the flag provides a symbol that facilitates national identification, young children in the first and second grades do not so much grasp the meaning of the pledge as they grasp a "basic tone of awe for government" and that adults highly value it. The flag rituals operate as "indoctrinating acts that cue and reinforce feelings of loyalty," and "unquestioning patriotism." They "establish an emotional orientation toward country and flag even though an understanding of the meaning of the words and actions has not been developed.")

students from being required to participate in a flag salute but not from the burden of having to opt out, in one way or another, from such a ritual. The threat to democratic character inherent in patriotic ritual is greatly reduced when the element of legal compulsion is removed and the phenomenon of conscientious objection is legitimated by the constitutional regime. So long as school authorities take care to treat objecting students with respect, and insist that fellow students do the same, the loss of privacy and the sense of separation attendant to opting out of the ceremony are best treated as the natural, and not entirely unhealthy, incidents of dissent in a designedly contentious political culture. One might even consider the practice of dissenters publicly asserting their right to be excused from the patriotic catechism to be character building in the First Amendment sense, both for the dissenters themselves and for the other students who witness conscientious objection in action.

Do these grounds then suggest that *Engel* took too radical a turn? Why should the pledge be treated differently from prayer? To that question there is, in our judgment, a ready answer. The linchpin of the Supreme Court's school prayer jurisprudence holding that a right to be excused is insufficient under the Establishment Clause is the basic proposition that "it is no part of the business of government to compose official prayers."[159] As explained above, one cannot say that it is no part of the business of government to attempt to foster a widely shared, collectively articulated, even if not universally embraced, sense of national identity.

It was confidence that such a national identity could be achieved without compulsion, not indifference to whether it could be achieved, that led the Court in *Barnette* to say:

> [W]e apply the limitations of the Constitution with no fear that freedom to be intellectually and spiritually diverse or even contrary will disintegrate the social organization. To believe that patriotism will not flourish if patriotic ceremonies are voluntary and spontaneous instead of a compulsory routine is to make an unflattering estimate of the appeal of our institutions to free minds.[160]

This insistence that love of country and freedom of thought are complementary "even when a nation is at war"[161] may prove to be *Barnette's* most important legacy. The idea is hardly novel. Its roots go back at least as far as Pericles' Funeral Oration of 431 B.C.[162] Despite its appeal,

---

[159] *Engel v. Vitale*, 370 U.S. 421, 425 (1962).

[160] *West Va. State Bd. of Educ. v. Barnette*, 319 U.S. 624, 641 (1943).

[161] *See* Harry Kalven, Jr., *Foreword: Even When a Nation Is at War*, 85 Harv. L. Rev. 3 (1971).

[162] See Thucydides, *History of the Peloponnesian War* 146–50 (Rex Warner tr., M.I. Finley, ed., 1954); W. Robert Connor, *Thucydides* 70–71 (1984).

however, the claim is destined to remain controversial, especially in each new period of military mobilization. Sound but demanding ideas depend for their survival on articulate renewal. Justice Jackson's opinion for the Court in *West Virginia State Board of Education v. Barnette* is best read not as a doctrinal breakthrough or a justificatory tour de force but rather, and more impressively, a timely and memorable reiteration of an ancient truth.

*

13

Garrett Epps

The Story of Al Smith: The First Amendment Meets Grandfather Peyote

Americans pride themselves on living in a land of religious freedom, where rights of conscience are respected. But when does the First Amendment's guarantee of "the free exercise" of religion prevent the majority from burdening, or even outlawing altogether, the practices of minority faiths? When does the Constitution require government to exempt religious believers from its laws?

For years, the Court's answer to these questions was unclear, although language in the Warren and Burger Courts' opinions suggested that the Constitution required government to show a "compelling interest." In 1990, however, the Rehnquist Court unexpectedly announced a new rule: the Free Exercise Clause provided no protection at all to religious believers facing regulation—even, potentially, imprisonment—under "neutral, generally applicable" laws.

Employment Division v. Smith[1] was a radical and surprising decision, one of the earliest indications that a majority on the Rehnquist Court was prepared to rewrite, not just narrow or refine, the broad protections of civil liberties found by the Warren and Burger Courts. In *Smith,* the Court's majority held that religious believers facing criminal punishment for following their beliefs could find no protection in the First Amendment's Free Exercise Clause[2]—as long as the law that burdened their beliefs was not drawn with the purpose of penalizing religion.[3] The case sparked a nationwide outcry by religious groups

---

[1] 494 U.S. 872 (1990).

[2] U.S. Const. amend. I.

[3] *Smith,* 494 U.S. at 878–9.

across the political and theological spectrum, and spurred Congress to seek to overrule the decision not once but twice. Almost two decades after *Smith,* the case remains controversial, and both the Court and Congress continue to struggle with the problems of minority religions in a democratic, pluralistic nation. The Court's *Smith* rule presents a profound challenge to many Americans' image of their country as a land of tolerance and religious freedom.

But *Smith* was not seen as a landmark case at the time the Court reviewed it. The Court's radical holding came as a surprise to observers and to the parties themselves, none of whom had asked the Court to redraw the system of religious freedom. And the dispute itself arose in the most obscure of circumstances: an administrative challenge to a decision denying unemployment benefits to alcohol and drug abuse counselors. It was largely powered by the sheer stubbornness and grit of two remarkable men, who held diametrically opposite positions on the constitutional status of the Native American Church, a traditional Native American religion that worships peyote as the messenger and embodiment of the Creator. Each man believed his position was right; each man believed the issues in the case were matters of life and death. One of the two antagonists was Oregon's attorney general, Dave Frohnmayer; the other was a little-known Native American named Alfred Leo Smith Jr. In the end, Smith's determination wrote his name into constitutional history. By losing his case, Al Smith emerged a winner.

Background to the Dispute

Peyote is a small, spineless cactus that grows in dry areas of Northern Mexico and Southern Texas.[4] The "buttons" contain a potent blend of naturally occurring hallucinogens. Their taste, however, is bitter and often nauseating, which has limited the popularity of peyote as a recreational drug.

Spanish explorers in Mexico reported seeing peyote worshipers engaged in ecstatic dancing and ritual scarification with knives and hooks. In 1620 the Inquisition banned this "pagan" rite. But peyotism survived, and sometime in the nineteenth century it crossed the Rio Grande and moved into what was then Indian Territory (present-day Oklahoma). By 1890, a new rite had evolved, which blended aspects of Christian ritual and theology with the music and ceremonies of the tribes of the Southwest.

A peyote service is usually held in a Plains-style tipi and is supervised by a peyote priest, or "Road man." The participants gather at

---

[4] For details on the history and pharmacology of peyote, see generally Omer Stewart, *Peyote Religion: A History* (1987); Weston La Barre, *The Peyote Cult* (5th ed. 1989); and Edward Anderson, *Peyote: The Divine Cactus* (2d ed. 1996).

sundown to sit all night in the tipi around a ceremonial fire. Participants are offered the chance to eat peyote buttons (or drink the sacrament in the form of tea) several times during the night. The rest of the service involves song, prayer, and meditation. The peyote increases concentration and also allows participants to ignore the discomfort of sitting cross-legged with no back support for twelve to fifteen hours. Actual hallucinations, or visions, are relatively rare. Once the sun has risen, the participants leave the tipi, eat breakfast together, and disperse.

Peyotists are urged to be faithful to their spouses, to be self-supporting, and to care for their families. Peyote itself is to be used only in the ritual context, and alcohol in any form, or any kind of illegal drug (other than peyote itself), is strictly off-limits. By 1970, a significant scientific literature had emerged suggesting that peyote religion was a powerful force in helping its adherents maintain sobriety and abstain from drug use.

Partly as a result of the Church's caution, peyote religion remains an obscure faith to most Americans today, vaguely though inaccurately associated with the psychedelic experiments of the 1960s counterculture. The issue reached the Court over the strenuous objections of Church leaders themselves; that it did so was because of the insistence of Al Smith that Native traditions were entitled to the same level of respect as "mainstream" faiths like Protestant Christianity.

Alfred Leo Smith Jr.—a full-blooded Native American and an enrolled member of the Klamath tribe of Southwestern Oregon—was born in 1920. Klamath people have lived for nearly 10,000 years in the marshy areas around the great Upper Klamath Lake, a vast shallow body of water that is home to the largest migratory bird population in the lower forty-eight states. For generations, Klamath people have harvested the sucker fish that teem the region's rivers and the berries, fruit, and pond-lily seeds that grow around the lake.[5]

But throughout the twentieth century, the Klamath way of life faced unremitting pressure from white culture, which opposed its traditional ways as primitive and pagan and coveted the valuable timber that grew on the tribe's reservation. Federal Indian agents pressed Klamath parents to send their children to boarding schools to learn to be "Americans." So, when Al was only seven, his mother, Delia, sent him to St. Mary's Academy, a Catholic boarding school in nearby Klamath Falls. At boarding school, Smith quickly displayed the stubborn and independent streak that would characterize his whole life. He falsely told the nuns that he was already baptized, thus avoiding the Christian rite. But the religious instruction he received there, which he found insensitive and

---

[5] For a general ethnography and history of the Klamath people, see Theodore Stern, *The Klamath Tribe: A People and Their Reservation* (1965).

bigoted, inspired a lifelong distaste for white Christianity and what he considered to be the white man's God.

Al resisted Church teaching, and repeatedly ran away from his Catholic teachers. Finally, a priest administered a beating as punishment; outraged, Smith ran away again and convinced his mother to send him to the Stewart School, a government-run boarding school in Nevada for Indian students. He finished his education there and at the Chemawa Indian School near Salem, Oregon. Though he had been a good student and a star athlete, Al left school without graduating and quickly found himself living on the street, surviving by petty crime and seeking solace in alcohol. His drinking spun out of control, and after being drafted into the Army during World War II, he was found drinking on duty and sentenced to federal prison. Upon his release, he resumed his life as an alcoholic until, one day in 1957, he hit what alcoholism counselors called his bottom—a point at which he realized that the only two choices were sobriety or death. He chose sobriety.[6]

That choice, however, required membership in Alcoholics Anonymous, which was then as now almost the only significant treatment option that offered a chance at long-term success. To work the "Twelve Steps" of AA, Smith had to accept a "Higher Power" that would provide him with the strength to face life without the refuge of alcohol. But as Al later recalled, he had spent his life running from the white idea of God, and had no concept of the Divine that would speak to his soul and his Native American heritage. Then he remembered his grandmother, who had made a habit of praying every night before bed in her Klamath language. Al did not know Klamath and he did not know what the prayers had meant. But he decided to adopt her God, whoever that was—"a God that I didn't even understand."[7]

In the quarter century after his turning point, Al Smith rebuilt his life. He learned to hold a job, and became a sought-after speaker at AA meetings. In the 1970s, alcoholism expertise became a valuable commodity, and Smith found work as a full-time professional alcohol and drug-abuse counselor, first at the Alcohol Counseling and Recovery Program in Portland and then with the American Indian Council on Alcohol and Alcohol Abuse in Denver, Colorado, where he gained renown in Indian country for his work with tribal governments and health agencies in attacking the plague of alcoholism and drug abuse that afflicts Native peoples.[8] As he did so, he began to learn about the spiritual traditions of

---

[6] Garrett Epps, *To an Unknown God: The Hidden History of* Employment Division v. Smith, 30 Ariz. St. L.J. 953, 961 (1998) [hereinafter *Hidden History*].

[7] *Id.* at 955.

[8] Garrett Epps, *To an Unknown God: Religious Freedom on Trial* 42–43 (2001) [hereinafter *Unknown God*].

the many tribes he visited, and to incorporate distinctly Indian concepts of God—whom many Native people call "the Creator"—into his own spiritual life.

Native people were undergoing a spiritual awakening in the 1970s, as members of diverse tribes shared their rituals and traditions. A kind of "pan-Indian" religion was being born out of the old tribe-specific religions. Its key elements were the Sweat Lodge, in which worshipers purify themselves by praying and sweating in a kind of sauna made of wooden boughs, and the Sun Dance, a profoundly sacred ceremony that can last days or weeks. Another element that had begun to spread from its base in the Southwest was the tipi ritual of the Native American Church.

Al Smith first heard about the ritual when he was working at Sweat House Lodge, an inpatient treatment facility for Native Americans with drug and alcohol problems. When he was offered a chance to participate, he reacted the way most recovering alcoholics would. Peyote, he had heard, was a drug; getting "high" in any setting would threaten his hard-won sobriety. But after talking with a peyote priest, or "Road man," Smith realized that peyote religion was not thinly veiled drug abuse, and that many Church members found the tipi ritual a profound aid to their sobriety. Once he had participated, he discovered he agreed—though, he later said, he never considered himself a "member" of the Church.

Smith left Sweat House Lodge in April 1981.[9] He married again and he and his wife, Jane Farrell–Smith, had a new baby, Kaila, in 1982. To support the family, Smith took a job as an outpatient counselor at the Douglas County Council on Alcohol and Drug Abuse Prevention and Treatment (ADAPT), a private rehabilitation facility in Roseburg, Oregon. ADAPT, unlike Sweat House Lodge, had no Native orientation, and it took a strongly orthodox position on "relapses" into drinking or drug use—even one drink, even one incident of illicit drug use by "recovering" staff members was grounds for dismissal. But ADAPT encouraged Al Smith to offer traditional native Sweat Lodges and to introduce clients to other forms of Native spirituality.

One enthusiastic convert was Galen W. Black, a white man who was a recently recovering alcoholic just hired by ADAPT to work in its inpatient facility. Black, who was thirty-four, had grown up in Kansas, served in the Navy, and then eked out a living as an itinerant car mechanic while alcohol consumed more and more of his time and energy. Unlike Al Smith, Black had not spent years recovering. His commitment to sobriety, AA and the Twelve Steps was recent, and his soul burned with the zeal of a classic convert. The Sweat Lodge seemed to Black to

---

[9] *Hidden History, supra* note 6, at 963.

open a door to a whole new world of spirituality, untainted by the baggage his own Protestant upbringing carried. He began reading books about Native American religion and attending Indian ceremonials and pow-wows.[10]

At some point in this process Black heard about the Native American Church. Peyote religion, he thought, might offer both spiritual solace and a step forward in his new career as a rehabilitation counselor. Authorities seemed to agree that the Church offered powerful support to Native alcoholics and drug addicts. If it could be incorporated into the treatments available at ADAPT, it might help broaden the program's appeal.

Black went to Al Smith and asked him about peyote. Smith, however, was a bit unclear on who this white enthusiast was. He thought Galen was a recovering client seeking spiritual advice, not a colleague conferring on treatment methods. Smith later said that he knew from the time he went to work at ADAPT that his white superiors would consider peyote a drug. But when a client asked him about the Church, he could not truthfully say that it was harmful. Should I try it? Galen asked. That's up to you, Smith replied.

In September 1983, Galen attended a tipi ceremony in Salem, Oregon, and ate some of the sacred peyote.[11] He found the experience powerful, and when he returned he told one of his co-workers about the potentially important treatment method he had discovered. But in the zealously anti-drug atmosphere of the rehab center, the news traveled like lightning back to his bosses. They called Black in and ordered him to report to a treatment facility for a new round of rehabilitation. His ingestion of peyote was drug use, they said, and drug use constituted "relapse." When Black refused, they fired him.

ADAPT's director called in Al Smith as well and warned him in no uncertain terms that his own job was on the line if he used peyote again. Smith had not been to a ceremony since joining ADAPT; but now he felt that the agency's position showed disrespect to him—a man with a quarter century of sobriety—and to Native religion. After long deliberation, he went to a ceremony in March 1984 and took the sacrament. The next Monday, he told his boss what he had done, and he was fired.[12]

So far the dispute had been about treatment philosophy and the meaning of "abstinence" for recovering alcoholics. But now the state of Oregon became involved. When Smith and Black applied for unemployment compensation, the state's unemployment board, at the urging of

---

[10] *Unknown God, supra* note 8, at 98–99.

[11] *Hidden History, supra* note 6, at 100–01.

[12] *Id.* at 109.

ADAPT management, rejected their claims. They had been fired for "misconduct," the state said. At this point the fight, for Al Smith, became personal. "Do you want to fight?" he remembered thinking. "Okay."

Proceedings in the Oregon Courts

Oregon's state drug laws, unlike those of most Western states, made no exception for religious peyote use. The omission made little practical difference: not many Oregonians, Native or not, were involved in the Native American Church, and state authorities had made little effort to enforce the law against religious peyote users. In 1973, one Native peyotist had been convicted of possession, when a police officer during a routine traffic stop spotted a peyote button hanging from his rear-view mirror. The Oregon courts had rejected the man's defense—the state constitution required religious "neutrality," they held, which meant that no religion could be given special treatment under the law.[13]

Now, the state worried, the Department of Human Resources might allow an exemption from its misconduct rules for religious users of peyote. That might be a problem down the road—if "neutrality" among religions was the rule, then others might demand religious exemptions for use of other drugs, most particularly marijuana. Some of the world's most potent pot was grown in Southern Oregon, and at least one religious group, colorfully known as the Universal–Industrial Church of the New World Comforter, had recently switched its theology from worship of flying saucers to religious marijuana use.[14]

ADAPT wanted the state to defend against Smith's and Black's claims on the grounds that even occasional religious use of peyote violated the agency's philosophy of "total abstinence." But the state also chose to argue that Black and Smith had been fired for breaking the law. Even though neither man had been prosecuted (the state took no action to investigate them for criminal purposes), the state argued that this made their cases different from earlier cases in which the federal courts had required states to pay unemployment compensation to individuals who were out of work because of their religious practices.

The leading Supreme Court case was *Sherbert v. Verner*.[15] In *Sherbert,* South Carolina refused unemployment payments to a Seventh–Day Adventist who could not find a job that would permit her to remain at home on Saturday, which is the Adventist's Sabbath. In a famous

---

[13] *State v. Soto*, 537 P.2d 142 (Or. App. 1975).

[14] *See State v. Venet*, 797 P.2d 1055 (Or. App. 1990).

[15] 374 U.S. 398 (1963).

opinion by Justice Brennan, the Court had ordered the state to pay her anyway. The state system allowed payment to those who refused offered work for "good cause." Thus, the Court reasoned, the state could not discriminate against religious reasons in determining what constituted cause. In deciding the case, the Court laid down what came to be called "the *Sherbert* rule," or the "compelling interest test." Government, the court said, could not burden a citizen's religious belief or practice—at least by withholding benefits otherwise due—unless it had a "compelling interest" for doing so, and the refusal to pay was further "narrowly tailored" (which in practice meant just about absolutely necessary) to further that interest.

For that reason, the Oregon administrative law judge held that the First Amendment required payment to Smith and Black. An appeals board reversed him; from there the case went to the Oregon Court of Appeals and then the Oregon Supreme Court. Before both courts, the state (which now had sole charge of the case) argued that the case was different from *Sherbert*. There was no criminal law against observing Saturday as the Sabbath, it argued. But there was a valid criminal statute forbidding peyote possession. The First Amendment did not require the state to subsidize behavior that it had made illegal—particularly when the state's own constitution might require sharing that subsidy with many other users of illegal drugs.

The state courts agreed that the state constitution required "neutrality." But the federal First Amendment, as interpreted in *Sherbert,* went further, the Oregon judges said. Federal precedent imposed the "compelling interest" test. The state argued that it met that test—state laws designed to deal with the epidemic of drug use were vitally important to public health and safety. But the Oregon courts rejected that argument. The state unemployment compensation statute itself said nothing about criminal law enforcement or drug abuse prevention, and, as they read *Sherbert,* the "compelling interest" had to be stated in the law itself. The only interest the Oregon courts could find in the law was that of protecting the state treasury against false unemployment claims, and the courts found that this interest did not rise to the level required by *Sherbert.*[16]

At this point, the state had a choice. It could pay Smith and Black their unemployment and forget the matter, or it could seek review by the United States Supreme Court—the only federal court that can review a civil judgment of a state supreme court. And just as Al Smith's stubborn-

---

[16] *Black v. Employment Div.*, 721 P.2d 451 (Or. 1986), *aff'g* 707 P.2d 1274 (Or. App. 1985); *Smith v. Employment Div.*, 721 P.2d 445 (Or. 1986), *aff'g* 709 P.2d 246 (Or. App. 1985).

ness had fueled the dispute so far, at this point Dave Frohnmayer's own stubbornness came into play.

Frohnmayer, an Oregon native, was born in 1940. After graduating from high school in Medford, Oregon, he attended Harvard College, where he won a Rhodes Scholarship to Oxford, then studied law at the Boalt Hall School of Law at the University of California at Berkeley. After a brief stint as a special assistant in the Nixon administration, he returned to Oregon as a law professor at the University of Oregon. From there he won election to the state legislature and then, in 1980, as Oregon's attorney general. By the time the Smith and Black cases crossed his desk, his name was being mentioned as a future governor or senator from the state.

During his years as attorney general, Frohnmayer had been shaped by two experiences, one professional, the other personal. The first experience was the rise and fall of Rajneeshpuram, a religious commune established in the desert of eastern Oregon in 1981 that created a statewide crisis by the time of its collapse in 1985. Rajneeshpuram was established by Bhagwan Shree Rajneesh, a renegade Hindu holy man who had been more or less driven from his ashram in Poona, India, because of his practice of ridiculing his fellow Hindus—and because of the radical sexual freedom he permitted among his mostly American and European disciples, whom he called *sanyassins*. Because his followers were largely educated and well-to-do, the guru had amassed considerable wealth (at the height of the movement he owned nearly 100 Rolls Royce automobiles), and he used some of it to purchase the Big Muddy Ranch, a 64,000–acre expanse of arid grazing land located in the desert along the John Day River in Eastern Oregon, not far from the sleepy hamlet of Antelope. Here the guru planned a new Jerusalem, complete with hotel, shopping mall, restaurant, convention center, and other facilities of a modern city.[17]

But Bhagwan had not reckoned with Oregon's strict land-use laws, which forbade this kind of development outside an established city. Faced with opposition to his plans, he first sent followers to live in Antelope, where they quickly took over the city government and changed its name to Rajneesh. He also got permission from county authorities to incorporate the Ranch as a city on its own, named Rajneeshpuram. This legal maneuver would give him control of the land-use decisions in both communities—and, among other things, access to state law-enforcement information and resources for his private security force, which now became the police of the two cities.

But neighbors objected to the growth of this massive enterprise in the fragile desert environment. They persuaded a legislator to ask

---

[17] *Unknown God, supra* note 8, at 66–89.

Frohnmayer's office to examine the legality of Rajneeshpuram's incorporation, and in 1983, the attorney general issued an opinion that the city
itself violated the state and federal constitutions. Because all the land
within Rajneeshpuram was owned by a religious commune, the Rajneesh
Neo–Sannyas International Foundation, the incorporation of the city
amounted to state delegation of government authority to a religious
body. "The federal and state constitutions," Frohnmayer wrote, "do not
permit the road to Damascus to be paved with public funds."[18] After
releasing the opinion, Frohnmayer's office began legal proceedings to
disincorporate Rajneeshpuram.

This move made the attorney general the commune's Public Enemy
Number One. The Rajneesh daily newspaper began calling him "Herr
General Frohnmayer," in derision of his father's German birth. They
branded him a bigot, a fundamentalist, a foe of religious freedom
prosecuting a harmless band of pilgrims on their search for salvation.
More sinister signs of disfavor appeared as well: mysterious late-night
phone calls; strange visitors to the house on pretended errands; and
animal entrails wrapped in Rajneesh leaflets and left for the Frohnmayer
children to find. Eventually, as the conflict heated up, forces inside the
Ranch sent teams of assassins to plan the murders of a federal prosecutor, a top investigative reporter, and Dave Frohnmayer.

It was not generally known, in fact, but the state's opposition and
the internal tensions within the Rajneesh movement had led the commune to take a sharp turn into madness. Followers of Bhagwan were
amassing assault weapons, and a secret lab on the ranch was researching
germ and biological warfare, including attempts to culture the AIDS
virus as a potential weapon. In fact, in the fall of 1984, Rajneesh
followers carried out the first modern attempt at bioterrorism on American soil.[19]

Their aim was to take over Wasco County, which partially contained
the ranch, by disabling voters on election day with salmonella poisoning.
Widespread illness would reduce the turnout of ordinary voters, permitting the Rajneesh followers—who had imported some 3,000 homeless
people from around the country to the ranch in advance of the election—
to elect their own write-in candidates to the county's Board of Commissioners. On September 9, 1984, dozens of disciples fanned out across the
county on a dry run, introducing salmonella into the salad bars of local
restaurants. As a result, nearly 700 citizens were sickened, some seriously, and state law-enforcement authorities became suspicious. The Oregon

---

[18] 44 Or. Op. Att'y Gen. 20 (1983).

[19] *See* Stephen Engelberg & Judith Miller, *Germs: Biological Weapons and America's
Secret War* (2001).

Secretary of State stepped in to monitor voter registration, foiling the plan to register the homeless, and the plot unraveled.[20]

After its failure, Rajneeshpuram's internal tensions boiled over. Bhagwan's top follower, Ma Anand Sheela, fled the ranch with her inner circle of advisers, and Bhagwan accused her of plotting to poison him. State police swarmed the ranch, finding the germ lab, the weapons, an extensive secret taping system for spying on residents and guests, and evidence of plans for mass immigration fraud through phony marriages between non-citizen Rajneesh followers and American disciples. Bhagwan attempted to flee the country, but authorities arrested him in North Carolina when his plane, laden with cash and jewels, stopped to refuel there. The guru agreed to leave the U.S.; Sheela and others pleaded guilty to charges of immigration fraud and attempted murder.[21]

The Rajneesh experience left the state shaken. It left Dave Frohnmayer in particular skeptical about claims for religious exemption from the law.

At the same time this drama was unfolding, Frohnmayer's personal life took a tragic turn. He and his wife Lynn discovered that of their five children, three—their daughters Kirsten, Katy, and Amy—were all suffering from Fanconi Anemia, a rare, fatal genetic disease. The gene had come to them from both parents, though because it was so rare neither family had ever before experienced a case. The girls' only hope was a bone-marrow transplant. The Frohnmayer family became deeply involved in trying to promote research on the disease and on bone-marrow transplantation generally. They started a foundation to fund scientific efforts and began a personal quest to find a distant relation whose bone marrow might be compatible with one of the girls. Though foundation-funded research made progress in treating the disease, no cure has been found, and the search for donors proved fruitless. Eventually two of the girls, Katie and Kirsten, would die.

Frohnmayer's response to tragedy was a ferocious, single-minded determination to fight the disease. To a lawyer's ordinary stubbornness—any good lawyer hates to lose—he now brought an unusual reserve of resolve.[22]

Perhaps these experiences played into the attorney general's decision to seek review of Smith and Black's case by the United States Supreme Court. Many Court-watchers were surprised, however, when the petition for certiorari was granted. The issue was hardly one of national importance—almost every state with a significant Native popu-

---

[20] *Unknown God, supra* note 8, at 83.

[21] *Id.* at 84–89.

[22] *Id.* at 20–41.

lation exempted peyote religion from its drug laws, and even in Oregon the issue had come up only once previously. Frohnmayer consulted a national expert, Berkeley professor Jesse Choper, who cautioned the attorney general that the Court was firmly committed to the *Sherbert* rule, and that the state of Oregon should make sure to couch all its arguments in terms of the compelling interest test.[23]

The Supreme Court's Two Smith *Decisions*

The Supreme Court's first consideration of *Smith* produced little clarity. Argument before the high court on December 8, 1987 centered around the meaning of Oregon's drug law. Smith and Black's legal aid lawyer (who had never handled an appellate case in front of any federal court) filed a brief arguing that, properly interpreted, Oregon's drug-abuse statutes did not even forbid the consumption of peyote, only its possession. Since the two men had not owned the peyote, she insisted, the statute could not be applied to them. And even if it could, Oregon's state unemployment statute did not permit the state to use illegality of employee conduct as a basis for denying compensation claims.[24]

It was a clever argument, but the attorney had waited too long to raise it. The Supreme Court of the United States has no jurisdiction over interpretation of state statutes, and Court rules require attorneys offering such an argument to raise it no later than in their brief in opposition to a grant of certiorari.[25] Smith and Black's attorney, however, had argued against certiorari only on federal constitutional grounds, citing *Sherbert* and succeeding cases on the compelling interest test. Only in her reply brief on the merits did the lawyer unveil the statutory arguments.

In oral argument, the Justices harshly criticized the attorney for this omission, and suggested that this defense was waived. Or, the Justices suggested in questions, perhaps they should simply remand the case to the Oregon courts for a ruling on the statutory issue. The state of Oregon insisted that peyote possession and use were illegal under Oregon law and that the state had the right to take this into account for purposes of unemployment benefits. And so the Free Exercise issue was clouded by a confusion over state law—a confusion the Court was neither equipped nor inclined to resolve.

---

[23] *Id.* at 149–50.

[24] *Id.* at 174–75

[25] Sup. Ct. R. 15(2).

On April 20, 1988, the Court issued its first opinion in *Employment Division v. Smith*,[26] a decision which would come to be known as *Smith I*. The Court remanded the case to the Oregon Supreme Court for clarification of state law. In a majority opinion written by Justice Stevens, the Court said:

> Neither the Oregon Supreme Court nor this Court has confronted the question whether the ingestion of peyote for sincerely held religious reasons is a form of conduct that is protected by the Federal Constitution from the reach of a State's criminal laws. It may ultimately be necessary to answer that federal question in this case, but it is inappropriate to do so without first receiving further guidance concerning the status of the practice as a matter of Oregon law. A substantial number of jurisdictions have exempted the use of peyote in religious ceremonies from legislative prohibitions against the use and possession of controlled substances. If Oregon is one of those States, respondents' conduct may well be entitled to constitutional protection. On the other hand, if Oregon does prohibit the religious use of peyote, and if that prohibition is consistent with the Federal Constitution, there is no federal right to engage in that conduct in Oregon. If that is the case, the State is free to withhold unemployment compensation from respondents for engaging in work-related misconduct, despite its religious motivation. Thus, paradoxical as it may first appear, a necessary predicate to a correct evaluation of respondents' federal claim is an understanding of the legality of their conduct as a matter of state law.[27]

Justice Brennan wrote a dissent, in which Justices Marshall and Blackmun joined. Brennan argued that the Oregon Supreme Court's opinion had not even raised the issue of illegality under state law, and thus by implication had held it to be irrelevant to its First Amendment conclusion. The remand was a waste of time, he argued, and he then dropped a broad hint to the Oregon court that a properly worded opinion would insulate the result in *Smith* from further review by the Supreme Court:

> The Court merely remands these cases to the Oregon Supreme Court for further proceedings after concluding that a "necessary predicate" to its analysis is a pronouncement by the state court on whether respondents' conduct was criminal. It seems to me that the state court on remand could readily resolve these cases without reaching that issue. The Court has expressed no intention to depart from the longstanding rule that, in strictly scrutinizing state-imposed burdens on fundamental rights, courts may not assert on a State's behalf interests that the State does not have. Accordingly, I must assume that the Court has tacitly left the Oregon Supreme

---

[26] 485 U.S. 660 (1988) [hereinafter *Smith I*].

[27] *Id.* at 672 (footnotes omitted).

Court the option to dispose of these cases by simply reiterating its initial opinion and appending, "And we really mean it," or words to that effect.[28]

The Oregon Supreme Court, however, did not accept Justice Brennan's invitation. During the 1980s, the Oregon court had become nationally renowned for its independence and its insistence that the state courts must construe Oregon's constitution before reaching any issues of federal constitutional interpretation. Under the leadership of Justice Hans Linde, a former law professor, the Oregon court was in the forefront of a revolution in state constitutional law that had spread far beyond the state's borders. In Linde's view, state courts had fallen too deeply under the sway of the Warren and Burger Courts, with their often-vague "balancing" tests which posed state "interests" against individual rights. State courts were not simply a junior version of the federal judiciary, Linde contended, and each state's own history and law mandated an independent consideration of the text and history of its own constitution.[29]

Often, state constitutions could provide more protection for individual rights than did the federal charter. Thus, in Oregon, the courts had held that the state's guarantee against search and seizure was broader than that provided by the federal Fourth Amendment,[30] and the state's free speech clause provided protection for expression that could be outlawed as obscene under First Amendment caselaw.[31]

Such was not the case with Oregon's religious-liberty clauses, however, which were quite different in language from the federal First Amendment. The U.S. Constitution provides that "Congress shall make no law respecting an establishment of religion or prohibiting the free exercise thereof."[32] Oregon's Constitution, which was written seventy years later by a band of frontiersmen who were suspicious of organized religion (and somewhat unorthodox in their spelling), provides:

> All men shall be secure in the Natural right, to worship Almighty God according to the dictates of their own consciences[, and] [n]o law shall in any case whatever control the free exercise, and enjoyment of religeous (sic) opinions, or interfere with the rights of conscience.[33]

---

[28] *Id.* at 678–79 (Brennan, J., dissenting).

[29] *See, e.g.,* Hans A. Linde, *First Things First: Rediscovering the States' Bill of Rights,* 9 U. Balt. L. Rev 379 (1980).

[30] *State v. Caraher,* 653 P.2d 942 (Or. 1982).

[31] *State v. Robertson,* 649 P.2d 569 (Or. 1982).

[32] U.S. Const. amend I.

[33] Oregon Const. Art. I, §§ 2–3.

This language, the Oregon Court had previously held, meant that the state must be neutral in all religious or denominational questions—even when the requirement of neutrality meant the state could not provide religious exemptions that were otherwise compatible with federal law.[34] This suggested that the state constitution would not protect Smith and Black.

But the Oregon court's independent streak meant something else: The U.S. Supreme Court had rather peremptorily ordered it to decide whether Oregon's laws and constitution protected peyote religion from criminal prosecution under state law. But the state was not prosecuting Al Smith and Galen Black. So any such opinion would be hypothetical, an "advisory" opinion about a question that had not arisen in fact. Federal courts are adamant that legislators and the litigants may not use federal litigation simply to get advice. Courts would authoritatively construe the U.S. Constitution only when required to do so in the context of an actual "case or controversy."[35] Some state courts follow a different practice, and will advise the legislature in advance about the potential constitutionality of a bill.[36] But Oregon was not one of those states. The Oregon courts followed a "case or controversy" rule as strict in its way as the federal one.[37] And the Oregon Supreme Court was the highest court in the state system, independent of the federal judiciary. What the justices would not do for their own state legislature, they would not do for the nine oracles in Washington, however sternly the U.S. Supreme Court might instruct them to.

Thus, on remand, the Oregon court issued a truculent per curiam opinion. It stated once again that its own reading of federal caselaw—and the will of Congress as expressed in the legislative history of federal drug statutes—led to the conclusion that the federal First Amendment protected religious peyote use from criminal prosecution. It further affirmed that as written Oregon's statutes did not exempt religious peyote use from criminal prohibition. Under Oregon's constitution, that might mean that the state could jail peyote worshipers—or it might not:

> If disqualification from unemployment compensation hinged on guilt or innocence of an uncharged and untried crime, it would raise issues of the applicable mental state and of changing burdens of proof for which the compensation procedure is neither designed nor equipped. Because no criminal case is before us, we do not give an advisory opinion on the circumstances under which prosecuting

[34] *Salem Coll. & Acad., Inc. v. Employment Div.*, 695 P.2d 25 (Or. 1985).

[35] *Flast v. Cohen*, 392 U.S. 83, 107 (1968).

[36] *See* Erwin Chemerinsky, *Constitutional Law* § 2.4 at 53 n.1 (3rd ed. 2006).

[37] *In re Ballot Title*, 431 P.2d 1 (Or. 1967).

members of the Native American Church [under state law] for sacramental use of peyote would violate the Oregon Constitution.[38]

The U.S. Supreme Court had tried to pass the case back to the Oregon court. But the Oregon justices refused to play. *Sherbert* and its test were federal law, which they would apply as best they understood it. Under the "compelling interest" test, Smith and Black would win.

But Dave Frohnmayer could not live with that result. "If we couldn't take that case off the books," he said later, "we were in a major world of hurt."[39] Many outside observers disagreed with that suggestion—newspapers and religious leaders in the state urged the attorney general not to seek certiorari again. But Frohnmayer was determined. He believed that the Oregon Supreme Court was wrong; crafting an exemption from the law for one church or one faith, he argued, was a violation of the Establishment Clause, just the way creating a city for Bhagwan had been. But beyond that, he had a practical worry. If religious peyote use was exempt from state law, how long would it be before demands were made for the same exemption for religious marijuana use?

The idea was not fanciful. By the time of the second Oregon Supreme Court decision, there was an actual case involving that issue in the Oregon courts. The defendant was Alan Venet, a calm, well-spoken ex-hippy from New Jersey who had taken up residence on a farm near Grants Pass, Oregon. Venet was an ordained cleric, or "Boo-hoo," of a sect called the Universal–Industrial Church of the New World Comforter, mentioned earlier. The Church had been founded in the late 1940s by one of the first Americans to report having been abducted by aliens in a UFO. But Venet's branch of the Church, at least, had evolved into the worship of cannabis. Venet had been arrested for growing marijuana on his farm, and at his trial he had argued that the First Amendment protected his worship.[40] A decision for Al Smith and Galen Black would not necessarily mean that Venet would win. But it would make prosecuting Venet more complicated, and perhaps encourage other defendants to raise the same defense. And while peyote was not a problem in Oregon, Frohnmayer did believe that marijuana use was. In his certiorari petition, Frohnmayer suggested that the issue now was whether "the federal constitution protects religious use of dangerous drugs." In fact, the petition suggested the Court should hold that the federal government's exemption for the Native American Church was itself unconstitutional.

---

[38] *Smith v. Employment Div.*, 763 P.2d 146 (Or. 1988) (per curiam).

[39] *Hidden History*, supra note 6, at 1003.

[40] *Id.* at 995.

When the Court granted certiorari on March 20, 1989, alarm bells went off across Indian country. Before, the issue had been unemployment compensation, and the consequences of a loss for Smith and Black would probably have been confined to Oregon. Now the issue was jail time for peyotists. A victory for Oregon this time around could mean that other states would decide to repeal their own protection of the Church, and even set off a wave of persecution in places like Oklahoma or Arizona with substantial Native populations.

And the grant of certiorari wasn't a good sign. The Court had become markedly more conservative since the ascension of William Rehnquist to the Chief Justice position in 1986. Where the Warren Court, and, to a lesser extent, the Burger Court, had shown some solicitude for the special problems of Indian culture and tribal rights, the new conservative majority was visibly impatient with Native claims. Just the year before, in 1988, the Court's majority had dismissed summarily a challenge by a group of California Indians to a plan by the U.S. Forest Service to build a logging road near sacred sites inside a national forest that the tribes believed to be the center of the world. The Service's own anthropological consultant had concluded that the logging road would destroy the Native people's traditional religion. But the majority, in an opinion by Justice Sandra Day O'Connor, declined even to engage in a process of balancing between the harm to the Indians and the gain to the government. The government could do whatever it liked with "what is, after all, its land."[41] That the land had belonged to the Indians for thousands of years before the United States took it simply did not matter; nor did the consequences for traditional culture and freedom of religion.

Now the Native American Church was facing the same fate. For the first time, leaders of the organized peyote religion became involved in the case. The Church's strategy for most of the twentieth century had been to avoid conflict where possible and to work for informal settlements or legislative accommodation when necessary. Many Church elders wanted no part of a fight to the death against the state and federal anti-drug establishments. The Native American Church of North America (NACNA), one of the largest organized denominations within the broader peyotist movement, now decided the time had come to end Smith and Black's challenge.

NACNA was represented by the Native American Rights Fund (NARF), probably the most formidable of the many public-interest groups that represent Native American interests in the courts. NARF was founded in the early 1970s by John Echohawk, a Pawnee Indian who had been the first Native American to graduate from the University

---

[41] *Lyng v. Northwest Indian Cemetery Protective Ass'n*, 485 U.S. 439, 453 (1988).

of New Mexico School of Law.[42] NARF had been involved for years in negotiations and litigation with Western state governments over the interests of the tribal governments who were its clients. During those years, Echohawk had become a friend of Frohnmayer's.

Now Echohawk came to Oregon to seek a way out of the looming showdown. He asked Al Smith's permission to try to negotiate a settlement with the state, and Smith agreed to let him try. Echohawk then went to Frohnmayer and pleaded with him to make this case, with its mortal danger for an ancient Indian faith, somehow disappear from the Court's docket.

Frohnmayer agreed to talk. He had little incentive to settle; most Court observers on both sides of the issue believed that the Justices had granted certiorari in order to reverse the Oregon Supreme Court. When settlement talks began on October 24, 1989, the attorney general was in a strong position. He had no desire to prosecute Church members; but he believed strongly that the *Smith* precedent must be taken off the books if Oregon was to avoid the danger of constant litigation over religious claims for drug-use exemptions. During all-night negotiations over pizza and coffee, state lawyers, NARF attorneys, and Al Smith's Legal Aid lawyer, Craig Dorsay, worked out an agreement. Under its terms, Oregon would inform the Supreme Court that it was withdrawing its cert. petition (an unusual and somewhat embarrassing move, since the petition had been granted and oral argument was only weeks away). In exchange, Smith and Black would petition the Oregon Supreme Court to vacate its decision in their favor. The two men would also repay the unemployment compensation they had already received under the Oregon court's original judgment.[43]

The agreement satisfied the Church, which would avert a mortal danger. It satisfied the state, which would wipe out a precedent it regarded as dangerous. But it didn't do much for Al Smith. The repayment would not come out of his pocket—NARF and Church officials assured him that wealthy donors would happily write the check—but it was a surrender, a humiliation, and an admission that he had been wrong and white culture had been right all along. NARF representatives told him in no uncertain terms that it was his duty to accept the deal, like it or not. And Smith began to receive messages and calls from Church leaders elsewhere in the country begging him not to "take our medicine away."

But the pressure backfired in the end. Al Smith had never been one to take orders from anyone, white or red. And Smith and his family felt

---

[42] *Hidden History*, supra note 6, at 1004.

[43] *Id.* at 1007–08.

that Church leaders had been disrespectful in their approach. In the end, Smith was left with only a few advisers: his wife, Jane Farrell–Smith, and a Road man, Stanley Smart, who had introduced him to peyote religion. Smart in particular counseled Smith to stay the course. Grandfather Peyote had lived on the edge of the law long enough, Smart said. Perhaps it was time to find out if the white man's First Amendment was big enough to include this Indian tradition. And Smith, now nearly seventy years old, was troubled by the message that the settlement would send to his children, two of whom were still in elementary school. Some day he would be gone, and perhaps this was all they would remember—that their father had lost his nerve and run from the final battle. "I can't lay that on my kids," he later remembered thinking. "So I got a couple of hours sleep. I phoned [Craig Dorsay] and told him, 'Well, let's go to court.' "[44]

The Court's Second Decision

The Court heard oral argument in what came to be known as *Smith II* on November 6, 1989. Frohnmayer himself, a veteran of six earlier Supreme Court hearings, argued for the state.[45] He contended that an exemption for peyote religion would open the door for countless religious claims for other drugs. He conceded that peyote use by Church members had been safe and responsible so far. But what about the future? "[D]enominational practices, and indeed individual believers, in long-standing religions, can and do change.... [I]f the denominational or church controls weaken or change, there [will be] still enshrined in the Bill of Rights a permanent exemption for the practices of that religion."[46]

Craig Dorsay argued for Smith and Black. He found the Justices skeptical of his argument that this case was no different from others decided under the *Sherbert* test. Justice O'Connor, the author of the *Lyng* decision, asked him whether a decision for Smith and Black would require a religious exemption for marijuana too. "I don't want to go down that road too far," Dorsay began. "I'll bet you don't," O'Connor quipped, drawing laughter from the bench and audience. Justice Scalia asked whether Aztecs would be entitled to exemptions from murder laws if they wanted to practice human sacrifice. Dorsay controlled his irritation at the question, which seemed to equate the Church with murder.[47]

Interestingly enough, during the entire argument—as indeed in the briefing of the case by the parties and by amici—no one on either side,

---

[44] *Id.* at 1010 (brackets omitted).

[45] *Id.* at 967 n.58.

[46] Transcript of Oral Argument at 24–25, *Smith II*, 494 U.S. 872 (1990).

[47] *Id.* at 42–45.

and no Justice from the bench, suggested that the case would be decided under any other standard but *Sherbert*. Oregon argued that it had a compelling interest that made an exemption impossible; Smith and Black argued that the Church could be exempted without compromising the integrity of drug laws.

When the Court announced its decision on April 17, 1990, however, the parties—and much of the religious community nationwide—were shocked to find that five Justices had decided to use the occasion to virtually eliminate the compelling interest test. "In recent years we have abstained from applying the *Sherbert* test (outside the unemployment compensation field) at all," Scalia wrote.[48] That would seem to favor Smith and Black; their claim was for unemployment compensation. But the Court decided to treat their claim as a request for exemption from criminal prosecution—an issue that had been argued only at the Court's request. In cases involving "across-the-board criminal prohibition on a particular form of conduct," the majority now said, *Sherbert* did not apply.[49] The better rule was that "the right of free exercise does not relieve an individual of the obligation to comply with a 'valid and neutral law of general applicability on the ground that the law proscribes (or prescribes) conduct that his religion prescribes (or proscribes).' "[50]

True, religious claimants had won other cases—but Scalia now explained that those victories weren't based solely on free exercise, but were in a category (unheard of until the *Smith* opinion) called "hybrid cases," which "involved not the Free Exercise Clause alone, but the Free Exercise Clause in conjunction with other constitutional protections, such as freedom of speech and of the press . . . or the right of parents . . . to direct the education of their children."[51]

The new rule seemed to relegate free exercise to a second-rung status in the scale of constitutional values. Justice Scalia argued that courts should not be in the business of assessing individual religious claims. The United States was a land of many faiths, he explained, and "precisely because we value and protect that religious divergence, we cannot afford the luxury of deeming *presumptively invalid*, as applied to the religious objector, every regulation of conduct that does not protect an interest of the highest order."[52]

---

[48] 494 U.S. at 883.

[49] *Id.* at 884.

[50] *Id. at* 879 (quoting *United States v. Lee*, 455 U.S. 252, 263, n.3 (1982) (Stevens, J., concurring in judgment)).

[51] *Id.* at 881 (citations omitted).

[52] *Id.* at 888.

That language shocked many non-lawyers, who took it to mean that the cherished American ideal of equality and respect for all faiths was now considered something government should not be obliged to observe. To lawyers, something else about the opinion was almost equally shocking[53]: Scalia seemed to juggle precedents rather cavalierly to make them fit his analysis. For example, he relied heavily on citations of *Minersville School District v. Gobitis,*[54] a 1940 case in which the Court had held that Free Exercise did not excuse Jehovah's Witness children in the public schools from a required salute to the flag and recitation of the Pledge of Allegiance, even though under their religious beliefs, such obeisance to a "graven image" was idolatry punishable by eternal damnation. *Gobitis,* though, isn't good law—the Court had specifically overturned it three years later in *West Virginia Board of Education v. Barnette*[55] (discussed in Chapter Twelve). Scalia acknowledged *Barnette* in a brisk string citation elsewhere in the opinion. Because in *Barnette* the Court had relied on the Free Speech Clause to hold that school authorities could not require any child, no matter his or her religion, to recite words he or she didn't believe, Scalia implied, *Barnette* was a "hybrid" case, leaving *Gobitis* a valid precedent even though its result had been erased. Even lawyers who specialize in religious freedom had to read and reread the two cases to understand what Scalia had done.

Justice O'Connor concurred in the result, though her separate opinion read like a dissent. She criticized the "neutral, generally applicable" test as without foundation in the Court's precedent. "Our free exercise cases have all concerned generally applicable laws that had the effect of significantly burdening a religious practice. If the First Amendment is to have any vitality, it ought not be construed to cover only the extreme and hypothetical situation in which a State directly targets a religious practice."[56]

Justice O'Connor insisted that retaining the compelling interest test was essential for the continued protection of free exercise.

> In my view ... the essence of a free exercise claim is relief from a burden imposed by government on religious practices or beliefs, whether the burden is imposed directly through laws that prohibit or compel specific religious practices, or indirectly through laws

---

[53] *See, e.g.,* Michael W. McConnell, *Free Exercise Revisionism and the* Smith *Decision,* 57 U. Chi. L. Rev. 1109, 1125 (1990). McConnell's criticism is particularly striking because he is a committed legal conservative who has since been appointed to the appellate bench by President George W. Bush. (He is also the author of Chapter One of this book.)

[54] 310 U.S. 586 (1940).

[55] 319 U.S. 624 (1943).

[56] *Smith II,* 494 U.S. at 894 (O'Connor, J., concurring).

that, in effect, make abandonment of one's own religion or conformity to the religious beliefs of others the price of an equal place in the civil community.[57]

O'Connor defended the test in ringing terms, quoting Justice Robert Jackson on the meaning of the Bill of Rights in *Barnette* (which she pointedly noted, had overruled *Gobitis*):

> The very purpose of a Bill of Rights was to withdraw certain subjects from the vicissitudes of political controversy, to place them beyond the reach of majorities and officials and to establish them as legal principles to be applied by the courts. One's right to life, liberty, and property, to free speech, a free press, freedom of worship and assembly, and other fundamental rights may not be submitted to vote; they depend on the outcome of no elections.[58]

The ringing tones of Justice O'Connor's opinion won her applause from many commentators, who almost seemed not to notice that in her view the result should still have been defeat for Al Smith and Galen Black. Justice O'Connor was a hard-liner on criminal justice, and she was the author of the *Lyng* opinion that dismissed Native religious claims as meddlesome interference with the government's prerogatives. Now she noted that protecting the Native American Church would require disturbing the state of Oregon's judgment that peyote was a drug and that no exceptions should be made in its drug abuse laws. "I believe that granting a selective exemption in this case would seriously impair Oregon's compelling interest in prohibiting possession of peyote by its citizens. Under such circumstances, the Free Exercise Clause does not require the State to accommodate respondents' religiously motivated conduct."[59]

Justice Blackmun, joined by Justices Brennan and Marshall, wrote an impassioned dissent, arguing that the majority opinion "effectuates a wholesale overturning of settled law concerning the Religion Clauses of our Constitution. One hopes that the Court is aware of the consequences, and that its result is not a product of overreaction to the serious problems the country's drug crisis has generated."[60]

Aftermath of Smith

If the majority was unaware of the consequences, it did not remain so for long. The *Smith II* opinion sparked a flood of hostile comment

---

[57] *Id.* at 897.

[58] *Id.* at 903 (quoting *Barnette*, 319 U.S., at 638).

[59] *Id.* at 906.

[60] *Id.* at 908 (Blackmun, J., dissenting).

from the nation's press.[61] Mainstream religious leaders, too, reacted to the opinion—which seemed to demote religious liberty to a secondary status among the nation's individual rights—with outrage. A coalition of religious leaders filed an immediate petition with the Court asking the Justices to vacate the *Smith II* decision and hear reargument, this time with the question of the "compelling interest" test explicitly among the issues to be considered.[62] The Court rejected the petition in a one-sentence order issued a few months after the original decision.[63]

Once mobilized, the coalition began to lobby for a legislative override of the decision. The group that backed legislation was unusually broad, stretching from the American Civil Liberties Union and People for the American Way on the left all the way to such religious-right stalwarts as the American Center for Law and Justice, sponsored by Pat Robertson, and the National Home–School Defense Association. It was not, however, quite wide broad enough to include the Native American Church. Coalition leaders told the Church that peyote was controversial and should perhaps be addressed at another time. In their work with legislative leaders, they did not object to legislative history indicating that Congress did not necessarily intend to overturn the *result* in *Smith II*. Peyote might still be outlawed under the compelling interest test, as Justice O'Connor's concurrence suggested.[64] Church leaders and their lawyers resented the way they were shunted aside during the drafting of the proposed remedial legislation.[65]

The result of the lobbying effort came to be known as the Religious Freedom Restoration Act, and it was passed, nearly unanimously, by Congress in 1993.[66] The Act was based on Congress's power under § 5 of

---

[61] *See, e.g.*, Nat Hentoff, *Justice Scalia vs. the Free Exercise of Religion*, Wash. Post, May 19, 1990, at A25 (stating generally that the *Smith* decision casts a pall over the bicentennial of the Bill of Rights); *Indian Religion; Must Say No*, Economist, Oct. 6, 1990, at 25 (U.K. ed. p. 51) (decision "stunned church leaders, both Christian and Jewish"); Samuel Rabinove, *The Supreme Court and Religious Freedom*, Christian Sci. Monitor, June 25, 1990, at 19 (recalling Madison's warning that "[i]t is proper to take alarm at the first experiment on our liberty."); Edwin Yoder, *A Confusing Court Ban on Peyote's Ritual Use*, St. Louis Post–Dispatch, Apr. 24, 1990, at 3C ("In theory, all religions are equal under the First Amendment; but in the eyes of the court some are clearly more equal than others.").

[62] Douglas Laycock, *The Supreme Court's Assault on Free Exercise, and the Amicus Brief That Was Never Filed*, 8 J. L. & Religion 99 (1990).

[63] 496 U.S. 913 (1990).

[64] *See, e.g.*, H.R. 103–88, "Religious Freedom Restoration Act of 1993" (May 11, 1993) (noting that RFRA "will not mandate that all states permit the ceremonial use of peyote")

[65] *Unknown God, supra* note 8, at 230–31.

[66] *Id.* at 233.

the Fourteenth Amendment[67] to enforce the national constitutional values of Equal Protection and Due Process of Law. It directed courts to apply the compelling interest test whenever neutral laws burdened an individual right of Free Exercise, whether that burden resulted from federal or state law or from the action of state or federal administrative agencies.[68] President Clinton, who had enthusiastically supported the law, signed it in November 1993, saying, "Let us respect one another's faiths, fight to the death to preserve the right of every American to practice whatever convictions he or she has, but bring our values back to the table of American discourse to heal our troubled land."[69]

The Native American Church, meanwhile, had looked elsewhere for relief. Senator Daniel Patrick Inouye (D–HI), a decorated veteran of World War II, was outraged by the intolerance he saw in lumping peyote religion together with criminal drug use. His statute, passed a year after the enactment of RFRA, was called the American Indian Religious Freedom Act Amendments of 1994.[70] The Act provided that peyotists who are members of Indian tribes may not be "penalized or discriminated against" by state or federal governments on the basis of "use, possession or transportation" of peyote "in connection with the practice of a traditional Indian religion." In particular, government could not penalize peyotists by "denial of otherwise applicable benefits under public assistance programs."[71] The Act, for the first time, placed the Church, and peyote religion generally, on firm legal ground. But a few observers noted that the law's protection was limited to enrolled members of Indian tribes. Under its provisions, Al Smith would have received his unemployment compensation; Galen Black would receive no protection.

In Oregon, the public reaction to *Smith II* was even more negative than in the nation as a whole. Having fought to vindicate the state's right to control its own drug laws, Dave Frohnmayer now found himself repudiated by his own legislature. Only a few months after *Smith II* was decided, that body amended the state's Controlled Substances Act to provide that criminal charges could not be brought against a defendant who possessed peyote as part of a "good faith practice of a religious

---

[67] U.S. Const. amend. XIV, § 5 (granting Congress power "by appropriate legislation to enforce the provisions" of the Amendment).

[68] 42 U.S.C. § 200bb (1993).

[69] *Unknown God, supra* note 8, at 233–34.

[70] Pub.L. No. 103–344 § 2, 108 Stat. 3125 (codified as amended at 42 U.S.C. § 1996a (2000)).

[71] *Id.*

belief."[72] The attorney general's office, which had expressed concern about possible implications of an exemption under Oregon's constitution, took no position for or against the legislation.

RFRA was one of the most controversial laws Congress passed during the 1990s. It is unusual for Congress to try to overturn a constitutional decision of the Supreme Court. Under Chief Justice Rehnquist, the Court had become aggressive in its review of congressional action, invalidating more federal statutes in any given term than most previous Courts had struck down in a decade. In 1997, it reacted sharply to Congress's challenge. In a case called *City of Boerne v. Flores*,[73] (discussed at length in Chapter Fourteen) the Court held that Congress had no power under the Fourteenth Amendment to protect religious freedom to a greater extent than the Court deemed to be constitutionally required. "RFRA was designed to control cases and controversies," Justice Anthony Kennedy wrote for the majority, "but as the provisions of the federal statute ... are beyond congressional authority, it is this Court's precedent, not RFRA, which must control."[74]

But *Boerne* was more of a defense of states' rights than of the decision in *Smith II*. The Court seemed uneasy with the *Smith* rule, and Justices O'Connor and Souter (who had not been on the Court when the case was decided) called for a re-examination of the decision.[75] In a case called *Church of the Lukumi Babalu Aye v. City of Hialeah*,[76] the Court's majority had already indicated that the "neutral, generally applicable" requirement of *Smith II* had a good deal more bite than had been imagined at the time it was announced.

Lukumi Babalu Aye concerned an "animal cruelty" ordinance passed by the city of Hialeah, Florida. The law had been challenged by a congregation of Santerists, followers of an ancient Afro–Cuban religion that worshiped by sacrificing small animals like goats and chickens. Because of the law, the Santerists had been forced to abandon plans to build a new temple in an old auto dealership in Hialeah. In *Smith*, Justice Scalia had cited the case, then in the lower federal courts, as an example of a law that should be exempt from Free Exercise scrutiny.[77]

---

[72] Or. Rev. Stat. § 475.992(5) (2001).

[73] 521 U.S. 507 (1997).

[74] *Id.* at 536.

[75] *See Boerne*, 521 U.S. at 544–45 (O'Connor, J., dissenting); *id.* at 565 (Souter, J., dissenting).

[76] 508 U.S. 520 (1993).

[77] *Smith II*, 494 U.S. 872, 889 (1990).

But when the case made its way to the Supreme Court, the Justices decided that the ordinance was not neutral or generally applicable at all.

The decision was unusually thorough, which was surprising because the Hialeah ordinance (although Justice Scalia, perhaps writing in haste, had not noticed this) was clearly on its face not neutral. It did not ban animal cruelty generally, but simply outlawed "ritual slaughter" of animals—thereby facially singling out religion. The Court could simply have relied on this lack of facial neutrality. But the majority rather systematically canvassed the structure of the law, noting that it was written to single out one religious practice (thus violating the "neutrality" requirement), and that it carefully exempted scientific research, pest control, hunting for sport, and even slaughter of animals for Kosher food (and thus was not "generally applicable").[78]

Thus, in an oblique way, the Court had retreated from the sweeping nature of the *Smith II* rule. *Lukumi Babalu Aye* provided a road map for litigators seeking to challenge state or federal laws that burdened religious minorities. Justice Scalia, the author of *Smith II*, objected to the *Lukumi* Court's careful scrutiny of the law's structure. He interpreted his own opinion to give the state legislatures broad discretion to exempt religious minorities—or to refuse such accommodation. But after *Lukumi,* the Courts were back in the free-exercise business, and any law that failed the stern test of *Lukumi* would be judged by the compelling interest test, which was now held to be applicable to many areas outside unemployment compensation.[79]

If *Lukumi* showed that the domain of *Smith* was limited, a 2006 case showed that *Boerne* too had its limits. The Supreme Court had held Congress without power to impose the compelling interest test on the states, but RFRA remained valid as a constraint on the federal government. Therefore, in *Gonzales v. O Centro Espirita Beneficente Uniao do Vegetal,*[80] the Court applied RFRA to facts reminiscent of *Smith*. In a unanimous opinion authored by Chief Justice Roberts, the Court held that the compelling interest test required the federal government to exempt a Brazil-based Christian Spiritist sect from a neutral federal drug law that would have forbidden access to *hoasca*, a hallucinogenic tea. The government contended that the federal enforcement policy could not tolerate any exemptions, but in an ironic twist, the Court found this contention belied by an exemption for ritual peyote.[81]

---

[78] 508 U.S. at 532–46.

[79] *Id.* at 546.

[80] 546 U.S. 418 (2006).

[81] *See id.* at 433.

Meanwhile, in 2000, Congress partially filled the gap left by the invalidation of RFRA by passing the Religious Land Use and Institutionalized Persons Act,[82] which applied the compelling interest test to state and federal actions in two specific contexts—zoning decisions (such as the one at stake in *Boerne)* and the rights of prisoners to religious observances. In losing the *Smith* and RFRA battles, the advocates of free exercise had nonetheless won other important victories. And the long fight over Free Exercise went on.

The Aftermath for the Parties

Despite the scorn heaped on Al Smith by officials of NACNA during the settlement crisis, Smith is now seen by many Native Americans as something of a hero, who persevered in a lonely and stressful quest to win protection for peyote religion. He retired to Eugene, Oregon, with his wife, Jane Farrell–Smith. In 2000, he celebrated his eightieth birthday with a massive Indian feast at the University of Oregon Long House, the Native American student center. Not long afterwards, he was also the guest of honor at a NAC tipi ceremony.

Dave Frohnmayer ran for governor of Oregon in 1990. Though he entered the election as the favorite, a breakaway group of conservative Republicans refused to support him because of his pro-choice stance on abortion and his moderate orientation generally. They ran an independent candidate who drained off just enough votes in November to swing the election to Barbara Roberts, Frohnmayer's Democratic opponent. Not long after the election, on September 21, 1991, Katie Frohnmayer died of complications from Fanconi Anemia. Frohnmayer left politics to become dean of the University of Oregon Law School in 1992, and in 1994, he was made president of the University, a position he held through the end of the 2008–09 academic year. After a long and gallant struggle, Kirsten Frohnmayer, too, died of FA on June 20, 1997.

---

[82] P.L. 106–274, 114 Stat. 803 (codified at 42 U.S.C. § 2000cc (2000)).

*

14

Mark Tushnet

The Story of *City of Boerne v. Flores*: Federalism, Rights, and Judicial Supremacy

Introduction

The Supreme Court's decision in *Employment Division v. Smith*[1] (Chapter 13) was met with a storm of protest from a wide range of religious and civil liberties organizations. They assembled a coalition to support the enactment of a federal statute that would direct the courts to apply to state and federal laws that placed burdens on the exercise of religion the "compelling state interest" test that prevailed before the *Smith* decision. Congress responded with the Religious Freedom Restoration Act of 1993[2] (RFRA—pronounced "riffra").

The RFRA coalition included over fifty interest groups, ranging from church lobbying entities to the American Civil Liberties Union and People for the American Way, two organizations that frequently opposed the initiatives supported by religious interest groups. The coalition pointed to state and local actions that, it argued, unjustifiably interfered with religious liberty. The examples ranged from zoning decisions in which cities refused to allow congregations to meet in the most convenient locations, to the denial of religious materials to prisoners, to cases in which seemingly unnecessary autopsies were performed on people whose religion saw autopsies as desecrations of the body.

State and local government officials found it politically difficult to oppose RFRA, which the House of Representatives passed on a voice

---

[1] 494 U.S. 872 (1990).

[2] 42 U.S.C. § 2000bb et seq. (2000).

vote, with no opposition recorded, in May 1993. State correctional officials did mobilize to seek an exemption for their operations. However, the coalition took an all-or-nothing position, because its organizers believed in the statute's general principle and thought that political support for the proposal would erode if portions of the larger statute were chipped away. The Senate rejected the exemption for prisons by a vote of fifty-eight to forty-one, and President Clinton signed the statute into law on November 16, 1993.

RFRA begins with a series of "findings," but they are not ordinary factual findings. Instead, the statute recites that Congress "finds" that "the framers of the Constitution, recognizing free exercise of religion as an unalienable right, secured its protection in the First Amendment," that neutral laws might nonetheless burden religion, that "governments should not substantially burden religious exercise without compelling justification," that the *Smith* case "virtually eliminated" such a requirement, and that "the compelling interest test as set forth in prior Federal court rulings is a workable test for striking sensible balances between religious liberty and competing prior government interests."[3]

RFRA also states that its goal is to "restore the compelling interest test as set forth" by the Supreme Court in cases before *Smith*. It provides that government—defined to include federal, state, and local bodies—shall not substantially burden a person's exercise of religion, even through the enforcement of a neutral law of general applicability, unless the government demonstrates that "application of the burden" advances "a compelling government interest" and is "the least restrictive means" of doing so.[4]

Congress relied on its power under Section Five of the Fourteenth Amendment as the basis for RFRA. Section One of the Fourteenth Amendment provides, "No State shall ... deprive any person of life, liberty, or property without due process of law." Section Five provides, "The Congress shall have power to enforce, by appropriate legislation, the provisions of this article."[5] *City of Boerne v. Flores*[6] asked whether Section Five gave Congress the power to enact RFRA. (The city's name is pronounced "Bernie.")

That question lies at the intersection of the Constitution's structural provisions and its individual rights provisions. Principles of federalism dictate that Congress has only those powers enumerated in the Constitution. If Congress cannot rely on an enumerated power, such as Section

---

[3] *Id.* § 2000bb(a).

[4] *Id.* § 2000bb–1.

[5] U.S. Const. amend. XIV.

[6] 521 U.S. 507 (1997).

Five, as the basis for RFRA, the statute is unconstitutional, legislating in an area the Constitution does not commit to Congress. The question in *Boerne* thus becomes: "What is appropriate legislation enforcing the provisions of Section One of the Fourteenth Amendment?"

Section One, in turn, declares that states may not deprive persons—including, the Court's precedents confirm, corporations—of liberty without due process. However, *Smith* held that a neutral law of general applicability did not deprive anyone of a right to free exercise of religion. RFRA purported to require the national government and, more important, state and local governments, to have only compelling reasons for the burdens they placed on free exercise—even though *Smith* held that Section One did not require them to have such reasons. How then can RFRA be said to be a statute "enforcing" rights protected by Section One?

RFRA poses a federalism question directly. Indirectly, it presents two questions of separation of powers as well. Congress purported to direct courts to apply a test that the Supreme Court had itself rejected, at least in part because the Court believed that administering a "compelling interest" test in this context was beyond the capacity of the judiciary. Can Congress direct the courts to use a test that the courts themselves say they lack the capacity to administer? And, more important, can Congress specify what rights are protected by Section One of the Fourteenth Amendment, even if the Supreme Court disagrees?

The Facts

The city of Boerne, Texas, is a bedroom suburb thirty miles northwest of San Antonio. In 1992, the city created a historic preservation district, hoping to attract tourists and provide the right atmosphere for local antique dealers. St. Peter's Catholic Church is within the historic preservation district. Erected in 1923 and modeled on a Spanish mission church in San Antonio, the church is a prominent feature on the hillside as drivers approach Boerne. Phillip Bell, the chair of the city's Historic Landmark Commission, called the church "a drawing card for the whole city."[7]

As San Antonio's population grew, so did its suburbs and, more importantly, so did the congregation at St. Peter's. The church seated about 230 people, but by the early 1990s, another forty to sixty people regularly attended Mass, a number that Archbishop P. F. Flores of San Antonio expected only to increase. Archbishop Flores authorized the parish to expand the church. At the end of 1993, the church applied for a

---

[7] Thaddeus Herrick, *Preservation Law Pits Church Versus State*, Hous. Chron., Aug. 27, 1995, at 1.

building permit. Under the church's proposal, the church's façade would be preserved, but 80% of the structure behind the façade would be demolished and 700 seats added for the congregation. The city's Historic Landmark Commission refused to approve the plans after a public hearing, and the city council voted to deny the application, with Bell saying, "We would like you to build a new church, but don't touch a rock of the old one."[8] The church's architect estimated that following that course would add $500,000 to the project's cost.

The Archbishop, who had applied for the building permit, sued the city in federal court. The lawsuit made a number of constitutional claims, including that the denial of a building permit was a "taking" of the church's property, but its primary focus was on RFRA. The Archbishop argued that the permit denial violated RFRA because it imposed a substantial burden on the church, and was not justified by any compelling interest. The city replied that RFRA was unconstitutional. Ruling only on the RFRA question, the district court held the statute unconstitutional.[9] The city appealed to the Court of Appeals for the Fifth Circuit, which reversed the district court and upheld the statute.[10]

The Precedents

Supreme Court opinions defining the scope of Congress's power under Section Five are rare. The reason: For decades after the end of Reconstruction, Congress was uninterested in enforcing constitutional rights. The civil rights movement of the 1960s prodded Congress into action. But much of what Congress did—such as enacting federal laws against discrimination in employment, housing, and places of public accommodation[11]—was directed at private parties. Concerned that the 1883 *Civil Rights Cases*[12] barred Congress from invoking its power under Section Five to act against such parties, Congress relied on its power to regulate interstate commerce. The Supreme Court upheld this legislation on that basis, avoiding the Section Five issue.[13] The civil rights move-

---

[8] Zeke MacCormack, *Church Versus State*, San Antonio Express–News, Feb. 16, 1997, at 1.

[9] 877 F.Supp. 355, 357–58 (W.D. Tex. 1995).

[10] 73 F.3d 1352, 1364 (5th Cir. 1996).

[11] *See* Civil Rights Act of 1964, 42 U.S.C. §§ 2000a–2000h–6 (2000); Fair Housing Act of 1968, *id*. §§ 3601–3619, 3631.

[12] 109 U.S. 3 (1883).

[13] *See Katzenbach v. McClung*, 379 U.S. 294 (1964); *Heart of Atlanta Motel v. United States*, 379 U.S. 241 (1964). Justice Douglas would have upheld this congressional action

ment challenged discrimination in voting rights as well, and there Congress's power under Section Five of the Fourteenth Amendment was clearly applicable. Similarly, Congress had power under the parallel Section Two of the Fifteenth Amendment to enforce that Amendment's ban on abridgements of the right to vote on the basis of race.

The Voting Rights Act of 1965[14] gave the Court its first modern opportunity to examine the scope of Congress's power to enforce the Reconstruction Amendments. Civil rights activists challenged the widespread exclusion of African Americans from voting in the South. One of their primary targets was the use of literacy tests to disqualify African–American voters. In the 1959 decision in *Lassiter v. Northampton County Board of Elections*,[15] the Court had rejected the claim that literacy tests for voting were invariably unconstitutional. But, civil rights activists said, Southern voting officials were administering literacy tests in a discriminatory way; African–American voters were asked questions no white voter was, and voting registration officials accepted answers from white applicants that they rejected from African–American ones. Discriminatory administration of a statute that is constitutional when administered fairly is unconstitutional under the old precedent of *Yick Wo v. Hopkins*.[16]

The problem facing civil rights activists, and Congress, was that it was difficult to prove in any individual case that a voting official had discriminated against African–American applicants, and even harder to do so in enough cases to have a real impact on the registration of African Americans in the South. Case-by-case litigation required large commitments of time—the Supreme Court quoted one case in which it took 6,000 man-hours to go through registration records to prepare a challenge. And so, such litigation moved slowly, particularly because Southern voting officials dragged their feet. Even more, a successful challenge to one state tactic would be met by the ingenious development of some new requirement, thereby setting in course the same long litigation process.

The Voting Rights Act addressed the problem of discriminatory administration of literacy and other tests, not by banning such tests outright, but by banning them when there was some reason to think that they had been used to discriminate. The mechanism was this: Federal officials would look at voting rates and the statute books. If they

---

under Section 5. *See Heart of Atlanta Motel*, 379 U.S. at 279 (Douglas, J., concurring in part and dissenting in part).

[14] 42 U.S.C. §§ 1971–1974 (2000).

[15] 360 U.S. 45 (1959).

[16] 118 U.S. 356 (1886).

found that literacy tests had been used in jurisdictions where fewer than fifty percent of the voting age population was registered to vote, or had voted, the use of the tests had to be suspended. In addition, states covered by the Act could not impose *new* standards or procedures without submitting those standards to the United States Attorney General and receiving clearance that the new standards were not racially motivated and would not have the effect of discriminating on the basis of race.

South Carolina challenged these provisions in an original action brought directly in the Supreme Court under the provision in Article III giving the Court original jurisdiction in cases "in which a State shall be a Party." (Three justices voted against taking the case up; they would have preferred to let lower courts consider the constitutional challenge first.) Instead of appointing a special master as it usually does in such cases, the Court heard the case immediately. It also invited every state to participate in the proceeding. Five Southern states filed *amicus* briefs supporting South Carolina's challenge. Twenty-one states filed briefs supporting the Voting Rights Act's constitutionality.

The Supreme Court, in an opinion by Chief Justice Earl Warren, upheld the Voting Rights Act.[17] (Justice Hugo Black dissented, but only with respect to the "preclearance" requirement, which he regarded as inconsistent with the principle that states could not be required to "beg federal authorities to approve their policies." This argument anticipates the Supreme Court's more recent decisions finding unconstitutional federal statutes that commandeer state legislatures or executive officials.[18])

Chief Justice Warren's opinion opened by saying that the Act "was designed by Congress to banish the blight of racial discrimination in voting," and asserted that the Act "creates stringent new remedies for voting discrimination where it persists on a pervasive scale." As his analysis developed, the pervasiveness of the problem justified the stringency of the remedies. The opinion examined the extensive hearings Congress held before adopting the Act, and found that "Congress felt itself confronted by an insidious and pervasive evil which had been perpetuated in certain parts of our country through unremitting and ingenious defiance of the Constitution." And "it concluded that the unsuccessful remedies which it had prescribed in the past would have to be replaced by sterner and more elaborate measures in order to satisfy the clear commands of the Fifteenth Amendment."[19]

---

[17] *See South Carolina v. Katzenbach*, 383 U.S. 301, 308 (1966).

[18] *See Printz v. United States*, 521 U.S. 898 (1997); *New York v. United States*, 505 U.S. 144 (1992).

[19] *See* 383 U.S. at 309.

The opinion recounted the history of voting rights litigation. It observed that exclusion of African–American voters occurred through discriminatory administration of literacy tests, and that case-by-case litigation was quite difficult. Congress, the opinion noted, had tried to facilitate such litigation in earlier Civil Rights Acts in 1957 and 1960, but those statutes had "done little to cure the problem of voting discrimination."[20] As the Chief Justice had put it to his colleagues in their discussion of the case, "Congress knows what the problem is. It knows that the case by case method was ineffectual, so it changed its tactics and used drastic means."[21]

According to Chief Justice Warren, the "ground rules" for deciding the case were "clear."[22] His crisp statement when he discussed the case with the other justices captures his position: "As long as the act is aimed at [eliminating discrimination], Congress can legislate any way it chooses."[23] His written opinion was more formal. As a matter of "fundamental principle," it said, Congress could "use any rational means to effectuate the constitutional prohibition of racial discrimination in voting."[24] The Court adopted the well-known test from *McCulloch v. Maryland* (Chapter 2): "Let the end be legitimate, let it be within the scope of the constitution, and all means which are appropriate, which are plainly adapted to that end, which are not prohibited, but consist with the letter and spirit of the constitution, are constitutional."[25] Indeed, for the Court, the framers of the Reconstruction Amendments "indicated that Congress was to be chiefly responsible for implementing the rights" created in Section One of the Fifteenth Amendment. Congress's "inventive" response to the problems it identified was "clearly a legitimate" one.[26]

South Carolina v. Katzenbach can be read broadly or narrowly. The broad reading is that Section Two of the Fifteenth Amendment (and by analogy, Section Five of the Fourteenth Amendment) gives Congress the power to "enforce" voting rights (and again by analogy other constitutional rights) by any means it—and the courts—find rational. The narrow reading is that Section Two and Section Five give Congress the power to develop *complex remedies* where it finds a *pervasive* problem. In

---

[20] *Id*. at 313.

[21] *The Supreme Court in Conference (1940–1985)*: The Private Discussions Behind Nearly 300 Supreme Court Decisions, at 831 (Del Dickson ed., 2001) [hereinafter *Court in Conference*].

[22] 383 U.S. at 324.

[23] *Court in Conference, supra* note 21, at 831.

[24] 383 U.S. at 324.

[25] 17 U.S. (4 Wheat.) 316, 421 (1819).

[26] 383 U.S. at 326–27.

considering another provision of the Voting Rights Act of 1965, the Supreme Court developed two additional accounts of congressional power—a *preventive* one and a *substantive* one.

Section 4(e) of the Voting Rights Act was added on the floor during the debates on the Act. It was sponsored by New York's Senators and by two Representatives from New York. The section provided that no one who had received a sixth grade education in a school in Puerto Rico could be denied the right to vote because that person was not literate in English. The statute was designed to ensure that several hundred thousand U.S. citizens who had moved from Puerto Rico to New York could vote, notwithstanding a New York statute making English-language literacy a prerequisite to voting. The New York statute was quite clearly constitutional under *Lassiter*. And, unlike the ban on literacy tests in South Carolina and other Southern states the Court upheld in *South Carolina v. Katzenbach*, there was no indication that New York's voting registrars administered the English-language literacy test unfairly, or to bar only people educated in schools in Puerto Rico from voting because of their race. (That meant, among other things, that the Fifteenth Amendment was irrelevant; the Court considered only Congress's power under Section Five of the Fourteenth Amendment, and so whether Section 4(e) was appropriate legislation to enforce the equal protection clause of Section One.)

Justice William Brennan, writing for the Court in *Katzenbach v. Morgan*,[27] first rejected the proposition that Congress's Section Five power came into play only when the courts themselves would decide— perhaps "with the guidance of a congressional judgment"—that the English-language literacy requirement violated the Equal Protection Clause. For Justice Brennan, that position would give Congress only the "insignificant role of abrogating only those state laws" that the courts themselves would find unconstitutional once the courts got around to it. Such a small role was, he thought, inconsistent with the vision the drafters of the Fourteenth Amendment had of a Congress substantially empowered by the new amendment.[28]

As in *South Carolina v. Katzenbach*, the Court applied *McCulloch v. Maryland*'s test. Why was Section 4(e) "appropriate" and "plainly adapted" to the end of protecting rights guaranteed by Section One of the Fourteenth Amendment? First, Justice Brennan said, Section 4(e) might promote the nondiscriminatory provision of public services to those who migrated from Puerto Rico to New York—including public housing, public schools, and law enforcement. (Call this the *preventive* interpretation of Section Five.) The idea was that, absent the federal

---

[27] 384 U.S. 641 (1966).

[28] *Id*. at 648–49.

legislation, members of that community would be unable to vote in New York, and so would be unable to influence legislators to provide public services to them to the same extent that such services were provided to voters. As Justice Brennan put it, "This enhanced political power will be helpful in gaining nondiscriminatory treatment in public services for the entire Puerto Rican community."[29] One might, of course, be skeptical about the claim that the community did in fact receive *discriminatory* treatment because of its lack of voting power. But, Justice Brennan wrote, "It was for Congress ... to assess and weigh the various conflicting considerations—the risk or pervasiveness of the discrimination in governmental services [and] the effectiveness of eliminating the state restriction on the right to vote as a means of dealing with the evil.... "[30]

Justice Brennan continued by articulating an alternative justification, which has come to be known as the *substantive* account of Congress's Section Five power. Here the question was whether *Congress* could decide that the English-language literacy requirement violated the Equal Protection Clause. Justice Brennan began the analysis of this question by describing New York's interest as providing an incentive to learn English and to ensure that voters would be adequately informed. But, he wrote, "Congress *might well have questioned* ... whether these were actually the interests being served."[31] And, "Congress *might have also questioned* whether denial of a right deemed so precious and fundamental in our society was a necessary or appropriate means of encouraging persons to learn English, or of furthering the goal of an intelligent exercise of the franchise."[32] And, once again, "Congress *might well have concluded* that as a means of furthering the intelligent exercise of the franchise, an ability to read or understand Spanish is as effective as ability to read English for those to whom Spanish-language newspapers and Spanish-language radio and television programs are available to inform them of election issues and governmental affairs."[33]

The conditional formulation indicates the Court's willingness to accept from Congress conclusions reflecting the latter's own independent equal protection analysis. That is, if *the Court* thought that the interests asserted were not the ones actually being served, that the denial of the right was unnecessary, and that Spanish-language literacy was as effective as English-language literacy, it might well have found the English-language literacy requirement unconstitutional itself. The Court's condi-

---

[29] *Id.* at 652.

[30] *Id.* at 653.

[31] *Id.* at 654 (emphasis added).

[32] *Id.* (emphasis added).

[33] *Id.* at 654–55 (emphasis added).

tional language shows that, even though the Court might not make the judgments that would lead to a finding of unconstitutionality, Section Five gave Congress the power to make such judgments and to draw the conclusion that the requirement was unconstitutional.

Justices Potter Stewart and John Marshall Harlan dissented, in an opinion written by Justice Harlan. The Court's decision, according to Harlan, "sacrifice[d] ... fundamentals in the American constitutional system—the separation between the legislative and judicial function and the boundaries between federal and state political authority."[34] The Court's analysis, according to Justice Harlan, "confused the issue of how much enforcement power Congress possesses under Section Five with the distinct issue of what questions are appropriate for congressional determination and what questions are essentially judicial in nature."[35]

For Justice Harlan, Section Five should be given a purely remedial interpretation. Congress could develop "appropriate remedial mechanisms" for acknowledged state violations of the Constitution—presumably including remedies that the courts themselves might be unable or unwilling to develop (because otherwise, Section Five would give Congress no meaningful power at all). But, he said, "it is a judicial question whether the condition with which Congress has thus sought to deal is in truth an infringement of the Constitution, something that is the necessary prerequisite to bringing the § 5 power into play at all."[36]

As Justice Harlan saw it, the courts defined the rights protected by Section One. Congress could then intervene to provide remedies for rights violations. Justice Harlan also acknowledged a somewhat greater role for Congress. It might be able to investigate and make factual determinations relevant to the courts' own assessment of the Constitution's meaning. So, for example, Justice Harlan would have had no problem if the Court had added to its conditional phrasing about what Congress "might have believed," something like, "And we agree." But, he remarked, Congress had made no such factual determinations about the condition of citizens educated in Puerto Rican schools. All Congress had done, in Justice Harlan's eyes, was to declare that New York's statute was unconstitutional in Congress's own judgment. He insisted that the Court should give that declaration "the most respectful consideration," but that Congress's views could not relieve the Court of the duty to make its own determination of whether New York's statute denied equal protection of the laws.[37]

---

[34] *Id.* at 659 (Harlan, J., dissenting).

[35] *Id.* at 666.

[36] *Id.*

[37] *Id.* at 670.

One of Justice Harlan's most powerful objections has become known as the "ratchet" problem. Suppose, he said, that Congress *did* have a substantive power to define constitutional violations in a manner inconsistent with the courts' definition. Then, he wondered, why couldn't Congress *dilute* the protections the courts provided, in the form of specifying what the Constitution means notwithstanding the courts' determinations? That is, if Congress could ratchet *up* constitutional protections (relative to what the courts had said), why couldn't it ratchet them *down* as well? Justice Brennan responded to this concern in a footnote that distinguished between "enforcing" rights and "restricting" or "diluting" them.[38] Another metaphor is that judicial determinations provide a floor for constitutional rights, which Congress can raise but may not lower. This distinction may make sense, as we will see. It needed more in the way of defense than Justice Brennan provided, though.

Lurking behind the substantive account of Congress's power in *Katzenbach v. Morgan* is the specter of *Marbury v. Madison*[39] (Chapter 1). There Chief Justice John Marshall asserted that it was *"emphatically the province and duty of the judicial department to say what the law is."*[40] The substantive account in *Katzenbach v. Morgan* seems to mean that Congress has the power to say what the law—here, the Constitution—is. Where Congress and the Court agree, of course, no problem will arise. But what of the situation in which the Court says that the Constitution means one thing and Congress says that it means another? In one sense, *Marbury* itself presented that problem: Congress proclaimed that the Constitution gave it the power to expand the Supreme Court's original jurisdiction, the Supreme Court declared that the Constitution did not give Congress that power, and the Supreme Court's view prevailed. *City of Boerne v. Flores*[41] thus presented the Court with a modern version of *Marbury*.

The Supreme Court Opinions

The Supreme Court held that RFRA was not a constitutional exercise of Congress's Section Five power to enforce Section One rights. Justice Anthony Kennedy's opinion for the Court began by emphasizing that "the Federal Government is one of enumerated powers."[42] After

---

[38] *Id*. at 651 n.10.

[39] 5 U.S. (1 Cranch) 137 (1803).

[40] *Id*. at 177 (emphasis added).

[41] 521 U.S. 507 (1997).

[42] *Id*. at 516.

summarizing the parties' contentions, the opinion endorsed the remedial and prophylactic accounts of Section Five, relying on *South Carolina v. Katzenbach*: "Legislation which deters or remedies constitutional violations can fall within the sweep of Congress' enforcement power even if in the process it prohibits conduct which is not itself unconstitutional."[43] But the enforcement power was not unlimited.

The Court started its search for the limits with Section Five's text. Section Five clearly means that Congress can enforce the right to free exercise of religion. But, the Court insisted, Congress can only *enforce* Section One rights, not define them. The line between *enforcing* and *defining* might be difficult to locate, and "Congress must have wide latitude in determining where it lies," but the line must be respected. According to the Court, it is defined by a test of congruence and proportionality. Because congressional statutes must be remedial or preventive, they must identify a constitutional violation and then provide a remedy that is commensurate to the violation, for otherwise the statute would "become substantive in operation and effect."[44]

Justice Kennedy turned to the drafting history of the Fourteenth Amendment for support. (Justice Antonin Scalia, an inveterate opponent of using drafting history as the basis for interpreting statutes and the Constitution, did not join this portion of the Court's opinion.) Representative John Bingham's initial proposal was this: "The Congress shall have power to make all laws which shall be necessary and proper to secure to the citizens of each State all privileges and immunities of citizens in the several States, and to all persons in the several States equal protection in the rights of life, liberty, and property."[45] According to Justice Kennedy, this proposal met with "immediate opposition," sounding a "common theme": The proposal "gave Congress too much legislative power at the expense of the existing constitutional structure." Several months later Congress took the matter up again, this time with a draft that listed "self-executing limits on the States" in one section, and a congressional enforcement power in another. Justice Kennedy described the proposal as making Congress's power "no longer plenary but remedial."[46]

According to Justice Kennedy, this design "has proved significant also in maintaining the traditional separation of powers between Congress and the Judiciary."[47] The Bill of Rights "set forth self-executing

---

[43] *Id.* at 518.

[44] *Id.* at 520.

[45] *Id.* at 520.

[46] *Id.* 522.

[47] *Id.* at 523–24.

prohibitions," which the Court "has had primary authority to interpret."[48] Opponents of Representative Bingham's proposals thought that the proposal "departed from that tradition by vesting in Congress primary power to interpret and elaborate on the meaning of the new Amendment through legislation."[49] Justice Kennedy then examined the Court's prior cases, from which he assembled quotations expressing the view that the Section Five power was remedial and preventive rather than substantive. He acknowledged that "[t]here is language in our opinion in *Katzenbach v. Morgan* which could be interpreted" to support the substantive account of Section Five.[50] But, Justice Kennedy continued, "[t]his is not a necessary interpretation . . . or even the best one."[51] It was not the best, he explained, because (quoting *Marbury*) "If Congress could define its own powers by altering the Fourteenth Amendment's meaning, no longer would the Constitution be 'superior paramount law, unchangeable by ordinary means.' It would be 'on a level with ordinary legislative acts, and, like other acts, . . . alterable when the legislature shall please to alter it.' . . . Shifting legislative majorities could change the Constitution and effectively circumvent the difficult and detailed amendment process contained in Article V."[52]

The question then was whether RFRA could be justified as remedial legislation. The statute's defenders maintained that it was. They saw a problem with free exercise doctrine akin to the problems associated with case-by-case litigation against voting discrimination. Even after *Smith*, the free exercise clause prohibits statutes "targeting religious beliefs and practices."[53] But, the statute's defenders argued, proving unconstitutional motivation is quite difficult, and the broad ban enacted in RFRA is a sensible method of ensuring that no laws targeting religion take effect, even if it prevents some, even many, constitutionally legitimate laws from being enforced as well.

The Court responded by applying its test of congruence and proportionality. Citing *South Carolina v. Katzenbach*, the Court said that the "appropriateness of remedial measures must be considered in light of the evil presented. Strong measures appropriate to address one harm may be an unwarranted response to another, lesser one."[54] Justice

---

[48] *Id.* at 524.

[49] *Id.*

[50] *Id.* at 527.

[51] *Id.* at 528.

[52] *Id.* at 529.

[53] *Id.*

[54] *Id.* at 530.

Kennedy then compared RFRA to the Voting Rights Act, where Congress had a substantial record of constitutional violations. In contrast, he wrote, "RFRA's legislative record lacks examples of modern instances of generally applicable laws passed because of religious bigotry."[55] There were references to burdensome general laws, without express statements that such laws were targeted at religious exercise, and "anecdotal evidence" about autopsies, zoning regulations, and historic preservation laws. These were not, according to the Court, "examples of legislation enacted or enforced due to animus or hostility" to religion. "Congress' concern was with the incidental burdens imposed, not the object or purpose of the legislation."[56]

The Court did not rely entirely on what was—or was not—in the legislative record, though, in part because of its concern that doing so would impose as a matter of constitutional law some procedural requirements upon Congress. Such a course, the Court feared, might not be sufficiently respectful of Congress's prerogatives, and might commit the Court to upholding statutes enacted after the procedures were followed without the Court considering the statutes' substance, something the Court might not want to do.

Rather, Justice Kennedy emphasized RFRA's breadth. It was "so out of proportion to a supposed remedial or preventive object that it cannot be understood as responsive to, or designed to prevent, unconstitutional behavior."[57] A broad statute might be remedial if there were many unconstitutional statutes it addressed and only a few constitutionally permissible ones that were incidentally swept in. But, where there appeared to be only a few unconstitutional statutes, a broad ban is not congruent with and proportional to the underlying problem. "Laws valid under *Smith* would fall under RFRA without regard to whether they had the object of stifling or punishing free exercise."[58] Justice Kennedy emphasized the "substantial costs RFRA exacts," which "far exceed any pattern" of unconstitutional conduct. It was, in short, not proportional to the underlying problem.[59]

Much of this portion of the opinion amounts to overkill. No one could reasonably think that RFRA was geared in any substantial way to eliminating only unconstitutionally motivated statutes, and just happened to sweep in a good deal of other statutes that unintentionally imposed burdens on religious exercise. As Justice Kennedy accurately

---

[55] *Id.*

[56] *Id.* at 531.

[57] *Id.* at 509.

[58] *Id.* at 534.

[59] *Id.* at 534.

said, "In most cases, the state laws to which RFRA applies are not ones which will have been motivated by religious bigotry."[60] Congress adopted RFRA believing that it had substantive power under Section Five. The attempt to defend it as remedial was a litigation strategy that emerged in light of the Supreme Court's newfound interest in federalism and, perhaps, marked an effort to deflect concern on the Court over Congress's in-your-face repudiation of *Smith*.

Justice Kennedy contrasted RFRA, applicable to nearly every law and at every level of the government throughout the nation, with the Voting Rights Act, which, at least as initially enacted, was confined to regions where problems with unconstitutional restrictions on voting were "most flagrant," and was limited to "a discrete class of state laws."[61] The provisions dealing with literacy tests addressed "a particular type of voting qualification, one with a long history" of abuse.[62] Perhaps to address concern that the re-enactment of the Voting Rights Act, which extended its geographic reach and eliminated a statutory termination date, might have made the Act unconstitutional under this analysis, Justice Kennedy added that Section Five legislation did not require "termination dates, geographic restrictions, or egregious predicates."[63] But, he said, such limitations are an indication that the legislation uses means that are proportionate to the remedial and preventive ends authorized by Section Five.[64]

Justice Kennedy concluded the Court's opinion with three paragraphs on the meaning of judicial review. The first asserted, "When Congress acts within its sphere of power and responsibilities, it has not just the right but the duty to make its own informed judgment on the meaning and force of the Constitution."[65] That duty gives rise to the presumption of validity that courts accord congressional enactments. But, of course, the very decision in *Boerne* shows why this duty may have little meaning. According to *Boerne*, it is up to the courts to determine the boundaries of Congress's "sphere of power and responsibilities." If they conclude that Congress has acted outside that sphere, Congress's action is unconstitutional—that is, deserves no deference. Yet, if Congress acts within the sphere that the courts define as Congress's own, deference is irrelevant because Congress, by the courts' own acknowledgement, has done nothing unconstitutional.

---

[60] *Id.* at 535.

[61] *Id.* at 533.

[62] *Id.*

[63] *Id.*

[64] *Id.* at 533.

[65] *Id.* at 535.

The opinion's penultimate paragraph returned to the separation of powers theme. "Our national experience teaches that the Constitution is preserved best when each part of the government respects both the Constitution and the proper actions and determinations of the other branches."[66] Alluding to *Smith* without citing it, Justice Kennedy said that the political branches often "act against the background of a judicial interpretation of the Constitution already issued," and that when they did, the political branches should expect that "the Court will treat its precedents with the respect due them under settled principles, including *stare decisis....*"[67] This responds to a suggestion made in some of the commentary on RFRA, that the Court should take the statute's enactment as an occasion for overruling *Smith*, but it does not address arguments in favor of giving Section Five the substantive interpretation.

The opinion's final paragraph stressed that Congress did not have unlimited discretion to determine what sort of legislation is needed to protect Fourteenth Amendment rights. But, the Court said, "the courts retain the power, as they have since *Marbury v. Madison*, to determine if Congress has exceeded its authority under the Constitution."[68] Finding that Congress had done so in enacting RFRA, the Court reversed the Court of Appeals and held RFRA unconstitutional.

Justice Stevens concurred, saying that RFRA was an unconstitutional establishment of religion because "the statute has provided the Church with a legal weapon that no atheist or agnostic can obtain."[69] Such governmental preferences for religion were, he said, barred by the First Amendment.[70]

Justices Sandra Day O'Connor, Stephen Breyer, and David Souter dissented, but their dissents focused on their disagreement with *Smith* (and Justice Scalia, who, in a concurring opinion joined by Justice Stevens, responded with a defense of *Smith*). Only Justice Breyer briefly suggested some misgivings, which he did not develop in any detail, about the Court's treatment of the basic question of Congress's power under Section Five. Justice Kennedy's discussion of the scope of the Section Five power thus went essentially unchallenged from within the Court.

A historical perspective helps in understanding the difference between the Court's vision of congressional power during the civil rights era and the vision it evidenced in *Boerne*. During the 1960s, the Court

---

[66] *Id.* at 535–6.

[67] *Id.* at 536.

[68] *Id.*

[69] *Id.* at 537 (Stevens, J., concurring).

[70] *Id.*

saw itself as collaborating with Congress to develop a set of fundamental principles that would permanently order U.S. society. Sometimes Congress would push the ball forward, and the Court would approve, as in its holding that the Commerce Clause gave Congress the power to enact the Civil Rights Act of 1964. On other occasions, Congress would actively seek out the Court's assistance, as when Congress directed the president to file a lawsuit challenging the constitutionality of the poll tax (the Attorney General intervened in a pending case, *Harper v. Virginia State Board of Elections*[71], supporting the ultimately successful plaintiff). And sometimes, conversely, the Court would creatively rely on congressional action to bail itself out of difficulty, as when the Court invoked an obscure provision of the 1964 Civil Rights Act to invalidate convictions in a number of sit-in cases,[72] thus avoiding the hard question, posed by the state action doctrine, of whether government enforcement of private discrimination was unconstitutional. *South Carolina v. Katzenbach* and, even more, *Katzenbach v. Morgan*, reflect this effort at collaboration. Congress was constructing a set of new constitutional arrangements, generally consistent with the Court's own construction, although perhaps moving to a point the Court was not yet prepared to reach on its own.

Boerne, in contrast, emerges out of a context in which Congress regarded the Court as its adversary, and the Court reciprocated the sentiment. The difference in context is basically political. In the 1960s, the center of the liberal Court—what political scientists refer to as the "median Justice"—was not far from the center of the liberal Congress. In the 1990s, both Congress and the Court had become more conservative, but the Court's median Justice was rather more conservative than the median member of Congress. Although RFRA itself was enacted with support from both ends of the political spectrum, the center of the Rehnquist Court was generally inclined to view Congressional output skeptically during the Clinton years, and *Boerne*—along with other clashes over the scope of federal power—simply provided an outlet for the Court's skepticism. Unless President Obama has an opportunity to name a successor to one of the five conservative Justices, a joint collaboration in creating new constitutional arrangements is unlikely. (More generally, the unpredictable timing of Superme Court vacancies ensures that the Court and Congress will only sometimes regard each other as allies.)

---

[71] 383 U.S. 663 (1966).

[72] *See, e.g., Hamm v. City of Rock Hill*, 379 U.S. 306 (1964).

Analysis and Critique

In an important passage summarizing the Court's analysis of Section Five's meaning, Justice Kennedy wrote:

> Legislation which alters the meaning of the Free Exercise Clause cannot be said to be enforcing the Clause. Congress does not enforce a constitutional right by changing what the right is. It has been given the power "to enforce," not the power to determine what constitutes a constitutional violation. Were it not so, what Congress would be enforcing would no longer be, in any meaningful sense, the "provisions of [the Fourteenth Amendment]."[73]

Some of the words used in this passage open the way to a deeper understanding of what was at stake in the case. Justice Kennedy says that RFRA *alters* the meaning of the Free Exercise Clause; this phrasing assumes that the Court's decision in *Smith* determined that meaning. He says that Congress *changed* the right to free exercise of religion; this phrasing assumes that the Court's decision in *Smith* is unalterable except by the Court itself (or by the arduous process of constitutional amendment). The deepest issues in *Boerne* deal with the relation between the Court and Congress in determining what the Constitution means. As noted above, in this regard the case is a contemporary version of *Marbury v. Madison*.

Begin with the terms *changing* and *altering*. Justice Kennedy assumes that the Constitution's words must mean what the Supreme Court says they mean, and not what Congress says they mean. Consider, though, the constitutional language at issue in *Marbury*. There the Court held that the Constitution's enumeration of subjects within the Supreme Court's original jurisdiction precluded Congress from adding other subjects to that jurisdiction. Yet, as a matter of simple textual interpretation, the Constitution's language is susceptible of another reading: that the Court *must* have original jurisdiction of the listed subjects, but that Congress *may* add subjects, exercising its power to make exceptions to the Court's appellate jurisdiction. Many commentators believe that the latter reading is better than John Marshall's, but no matter what, it is clear that both readings are reasonable ones.

The real question is this: Given alternative reasonable interpretations of the Constitution's language, should the Court's interpretation prevail over Congress's? Marshall got some mileage in *Marbury* by posing hypotheticals where Congress's reading was plainly unreasonable. He asked us to imagine, for example, a statute enacted by Congress making testimony by one witness in open court sufficient to convict for treason, in the face of the Constitution's explicit requirement that conviction be obtained only on the basis of testimony of two witnesses.

---

[73] 521 U.S. at 519.

That is a distraction, a "strawman": Congress no more enacts legislation in clear violation of the Constitution than the Supreme Court issues clearly unconstitutional rulings.

Boerne poses the problem as it usually arises. RFRA enacts an interpretation of what the Free Exercise Clause means that we *know* is reasonable because it was an interpretation that the Supreme Court itself articulated and applied for two decades. True, the Court today thinks that the older Court's interpretation—and Congress's—is not the best one. But, again, why should the Court's interpretation prevail?

One rationale is that, as a purely practical matter, the Court has the final word. If it does not agree with Congress's interpretation—in a context, like RFRA, where litigants are able to invoke the judicial power to resolve their dispute—what the Court says (last), goes. Yet this answer is inadequate. For one thing the Court could say is: "Were we to exercise our independent judgment about what the Constitution means, we would say that the Free Exercise Clause does not require states to exempt religious exercises from their neutral laws of general applicability, but we think it appropriate to defer to Congress's reasonable judgment otherwise." The Court has the last word, true. But in speaking that word, the Court might well decide to acquiesce in Congress's decision.

A related possibility is that stability in the law requires that *someone* have the last word, and that giving the last word to the Court will get us more stability than giving it to Congress. Providing Congress room to interpret the Constitution would, as Marshall put it in *Marbury*, convert the Constitution into ordinary law, alterable at will by a temporary majority. The idea is something like this: If Congress has the last word, what it says will only be provisional. People who do not like what Congress says will try to elect new representatives, lobby vigorously, and do all the usual things needed to get the law changed. When the Court says what the Constitution means, in contrast, people who don't like it don't have much recourse. True, the Court can change its mind—as *Smith* itself shows—but it does so less often, and less dramatically, than Congress does when control shifts from one party to another.

That the Court can change its mind shows, of course, that our concern here is with a comparison between the stability we get when Congress has the last word, and can change its mind through the usual operations of ordinary politics, and the stability we get when the Court has the last word, and can change its mind through the operations of ordinary litigation. No one has done a serious comparison of this sort. But one note of caution: We are concerned here not with what Congress does when considering the budget or providing medical care for the needy, but what it does—or would do—when considering fundamental questions of constitutional interpretation. The fact, if it is one, that policies of the first sort may shift dramatically in a short time does not necessarily imply that decisions about what the Constitution means would shift equally dramatically.

A third possibility is that the Court is simply better at interpreting the Constitution than Congress is. Members of Congress are politicians after all, and only some of them are lawyers. Politicians' constitutional interpretations will almost inevitably be influenced by purely partisan concerns. Modern Supreme Court justices, by contrast, are all lawyers, and the grant of life tenure makes it more likely (though not guaranteed, of course) that they will take a longer view of what a good constitutional interpretation is than will members of Congress.

The justices' disinterestedness does provide them some advantages in constitutional interpretation, but it also has some costs. In particular, the justices are less likely than members of Congress to have a good sense of how legal rules operate in the real world. Members of Congress hear from constituents all the time, and they are likely to appreciate what it means to real people for the Constitution to have one rather than another interpretation. The justices' dispassion means that they have a more remote and abstract understanding of the Constitution. It is unclear whether, on balance, the mix of interestedness and disinterestedness on the Court will produce better constitutional interpretations than the different mix in Congress.

So far we have considered the question: Why should the Supreme Court's interpretations be final? We could flip the question around, and ask: Why should *Congress's* constitutional interpretations be final? Here the answer is straightforward. Making congressional constitutional interpretation final advances democratic self-government. There may of course be problems in saying that Congress is a perfect representative of the democratically expressed will of the American people. But, as John Hart Ely quipped, whatever the problems there are with Congress as the people's representative, it's hard to see how the Supreme Court is a *better* representative.[74] So, switching final authority to interpret the Constitution from the Supreme Court to Congress would increase democratic inputs into constitutional interpretation. And, on the assumption made throughout that the congressional interpretation is a reasonable one, giving Congress the last word would not impair any definitive commitments expressed in the Constitution.

Suppose, then, we rejected the judicial supremacy position *Boerne* adopts. How could we design our institutions to give Congress an

---

[74] John Hart Ely, *Democracy and Distrust: A Theory of Judicial Review* 67 (1980) ("[W]e may grant until we're blue in the face that legislatures aren't wholly democratic, but that isn't going to make courts more democratic than legislatures.").

important role in interpreting the Constitution? The tradition of giving the Supreme Court the last word on constitutional interpretation is deeply entrenched in U.S. constitutional law. No changes in that tradition are at all likely. Still, thinking about institutional alternatives helps us think about the most fundamental questions in constitutional law.

Perhaps the most modest independent role Congress could have is envisaged by Justice Brennan's ratchet theory. Under that theory the Court retains the ultimate power to say what the law is, inasmuch as the Court will invalidate congressional legislation that purports to enforce Section One rights but that, in the Court's view, actually *reduces* their reach.

There is one obvious difficulty with the ratchet theory, though it is less important than some critics suggest. Sometimes a statute expanding one person's rights simultaneously contracts another's. Some applications of RFRA might provide an illustration. Consider, for example, a municipal ordinance banning discrimination on the basis of, *inter alia*, religion by all employers in the city. Some employers may believe, for reasons predicated on their religion, that they should employ only co-religionists, even for positions having nothing to do with preaching or otherwise disseminating the employers' religious views. RFRA might have been interpreted to preempt the city's nondiscrimination ordinance as applied to such employers. And yet, it is plausible to maintain that providing employers with an exemption from the non-discrimination ordinance violates the *constitutional* rights of those individuals the employer discriminates against. (This argument would be based on *Romer v. Evans*[75] and is by no means iron-clad.)

More commonly, though, expansions of one person's rights contract not the constitutional *rights* of another person, but the statutory or other *interests* of that person. Consider a city ordinance banning discrimination in employment on the basis of marital status, as applied to an employer who has a religious basis for his belief that married women with children should not be employed outside the home. Again, RFRA might have been interpreted to require that this employer be exempted from the ordinance's application. Doing so would clearly impair the married woman's interests, and would take away her rights under the ordinance. But—unless we developed a pretty fancy argument—the exemption would not violate the woman's *constitutional* rights. It should not be a problem for Congress to have the power to expand someone's rights while adversely affecting another's *interests*; indeed, that's precisely analogous to what Congress does all the time with respect to non-constitutional rights, when it enacts a statute giving workers some benefit and requiring employers to pay for it.

---

[75] 517 U.S. 620 (1996).

The usual charge leveled against the ratchet theory draws a parallel to Congressional overruling of other Court decisions. Suppose, critics of the ratchet theory say, Congress repudiates *Miranda v. Arizona*,[76] insisting that it is doing so to expand the rights of victims of crime. Of course, in expanding those rights it contracts the rights of criminal defendants, but how does that differ from the one-way ratchet Justice Brennan approved? The answer is that a congressional repudiation of *Miranda* would promote the *interests* of victims of crime, but not their constitutional rights. Victims of crimes do not have any rights under Section One as conventionally understood because the *state* has done nothing to deprive them of life, liberty, or property—the criminals have. So, on this view, the congressional action ratchets down the constitutional rights of criminal defendants without ratcheting up anyone else's constitutional rights, and should thus fail Justice Brennan's test.

In response, one could argue that Congress might be advancing the following interpretation of Section One: Section One prohibits states from depriving people of life, liberty, and property without due process. States that have inadequate systems of law enforcement are thereby depriving crime victims of life, liberty, and property. Repudiating *Miranda* enforces Section One, so interpreted, by enhancing the effectiveness of the states' systems of law enforcement.

In principle, this response is entirely adequate, and would indeed support the argument that a congressional repudiation of *Miranda* could be seen as an enforcement of Section One rights. Note, though, how the response interacts with the *judicial* role in enforcing Section One rights. A court that upheld the congressional action would have to accept the proposition that Congress could reasonably conclude that inadequate systems of law enforcement violated Section One rights. Having accepted that proposition, the court would be able to act on its own to ensure that states had adequate systems of law enforcement—which might entail far greater intervention than the one *Miranda* represented. (A court that accepted the congressional repudiation of *Miranda* on the theory developed here *could* start using its own authority to enforce Section One rights, but it would not *have* to do so. Its decision approving the congressional action might indicate that, although Congress's conclusion that Section One guaranteed adequate law enforcement systems was reasonable, the court did not draw the same conclusion and so would not enforce Section One rights by attempting to improve state law enforcement systems.)

Under the ratchet theory, the Supreme Court continues to have a role in constraining Congress (beyond the constraint imposed by the requirement that congressional constitutional interpretations be reason-

---

[76] 384 U.S. 436 (1966).

able ones). Other institutional designs would give Congress an even larger role.

These designs would give Congress the last word, but would impose various procedural requirements before that word was spoken. The simplest requirement is perhaps the most obvious: The courts could act on their own interpretations of the Constitution unless Congress explicitly indicated that it had a different view of what the Constitution meant. The courts would not infer from the simple enactment of a statute that Congress believed it to be constitutional. So, the courts could find a statute unconstitutional, based on their independent constitutional analysis, even though the statute *might* be constitutional on one reasonable interpretation of the Constitution that differed from the courts' interpretation. For Congress to have the last word, it must at least *say* something about what it thinks the Constitution means.

Some commentators have directed attention to an ingenious provision in Canada's Charter of Rights as a model for giving both legislatures and the courts important roles in constitutional interpretation. Section 33 of the Charter gives the Canadian national and provincial parliaments the power to override a list of specific constitutional rights—but not voting, equality, or mobility rights—by enacting a statute with a sunset period of five years (a period that ensures that there is an opportunity for the statute to become an issue in the next parliamentary election). This so-called "notwithstanding" clause might be used as part of a dialogue between Canada's courts and its legislatures: The legislature enacts a statute, its constitutionality is challenged, the courts invalidate the statute, and the legislature considers whether it wants to re-enact the statute notwithstanding the courts' interpretation that it violated the constitution.

Scholars of Canadian constitutional law disagree about whether the notwithstanding clause has actually promoted this sort of inter-branch dialogue. The Canadian Supreme Court has allowed legislatures to invoke Section 33 prospectively, before the courts have said anything about a particular statute, which stops the dialogue before it begins. (Judge Robert Bork's proposal that Congress be allowed to overrule the Supreme Court's constitutional decisions by majority vote addresses the problem of stopping a dialogue before it begins, because under his proposal Congress can act only after the Court has spoken. Bork's proposal does not include an analogue to the Canadian sunsetting requirement.[77]) Canada's legislatures have been quite reluctant to use the override power, in part because the most prominent case upholding its use involved questions bound up with Quebec separatism and so

---

[77] *See* Robert H. Bork, *Slouching Towards Gomorrah: Modern Liberalism and American Decline* 117 (1996).

tarnished the notwithstanding clause in the eyes of many Canadians outside Quebec. Yet, considered as a model for institutional design, the notwithstanding clause is quite interesting.

A Simpler Separation of Powers Question

RFRA raises another separation of powers question that received surprisingly little attention in the course of the litigation. *Smith* held that the Free Exercise Clause did not require governments to exempt religious practices from their neutral laws of general applicability. One reason the *Smith* Court gave went to judicial capacity. Justice Scalia argued that any other rule, such as the compelling interest/least restrictive means rule *Smith* repudiated, inevitably required the courts to assess the importance of a practice to religious believers, and then to balance that importance against the importance of the public interest served by the neutral law. Such balancing, the Court indicated, was beyond the capacity of courts. It entailed intrusive inquiries into the details of religious belief, and required the courts to balance incommensurable values.

One can describe this as a suggestion that the rule applied before *Smith* required judges to engage in non-judicial tasks—to behave as policy-makers rather than as judges. Whatever one thinks of the cogency of this argument, it is as applicable to the statutory duty RFRA imposed on judges as it is to the pre-*Smith* rule the Court rejected. And, one might say, it is hornbook separation of powers law that Congress cannot direct the courts to engage in non-judicial tasks.

This separation of powers question continues to matter even after *Boerne*. The reason is that *Boerne* rests on an analysis of Congress's power under Section Five to enforce Section One. It is, in that sense, primarily a decision about federalism. But, RFRA applies to *federal* laws as well. The open question is whether *Boerne* means that RFRA is unconstitutional as applied to federal laws. For example, does RFRA mean that federal land-management programs that place substantial burdens on religious exercises by Native Americans must satisfy the compelling interest/least restrictive means test? Must federal bankruptcy law take into account the impact of some of its provisions on charitable donations to religious institutions made in the year preceding bankruptcy?

The Supreme Court *applied* RFRA to a federal statute in *Gonzales v. O Centro Espirita Beneficente Uniao do Vegetal* (UDV) but mentioned a separation-of-powers concern only obliquely.[78] UDV is a religious group of Brazilian origin. Like the Native American Church in *Smith*, O Centro

---

[78] 546 U.S. 418 (2006).

uses a psychoactive drug in the form of a tea, called hoasca, in its sacraments. And, like peyote, the psychoactive ingredients in hoasca are controlled substances under federal law, making their importation and use unlawful. Invoking RFRA, UDV sought an injunction against enforcement of the federal drug laws against its use of hoasca. The government argued that the ban was consistent with RFRA because it had compelling reasons to refuse to exempt hoasca from the general laws regulating controlled substances. The Court, in a unanimous opinion written by Chief Justice John Roberts, held that the government failed to show that a complete ban was the least restrictive means of controlling access to the drugs in hoasca. The government's strongest argument was that a complete ban was the only way to ensure that the psychoactive ingredients would not leak out into a broader market. But, the Court said, the fact that federal statutory law provided an exemption for sacramental use of peyote "fatally undermine[d]" that argument.[79] In Chief Justice Roberts's words, "The Government's argument echoes the classic rejoinder of bureaucrats throughout history: If I make an exception for you, I'll have to make an exception for everyone, so no exceptions."[80] The exemption for peyote showed that a substance-by-substance approach to leakage was possible, and so the government's argument failed.

The *UDV* decision seems sensible enough, as far as it goes. As a matter of *power*, it would seem clear that Congress could, as an initial matter, limit the reach of its land-management, bankruptcy, and drug statutes out of a policy-based concern (not one necessarily compelled by an interpretation of the free exercise clause) about its statutes' impact on religious believers. And so, it would seem, Congress could impose such limits on all existing statutes, through a general statute like RFRA. And, finally, the enactment of such a statute would seem to provide a good reason for interpreting later-enacted statutes to incorporate similar limitations, unless Congress made it clear that it didn't want those limitations imposed on some particular new statute.

The analysis so far has dealt with the question of Congress's power. But, it does not address the simpler separation of powers question *Smith* raises. RFRA may fall within the scope of Congress's power to enact statutes dealing with drugs, land management, and everything else within its enumerated powers. It may, however, violate the separation of powers insofar as it purports to require that federal courts perform nonjudicial tasks. The *UDV* decision dealt solely with statutory interpretation, but at its conclusion Chief Justice Roberts observed, "We have no cause to pretend that the task assigned by Congress to the courts is an

---

[79] *Id.* at 421.

[80] *Id.* at 436.

easy one."[81] The Court had no occasion to consider whether the task was so difficult as to be beyond judicial capacity because the issue had not been raised, but the tone of the decision tilts strongly against the separation-of-powers objection.

That the Court in *Boerne* did not rely more heavily on *Smith* itself is less surprising than it might seem, however. Only Justice Breyer refused to endorse the Court's account of judicial supremacy. Invalidating RFRA as inconsistent with *Smith*'s account of the judicial role would have been more controversial among the justices. Notably, Justice Kennedy's discussion of the relation between RFRA and *Smith* included the phrase, "We make these observations *not to reargue the position of the majority in Smith*",[82] suggesting that a more direct reliance on *Smith* would have lost him some votes.

The Establishment Clause

Justice Stevens argued that RFRA violated the Establishment Clause because it gave a benefit to churches—the application of the compelling interest/least restrictive means test—that, as he put it, "no atheist or agnostic can obtain."[83] RFRA is a statute falling into a class of *accommodations of religion*. Such statutes embody legislative choices to relieve religious exercise of burdens that neutral laws of general applicability may impose. The class has two components. First, there are accommodations that are constitutionally *compelled*. *Smith* substantially reduced the size of this class. Notwithstanding *Smith*, however, most scholars believe that some accommodations remain constitutionally required. The primary example offered is the ministerial exemption from anti-discrimination laws: Federal anti-discrimination law expressly exempts ministers from its reach, and no respected constitutional scholar thinks that this exemption is an unconstitutional establishment of religion. The prevailing view is just the opposite, namely that it would violate the free exercise clause to hold the Catholic Church liable for refusing to employ women as priests.[84]

Smith recognized that legislatures could voluntarily exempt religious institutions and believers from generally applicable requirements. The Court noted that nothing in its holding precluded Oregon from

---

[81] 546 U.S. at 439.

[82] 521 U.S. at 534.

[83] *Id.* at 537 (Stevens, J., concurring).

[84] *But see* Caroline Mala Corbin, *Above the Law? The Constitutionality of the Ministerial Exemption from Antidiscrimination Law*, 75 Fordham L. Rev. 1965 (2007)(questioning the prevailing wisdom).

exempting the use of peyote in religious practices from its drug abuse laws. Such exemptions form the second component of the category of accommodations of religion. These are *permissible* accommodations. Justice Stevens's opinion in *Boerne* raises the question: Why don't such accommodations violate the Establishment Clause? As he points out, the accommodations provide a benefit for religious exercise because it is religious exercise, which seems to be precisely what the Establishment Clause prohibits.

The Supreme Court's opinions do not provide a fully satisfactory answer to the question raised by Justice Stevens. They clearly do recognize, as he might not, that some accommodations of religion, while not constitutionally compelled, are nonetheless constitutionally permissible.

One reason may be the Court's recognition that the expanded role of government in the modern era creates a far larger number of burdens on religious exercise than occurred in the past. A constitutional rule barring legislatures from adjusting their regulatory statutes to take account of these burdens, while allowing it to draw all sorts of other lines (such as exempting small businesses from laws prohibiting discrimination in employment), would be in practice *hostile* to religion.

Another rationale, to which the Court has sometimes referred, considers the prohibition of establishments of religion in light of its purposes and contemporary politics. The Establishment Clause responds to a historic concern that allowing government to support religion has bad effects on politics as religious believers fight with each other over who gets the government's support (and, though this is less important in the present context, bad effects on religion, which comes to depend on the government for its vitality rather than on God or on believers). However, barring legislatures from accommodating religion would not necessarily address this concern. Indeed, it might alienate religious believers, thereby creating the very social discord based on religious belief that the Establishment Clause was designed to reduce. And, moreover, in a world of substantial religious pluralism, the risk that accommodations of religion will turn into sectarian domination of the government is small.

The exemption for religious uses of peyote and RFRA illustrate the two main facets of this argument. Those who use peyote in religious exercises are, of course, a tiny minority in today's society. They may be able to assemble political support for an accommodation of their religious belief, but they are surely not going to be able to assemble political support for any other practice that distinguishes their religion from the majority's religions. The RFRA coalition, in contrast, did span the religious spectrum. But, precisely because it did so, it could support only something that benefited *all* religions. A sufficiently broad exemption, that is, does not raise the threat of sectarian contention for government's favoritism.

On the view presented here of the politics associated with Establishment Clause fears, two kinds of accommodations of religion should be permissible: Those that are targeted quite narrowly at religious practices of a tiny minority, and those that are targeted broadly at practices common to a wide range of religions. The Supreme Court has not developed a theory of permissible accommodations, but the view presented here captures much of what the Court has done and said. (It does not, however, explain one widely held intuition: That it was constitutionally permissible for governments during the period when consumption of alcohol was prohibited to exempt from the prohibition the sacramental use of wine.)

The Aftermath

While litigation proceeded, the St. Peter's Catholic Church held Mass in a nearby gymnasium. Some city residents said that the lawsuit divided the city, pitting "friend against friend, relative against relative."[85] Negotiations produced a proposal that would have allowed an expansion at the Church that would have left seventy-five percent of the building intact. After the Supreme Court's decision in the city's favor, the parties agreed on a plan that preserved eighty percent of the church building, while allowing an increase in seating to 800.

The coalition that supported RFRA assembled again in response to *Boerne*. In 2000 Congress passed the Religious Land Use and Institutionalized Persons Act.[86] RLUIPA (pronounced raloopa), like RFRA, requires that courts apply the "compelling interest" and "least restrictive means" tests to statutes that substantially burden religious practices, but it confines itself to the areas of land use and imprisonment, areas where the coalition's members found the most extensive examples of state actions they thought inappropriate. RLUIPA limits its reach to situations in which the burden "is imposed in a program or activity that receives Federal financial assistance," when the burden—or its removal—affects interstate commerce, or when the burden arises in connection with a land use program where the government has in place a system for making "individualized assessments" of proposed land uses. These jurisdictional triggers aim to get around the federalism problems the Court found with RFRA. RLUIPA provides, in addition, that "No government shall impose or implement a land use regulation in a manner that treats

---

[85] MacCormack, supra note 8.

[86] 42 U.S.C. § 2000cc (2003).

a religious assembly or institution on less than equal terms with a nonreligious assembly or institution."

Cutter v. Wilkinson upheld RLUIPA against a facial constitutional challenge.[87] Several Ohio prisoners alleged that the state's prisons did not accommodate their religious beliefs as required by RLUIPA. A court of appeals held the statute unconstitutional on its face, and did not consider whether the prisons could accommodate the inmates' religious beliefs without excessive difficulty. The Supreme Court reversed that decision in a unanimous opinion written by Justice Ruth Bader Ginsburg. The statute was constitutional because it "alleviates exceptional government-created burdens on private religious exercise"—the burdens being those that flowed from the fact of incarceration itself.[88] Justice Ginsburg's opinion relied on pre-*Smith* law in observing that RLUIPA should be applied sensibly, to take into account the burdens accommodation might place on others and, particularly, security concerns inevitable in a prison setting. Were accommodations required by the statute to "jeopardize an institution's effective functioning," it might succumb to an as-applied challenge.[89]

Boerne's doctrine had a significant impact in other settings. Relying on its requirement that Section Five legislation be proportional to and congruent with state actions that were inconsistent with the Constitution as interpreted by the courts, the Supreme Court held that Congress could not use its Section Five power to impose financial liability (inconsistent with the Eleventh Amendment) on state governments under the Americans with Disabilities Act and the Age Discrimination in Employment Act.[90] Both cases involved discrimination against members of groups that receive only "rational basis" scrutiny, and the Court held that the statutes imposed liability with little evidence that irrational discrimination was widespread. In contrast, the Court upheld the imposition of similar liability under the Family and Medical Leave Act, which it treated as addressing sufficiently widespread discrimination against women on the basis of stereotypes about their roles as homemakers and caretakers.[91] In these cases no questions arose about the states' obligation to comply with the federal statutes' *substantive* requirements, because all involved activities that Congress could regulate under the Commerce Clause. The implications of the *Boerne* doctrine for states'

---

[87] 544 U.S. 709 (2005).

[88] *Id.* at 709.

[89] *Id.* at 711.

[90] *Board of Trustees of University of Alabama v. Garrett*, 531 U.S. 356 (2001); *Kimel v. Florida Board of Regents*, 528 U.S. 62 (2000).

[91] *Nevada Department of Human Resources v. Hibbs*, 538 U.S. 721 (2003).

more distinctively sovereign activities remain unclear. The Court upheld the application of accommodation requirements on the facts presented in *Tennessee v. Lane*,[92] which involved alleged restrictions on access to courthouses that in the Court's view amounted to violations of the Sixth Amendment, and in *United States v. Georgia*,[93] where the failure to accommodate a prisoner's disabilities was alleged to violate the Eighth Amendment's ban on cruel and unusual punishment. These holdings are consistent with the narrowest possible interpretation of Section Five— that it gives Congress the power to create remedies for violations of Section One rights as the courts define those rights. Pending litigation deals with broader interpretations.[94]

---

[92] 541 U.S. 509 (2004).

[93] 546 U.S. 151 (2006).

[94] For example, does the Americans with Disabilities Act make it unlawful for states to charge special fees for drivers to obtain "Handicapped" stickers and, if it does, does Congress have the power under Section 5 to limit the states' power to set such fees?

15

Benjamin Wittes and Hannah Neprash

The Story of the Guantánamo Cases: Habeas Corpus, the Reach of the Court, and the War on Terror

American forces deployed to Afghanistan in the fall of 2001 faced a mission unlike that confronting any military force in prior history: preventing unspecified catastrophes at the hands of unspecified people using unspecified means in unspecified locations at unspecified times in the future. In pursuit of this task, they removed the de facto government of the country and installed a new one. They bombed targets, attacked Taliban installations, and armed and supported Northern Alliance forces. They also began capturing people—and, in still greater numbers, assuming custody of people captured by allied militias and by the Pakistani army. Suspected Taliban fighters, Arab foreigners suspected of al Qaeda and Taliban ties, and other foreign men fleeing the country all fell into American hands. Unlike detainees in more conventional conflicts, no uniforms distinguished these fighters from the innocent civilians many of the detainees claimed to be. Bounty hunters captured some and turned them over to American forces. Consequently, within weeks of the September 11 attacks, everyone from soldiers in the field to the President of the United States faced fateful decisions with wrenching consequences for the safety of American civilians and the liberty of those in custody. Who were these detainees? What legal status did they occupy? Were they criminal suspects or captives in a war? If the former, under what rules should they face trial, in what forum, and where? If the latter, what should be done with those who denied being combatants at all?

These questions required immediate answers, and in the earliest months of the global war on terrorism—with the World Trade Center rubble still smoldering, passions running high, and fear running high-er—the Bush administration made a series of fateful decisions concerning them. By the end of President Bush's second term, these decisions had led to unceasing political controversy, seven years of continuous litigation, and four major Supreme Court cases.[1] First, the President decided that war crimes trials would take place not in American federal courts but in military commissions—tribunals of a type the military had not convened since the years immediately following World War II. On November 13, 2001, he issued an order authorizing commissions to try any non-United States citizen who had "engaged in, aided or abetted, or conspired to commit, acts of international terrorism" against "the United States, its citizens, national security, foreign policy, or economy."[2] These tribunals lacked many of the safeguards of either the American domestic criminal justice or the courts martial which the military uses to try American soldiers accused of crimes. At least in theory, they could admit hearsay evidence and evidence obtained by coercion; they could use secret evidence; and their verdicts lacked any appeal to the civilian courts.

Second, President Bush decided to hold particularly significant detainees at the Guantánamo Bay Naval Station in Cuba, in a deliberate effort to create an operationally secure detention site outside of the zone of hostilities yet shielded from the jurisdiction of American courts. The choice of Guantánamo, a site leased in perpetuity to exclusive American jurisdiction and control, yet subject to the ultimate sovereignty of Cuba, aimed to prevent judicial review of both the legal propriety of detentions and the factual judgments that lay beneath them.

Finally, President Bush decided to hold these detainees neither as prisoners of war nor as criminal suspects but as "unlawful enemy combatants," a status of enemy detainee held without criminal process yet also not entitled to the considerable benefits due to prisoners of war under the Geneva Conventions. The administration also argued that Common Article 3 of the Geneva Conventions, which provides for a baseline of humane treatment to detainees not covered by the conventions' other provisions, did not apply to the conflict either on grounds that the provision, by its terms, applies only to conflicts "not of an international character" and that this language refers only to civil wars, not to global struggles like the War on Terror.

---

[1] This chapter tells the story of only three of those decisions, the ones concerning the detainees held at the Guantánamo Bay Naval Station. We do not include the related story of the Supreme Court's decision in *Hamdi v. Rumsfeld*, 542 U.S. 507 (2004).

[2] Military Order of Nov. 13, 2001: Detention, Treatment, and Trial of Certain Non–Citizens in the War Against Terrorism, 66 Fed. Reg. 57833 (2001), *reprinted in* 10 U.S.C. § 801 (2006).

Each of these decisions, the administration contended, had ample precedent in American law and practice, and each sported—at least at the outset—a broad political constituency. Indeed, the contours of the controversy over them developed slowly. The presidential order establishing military commissions generated some anxiety from its inception, for example, but the day after it came down, only one of the major newspapers led with the story. Other events dominated the news that day. In Crawford, Texas, Russian President Vladimir Putin and President Bush had agreed to cut their nuclear stockpiles by two-thirds. The Taliban's retreat from Afghan cities and the Northern Alliance's arrival in Kabul seemed imminent. Several Americans were dying of anthrax, which had just shown up in government mail rooms and at media organizations. Indeed, military commissions did not even dominate the debate over liberty and security in the new world in which America suddenly found itself. Civil libertarian anxieties about the administration's conduct tended to focus on the just-passed USA Patriot Act instead.[3]

Similarly, when the military opened the Guantánamo facility in the winter after the attacks, human rights groups leveled only relatively modest criticisms. They too saw the conflict in terms of the laws of war and its permissive standards for detention, arguing only about a narrow range of questions related to conditions of confinement for detainees, the status of Taliban fighters, and the necessity of holding cursory tribunals before denying any fighters treatment as POWs. Human Rights Watch, for example, did not question the authority of the military to hold the detainees as unlawful enemy combatants but argued only that it should not hold them in wire cages, that Taliban fighters might in principle be entitled to POW status, and that under international law, the administration must make such status decisions on an individual—rather than a blanket—basis.[4]

But the administration's insistence on a pure war paradigm, in which the executive could act on its own in detaining and trying suspected enemies and in which the courts and Congress sat on the sidelines, set up a conflict among the branches of American government that, even after seven years and landmark rulings in *Rasul v. Bush*,[5]

---

[3] *See* Uniting and Strengthening America by Providing Appropriate Tools Required to Intercept and Obstruct Terrorism Act (USA PATRIOT Act) of 2001, Pub. L. No. 107–56, 115 Stat. 272 (codified in scattered sections of 8, 12, 15, 18, 22, 28, 31, 42, 49, 50 U.S.C. (2006)).

[4] *See* Letter from Kenneth Roth, Executive Director, Human Rights Watch, to Condoleezza Rice, National Security Advisor (Jan. 27, 2002) *available at* http://hrw.org/press/2002/01/us012802–ltr.htm.

[5] 542 U.S. 466 (2004).

Hamdan v. Rumsfeld,[6] and *Boumediene v. Bush,*[7] has only the dimmest outlines of a resolution. Each of these cases involved a showdown—in equal part policy dialogue, power struggle, and debate over the nature of America's conflict with al Qaeda and the proper role of the branches of government within that struggle. In each instance, executive action led to judicial rejection, and that rejection in turn provoked an executive and legislative response that then led to the next round of litigation and confrontation. And so far, at least, this unending string of actions and reactions has left the central questions open: the high court's Guantánamo cases have established a major presence for the judiciary in global counter-terrorism. But they have not yet answered those vexing questions that American forces faced in the conflict's earliest days.

How the Detainees Ended up at Guantánamo

The detainee population that began arriving at Guantánamo in February 2002 varied enormously. As later hearings revealed, some detainees made no secret of their affiliations with al Qaeda or involvement in terrorist actions. For example, Abdul Rahman Al Zahri, whom the government accused of advance knowledge of the September 11 attacks, announced at one hearing: "I do pose a threat to the United States and its allies. I admit to you it is my honor to be an enemy of the United States. I'm a Muslim jihadist...." Al Zahri denied membership in al Qaeda but proudly declared that he trained at al Qaeda camps and met with Bin Laden many times. "I will kill myself for him and will also give my family and all of my money to him," he said. "With the help of God, we will stand Mujahedin and terrorists against Americans."[8] Some detainees admitted to Taliban affiliations, but minimized their role within the organization or described relatively low-level roles. Other detainees denied any involvement with the Taliban or al Qaeda whatsoever. For many of the detainees, the evidence on the public record simply does not definitively establish whether the captives ever posed a genuine threat to the security of the United States, were victims of mistaken identity, or fell somewhere in between.[9]

The detainees whose names grace the captions of the high court's Guantánamo cases reflect the diversity of the larger detainee population.

---

[6] 548 U.S. 557 (2006).

[7] 128 S.Ct. 2229 (2008).

[8] Summary of Administrative Review Board Proceedings for ISN 441 (Abd Al Rahman Al Zahri), http://www.dod.mil/pubs/foi/detainees/csrt_arb/ARB_Transcript_2196–2293.pdf. The military has made certain hearing transcripts available at http://www.dod.mil/pubs/foi/detainees/csrt_arb/index.html.

[9] For a general discussion of the detainee population at Guantánamo, see Chapter 3 of Benjamin Wittes, *Law and the Long War: The Future of Justice in the Age of Terror* (2008).

By no accounts does it seem likely that Shafiq Rasul presented any profound threat to the United States. Born on April 15, 1977 in Dudley, West Midlands, England, he lived, prior to his capture in Afghanistan and subsequent detention at Guantánamo, in Tipton, a town of 50,000 in which roughly 14 percent of the population was of Asian descent. After flunking out of law school, Rasul worked as a stockroom clerk for an electronics store. He led a thoroughly Westernized lifestyle, following professional sports, going out to nightclubs, and wearing designer clothes. Six feet, two inches tall and purportedly handsome, he was, according to family members, mild-mannered and apathetic religiously speaking, a Muslim who attended services only reluctantly. This lifestyle changed, according to the *New York Times*, when Rasul and a few of his friends began studying with a hard-line cleric who espoused jihad against the West. Rasul withdrew from his family and friends, judging them negatively for having assimilated to Western culture and warning of the consequences that their nightclubbing would have in their afterlives.[10]

Despite this change in behavior, the news that Rasul had been captured along with Taliban forces shocked his family. When he left Tipton, he had told his relatives that he was enrolling in a computer class in Pakistan because it cost less than did a similar class in England. He traveled to Pakistan with two friends, Asif Iqbal and Ruhal Ahmed, who gave their families the excuses of an arranged marriage and a vacation respectively. Together, these three men became known as the Tipton Three when the story of their capture and detention became public.[11] Rasul's family heard from him in October 2001, when he emailed his older brother with a computer-related question. Three months later, relatives learned that he had been captured in Afghanistan with Taliban fighters, and was being held as an unlawful combatant in Cuba.[12]

It is not hard to imagine how the military would have regarded radicalized British youth captured in Afghanistan with Taliban fighters as a threat. But there exists little suggestion that the three were ever more than foot soldiers. And they did not concede even being that. In statements following their release, they denied ever having been part of the Taliban or even sympathetic to its brand of radical Islam.[13] As

---

[10] *See* Warren Hoge, *Hometown of British Prisoners Known for Tranquil Diversity*, N.Y. Times, Jan. 29, 2002, at A14; Sarah Lyall, *English Town Whispers of a Taliban Connection*, N.Y. Times, Feb. 3, 2002, at A14; Amy Waldman, *How in a Little English Town Jihad Found Young Converts*, N.Y.Times, Apr. 24, 2002, at A1.

[11] *See* Waldman, *supra* note 10.

[12] *Id.*

[13] *See* David Rose, *How We Survived Jail Hell*, The Observer (London), Mar. 14, 2004, at 5; David Rose, *Guantánamo: The War on Human Rights*, 11–16 (2004); *see also Rasul v. Myers*, 512 F.3d 644 (D.C. Cir. 2008).

British journalist Andy Worthington summarized:

> Iqbal was making arrangements for his forthcoming marriage to a young woman in Pakistan, Ahmed was his best man, and Rasul was planning to do a computer course once the wedding was over, but soon after their arrival, when the invasion of Afghanistan began, they made the fateful decision that exciting adventure awaited them over the border, just a short bus-ride away.... [T]hey planned to provide humanitarian aid to Afghan villagers, a mission that also involved the adrenaline rush of being in a war zone, and they hoped, the opportunity to sample the Afghans' enormous naan breads. At risk from both US bombing raids and the Taliban, who were deeply suspicious of young men wandering around without beards, they tried to return to Pakistan in a taxi, but were instead taken to Kunduz. As the first groups of Taliban soldiers began to surrender, they clambered onto a truck that was leaving the city, but the vehicle was immediately shelled, and almost everyone on board was killed. With nowhere else to turn, they surrendered to [Northern] Alliance soldiers....[14]

Whatever story one chooses to believe, Rasul was at most a marginal figure among America's foes.

By contrast, Salim Ahmed Hamdan clearly attached himself to al Qaeda at the group's highest levels, although he does not appear to have played any sort of role in planning its operations. Hamdan arrived at Guantánamo around the same time as Rasul did, but he traveled a very different road to the American detention camp. Journalist Jonathan Mahler provides the richest description of Hamdan's background and recruitment into al Qaeda, from which the following account is distilled.[15] Born in 1970 in Wadi Hadhramaut, Yemen, a rural village in the southern region of the country, he neither frequented night clubs nor wore designer clothing. His father worked as a farmer and a shopkeeper, and both of Hamdan's parents died while he was still a child. Soon after his parents' death, Hamdan quit school, never having achieved more than a fourth grade education, and he went to live with relatives in Mukalla, a port city on Yemen's southern coast. By the time he turned 26, he was working part time as a cab driver in Yemen's capital city of Sana, spending his discretionary income on khat, the amphetamine-like stimulant chewed by many young Yemeni men. He had a heavy mustache and densely curly black hair, but no prospects and limited income or education in a country in which economic opportunities were not

---

[14] See Andy Worthington, *The Guantánamo Files: The Stories of the 759 Detainees in America's Illegal Prison* 19–20 (2007).

[15] See Jonathan Mahler, *The Challenge:* Hamdan v. Rumsfeld *and the Fight over Presidential Power* 3–11 (2008)

abundant. Hamdan had never been devout, but when a group of jihadists recruited him in 1996 to travel to Tajikistan with them to fight in solidarity with that country's small Islamic uprising against the Russian-backed government, he jumped at the chance. It surely did not hurt that they offered travel expenses and promised a generous salary.

The group traveled northwards from Jalalabad, Afghanistan toward Tajikistan, but found the roads nearly impassible by car or on foot. What's more, the Tajik border authorities turned the fighters away from the Afghan border. So instead of fighting in Tajikistan, the group sought out Osama Bin Laden, who had recently settled in Afghanistan after his expulsion from Sudan. Hamdan's group arrived at Bin Laden's camp in late 1996. After hearing Bin Laden's anti-American rhetoric, 17 members of the 35–person group—including Hamdan—chose to stay.

Hamdan took a position as a driver for Bin Laden and other al Qaeda associates on an agricultural complex near Kandahar. He later maintained that he took the job not out of ideological sympathy but because he needed the $200 monthly salary. With Bin Laden's encouragement and financial assistance, Hamdan married a Yemeni woman in Sana and returned with her to Afghanistan. There they lived in a mud house with dirt floors and no running water. When she complained about their living conditions, Hamdan urged patience, for one day they would return to Yemen.

In November following the attacks on September 11, Hamdan borrowed a car to take his daughter and his wife—then pregnant with his second daughter—to Pakistan, where he thought they would be safe. On the return trip, he was captured by Northern Alliance soldiers and turned over to the Americans days later. He spent the next six months detained in the Bagram and Kandahar prison camps, before his transport to Guantánamo Bay in May 2002.

Two and a half years later, Hamdan became one of the first defendants in the military commission system laid out in President Bush's executive order. On July 14, 2004, the Department of Defense prosecutors charged him with conspiracy, alleging that he had served as a bodyguard and driver for Bin Laden between 1996 and 2001. During that time, he allegedly picked up and delivered weapons to al Qaeda members and associates. He also allegedly received extensive firearms training at the al Qaeda-sponsored Al Farouq camp in Afghanistan.[16]

---

[16] The original military commission charge sheet for *U.S. v. Salim Ahmed Hamdan* can be found at http://www.defenselink.mil/news/Jul2004/d20040714hcc.pdf. A revised version that followed the enactment of the Military Commissions Act of 2006 can be found at http://www.defenselink.mil/news/d2007Hamdan%20–%20Notification%20of%20Sworn%20 Charg es.pdf.

Lakhdar Boumediene and the group of Algerian-born men collective-ly known as the Algerian Six represented still another category of detainee. Unlike Hamdan and Rasul, they were—if the government's suspicions about them are correct—neither low-level fighters nor hired hands for the big guns. Rather, they constituted a dangerous terrorist cell in the heart of Europe. Yet in several respects, their case also presented the most troubling procedural issues, for these men looked the least like soldiers subject to conventional military detention—and their capture took place thousands of miles from any battlefield. They repre-sented, in short, that category of captives who may have threatened the greatest havoc yet whose detention also threatened the gravest damage to liberty. Seven years after their capture, it remained unclear who they were or what they might have done.

A native of Algeria, Boumediene traveled to Bosnia in the wake of the civil war that tore that country apart in the 1990s. Many foreign Muslim volunteers migrated to Bosnia to help fight Serbian forces, and the military has intimated that Boumediene may have been one of them.[17] What is clear, however, is that like many of these foreigners, he became a naturalized Bosnian citizen. He was married and had two children in Bosnia. After the war, many of these foreign fighters began working for Muslim charitable organizations; Boumediene worked for the Red Crescent of the United Arab Emirates. Because American intelligence agencies had long suspected that some of these Islamic charities in Bosnia were acting as terrorist fronts, they kept close tabs on them and their employees.

In the fall of 2001, the United States asked Bosnian authorities to investigate several alleged al Qaeda associates. The investigation led to the arrest of Bensayah Belkacem, the first member of the Algerian Six to end up in jail. Belkacem was living with his wife and two daughters near the town of Zenica, when police picked him up for using a falsified Yemini passport to enter Bosnia. While searching his home, authorities found the name "Abu Zubeida" and a Pakistani phone number scrawled on a piece of paper inside a library book. Authorities assumed this to be contact information for Abu Zubaydah, the prominent al Qaeda opera-tive.[18] Subsequently, U.S. officials accused Belkacem of being "the pri-mary [al Qaeda] facilitator" in Bosnia, in part citing phone records and

---

[17] *See* Unclassified Summary of Evidence for Administrative Review Board in the case of Boumediene, Lakhdar (ISN 10005), http://www.dod.mil/pubs/foi/detainees/csrt_arb/ARB_Round_2_Factors_900–1009.pdf. The military states in this document that "A source stated the detainee was a former Bosnian Mujahedin who had planned to travel to Afghanistan." *Id.*

[18] *See* Marc Perelman, *From Sarajevo to Guantánamo: The Strange Case of the Algerian Six*, Mother Jones, Dec. 4, 2007, http://www.motherjones.com/news/feature/2007/12/gitmo-sarajevo-guantanamo-algerian-six.html.

the 70 calls he had allegedly placed to Afghanistan in the month following September 11.[19]

Having taken Belkacem into custody, U.S. officials focused their attention on his acquaintance, another Algerian man named Saber Lahmar. Lahmar had a suspicious connection: his father-in-law, with whom he lived, worked as a janitor at the U.S. Embassy in Sarajevo. According to the *Washington Post*, an October 16 wiretap on Lahmar's phone revealed a coded reference to what sounded like a plan to attack the U.S. and British embassies in Sarajevo.[20] Within a week, Bosnian police had arrested Lahmar and four others, including Ait Idr, Hadj Boudella, Mohamed Nechle, and Boumediene.[21]

These men, who said they knew each other through charity work, remained in Bosnian custody for three months. But during that time, Bosnian investigators could not find evidence to justify their continued detention. Phone records did not indicate that Bensayah had ever called the number listed as Abu Zubaydah's, and the U.S. declined to share any evidence in its possession suggesting that he did. The Bosnian Supreme Court ultimately ruled that there was not sufficient evidence to justify the detention of the six Algerians and ordered their release on January 17, 2002.[22] The Bosnian government tried unsuccessfully to strip the men of their citizenship and deport them to Algeria, but when that effort failed, it turned them over to U.S. military personnel instead of setting them free. Three days after leaving Bosnian custody, the six men arrived handcuffed and blindfolded at Guantánamo.

Like Hamdan, each of the Algerian Six waited more than two years for a military tribunal to review the basis for his detention. Boumediene made no statement at his administrative hearings, although his lawyers later submitted a significant volume of material detailing his denial.[23] Each tribunal declared its subject an enemy combatant. And while

---

[19] Unclassified Summary of Evidence for Administrative Review Board in the case of Belkacem, Bensayah (ISN 10001), http://www.dod.mil/pubs/foi/detainees/csrt_arb/ARB_Round_2_Factors_900–1009.pdf. *See also* Perelman, *supra* note 18.

[20] *See* Craig Whitlock, *At Guantánamo, Caught in a Legal Trap*, Wash. Post, Aug. 21, 2006, at A1.

[21] *Id.*

[22] *See Boudellaa, et al. v. Bosnia and Herzegovnia, et al.,* Nos. CH/02/8679; CH/02/8689; CH02/8690; CH/02/8691, Human Rights Chamber for Bosnia and Herzegovina (Oct. 11, 2002).

[23] *See* Classified Annual [sic] Review Board Submission on behalf of Lakhdar Boumediene (ISN 10005), http://www.dod.mil/pubs/foi/detainees/csrt_arb/ARB_Transcript_Set_15_22683–22733.pdf; *see also* Memorandum in Support of the Release and the Return to Bosnia of Detainees Bensayah, Lahmar, Nechla, Ait Idir, Boumediene and Boudella, http://www.dod.mil/pubs/foi/detainees/csrt_arb/ARB_Transcript_Set_12_22011–22244.pdf.

subsequent administrative reviews have continued to regard the men as a threat to the United States, the charges themselves have evolved. Tribunal records from 2005 show that the military had dropped its accusations of conspiracy to attack the U.S. Embassy in Sarajevo, and the government in their habeas case in 2008 proceeded on other grounds.

Both the Bush administration and its legion of critics have tended to treat detainees at Guantánamo as a block, but the cases of these three men presented very different, though overlapping problems. Rasul was an example of hundreds of alleged foreign fighters captured and held at Guantánamo. Most of them were likely relatively harmless foot soldiers, though potentially convertible to terrorist causes, and some of their denials were probably true. This group of detainees presented the question of what role the courts should play in reviewing the cases of low-level fighters against whom the government may have strong, imperfect, or utterly weak evidence of belligerency. Hamdan, whom the administration wanted to try for crimes, raised the question of the lawfulness and integrity of the new system of military commissions and the broader policy question of what the appropriate forum is for trying foreign nationals for overseas misconduct hostile to the United States. The Algerian Six represented a still more difficult series of questions: Does the government possess any detention power other than the criminal process for terrorists outside of the battlefield setting? If so, whom does this process cover and what are the rules? What constitutes an appropriate burden of proof and who bears it? And what role should the courts play in adjudicating these cases in the first place?

How the Bush Administration Read the World War II–Era Precedents

From the White House's point of view, the pre–2004 Supreme Court precedents solidly backed all three of the major judgments underlying the president's policies. Indeed, historically speaking, the administration's position, at least superficially, had a lot going for it. For starters, the Court in 1950 had confronted the question of whether the federal courts had habeas jurisdiction over aliens detained overseas and it seemed to give an emphatic answer: they don't. During World War II, Lothar Eisentrager, a German intelligence officer in Shanghai, spearheaded Nazi espionage operations in the Far East. An American military commission convicted him as a war criminal and American forces subsequently imprisoned him in occupied Germany. He filed a petition for a writ of habeas corpus, but the Supreme Court ruled that the constitutional guarantee of habeas corpus did not reach enemy aliens detained by the United States on foreign soil. In his majority opinion, Justice Robert Jackson wrote:

> We are cited to no instance where a court, in this or any other country where the writ is known, has issued it on behalf of an alien enemy who, at no relevant time and in no stage of his captivity, has been within its territorial jurisdiction. Nothing in the text of the Constitution extends such a right, nor does anything in our statutes.[24]

In some places, Jackson's opinion seems somewhat equivocal on the jurisdictional point. Elsewhere in the opinion, for example, he seems to rule affirmatively on the legality of Eisentrager's tribunal, implying that he had reached the case's merits. Still, his language leaves little room for doubt that he imagined such questions beyond the court's ken:

> [E]ven by the most magnanimous view, our law does not abolish inherent distinctions recognized throughout the civilized world between citizens and aliens, nor between aliens of friendly and of enemy allegiance, nor between resident enemy aliens who have submitted themselves to our laws and nonresident enemy aliens who at all times have remained with, and adhered to, enemy governments.[25]

Jackson was thinking in terms of his era, when enemy aliens were necessarily citizens of enemy countries. But it's not hard to understand how the Bush administration could apply the principles he articulated and conclude that the courts would keep their noses out of wartime detentions as long as they involved aliens held overseas. Guantánamo was a clever solution: overseas in a technical sense, domestic in all practical senses. It proved too clever by half.

Eisentrager was not the only World War II-era arrow in the administration's quiver.

In *Ex Parte Quirin* the Court considered the propriety of using military commissions stripped of some of the procedural generosity of America's normal justice to try unlawful enemy combatants—and it upheld the practice, even as applied to an American citizen.[26] Along the way, the Justices had seemed unambiguously to validate the administration's premise that it could detain enemy fighters who don't follow the laws of war without giving those detainees the privileges of prisoners of war.

At the height of World War II, President Franklin Delano Roosevelt established a military commission to try eight Nazis operatives who had conspired unsuccessfully to commit acts of sabotage against American

---

[24] *Johnson v. Eisentrager*, 339 U.S. 763, 768 (1950).

[25] *Id.* at 769.

[26] *See Ex parte Quirin*, 317 U.S. 1 (1942).

industry. Six months after Adolf Hitler's declaration of war against the United States, these Nazi operatives traveled by submarine from France and landed in New York and Florida. Two were naturalized American citizens, and all had lived previously in the United States. Their mission, orchestrated by Hitler himself, was to blow up aluminum plants, hydro-electric plants, railroad lines and terminals, bridges, and Jewish-owned department stores. When two of the saboteurs betrayed their mission to American authorities, the FBI took all of the operatives into custody.[27]

On June 27, 1942, J. Edgar Hoover announced the capture of the Nazi operatives, and a week later, Roosevelt issued two proclamations that jointly established the military commission's structure and jurisdiction and named the eight defendants. Soon after, the trial began in near-total secrecy; except for a few pictures of the trial and the defendants, it was off-limits to the public. Before it could conclude, however, the Supreme Court announced at the request of lawyers for the saboteurs that it would hold an unprecedented summer session to hear their habeas corpus petitions questioning the legality of the military commission. Barely a month later, the Justices unanimously decided that the President had legally constituted the commission and that the government had acted lawfully in detaining the petitioners. At the time it issued its judgment, the Court made clear that it would explain its reasoning at a later date. Three months later, after the government had executed six of the saboteurs, the Court released its opinion.[28]

For President Bush's purposes, *Quirin* established two important points. First, the Justices had made clear that not all enemy belligerents qualify as POWs, but that a lesser-category of wartime detainee exists:

> By universal agreement and practice the law of war draws a distinction between the armed forces and the peaceful populations of belligerent nations and also between those who are lawful and unlawful combatants. Lawful combatants are subject to capture and detention as prisoners of war by opposing military forces. Unlawful combatants are likewise subject to capture and detention, but in addition they are subject to trial and punishment by military tribunals for acts which render their belligerency unlawful. The spy who secretly and without uniform passes the military lines of a belligerent in time of war, seeking to gather military information and communicate it to the enemy, or an enemy combatant who without uniform comes secretly through the lines for the purpose of waging war by destruction of life or property, are familiar examples of belligerents who are generally deemed not to be entitled to the

---

[27] *See* Jack Goldsmith & Cass R. Sunstein, *Military Tribunals and Legal Culture: What a Difference Sixty Years Makes*, 19 Const. Comment., 261, 263–266 (2002).

[28] *Id.*

status of prisoners of war, but to be offenders against the law of war subject to trial and punishment by military tribunals.[29]

Second, the Justices upheld the use of military commissions for war crimes trials of this latter category of detainee.[30]

During World War II, public solicitude for the plight of captured Nazis ran pretty low, and the Supreme Court's intervention in Roosevelt's military commission met with broad disapproval from Congress and the general public. The *New York Times* reported at the time that, the "decision to seek recourse in the Supreme Court did not meet popular approval in Washington. On the contrary, there is great dissatisfaction here with the length to which the [three-week military trial] has already proceeded."[31] The *Los Angeles Times* described the hearing as, "totally uncalled for. . . . [T]he Supreme Court should never have been drafted into this war time military matter."[32]

By contrast, the press reacted enthusiastically to the Court's expedited rubber-stamping of the trials. The *Washington Post* wrote:

> In denying civil justice to the eight Nazi saboteurs, the Supreme Court did the expected thing. The full ruling still has to be published. It will be awaited with great interest because it involves issues which are vital both to our territorial and political security... To handle [the Nazi saboteurs] in the civil courts would be to help Hitler immensely, and that would be intolerable.[33]

To a White House predisposed to enthusiasm for presidential power and thrust into the cauldron of post-September 11 policymaking, *Quirin* and *Eisentrager* were irresistible precedents—a nearly blank check for presidential justice against the country's enemies. Applied to the enemy belligerents in the War on Terror, all of whom the administration regarded as unlawful combatants, the precedents meant a powerful detention authority leading to streamlined military justice, and all unreviewable by the federal courts. The beauty of it, from the White House's point of view, was that the Supreme Court had already signed off. "We relied on the same language in FDR's order, the same congressional statute that FDR did, and we had a unanimous Supreme Court precedent on point," recalled Bradford Berenson, a lawyer who served in the

---

[29] *Ex parte Quirin*, 317 U.S. at 30–31.

[30] *See id.* at 35–36.

[31] Lewis Wood, *Supreme Court is Called in Unprecedented Session to Hear Plea of Nazi Spies*, N.Y. Times, July, 28, 1942, at 1.

[32] Editorial, *The Saboteurs Seek Civil Court Relief*, L.A. Times, July 29, 1942, at A4.

[33] Editorial, *Saboteur Case*, Wash, Post, Aug. 1, 1942, at 8.

White House Counsel's office, of the military commissions. "As a lawyer advising a client, it doesn't get much better than that."[34]

But times had changed. The reaction to President Bush's November 13, 2001 military order differed dramatically from the public response to Roosevelt's. Three days after President Bush issued the order, the *New York Times* editorialized:

> The administration's action is the latest in a troubling series of attempts since Sept. 11 to do an end run around the Constitution.... [B]y ruling that terrorists fall outside the norms of civilian and military justice, Mr. Bush has taken it upon himself to establish a prosecutorial channel that answers only to him. The decision is an insult to the exquisite balancing of executive, legislative and judicial powers that the framers incorporated into the Constitution. With the flick of a pen, in this case, Mr. Bush has essentially discarded the rulebook of American justice painstakingly assembled over the course of more than two centuries. In the place of fair trials and due process he has substituted a crude and unaccountable system that any dictator would admire.[35]

Where liberal opinion had once looked to the courts to validate the exertion of presidential justice against Nazi saboteurs, it now looked to them to limit the exercise of presidential justice against al Qaeda and Taliban suspects.

The source of this shift in elite attitudes is tricky to pin down. Cass Sunstein and Jack Goldsmith, in a perspicacious early article on the subject that first identified the shift in elite reaction to military commissions, highlight several differences in the context in which the presidents in question acted. But these, they argue, do not quite account for the dramatic difference in the response, which they ultimately attribute to changes in the political and legal culture and the average American's experience of the war at hand.[36] World War II had a vastly different impact on most Americans than did the events following September 11. During the Second World War, the entire nation mobilized, and people believed that the future of the United States was uncertain. Gas rationing, rubber shortages, and wage and price controls reminded Americans daily of the threat to their country. By contrast, in the months following September 11, the administration asked Americans to change their lifestyles merely by spending more money.[37] Sunstein and Goldsmith

---

[34] Jack Goldsmith, *The Terror Presidency* 109 (2007).

[35] Editorial, *A Travesty of Justice*, N.Y. Times, Nov. 16, 2001, at A24.

[36] *See* Goldsmith & Sunstein, *zupra* note 27.

[37] *See, e.g.*, President Bush's statement at O'Hare International Airport on September 27, 2001: "And one of the great goals of this nation's war is to restore public confidence in

argue that the "widespread perception [in 1942] of a threat to national survival made it far harder for people to insist on the use of those [civil] courts."[38] Without the daily reminder that the nation was at war in 2001, military trials seemed inappropriate to many people when civilian courts remained both available and functioning.

Sunstein and Goldsmith also suggest that the nation's social attitudes towards government, the military, and the law had evolved between 1942 and 2001. Between the two military orders, the United States experienced Vietnam and Watergate. These events and others eroded the high regard held in the press, in Congress, and in academia for the executive branch and the military. Yet even as this respect dissipated, Sunstein and Goldsmith suggest that the commitment to individual rights strengthened within the public and the legal system. The Court that wrote the *Quirin* opinion was the same Court that supported the Japanese exclusion in *Korematsu v. United States.*[39] Between 1942 and 2001, federal constitutional law and habeas corpus review had changed significantly.

Public expectations of the courts had changed too. Americans have long reposed great political power in their judiciary, but that power has grown enormously in the years since *Quirin* and *Eisentrager*. Those decisions predated *Brown v. Board of Education.*[40] They predated the Warren Court more generally. The idea of keeping a large group of men under lock and key for many years outside of the oversight of the court system seems far more alien to a culture that delegates abortion policy,[41] firearms policy,[42] campaign finance rules,[43] the permissible use of race in university admissions and public school placement,[44] even the rules of professional golf[45] to judicial review—to name a few randomly selected examples—than it must have seemed in an America that had not yet

---

the airline industry. It's to tell the traveling public: Get on board. Do your business around the country. Fly and enjoy America's great destination spots. Get down to Disney World in Florida. Take your families and enjoy life, the way we want it to be enjoyed." *available at* http://www.whitehouse.gov/news/releases/2001/09/20010927–1.html.

[38] Goldsmith & Sunstein, *supra* note 27, at 281.

[39] 319 U.S. 432 (1943).

[40] 347 U.S. 483 (1954).

[41] *See, e.g., Roe* v. *Wade,* 410 U.S. 113 (1973).

[42] *See, e.g., District of Columbia v. Heller,* 128 S.Ct. 2783 (2008).

[43] *See, e.g., McConnell v. Federal Election Comm'n,* 540 U.S. 93 (2003).

[44] *See, e.g., Gratz v. Bollinger,* 539 U.S. 244 (2003); *Grutter v. Bollinger,* 539 U.S. 306 (2003); *Parents Involved in Cmty. Sch. v. Seattle Sch. Dist. No. 1,* 127 S.Ct. 2738 (2007).

[45] *See, e.g., PGA TOUR, Inc. v. Martin,* 532 U.S. 661 (2001).

submitted such questions to resolution by judges. Bush administration critics constantly accused the administration of lawlessness in its confrontation with al Qaeda. Yet the administration understood the legal landscape far better than it grasped the cultural and political changes in the decades since *Quirin* and *Eisentrager* had come down. As Goldsmith, a former Bush administration Justice Department official, has written: "On issue after issue, the administration had powerful legal arguments but ultimately made mistakes on important questions of policy. It got policies wrong, ironically, because it was excessively legalistic, because it often substituted legal analysis for political judgment, and because it was too committed to expanding the President's constitutional powers."[46] Given the magnitude of the changes that had taken place since World War II, the administration's reliance on doctrine from that era smacked of delusion. In modern America, the President cannot run his own justice system without provoking a legal challenge and great skepticism from the courts—which is exactly the response that President Bush's policies provoked.

The Lawyers Behind the Legal Challenges

The lawyers who assembled to launch these challenges were a motley crew. They ranged from the sort of left-leaning legal advocates who make a career out of using unpopular clients to challenge government policies to fixtures of Washington's white shoe law firm culture to at least one law professor who believed in strong governmental antiterrorism powers. These lawyers acted sometimes in conjunction, sometimes separately, sometimes even in tension as the interests of their clients converged and separated.

The ideological component of the coalition mobilized early. Michael Ratner, head of the Center for Constitutional Rights (CCR), got involved with the Guantánamo detainees after reading about the November 13 military order, which added another puzzle piece to what he saw as the "underpinnings of a police state."[47] He later described his astonishment at what he considered a blatant stab at a conservative political agenda using legal tools. In response, he took on David Hicks as his first Guantánamo client. Hicks, an Australian former kangaroo-skinner who converted to Islam and fought for the Taliban, had arrived at Guantánamo in early 2002.[48] As habeas litigation began proliferating, CCR played

---

[46] Goldsmith, *supra* note 34, at 102.

[47] Joshua Holland, *Human Rights Crusader Michael Ratner: We'll Keep Going After Bush and Cheney When They Leave Office*, AlterNet, Dec. 3, 2007, http://www.alternet.org/waroniraq/69421/?page=1.

[48] *See* Raymond Bonner, *Australian Detainee's Life of Wandering Ends With Plea Deal*, N.Y. Times, Mar. 28, 2007, at A17.

an important role in coordinating the many cases and the many lawyers shepherding them.[49] Another early player was Joseph Margulies, a lawyer used to dealing with "really unpopular clients." When he joined forces with Ratner in 2001, he was living in Minneapolis and working as a private practice attorney specializing in civil rights and capital defense cases. Margulies had worked for a time at the Texas Capital Resource Center, mostly defending Mexican citizens on death row in the United States; he had, as he later put it, "gone face-to-face with Bush justice before" when Bush was serving as governor of Texas. Discussing his reaction to the November 13 military commission order, Margulies later wrote, "the risk of error in the outcome is not the only evil to be avoided. It is not even the greatest evil. Respect for the rule of law is a virtue in its own right, a virtue that becomes *more* important, rather than less, as the stakes increase."[50] Upon hearing of the order, Margulies arranged a conference call with colleagues nationwide, including Ratner. Their group soon expanded to include Clive Stafford Smith, a British death penalty lawyer who had defended more than 300 clients on death row in Louisiana and Mississippi—not one of whom had been executed.[51]

Most of the Guantánamo lawyers, however were not political activists. Tom Wilner was one of the more unlikely lawyers to defend Guantánamo detainees at the outset of the War on Terror. He had attended the elite St. Albans School in Washington with Al Gore, shared a fraternity with George W. Bush at Yale, and lived two doors away from Teresa Heinz Kerry in a posh neighborhood of Washington, DC. When he became involved in the Guantánamo litigation, he was working as an international trade partner at Shearman & Sterling, a law firm in Washington with significant business in Kuwait and around the Persian Gulf. His firm was originally one of ten contacted by relatives of Kuwaiti detainees in early 2002. Seven of these firms rejected the requests for representation, but Wilner traveled to Kuwait to hear the detainees' stories from their families. Despite initial reluctance on behalf of his firm and his wife, he agreed to represent them.[52] Unlike the more ideological lawyers, Wilner seems to have received compensation for defending the Guantánamo detainees—much of it from the Kuwaiti government itself.[53]

---

[49] *See* Michael Ratner & Sara Miles, *Keep the Great Writ Alive*, Salon, Sept. 26, 2006, http://www.salon.com/opinion/feature/2006/09/26/habeas/.

[50] Joseph Margulies, *Guantánamo and the Abuse of Presidential Power* 8 (2007).

[51] *See* Jane Mayer, *The Dark Side* 91 (2008).

[52] *See id.*, at 205–206.

[53] *See* Debra Burlingame, Op–Ed, *Gitmo's Guerilla Lawyers*, Wall St. J., Mar. 8, 2007, at A17.

Ultimately a large number of firms took on Guantánamo clients, most of them on a *pro bono* basis. This wave of legal activism on behalf of people the government regarded as the enemy angered officials—some of whom did not hide their anger. At one point, the Deputy Assistant Secretary of Defense for Detainee Affairs, Charles Stimson, expressed his anger a little too candidly in an interview with Federal News Radio. Referring to a list of major law firms representing Guantánamo detainees, Stimson said, "I think, quite honestly, when corporate C.E.O.'s see that those firms are representing the very terrorists who hit their bottom line back in 2001, those C.E.O.'s are going to make those law firms choose between representing terrorists or representing reputable firm. . . ."[54] Following a public outcry, Stimson resigned.[55]

In some cases, the line between the firm lawyers and the ideological ones blurred. David Remes, a Harvard Law-educated attorney who had previously represented tobacco firms, took on the cases of 15 Yemeni detainees at Guantánamo. After years of handling their cases, he resigned from his firm, Covington & Burling, in the summer of 2008 to devote himself full-time to human rights work that had become, as he put it "a consuming passion." Remes adopted a particularly flamboyant style of public relations on behalf of his clients. At a 2008 press conference in Yemen, he went so far as to remove his pants to demonstrate the sexually humiliating treatment that detainees had received at Guantánamo.[56]

The crowd also included some evident misfits. Neal Katyal, a young Georgetown law professor and former official in the Justice Department during the Clinton administration, was known prior to September 11 as something of a national security hawk. Even after the attacks, he largely defended the administration's response to September 11—including the Patriot Act—until the November military order.[57] Shocked by that order, however, he began looking for avenues to challenge the military commissions. Although he never took on the administration's detention policies, he ended up approaching Salim Hamdan's military attorneys—appointed to defend him in the planned commission trial—and filed a brief on their behalf. He eventually took on the bin Laden driver as a client for a federal court challenge to the new system.

---

[54] Neil A. Lewis, *Official Attacks Top Law Firms Over Detainees*, N.Y. Times, Jan. 13, 2007, at A1.

[55] *See Pentagon Official Who Criticized Detainee Lawyers Quits*, Wash. Post, Feb. 3, 2007, at A6.

[56] *See* Dan Slater, *Covington Partner Demonstrates Treatment of Detainees*, Wall Street Journal Law Blog, http://blogs.wsj.com/law/2008/07/16/to-protest-gitmo-punishment-covington-parnter-drops-trou-in-yemen/ (July 16, 2008, 9:53 EST).

[57] *See* Mahler, *supra* note 15, at 76–80.

These lawyers faced significant social pressures but also received support—from both predictable and surprising places. Katyal's professional mentors advised him to stay away from Hamdan's case, arguing that he would lose, embarrass himself, and damage his long-term career prospects.[58] And other lawyers faced pressures within their firms, particularly early on, to stay away from Guantánamo cases. On the other hand, lawyers representing Guantánamo clients could expect sympathetic press coverage.[59] Such praise was not limited to the press. When a prominent defense lawyer in Washington, D.C., criticized Wilner at a dinner party for choosing to defend terrorists at Guantánamo, another guest at the table spoke up for him: FBI Director Robert Mueller broke the tense silence that followed, raising his wineglass and saying, "I toast Tom Wilner. He's doing what an American should."[60]

The government side of the battle sported a less colorful team, but it too saw its share of drama. Leading the fight early in the administration was Solicitor General Theodore Olson, whose wife Barbara had died on American Airlines flight 77 when it crashed into the Pentagon on September 11. Olson, a famed Supreme Court advocate, never made reference in court to what must have been a great personal stake in the War on Terror. Yet his own tragedy necessarily added a measure of immediacy to any case he argued. Olson's field general from early on in all of the enemy combatant cases was his deputy, Paul Clement, who later succeeded him as Solicitor General. The Solicitor General's office made the unusual decision at the outset of the litigation to manage much of it directly in the lower courts and not—as it usually does—wait until the cases arrived at the Supreme Court to take them over. As a result, Clement and a group of assistants in the Solicitor General's office found themselves arguing detention cases in federal district courts in New York, Virginia, Washington D.C, and even Seattle, and following those cases into the Supreme Court chamber. Clement, a young appellate advocate who sprang to the front ranks of Supreme Court advocacy during his years first as Olson's deputy and later as his successor, is one of the few prominent politically appointed lawyers in the Bush administration to see his reputation enhanced by the exercise. Clement left office in 2008, having argued and lost three major enemy combatant cases and widely acclaimed as the greatest oral advocate of his generation.

---

[58] *Id.*

[59] Mahler's book about the *Hamdan* case, *supra* note 15, which elaborates on a *New York Times Magazine* feature story he wrote earlier, is a typical example. Its heroes are the lawyers who represented Hamdan, and it offers neither a critical appraisal of their arguments nor any account of the government side of the litigation that seriously engages the other side of the battle over the commissions.

[60] *See* Mayer, *supra* note 51, at 204–205.

As habeas litigation proliferated after 2004, it became impractical for the Solicitor General's office to run the show, so the litigation reverted to a more traditional arrangement. Career attorneys in the Justice Department's Civil Division handled the many cases in the lower courts, with the Solicitor General's office keeping a watchful eye and handling the high court appeals. Like many of the corporate lawyers who took on Guantánamo clients, the lawyers who handled the government end of these cases were not ideological; they were simply attorneys who defended the government for a living. In fact, the leader of the Civil Division team, a career lawyer named Douglas Letter, had spent time detailed to the White House Counsel's office during the early years of the Clinton administration.

The pressures on the government litigation team were less visible than those on outside lawyers who had taken on accused terrorists as clients, but they were very real and came from multiple sources. For one thing, the lawyers defending the administration's policies had to contend with the lawyers who had formulated those policies. As often happens, attorneys who have to defend challenged policies in front of courts likely to view them suspiciously pushed the group that had made those policies to moderate the government's stance in ways that would make their position more defensible in court. Yet in this case, the group that had formulated the policies included some of the most powerful and ideological people in the federal government: Vice President Cheney's counsel, David Addington, the de facto head of the Justice Department's Office of Legal Counsel, John Yoo, and White House Counsel and later Attorney General Alberto Gonzales. The result was a constant tension that led to a strange paralysis, in which the government could not shift gears to defend cases in which it was clearly heading towards defeat despite warnings from its own lawyers that defeat was coming.

Mirroring this top-down pressure, the Civil Division also faced pressure from the staff level—in the opposite direction. A number of staff attorneys declined to participate in defending Guantánamo habeas claims, on grounds that they disagreed too fundamentally with the positions the government was taking in them.[61] As these cases proliferated, they became an enormous workload burden for the government, one exacerbated for a time by those whose conscientious objections kept them out of the action. But this was later. The Guantánamo cases did not begin as a flood. With the very jurisdiction of the courts to hear Guantánamo cases in doubt, they began as a trickle.

---

[61] See Emma Schwartz, *Respectfully Disagreeing; Justice Lawyers Refuse to Take Detainee Cases,* U.S. News & World Report, Sept. 10, 2007, at 28.

The First Round of Legal Challenges

On February 19, 2002, months after Rasul's capture in Afghanistan, Joseph Margulies, Michael Ratner, Clive Stafford Smith, and others filed a petition in the federal district court in Washington for a writ of habeas corpus on behalf of him, Asif Iqbal—another of the Tipton Three—and David Hicks, the Australian. The petition alleged that the government was holding the three in "prolonged, indefinite, and arbitrary detention ... without Due Process of Law."[62] It sought, among other things, the detainees' release "from [the military's] unlawful custody," an order "to allow counsel to meet and confer with detained petitioners, in private and unmonitored attorney-client conversations," and an order ceasing "all interrogations of the detained petitioners, direct or indirect, while this litigation is pending."[63] A few months later, Wilner filed a suit on behalf of twelve Kuwaiti detainees; unlike the *Rasul* petition, this case did not seek their release but, rather, an order allowing meetings with family and counsel and forcing the government to inform them of any charges against them and grant them access to "courts or some other impartial tribunal."[64] The two cases, *Rasul v. Bush* and *Al Odah v. United States*, were quickly consolidated before Judge Colleen Kollar–Kotelly, a moderately liberal judge appointed by President Bill Clinton.

The reaction of the lower courts, where Supreme Court precedent is binding, to the early Guantánamo cases testifies both to the relative strength of the administration's legal position under *Eisentrager* and to the extreme caution judges felt about interfering in the war effort in the period immediately following the attacks. Kollar–Kotelly dismissed the case for lack of jurisdiction, on grounds that Guantánamo Bay "is outside the sovereign territory of the United States. Given that under *Eisentrager*, writs of habeas corpus are not available to aliens held outside of the sovereign territory of the United States, this Court does not have jurisdiction to entertain the claims made by Petitioners in *Rasul* or Plaintiffs in *Odah*."[65] When a philosophically mixed panel of the U.S. Court of Appeals for the D.C. Circuit reviewed her opinion, it affirmed unambiguously.[66] No judge on the D.C. Circuit recorded a vote to review the panel opinion *en banc*.

Indeed, when *Rasul* went to the Supreme Court, no lower court judge anywhere in the country had written an opinion accepting the

---

[62] Petition for Writ of Habeas Corpus at 15, *Rasul v. Bush*, 215 F.Supp.2d 55 (D.D.C. 2002) (No. 02 Civ. 0299).

[63] *Id.* at 18.

[64] *Rasul v. Bush*, 215 F.Supp.2d at 58 (D.D.C. 2002).

[65] *Id.* at 72–73.

[66] *See Al Odah v. U.S.*, 321 F. 3d 1134 (D.C. Cir. 2003).

proposition that a federal court had habeas jurisdiction over Guantánamo. While a conflict in the circuits did develop later, when a panel of the
U.S. Circuit Court of Appeals for the Ninth Circuit held that jurisdiction
did lie over Guantánamo, this happened only after the Supreme Court
granted certiorari in *Rasul*.[67] The absence in November 2003, when the
Justices took up *Rasul*, of any lower court dispute over Guantánamo
jurisdiction made the Court's action a particularly striking expression of
anxiety about the government's position. The more insightful lawyers in
the administration knew they were heading for trouble, but the government as a whole ignored the Court's anxiety.[68]

The Justices were not the only ones anxious over the government's
stance in *Rasul*. For Katyal, who was then preparing to challenge the
military commissions, a Supreme Court decision barring habeas jurisdiction over Guantánamo would cut him off at the knees. Katyal did not
mean to challenge Hamdan's detention, so he could potentially live with
a decision blocking suits like Rasul's. But a broad decision would be a
disaster for him, and he wanted to make sure the court did not throw his
baby out with the larger litigation bath water. So he filed an amicus
brief on behalf of the military lawyers then gearing up to represent the
still-uncharged military commission defendants, asking the Court—
whatever it did to Rasul's suit—to leave open the possibility of hearing a
suit attacking commissions. Katyal conspicuously filed the brief "on
behalf of neither party":

> *Amicus* does not challenge or expect to challenge the power of the
> United States to wage war as its civilian and military leaders see fit.
> It does not challenge or expect to challenge the government's
> temporary detention of enemy combatants while military activities
> are underway abroad. What *Amicus* does challenge is the attempt by
> the Executive to oust Article III courts of jurisdiction over the
> military prosecution of individuals whom the President deems "ene-
> my combatants." Although military commissions will likely take
> place at Guantánamo, this sensitive jurisdictional issue is not within
> the question presented in this case, and the Court should not
> foreclose its consideration.[69]

Shortly before the Court heard oral arguments in *Rasul*, Katyal—
along with Hamdan's military counsel, Lt. Commander Charles Swift

---

[67] *See Gherebi v. Bush*, 352 F.3d 1278 (9th Cir. 2003).

[68] *See, e.g.*, Jack Goldsmith's comments to Benjamin Wittes, quoted in Wittes, *supra*
note 9, at 63 ("When was the last time the Supreme Court granted [review] in order to
decide that it *didn't* have jurisdiction over something?").

[69] Brief of the Military Attorneys Assigned to the Defense in the Office of Military
Commissions as Amicus Curiae in Support of Neither Party at 3, *Rasul v. Bush*, 542 U.S.
466 (2004) (Nos. 03–334, 03–343).

and attorneys from a Seattle firm—filed a petition in federal district court in Washington state. They argued that holding Hamdan "incommunicado in pre-trial custody" violates "the U.S. Constitution, U.S. law, and U.S. treaty obligations." They sought an order prohibiting the military "from using a military commission to try Mr. Hamdan" and barring also "the indefinite detention of Mr. Hamdan for an unscheduled trial before such a commission, when such a commission will be held far beyond the theater of military operations and at a time when Congress has not declared war."[70]

If there was any doubt that times had changed since *Eisentrager*, that doubt faded considerably on April 20, 2004, the day the Supreme Court heard oral arguments in *Rasul*. The Justices clearly struggled both with the continuing vitality of Justice Jackson's decades-old precedent and with its application to Guantánamo, where foreign sovereignty was something of a fiction. Whereas the lower courts heard *Rasul* with September 11 in the recent past and with little information about the detainees and their treatment, the Justices heard the case with the attacks more remote and within days of the Abu Ghraib prisoner-abuse scandal's breaking. While lower court judges faced the question of whether *Eisentrager* controlled the case, the Justices faced a somewhat broader set of questions: Should *Eisentrager* control the case and define the judicial role at Guantánamo? Did it make sense in the War on Terror for the executive to be able to make its own rules at an off-shore detention site?

John J. Gibbons argued the case on behalf of the petitioners. Gibbons, a former chief judge of the Third Circuit Court of Appeals, had had limited involvement in the case prior to its arrival at the high court.[71] And it showed. He badly misstated the terms of the Guantánamo lease at one point, a matter on which Justice Antonin Scalia was happy to correct him. And he largely failed to frame the case effectively, veering from the jurisdictional questions at its heart to the substantive and international law matters that still lay several steps down the road.

Several Justices tipped their hands relatively swiftly as to the contours of the opinions they would ultimately write.[72] Justice Sandra Day O'Connor hinted early on that she was looking for a narrow holding, not a broad one. "[Y]ou don't raise the issue of any potential jurisdiction

---

[70] Petition for Writ of Mandamus Pursuant to 28 U.S.C. § 1361 or, in the Alternative, Writ of Habeas Corpus at 5, 7, 8, *Hamdan ex rel. Swift v. Rumsfeld*, No. 04 Civ. 0777 (W.D. Wash. 2004).

[71] *See* Vanessa Blum, *A Veteran Gives Voice to Guantánamo Case*, Legal Times. Apr. 12, 2004.

[72] For all quotations, see Transcript of Oral Argument, *Rasul v. Bush.*, 542 U.S. 466 (2004).

on the basis of the Constitution alone," she clarified to Gibbons. "We are here debating the jurisdiction under the habeas statute, is that right?" And in a telling foreshadowing of his coming majority opinion, Justice John Paul Stevens sportingly tried to help Gibbons by pointing out that the court had decided *Eisentrager* in part relying on *Ahrens v. Clark*,[73] a case which had since been largely overruled. Gibbons did not pick up the thread.

Tension escalated as the argument shifted to the nature of Guantánamo itself and whether it really was overseas in the sense *Eisentrager* contemplated. Gibbons got into the aforementioned messy colloquy with Justice Scalia over the terms of the lease and whether it truly reserved ultimate sovereignty to Cuba. After conceding that Scalia was correct on this point and that he had misspoken, he brushed the point aside: "it doesn't make any difference.... Queen Elizabeth is the nominal sovereign of Canada. That doesn't determine whether or not Canadian courts can grant a writ of habeas corpus. She's also the nominal sovereign of Australia."

Scalia wasn't buying it. "I don't think sovereignty is being used in the same sense," he said. "I mean, it would be a good point ... if you said that England was sovereign over Canada, [but] I don't think anybody would say that."

Gibbons clarified that the salient point for him was that Cuba's residual sovereignty does not imply that Cuban law has "any application inside that base" or could be used to adjudicate the cases of the detainees there. "A stamp with Fidel Castro's picture on it wouldn't get a letter off the base," he said. It was Gibbons' best moment of the day.

Solicitor General Olson opened his argument with a reminder that as he spoke, the United States remained at war, with more than 10,000 American troops stationed in Afghanistan. He made no mention of his wife, and quickly made clear that he had shown up not in his capacity as the American government's most senior victim of the September 11 attacks but to defend his client's position that *Eisentrager* controlled the case and precluded federal court involvement in Guantánamo.

Under questioning from Justice Stevens, he quickly conceded that his position did not depend on the current state of war, that the courts would have no role even had the war already ended. Justices Souter and Ginsburg pushed him on whether *Eisentrager* was really unambiguously jurisdictional in nature. But Olson stood firm. Justices Souter and Stevens pushed him on whether *Eisentrager*'s predicate had been eroded by the subsequent overruling of *Ahrens*, but Olson gave no ground on that point either.

---

[73] 335 U.S. 188 (1948).

Justice Breyer then turned the discussion to matters of high constitutional policy. Acknowledging that language in *Eisentrager* supported the government, he agreed that it "has the virtue of clarity, the clear rule: not a citizen, outside the United States, you don't get your foot in the door. But against you is that same fact. It seems rather contrary to an idea of a Constitution with three branches, that the executive would be free to do whatever they want, whatever they want without a check." Olson responded that the executive branch had had a check: Congress had 54 years to change the habeas statute, had even considered doing so after *Eisentrager*, but had never done it.

Like Gibbons, Olson had some of his sharpest exchanges with the Justices over the nature of the American presence at Guantánamo. Justice Ginsburg tried to analogize American control there to the Panama Canal Zone; Olson resisted. "Why isn't this like, as I asked Mr. Gibbons, a Federal enclave with a state?" Justice Ginsburg pressed. Answered Olson, "Because ... in the first place, the question of sovereignty is a political decision. It would be remarkable for the judiciary to start deciding where the United States is sovereign." The issue, Justice Ginsburg retorted, is "physical control, power."

"We have that, Justice Ginsburg, in every place where we would put military detainees, in a field of combat where there are prisons in Afghanistan where we have complete control," Olson said.

But Afghanistan, Justice Souter objected, "is not a place where American law is and for a century has customarily been applied to all aspects of life. We even protect the Cuban iguana [at Guantánamo].... In bringing people from Afghanistan or wherever they were brought to Guantánamo, we are doing in functional terms exactly what we would do if we brought them to the District of Columbia...."

The Supreme Court Opinion in Rasul

Ultimately, all doctrine aside, this functional analysis was the guiding spirit that led the Court to its opinion in *Rasul*. As Justice O'Connor had intimated, the five-Justice majority—along with Justice Anthony Kennedy, who concurred separately—sought a narrow ruling affirming their jurisdiction on the basis of the habeas statute alone. As Justice Stevens, who wrote the opinion, had suggested at oral argument, it hinged not on overturning *Eisentrager* but on the notion that the *Eisentrager* Court's reading of the statute had been eroded by the overturning of *Ahrens*. And as several Justices had hinted, changed facts had made all the difference. Wrote Justice Stevens:

They [the *Rasul* petitioners] are not nationals of countries at war with the United States, and they deny that they have engaged in or plotted acts of aggression against the United States; they have never been afforded access to any tribunal, much less charged with and convicted of wrongdoing; and for more than two years they have been imprisoned in territory over which the United States exercises exclusive jurisdiction and control.[74]

Over Justice Scalia's vigorous dissent, the majority adopted a new test for statutory habeas jurisdiction—at least as applied to Guantánamo: "Petitioners contend that they are being held in federal custody in violation of the laws of the United States. No party questions the District Court's jurisdiction over petitioners' custodians.... [The habeas law] by its terms, requires nothing more."[75]

On the surface, *Rasul* seemed like an unambiguous rebuke to the administration. The President had urged the Court to refrain from asserting jurisdiction over Guantánamo, yet the court had done the opposite in unequivocal terms. The opinion, however, actually posed more questions than it answered. Announcing the courts' jurisdiction to hear habeas cases, after all, gives no guidance about what those cases might look like or how they should proceed. For a landmark case, *Rasul* was strangely non-substantive. It didn't say what conduct on the government's part was legal, what a proper basis for detention would look like, what rights detainees had, what evidence the government might introduce against them, who should bear the burden of proof, or what that burden should be. Moreover, by acting on the basis of statutory law alone and not addressing the underlying question of whether the Constitution itself requires that detainees have access to habeas review, the Court left open the door for Congress to amend the statute. Finally, *Rasul* also struck an ambiguous note on the question of whether jurisdiction extended beyond Guantánamo or whether it depended on the unique status of that particular American base. These questions and others the Justices kicked down the road.

Rasul, however, did not lack for hints as to the Court's instincts on some of these questions. Most critically, while the Justices rooted the decision on statutory grounds only, certain passages indicated the existence of a more fundamental constitutional basis for jurisdiction. Justice Stevens, having determined that the habeas statute reached Guantánamo, added the following curious paragraph:

Application of the habeas statute to persons detained at the base is consistent with the historical reach of the writ of habeas corpus. At common law, courts exercised habeas jurisdiction over the claims of aliens detained within sovereign territory of the realm, as well as

---

[74] *Rasul*, 542 U.S. at 476.

[75] *Id.* at 483–84.

the claims of persons detained in the so-called "exempt jurisdictions," where ordinary writs did not run, and all other dominions under the sovereign's control. As Lord Mansfield wrote in 1759, even if a territory was "no part of the realm," there was "no doubt" as to the court's power to issue writs of habeas corpus if the territory was "under the subjection of the Crown." ... Later cases confirmed that the reach of the writ depended not on formal notions of territorial sovereignty, but rather on the practical question of "the exact extent and nature of the jurisdiction or dominion exercised in fact by the Crown."[76]

This passage proved to be—and may have been intended as—a kind of ticking time bomb. While it did nothing in the short run, in the longer term it laid down a marker that the Court's power over Guantánamo would not depend on a mere statute. If the habeas statute did not reach overseas detainees like those at Guantánamo, the Court seemed to be saying, the Constitution might create jurisdiction over them anyway. On its face, however, *Rasul* did not go that far. Rather, it seemed to dare Congress to adjust a single statute and thereby erase the problem it had created for the executive branch: court oversight of hundreds of individual detentions. The temptation proved too much for the administration.

Congress Responds with the Detainee Treatment Act

In the months that followed *Rasul*, two important developments took place. Habeas lawsuits almost immediately began proliferating. Lawyers at the Washington firm of Wilmer Hale filed on behalf of the "Algerian Six" within weeks of the decision, for example, arguing that "The Detained Petitioners are not, nor have they ever been, enemy aliens, lawful or unlawful belligerents, or combatants in any context involving hostilities against the citizens, government or armed forces of the United States." They argued that the "prolonged, indefinite, and arbitrary detention of the Detained Petitioners, without Due Process of Law" violated the Fifth Amendment, various international law instruments, military regulations, and the War Powers Clause of the Constitution—and amounted to an unconstitutional suspension of the writ of *habeas corpus* to boot.[77] David Remes quickly filed on behalf of a group of Yemeni detainees. All told, the government found itself litigating roughly 300 cases.

The second major development was that the military convened panels, known as the Combatant Status Review Tribunals (CSRTs), to

---

[76] *Id.* at 481–82.

[77] First Amended Petition for a Writ of Habeas Corpus at 6, 13, Boumediene v. Bush, 355 F.Supp.2d 311 (D.D.C. 2005) (No. 04 Civ. 1166).

review each detainee's case and determine whether previous review
mechanisms had properly deemed him an "enemy combatant." The
CSRTs were designed to shore up the administration's litigation position
by offering a measure of due process to which courts might defer. In a
case handed down the same day as *Rasul*, a plurality of the Justices had
seemed to describe a non-judicial process within the military as adequate
due process in a wartime setting even to justify the detention of an
American citizen.[78] So the idea was to buy the respect of the courts by
giving detainees a review system the military might keep under tight
control.

But the CSRTs triggered fierce controversy, for they fell far short of
the sort of hearings that would take place in federal court. Though they
ultimately freed 39 people as "no longer enemy combatants," detainees
had no access to counsel to represent them in the process; they received
only the barest summaries of the evidence against them and had highly
limited ability to put on evidence of their own and call their own
witnesses; and they bore the burden of proof under a broad definition of
"enemy combatant." What's more, as the habeas litigation progressed,
the CSRTs began to look in some cases as though they might have erred
badly.[79]

Even as this process was playing out, Katyal's case on Salim
Hamdan's behalf was getting moving. The government charged Hamdan
shortly after *Rasul* came down, and a month later, the district court in
Seattle transferred his petition to federal district court in Washington
D.C. In November 2004, U.S. District Judge James Robertson ruled in
Hamdan's favor, finding that under the Geneva Conventions, the military could not try Hamdan by military commission without first showing
he was not a prisoner of war. Moreover, the judge held that the
commission convened to try Hamdan in any event violated the Uniform
Code of Military Justice, because its rules could permit his conviction
based on evidence he might never see.[80]

Robertson's decision, however, did not last long. Even after *Rasul*,
the way was tough for plaintiffs in the lower courts; the residual power
of the World War II-era precedents on which the government relied
remained strong. And on July 15, 2005, a three-judge panel of the D.C.
Circuit that included soon-to-be-named Chief Justice John Roberts Jr.,
unanimously reversed Robertson, holding that "on the merits there is

---

[78] See *Hamdi v. Rumsfeld*, 542 U.S. 507 (2004).

[79] See, e.g., *In re Guantánamo Detainee Cases*, 355 F.Supp.2d 443 (D.D.C. 2005)
(granting, *inter alia*, a protective order governing attorney-client communications, and
granting the detainee petitioners' requests for access to counsel, both of which had been
previously denied by the government).

[80] See *Hamdan v. Rumsfeld*, 344 F.Supp.2d 152 (D.D.C. 2004).

little to Hamdan's argument."[81] Congress had authorized Hamdan's commission, the court ruled, citing *Quirin*; trying him by military commission would not violate the Geneva Conventions, which in any event are not enforceable in court; and the courts, to top it off, could not properly hear Hamdan's other complaints about the fairness of the tribunal before he had even gone through a trial.[82] Persuading the Supreme Court to overturn the military commissions would require convincing the Justices not just that the commissions were unfair but that they were so inherently unfair that the courts need not wait until their unfairness manifested itself in Hamdan's actual trial to say so. On November 7, 2005, the Justices agreed to consider the matter.

By the time they actually heard the case, however, Katyal faced an additional complication. A year and a half after *Rasul* and after the high court had granted certiorari in *Hamdan*, the administration prevailed on Congress to pass the Detainee Treatment Act of 2005 (DTA),[83] whose key provision stripped the federal courts of jurisdiction to hear habeas corpus petitions or other claims filed against the government by Guantánamo detainees.[84] The provision responded both to *Hamdan* itself and to the larger problem—from the government's point of view—of the huge volume of habeas cases it found itself defending. The Court in *Rasul* had pointedly not gone beyond the habeas statute. Congress can amend statutes, so what the Court had given, Congress could, at least in theory, take away.

The DTA did not seek to strip the courts of all jurisdiction over Guantánamo detentions. It set up a direct appeal from both the CSRTs and the military commissions to the D.C. Circuit. But it otherwise stipulated that,

> no court, justice, or judge shall have jurisdiction to hear or consider (1) an application for a writ of habeas corpus filed by or on behalf of an alien detained by the Department of Defense at Guantánamo Bay, Cuba; or (2) any other action against the United States or its agents relating to any aspect of the detention by the Department of Defense of an alien at Guantánamo Bay, Cuba.... [85]

From the government's point of view, the DTA represented an effort to restore the pre-*Rasul* status quo while granting detainees direct access

---

[81] *Hamdan v. Rumsfeld*, 415 F.3d 33, 37 (D.C. Cir. 2005).

[82] *See id.*

[83] Pub. L. No. 109–148, 119 Stat. 2739 (codified as amended in scattered sections of 10, 26, and 42 U.S.C.).

[84] *See* Detainee Treatment Act § 1005(e).

[85] *Id.*

to the courts. To the habeas petitioners, however, it was a disaster—a law that could force all challenges into appeals based on a fixed record, rather than civil lawsuits with potentially far broader opportunities for discovery of evidence. Many critics saw it as a backdoor suspension of the writ of habeas corpus.

For Katyal, the DTA, if taken at face value, would mean the end of Hamdan's case and would require him to go through trial and challenge his client's conviction—rather than frontally attacking the system as a system. Katyal had lobbied Congress on the DTA in an effort to muddy the waters concerning the effective date of the provision and leave some measure of ambiguity regarding the court stripping language's application to pending cases.[86] But on its face, the language added another big obstacle.

Oral Argument in Hamdan

The initial questioning in a special 90–minute argument on the morning of March 28, 2006 focused substantially on this new obstacle. The arguments took place with the Chief Justice absent—recused as a consequence of his participation in the lower court decision his colleagues would be reviewing. Katyal opened with an argument for the Court's continued jurisdiction in spite of the DTA, citing the congressional debate over the law's effective date and the resulting change in the legislative language.[87] The original language, he observed, said that it "shall apply to any application or other action that is pending on or after the date of enactment of this act," which clearly included Hamdan. As ultimately enacted, however, the key provision lacked such a clear statement of application to pending cases and thereby, as Katyal put it, "grandfathered pending cases such as this one." Once again trying to sever *Hamdan* from the mass of other habeas litigation, Katyal acknowledged that "it's certainly possible ... to read the DTA as truncating the vast majority of claims at Guantánamo in current pending cases" based on other language in the statute. But, he argued, "that isn't the issue before you here. The issue before you here is simply the *Hamdan* case, and there was ... the strong desire by the Congress not to interfere with this Court's traditionally exercised jurisdiction."

The newly-confirmed Justice Samuel Alito, in one of his only comments that morning, inquired why Hamdan couldn't wait to raise his claims until a final commission decision, the way one would after a criminal proceeding. Katyal explained that unlike criminal proceedings,

---

[86] *See* Mahler, *supra* note 15, at 218–20.

[87] For all quotations, see Transcript of Oral Argument, *Hamdan v. Rumsfeld*, 548 U.S. 557 (2006).

the DTA means that "you can't walk into court right after you're convicted ... you can only walk into court after a final decision. And a final decision requires the sign-off of the President of the United States. And so, effectively, this reading would give a litigant the ability to block Federal Court review for all time." As he later put it, "the predicate for abstention has always been that Congress, or some other entity, has fairly balanced the rights of both sides. Here, you don't have that fundamental guarantee."

Turning to the case's merits, Katyal pointed out that the only charge against his client was conspiracy, which he argued had been rejected as a violation of the laws of war in every tribunal since World War II. Justice Kennedy queried why the court could not treat the question of the integrity of the charge as subordinate to that of the lawfulness of the tribunal. If the tribunal is not lawfully constituted, he suggested, the point is moot; if it is lawful, the tribunal itself should decide in the first instance whether the charge is proper.

Katyal responded, "even if we assume that the tribunal is authorized and that all of its microprocedures are authorized under the act of Congress, allowing this charge, conspiracy, is to open the floodgates to give the President the ability to charge whatever he wants in a military commission."

Returning again to the propriety of pre-trial review of the tribunal's integrity, Justice Alito observed that prosecutors could amend the charges against Hamdan before they went to trial. Why, he asked, "should there be review, before trial, of a charge that could be amended?" Katyal responded that the government had already had four years to assemble its charges against Hamdan. "[T]hey've stuck with this charge, of conspiracy, which is not a violation of the laws of war," he argued. "Indeed, Justice Alito, all ten people facing military commissions today, all ten indictments charge conspiracy right now. Seven only charge conspiracy." He pointed out that the court in *Quirin* had reviewed both the tribunal's legality and the propriety of the charge under the laws of war without waiting for an appeal from a verdict.

After additional back-and-forth with the Justices over the conspiracy charge, Katyal turned to the grounds on which Judge Robertson had initially sided with him: that the commission violated the Uniform Code of Military Justice. Hamdan, he argued had already been excluded from portions of his commission proceedings, something the UCMJ forbids in courts martial. "We're asking this Court to apply the minimal rules of the UCMJ to the military commissions that operate at Guantánamo Bay," he said. "And one of its protections is the right to be present, and that has been fundamentally violated."

Justice Scalia cut him off. "You acknowledge the existence of things called commissions. Or don't you?"

"We do."

"What is the use of them if they have to follow all of the procedures required by the UCMJ? I mean, I thought that the whole object was to have a different procedure."

Katyal replied, "Justice Scalia, that's what the Government would like you to believe. I don't think that's true. The historical relationship has been that military commissions [and] courts-martial follow the same procedures.... Now, to be clear, our position is not that military commissions must follow all the rules for courts-martial.... They must ... follow the minimal baseline rules set in the Uniform Code of Military Justice by Congress."

Katyal concluded by arguing that the tribunal also violated Common Article 3 of the Geneva Conventions "and its minimal baseline requirements that a regularly constituted court be set up, and one that ... affords the rights indispensable to civilized peoples."

Solicitor General Paul Clement opened his argument with a history lesson on past uses of military commissions; their use goes back to George Washington, he observed, and "Congress has repeatedly recognized and sanctioned that authority. Indeed, each time Congress has extended the jurisdiction of the [courts-martial], Congress was at pains to emphasize that that extension did not come in derogation of the jurisdiction of military commissions."

Justice Stevens took the historical bait and inquired into "sources of law [that] the commissions [have] generally enforced over the years." Clement answered that military commissions have, with certain exceptions, basically enforced the "laws of war." What's more, Clement argued, the UCMJ does not require that military commissions follow the norms of courts-martial. Under past precedent, rather, "only those nine provisions of the UCMJ that expressly reference military commissions will apply, and the rest is left to a much more common-law, war-court approach, where there's much greater flexibility."

Justice Souter then asked if the Geneva Conventions applied in this context, since the commission system operated under the laws of war. He pointed out a tension between citing the laws of war as the domestic authority to establish the military commission and rejecting the laws of war to determine the procedural rights therein. "I mean, ... why don't you go from the frying pan into the fire, in effect, when you take the position that the laws of war are what the tribunal is applying?"

"Well, Justice Souter," Clement replied, "I don't think there's any frying pan effect or fire effect." The executive, he said, is not "trying to have it both ways. The fact that the Geneva Conventions are part of the law of war doesn't mean that Petitioner is entitled to any protection under those conventions." Moreover, to the extent that Hamdan has claims under the Geneva Conventions that exempt him from the jurisdiction of the commission, he is free to make those arguments to the tribunal itself. This point led to a colloquy with several of the Justices over the propriety of pre-trial review, with Clement arguing that "Congress has made it clear that, whatever else is true, these military commission proceedings can proceed, and exclusive review can be done after the fact, after conviction, in the D.C. Circuit."

Justice Breyer then transitioned to the jurisdictional question, asking how the court could, "if we accepted your interpretation, possibly avoid the most terribly difficult and important constitutional question of whether Congress can constitutionally deprive this Court of jurisdiction in habeas cases?" Clement, after some intervening questions, responded that "this case, and most of the cases, don't raise a serious Suspension Clause problem, for the simple reason that I think deferring review or channeling it to the court of appeals does not amount to a suspension." All Congress did in the DTA, he contended, was to "restore the law to the understanding of the law that had prevailed for 200 years."

Justice Souter wasn't buying this. Should not Congress have to be crystal clear about what it is doing before the Court interprets a provision as affecting a potential suspension, he asked.

Clement concluded his argument with a race through the merits of the case—arguing that the commissions were authorized by the UCMJ and consistent with international law and that the charge of conspiracy had been long recognized as a war crime.

The Supreme Court Ruling in Hamdan

The day the Justices handed down *Hamdan* in June 2006,[88] few people doubted its momentousness. Linda Greenhouse, the normally sober Supreme Court correspondent for *The New York Times*, described it "as a sweeping and categorical defeat for the administration," and as "a defining moment in the ever-shifting balance of power among branches of government."[89] Walter Dellinger, a former Solicitor General, called the case "simply the most important decision on presidential power and the rule of law ever. Ever."[90] While on the surface, the case may be about

---

[88] *See Hamdan v. Rumsfeld*, 548 U.S. 557 (2006).

[89] Linda Greenhouse, *Justices, 5–3, Broadly Reject Bush Plan to Try Detainees*, N.Y. Times, June 30, 2006, at A6.

[90] Walter Dellinger, *The Most Important Decision on Presidential Power Ever*, Slate, June 29, 2006, http://www.slate.com/id/2144476/entry/2144825/.

military commissions, he said, up close *"Hamdan* is about the OLC [Office of Legal Counsel] torture memo; and it's about whether the President can refuse to comply with the McCain Amendment [on interrogation techniques]. It's about all those laws the President says, as he signs them, that he will not commit to obey."[91] The Court's critics decried the decision, and the administration's foes cheered it; but almost nobody questioned *Hamdan*'s importance, or the scope of its impact, or the certainty that it signaled a big shift.

The decision, which came down on a 5–to–3 vote because of Chief Justice Roberts' recusal, swept past the jurisdictional barrier Congress had erected in the DTA, ruling that Congress had not clearly stated an intention to preclude pending, as well as prospective cases. It struck down the system of military commissions. And it established that at least one key provision of the Geneva Conventions—Common Article 3— applies to the American conflict with al Qaeda and thereby creates a floor of humane treatment for all detainees American forces may hold. On the surface, at least, it seemed like a huge watershed.[92]

Yet, once again, the Court left key questions unanswered and avoided ruling on the basis of the Constitution. On the jurisdictional side, rather than ruling that Congress lacked the power to throw out cases from Guantánamo, it merely ruled that Congress had not in the DTA clearly ordered the courts to dismiss pending lawsuits. The result was that, as it did in *Rasul*, the Court left Congress free to change the law. As to the commissions, it held that they violated statutory and treaty law, but it stopped well short of either ruling that the Bill of Rights applied to these trials or that if it did, the commissions violated any of its provisions. And while the holding concerning Common Article 3 was a dramatic repudiation of the administration's contention that the Geneva Conventions did not apply to the conflict, Common Article 3's protections against inhumane treatment were ripe for interpretation through implementing legislation. For this reason, much of the practical importance of the decision proved short-lived.

The Military Commissions Act

Within only a few months, at the administration's behest, Congress had undone most of the new reality that the Court had crafted. The Military Commissions Act of 2006 (MCA),[93] passed in the run-up to the 2006 midterm elections, responded to each of *Hamdan*'s major compo-

---

[91] Walter Dellinger, *Still "the Most Important Decision on Presidential Power Ever"*, Slate, June 30, 2006, http://www.slate.com/id/2144476/entry/2144911/.

[92] *See Hamdan*, 548 U.S. 557 (2006).

[93] Pub. L. No. 109–366, 120 Stat. 2600 (codified in scattered sections of 10 U.S.C.).

nents. It re-created the military commissions system. And while the new statutory commissions differed in some respects from the old ones, they were in most respects more similar to than different from them—much to the frustration of critics of the old system. While the MCA did not overturn the holding that Common Article 3 governed the War on Terror, it did delegate the interpretation of all but the gravest violations of the provision to the president, meaning that President Bush retained a great deal of flexibility in defining the "inhumane treatment" which the conventions now required him to eschew. And, once again, Congress also moved to strip the courts of jurisdiction over Guantánamo cases, this time unambiguously applying the bar to "all cases, without exception, pending on or after the date of the enactment of this Act which relate to any aspect of the detention, transfer, treatment, trial, or conditions of detention of an alien detained by the United States since September 11, 2001."[94]

The MCA set up the third Supreme Court conflict over jurisdiction at Guantánamo, for it posed directly the question the court had avoided in the first two rounds: does the Constitution itself guarantee habeas jurisdiction over Guantánamo—jurisdiction Congress cannot strip away without invoking its power to suspend the Great Writ, which it can only do in circumstances of rebellion or invasion?[95] If some federal court jurisdiction is constitutionally mandated, is the system of CSRT hearings followed by judicial review in the D.C. Circuit, as Clement argued, a permissible deferral and channeling of judicial review or is it a squelching of the writ? Must a detainee at Guantánamo have as a matter of constitutional law access to a full-fledged habeas corpus proceeding of the type a majority of the Court had envisioned in *Rasul*?

The Algerian Six case and the cases of hundreds of other detainees had been kicking around in the lower courts since *Rasul*, following differing but ultimately converging paths. The paths differed, because district judges read the applicable substantive law completely differently. In the Algerian Six case, for example, Judge Richard Leon ruled that the detainees had no cognizable rights in American courts and therefore granted the government's motion to dismiss the case. Jurisdiction, in his reading of the law, meant little for the detainees, because they had at the end of the day no rights to vindicate.[96] By contrast, Judge Joyce Hens Green, hearing a group of consolidated cases covering 56 other detainees, refused to dismiss claims brought under the Fifth Amendment's Due Process Clause and the Third Geneva Convention.[97] Yet the cases ulti-

---

[94] *Id.* at § 7(b).

[95] *See* U.S. CONST. art. I, § 9, cl. 2.

[96] *See Khalid v. Bush*, 355 F.Supp.2d 311 (D.D.C. 2005).

[97] *See In re Guantánamo Detainee Cases*, 355 F.Supp.2d 443 (D.D.C. 2005).

mately converged because the merits took a back seat to Congress's efforts to throw the cases out of court altogether. Because of the changes in the jurisdictional statute, the D.C. Circuit took a long time to review these cases—two whole years—during which period it held oral arguments twice and had four separate rounds of briefing. When it finally ruled in February 2007, it once again held that *Rasul* had not disturbed *Eisentrager*'s constitutional holding, which still therefore required the lower courts to dismiss the cases.[98] While Judge Judith Rogers dissented, the World War II-era precedents, at least in the lower courts, had proven robust enough to prevail yet a third time.

The Supreme Court initially denied certiorari. While several of the Justices dissented from the denial, Justices Stevens and Kennedy wrote that "our practice of requiring the exhaustion of available remedies as a precondition to accepting jurisdiction over applications for the writ of habeas corpus ... make[s] it appropriate to deny these petitions at this time."[99] The provisions of the DTA providing for D.C. Circuit review of CSRT judgments should be given a chance to play out, they wrote. But that changed a few weeks later, after a military officer who had participated in CSRT hearings filed a devastating affidavit alleging inadequacies in the CSRT process.[100] In June 2007, the Court shifted gears and suddenly agreed to hear the case. One more time, the Justices would consider the rules of the road at Guantánamo—or, to put it more precisely, they would consider the scope of their own role in making and overseeing those rules.

Seth Waxman, a former Solicitor General, opened oral argument by reminding the Justices that the 37 petitioners had been imprisoned for the six years that the Court had spent hearing the Guantánamo cases, that "not one has ever had meaningful notice of the factual grounds of detention or a fair opportunity to dispute those grounds before a neutral decision-maker," that "under the decision below, they have no prospect of getting that opportunity," and that "each maintains ... that he is ... 'innocent of all wrongdoing.' "[101] While Waxman conceded that some of these men might be found in habeas proceedings to be detainable after all, he insisted that "limited DTA review of the structurally flawed CSRT process cannot provide any reliable examination of the Executive's

---

[98] *See Boumediene v. Bush*, 476 F.3d 981 (D.C. Cir. 2007).

[99] *Boumediene v. Bush*, 127 S.Ct. 1478 (2007).

[100] *See* Declaration of Stephen Abraham, filed as part of Reply to Opposition to Petition For Rehearing On Petition for Writ of Certiorari, *Al Odah v. United States*, 128 S.Ct. 2229 (2008) (No. 06 Civ. 1196).

[101] For all quotations, see Transcript of Oral Argument, *Boumediene v. Bush*, 128 S.Ct. 2229 (2008).

asserted basis for detaining these Petitioners, let alone an adequate substitute for traditional habeas review."

Waxman parried with Chief Justice Roberts over the adequacy of the CSRTs under the court's 2004 *Hamdi* decision and with Justice Ginsburg over the proper remedy. But argument heated up when Justice Scalia challenged his history: "Do you have a single case in the 220 years of our country or, for that matter, in the five centuries of the English empire in which habeas was granted to an alien in a territory that was not under the sovereign control of either the United States or England?"

"The answer to that is a resounding yes," replied Waxman, who then repeatedly attempted to convince the skeptical Justice that his examples actually met Justice Scalia's conditions. The two went back and forth, arguing about hundreds of years of habeas cases. The other Justices piped in now and then with less esoteric questions, but it was a Scalia–Waxman show. Waxman gave no ground, but also clearly did not move Justice Scalia. "I am still waiting for a single case . . . in which an alien . . . in a territory not within the Crown, was granted habeas corpus," Justice Scalia later said. Waxman finally pleaded exhaustion, much to the amusement of the audience. He clearly had a majority of the Justices on his side, but Justice Scalia would not be one of them.

Clement had a losing argument before the Justices, and he knew it. He had watched for years as the court's deference to the executive had eroded. Yet he jumped into the ring gamely, arguing that the detainees had access to a CSRT tribunal modeled on earlier army regulations and to judicial review of CSRT findings.

He immediately faced tough questioning, in which the Justices foreshadowed their coming rejection of DTA review as a substitute for habeas corpus rights. Justice Souter observed that in some cases in which a detainee had been found not to be an enemy combatant, the government had simply remanded the result to another tribunal, which frequently reversed the decision on enemy combatant status. How could the CSRTs be called a satisfactory substitute for habeas review if they didn't permit release of the detainee when appropriate?

Clement responded, "if what the Constitution requires to make the DTA . . . an adequate substitute is the power to order release, there is no obstacle in the text of the DTA to that."

Clement posited that the baseline year for interpreting the writ should be 1789. And compared to habeas rules at common law, he argued, detainees at Guantánamo have far *greater* judicial review under the DTA framework. "It is not even close. This is [a] remarkable liberalization of the writ, not some retrenchment or suspension of the writ" he said.

Justice Souter responded, "but aren't you simply rearguing *Rasul*?" The time bomb the majority had planted in *Rasul* had exploded. The statutory interpretation adopted in that case was now defining constitutional norms.

Chief Justice Roberts attempted to throw Clement a bone, pointing out that the adequacy of available judicial review couldn't be ascertained fully because the D.C. Circuit Court hadn't ruled on a relevant case yet. Clement took up this point, agreeing that, "there's a sense in which this is really a facial challenge." But by the end of the argument, it appeared to be a facial challenge destined to succeed. The World War II-era precedents had reached the end of their run.

The Supreme Court Ruling in Boumediene

The *Boumediene* decision, handed down on a 5-to-4 vote on June 12, 2008, marked the first time the Court took a step with respect to Guantánamo that Congress could not undo.[102] Ruling on a constitutional basis for the first time in the nearly seven-year trajectory of Guantánamo litigation, the Court declared that neither the executive branch nor the legislature could deny access to the federal courts for habeas petitioners from Guantánamo—and they left ambiguous the question of how far beyond Guantánamo their jurisdiction might reach. The Justices held that DTA review did not offer an adequate substitute for habeas. And they made clear that some measure of constitutional protection attended detention at Guantánamo. Justice Kennedy, writing for the majority, announced:

> We hold that petitioners may invoke the fundamental procedural protections of habeas corpus. The laws and Constitution are designed to survive, and remain in force, in extraordinary times. Liberty and security can be reconciled; and in our system they are reconciled within the framework of the law. The Framers decided that habeas corpus, a right of first importance, must be a part of that framework, a part of that law.[103]

In his concurring opinion, Justice Souter observed that the decision was, "no bolt out of the blue," but framed *Boumediene* as the continuation of what the Court started in *Rasul* and *Hamdan*.[104]

If Justice Souter saw the case as finishing what the Court had started, Justice Scalia—who had also dissented from the jurisdictional holdings of both *Rasul* and *Hamdan*—saw the decision as an abandon-

---

[102] *See Boumediene v. Bush*, 128 S.Ct. 2229 (2008).

[103] *Id.* at 2277.

[104] *See id.* at 2288 (Souter, J., concurring).

ment of precedent and a security risk for America. In his dissent, he wrote:

> The game of bait-and-switch that today's opinion plays upon the Nation's Commander in Chief, will make the war harder on us. It will almost certainly cause more Americans to be killed. That consequence would be tolerable if necessary to preserve a time-honored legal principle vital to our constitutional Republic. But it is this Court's blatant abandonment of such a principle that produces the decision today.[105]

Chief Justice Roberts, while joining Scalia's dissent, dissented on a different point as well. In his view, the Court's most significant error lay in tossing out the D.C. Circuit review system created by the DTA, which he termed "the most generous set of procedural protections ever afforded aliens detained by this country as enemy combatants" without even seeing how it worked in practice.[106] "The Court does eventually get around to asking whether review under the DTA is, as the Court frames it, an 'adequate substitute' for habeas ... but even then its opinion fails to determine what rights the detainees possess and whether the DTA system satisfies them. The majority instead compares the undefined DTA process to an equally undefined habeas right—one that is to be given shape only in the future by district courts on a case-by-case basis."[107]

An ironic coda to the decision arrived a few days after *Boumediene* came down, when the D.C. Circuit handed down its first decision in a DTA review case. The decision, in a review process the high court had declared inadequate, overturned a CSRT judgment that an ethnic Turkic Chinese detainee was an enemy combatant.[108] It was the first time in the War on Terror a court had done so.

The Uncertain Legacy of the Guantánamo Cases

As the presidency of George W. Bush drew to a close, the Guantánamo cases had not ended. In many respects, they had hardly begun. Seven years into the litigation, the Justices had established the principle that the government cannot insulate detentions at the base from judicial review. They had raised the possibility of extraterritorial application of the Constitution and of judicial power that extends beyond Guantánamo. They had insisted that a step as fateful as the design of a trial regime

---

[105] *Id.* at 2294 (Scalia, J., dissenting).

[106] *Id.* at 2279 (Roberts, C.J., dissenting).

[107] *Id.* at 2279–80.

[108] *See Parhat v. Gates*, 532 F.3d 834 (D.C. Cir. 2008).

must proceed with congressional involvement. And they had bound the executive branch a little tighter to the Geneva Conventions. What they had not done, however, was answer the questions at the core of the American debate over the detention of the enemy.

Except in the vaguest terms, the enemy combatant cases have not answered the question of when the president has the authority to detain terrorist suspects outside the criminal justice system. They have barely begun defining who counts as an "enemy combatant" subject to detention. They have not decided the scope of the procedural rights such a person has in a habeas case, the extent of the showing required of the government to justify detention, or what sort of evidence a court might admit to support a detention. They have not spelled out how classified evidence should be handled. They have not, in short, defined the system under which America will detain its foes in a worldwide conflict that has aspects of criminal justice and aspects of warfare but all of the hallmarks of neither. And despite President Obama's decision to close the Guantánamo Bay detention facility and to revise the military commission process, there is no reason to believe that the underlying conflict will end soon.

The government released Shafiq Rasul in March 2004, shortly before the Court's ruling that bears his name. Along with Asef Iqbal and Ruhal Ahmed—the other members of the Tipton Three—he has since returned to Britain and spoken and written about his experiences at Guantánamo, alleging physical and mental abuse there. Their story was dramatized in a film entitled *The Road to Guantánamo*. And along with the other members of the Tipton Three and another British detainee, he filed a civil suit alleging torture and other abuse. In 2008, the Supreme Court ordered the D.C. Circuit to reconsider its rejection of his claims in light of *Boumediene*.[109]

In the summer of 2008, Salim Ahmed Hamdan became the first Guantánamo detainee to face a full trial before a military commission. (One previous detainee, David Hicks, reached a plea deal.) He pled not guilty to charges of conspiracy and providing material support for terrorism. The panel of six military officers delivered a split verdict, clearing him of the conspiracy charge and convicting him of material support. On August 7, 2008, the same panel of officers sentenced him to 66 months of imprisonment and gave him credit for time served at Guantánamo—a dramatically lighter sentence than lesser terrorist figures had received in federal court trials. A few months later, the military sent him home to Yemen to serve the remaining weeks of his sentence.[110]

---

[109] *See Rasul v. Myers*, No. 08–235 (Dec. 15, 2008) (Order granting certiorari and vacating *Rasul v. Myers*, 512 F.3d 644 (D.C. Cir. 2008)).

[110] *See* Robert F. Worth, *Bin Laden Driver to Be Sent to Yemen*, N.Y. Times., Nov. 25, 2008.

The Algerian Six saw their habeas case go to trial in federal district court in Washington in November 2008. Judge Richard Leon, who had three years earlier held that they had no cognizable rights in court, heard a week's worth of classified evidence. The government was no longer arguing that the six had plotted to blow up the U.S. embassy in Sarajevo, merely that one—Bensayah—was an al Qaeda member and "facilitator," and that all six had, as Leon summarized it, "planned to travel to Afghanistan in late 2001 and take up arms against the U.S. and allied forces."[111] After hearing the evidence, however, Leon was unpersuaded about all save Bensayah. The government, he wrote, had not shown by a preponderance of evidence that such a plot existed. Its information all came from "a classified document from an unnamed source" whose credibility and reliability he could not evaluate. He ordered five of the six, including Lakhdar Boumediene, released. Of Bensayah, by contrast, Leon determined that the government had "met its burden" by putting forth "a series of other intelligence reports based on a variety of sources and evidence."[112] As of the beginning of 2009, the government had released three of the six; Boumediene, however, remained at Guantánamo.

In the end, whether history comes to view these cases as great victories for the rule of law or as a series of hubristic bait-and-switches by courts that fail to honor the safe harbors their precedents offered the executive probably depends on functional questions: For how many detainees will they mean release? How many will go on to make Americans regret their release? Is Justice Scalia correct that we will pay for these decisions in blood or is Justice Kennedy correct that security and rich habeas rights for unlawful combatants can coexist? These questions America will not answer in court.

---

[111] *Boumediene v. Bush*, 579 F.Supp.2d 191, 196 (D.D.C. 2008).

[112] *Id.* at 198.

*

Biographies of *Constitutional Law Stories* Contributors

Stephen Ansolabehere is Professor of Government at Harvard University. The chapter in this book grew out of an empirical study he conducted on the effect of *Baker v. Carr* on public policy: *Equal Votes, Equal Money: Court Ordered Redistricting and the Distribution of Public Expenditures in the American States*, 96 Am. Pol. Sci. Rev. 767 (2002) (with Alan Gerber and Jim Snyder). This work eventually grew into his book *The End of Inequality: One Person, One Vote, and the Transformation of American Politics* (2008). Professor Ansolabehere's research focuses broadly on issues of electoral politics and representation, including campaign finance, campaign advertising, roll call voting analysis, and legislative coalition formation. He has published on these topics in communications, economics, law, political science, and statistics journals. He is co-author of *The Media Game* (1993), *Going Negative* (1996), winner of the Goldsmith Book prize, *The End of Inequality* (2008), and *American Government* (2009). Professor Ansolabehere directed the Caltech/MIT Voting Technology Project, a team of engineers and social scientists seeking to improve voting technology and election systems in the United States, from its inception through the 2004 election.

David E. Bernstein is a Professor at the George Mason University School of Law in Arlington, Virginia, where he has been teaching since 1995. Professor Bernstein is the author of *You Can't Say That! The Growing Threat to Civil Liberties from Antidiscrimination Laws* (2003), *The New Wigmore: Expert Evidence* (2003) (with Kaye and Mnookin); *Only One Place of Redress: African–Americans, Labor Regulations, and the Courts from Reconstruction to the New Deal* (2001); and co-editor of *Phantom Risk: Scientific Inference and the Law* (1993). Professor Bernstein's next book, *Rehabilitating* Lochner, will be published by the University of Chicago Press.

Ashutosh A. Bhagwat is Professor of Law at the University of California, Hastings College of the Law in San Francisco. His research and teaching interests focus on the areas of constitutional law, economic regulation, and administrative law. His publications in scholarly journals include: *The Test That Ate Everything: Intermediate Scrutiny in First Amendment Jurisprudence*, 2007 U. Ill. L. Rev. 783; *What If I Want My Kids to Watch Pornography?: Protecting Children from "Indecent" Speech*, 11 Wm. & Mary Bill of Rts. J. 671 (2003); *Institutions and Long Term Planning: Lessons from the California Electricity Crisis*, 55 Admin. L. Rev. 95 (2003); *Affirmative Action and Compelling Interests: Equal Protection Jurisprudence at the Crossroads*, 4 U. Penn. J. Con. L. 260 (2002); *Separate But Equal?: The Supreme Court, the Lower Federal Courts, and the Nature of the "Judicial Power,"* 80 B.U. L. Rev. 967 (2000); and *Purpose Scrutiny in Constitutional Analysis*, 85 Cal. L. Rev. 297 (1997). Professor Bhagwat holds a B.A., *summa cum laude*, from Yale University and a J.D. from the University of Chicago Law School. He clerked for Judge Richard A. Posner of the United States Court of Appeals for the Seventh Circuit, and for Associate Justice Anthony M. Kennedy of the United States Supreme Court.

Vincent Blasi is Corliss Lamont Professor of Civil Liberties at Columbia Law School. Among his recent writings are: *Free Speech and Good Character: From Milton to Brandeis to the Present*, in Lee Bollinger & Geoffrey Stone, eds.; *Eternally Vigilant: Free Speech in the Modern Era* (2002); *School Vouchers and Religious Liberty: Seven Questions From Madison's Memorial and Remonstrance*, 87 Cornell Law Rev. 783 (2002); and *Holmes and the Marketplace of Ideas*, 2004 Supreme Court Review 1 (2005). Earlier articles include: *The Checking Value in First Amendment Theory*, 1977 Am. Bar Foundation Res. J. 521; and *The Pathological Perspective and the First Amendment*, 85 Colum. L. Rev. 449 (1985). He edited *The Burger Court: The Counter–Revolution That Wasn't* (1983) and *Ideas of the First Amendment* (2006). In 1998 Professor Blasi was elected a fellow of the American Academy of Arts and Sciences.

Jim Chen became dean of the University of Louisville School of Law in January 2007. Dean Chen is a prolific and influential scholar whose works span subjects such as administrative law, agricultural law, constitutional law, economic regulation, environmental law, industrial policy, legislation, and natural resources law. He is the coauthor of *Disasters and the Law: Katrina and Beyond* (2006), the first book to provide comprehensive coverage of the legal issues surrounding natural disasters. He clerked for Justice Clarence Thomas of the Supreme Court of the United States and Judge J. Michael Luttig of the United States of Appeals for the Fourth Circuit. A Fulbright Scholar and a *magna cum laude* graduate of Harvard Law School, Dean Chen served as an executive editor of the *Harvard Law Review*.

Michael C. Dorf is the Robert S. Stevens Professor of Law at Cornell Law School. His recent works include *How the Written Constitution Crowds Out the Extraconstitutional Rule of Recognition*, in Matthew

D. Adler & Kenneth Einer Himma, eds., *The Rule of Recognition and the U.S. Constitution* (2009); *Dynamic Incorporation of Foreign Law*, 157 U. Penn. L. Rev. 103 (2008); and *Fallback Law*, 107 Colum. L. Rev. 303 (2007). With Laurence H. Tribe, Professor Dorf is the co-author of *On Reading the Constitution* (1991). He is also the author of *No Litmus Test: Law Versus Politics in the Twenty–First Century* (2006) and the co-author, with Trevor Morrison, of a forthcoming book tentatively titled *Constitutional Law: An Overview*. Professor Dorf's bi-weekly legal affairs column appears on the website Writ.FindLaw.com and he blogs at dorfonlaw.org. A graduate of Harvard College and Harvard Law School, he was a law clerk for Judge Stephen Reinhardt of the United States Court of Appeals for the Ninth Circuit and Justice Anthony M. Kennedy of the Supreme Court of the United States. Before joining the Cornell faculty, Professor Dorf taught at Rutgers–Camden Law School for three years and at Columbia Law School for thirteen years.

Christopher L. Eisgruber is the Provost of Princeton University, where he also serves as the Laurance S. Rockefeller Professor of Public Affairs in the Woodrow Wilson School and the University Center for Human Values. His books include: *The Next Justice: Repairing the Supreme Court Appointments Process* (2007); *Religious Freedom and the Constitution* (2007) (co-authored with Lawrence G. Sager); and *Constitutional Self–Government* (2001). He is the co-editor (with Andras Sajo) of *Global Justice and the Bulwarks of Localism: Human Rights in Context* (2005). Chapter 5 of this book incorporates and revises material originally published in *Dred Again: Originalism's Forgotten Past*, 10 Constitutional Commentary 37 (1993).

Garrett Epps is Professor of Law at the University of Baltimore. A former reporter for The Washington Post, he is also the author of two published novels, *The Shad Treatment* (1977) and *The Floating Island: A Tale of Washington* (1985). His most recent book, *Democracy Reborn*, is a narrative of the framing of the Fourteenth Amendment. His work has appeared in The New York Review of Books, The Nation, The New Republic, The American Prospect, The New York Times Magazine and The New York Times Book Review. Professor Epps is the editor of *First Amendment Freedom of the Press: Its Constitutional History and the Contemporary Debate* (2009). His book-length study of *Employment Division v. Smith* will be reissued in 2009 under the title *Peyote v. The State*.

Daniel Farber is Sho Sato Professor of Law at the University of California, Berkeley. He received a B.A. in philosophy with high honors in 1971 and an M.A. in sociology in 1972, both from the University of Illinois. In 1975 he earned his J.D. *summa cum laude* from the University of Illinois, where he was Editor in Chief of the *University of Illinois Law Review* and class valedictorian. Professor Farber clerked for Judge Philip W. Tone of the United States Court of Appeals for the Seventh

Circuit and for Justice John Paul Stevens of the United States Supreme Court. Prior to Berkeley, he taught at the University of Minnesota and the University of Illinois. He has also been a visiting professor at the University of Chicago, Harvard, Bocconi University in Milan, Catholic University in Lisbon, and Stanford. He is a member of the American Law Institute and the American Academy of Arts and Sciences. Professor Farber's books on constitutional topics include: *Desperately Seeking Certainty: The Misguided Quest for Constitutional Foundations* (with Suzanna Sherry, 2002); *Constitutional Law: Themes for the Constitution's Third Century* (with Philip Frickey and William Eskridge, 4th ed., 2009); *A History of the American Constitution* (with Sherry, 1990, 2d ed. 2006); *Lincoln's Constitution* (2003); and *Judgment Calls* (2008)(with Sherry). He has also written many articles on environmental and constitutional law as well as about contracts, jurisprudence and legislation.

Lucinda Finley is the Vice Provost for Faculty Affairs at the University of Buffalo, State University of New York, where she also serves on the Law School faculty as the Frank Raichle Professor. She has taught at Yale Law School, Cornell Law School, and DePaul Law School, and lectured at the University of Sydney Law School. She teaches in the areas of reproductive rights, women and the law, and torts. She has published articles on gender equality and feminist legal theory in leading law reviews, and is co-author of a Torts casebook that incorporates issues of how tort law affects people based on gender, race and sexual orientation. Professor Finley has frequently testified before federal and state legislatures on issues of tort reform and gender fairness. She is a leading expert on the Freedom of Access to Clinic Entrances Act, which prohibits violence and obstruction aimed at reproductive health providers and patients, and she has litigated major cases under this law. She has also represented reproductive health providers before the United States Supreme Court in *Schenck v. Pro-Choice Network of Western New York*, 519 U.S. 357 (1997), a case about limits on anti-abortion protest and the First Amendment.

Michael Gerhardt is the Samuel Ashe Distinguished Professor of Constitutional Law & Director of the UNC Center on Law & Government at the University of North Carolina at Chapel Hill. He has written over fifty law review articles and essays on various topics in constitutional law. He is also the author of several books, including most recently *The Power of Precedent* (2008). He is the co-author of the book, *Constitutional Theory: Arguments and Perspectives* (3rd ed., 2007). Professor Gerhardt has testified many times before Congress, including as the only joint witness in the House Judiciary Committee's historic 1998 hearing on the background and history of impeachment and in 2003 as an expert on the constitutionality of the filibuster before the Senate Rules and Judiciary Committees. He has served as a special consultant to the

National Commission on Judicial Discipline and Removal, the Presidential Transition in 1992–93, and the White House on the nomination of Stephen Breyer to the Supreme Court.

Neil Gotanda is Professor of Law at Western State University College of Law in Fullerton, California. He has written extensively in the areas of racial theory and Asian American studies. He was an original participant in the Conference on Critical Legal Studies, co-founded the Conference on Critical Race Theory, and developed the earliest courses on Asian American jurisprudence. He is co-editor with Kimberle Crenshaw, Gary Peller and Kendall Thomas of *Critical Race Theory: The Key Writings that Formed the Movement* (1995). His other publications include *Comparative Racialization: Racial Profiling and the Case of Wen Ho Lee*, 47 UCLA L. Rev. 1689 (2000); *Failure of the Color–Blind Vision: Race, Ethnicity, and the California Civil Rights Initiative*, 23 Hastings Const. L.Q. 135 (1996); *Towards Repeal of Asian Exclusion, 1943–1950*, in Hyung-chan Kim, ed., *Asian Americans and Congress* (1996); *The Assertion of Asian-American Rights and the "Miss Saigon Syndrome"* in Hyung-chan Kim, ed., Asian Americans and the Supreme Court, (1992); *A Critique of "Our Constitution is Color–Blind,"* 44 Stan. L. Rev. 1 (1991); and *Other Non–Whites in American Legal History: A Review of "Justice at War,"* 85 Colum. L. Rev. 1186 (1985).

Cheryl I. Harris is Professor of Law at UCLA School of Law, teaching in the areas of constitutional law, civil rights, critical race theory, and employment discrimination. Her publications include the groundbreaking *Whiteness as Property*, 106 Harv. L. Rev. 1707 (1993), a work that has been heavily cited and widely acclaimed; *Finding Sojourner's Truth: Race, Gender and the Institution of Property*, 18 Card. L. Rev. 309 (1996); *Equal Treatment and the Reproduction of Inequality*, 69 Ford. L. Rev. 1753 (2001), as well as most recently, *The New Racial Preferences*, 96 Cal. L. Rev. 1139 (with Devon W. Carbado 2008), which examines how efforts to erase race from the admissions process and from personal statements in particular can impose racial burdens and create racial preferences. Professor Harris's work has appeared in a number of anthologies on Critical Race Theory as well as other media and journals. She has served as consultant to the MacArthur Foundation, Program in Peace and International Cooperation and has lectured in numerous fora and leading academic institutions on race and American law, more broadly. In 2003 Harris was a fellow at the University of California Humanities Research Institute focusing on issues of redress.

Samuel Issacharoff is the Reiss Professor of Constitutional Law at New York University School of Law. His publications cover topics in constitutional law, the law of the political process, procedural issues of complex litigation, employment law, and law and economics. His publications have appeared in all the leading American law reviews, as well as in social science and economics journals. Professor Issacharoff is an author of the *Law of Democracy* (with Pamela Karlan and Richard Pildes, (2d. ed., 2001)), the leading text on the law governing the political process. Professor Issacharoff is a 1983 graduate of Yale Law School. He began his teaching career at the University of Texas, where he held the Joseph Jamail Centennial Chair in Law, before becoming the Harold R. Medina Professor of Procedural Jurisprudence at Columbia Law School, and then moving to NYU. He is a Fellow of the American Academy of Arts and Sciences.

Michael W. McConnell is a Circuit Judge on the U.S. Court of Appeals for the Tenth Circuit. Before his appointment to the bench in 2002, Judge McConnell taught constitutional law and related subjects at the University of Chicago and later the University of Utah. He continues to teach part time as Presidential Professor at the S.J. Quinney College of Law at the University of Utah and as a visiting professor at Harvard and Stanford Law Schools. In his academic work, Judge McConnell has written widely on such subjects as freedom of religion, segregation, unenumerated rights, and constitutional history and theory. He is co-editor of *Religion and the Law* (2002) and *Christian Perspectives on Legal Thought* (2002). Judge McConnell graduated from Michigan State University and the University of Chicago Law School. He served as law clerk to Chief Judge J. Skelly Wright on the United States Court of Appeals for the D.C. Circuit and for Associate Justice William J. Brennan, Jr., on the United States Supreme Court, as Assistant General Counsel of the Office of Management and Budget, and as Assistant to the Solicitor General of the United States. Before becoming a judge, McConnell argued eleven cases in the Supreme Court, and served as Chair of the Constitutional Law Section of the Association of American Law Schools, Co–Chair of the Emergency Committee to Defend the First Amendment, member of the President's Intelligence Oversight Board, and special counsel to Mayer, Brown, Rowe & Maw. In 1996, he was elected a Fellow of the American Academy of Arts and Sciences. In 2008, he was awarded an honorary Doctorate of Laws by the University of Notre Dame.

Hannah Neprash is a Research Assistant at the Medicare Payment Advisory Commission. She is a graduate of Oberlin College. The views expressed here are her own and do not reflect the views of MedPAC.

Seana V. Shiffrin is Professor of Law and Professor of Philosophy at the University of California, Los Angeles. She writes primarily about issues at the intersection of law and moral and political philosophy. Among her articles are: *The Divergence of Contract and Promise*, 120 Harv. L. Rev. 708 (2007); *What Is Really Wrong With Compelled Association?*, 99 Nw L. Rev. 839 (2005); *Speech, Death and Double Effect*, 78

NYU L. Rev. 1135 (2003); *Egalitarianism, Choice Sensitivity, and Accommodation*, in Philip Pettit et al., ed., *Reasons and Values: Themes from the Work of Joseph Raz* (2004); *Lockean Theories of Intellectual Property*, in Stephen R. Munzer, ed., New Essays in the Political Theory of Property (2001); and *Paternalism, Unconscionability Doctrine, & Accommodation*, 29 Phil. & Pub. Aff. 205 (2000) (winner of the 2002 American Philosophical Association's Berger Prize for best essay in philosophy of law). Professor Shiffrin is also an associate editor of Philosophy and Public Affairs.

Mark Tushnet is William Nelson Cromwell Professor of Law, Harvard Law School. He is the co-author of several casebooks, including the most widely used casebook on constitutional law, has written more than fifteen books, including a two-volume work on the life of Justice Thurgood Marshall, and has edited ten others. He was President of the Association of American Law Schools in 2003. In 2002 he was elected a Fellow of the American Academy of Arts and Sciences.

Benjamin Wittes is a senior fellow in Governance Studies at The Brookings Institution. He is the author of *Law and the Long War: The Future of Justice in the Age of Terror* (2008). His previous books include *Starr: A Reassessment* (2002) and *Confirmation Wars: Preserving Independent Courts in Angry Times* (2006). Between 1997 and 2006, he served as an editorial writer for *The Washington Post* specializing in legal affairs. Before joining the editorial page staff of *The Washington Post*, Wittes covered the Justice Department and federal regulatory agencies as a reporter and news editor at *Legal Times*. His writing has also appeared in a wide range of journals and magazines, including *Slate, The New Republic, The Wilson Quarterly, The Weekly Standard, Policy Review*, and *First Things*. Wittes is a graduate of Oberlin College.

†